A HANDBOOK OF CONTEMPOR

SPANISH GRAMMAR

Ana Beatriz Chiquito

Professor, University of Bergen, Norway
Visiting Researcher, MIT

VISTA
HIGHER LEARNING

Boston, Massachusetts

Publisher: José A. Blanco
Managing Editors: Eugenia Corbo, Paola Rios Schaaf (Technology)
Project Manager: Patricia Ravetto
Editors: John DeCarli (Technology), Lauren Krolick, Paula Orrego,
Raquel Rodríguez Muñoz, Carolina Zapata Pérez
Production and Design Director: Marta Kimball
Senior Designer: Sarah Cole
Production and Design Team: María Eugenia Castaño, Oscar Díez, Mauricio Henao,
Jhoany Jiménez, Erik Restrepo, Hamilton Zuleta

Library of Congress Card Number: 2010942655

2 3 4 5 6 7 8 9 TC 17 16 15 14 13 12 11

The Vista Higher Learning Story

Your Specialized Foreign Language Publisher

Independent, specialized, and privately owned, Vista Higher Learning was founded in 2000 with one mission: to raise the teaching and learning of world languages to a higher level. This mission is based on the following beliefs:

- It is essential to prepare students for a world in which learning another language is a necessity, not a luxury.
- Language learning should be fun and rewarding, and all students should have the tools necessary for achieving success.
- Students who experience success learning a language will be more likely to continue their language studies both inside and outside the classroom.

With this in mind, we decided to take a fresh look at all aspects of language instructional materials. Because we are specialized, we dedicate 100 percent of our resources to this goal and base every decision on how well it supports language learning.

That is where you come in. Since our founding, we have relied on the continuous and invaluable feedback from language instructors and students nationwide. This partnership has proved to be the cornerstone of our success by allowing us to constantly improve our programs to meet your instructional needs.

The result? Programs that make language learning exciting, relevant, and effective through:

- an unprecedented access to resources
- a wide variety of contemporary, authentic materials
- the integration of text, technology, and media, and
- a bold and engaging textbook design

By focusing on our singular passion, we let you focus on yours.

The Vista Higher Learning Team

VISTA
HIGHER LEARNING

31 St. James Avenue Boston, MA 02116-4104 TOLLFREE: 800-618-7375
TELEPHONE: 617-426-4910 FAX: 617-426-5209 www.vistahigherlearning.com

Foreword

Spanish is spoken by close to half a billion people around the world and is the official language in most countries in Central and South America, as well as in Mexico and Spain. For a long time, it has also been an important language in teaching institutions around the world.

In 2009, the United States Census Bureau conducted the American Community Survey, which shed some light on the situation of the Spanish language in the United States. According to the survey, there are 45 million people in the United States who speak Spanish as a first or second language. Over 35 million use Spanish as their primary language. The number of students of Spanish in schools and colleges has surpassed six million.

A Handbook of Contemporary Spanish Grammar was developed taking into account the heterogeneous nature of Spanish-language communities in the United States. It provides the support that English speakers and heritage speakers need to master Spanish grammar up to an advanced level.

Grammar topics are presented and reviewed in a clear and logical manner. The text covers basic pronunciation and spelling, parts of speech, verb tenses and moods, tense sequencing, subordinate clauses, and all grammar topics that a student of Spanish needs to master. All concepts and structures are presented in a step-by-step manner, with charts and examples. The handbook also presents regional variations in both the explanations and the examples.

The handbook incorporates significant key updates from the **Real Academia Española**, as presented in the *Nueva gramática de la lengua española* published in 2010. While the *Nueva gramática* targets linguists and scholars, the handbook presents these updates in an accessible, easy-to-follow format.

A glossary of collocations is included to help students improve their vocabulary and deepen their understanding of the subtle differences between terms. The glossary includes grammatical collocations (such as *verb + preposition* combinations), which students will refer to in order to gain mastery over more complex structures.

At the end of the text, hundreds of activities give students ample opportunity to practice and check their understanding.

A Handbook of Contemporary Spanish Grammar is an indispensable tool for anyone with a keen interest in furthering their knowledge of Spanish grammar and achieving a higher level of practical, day-to-day fluency.

Miguel Ángel Quesada Pacheco
Academia Costarricense de la Lengua
Correspondiente de la Real Academia Española

To the student

A Handbook of Contemporary Spanish Grammar is your one-stop source for Spanish grammar reference and practice. Through comprehensive and accessible presentations, detailed charts and diagrams, a *Glosario combinatorio* (glossary of collocations), and substantial auto-gradable practice, this useful reference tool will reinforce and expand your knowledge of Spanish grammatical concepts.

Here are some of the features you will encounter in **A Handbook of Contemporary Spanish Grammar:**

- Grammar presentations that incorporate key updates from the *Nueva gramática*, published in 2010 by the **Real Academia Española**

- Coverage of standard usage in Spain and Latin America, including the use of the *voseo*

- Presentation of regional variations

- An abundance of examples that demonstrate contemporary, real-world usage

- A highly structured, easy-to-navigate design that facilitates the learning of grammar concepts

- A thorough glossary of grammatical and lexical collocations to expand your vocabulary and improve oral and written communication

- Abundant online, auto-gradable activities that practice the concepts

A Handbook of Contemporary Spanish Grammar serves multiple course configurations:

- Stand-alone textbook for advanced Spanish grammar courses

- Companion grammar reference for any advanced Spanish class

- Reference and practice book for heritage speakers and Spanish majors

- Self-study book for students who want to go beyond the grammar taught in introductory and intermediate courses

We hope that **A Handbook of Contemporary Spanish Grammar** will be an invaluable tool as you advance in your study of Spanish.

Table of contents

Organization

A Handbook of Contemporary Spanish Grammar includes the following sections:

Grammar presentations

- 31 chapters divided into clearly marked sections and subsections
- Complete verb tables for easy reference

Glosario combinatorio

- See pp. xvii and 279 for more details.

Activities

- More than 400 activities
- Immediate feedback provided when practice is done on the Supersite
- Additional practice available online (See p. xviii.)

Answer key

- Built-in answer key for checking your work when practice is done manually

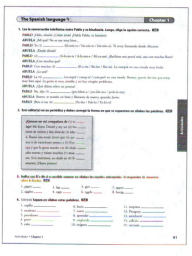

Sidebars and icons

- On the first page of every chapter, a sidebar summarizes the chapter's contents.

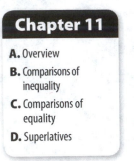

Chapter 11

A. Overview
B. Comparisons of inequality
C. Comparisons of equality
D. Superlatives

- Clearly marked and numbered headings help you navigate the grammar explanations and easily locate cross-references.

19.B Use of the present perfect

19.B.1 Life experiences – *nunca, alguna vez, hasta ahora*

- A sidebar at the end of the chapter includes the specific activity sequence with its corresponding page numbers. The Supersite icon indicates that these activities are also available online.

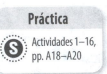

Práctica

(S) Actividades 1–16, pp. A18–A20

- In the *Actividades* section, a mouse icon 🖱 indicates when activities are also on the Supersite.

Adverbs 🖱   **Chapter 10**

- Each activity identifies the chapter (**2**) and section(s) (**A–D**) where the material is presented.

16. Síntesis Elige la palabra que no pertenece al grupo. **2.A–2.D**

- Additional practice on the Supersite, not available in the text, is indicated at the end of each practice section.

🖱 Practice more at **vhlcentral.com.**

Glosario combinatorio

A Handbook of Contemporary Spanish Grammar features a practical glossary of collocations, or common word combinations. The glossary functions as:

- An invaluable tool for expanding vocabulary and increasing grammatical accuracy
- An excellent reference for improving fluency by learning word combinations commonly used by native speakers

For a detailed description, see p. 279.

Glosario combinatorio

In English, you can see somebody *in the flesh*, while in Spanish, you can see someone **en carne y hueso** (lit. *in flesh and bone*). In English, you are *fed up with something or someone* and in Spanish, you can be **harto de algo o alguien**. This glossary provides a sample of word combinations like these, which will help expand your vocabulary by giving a glimpse of the common, established word combinations that native speakers use. It will also help you with your grammar by showing that certain verbs take different prepositions from the ones used in English, or that no preposition is needed at all.

These types of word combinations are commonly called *collocations*. Not all of these word combinations are considered collocations. Many are free combinations with countless options. For example, the phrase **un hermano joven** is a free combination. The adjective, **joven**, can be used together with countless nouns (**un niño joven, una muchacha joven, un profesor joven, una estudiante joven**, etc.). **Un hermano gemelo**, on the other hand, is a collocation. The use of the adjective **gemelo** is restricted to a limited number of nouns.

Lexical collocations usually involve nouns, adjectives, adverbs, and verbs. *Grammatical* collocations usually involve a main word and a preposition or a dependent clause.

Compare these other examples. You can look up these collocations in the glossary!

Free combinations	Collocations
caer en un pozo, caerse en la calle	caer en la cuenta
surtir gasolina, surtir un medicamento	surtir efecto
va al cine, va a la escuela	va de veras

Compare these Spanish and English collocations:

Spanish collocations	English collocations
fuego lento	low heat
trabajar **en** algo	to work **on** something
hacer la vista gorda	to turn a blind eye

How to find collocations in this glossary

Follow these simple rules:

- If there is a noun, look under the noun.
- If there are two nouns, look under the first.
- If there is no noun, look under the adjective.
- If there is no adjective, look under the verb.

In addition, common expressions that are introduced by prepositions are also cross-listed under the preposition so students can benefit from lists of expressions organized by preposition.

Abbreviations

adj.	adjective	*f.*	feminine noun	*p.p.*	past participle
adv.	adverb	*fam.*	familiar	*prep.*	preposition
algn	alguien	*form.*	formal	*pron.*	pronoun
Am. L.	Latin America	*m.*	masculine noun	sb	somebody
Arg.	Argentina	*Mex.*	Mexico	sth	something
Esp.	Spain	*pl.*	plural	*v.*	verb

Glosario combinatorio

279

---

atractivos de la ciudad. María está a la izquierda de Juana.)

a la larga in the long run (Estoy segura de que Pedro, a la larga, comprenderá que es por su bien.)

a la manera de algn sb's way (Hagámoslo a mi manera.)

a la primera de cambio at the first opportunity

a la sombra de in the shadow of

a la vez at the same time

a la vista in sight, on view

a las mil maravillas wonderfully (¡Todo salió a las mil maravillas!)

a lo grande luxuriously, in style (Festejaremos tu cumpleaños a lo grande.)

a lo largo de throughout

a lo loco in a crazy way (Está gastando el dinero a lo loco.)

a lo mejor probably, likely

a los efectos de algo in order to do sth

a manera de algo by way of / as (Traje este dibujo a manera de ejemplo.)

a mano by hand

a (la) mano close at hand (¿Tienes tu planilla a (la) mano?)

a más tardar at the very latest

a mediados de in mid-/by mid- (Voy a retirar las cosas que faltan a mediados del mes que viene.)

a medias halfway/half

a medida que as/when/only (Resolveremos los problemas a medida que vayan surgiendo.)

a menos que unless

a menudo often

a modo de by way of, as (Usó su cuaderno a modo de pantalla.)

a no ser que if not

a nombre de algn addressed to sb

a oscuras in the dark

a partir de from, starting from

a pesar de in spite of

a pie on foot

a poco de algo shortly after sth

a por *Esp.* to go and get (Iré a por ti en dos horas.)

280

Glosario combinatorio

xvii

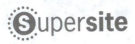

The Supersite for **A Handbook of Contemporary Spanish Grammar** provides a wealth of resources for both students and instructors.

For students

Student resources, available with a Supersite code, are provided free-of-charge with the purchase of a new student text. Here is what you will find at **vhlcentral.com**:

- All activities from the student text, with auto-grading

- Additional practice for each chapter

- Quizzes for self-assessment

- Oxford Spanish Mini Dictionary **OXFORD**
  UNIVERSITY PRESS

- Wimba Voice Board

For instructors

Instructors have access to the entire student site, as well as to these additional resources:

- A robust course management system

- Voice Board capabilities for creating custom oral activities

Supersite Plus includes the Supersite for **A Handbook of Contemporary Spanish Grammar**, plus **Wimba Pronto** for online communication and collaboration.

- Audio and video conferencing

- Instant messaging

- Online whiteboard to synchronously view and modify a shared canvas

- Application sharing—perfect for online tutoring

- Online office hours

- Instructor control of Pronto activation/deactivation

To the instructor

A Handbook of Contemporary Spanish Grammar combines thorough, accessible grammar explanations with a unique online component that offers Spanish students an invaluable reference tool. The text's content and organization enable its use as a standalone textbook for grammar courses, as a companion text for language, composition, literature, and culture courses, or as a reference for independent study. The **Handbook** incorporates key updates from the *Nueva gramática* and the *Nueva ortografía,* published in 2010 by the **Real Academia Española**.

Program features

- A topical structure that is flexible and simple to navigate

- Coverage of all major grammar topics, incorporating key updates and revisions from the *Nueva gramática* published by the Real Academia Española

- Concise, comprehensive explanations that include detailed tables and relevant examples

- Presentation of lexical and regional variations

- An abundance of examples of contemporary, real-world usage

- A glossary of collocations (*Glosario combinatorio*)

- Activities that allow students to practice and apply the grammar concepts

- An answer key that allows students to check their work

- Additional online practice and assessment (See p. xviii.)

The *Nueva gramática* and the *Nueva ortografía*

This **Handbook** incorporates key updates from the *Nueva gramática*, published by the **Real Academia Española** (RAE) in conjunction with all the regional Spanish language academies (see p. 18). The nomenclature used by the RAE often differs from that used throughout North America. Though the RAE's nomenclature is standard in this book, other naming conventions are acknowledged and presented.

The same approach has been applied to the grammar explanations. When relevant, both the RAE explanation and the traditional explanation are presented. For an example, see the case of demonstratives on p. 63. As you use the **Handbook**, you will see many instances like this.

The *voseo* conjugations covered correspond to those presented in the verb tables in the *Nueva gramática*. Verb tense presentations and verb tables include the *voseo* form for the present indicative and the affirmative imperative (*salís, salí*). The *voseo* forms for the present subjunctive and the negative imperative that do not match the *tú* forms (*salgás, no salgás*) are acknowledged in the verb presentations, but not included in verb tables.

Reviewers

On behalf of the author and its editors, Vista Higher Learning expresses its sincere appreciation to the many professors nationwide who participated in the preliminary surveys that led to the development of **A Handbook of Contemporary Spanish Grammar**. Their insights, ideas, and detailed comments were invaluable to the final product.

Robert Baah
Seattle Pacific University, WA

Lisa Barboun
Coastal Carolina University, SC

Servio Becerra
Youngstown State University, OH

Karen Berg
College of Charleston, SC

Peggy Buckwalter
Black Hill State University, SD

Vanessa Burch-Urquhart
Western Nevada College, NV

Bonnie Butler
Rutgers University, NJ

Jessie Carduner
Kent State University, OH

Debora Cordeiro Rosa
University of Central Florida, FL

Norma Corrales-Martin
Temple University, PA

Rocío Cortés
University of Wisconsin-Oshkosh, WI

Gerardo Cruz
Cardinal Stritch University, WI

Richard P. Doerr
Metropolitan State College of Denver, CO

Deborah Dougherty
Alma College, MI

Dina A. Fabery
University of Central Florida, FL

Elizabeth Fouts
Saint Anselm College, NH

Jose García
Eastern Washington University, WA

Próspero N. García
Amherst College, MA

Iria González-Liaño
University of Nevada
Las Vegas, NV

Kim Hernandez
Whitworth University, WA

Mary Kempen
Ohio Northern University, OH

Phil Klein
University of Iowa, IA

Iana Konstantinova
Southern Virginia University, VA

Kevin Krogh
Utah State University, UT

Lisa Kuriscak
Ball State University, IN

Joanna Lyskowicz
Drexel University, PA

Jeffrey Mancilla
De Anza College, CA

Francisco Manzo-Robledo
Washington State University, WA

Frank R. Martinez
Lipscomb University, TN

Mark J. Mascia
Sacred Heart University, CT

Collin McKinney
Bucknell University, PA

David Migaj
Wright College, IL

Lee Mitchell
Henderson State University, AR

Evelyn Nadeau
Clarke College, IA

James J. Pancrazio
Illinois State University, IL

Wendy Pilkerton
Linn Benton Community College, OR

Eve Pujol
University of Wisconsin
Madison, WI

George Robinson
Montana State University at Billings, MT

Shelli Rottschafer
Aquinas College, MI

Francisco Salgado-Robles
University of Florida, FL

Rachel Shively
Illinois State University, IL

José I. Suárez
University of Northern Colorado, CO

Sixto E. Torres
Metropolitan State College of Denver, CO

Maria Eugenia Trillo
Western New Mexico University, NM

Dr. Nick Uliano
Cabrini College, PA

Clara L. Vega
Alamance Community College, NC

Mariana Zinni
Queens College CUNY, NY

España y Guinea Ecuatorial

Mar Cantábrico

FRANCIA

La Coruña
Galicia · Lugo
Oviedo
Asturias
Santander
País Vasco · San Sebastián
Cantabria
Bilbao
Vizcaya Guipúzcoa
Golfo de Los Leones

Pontevedra
Orense
León
Castilla y León
Burgos
Álava
Vitoria
Navarra
La Rioja
Logroño
Pamplona
ANDORRA

Huesca
Palencia
Soria
Zaragoza
Aragón
Lérida
Cataluña
Gerona

Zamora
Valladolid
Barcelona
Tarragona

Salamanca
Segovia
Ávila
MADRID
Guadalajara
Teruel
Castellón
Menorca

Extremadura
Cáceres
Toledo
Castilla – La Mancha
Cuenca
Castellón de la Plana
Mallorca
Palma de Mallorca

PORTUGAL
Océano Atlántico
Valencia
Comunidad Valenciana
Islas Baleares
Ibiza
Formentera

Badajoz
Ciudad Real
Albacete
Alicante
Mar Mediterráneo

Andalucía
Córdoba
Jaén
Murcia
Murcia

Huelva
Sevilla
Granada
Golfo de Cádiz
Málaga
Almería
Cádiz

Estrecho de Gibraltar
Ceuta (España)
MARRUECOS

Islas Canarias

La Palma
Lanzarote
La Gomera
Tenerife
Fuerteventura
Gran Canaria
El Hierro

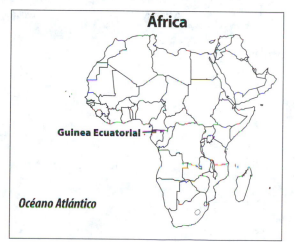

África

Guinea Ecuatorial

Océano Atlántico

América del Sur

Mar Caribe

Barranquilla

Caracas ✪

VENEZUELA

Cúcuta
•San Cristobal

Océano Atlántico

GUAYANA

SURINAME

GUAYANA FRANCESA (FRANCIA)

•Medellín

•Bogotá

•Cali

COLOMBIA

Mitú•

✪ Quito

ECUADOR

•Guayaquil

BRASIL

ISLAS GALÁPAGOS

•Iquitos

•Piura

PERÚ

•Trujillo

✪ Lima

•Cusco

BOLIVIA

•Ica

•Trinidad

Océano Pacífico

Arequipa•

✪ La Paz

•Cochabamba

Arica•

•Santa Cruz

✪ Sucre

PARAGUAY

•Antofagasta

✪ Asunción

CHILE

San Miguel de Tucumán•

Resistencia•

•Córdoba

•Salto

Rosario•

URUGUAY

Mendoza•

Montevideo

Valparaíso•

✪

Santiago•

Buenos Aires ✪

Océano Atlántico

ARGENTINA

•Concepción

•Mar del Plata

•Valdivia

•San Carlos de Bariloche

ISLAS MALVINAS (R.U.)

500 km

500 mi.

México, América Central y el Caribe

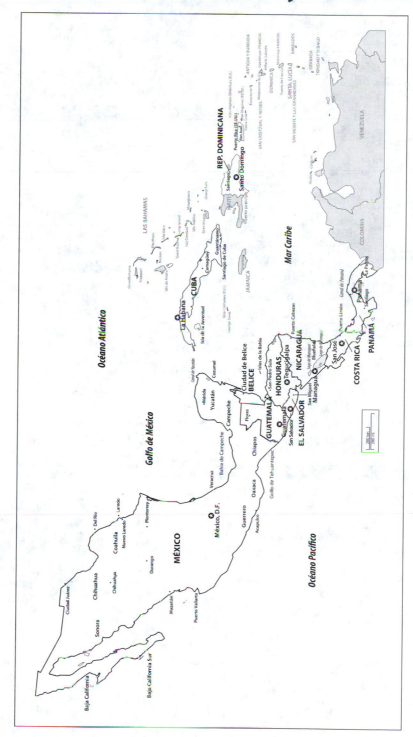

El español en los Estados Unidos

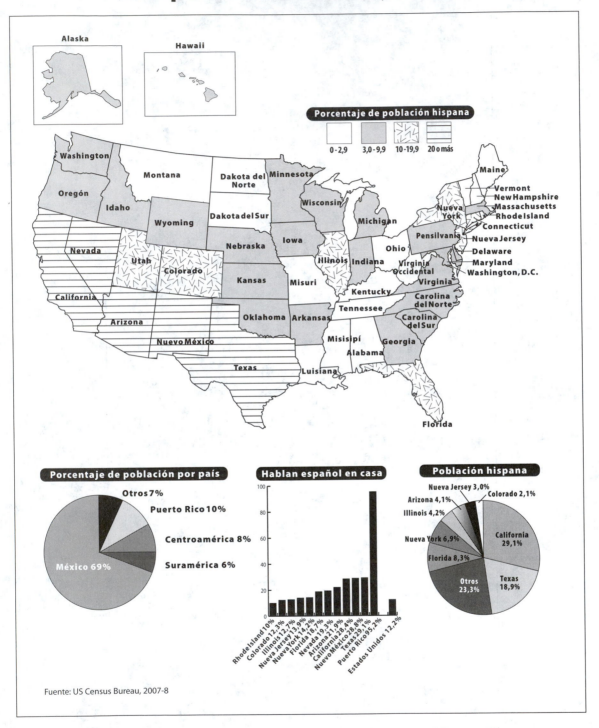

Porcentaje de población hispana

0-2,9 | 3,0-9,9 | 10-19,9 | 20 o más

Porcentaje de población por país

- Otros 7%
- Puerto Rico 10%
- Centroamérica 8%
- Suramérica 6%
- México 69%

Hablan español en casa

Rhode Island 10%
Colorado 12,3%
Illinois 12,7%
Nueva Jersey 13,9%
Nueva York 14,2%
Florida 18,7%
Nevada 19,3%
Arizona 21,9%
California 28,4%
Nuevo México 28,8%
Texas 29,1%
Puerto Rico 95,2%
Estados Unidos 12,2%

Población hispana

- Nueva Jersey 3,0%
- Colorado 2,1%
- Arizona 4,1%
- Illinois 4,2%
- Nueva York 6,9%
- Florida 8,3%
- Otros 23,3%
- California 29,1%
- Texas 18,9%

Fuente: US Census Bureau, 2007-8

The Spanish language
La lengua española

1.A Letters

Las letras

Letters represent *phonemes*: distinct sounds in a language which are capable of conveying differences in meaning. One letter can represent multiple phonemes, which in turn can change meanings of words. For example, in English the letter **i** in *wind* (as in weather) and *wind* (the act of twisting, as in winding a clock) represents two different phonemes —sounds— that give the words different meanings. This example shows there is no direct correlation between letters and phonemes.

1.B The alphabet

El alfabeto

The Spanish alphabet, or **abecedario**, has twenty-seven letters. It has five vowels and twenty-two consonants. One of the consonants is silent: **h**. **Ch** and **ll** are not letters but **dígrafos** (digraphs). Digraphs are combinations of two letters that represent a single sound, like the English *th* in *those*.

a	a	g	ge	m	eme	s	ese
b	be	h	hache	n	ene	t	te
c	ce	i	i	ñ	eñe	u	u
(ch)	(che)	j	jota	o	o	v	uve/ve
d	de	k	ka	p	pe	w	doble uve / doble ve
e	e	l	ele	q	cu	x	equis
f	efe	(ll)	(elle)	r	erre	y	ye (i griega)
						z	zeta

In the past, **ch** and **ll** had their own entries in dictionaries and reference books, just like the other letters. In 1994, the language academies in Spanish-speaking countries voted to follow the international guidelines for alphabetization. Subsequently, **ch** and **ll** were included under **c** and **l**, respectively. The letter **ñ** retained its own entry. Recent reforms have eliminated **ch** and **ll** from the alphabet.

1.C Pronunciation

Pronunciación

In English and Spanish, spelling, sound, and meaning are interconnected. In English, the vowel often differentiates meaning, as in *pop/pope* or *dove* (a bird)/*dove* (past of *to dive*). In Spanish, the stressed syllable can determine the meaning of a word. Most Spanish words carry the stress on the penultimate syllable.

Stress and accents: 1.E

habl**o**   *I speak*   habl**ó**   *he spoke*   cant**o**   *I sing*   cant**ó**   *he sang*

Vowels and consonants

The charts on the next few pages outline how Spanish vowels, consonants, and digraphs are pronounced.

Vocales
a
e
i
o
u

1.C.1 Vowels

The pronunciation of Spanish vowels (**vocales**) is similar to some English vowel sounds. Unlike English, each vowel in Spanish has only one sound.

Spanish vowels	Similar to the following English vowel sounds		Examples	
			Spanish	English meaning
a	**ah** sound	*father*	c**a**sa, **a**la	*house, wing*
e	long **a**	*tell, west*	m**e**sa, p**e**sa	*table, weight*
i	long **e**	*bee, meat*	s**í**, m**i**	*yes, my*
o	long **o**	*more, floor*	y**o**, c**o**c**o**	*I, coconut*
u	long **u**	*food, rude*	l**u**na, t**u**	*moon, your*

1.C.2 Diphthongs

In Spanish, there are strong vowels and weak vowels. **A, e,** and **o** are strong vowels, and **i** and **u** are weak. A diphthong (**diptongo**) is a combination of a strong and a weak vowel, or two weak vowels, in a single syllable. A syllable ending in a vowel + **y** is also considered a diphthong.

Diptongos
ai, ay, au
ia, ua
ei, ey, eu
ie, ue
oi, oy, ou
io, uo
iu, ui, uy

Diphthongs with *a*			Diphthongs with *e*		
ai	b**ai**le	*dance*	ei	s**ei**s	*six*
ay	h**ay**	*there is/are*	ey	r**ey**	*king*
ia	famil**ia**	*family*	ie	c**ie**n	*one hundred*
au	**au**la	*classroom*	eu	**Eu**ropa	*Europe*
ua	c**ua**tro	*four*	ue	b**ue**no	*good*

Diphthongs with *o*			Diphthongs with *u, i*		
oi	**oi**go	*I hear*	iu	c**iu**dad	*city/town*
oy	s**oy**	*I am*	ui	r**ui**do	*noise*
io	qu**io**sco	*kiosk/newsstand*	uy	m**uy**	*very*
ou	b**ou**	*little boat*			
uo	c**uo**ta	*payment/installment*			

Division of words: 1.D.3 ▶
Accents on vowel combinations: 1.E.4
Hiatus and accentuation: 1.E.5

1.C.3 Triphthongs

When three vowels are pronounced together as one syllable, they create a triphthong (**triptongo**). Triphthongs begin and end with an unstressed **i** or **u** and have a stressed **a, e,** or **o** in the middle: **buey, guiais**. Most triphthongs with **i** or **u** carry a written accent over the letter in the middle. Most words with triphthongs are verb forms used with **vosotros** (*you, pl.*): **enviáis** (*you send*), **continuáis** (*you continue*).

Division of words: 1.D.3 ▶
Accents on vowel combinations: 1.E.4
Hiatus and accentuation: 1.E.5

1.C.4 Combinations: *a, e, o*

When any of the vowels **a, e,** or **o** are paired together, they do not form a diphthong or a triphthong. These combinations always form two syllables: hé-**ro**-e, ca-**o**s, le-**e**r.

1.C.5 *g, c, d, p,* and *t*

The consonants (**consonantes**) **g** and **c** (both before **a, o,** or **u**), and **d** are pronounced with a short aspiration in English. This aspiration does not occur in Spanish. At the beginning of a phrase or after the letter **n**, the Spanish **g** is pronounced like the *g* in *girl*. In any other position, the Spanish **g** has a somewhat softer sound. The consonants **p** and **t** are also pronounced with a short aspiration in English, but not in Spanish.

	Consonants	Examples
b, v	represent the same sound. They are pronounced roughly like the English *b* at the beginning of a word and after **m** and **n**. Between vowels, **b** and **v** are pronounced like a soft English *b* sound; the lips do not close.	**b**ueno (*good*) tam**b**ién (*also*) u**v**a (*grape*)
c	is pronounced like the English *k* in *keep* before **a**, **o**, and **u**, but without aspiration. In most of Spain, **c** is pronounced like an English *th* before **e** and **i**. In Latin America and southern Spain, it is pronounced like an **s**.	**c**asa (*house*) **c**olonia (*colony*) **c**ielo (*sky*) **c**ena (*dinner*)
d	is pronounced roughly like the English *d* at the beginning of a word and after **l** or **n**. Between vowels and in other positions the **d** has a soft sound (almost like an English *th*).	**d**iez (*ten*) fal**d**a (*skirt*) bo**d**a (*wedding*) Pe**d**ro
f	is pronounced like the English *f*.	**f**in (*end*)
g	is pronounced like the English *g* in *go* before **a**, **o**, or **u**, and **-ui** or **-ue** (**gue**, **gui**). Before **e** and **i**, the **g** is pronounced like the Spanish **j**. (See below.)	**g**ato (*cat*) **g**uerra (*war*) **g**igante (*giant*) **g**ente (*folk*)
h	is silent.	**h**ola (*hello*) a**h**ora (*now*)
j	is pronounced in Spanish like a *guttural sound* with varying strength depending on the region. In Latin America, the pronunciation varies from a strong to a very weak English *h*.	**j**efe (*boss*) a**j**o (*garlic*) **j**oven (*young*)
k	is pronounced like the English *k* without aspiration.	**k**ilo (*kilogram*)
l	is pronounced like the English *l*.	**l**indo (*pretty*)
m	is pronounced like the English *m*.	a**m**or (*love*)
n	is pronounced with the tongue a little higher up (towards the back of the teeth) than the English *n*, which is more dental (a little further down).	**n**ada (*nothing*) **n**osotros (*we*) A**n**a
ñ	is pronounced like the *ny* sound in the English word *canyon* or the *ni* sound in the English word *onion*.	ni**ñ**a (*girl*) ma**ñ**ana (*morning*) sue**ñ**o (*dream*)
p	is pronounced like the English *p* without aspiration.	**p**a**p**á (*dad*)
q	is pronounced like the English *k* without aspiration; the letter **q** occurs in Spanish only in the combinations **que** and **qui**.	**q**ueso (*cheese*) a**q**uí (*here*)
r	is pronounced as a strong trill at the beginning of words and after **n, l,** and **s**. Otherwise the **r** is pronounced with a very short, loose, and simple hit of the tongue. Note that a **rr** combination represents a strong trill between vowels. See the digraphs chart on the next page.	**r**osa (*rose*) al**r**ededor (*around*) hon**r**ado (*honest*) co**r**o (*choir*)
s	is pronounced like the English *s* in *summer*, but can vary regionally. In parts of Latin America, southern Spain, and the Caribbean the **s** is aspirated—it is pronounced very soft or it is omitted at the end of a word and before a consonant. In Madrid, the **s** is pronounced with a whistling sound.	**s**ala (*sitting room*) ca**s**a (*house*)
t	is pronounced roughly like the English *t*, but without aspiration.	**t**aza (*cup*)
w	is found only in foreign words and can be pronounced like the English *w* or like the Spanish **b/v**.	**W**ashington

Consonantes

b
v
c
d
f
g
h
j
k
l
m
n
ñ
p
q
r
s
t
w

◀ Omission of the letter **p**: 1.G.3

Variations in the pronunciation of the letter **x**: 1.D.5, 1.G.2a, 3.F.4

x	varies in pronunciation regionally. It can be pronounced like an English *ks*, *gs*, or *s* between vowels. Before a consonant, it is usually pronounced like an **s**. When **x** appears in the name of a Mexican town, it is pronounced like the Spanish **j** or English *h*.	e**x**amen (*exam*) e**x**acto (*exact*) me**x**icano (*Mexican*) Mé**x**ico, Oa**x**aca
y	acts as a vowel with the Spanish **i** sound when it is part of a diphthong. At the beginning of words and between vowels, **y** sounds like the English *y* in *yes*. (See also **ll** for regional variations.)	ho**y** (*today*) **y**uca (*yucca*) pla**y**a (*beach*)
z	is pronounced like the English *th* in most parts of Spain. In Latin America, southern Spain, and the Canary Islands, **z** is pronounced like an **s**. Pronouncing the **z** like an **s** is called **seseo**. (See also **c**.)	**z**apato (*shoe*) a**z**ul (*blue*)

Yeísmo is pronouncing **ll** and **y** like the English *y* in *yes*. It is a common feature in Latin America and in Spain.

	Digraphs	Examples
ch	is pronounced like the English *ch* in chocolate.	**ch**ocolate
ll	is pronounced very much like the English *y* in most parts of Latin America and in many areas of Spain. This is called **yeísmo**. (See also the pronunciation of **y**.) In Argentina, Uruguay, and parts of Paraguay, the **ll** is pronounced similarly to the English *sh*. In central parts of Spain and in some Andean regions of Latin America, the **ll** is pronounced like a continuous **lj** sound.	ca**ll**e (*street*) **ll**ave (*key*)
rr	is a strong rolling **r** sound that occurs between vowels, and it is written with a double **rr**.	ba**rr**o (*mud*) a**rr**oz (*rice*)

1.D Division of words

Separación de las palabras

In writing, it is sometimes necessary to hyphenate words at the end of a line. According to style conventions in Spanish, the words must be divided into syllables; the syllables themselves cannot be divided.

1.D.1 Formation of syllables

a. A consonant between two vowels forms a syllable with the second vowel.

ca-**m**a-**r**o-te	*boat cabin*	Ca-**t**a-**l**i-**n**a	*Catalina*
gra-**m**á-**t**i-**c**a	*grammar*	co-**l**e-**g**io	*school*

b. The consonants **b, c, f, g,** and **p** followed by **l** or **r** form syllables with the subsequent vowel.

a-**cr**í-li-co	*acrylic*	en-**cr**ip-ta-do	*encrypted*	an-**gl**o-sa-jo-na	*Anglo-Saxon*
a-**br**a-si-vo	*abrasive*	a-**fr**i-ca-no	*African*	em-**pl**e-a-do	*employee*

c. The consonants **t** and **d** followed by **r** form syllables with the subsequent vowel.

Pe-**dr**o	*Pedro*	ras-**tr**i-llo	*rake*	a-**tr**o-ci-dad	*atrocity*

d. The combination **tl** stays united in one syllable in Latin America and the Canary Islands; it is split between two syllables in the rest of Spain.

Latin America	Spain	
a-**tl**e-ta	a**t-l**e-ta	*athlete*
a-**tl**as	a**t-l**as	*atlas*

e. Other consonant pairs are split between two syllables when they occur in the middle of a word.

pri**s-m**a	*prism*	a**c-c**ión	*action*	co**n-s**o-na**n-t**e	*consonant*

f. When **l** or **r** occur last in a group of three consonants, the last two consonants stay together.

co**m-pr**o-mi-so	*compromise*	si**m-pl**e	*simple*
si**n-cr**o-ni-zar	*to synchronize*	a**m-pl**iar	*to enlarge/extend*

1.D.2 Diphthongs and triphthongs

Vowel groups which form a diphthong or a triphthong cannot be split.

ja-**guar**	*jaguar*	qu**ie**-ro	*I want*	v**iei**-ra	*scallop*
s**ue**l-do	*salary*	d**ue**r-mo	*I sleep/am sleeping*	U-ru-**guay**	*Uruguay*

1.D.3 Other vowels

Vowel groups that do not form a diphthong or triphthong can be split into syllables, but stylistically they should stay together.

a-ho-ra	*now*	ca-os	*chaos*	ca-er	*to fall*
le-er	*to read*	cre-o	*I believe*	ca-ca-o	*cocoa*

> However, when hyphenating at the end of a line of text, vowel groups that do not form a diphthong should not be divided: **aho-ra, ca-cao.**

1.D.4 *ch, ll, rr*

These letter pairs cannot be split.

an-**ch**o	*wide*	a-**ll**í	*there*	ca-**rr**e-ta	*wagon*
te-**ch**o	*ceiling/roof*	ca-**ll**e	*street*	pe-**rr**o	*dog*

> Digraphs: 1.C.6

1.D.5 The letter *x*

X represents two phonemes [ks]. When it occurs between vowels, **x** forms a syllable with the second vowel. If **x** is followed by a consonant, it forms a syllable with the previous vowel.

> Variations in the pronunciation of the letter **x**: 1.C.6, 1.G.2a, 3.F.4

Division of words with *x*			
e-**xa**-men	*exam*	tó-**xi**-co	*toxic*
[e-**ksa**-men]		[tó-ksi-ko]	
ex-cep-ción	*exception*	**ex**-plicar	*explain*
[e**ks**-cep-ción]		[e**ks**-pli-kar]	

1.E Stress and accents

Acentuación

In Spanish, there are two kinds of accents. The accent that indicates the stressed syllable of a word is the **acento prosódico** (*prosodic accent*). The **acento diacrítico** (*diacritical accent*) distinguishes two words that are otherwise spelled the same: **mi** (*my*), **mí** (*me*).

The following rules explain the regular pronunciation of Spanish words, when to use the **tilde** or **acento gráfico**, and the accentuation of diphthongs and triphthongs.

Acentos
(á)
(é)
(í)
(ó)
(ú)

> Pronunciation: 1.C

1.E.1 Stress on the final syllable: *Palabras agudas*

Most words that end in a consonant other than **n** or **s** are stressed on the final syllable. No accent is needed in these cases.

pa-pe**l**	*paper*	ciu-da**d**	*city/town*	es-cri-bi**r**	*to write*

If a word ends in **n, s,** or a vowel and is stressed on the final syllable, a written accent is needed.

ha-bl**é**	*I spoke*	ca-j**ó**n	*box*	qui-z**á**s	*maybe*

One exception is when a word ends in *consonant* + **-s**; a written accent is not needed in this case. This rule usually affects technological or foreign words, such as **robots**.

1.E.2 **Stress on the penultimate syllable:** *Palabras llanas o graves*

Most words that end in **n, s,** or a vowel are stressed on the penultimate syllable. No accent is needed in these cases.

me-sa   *table*   **can**-tan   *they sing/are singing*   lec-**cio**-nes   *lessons*

If a word ends in any consonant other than **n** or **s**, and is stressed on the penultimate syllable, a written accent is needed.

fá-cil   *easy*   **ál**-bum   *album*   a-**zú**-car   *sugar*

Words in this group that end in **-s** preceded by another consonant carry a written accent (**bíceps**), as do plurals of some foreign words, such as **cómics.**

1.E.3 **Other cases:** *Palabras esdrújulas y sobreesdrújulas*

If the stress falls before the penultimate syllable, the stressed syllable must always be marked with a written accent, regardless of the word's ending or length.

cá-ma-ra   *camera*   ce-**rá**-mi-ca   *ceramic*   e-**léc**-tri-co   *electric*
rá-pi-do   *fast*   **más**-ca-ra   *mask*   **sá**-ba-na   *sheet*

When one or more pronouns are added to an imperative, the number of syllables increases and usually the word will need a written accent on or before the third-to-last syllable.

es**crí**beme   *write to me*   **llá**melos   *call them*
cómpratelos   *buy them for yourself*   ex**plí**camelo   *explain it to me*
de**mués**tranoslo   *show it to us*   **dí**gaselo   *tell it to him*

1.E.4 **Accents on vowel combinations**

Diphthongs: 1.C.2
Triphthongs: 1.C.3

Diphthongs and triphthongs follow the accentuation rules of **palabras agudas, palabras llanas,** and **palabras esdrújulas.** When the stress falls on the syllable with the diphthong or triphthong, there are rules that dictate which vowel will carry the accent mark. In these cases, it is useful to remember that the vowels **a, e,** and **o** are considered **fuertes** (*strong*) and the vowels **u** and **i** are **débiles** (*weak*). Diphthongs and triphthongs are either a combination of strong vowels and unstressed weak vowels (**ai, eu,** etc.) or a combination of weak vowels (**ui, uy, iu**). The combination of two strong vowels never forms a diphthong.

a. When a syllable with a diphthong or triphthong requires an accent for stress, the strong vowel carries the written accent and the pronunciation of the diphthong or triphthong is usually maintained. In the following list, we see that **cuen-ta** does not carry a written accent because it ends in a vowel and the stress is on the penultimate syllable (**llana**). **Cuén-ta-me** does have a written accent because the stress is on the third-to-last syllable (**esdrújula**); the accent goes over the strong vowel, **e.**

<u>cue</u>n-ta   <u>cué</u>n-ta-me   can-<u>tas</u>-t<u>ei</u>s   can-<u>téi</u>s   U-ru-g<u>uay</u>   en-v<u>iái</u>s
a-<u>ma</u>-b<u>ai</u>s   a-<u>mái</u>s   fun-<u>cio</u>-na   fun-<u>ció</u>n   <u>buey</u>   a-ve-ri-g<u>üéi</u>s

b. If the stress falls on the weak vowel of a *weak vowel + strong vowel* combination that would normally form a diphthong or triphthong, the vowels split to form part of different syllables. This break in the vowels is called **hiato** (*hiatus*). In this case, the stressed weak vowel always carries a written accent.

Hiatus and accentuation: 1.E.5

Regional differences in pronunciation can create a diphthong or hiatus; for example, **mie-do** is pronounced with a diphthong, while the same combination of vowels can be pronounced with a hiatus in some regions of Spain and Latin America: **su-fri-e-ron.** 1.C.2, 1.C.3, 1.E.5

One syllable	Hiatus: Different syllables
La serie es continua. (con-<u>ti</u>-n<u>ua</u>)	La fiesta continúa. (con-ti-n<u>ú</u>-a)

When the first weak vowel in a combination of three vowels that would normally form a triphthong is stressed, it stands as a separate syllable while the other two vowels form a diphthong.

oiríais (oi-<u>rí</u>-<u>ai</u>s)   salíais (sa-<u>lí</u>-<u>ai</u>s)   comprendíais (com-pren-<u>dí</u>-<u>ai</u>s)

c. The combination of the weak vowels **i** and **u** forms a diphthong for the purpose of spelling, although it can sometimes be pronounced as either a diphthong or a hiatus.

ciudad (c**iu**-dad) cuidado (c**ui**-da-do) ruido (r**ui**-do)
construir (cons-tr**uir**, also pronounced cons-tru-**ir**)

d. When two weak vowels are combined and the stress falls on the second vowel in the pair, a diphthong is formed and the word follows the regular rules of accentuation. For example, if the diphthong appears in the third-to-last syllable, the second vowel carries a written accent. Note that the accent is always written on the second vowel.

cuídate (c**uí**-da-te) lingüística (lin-g**üís**-ti-ca)

1.E.5 Hiatus and accentuation

A *hiatus* (**hiato**) is formed when two or more sequential vowels in a word are not pronounced together as one syllable. In Spanish, a hiatus occurs in the following cases:

a. When the vowels **a**, **e**, and **o** are combined in pairs, they *always* form a hiatus. This also applies when the letter **h** occurs between two of those vowels.

Combinations: *a, e, o*: 1.C.4
Accents on vowel combinations: 1.E.4

ah**o**ra	a-h**o**-ra	*now*	real**i**dad	re-a-li-dad	*reality*
p**oe**ta	po-**e**-ta	*poet*	te**o**rema	te-o-re-ma	*theorem*

b. Double vowels or double vowels separated by an **h** also form a hiatus.

albah**a**ca	al-ba-h**a**-ca	*basil*	micr**oo**ndas	mi-cro-**on**-das	*microwave*
ch**ii**ta	chi-**i**-ta	*Shiite*	pos**ee**r	po-se-**er**	*to own*
c**oo**rdinar	co-**o**r-di-nar	*to coordinate*			

c. The words that appear in the two previous points do not require a written accent according to the rules of accentuation. For example, **poeta** does not carry a written accent because its pronunciation is regular. The stress falls on the vowel **e** (the penultimate syllable) and the word ends in a vowel. The following words, however, require a written accent because they are **esdrújulas** (stress on the third-to-last syllable).

Palabras agudas: 1.E.1
Palabras esdrújulas: 1.E.3

a**é**reo	a-**é**-re-o	*aerial*	cr**é**eme	cr**é**-e-me	*believe me*
ca**ó**tico	ca-**ó**-ti-co	*chaotic*	te**ó**rico	te-**ó**-ri-co	*theoretic*

d. Words that have a strong vowel combined with a weak, stressed vowel always form a hiatus and require a written accent over the stressed vowel. Because the accent is breaking a diphthong, it is required even if other rules for accentuation do not call for it. For example, the word **increíble** is **llana** (stressed on the penultimate syllable) and ends in a vowel, a case which normally does not call for an accent. However, because the **i** is stressed, an accent is required to reflect the correct pronunciation.

Palabras llanas o graves: 1.E.2

ba**ú**l	ba-**ú**l	incre**í**ble	in-cre-**í**-ble	o**í**r	o-**í**r
b**ú**ho	b**ú**-ho	m**í**o	m**í**-o	pa**í**s	pa-**í**s
d**í**a	d**í**-a	proh**í**be	pro-h**í**-be	sonr**í**e	son-r**í**-e

1.E.6 Diacritical marks

The written accent, or **tilde**, indicates the stressed syllable of a word and visually marks the stressed vowel. In speech, the stress on a syllable is called the **acento prosódico** (*prosodic accent*). The **acento diacrítico** (*diacritical accent*) is a written accent mark used to distinguish two words that are otherwise spelled the same.

Spanish relative pronouns: 15.A.2, Question words and exclamations: 1.E.7

a. One-syllable words (**palabras monosílabas**) have only one vowel, or, if they have more than one, they do not have a hiatus (**hiato**). One-syllable words usually do not carry a written accent.

bien mal no si un cien muy pie sol vas

b. A diacritical accent is necessary to differentiate these pairs of words:

de	of, from	dé	imperative of **dar** (to give)
el	definite article	él	he
mi	my	mí	me/myself
se	himself, herself, itself, themselves, yourself (formal)	sé	I know; imperative of **ser** (to be)
si	if	sí	yes; yourself/yourselves/him/himself/her/herself/themselves (object of a preposition)
tu	your	tú	you
te	you/yourself	té	tea
mas	but	más	more

Somos **de** Nueva York.   We are from New York.
Por favor, **dé** usted una donación.   Please give a donation.
El chico habla francés y español.   The boy speaks French and Spanish.
Hoy viene **él**, ella no.   He is coming today, but she is not.
Mi padre es Lorenzo.   My father is Lorenzo.
Nora siempre me llama a **mí**.   Nora always calls me.
Viviana **se** mira en el espejo.   Viviana is looking at herself in the mirror.
Sé mucho español.   I know a lot of Spanish.
Sé un buen chico.   Be a good boy.
Si vas a viajar, llámame.   If you're going to travel, call me.
—¿Quieres viajar a Madrid? —¡**Sí**!   —Do you want to go to Madrid? —Yes!
Sólo piensa en **sí** mismo.   He only thinks of himself.
Yo soy **tu** amigo.   I am your friend.
¿Quién eres **tú**?   Who are you?
¿**Te** gusta el **té**?   Do you like tea?
Quiero ir, **mas** no puedo.   I want to go, but I can't.
No hay nada que me guste **más**.   There's nothing I like better.

Aun/aún: 10.B.4, 16.C.6

c. *Aun, aún*
The word **aun** can mean *even, until, also,* or *including,* but the written accent on **aún** changes the meaning to *still* or *yet.*

Estoy cansado, **aun** después de pasar una buena noche.   *I am tired even after a good night´s sleep.*

¡**Aún** estoy esperando a Luisa!   *I am still waiting for Luisa!*

d. *Solo, sólo*
The word **solo** can be an adjective or an adverb. As an adjective, it never carries a written accent. The adverb can carry an accent in case of ambiguity; however, according to the *Nueva ortografía*, it is not required. As an adverb, a synonym can also be used: **solamente**, **únicamente**.

¿Estás **solo** en casa?   *Are you home alone?*   **Sólo/Solo** estaré en casa hoy.   *I will only be home today.*

Demonstratives: Ch. 8

e. The demonstratives **este, ese,** and **aquel** and their feminine and plural forms used to carry an accent when they functioned as pronouns and there was risk of ambiguity. It is still possible to use the written accent in case of ambiguity, but it is not required.

1.E.7 Question words and exclamations

a. The following words always carry a written accent when their function is interrogative or exclamative:

cómo	*how*	dónde	*where*	quién(es)	*who*	cuánto/a(s)	*how much/many*
qué	*what*	cuándo	*when*	cuál	*which*	cuáles	*which*

¿**Cómo** estás? — *How are you?*

¿**Qué** estudias? — *What are you studying?*

¿**Dónde** estudias? — *Where are you studying?*

¿**Cuándo** vas a la clase? — *When are you going to class?*

¿**Quién** es tu profesor? — *Who is your teacher?*

¿**Cuál** es tu asignatura favorita? — *What is your favorite subject?*

¿**Cuánto** pagas en la universidad? — *How much do you pay at the university?*

¿**Cuáles** son tus libros? — *Which books are yours?*

¡**Qué** hermoso día! — *What a beautiful day!*

¡**Cómo** puedes decir eso! — *How can you say that!*

¡**Cuántos** libros tienes! — *You have so many books!*

Diacritical marks: 1.E.6
Spanish relative pronouns: 15.A.2
Questions and question words: Ch. 14

b. These words also carry a written accent in sentences with an indirect question:

No sé **cuánto** cuesta el libro. — *I don't know how much this book costs.*

Dime **dónde** vives. — *Tell me where you live.*

En las noticias dicen **qué** sucedió. — *They explain what happened on the news.*

En *Google* encuentras **cómo** llegar aquí. — *You can use Google to find out how to get here.*

No recuerdo **cuándo** es su cumpleaños. — *I don't remember when her birthday is.*

Indirect questions: 31.B.6d

1.E.8 Adverbs ending in *-mente*

Adverbs ending in **-mente** are formed using the feminine adjective as the base. These words are special in Spanish because they have two prosodic accents: that of the adjective and that of the ending **-mente.** In order to determine whether the adverb needs an accent mark, look at the adjective base. If the adjective has an accent, as in **fácil**, the adverb keeps it: **fácilmente.** If the adjective does not have an accent, as in **tranquila**, the adverb does not either: **tranquilamente.**

Adverbs ending in **-mente**: 10.G

Stress and accents: 1.E

bueno	buenamente	cortés	cortésmente
claro	claramente	difícil	difícilmente
preferible	preferiblemente	pésimo	pésimamente
terrible	terriblemente	rápido	rápidamente

1.E.9 Accentuation of plurals and compound words

Most nouns and adjectives conserve the accent on the same stressed syllable in both the singular and plural form: **fácil/fáciles, cámara/cámaras.** However, the use of a written accent can also vary when forming the plural.

a. Some words gain a syllable in the plural and become **esdrújulas**. The accented syllable remains the same, but a written accent must be added in the plural to reflect the correct stress.

Plural formation: 2.B

Palabras esdrújulas: 1.E.3

crimen	crímenes	joven	jóvenes
examen	exámenes	orden	órdenes
imagen	imágenes	origen	orígenes

Irregular plurals: 2.B.2c ▶

b. The following are examples of words that are irregular because the accented syllable, either written or spoken, is different in the singular and plural.

carácter	caracteres
régimen	regímenes
espécimen	especímenes

In the plural, these words ▶ are no longer **agudas**. Since they are now **llanas** and end in **-s**, a written accent is not required: 1.E.1, 1.E.2, 2.B.1d

c. When a word ends in a stressed syllable with a written accent, as in **televisión, revés,** and **corazón,** the written accent is not necessary in the plural.

revés	reveses	ecuación	ecuaciones
cortés	corteses	nación	naciones
faisán	faisanes	sillón	sillones
confín	confines	fusión	fusiones
delfín	delfines	misión	misiones
jardín	jardines	pensión	pensiones
pequeñín	pequeñines	televisión	televisiones
sillón	sillones	versión	versiones
belén	belenes	corazón	corazones
sartén	sartenes	razón	razones
edición	ediciones	atún	atunes

Hyphen: 1.F.6a ▶

d. Compound words written as one word follow Spanish rules of accentuation. When the words are separated by a hyphen, they conserve their original accentuation.

tragicómico	político-social
lavaplatos	socio-económico
hispanoamericano	técnico-administrativo

1.E.10 Words with varied accentuation

In Spanish, some words allow for different accentuation without changing meaning. Using one form over the other can be regional or personal preference. Some common examples are:

básquetbol	basquetbol	maníaco/a	maniaco/a
chófer	chofer	olimpíada	olimpiada
cóctel	coctel	paradisíaco/a	paradisiaco/a
fríjol	frijol	período	periodo
fútbol	futbol	policíaco/a	policiaco/a
hipocondríaco/a	hipocondriaco/a	vídeo	video
ícono	icono	zodíaco	zodiaco

1.E.11 Accentuation of capital letters

Use of capital letters: 1.G.1 ▶

Capital letters require a written accent according to the rules of accentuation, whether the capital letter is the first letter of the word or the word is written entirely in capitals. Due to past typographical and printing constraints, this rule was not always possible to follow. Therefore, there are still older signs or books that do not follow it.

Él se llama Héctor.   Me llamo Miguel **Á**ngel.   ¡DETÉNGASE!

1.F Punctuation

Puntuación

Punctuation in Spanish is very similar to English. Note these uses:

1.F.1 [.] Period

a. Sentences

As in English, the period (**punto**) marks the end of a sentence. If you are dictating, say **punto [y] seguido** to indicate that the sentence should end and the paragraph should continue. To indicate that the sentence and the paragraph should end, say **punto [y] aparte**.

Sentences ending with an abbreviation do not need an additional period.

Visitaremos los EE.UU.	*We will visit the U.S.*

Sentences ending with an ellipsis, or exclamation or question marks, do not need a period unless the sentence is enclosed in parentheses or quotes.

¡Iremos al Cañón del Colorado! Es un sitio majestuoso... Llegaremos allí mañana.	*We will go the Grand Canyon! It's a majestic site... We will arrive there tomorrow.*

b. Abbreviations, acronyms, and symbols

Abbreviations are always followed by a period. Symbols never are; acronyms in all capital letters may or may not be.

 Use of capital letters: 1.G.1g

Abbreviation	Symbol	Acronym
Sr. (señor)	kg (kilo)	ONU (Organización de las Naciones Unidas) *UN*
Ud. (usted)	lb (libra, *pound*)	EE. UU. (Estados Unidos de América) *USA*

Abbreviations of ordinal numbers: 6.D.5

Spanish abbreviations of ordinal numbers have a period before the small superscript sign showing the noun's number and/or gender ending.

1.er piso   *first floor*   3.^{a} salida   *third exit*

c. Numbers

Hours and minutes are separated by a period or a colon. Number-only dates are separated by slashes, periods, or hyphens (less common).

La fecha y hora de nacimiento de las gemelas fue: 9.10.2010 a las 5:27 p.m.	*The date and time of the twin girls' birth was: October ninth 2010 at five twenty-seven in the afternoon.*

The standard date format in Spanish is day/month/year: 6.G.1

Thousands and millions are notated by a period in some countries and by a comma in others. The formal rule requires a space to separate the thousands when the number has five or more digits. The comma is the most common sign used to separate decimals in Spanish, although the decimal point is also used in some countries.

Writing styles for numbers: 6.A.1 Numbers and counting expressions: 6.C.2

Current norm		Period	Comma	Decimals	
1000	10 000	10.000	10,000	10,2	10.2
mil	diez mil			diez coma dos	diez punto dos

A period should not be used in the numerical expression of years, page numbers, street numbers, or zip codes, nor in articles, decrees, or laws.

el año 2012   página 2345   calle Príncipe, 1034   28010 Madrid

d. Addresses

Street numbers and postal codes do not have a period, except when there is an abbreviation.

La dirección del Hospital General de México es: Calle Dr. Balmis N.º 148, Col. Doctores, Delegación Cuauhtémoc, C. P. 06726, México, D. F.

Internet URLs and e-mail addresses use periods to separate elements. Note how they are read in Spanish.

Spain: **uve doble** (w) ▶
Lat. Am.: **doble ve** (w)

http://www.whitehouse.gov	*Hache-te-te-pe-dos puntos-barra doble-uve doble-uve doble-uve doble (o triple uve doble)-punto-white house-punto-gov*
minombre.miapellido@miservidor.com	*Mi nombre-punto-mi apellido-arroba-mi servidor-punto-com*

`1.F.2` [,] Comma

Non-defining relative ▶
clauses: 15.B.1

a. Inserted clauses that are not essential for the meaning of a sentence start and end with a comma (**coma**), as in English.

El profesor, **que es joven**, trabaja mucho.   *The teacher, who is young, works a lot.*

Defining relative clauses: ▶
15.B.2

b. Clauses that are necessary for the meaning of a sentence do not have a comma.

El profesor **que es joven** trabaja mucho; el otro profesor, no.   *The young teacher works a lot; the other doesn't.*

c. Use a comma to separate a person's name from an inverted exclamation or question mark.

Hola, **Patricia**, ¿cómo estás?   *Hi, Patricia, how are you?*
Martín, ¡bienvenido a casa!   *Welcome home, Martin!*

d. Use a comma after a **si** clause at the beginning of a sentence.

Conditional *si* clauses: 23.E.8 ▶

Si vas al mercado, compra manzanas.   *If you go to the market, buy apples.*
Compra manzanas si vas al mercado.   *Buy apples if you go to the market.*

e. A comma may be used to replace an implied verb.

Ana fue al parque; **Paula**, al cine.   *Ana went to the park; Paula, to the movies.*

f. A comma is used before the words **como** and **pero**.

Quiero algo dulce, **como** chocolate.   *I want something sweet, like chocolate.*
Tengo sueño, **pero** quiero jugar.   *I'm tired, but I want to play.*

g. Commas are used to separate items in enumerated lists. In Spanish, it is incorrect to use a comma before the last item in the series.

Tengo **libros, papel y lápices.**   *I have books, paper, and pencils.*

`1.F.3` [;] Semicolon

a. The semicolon (**punto y coma**) is used to enumerate groups of things which are separated internally by a comma and/or **y**.

Tengo papel, libros y lápices; cuadernos y computadoras.   *I have paper, books, and pencils; notebooks and computers.*

b. A semicolon is used to link two independent clauses without connecting words.

Voy a la fiesta; no me voy a quedar mucho tiempo.   *I am going to the party; I am not going to stay long.*

c. A semicolon is used before a dependent clause that begins with a conjunction or phrase such as **sin embargo, por lo tanto, no obstante, por consiguiente, en cambio,** and **en fin.**

Llovió mucho; sin embargo, fuimos al parque.   *It rained heavily; however, we went to the park.*

1.F.4　[:] Colon

a. Colons (**dos puntos**) are used after the person's name in a salutation for a letter or e-mail. The colon is more formal than a comma.

Direct discourse: 31.A.1

Querida Paula**:** Espero que estés muy bien.　　*Dear Paula: I hope all is well with you.*

b. A colon is also used before the enumeration of several elements.

Tengo muchos amigos: Luis, Marta, Patricia, Frank, Adam y Sarah.　　*I have many friends: Luis, Marta, Patricia, Frank, Adam, and Sarah.*

c. A colon is used to separate a clarification, explanation, cause, consequence, summary, conclusion, or example from a preceding independent clause.

Siempre me dice lo mismo: que busque trabajo.　　*He always tells me the same thing: to get a job.*

1.F.5　Questions and exclamations

In Spanish, questions can be asked without changing the sentence structure, as is done in English. The opening question mark conveys the intonation that must be used in order to pronounce the statement as a question. The same occurs with an opening exclamation mark. Opening exclamation marks can be placed anywhere you wish to start an exclamation and where the voice must be raised, even if it is in the middle of the sentence.

Questions and question words: Ch. 14

a. [¿ ?] Question marks – *Signos de interrogación*
The beginning of a question is marked with an inverted question mark. As in English, if the question is part of a longer sentence, a comma separates it.

¿Qué día es hoy**?**　　*What day is it today?*　　Hace frío, ¿verdad**?**　　*It's cold, isn't it?*

b. [¡ !] Exclamation marks – *Signos de admiración o exclamación*
Exclamation marks are always placed at the beginning and end of an exclamation and follow a comma when placed within a sentence.

¡Qué bonito día**!**　　*What a lovely day!*　　Me gusta la paella, ¡es deliciosa**!**　　*I like paella. It's delicious!*

1.F.6　[-] Hyphen

The hyphen (**guión corto**) is a short dash that is used in writing to join or separate words.

a. The hyphen joins words to form a compound word. When two adjectives are joined, only the last one agrees with the noun in gender and number; the first is always singular and masculine.

Accentuation of plurals and compound words: 1.E.9d

tareas teórico-prácticas　　*theoretical and practical homework*
textos histórico-religiosos　　*texts about history and religion*

Words that indicate origin (**gentilicios**) can be written with or without a hyphen.

colombo-irlandés/irlandesa　　*of Colombian and Irish origin*
franco-alemán/alemana　　*of French and German origin*
afroamericano/a　　*Afro-American*

It is also possible to use a hyphen to create new concepts.

¡Luis tiene una **casa-mansión** enorme!　　*Luis has a huge mansion-like house!*

b. The hyphen separates syllables of a word when the word does not fit on a line of text. In order to divide the word, it is necessary to follow the Spanish rules for dividing words into syllables.

Division of words: 1.D. Abbreviations, acronyms, and symbols: 1.F.1b

pan-ta-lla　　co-rres-pon-den-cia　　sal-chi-cha　　com-pren-sión　　cons-ti-tu-ción
(*screen*)　　(*correspondence*)　　(*sausage*)　　(*comprehension*)　　(*constitution*)

Stylistically, it is preferable not to leave one letter alone on a line. Also, abbreviations (**Srta.**) and acronyms (**ONU, EE.UU.**) should not be divided.

c. The hyphen indicates part of a word in grammar texts, word lists, and dictionaries. The position of the hyphen indicates whether the segment goes at the beginning, middle, or end of a word.

El sufijo **-ito** se usa en los diminutivos: libr**ito**.	*The suffix **-ito** is used in diminutives: libr**ito**.*
La palabra **ante**pasado contiene el prefijo **ante-**.	*The word **ante**pasado (ancestor) has the prefix **ante-**.*
Las consonantes **-zc-** aparecen en varios verbos: cono**zc**o.	*The consonants **-zc-** appear in several verbs: cono**zc**o.*

d. Time periods or ranges are specified with a hyphen.

Tenemos que estudiar los capítulos 1-3.	*We have to study chapters 1–3.*
El Quijote fue escrito por Miguel de Cervantes (1547-1616).	*El Quijote was written by Miguel de Cervantes (1547–1616).*
Estudié tres años en la universidad (2011-13).	*I studied three years at the university (2011–2013).*

`1.F.7` [——] Dash

The dash (**guión largo** o **raya**) is longer than the hyphen. Its main function is to mark the beginning or end of a segment of text in the following cases:

a. Dashes separate comments that interrupt the text. Commas and parentheses can also serve this function.

Celeste —pensativa— contestó mi pregunta.	*Celeste—thoughtful—answered my question.*

b. Dialogues are indicated with a dash at the beginning of each intervention.

> Notice that in English there is no space in between the dash and the text. However, in Spanish, the dash is separated by one space from the word that precedes it and attached to the first word of the text that interrupts the sentence.

—¿Quieres café?	*"Do you want some coffee?"*
—Sí, muchas gracias.	*"Yes, thank you very much."*

c. In narrations with dialogue, the dash separates dialogue from narration.

—Tengo miedo —dijo Pilar cuando escuchó que alguien intentaba abrir la puerta.
—No tengas miedo —le dijo su madre, aunque ella sabía que no podrían escapar.
"I'm scared," said Pilar when she heard someone was trying to open the door.
"Don't be afraid," said her mother, though she knew they could not escape.

`1.F.8` Quotation marks

Spanish usually uses a different symbol than English to mark quotation marks (**comillas**): « ». However you may also see single or double straight quotes and smart quotes, as in English: ' ' and " ".

a. The main use of quotation marks is to indicate quotes taken from a text, to tell what a person has said, or to cite titles or names of book chapters, articles, reports, or poems. Punctuation of quotes remains inside the quotation marks, but if punctuation is not part of the quoted text, it falls outside the quotes. The period, however, always appears after the quoted text.

Gabriel García Márquez empieza su autobiografía diciendo «Mi madre me pidió que la acompañara a vender la casa».	*Gabriel García Márquez starts his autobiography saying: "My mother asked me to go sell the house with her."*
Según los estudiantes que han leído el libro, «¡Vale la pena leerlo!».	*According to students who have read the book, "It's worth reading it!"*
¿Leíste el artículo «Náufrago en tierra firme»?	*Have you read the article "Castaway on Land"?*

b. Quotation marks can call attention to a word in a text, for example, to explain a word or indicate that it is foreign, improper, wrong, or said with irony.

«**Hablar**» es un verbo regular.	"**Hablar**" (to speak) *is a regular verb.*
Las palabras «quiosco» y «kiosco» son igualmente aceptables.	*The words "**quiosco**" and "**kiosco**" are equally acceptable.*
¡Pablo dice que «sabe» escribir!	*Pablo says he "knows" how to write!*

`1.F.9` [...] Ellipsis

Ellipses (**puntos suspensivos**) may indicate that what is expressed in the sentence is uncertain or unknown, but it also has other uses.

a. Ellipses are used to mean *et cetera* in an incomplete list. A capital letter is used if the following phrase is a new sentence, and other punctuation marks may be used if necessary.

En el colegio tenemos que estudiar, escribir, leer… ¡No tengo tiempo para nada más!	*At school we have to study, we have to write, we have to read… I have no time for anything else!*
Tengo amigos mexicanos, peruanos, cubanos… de todas partes.	*I have friends from Mexico, Peru, Cuba… from all over the world.*

b. Ellipses can also express suspense or uncertainty in the message, for example, when writing letters, e-mails, text messages, etc.

Me gané la lotería y… bueno… no sé qué hacer…	*I won the lottery and… well… I don't know what to do…*
Pienso en ti…	*I think of you…*
Estoy esperando tu llamada…	*I'm waiting for your call…*

c. When quoting a text, ellipses in parentheses or brackets indicate that part of the text has been omitted.

Dice García Márquez en su autobiografía: "No nos tuteábamos, por la rara costumbre (…) de tutearse desde el primer saludo y pasar al usted sólo cuando se logra una mayor confianza (…)".

García Márquez says in his autobiography: "We did not use the tú *form of address, due to the strange custom (…) of using* tú *from the first greeting and switching to* usted *only upon becoming close friends (…)".*

`1.F.10` Parentheses and brackets

Parentheses (**paréntesis**) ( ) and brackets (**corchetes**) [ ] have similar functions.

a. Parentheses enclose text that expands on or clarifies what is said in a sentence, for example, data, dates, names, etc.

Me gusta mucho Nueva York (es una metrópoli impresionante) y quiero volver allí. Es extraño que no sea la capital del estado del mismo nombre (la capital es Albany).

I like New York very much (it is an impressive metropolis) and I want to go there again. It is strange it is not the capital of the state of New York (the capital is Albany).

b. When it is necessary to give alternatives in a text, they can be included in parentheses.

Los (Las) estudiantes tendrán vacaciones pronto.	*The students will be on break soon.*

c. Brackets can replace parentheses. They are also used to add comments or clarifications in a sentence that is already in parentheses. Notes about a text, such as notes from a translator or editor, also go in brackets.

El primer presidente afroamericano (se llama Barack Obama [nacido en Hawaii] de padre keniano y madre norteamericana) subió al poder en 2009.	*The first Afro-American president (called Barack Obama [born in Hawaii], his father was Kenyan and his mother, American) came into power in 2009.*

1.G Spelling

Ortografía

1.G.1 Use of capital letters

Accentuation of capital letters: 1.E.11

a. Days of the week and months are not capitalized in Spanish as they are in English.

lunes	domingo	viernes	mayo	abril	enero
Monday	*Sunday*	*Friday*	*May*	*April*	*January*

b. All proper nouns begin with a capital letter. Articles or nouns that are part of the proper noun are also capitalized. Adjectives formed from proper nouns are not written with a capital letter. This rule is also valid for names of religions and their followers (adjectives).

Pedro	Luisita	Júpiter	Google	Facebook
Venezuela	**venezolano/a**	La Habana	**habanero/a**	
Cristianismo	**cristiano/a**	Protestantismo	**protestantes**	

c. Prepositions that are part of a Spanish last name are not capitalized except when the last name appears alone. If only the definite article is present, it is always capitalized.

Alejandro de la Hoz   Sr. De la Hoz   Susana la Salle   Sra. La Salle

d. Only the first word in a title is capitalized in Spanish, unless the title includes a proper noun. However, capitals in all words of a title are becoming increasingly used in official settings.

La isla bajo el mar es una novela de Isabel Allende.	*Island Beneath the Sea* is a novel by Isabel Allende.
Instituto Nacional de Salud (Bogotá)	National Institute of Health (*Bogotá*)
Centro Nacional de Educación Básica a Distancia (Cenebad, Madrid)	National Center for Long-Distance Basic Education (*Cenebad, Madrid*)

e. As in English, the first letter of a sentence is always capitalized. After a colon, capitals are normally not used in Spanish. However, capitals are used after a colon in the salutation of a letter or e-mail or if the text that follows a colon is a full quote.

Esta es la primera oración de este párrafo. Continuamos con la segunda oración aquí y terminamos este texto con estas últimas palabras: ¡has leído hasta el final!
This is the first sentence in this paragraph. We continue with the second sentence here and we end this text with these final words: You have read to the end!

f. In Spanish, exclamation marks and question marks can end sentences, in which case the new sentence starts with a capital letter. However, unlike English, a comma can also separate a series of exclamations and/or questions.

¿Sabes cuándo es la fiesta? Creo que será pronto, ¿verdad?	*Do you know when the party is? I think it will be soon, won't it?*
¿Cómo estás?, ¿sigues viviendo en Miami?, ¡cuéntame toda la historia!	*How are you? Still living in Miami? Tell me everything!*

Abbreviations, acronyms, and symbols: 1.F.1b

g. All capitals are used for acronyms of four letters or less. When they are longer, usually only the first letter is capitalized. When acronyms become common nouns, the name is written with lowercase letters.

Insalud	Instituto Nacional de Salud
SIDA (*AIDS*)	Síndrome de inmunodeficiencia adquirida

1.G.2 Place names

a. The letter **x** in **México** and in other Mexican names and their adjectives, is pronounced like the Spanish **j** when it is the first letter of the word or occurs between vowels. Its pronunciation is /**ks**/ or /**s**/ in consonant combinations.

◀ México: 3.F.4

Name	Adjective	Name	Adjective
México	mexicano/a	Oaxaca	oaxaqueño/a
Xalapa	xalapeño/a / jalapeño/a	San Jerónimo Xayacatlán	xayacateco/a
Tlaxcala	tlaxcalteca	La Mixteca	mixteco/a

b. Names of cities and regions in Spain where other national languages are official may be written in the region's native language.

Catalunya	Euskadi	A Coruña	A Mariña
Cataluña	País Vasco	La Coruña	La Mariña

c. Many cities and geographical places in the world have their own Spanish names or spelling.

Nueva York   Estados Unidos   Venecia   Ginebra   Londres   Holanda   Inglaterra

d. Articles and geographical terms included in the *official* name of a place (city, mountain, river, gulf, etc.) are written in capital letters; otherwise, lowercase is used.

Official name		Description only
el Golfo de México	el Río Bravo	la cordillera de Los Andes
la Ciudad de México	el Río de la Plata	la ciudad de Miami
la Ciudad del Cabo	El Salvador	el río Amazonas
La Paz	El Cairo	la Argentina

e. The names of planets, stars, and constellations are written with a capital letter unless they are used as common nouns.

Los planetas giran alrededor del **Sol**.	Protégete del **sol**.	Los astronautas ven la **Tierra** desde el espacio.	En California, la **tierra** es fértil.
The planets orbit around the Sun.	*Protect yourself from the sun.*	*Astronauts look at the Earth from space.*	*In California, the land is fertile.*

1.G.3 Omission of the letter *p*

a. The letter **p** is silent in words beginning with combination **ps-** (**psicólogo, psiquiatra**). These words may also be spelled without the **p** (**sicólogo, siquiatra**). This spelling is accepted, but in formal texts, these words tend to keep the initial **p**. In words containing **-ps-** (**eclipse, cápsula**), the letter **p** is always kept.

b. Among the words that contain the consonant combination **-pt-**, only **septiembre** and **séptimo/a** (*seventh*) can be spelled **setiembre** and **sétimo/a**.

c. The past participles of many verbs ending in **-bir** end in **-to** in most Spanish-speaking countries, except Argentina and Uruguay, where they are spelled with **-pt-**. This is an archaic form that has remained in use in the **Río de la Plata** region.

◀ Irregular past participles: 19.A.2, 25.D.2

Infinitive	English	Past participle	Past participle (Arg./Uru.)
describir	*to describe*	descrito	descripto
inscribir	*to enroll*	inscrito	inscripto
suscribir	*to subscribe*	suscrito	suscripto

La lengua española

In the Spanish-speaking world, the terms **español** (*Spanish*) or **castellano** (*Castilian*) are used to refer to the Spanish language, which today is one of the most widely spoken languages in the world. Castilian was the language in **Castilla** (*Castile*), the powerful kingdom that united with the kingdom of **Aragón** to form **España** and reached the coasts of the New World in 1492. Castile's language spread quickly to the new continent and the word *Castilian,* therefore, demonstrates the origin of the Spanish language. The term is still associated in Spain with the language variant spoken in today's Castile, the government's center. Spain's constitution (1978) declares that **castellano** is the national language, but that the autonomous provinces can have their own official language in addition to **castellano**. Today **catalán** (*Catalan*), **euskera** (*Basque*), **gallego** (*Galician*), and **valenciano** (*Valencian*) are official languages, along with Castilian, in their regions. Furthermore, there are other languages which are not official, such as those spoken in Asturias and Mallorca.

In most parts of Latin America, **español** and **castellano** are used as synonyms, but the term **español** is more common than **castellano.** The Spanish variant, **español americano** or **español de América,** is the mother tongue of over 90% of the nearly 500 million Spanish-speaking people in the world (including the U.S.). Spanish in Latin America also exists in conjunction with other American languages, such as **maya** and **náhuatl** (in Mexico and Guatemala), **quechua** (in Ecuador, Peru, and Bolivia), **guaraní** (in Paraguay), and **English** (in the Caribbean), among others. In many new Latin American constitutions from the 1990s, the majority of countries declared themselves multicultural and multilingual nations, naming Spanish as their official language or as one of their official languages.

Ever since the 1700s, when the Royal Academy for the Spanish Language (**La Real Academia Española, RAE**) published its first standard works—a dictionary, *Diccionario de autoridades* (1726–1739); a text on spelling, *Ortografía* (1741); and one on grammar, *Gramática* (1771)— their rules have played an important role in retaining the Castilian variant as the norm in the whole of the Spanish-speaking world. Eventually, with the formation of the Association of Spanish Language Academies (**Asociación de Academias de la Lengua Española, ASALE**) in 1951, the Spanish-speaking world was finally treated as a whole in terms of the development and use of the Spanish language. A goal was set to maintain the Spanish-speaking community, but also to recognize and make known the different variations of the Spanish language. This goal led to the release of a common description of the Spanish language in the form of a spelling text (1999), a common dictionary, and a common grammar text (approved by the ASALE in 2007 and published in 2010). An updated spelling text, the *Nueva ortografía*, was approved in late 2010. **A Handbook of Contemporary Spanish Grammar** is written from this integral perspective of the Spanish language.

Asociación de Academias de la Lengua Española (ASALE), 1951: http://asale.org	
Real Academia Española (RAE), 1713	Academia Hondureña de la Lengua, 1948
Academia Argentina de Letras, 1931	Academia Mexicana de la Lengua, 1875
Academia Boliviana de la Lengua, 1927	Academia Nacional de Letras del Uruguay, 1943
Academia Chilena de la Lengua, 1885	Academia Nicaragüense de la Lengua, 1928
Academia Colombiana de la Lengua, 1871	Academia Norteamericana de la Lengua Española, 1973
Academia Costarricense de la Lengua, 1923	Academia Panameña de la Lengua, 1926
Academia Cubana de la Lengua, 1926	Academia Paraguaya de la Lengua Española, 1927
Academia Dominicana de la Lengua, 1927	Academia Peruana de la Lengua, 1887
Academia Ecuatoriana de la Lengua, 1874	Academia Puertorriqueña de la Lengua Española, 1945
Academia Filipina de la Lengua Española, 1924	Academia Salvadoreña de la Lengua, 1876
Academia Guatemalteca de la Lengua, 1887	Academia Venezolana de la Lengua, 1883

Práctica

 Actividades 1–24, pp. A1–A6

Nouns
Sustantivos

Chapter 2

A. Gender
B. Number
C. Appreciative suffixes
D. Regional variations

2.A Gender

Género

Nouns are words that refer to people, animals, objects, places, events, or abstract concepts. In Spanish, nouns are either feminine or masculine.

2.A.1 People and animals

a. The ending **-a** usually denotes feminine and the ending **-o** denotes masculine.

Masculine		Feminine	
el amig**o**	the (male) friend	**la** amig**a**	the (female) friend
el chic**o**	the boy	**la** chic**a**	the girl
el niñ**o**	the (male) child	**la** niñ**a**	the (female) child
el gat**o**	the (male) cat	**la** gat**a**	the (female) cat

Determiners and subjects: 1.B.1
Use of definite articles: 5.C

b. An **-a** is added to a noun that ends in **-or** to make it feminine.

Masculine		Feminine	
el profes**or**	the (male) teacher	**la** profes**ora**	the (female) teacher
el señ**or**	the man/lord	**la** señ**ora**	the lady

c. Nouns that end in **-ista** and **-al** can be either feminine or masculine. This is determined by the article or context.

el/la art**ista**	the artist	**el/la** intelectu**al**	the intellectual
el/la electric**ista**	the electrician	**el/la** profesion**al**	the professional
el/la correspons**al**	the correspondent	**el/la** riv**al**	the rival
el/la fisc**al**	the district attorney		

Poeta is both masculine and feminine. The feminine **poetisa** is also used.

d. Nouns that refer to people that end in **-ante, -ente** usually can be either masculine or feminine based on the article used.

Masculine	Feminine	
el ag**ente**	**la** ag**ente**	the agent
el cant**ante**	**la** cant**ante**	the singer
el pac**iente**	**la** pac**iente**	the patient
el particip**ante**	**la** particip**ante**	the participant
el represent**ante**	**la** represent**ante**	the representative

A number of nouns that end in **-ente**, the masculine form, have an **-enta** ending in the feminine form.

Masculine	Feminine	
el asist**ente**	**la** asist**enta**	*the assistant*
el depend**iente**	**la** depend**ienta**	*the shop assistant*
el ger**ente**	**la** ger**enta**	*the manager*
el presid**ente**	**la** presid**enta**	*the president*
el pari**ente**	**la** pari**enta**	*the relative*

e. A number of social roles and professions are either masculine or feminine based on the person's gender.

emperador (*emperor*) →
emperatriz (*empress*)

padrino (*godfather*) →
madrina (*godmother*)

Masculine		Feminine	
el actor	*the actor*	**la** actriz	*the actress*
el caballero	*the gentleman*	**la** dama	*the lady*
el hombre	*the man*	**la** mujer	*the woman*
el padre, **el** papá	*the father*	**la** madre, **la** mamá	*the mother*
el príncipe	*the prince*	**la** princesa	*the princess*
el rey	*the king*	**la** reina	*the queen*
el yerno	*the son-in-law*	**la** nuera	*the daughter-in-law*

f. Some nouns can only be masculine or feminine even though they can refer to both men and women.

Mi padre es **una** buena **persona**.   *My father is a good person.*

¡Tu hija es **un encanto**!   *Your daugher is a very charming girl.*

g. Regarding animals, the *noun* + **macho** is used for masculine, and the *noun* + **hembra** for feminine. Some animal names can be either masculine or feminine, while others can only be one or the other. Pets, such as **el** gat**o** or **el** perr**o**, usually follow gender rules and can take an **-a** in the feminine (**la** gat**a**, **la** perr**a**).

Masculine		Feminine	
la jirafa **macho**	*the male giraffe*	**la** jirafa **hembra**	*the female giraffe*
el os**o**	*the (male) bear*	**la** os**a**	*the (female) bear*
el león	*the lion*	**la** leona	*the lioness*
el caballo	*the horse*	**la yegua**	*the mare*
el toro	*the bull*	**la vaca**	*the cow*
el gallo	*the rooster*	**la gallina**	*the hen*

2.A.2 Things

a. Nouns that denote concrete things or abstract ideas are, with a few exceptions, masculine if they end in **-o** and feminine if they end in **-a**.

Singular feminine nouns that
begin with a stressed **a**
or **ha** take the masculine
singular article, but take an
adjective with a
feminine form.
**el agua clara, el alma
buena**: 5.A.3

Masculine		Feminine	
el calendari**o**	*the calendar*	la ros**a**	*the rose*
el flo0rer**o**	*the vase*	la calculador**a**	*the calculator*
el libr**o**	*the book*	la impresor**a**	*the printer*
el pensamient**o**	*the thought*	la ide**a**	*the idea*

Exceptions:

Masculine		Feminine	
el día	*the day*	**la** mano	*the hand*
el mapa	*the map*	**la** foto	*the photo*
el planeta	*the planet*	**la** moto	*the motorcycle*
el tranvía	*the tram*	**la** radio	*the radio*

La foto and la moto are feminine because they are short for **la fotografía** and **la motocicleta**.

b. Nouns that end in **-e** can be masculine or feminine. The same applies to the few nouns that end in **-i** or **-u**.

el cine	*the cinema*	**la** gen**te**	*the people*	**el** rub**í**	*the ruby*
la clas**e**	*the class*	**el** puen**te**	*the bridge*	**el** tab**ú**	*the taboo*

c. Nouns that end in **-aje, -al, -és, -in,** and **-or** are usually masculine.

el pas**aje**	*the fare/ticket*	**el** can**al**	*the canal*	**el** estr**és**	*the stress*
el sab**or**	*the taste*	**el** val**or**	*the value/worth*	**el** f**in**	*the end*

Exceptions:

la f**lor**	*the flower*	**la** lab**or**	*the task*

d. Many nouns that end in **-ma** are masculine. Most are of Greek origin and have cognates in English.

el cli**ma**	*the climate*	**el** proble**ma**	*the problem*
el dile**ma**	*the dilemma*	**el** progra**ma**	*the program*
el dra**ma**	*the drama*	**el** poe**ma**	*the poem*
el enig**ma**	*the enigma*	**el** sínto**ma**	*the symptom*
el idio**ma**	*the language*	**el** siste**ma**	*the system*
el panora**ma**	*the panorama*	**el** te**ma**	*the theme/topic*

e. Nouns that end in **-ción, -sión, -dad, -umbre, -tad, -tud, -is,** and **-z** are usually feminine.

la lec**ción**	*the lesson*	**la** televi**sión**	*the television*
la activi**dad**	*the activity*	**la** liber**tad**	*the freedom*
la sínte**sis**	*the synthesis*	**la** lu**z**	*the light*
la cost**umbre**	*the custom*	**la** juven**tud**	*the youth*

2.A.3 Other nouns

a. Names of colors are masculine.

el azul	*blue*	**el** negro	*black*
el amarillo	*yellow*	**el** rojo	*red*
el blanco	*white*	**el** verde	*green*

b. Names of days, months, trees, mountains, rivers, numbers, oceans, and lakes are masculine.

Trabajo **los** lunes.	*I work on Mondays.*
Enero es frí**o**.	*January is cold.*
El pino es bonit**o**.	*The pine tree is beautiful.*
El Aconcagua es alt**o**.	*The Aconcagua Mountain is high.*
El Amazonas es larg**o**.	*The Amazon River is long.*
El 13 no es peligros**o**.	*The number 13 is not dangerous.*
El Atlántico es inmens**o**.	*The Atlantic Ocean is enormous.*
El Titicaca es hermos**o**.	*Lake Titicaca is beautiful.*

City names that begin with **San/Santo** are masculine: San Francisco, Santo Domingo, Santo Tomás. City names that begin with **Santa** are feminine: Santa Marta, Santa Mónica: 3.D.2

c. The gender of town names varies. Names of towns are often feminine if they end in an unstressed **-a**, and if the town is considered a city (**una ciudad**). If you define a town as a place (**un sitio**), masculine is also possible.

la hermosa Barcelona	*beautiful Barcelona*	**la** misteriosa Machu Picchu	*the mysterious Machu Picchu*
la lejana Santiago	*remote Santiago*	**el** inmenso Yucatán	*the immense Yucatán*

d. Names of letters are feminine: **la letra** (*the letter*).

La eñe es española.   *The letter **ñ** is Spanish.*

e. Infinitives used as nouns are masculine.

el deber   *duty*   **el** atardecer   *dusk*

f. The meaning of some nouns changes based on its masculine or feminine form.

Masculine		Feminine	
el capital	*the capital (funds)*	**la** capital	*the capital (city)*
el cometa	*the comet*	**la** cometa	*the kite*
el cura	*the priest*	**la** cura	*the cure*
el editorial	*the editorial*	**la** editorial	*the publishing house*
el frente	*the front*	**la** frente	*the forehead*
el guía	*the tour guide*	**la** guía	*the tour guide/guide book*
el mañana	*the future*	**la** mañana	*the morning*
el modelo	*the model*	**la** modelo	*the model (fashion)*
el orden	*the order*	**la** orden	*the command; the religious order*
el Papa	*the Pope*	**la** papa/**la** patata	*the potato (Lat. Am.)/the potato (Spain)*
el policía	*the policeman*	**la** policía	*the policewoman/the police*
el pendiente	*the earring*	**la** pendiente	*the slope*

2.B   Number

Número

Accentuation of plurals and compound words: 1.E.9

2.B.1   Regular plurals

a. Nouns that end in an *unstressed vowel* form the plural with an **-s**.

Singular		Plural	
el amig**o**	*the friend*	los amig**os**	*the friends*
la cas**a**	*the house*	las cas**as**	*the houses*
el espírit**u**	*the spirit*	los espírit**us**	*the spirits*
la noch**e**	*the night*	las noch**es**	*the nights*

b. Nouns that end in a *stressed* **-a**, **-o**, or **-e** form the plural with an **-s**.

Singular		Plural	
la mam**á**	*the mother*	las mam**ás**	*the mothers*
el pap**á**	*the father*	los pap**ás**	*the fathers*
el sof**á**	*the sofa*	los sof**ás**	*the sofas*
el caf**é**	*the coffee/cafe*	los caf**és**	*the coffees/cafes*

Singular		Plural	
el pie	*the foot*	los pies	*the feet*
el dominó	*the domino*	los dominós	*the dominoes*
el buró	*the bureau*	los burós	*the bureaus*

c. Nouns that end in a *consonant* or a *stressed* -**i** or -**u** form the plural with -**es**. When the noun ends in -**z** in the singular, the -**z** changes to -**c** in the plural.

Singular		Plural	
la actividad	*the activity*	las actividades	*the activities*
el papel	*the paper*	los papeles	*the papers*
el monitor	*the monitor*	los monitores	*the monitors*
el esquí	*the ski*	los esquíes	*the skis*
el pez	*the fish*	los peces	*the fish [pl.]*

d. Words that have an accent on the last syllable and form the plural with -**es** do not have an accent in the plural.

Singular		Plural	
el salón	*the living room*	**los** salones	*the living rooms*
la transmisión	*the broadcast*	**las** transmisiones	*the broadcasts*

Note that there are also nouns that require an accent in the plural to maintain the correct stress, 1.E.9:

joven → jóvenes

lapiz → lápices

2.B.2 Irregular plurals

a. Nouns that end in an *unstressed* vowel followed by -**s** do not change form between singular and plural.

el lunes	*Monday*	los lunes	*Mondays*
el martes	*Tuesday*	los martes	*Tuesdays*
el miércoles	*Wednesday*	los miércoles	*Wednesdays*
el jueves	*Thursday*	los jueves	*Thursdays*
el viernes	*Friday*	los viernes	*Fridays*
el análisis	*the analysis*	los análisis	*the analyses*
la crisis	*the crisis*	las crisis	*the crises*
el oasis	*the oasis*	los oasis	*the oases*
la tesis	*the thesis*	las tesis	*the theses*

b. Some nouns are only used in the plural.

las afueras	*outskirts*	**los** anteojos	*glasses*
las esposas	*handcuffs*	**los** alrededores	*surroundings*
las gafas	*glasses*	**los** celos	*jealousy*
las nupcias	*wedding*	**los** enseres	*belongings*
las tijeras	*scissors*	**los** prismáticos	*binoculars*
las vacaciones	*vacation*	**los** víveres	*provisions*

The singular **la tijera** is also used.

c. The following nouns have irregular plural forms.

el carácter	*the character*	**los** caracteres	*the characters*
el régimen	*the regime*	**los** regímenes	*the regimes*
el arte	*the art*	**las** artes	*the arts*

Accentuation of plural and compound words: 1.E.9b

Sufijos apreciativos

2.C.1 Overview

There are three types of appreciative suffixes: *diminutives* (**diminutivos**), *augmentatives* (**aumentativos**), and *pejoratives* (**despectivos**). They are used to express sentiments or judgements about events, people, and things. While diminutives and augmentatives are generally used to express affection or size, pejorative suffixes attach negative meaning to a word. The use and meaning of appreciative suffixes varies greatly depending on context, intonation of the speaker, and regional differences. The formation of these suffixes also differs from region to region, but the most common rules are described below.

2.C.2 Structure of diminutives

The most common diminutive suffix is **-ito/a**. Other suffixes are **-illo/a, -ico/a,** and **-uelo/a**.

> The spelling changes if the word ends in a syllable with **-c-** or **-g-**: juego/jueg**uito**, barco/barq**uito**.

a. Generally, in nouns ending with an *unstressed* (**átona**) **-o** or **-a**, the vowel is dropped to add the diminutive **-ito/a**.

gat**o**/gat**ito**   *cat/kitten*   niña/niñ**ita**   *girl/little girl*

> In these cases, the ending **-cito/-cita** is more common in Latin America.
> Examples of other diminutives of **café**: cafe**tito**, cafe**tico**, cafe**tín**, cafe**tillo**.

b. If a word ends in a *stressed* vowel, the preferred ending is **-cito/a,** but the diminutive can vary depending on the region.

bebé → bebe**cito**, bebi**to**   papá → papa**cito**, papa**íto**, pap**ito**   café → cafe**cito**, cafe**íto**

c. The most common ending of two-syllable nouns that end in **-e** is **-ecito/a**: madr**ecita**. If the word has more than two syllables, the ending is usually **-ito/a**: compadr**ito**, comadr**ita**.

> In general, **-ecito/-ecita** and **-ecillo/-ecilla** are more common in Spain, but they are also used in several parts of Latin America.

d. When the word is a *monosyllable* (**monosílabo**) and ends in a consonant, both **-cito/-cita** and **-ecito/-ecita** can be used: pan**cito**, pan**cillo**, pan**ecito**, pan**ecillo**, flor**cita**, flor**cilla**, flor**ecita**, flor**ecilla**.

> Words ending in **-z** have a spelling change:
> luz → luce**cita**
> Beatriz → Beatri**cita**

e. Words with two or more syllables that end in **-n** or **-r** usually take the ending **-cito/a**: camion**cito**, amor**cito**, cancion**cita**. If they end in any other consonant, the ending is usually **-ito/-ita**: lapi**cito**, dificil**ito.**

2.C.3 Structure of augmentatives and pejoratives

Augmentatives (**aumentativos**) and pejoratives (**despectivos**) are formed similarly to diminutives, adding **-ote/a** (**-zote/-zota**), **-azo/a**, **-ón/ona**, and **-ucho/a, -aco/a, -ote/a, -ajo/a**, respectively.

casa/cas**ona**   *house/big house*   casa/cas**ucha**   *house/ugly house*

2.C.4 Grammatical category, gender, and number

Words with an appreciative suffix follow the rules for forming plurals. They also keep their grammatical category and gender, but some feminine nouns can also be converted to a masculine form with the ending **-ón** for greater emphasis.

noticia → notici**ón**/notici**ona**   lámpara → lampar**ón**/lampar**ona**

2.C.5 Accentuation

Palabras agudas: 1.E.1
Palabras llanas: 1.E.2

The suffix is always the stressed syllable of a word. For this reason, most diminutives form **palabras llanas** (words with the stress on the second-to-last syllable): television**cita**, cama**rita**. The endings **-ón, -ín,** form **palabras agudas** (words with the stress on the last syllable): camis**ón**, pequeñ**ín.**

2.C.6 Grammatical category

Throughout most of the Spanish-speaking world, appreciative suffixes are generally used with just nouns and adjectives. However, in Latin America, diminutives are also used in other grammatical categories such as adverbs, some quantifiers, interjections, and also demonstratives, possessives, plurals, and numbers. The diminutive of the **gerundio** is used mostly in Spain. Some examples of the different grammatical categories are listed in the following table.

Base word	Diminutive	Augmentative	Pejorative
camión *n.*	camion**cito**	camion**ón**, camion**zote**, camion**azo**	camion**ucho**, camion**ete**, camion**aco**
casa *n.*	cas**ita**	cas**ota**, cas**ona**	cas**ucha**
libro *n.*	libr**ito**	libr**ote**, libr**ón**, libr**azo**	libr**ucho**, libr**aco**, libr**ajo**
débil *adj.*	debil**ito/a**, debil**cito/a**	debil**ote/a**	debil**ucho/a**
fuerte *adj.*	fuerte**cito/a**	fuert**ote/a**, fuert**ón/ona**	fuert**ucho/a**
ahora *adv.*	ahor**ita**		
aquí *adv.*	aqui**cito**		
nada *determ.*	nad**ita**		
todo *determ.*	tod**ito/a**		
adiós *interj.*	adios**ito**		
callando *ger.*	calland**ito**		

Adjectives: 3.A.4
Adverbs: 10.J.1

2.C.7 Combinations

Many nouns and adjectives can combine various suffixes (often repeated), but the final result depends on phonetic factors, number of syllables, specific noun or adjective and, of course, on regional and personal preferences.

chico	chiqu**ito**, chiqu**itico**, chiqu**ititito**, chiqu**itiquitico**, chiqu**illo**, chiqu**illito**, chiqu**illico**, chiqu**illote**, chiqu**illazo**, chic**ucho**
joven	joven**citico**, joven**citito**, joven**zotote**
casa	cas**uchita**

2.C.8 Independent words

Some diminutives and augmentatives have been used for so long that they do not change. These are examples of words that are no longer diminutives: **ventanilla**, **bocadillo**.

2.C.9 Uses of diminutives

a. To indicate smaller size or brevity of events. They can also indicate less intensity when describing physical characteristics of people and things.

Tengo un **autito** muy pequeño.	*I have a very little car.*
Demos un **paseíto cortito**.	*Let's take a very short walk.*
¿Te da **miedito** conducir por esta carretera?	*Aren't you a little scared of driving on this road?*
¿Por qué estás **tristecita** hoy?	*Why are you a little sad today?*

b. To show affection when speaking to loved ones or talking about them: **mamita, papito, amorcito, abuelita, noviecita.** Diminutives are also common with proper names: **Susanita, Eduardito.**

c. To soften requests or orders:

| ¿Me sirve un **cafecito**, por favor? | *Can I get a coffee, please?* |
| ¿Me haces un **favorcito**? | *Can you do me a little favor?* |

d. To soften the meaning of strong words or characteristics:

Esos chicos son unos **ladroncitos**.   *Those boys are just a couple of little thieves.*

e. To diminish the importance of uncomfortable or disagreeable situations:

La **multita** por la infracción es de cien dólares.   *It's only a little one-hundred dollar fine.*
La **operacioncita** no tiene importancia.   *The little procedure is nothing.*

2.C.10   Uses of augmentatives

a. To intensify the positive or negative meaning of a noun or adjective:

¡Tu visita me dio un **alegrón** inmenso!   *Your visit (absolutely) made my day!*
Tenemos un **problemazo.**   *We have a very/really big problem.*

b. To express an exaggerated size. The ending **-azo/a** can be positive, but context and intonation are crucial for its meaning. When referring to age, the ending **-ón/ona** can be derogatory.

Talking about age: 6.H.3

Tienes unos **ojazos** que me encantan.   *I just love your big eyes.*
Él es un **cuarentón** sin futuro.   *He is a forty-something with no future.*

c. To communicate a "hard hit" with the object described:

machete → **machetazo**   balón → **balonazo**   bate → **batazo**   codo → **codazo**

Adjectives: 3.A.4

d. Both nouns and adjectives can be pejorative with augmentative suffixes.

¡Has escrito una **novelucha** sin valor!   *What a trashy piece of pulp fiction you have written!*
Esa pobre familia vive en una **casucha**.   *That poor family lives in (such) a dump.*

2.D   Regional variations

Variaciones regionales

2.D.1   Gender

The following nouns can be either masculine or feminine depending on the region:

el/la azúcar	*sugar*	**el/la** lente	*the lens*
el/la Internet	*the Internet*	**el/la** maratón	*marathon*
el/la interrogante	*query, question*	**el/la** sartén	*the frying pan*

2.D.2   Job titles for women

a. In Spanish-speaking countries, the masculine form is traditionally used for all job titles, even for women. Use of the feminine form is increasing, especially among young people.

la abogad**a**   *the lawyer*   **la** médic**a**   *the doctor*

b. Words referring to people, especially job titles, that have historically had only a masculine form can now be found in the feminine.

For a better understanding of the differences in pronunciation of the **c** and **z** between Spain and Latin America, see Consonants and digraphs: 1.C.6.

el general	**la** general**a**	*the general*	**el** ingeniero	**la** ingenier**a**	*the engineer*
el juez	**la** juez**a**	*the judge*	**el** ministro	**la** ministr**a**	*the minister*

2.D.3   Common word variations

The most common regional variations in Spanish are expressed through vocabulary, especially nouns. For example, *hunting* is called **caza** in Spain, while in Latin America it is called **cacería**. In Latin America, **caza** is pronounced the same as **casa** (*house*) and for that reason a different word is used. The same happens with the word **cocer** (*to cook*), which sounds the same as **coser** (*to sew*). Therefore a different word, **cocinar** (*to cook*), is used in Latin America.

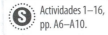

Práctica

Actividades 1–16, pp. A6–A10.

Adjectives
Adjetivos

Chapter 3
A. Gender and number
B. Agreement
C. Placement
D. Prenominal adjectives
E. Comparison
F. Regional variations

3.A   Gender and number

Género y número

An adjective describes the characteristics of a noun and agrees with the noun in gender and number.

3.A.1   Endings -o / -a

Adjectives that end in **-o** in the masculine form change to **-a** for the feminine form and add **-s** to form the plural.

	Singular		Plural	
Masculine	el libro blanco	*the white book*	los libros blancos	*the white books*
Feminine	la casa blanca	*the white house*	las casas blancas	*the white houses*

3.A.2   Endings -e / -ista

Adjectives that end in **-e** or **-ista** do not change in gender, but they do change in number.

	Singular		Plural	
Masculine	el libro grande	*the big book*	los libros grandes	*the big books*
	el país socialista	*the socialist country*	los países socialistas	*the socialist countries*
Feminine	la casa grande	*the big house*	las casas grandes	*the big houses*
	la nación socialista	*the socialist nation*	las naciones socialistas	*the socialist nations*

If the adjective is augmentative and ends in **-ote,** it forms the feminine with an **-a**.

grandot**ote,** grandot**ota**   *very big*

Diminutives, augmentatives, and pejoratives: 3.A.4

3.A.3   Other endings

a. For adjectives that end in **-or, -án, -ón, -ín,** add **-a** to form the feminine and remove the written accent. To form the plural, add **-es** to the masculine form and **-s** to the feminine form. Bear in mind that in the masculine plural form, the written accent is not needed for the endings **-anes, -ones, -ines.**

conservad**or(es)**	conservad**ora(s)**	*conservative*
encantad**or(es)**	encantad**ora(s)**	*charming*
trabajad**or(es)**	trabajad**ora(s)**	*hard-working*
holgaz**án**/holgaz**anes**	holgaz**ana(s)**	*lazy*
glot**ón**/glot**ones**	glot**ona(s)**	*gluttonous*
pequeñ**ín**/pequeñ**ines**	pequeñ**ina(s)**	*tiny*

b. The following comparative adjectives that end in **-or** do not change in gender, but do take **-es** in the plural.

Comparison of adjectives: 3.E
Comparisons: Ch. 11

anteri**or(es)**	*previous/front*	posteri**or(es)**	*subsequent/back*
mej**or(es)**	*better*	pe**or(es)**	*worse*
interi**or(es)**	*interior*	exteri**or(es)**	*exterior*
may**or(es)**	*older/larger*	men**or(es)**	*younger/smaller*
superi**or(es)**	*superior*	inferi**or(es)**	*inferior*

c. Many adjectives of nationality (**gentilicios**) that end in **-és** take **-a** in the feminine form. The feminine form and both the masculine and feminine plural forms lose the written accent.

Masculine	Feminine	
danés/daneses	danesa(s)	*Danish*
francés/franceses	francesa(s)	*French*
inglés/ingleses	inglesa(s)	*English*
portugués/portugueses	portuguesa(s)	*Portuguese*

Exception:

The adjective **cortés** (*polite*) retains the same form in the feminine. It has the same plural form for both masculine and feminine.

el chico cort**és**	*the polite boy*	**la** chica cort**és**	*the polite girl*
los chicos cort**eses**	*the polite boys*	**las** chicas cort**eses**	*the polite girls*

Many adjectives that form nouns come from art, science, and technology fields.
La **curva** es peligrosa.
La línea es **curva**.

d. Adjectives that end in **í, -a, -ú** do not change in gender, but do have a plural form. Adjectives that end in **-e** or in the consonants **-z, -r, -l, -s** act in the same way.

Singular		Plural	
problema **agrícola**	*agricultural problem*	problemas **agrícolas**	*agricultural problems*
persona **belga**	*Belgian person*	personas **belgas**	*Belgian people*
marinero **bengalí**	*Bengali sailor*	marineros **bengalíes**	*Bengali sailors*
templo **hindú**	*Hindu temple*	templos **hindúes**	*Hindu temples*
estudiante **feliz**	*happy student*	estudiantes **felices**	*happy students*
clase **útil**, libro **útil**	*useful class, useful book*	clases y libros **útiles**	*useful books and classes*
círculo **polar**	*polar circle*	círculos **polares**	*polar circles*

3.A.4 **Diminutives, augmentatives, and pejoratives**

Appreciative suffixes: 2.C

a. Like nouns, adjectives are very flexible when it comes to adding appreciative suffixes. The most common diminutive endings are **-ito/a(s)** and in some cases **-cito/a(s), -ecito/a(s),** and **-illo/a(s), -ín(es)/ina(s).**

amarill**ito(s)**	*yellowish*	pequeñ**ín(es)**	*tiny*
gord**ito(s)**	*chubby*	verde**cilla(s)**	*greenish*

b. Augmentatives are less common in adjectives than in nouns. The endings are **-ote/a(s), -zote/a(s), -ón(es)/ona(s).**

dul**zón**	*"somewhat sweet"*	simpatic**ona**	*very friendly (derogatory)/ "somewhat" nice*
joven**zote**	*handsome young man*	grand**ote**	*very big*

c. The suffix **-ón(ones)/ona(s)** can also be added to nouns to turn them into adjectives. These tend to have a negative connotation.

boca	*mouth*	María, ¡no seas boc**ona**!	*María, don't be a big-mouth!*
barriga	*belly*	Juan es muy barrig**ón**.	*Juan has a big belly.*

d. Some pejorative suffixes are **-acho/a**, **-ucho/a(s)**, **-ote/a(s)**, **-ajo/a(s)**. In English, the translations may lack the negative connotation the Spanish provides.

fe**úcho**	*quite ugly*	fri**úcha**	*very cold*	peque**ñajo**	*very small*
flac**ucho**	*too thin*	gord**ote**	*too fat*	ric**acho**	*filthy rich*

3.B Agreement

Concordancia

3.B.1 Nouns with the same gender

When an adjective describes several nouns of the *same* gender, the adjective takes the same gender in the plural.

un lib**ro** y un cuadern**o** nuev**os**	*a new book and notebook*
una lámpar**a** y una mes**a** nuev**as**	*a new lamp and table*

3.B.2 Nouns of different gender

a. When an adjective describes several nouns of *different* gender and is placed *after* the nouns, it takes the masculine form in the plural.

una herman**a** y un herman**o** simpátic**os**	*a nice sister and brother*
un lib**ro** y una mes**a** nuev**os**	*a new book and table*

b. When an adjective describes several nouns of *different* gender and is placed *before* the nouns, it agrees with the nearest subsequent noun.

un**os** simpátic**os** amig**os** y amig**as**	*some lovely friends*
un**as** simpátic**as** amig**as** y amig**os**	*some lovely friends*

3.B.3 Nouns used as adjectives

Nouns can be used as adjectives to modify other nouns. In this usage, they are invariable in number.

la palabra **clave**	*the keyword*	las palabras **clave**	*the keywords*
el programa **piloto**	*the pilot program*	los programas **piloto**	*the pilot programs*
el coche **bomba**	*the car bomb*	los coches **bomba**	*the car bombs*

3.B.4 Colors

a. It is common to use names of flowers, plants, minerals, and seeds as color adjectives. In this case, they are normally considered invariable and they are commonly used with **(de) color**. Words in this category include **naranja** (*orange*), **lila** (*lilac*), and **rosa** (*pink*).

la(s) corbata(s) **café/(de) color café**	*the brown tie(s)*
el/los mantel(es) **naranja/(de) color naranja**	*the orange tablecloth(s)*

b. They can also be treated as regular adjectives, in which case they agree with the noun in number but the gender remains invariable: **calcetines lilas**. In the case of **naranja** and **rosa**, the adjectives **anaranjado/a(s)** and **rosado/a(s)** can also be used.

las camisas **rosas**/las camisas **rosadas**	*the pink shirts*

c. When colors are modified by other adjectives (**claro, oscuro, pálido**), both the color and the adjective are usually considered invariable. This usage assumes the omission of the masculine singular noun **color**.

medias **verdes**	*green socks*	medias **(color) verde claro**	*light-green socks*
piel **pálida**	*pale skin*	piel **(color) rosa pálido**	*pale pink skin*

3.C Placement

Posición

The adjective is often placed after the noun, but it can also be placed before.

3.C.1 Placement after the noun

a. An adjective placed after a noun distinguishes that particular noun from others within the same group. It is the most common position used in Spanish.

Me gustan las películas **cómicas.**   *I like funny movies.*

In this example, the adjective **cómicas** restricts the meaning of the noun by referring only to *funny* movies and excluding all other movies that are not funny.

Adjectives and determiners with fixed placement: 3.C.3c

b. "Relational" adjectives that either derive from a noun or classify a noun are always placed after the noun. Context determines whether an adjective is descriptive or relational. For example, **grave** can be placed before or after **enfermedad** to describe an illness. However, **mental** can only be placed after **enfermedad** because it describes the specific nature of the disease: one related specifically to the brain. These adjectives can usually be paraphrased as "related to" or, in Spanish, as **de** + *noun*: **enfermedad mental = enfermedad de la mente.**

una enfermedad **mental**	una enfermedad **de la mente**
economía **nacional**	economía **de la nación**
actuación **cinematográfica**	actuación **de cine**
ecuación **matemática**	ecuación **de matemáticas**
sitio **web**	sitio **de Internet**
cosas **técnicas**	cosas **de la tecnología**

3.C.2 Placement before the noun

a. Adjectives can be placed before a noun to emphasize or intensify a particular characteristic or suggest that it is inherent to the noun.

una **oscura** noche de invierno	*a dark winter night*
el **horrible** monstruo	*the horrible monster*

When the adjective is placed before a noun, the noun must be defined by a determiner. See Determiner placement in relation to the noun: 4.B.5

b. Adjectives that precede a noun can create a certain stylistic effect or tone. They can indicate how the speaker feels toward the person or thing being described.

el **talentoso** autor	*the talented author*
las **feas** casas	*the ugly houses*
unas **pequeñas** calles	*some small streets*
un **amplio** jardín	*a spacious garden*

c. Adjectives are also placed before the noun when we want to communicate that a characteristic is unique to the noun. This mostly happens in poetry and literature for stylistic effect. Such adjectives are called **epítetos** (*epithets*).

La **famosa** Manhattan con sus **altísimos** rascacielos.	*The famous Manhattan with its very tall skyscrapers.*

d. Adjectives describing known persons and things precede the noun to highlight an inherent quality or trait.

la **hermosa** ciudad de Madrid	*the beautiful city of Madrid*
mis **queridos** padres	*my dear parents*
el **increíble** hombre araña	*the incredible Spiderman*

3.C.3 Adjectives and determiners with fixed placement

a. The following determiners are always placed *before* the noun.

amb**o/a(s)**	*both*	plen**o/a(s)**	*full*
much**o/a(s)**	*a lot (of)/many/much*	poc**o/a(s)**	*little/few*
otr**o/a(s)**	*other/s*	tant**o/a(s)**	*as/so much, as/so many*

b. Adjectives that describe origin, nationality, and noun type are placed *after* the noun.

la casa **alemana**	*the German house*	un chico **cubano**	*a Cuban boy*
una caja **fuerte**	*a safe deposit box*	la calle **principal**	*the main street*

c. Technical and professional characteristics are described by an adjective placed *after* the noun.

Placement after the noun: 3.C.1b

el teléfono **celular**	*the cell phone*	la tesis **doctoral**	*the doctoral thesis*
la página **web**	*the web page*	la impresora **láser**	*the laser printer*

d. Certain adjectives that derive from a noun and convey a direct relationship to it *follow* the noun (**economía → económico; nación → nacional**).

La familia tiene problemas **económicos.**	*The family has economic problems.*
Solo vendemos productos **nacionales.**	*We only sell domestic products.*

e. With comparisons, the adjective is placed *after* the noun.

Quiero un café **caliente,** no un café **frío.**	*I want a hot coffee, not a cold coffee.*

f. Adjectives with appreciative suffixes are placed *after* the noun.

Diminutives, augmentatives, and pejoratives: 3.A.4

Pedro está conduciendo un coche **nuevecito.**	*Pedro is driving a newish car.*
No conozco ciudades **feúchas** en el país.	*I don't know any ugly cities in this country.*

3.C.4 Placement and meaning

A number of common adjectives change meaning depending on whether they are placed before or after the noun.

Determiners:
Agreement: 4.B.4
Placement: 4.B.5

Adjectives	Placed before		Placed after	
alto	un **alto** ejecutivo	*a senior executive*	un ejecutivo **alto**	*a tall executive*
bueno	un **buen** amigo	*a good friend*	un chico **bueno**	*a kind boy*
cierto	una **cierta** persona	*a certain person*	una cosa **cierta**	*a sure thing*
diferente	**diferentes** lugares	*several places*	lugares **diferentes**	*different places*
grande	una **gran** casa	*a grand house*	una casa **grande**	*a big house*
medio	**media** hora	*half an hour*	la clase **media**	*the middle class*
nuevo	mis **nuevos** zapatos	*my brand-new shoes*	mis zapatos **nuevos**	*my new shoes*
pobre	un **pobre** pueblo	*unlucky people*	un pueblo **pobre**	*poor/needy people*
puro	**puro** aire	*only air*	aire **puro**	*pure/clean air*
raro	una **rara** cualidad	*a rare quality*	una persona **rara**	*a rare/unusual person*
rico	un **rico** chocolate	*a delicious chocolate*	una familia **rica**	*a rich family*
triste	un **triste** caso	*a sad case*	una historia **triste**	*a sad history*
único	mi **único** amor	*my only love*	un amor **único**	*a unique love*
viejo	un **viejo** amigo	*an old friend*	un amigo **viejo**	*an elderly friend*

Bueno is shortened to **buen** when placed before a masculine singular noun. **Grande** is shortened to **gran** before both masculine and feminine singular nouns: 3.D

mismo, propio: 7.E.5

3.D Prenominal adjectives

Adjetivos antepuestos

Indefinite quantifiers **algún**, **alguno**; **ningún**, **ninguno**, **ninguna**: 7.B.2

3.D.1 Buen, mal, primer, tercer, algún, ningún

The forms **bueno, malo, primero, tercero, alguno, ninguno** drop the final **-o** and become **buen, mal, primer, tercer, algún, ningún** before masculine singular nouns. This does not occur before feminine and plural nouns.

un **buen** libro	*a good book*	un **mal** ejemplo	*a bad example*
el **primer** día	*the first day*	el **tercer** año	*the third year*

3.D.2 Gran, san

a. The adjective **grande** is shortened before both masculine and feminine singular nouns.

un **gran** momento	*a big moment*
una **gran** fiesta	*a grand party*

b. The adjective **santo** is shortened to **san** only when it precedes a proper noun that does not begin with *-to* or *-do*.

San Diego	**Santo To**más
San José	**Santo Do**mingo

3.E Comparison

Comparación

3.E.1 Structure

Adjectives have gradable inflections. Most adjectives have a basic form, called the *positive* form. The *comparative* form expresses higher and lower grades of a characteristic; the *superlative* form expresses the highest or lowest grades.

Determiners are not inflected: 4.B.3, 4.B.4
Comparison of adverbs: 10.I
Comparisons: Ch. 11

Positive form		Comparative		Superlative	
verde(s)	*green*	**más** verde(s)	*greener*	**el/la/los/las más** verde(s)	*the greenest*
verde(s)	*green*	**menos** verde(s)	*less green*	**el/la/los/las menos** verde(s)	*the least green*

Todo es **más** verde en verano.	*Everything is greener in the summertime.*
La casa blanca es **la más** alta.	*The white house is the tallest.*
Mis jardines son **los más** bonitos.	*My gardens are the most beautiful.*
Esta flor es **menos** roja que esa.	*This flower is less red than that one.*

3.E.2 Irregular inflection

a. Some common adjectives have irregular gradable inflection forms.

Comparative adjectives ending in **-or**: 3.A.3b

Positive form		Irregular comparative		Irregular superlative	
bueno/a(s)	*good/kind*	**mejor(es)**	*better*	**(el/la) mejor**	*(the) best*
malo/a(s)	*bad/evil*	**peor(es)**	*worse*	**(el/la) peor**	*(the) worst*
joven/jóvenes	*young*	**menor(es)**	*younger*	**(el/la) menor**	*(the) youngest*
viejo/a(s)	*old*	**mayor(es)**	*older*	**(el/la) mayor**	*(the) oldest*

Rosa es **la mayor** de todos.	*Rosa is the oldest of them all.*
Juan es **el menor** de la familia.	*Juan is the youngest in the family.*

b. The regular comparative forms of **bueno/a** and **malo/a** can be used as well. However, in this case, they exclusively emphasize character judgments.

Mario es **más bueno** que el pan.	*Mario is a very good person.*
Mario es **mejor** deportista que su hermano.	*Mario is a better athlete than his brother.*
Este perro es **más malo** que el diablo.	*This dog is more evil than the devil.*
El problema es **peor** de lo que pensaba.	*The problem is worse than I thought.*

c. Mayor and **menor** are used interchangeably with the regular comparative forms.

Juan es **más viejo** que su hermano.	*Juan is older than his brother.*
Juan es **mayor** que su hermano.	*Juan is older than his brother.*

d. When **pequeño** and **grande** refer to age, their comparative and superlative forms are the same as those for **joven** and **viejo/a**.

Mario es el **más grande/pequeño** de los tres hermanos.	*Mario is the oldest/youngest of the three brothers.*
Mario es el **más viejo/joven** de los tres hermanos.	*Mario is the oldest/youngest of the three brothers.*
Mario es el **mayor/menor** de los tres hermanos.	*Mario is the oldest/youngest of the three brothers.*

e. Grande and **pequeño** also use **mayor** and **menor** as comparative and superlative forms when describing the scope or importance of an issue.

California es el estado con el **mayor** número de hispanohablantes en los EE.UU.
California is the state with the greatest number of Spanish-speakers in the U.S.

3.E.3 Superlatives with -*ísimo/a(s)*

a. Spanish also forms superlatives with the endings **-ísimo/a(s).** This form is called the **superlativo absoluto.**

muchísimo, poquísimo: 7.C.1
Adverbs: Superlative
constructions: 10.I.2

La casa es **alta.**	La casa es **altísima.**	*The house is (very) tall.*
El problema es **fácil.**	El problema es **facilísimo.**	*The problem is (very) easy.*

b. Many **adjectives** have irregular superlatives.

antiguo/a	**antiquísimo/a**	*old/very old*
ardiente	**ardentísimo/a**	*passionate/very passionate*
cruel	**crudelísimo/a** (also **cruelísimo/a**)	*cruel/very cruel*
fiel	**fidelísimo/a**	*loyal/very loyal*

c. Adjectives ending in **-ble** form the superlative with the ending **-bilísimo/a**.

Pedro es **amable**.	Pedro es **amabilísimo**.	*Pedro is (very) kind.*

d. Some adjectives have two absolute superlative forms. However, the regular form is more commonly used.

bueno/a	**buenísimo/a, bonísimo/a**	*good/very good*
fuerte	**fuertísimo/a, fortísimo/a**	*strong/very strong*

e. Some adjectives can take the suffix **-érrimo/a** instead. This is only found in the formal register.

célebre	**celebérrimo/a**	*famous/very famous*
libre	**libérrimo/a**	*free/very free*
mísero/a	**misérrimo/a**	*miserable/very miserable*
pobre	**paupérrimo/a** (also, **pobrísimo/a**)	*poor/very poor*

3.F Regional variations

Variaciones regionales

There are not many grammatical differences in the use of adjectives in the Spanish-speaking world. The differences depend on which adjectives are used in the different regions. A few examples of the variations are illustrated below.

3.F.1 Colors

a. In Spain, it is more common to use **marrón** than **café** for *brown*, and in Latin America **castaño** is used for *dark hair* (**cabello/pelo castaño**).

b. In some regions of the Spanish-speaking world, **morado/a** is used instead of **violeta, colorado/a** is more common than **rojo/a**, and **bordó** is heard instead of **granate**.

3.F.2 Nationality

a. People from India are called **hindú** in Latin America and **indio/a** in Spain. The latter word is used in Latin America to refer to the indigenous people of the region. The adjective **indio/a,** however, also has some negative connotations in Latin America; therefore **indígena** is preferred, especially in written language. **Indiano/a** is used in Spain for the Spaniards who returned home after becoming wealthy in the former Spanish colonies.

b. The adjective **suramericano/a** is more usual in most of Latin America than **sudamericano/a,** which is more common in Spain and Argentina.

3.F.3 *¿Hispano, latino o latinoamericano?*

a. In North America, the terms **hispano/a** and **latino/a** are used interchangeably to refer to people from Spanish-speaking countries. Both terms are correct and the preference for one or the other comes from one's personal perception of subtle differences between the two words. Outside of North America, **hispano/a** is used more frequently since one meaning of the term **latino/a** technically refers to all of the peoples, both European and American, that speak any language derived from Latin.

b. Latinoamericano/a refers to anyone from the Americas that speaks Spanish, Portuguese or French, while **hispanoamericano/a** refers exclusively to Spanish-speaking individuals from the Americas. **Iberoamericano/a** describes anyone from Spanish- and Portuguese-speaking countries in the Americas, or from these countries as well as Spain and Portugal.

3.F.4 *México*

Variations in the pronunciation of the letter **x**: 1.C.6, 1.D.5, 1.G.2a

Although at some point the adjectives **mejicano** and **mexicano** coexisted, the official name of the country is **México** and the official adjective is **mexicano**. This use of the **x** is common in many Mexican place names and in their corresponding adjectives. Although some cities have lost the **x** spelling (such as **Jalisco**), most have retained it. In most cases, this **x** is pronounced like a **j**.

México   mexicano/a   Oaxaca   oaxaqueño/a

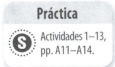

Práctica

Actividades 1–13, pp. A11–A14.

Determiners
Determinantes

4.A Overview

Aspectos generales

Determiners are words that precede a noun to indicate which object, person, or other entity the noun represents. They can be used to specify if a noun refers to something or someone nonspecific (**un** chico) or to something or someone very specific (like **el** coche or **esta** casa). Determiners can also refer to the quantitative nature of a noun, stating its exact number, as in **tres** amigos, or an indefinite amount: **varias** cosas, **muchas** chicas, **unos** estudiantes. Determiners state and clarify the nature of the noun.

Determiners		
	Groups	**Examples**
Articles *Artículos*	Specific reference: definite articles	**El** parque es grande.
	Non-specific reference: indefinite articles	**Unos** niños juegan.
Quantifiers *Cuantificadores*	Specific quantity: numbers	Hay **tres** árboles.
	Non-specific quantity: affirmative and negative quantifiers	Hay **muchas** personas; **algunos** chicos y **pocas** chicas.
Demonstratives *Demostrativos*	Three-level system for describing relative distance	**Este** árbol y **esas** flores me gustan. **Aquellas** no.
Possessives *Posesivos*	Prenominal and postnominal forms	**Mi** casa es **tuya**.

It is important to note that many determiners can have several functions in a sentence. For example, quantifiers are especially prone to becoming adverbs. The words **mucho, bastante, más, menos** are determiners that function like adjectives when they support the noun, but they are adverbs when they support the verb.

En verano hay **muchos** conciertos.   *There are many concerts in the summer.*

(**Muchos** is a determiner and modifies **conciertos** by stating its quantity.)

Los conciertos me gustan **mucho.**   *I like concerts very much.*

(**Mucho** is an adverb of quantity and modifies the verb **gustar** by stating how much the speaker likes concerts.)

En la Florida hay **bastantes** playas.   *There are a lot of beaches in Florida.*

(**Bastantes** is a determiner and modifies **playas** by stating its quantity.)

¡Cuando voy allí, nado **bastante**!   *When I go there, I swim a lot!*

(**Bastante** is an adverb of quantity and modifies the verb **nadar** by stating how much the speaker swims.)

¡No digas **más** mentiras!	*Don't tell any more lies!*
No voy a mentir **más**.	*I won't lie any more.*
Debes trabajar **menos**.	*You have to work less.*

Articles: Ch. 5

Quantifiers: Numbers: Ch. 6

Indefinite quantifiers and pronouns: Ch. 7

Demonstratives: Ch. 8

Possessives: Ch. 9

Most determiners agree in gender and/or number with the noun they modify. Adverbs never change form.
Agreement: 4.B.4
Determiners and adverbs: 4.B.7

Notice that **más** and **menos** do not change form.

4.B Common features

Características comunes

4.B.1 Determiners and subjects

a. One of the functions of a determiner is to designate the subject of a sentence.

Tu casa es bonita; **Las** casas son bonitas.

Such sentences without a determiner are grammatically incorrect in Spanish. This does not apply to proper nouns: **La** ciudad es hermosa. (*The city is beautiful.*), Madrid es hermosa. (*Madrid is beautiful.*)

b. When the subject is a *plural* noun, the determiner can be left out in specific written contexts such as newspapers, magazines, and commercials: **Investigadores** encuentran nuevo virus. (*Researchers find new virus.*), **Presos** se amotinan contra guardias. (*Prisoners riot against guards.*)

c. The determiner can be left out when an uncountable noun *follows* a verb that means (*not*) *to exist, to be lacking, to remain*: **Falta** azúcar. (*There's no sugar.*), **No hay** leche. (*There isn't any milk.*)

d. Countable nouns must have determiners when the quantity is specific: Queda **un** pan. (*There is one loaf left.*), Quedan **dos** panes. (*There are two loaves left.*)

e. Plural countable nouns can follow the verb without determiners when they have a non-specific reference. **Faltan** tenedores y cuchillos. (*There aren't any forks or knives.*)

f. The same rule applies to direct objects. A plural noun that functions as a direct object can also follow the verb without a determiner when it has a non-specific reference. Compré libros. (*I bought books.*), Comemos manzanas. (*We are eating apples.*)

g. Indirect objects, however, must always be specified by a determiner: Le compré un libro a **la niña.** (*I bought a book for the girl.*)

h. Personal pronouns and proper nouns can always be the subject without a determiner: **Ella** lee. (*She is reading.*), **Pedro** habla. (*Pedro is talking.*)

4.B.2 Determiners as pronouns

Indefinite pronouns: 7.C.3, 7.D ▶

a. When determiners stand alone, they act as pronouns. This only occurs when a noun is not present. The determiner's reference can often be understood from the context.

Algunos vienen, **otros** se van.	*Some are coming, others are going.*
Esta casa es cara, **esa** no.	*This house is expensive, but not that one.*
Tú tienes amigos; yo no tengo **ninguno.**	*You have friends; I have none.*

Demás: 7.C.10 ▶
Cada: 7.C.8

b. Some determiners can never stand alone as a pronoun and only appear next to other determiners. This applies to **demás,** which must always be preceded by a definite article and is often also used with **todo. Cada** must be followed by a noun.

Dame **las demás** cosas.	*Give me the rest of the things.*
Todo lo demás puede esperar.	*Everything else can wait.*
Cada persona tiene sus ideas.	*Every person has their own ideas.*
Os visitaremos **a cada uno** de vosotros.	*We're going to visit every/each one of you.*

c. The following words are always indefinite pronouns: **algo, alguien, nada, nadie.** They can never act as determiners.

¿Vais a hacer **algo** hoy?	*Are you [pl.] going to do anything today?*
¿Hay **alguien** en casa?	*Is anyone home?*

d. Negative indefinite pronouns and negative determiners require double negation when placed after the verb.

No tenemos **ningún** plan.	*We have no plans./We don't have (any) plans.*
No hay **nadie** en casa.	*There is nobody home.*

4.B.3 Determiners and adjectives

a. An adjective describes a noun and agrees with it in gender and number. Determiners are therefore related to adjectives, but illustrate other aspects of a noun. The main difference between them is that determiners belong to *closed word groups*. This means that there is a limited number of determiners of the same type in each group. It can take hundreds of years for new determiners to develop in a language. New adjectives, on the other hand, are forming continuously in order to describe new things. For example, by following the rules for adjective formation in Spanish, one can create new ones such as: ¡Mi hijo es **hispano-inglés, cibernavegante** y **chateadorcísimo**!

◀ Adjectives: Ch. 3

b. Suffixes and prefixes cannot be added to determiners, with the exception of **mucho** and **poco** (**muchísimo, poquísimo**). Suffixes and prefixes can be added to nouns and adjectives in Spanish: **superitalianísimo** (*unbelievably Italian*), **heladazo** (*gigantic ice-cream*), **colinita** (*little hill*).

◀ Appreciative suffixes: 2.C, 3.A.4

4.B.4 Agreement

The majority of determiners agree in gender and number with the noun they support, (**esta** casa, **algunos** libros, **pocas** chicas), but the determiners **cada, más,** and **menos** never change form (**menos** tiempo, **más** libros).

◀ Comparison of adjectives: 3.E

4.B.5 Placement in relation to the noun

a. It is common for a determiner to be placed before a noun: **este** chico, **el** estudiante. If the noun is described by an adjective preceding it, the determiner must be placed before the adjective: **este** simpático chico, **el** buen estudiante.

◀ Adjective placement before the noun: 3.C.2

b. Some determiners can be placed before or after the noun. Determiners placed after the noun highlight a feature of the noun or create a different emphasis.

◀ Demonstratives after a noun: 8.A.2b

El chico **ese** no es simpático.	*That boy is not nice.*
No soy una persona **cualquiera.**	*I'm not just anyone.*

4.B.6 Combination of two determiners

a. Determiners can be combined in pairs: **estos dos** libros (*these two books*), **mis otras** cosas (*my other things*). Three determiners together are rare, and in such cases the third one is usually a numeral: **los otros cinco** chicos.

b. Of all determiners, only **todo/a(s)** can *precede* a definite article: **todos los** días. The following determiners (with corresponding agreement forms) can *follow* the article: **el mucho** amor, **el poco** dinero, **la otra** vez, **los varios** países, **los tres** amigos.

◀ Use of definite articles: 5.C

c. The indefinite article **un(a)** must be placed after **todo/a** and can only be used in its singular form in this combination. **Un(a)** must be placed before **cierto/a(s),** and can be used in its singular or plural form. **Un(a)** can never be combined with **otro** like in English.

Eres **todo un** caballero.	*You're a real gentleman.*
Ellos pagaron **una cierta** suma.	*They paid a certain amount.*
Ahora vivo en **otra** ciudad.	*Now, I live in another town.*

Demás: 7.C.10

d. Demás always precedes the noun with the definite article in the plural: **los/las demás**. The article agrees with the noun's gender and number. It is common to add **todo/a(s)** to a definite or neuter article: **todas las demás** casas (*all those other houses*), **todo lo demás** (*all the rest*).

4.B.7 Determiners and adverbs

a. Determiners cannot be combined with quantifiers, gradable adverbs, or other expressions of quantity. One can say **muy tranquilo**, but not **muy este**. The exceptions are the determiners **más, menos,** and **poco,** which accept quantifiers: **muy poco** tiempo, **muchos más/menos** estudiantes. On some occasions, possessive pronouns can be placed after and modified by quantifiers or gradable adverbs.

Tiene una risa **muy** suya.   *His laugh is very distinctive.*

Indefinite quantifiers and pronouns: Ch. 7
Quantifying adverbs: 10.D.2

b. The following indefinite determiners which refer to a noun's quantity can also act as adverbs: **bastante, demasiado, más, menos, mucho, poco, tanto, todo.** Like all other adverbs, they can modify verbs, adjectives, or other adverbs.

¡Tú siempre te quejas **tanto**!	*You always complain so much.*
Trabajamos **demasiado**.	*We work too much.*
¡Chateas **bastante** en la red!	*You chat quite a bit online!*
Mi computadora es **un poco** lenta.	*My computer is a bit slow.*

c. Mucho can never be used with adjectives and adverbs; only **muy** can precede them.

El barco navega **muy** rápidamente.	*The boat is sailing very fast.*
El viento está **muy** fuerte hoy.	*The wind is very strong today.*

d. Only **tanto** and **todo** agree in gender and number when they occur before an adjective.

Ella está **toda** entusiasmada.	*She is all excited.*
Mis zapatos están **todos** mojados.	*My shoes are completely soaked.*

e. The abbreviation **tan** can only be used before adjectives and adverbs.

¡El tiempo es **tan** corto y pasa **tan** rápidamente!   *Time is so short and goes so fast!*

Comparisons: Ch. 11

4.B.8 Comparisons with *más, menos, mucho, tanto (tan)*

Comparative structures in Spanish use **que** or **como** and determiners.

El avión es **más** rápido **que** el tren.	*The plane is faster than the train.*
El rock británico es **tan** bueno **como** el estadounidense.	*British rock is just as good as American.*

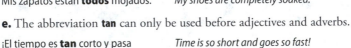

Práctica

(S) Actividades 1–2, p. A15

Articles
Artículos

Chapter 5

Determiners (2)
A. Definite and indefinite articles
B. Use of indefinite articles
C. Use of definite articles
D. Regional variations

5.A   Definite and indefinite articles
Artículos definidos e indefinidos

5.A.1   Forms of definite and indefinite articles

Both the definite and indefinite articles can be masculine or feminine, singular or plural. They are placed before a noun and take the same gender and number as that noun.

	Definite articles		Indefinite articles	
	Masculine	**Feminine**	**Masculine**	**Feminine**
Singular	el	la	un	una
Plural	los	las	unos	unas

el amigo	*the friend*	**un** amigo	*a friend*
los amigos	*the friends*	**unos** amigos	*some friends*
la escuela	*the school*	**una** escuela	*a school*
las escuelas	*the schools*	**unas** escuelas	*some schools*

◀ Note that **uno** is an *indefinite pronoun* and it can never be used with a noun: 7.C.4 and 7.D.3

5.A.2   *Lo*

The neuter article **lo** is used before adjectives, possessive pronouns, and gradable adverbs (**mejor**, **peor**) in order to express abstract concepts. The neuter article **lo** cannot be placed before nouns.

◀ Lo mejor, lo peor: 11.D.3

lo bueno	*the good (thing)*	**lo** mío	*my thing*

5.A.3   Use of *el* and *un* with feminine nouns

El and **un** are used before feminine nouns that begin with a stressed **a-** or **ha-**. The noun continues to be feminine in the plural: **el** agua, **las** aguas.

el águila bonit**a**	*the beautiful eagle*	**el ha**cha negr**a**	*the black axe*
un águila bonit**a**	*a beautiful eagle*	**un ha**cha negr**a**	*a black axe*

5.A.4   Abbreviating the article *el*

When the prepositions **a** or **de** precede the definite article **el**, they combine to form a contraction: **a + el = al** and **de + el = del**.

Viajo **al** Perú.	*I'm going to Peru.*	el libro **del** chico	*the boy's book*

◀ The article **el** does not form a contraction with the preposition when it is part of a proper name: **Viajo a El Salvador**: 5.C.6

5.B   Use of indefinite articles
Uso de los artículos indefinidos

◀ Indefinite determiners: 7.C.4

5.B.1   Placement and agreement of indefinite articles

a. Indefinite articles are always placed before the noun and agree with it in gender and number.

Tengo **un** libro.	*I have a book.*
Escribo **una** carta.	*I'm writing a letter.*

b. Nouns can become subjects accompanied by these determiners.

Unos turistas visitaron la Casa Blanca.	*(Some/A few) Tourists visited the White House.*
Un chico ya la había visitado.	*A boy had already visited it.*

c. No other determiners can appear together with indefinite articles, except for **poco/a(s)** and **cada**.

Tengo **un poco** de café.	*I have some coffee.*
Tengo **unas pocas** amigas mexicanas.	*I have a few Mexican friends.*
Cada uno debe cuidar sus cosas.	*Everyone should look after his/her possessions.*

5.B.2 Reference to quantity

Indefinite determiners: 7.C.4

a. The singular indefinite articles **un(a)** may refer to exactly one person or object, especially in contrasts and to stress the lack of something countable (*not even one, not a single one*).

No tengo **un** hermano, sino **tres**.	*I don't have **one** brother, but **three**.*
Voy a comprar **una** torta, no **dos**.	*I am going to buy **one** cake, not **two**.*
No hay ni **una** (sola) silla libre.	*There is not a single vacant seat.*

b. The plural indefinite articles **unos/as** refer to an undefined quantity and, with numbers, to an approximate one.

Hay **unas** estudiantes polacas.	*There are **some** Polish students.*
Me quedan **unos cuatro** dólares.	*I have **around** four dollars left.*

5.B.3 Exclamations

In exclamations, to add emphasis, it is common to use an article in cases where it may technically not be required.

Hace frío.	*It's cold.*
¡Hace **un** frío!	*It's so cold!*

5.B.4 *Otro/a(s)*

Uno/a are not used before **otro/a(s)** (*one more, another*).

¡Por favor, **otro** café!	*Another coffee, please!*	**¡Otra** vez!	*One more time!*

5.C | Use of definite articles

Uso de los artículos definidos

5.C.1 General uses

Unlike English, Spanish uses the definite article when talking about people, things, or events in general.

Los estudiantes son trabajadores.	*Students are hard-working.*
Me gusta **la** leche.	*I like milk.*

5.C.2 Days and dates

a. The definite article is *not* used with months or to tell which day it is.

Hoy es lunes.	*Today is Monday.*
Ayer fue jueves.	*Yesterday was Thursday.*
Voy a Medellín en noviembre.	*I'm going to Medellín in November.*

b. The definite article is used to refer to something on a specific day or date.

Estudio **los** martes.   *I study on Tuesdays.*
La Nochebuena es **el** 24 de diciembre.   *Christmas Eve is December 24.*

5.C.3 Time

Time is indicated by **ser** + **(a) las** + *number* for plurals, and **ser** + **(a) la una** for *one o'clock*.

La clase de español **es a las** tres.   *Spanish class is at three o'clock.*
Son las cuatro de la tarde.   *It is four o'clock in the afternooon.*
La cita es **a la una**.   *The appointment is at one o'clock.*

◄ **Ser** in calendar and time expressions: 29.C.2a

5.C.4 Vocative forms and titles

Articles are not used with titles or proper names when addressing someone directly. However, when talking about someone in the third person, the article is used and matches the person in gender and number. The polite vocative forms **don** and **doña** are used in the singular without an article and are followed by a first name.

Addressing someone	
Señora Gómez, ¿es usted peruana?	*Are you Peruvian, Mrs. Gómez?*
Doctor Medina, ¿cómo está usted?	*How are you, Dr. Medina?*
Don Pedro, ¿habla usted inglés?	*Do you speak English, Pedro?*

Talking about someone	
La señora Gómez es peruana.	*Mrs. Gómez is Peruvian.*
El doctor Medina está bien.	*Dr. Medina is well.*
Don Pedro no habla inglés.	*Pedro doesn't speak English.*

5.C.5 Names of languages

The names of languages take a definite article except after the preposition **en** or with the verbs **hablar** (*to talk*), **aprender** (*to learn*), **comprender** (*to understand*), **enseñar** (*to teach*), **escribir** (*to write*), **leer** (*to read*), and **saber** (*to know*).

El español es fácil.   *Spanish is easy.*
¿Cómo se dice eso **en** español?   *How do you say that in Spanish?*
John, ¿**hablas** español?   *Do you speak Spanish, John?*

5.C.6 Country names

a. The names of some countries and regions are used with the definite article. The article can be left out if it is not a part of the official name.

la Argentina	**los** Estados Unidos	**el** Paraguay
el Brasil	**la** Florida	**el** Perú
el Canadá	**la** India	**la** República Dominicana
el Ecuador	**el** Japón	**el** Uruguay

b. If the article is a part of the official name, it is capitalized. In this case, the masculine article is not abbreviated after the prepositions **a** or **de**.

Vivo en **El** Salvador.   *I live in El Salvador.*
Llegué a **El** Dorado, en Bogotá.   *I arrived in El Dorado in Bogotá.*

◄ Abbreviating the article **el**: 5.A.4

Prenominal possessives: 9.B ▶

5.C.7 Ownership expressions with an article

The definite article replaces prenominal (unstressed) possessive determiners when ownership is obvious, for example, when you talk about parts of the body or personal belongings.

Article instead of possessives: ▶
9.D.4

Me duelen **los** pies.	*My feet hurt.*
¡Ponte **los** zapatos!	*Put **your** shoes on!*

5.C.8 Position of the definite article

a. The definite article must always be placed before the noun. Adjectives and adjectival phrases (e.g. *adverb + adjective*) can come between the article and noun.

Combination of two ▶
determiners: 4.B.6

la hermosa Barcelona	*beautiful Barcelona*
los cada vez más altos precios	*ever-increasing prices*

b. No determiners other than **todo/a(s)** can be placed before the definite article.

todos los profesores	*all of the professors*

5.C.9 Articles without nouns

When the noun can be identified from context, the article can be used alone with an adjective, adverb, and/or pronoun.

No quiero tu bolsa azul; dame **la** roja.	*I don't want your blue bag; give me the red one.*
Nos gusta su auto, pero es mejor **el** nuestro.	*We like his car, but ours is better.*

5.C.10 Articles in exclamations

Lo: 5.A.2 ▶

The definite article and the neuter **lo** can be used before an adjective in exclamations. In English, you would normally use *how many/much* or *how + adjective*.

¡Es increíble **la** gente que hay!	*It's amazing how many people there are!*
¡**Lo** bien que estamos aquí!	*How great life is here!*

5.C.11 Family names

The definite article in the plural is used before last names (in the singular) to refer to the whole family.

Los Johnson están en Madrid.	*The Johnson family is in Madrid.*
Pronto vendrán **los** Romero.	*The Romero family will come soon.*

5.D Regional variations

Variaciones regionales

5.D.1 Proper names

In some regions of Latin America and Spain, the definite article is used before proper names in spoken language. Normally, it is used only when referring to close friends or family. In regions where this use of the definite article is less common, some native speakers may consider it incorrect.

Quiero mucho a **la** Juana.	*I'm very fond of Juana.*
¡Debemos visitar **al** Miguel!	*We must visit Miguel!*

Práctica

Actividades 1–4,
p. A16

Quantifiers: Numbers
Cuantificadores: Los números

Chapter 6
Determiners (3)
A. Cardinal numbers
B. Use of cardinal numbers
C. Collective numbers and counting expressions
D. Ordinal numbers
E. Fractions and multiples
F. Time
G. Dates
H. Age
I. Temperature
J. Idiomatic expressions

6.A Cardinal numbers

Números cardinales

0–199 Números del cero al ciento noventa y nueve

0	cero	10	diez	20	veinte	30	treinta
1	uno/a	11	once	21	veintiuno/a	40	cuarenta
2	dos	12	doce	22	veintidós	50	cincuenta
3	tres	13	trece	23	veintitrés	60	sesenta
4	cuatro	14	catorce	24	veinticuatro	70	setenta
5	cinco	15	quince	25	veinticinco	80	ochenta
6	seis	16	dieciséis	26	veintiséis	90	noventa
7	siete	17	diecisiete	27	veintisiete	100	cien
8	ocho	18	dieciocho	28	veintiocho	101	ciento uno/a
9	nueve	19	diecinueve	29	veintinueve	199	ciento noventa y nueve

200–1000 Números del doscientos al mil

200	doscientos/as	700	setecientos/as
300	trescientos/as	800	ochocientos/as
400	cuatrocientos/as	900	novecientos/as
500	quinientos/as	1000	mil
600	seiscientos/as		

1001–1 000 000 Números del mil uno a un millón

1001	mil un(o/a)	100 000	cien mil
1002	mil dos	200 000	doscientos/as mil
2000	dos mil	1 000 000	un millón

2 000 000 Números mayores de dos millones

2 000 000	dos millones
1 000 000 000	mil millones (*a billion*)
1 000 000 000 000	un billón (*a trillion*)

Spanish	U.S. English	U.K. English								
mil	*thousand*	*thousand*	1000							
un millón	*million*	*million*	1000	000						
mil millones/millardo	*billion*	*thousand million/milliard*	1000	000	000					
un billón	*trillion*	*billion*	1000	000	000	000				
mil billones	*quadrillion*	*billiard*	1000	000	000	000	000			
trillón	*quintillion*	*trillion*	1000	000	000	000	000	000		
mil trillones	*sextillion*	*trilliard*	1000	000	000	000	000	000	000	
cuatrillón	*septillion*	*quadrillion*	1000	000	000	000	000	000	000	000

España tiene alrededor de **cuarenta millones** de habitantes.	*Spain has approximately forty million inhabitants.*
México tiene más de **cien millones** de habitantes.	*Mexico has more than a hundred million inhabitants.*
Ecuador tiene **doscientos ochenta y tres mil quinientos sesenta y un** kilómetros cuadrados.	*Ecuador is 283,561 km².*

6.A.1 Writing styles for numbers

a. Numbers (not decimals) of four digits or fewer are written without a space, period, or comma: **1000; 230.** This also applies to years, pages, postal codes, law paragraphs, and line numbers.

b. Numbers (not decimals) of more than four digits are divided into groups of three, as in English. If the number of digits is not evenly divisible by three, the one or two digits left over form a separate group. Each group is separated by a space: **10 000 000; 23 005; 100 500.** The traditional spelling with a comma or a period as separator every three digits is no longer required. When the number is very large, it can be shortened in the text by writing digits and words: **3 trillones de euros.** Numbers with **mil**, however, cannot be written with both digits and words.

Numbers and counting expressions: 6.C.2
Ordinal numbers: 6.D.2

c. Decimals are marked with a comma, but a period can also be used. The convention varies between Spanish-speaking countries: 0.23 (**cero punto veintitrés**); 0,23 (**cero coma veintitrés**). This figure can also be read as (**cero con**) **veintitrés centésimos** (*zero and twenty-three hundredths*).

6.B Use of cardinal numbers

Uso de los números cardinales

6.B.1 Numbers combined

hay (*there is/are*): 29.B.1

Uno/un	**Un** is used before masculine nouns. *51 books:* cincuenta y **un** libros *541 books:* quinientos cuarenta y **un** libros The term **uno** is only used when it is not followed by a noun. —¿Cuántos estudiantes hay? *How many students are there?* —Hay **uno**. / Hay treinta y **uno**. *There is one. / There are thirty-one.*
Una	**Una** is used before feminine nouns. *31 pounds:* treinta y **una** libras *1001 pounds:* mil (y) **una** libras Note that **uno/una** do not have a plural form even if they are part of a number greater than 1.
Y	**Y** is used between the tens and ones. 1492: mil cuatrocientos noventa **y** dos 2 010 095: dos millones diez mil noventa **y** cinco But: 409 001: cuatrocientos nueve mil uno/a
21–29	Combinations of the number 20 are written as one word. It is less common to use three words. 21: **veintiuno/a** (**veintiún** before masculine nouns) / veinte y uno/a 26: **veintiséis** / veinte y seis 225: doscientos **veinticinco** / doscientos veinte y cinco
31–99	Combinations of numbers between 31 and 99 are written in three words. 32: **treinta y dos**; 92: **noventa y dos** 2255: dos mil doscientos **cincuenta y cinco**

100 **Cien**	**Cien** by itself expresses *a hundred/one hundred*. **Cien** does not agree in gender or number with the noun. *100 books*: **cien** libros *100 boxes*: **cien** cajas El cien es mi número favorito. *One hundred is my favorite number.* ¿Cuántos estudiantes hay? *How many students are there?* Hay **cien** estudiantes. *There are one hundred students.*
101–199 **Ciento**	**Ciento** is used between **101** and **199** before nouns and does not change in gender and number. *103 books*: **ciento** tres libros *169 boxes*: **ciento** sesenta y nueve cajas
200–999 **Cientos/as**	**Cientos/as** is used between **200** and **999** and agrees with the noun's gender. Unlike English, multiple hundreds are expressed in one word (though the subsequent numbers are separate). *200 schools*: **doscientas** escuelas *301 houses*: **trescientas** una casas *999 teachers*: **novecientos noventa y nueve** profesores
1000 **Mil**	**Mil** does not change in gender. In some Latin American countries, the indefinite article **un** can be used before **mil** in financial and legal documents when the number is exactly a thousand. *1000 dollars / girls*: (**un**) **mil** dólares / (**un**) **mil** niñas *2000 dollars / girls*: **dos mil** dólares / **dos mil** niñas
1 000 000 **Millón /** **Millones** **Millón de** **Millones de**	**Millón** is used in the singular when referring to a single million (**un millón, este millón**). When referring to two millions or more, always use **millones** (**dos millones** de personas; *two million people*). *1 021 101 pesos*: **un millón veintiún mil ciento un** pesos *2 100 341 rupees*: **dos millones cien mil trescientas cuarenta y una** rupias Round numbers in *whole millions* are followed by **de.** *1 000 000 pesos*: **un millón de** pesos *131 000 000 dollars*: **ciento treinta y un millones de** dólares But: *131 001 000 dollars*: **ciento treinta y un millones mil** dólares
Cientos de **Miles de** **Millones de**	**Cientos de** and **miles de** are not used for counting. The expressions are used similarly in English and Spanish. **Millones de** can also indicate an unspecified high number of countable nouns. Hay **cientos de / miles de /** *There are hundreds/thousands/* **millones de** personas en las calles. *millions of people on the streets.*

6.B.2   The word *número*

The word **número** is masculine and its article agrees in gender, no matter if the word **número** is explicit or not.

El (**número**) trece me gusta.   *I like the number thirteen.*
El **primer** trece de la lista tiene que ir en color rojo.   *The first (number) thirteen on the list must be in red.*

6.B.3   Plurals

a. Numbers' plural forms follow the same rules as other nouns.

¿Tienes billetes de **cinco** pesos?   *Do you have five-peso bills?*
No, solamente tengo **dieces** y **veintes.**   *No, I only have tens and twenties.*

b. As in English, the number **cero** is used with plural nouns, even with fractions.

Hace cero grados Celsius de temperatura.   *The temprature is zero degrees Celsius.*
El bebé creció solo 0,5 centímetros el último mes.   *Last month the baby grew only 0.5 centimeters.*

6.C Collective numbers and counting expressions

Expresiones numéricas colectivas y expresiones para contar

6.C.1 Decena, veintena

Collective numbers are followed by **de** before the noun.

Década and other words for periods of time: 6.J.2

decena(s)	*ten(s)*	**cincuentena**	*about fifty*
docena(s)	*dozen(s)*	**sesentena**	*about sixty*
veintena	*about twenty*	**setentena**	*about seventy*
treintena	*about thirty*	**centenar(es)**	*a hundred/hundreds*
cuarentena	*about forty*	**millar(es)**	*a thousand/thousands*

En la biblioteca hay **millares** de libros.   *There are thousands of books in the library.*
La **docena** de huevos cuesta dos dólares.   *A dozen eggs cost two dollars.*

6.C.2 Numbers and counting expressions

a. Percentages can be preceded by the definite article **el** or the indefinite article **un.**

Los precios suben (el/un) **2%** mañana.   *The prices go up 2% tomorrow.*
Mi casa vale hoy un **diez por ciento** más   *My house is worth about 10% more today than*
que cuando la compré.   *when I bought it.*

Writing styles for numbers: 6.A.1

b. In most Spanish-speaking countries, the period is still used after thousands (although it can be left out in newer writing styles) and the comma with decimals.

1.000   **mil**   **0,5**   **cero coma cinco**

c. The use of the comma for the thousands is still common in some countries, like México and Perú. The period is used for the decimals.

1,000   **mil**   **0.5**   **cero punto cinco**

d. The preposition **con** is used to indicate decimals in prices.

$ 45,60   cuarenta y cinco pesos **con** sesenta centavos   *forty-five pesos and sixty cents*

e. Although done in English, numbers over a thousand can not be read as hundreds in Spanish.

€ 1250   mil doscientos cincuenta euros   *twelve hundred and fifty euros*

f. The verb **ser** (**es/son**) and the following expressions are used to describe calculations in Spanish. The singular form (**es**) is used if the calculation is equal to the numbers 0 or 1 only. The symbols **:** and **/** are also used for division. The symbols **·** or **∗** are also used for multiplication.

	Mathematical operations		Examples
+	**La suma**	$1 + 2 = 3$	Uno **más/y** dos **es igual a / son** tres.
–	**La resta**	$2 - 2 = 0$	Dos **menos** dos **es igual a / es** cero.
×	**La multiplicación**	$3 \times 4 = 12$	Tres **por** cuatro **es igual a / son** doce.
÷	**La división**	$4 \div 2 = 2$	Cuatro **dividido (por/entre)** dos **es igual a / son** dos.
=	**El resultado:** *igual a*	$10 - 7 = 3$	Diez **menos** siete **es igual a / son** tres.

6.D | Ordinal numbers

Números ordinales

6.D.1 Ordinal numbers 1–99

a. The ordinal numbers between **1** and **10** are the most used in Spanish. In everyday speech it is also common to use **décimo primero/a** and **décimo segundo/a** instead of **undécimo/a** and **duodécimo/a**, which are not used in many countries. An ordinal number for the number zero does not exist. In most Spanish-speaking countries, the **planta baja** (*ground floor*) is not considered the first floor, whereas in English it is. Therefore, in Spanish the **primer piso** (*first floor*) is usually equivalent to the *second floor* in English, and so on.

Ordinal numbers 1–99			
primer(o/a)	first	**séptimo/a**	seventh
segundo/a	second	**octavo/a**	eighth
tercer(o/a)	third	**noveno/a**	ninth
cuarto/a	fourth	**décimo/a**	tenth
quinto/a	fifth	**undécimo/a**	eleventh
sexto/a	sixth	**duodécimo/a**	twelth

b. In formal situations, the following ordinal numbers are also used. However, in everyday language there is an increasing trend to avoid the usage of complex ordinal numbers, replacing them with the corresponding cardinal number.

vigésimo/a	twentieth	**sexagésimo/a**	sixtieth
trigésimo/a	thirtieth	**septuagésimo/a**	seventieth
cuadragésimo/a	fortieth	**octogésimo/a**	eightieth
quincuagésimo/a	fiftieth	**nonagésimo/a**	nintieth

Perdí la carrera en la **vigésima** vuelta.

I lost the race on the twentieth lap.

Hoy celebramos el **septuagésimo** aniversario de la escuela.

Today, we're celebrating the school's seventieth anniversary.

6.D.2 Centésimo, milésimo, millonésimo

The round numbers **centésimo/a(s)** (*hundredth[s]*), **milésimo/a(s)** (*thousandth[s]*), **millonésimo/a(s)** (*millionth[s]*), are mostly used for fractions or used figuratively to mean a large number.

◀ Writing styles for numbers: 6.A.1

Esta es la **milésima** llamada.

This is the thousandth call.

1/1000 es un(a) **milésimo/a.**

1/1000 is a thousandth.

6.D.3 Milenario, centenario, millonario

Milenario/a and **centenario/a** are terms for age, while **millonario/a** describes wealth, just like in English.

Machu Picchu es una ciudad **milenaria.**

Machu Picchu is a thousand-year-old city.

Roberta Martínez es **millonaria.**

Roberta Martínez is a millionaire.

Para el **bicentenario** de la Independencia hubo muchos actos oficiales.

There were many official ceremonies for the bicentennial anniversary of our Independence.

6.D.4 Agreement

Ordinal numbers are adjectives and agree in gender and number with the noun they modify. In the singular, **primero** and **tercero** are shortened before a masculine noun.

el décimo **tercer** aniversario	*the thirteenth anniversary*
el **tercer** puesto	*the third position*

6.D.5 Abbreviations

In written language, a superscript **a** or **o** is written to the right of the number to indicate the noun's gender and number. The superscript letter is separated from the number with a period. The superscript **-er** is used to abbreviate **primer** and **tercer.**

Viajo en **1.ª** clase.	*I travel in first class.*
Marta vive en el **10.º** piso.	*Marta lives on the tenth floor.*
Está en **3.ᵉʳ** grado.	*She is in third grade.*

6.D.6 Proper names

Royal names and other names in numerical order between **1–10** are written with Roman numerals and are read as ordinal numbers. Starting from the Roman numeral **XI,** the numerals are read as cardinal numbers.

Isabel II	Isabel **segunda**	*Elizabeth II*
Papa Juan Pablo II	Papa Juan Pablo **segundo**	*Pope John Paul II*
Luis XV	Luis **quince**	*Louis XV*
Papa Juan XXIII	Papa Juan **veintitrés**	*Pope John XXIII*

6.D.7 Ordinals used as nouns

With the definite article, ordinals may function as a noun.

Soy la **primera** de la fila y tú, el **tercero.**	*I am the first one in this line; you are the third.*

6.E Fractions and multiples

Números fraccionarios y multiplicativos

6.E.1 Numerators and denominators

a. The *numerator* (**numerador**) in Spanish is read as a cardinal number. *Denominators* (**denominadores**) are read as ordinal numbers, except in the case of 1/2, which is read **un medio**, or **la mitad**, and the masculine form for 1/3 or 2/3, for which the word **tercio(s)** is used. The ordinal number agrees in gender and number with the noun.

1/2	un medio, la mitad	1/10	un(a) décimo/a, una décima parte
2/3	dos tercios, dos terceras partes	1/7	un sé(p)timo, una sé(p)tima parte
1/4	un cuarto, una cuarta parte	4/8	cuatro octavos, cuatro octavas partes
3/5	tres quintos, tres quintas partes	2/9	dos novenos, dos novenas partes

b. Starting from 11, **-avo/a** is added to the cardinal numbers in denominators with the exception of **centésimo/a(s)**, **milésimo/a(s)**, **millonésimo/a(s)**.

Tenemos una **doceava** parte de la compañía.	*We own a twelfth of the company.*
Erré la estimación por sólo cinco **centésimas**.	*I misestimated by only five hundredths.*

c. Fractions are followed by **de** before a noun.

El corredor ganó por una **milésima de** segundo.   *The runner won by a thousandth of a second.*
Mil dólares es la **mitad del** precio.   *A thousand dollars is half the price.*

Medio is used without **de** before **kilo, litro**, etc. **De** can sometimes be omitted before **cuarto**.
Medio litro de leche.
Un **cuarto (de) kilo** de harina.

6.E.2 Multiples

a. The following words express multiple amounts and can function as nouns or adjectives.

Most used	
doble	*double*
triple	*triple*

Less used	
cuádruple	*cuadruple*
quíntuple	*quintuple*
séxtuple	*sextuple*

En el dormitorio hay una cama **doble.**   *There is a double bed in the bedroom.*
Por favor, dame un café expreso **triple.**   *Please, give me a triple espresso.*
Veinticinco es el **quíntuple** de cinco.   *Twenty-five is five times five.*

b. To express exponential quantities, use *number* + **veces más/menos** (*times more/less*).

Mi auto costó **cinco veces más** que el tuyo.   *My car cost five times more than yours.*

 Comparisons with **más/menos**: 11.B

6.F Time

La hora

6.F.1 *Es/son*

a. The time is given with the verb **ser** in the singular (**es**) for one o'clock, and in the plural (**son**) for the rest.

Use of **ser** with the time: 29.C.2

Es la una **en punto.**   *It's one o'clock.*
Son las ocho de la noche.   *It's eight at night.*
Son las cuatro de la mañana.   *It's four in the morning.*

b. It is the norm to ask about the time with the verb **ser** in the singular, but in some parts of Latin America the plural form is also used.

¿Qué hora es? / ¿Qué horas son?   *What time is it?*

6.F.2 Time after the hour

The time that has passed after the hour is expressed with the *hour* plus **y** and the *number of minutes*. **Cuarto** or **quince** can be used for *quarter past* and **media** or **treinta** for *half past*.

Son las ocho **y** diez.   *It's ten past eight.*
Es la una **y cuarto/quince.**   *It's quarter-past one.*
Son las seis **y media/treinta.**   *It's half-past six.*

6.F.3 Time before the hour

The minutes remaining until the next hour are expressed with **menos**, primarily in Spain. In Latin America, the expression **falta(n)** (*it's lacking*) is also used plus the number of minutes which remain until the next hour.

Son las dos **menos** diez.
Faltan diez **para** las dos.   *It's ten to two.*
Es la una **menos** cuarto.
Falta un cuarto **para** la una.   *It's a quarter to one.*

ser and estar with the calendar
and time: 29.C.2

6.F.4 Time (appointments)

The verb **ser** followed by **a** + **la(s)** + *clock time* expresses a time/appointment.

—¿**Es a las** dos de la tarde la cita?   *Is the appointment at 2 p.m.?*
—No, es **a la** una de la tarde.   *No, it's at 1 p.m.*

6.F.5 The 24-hour clock

In Latin America, the 12-hour clock is more commonly used in everyday speech. In Spain, the 24-hour clock sometimes called military time, is also used.

La conferencia es a las **19:30**   *The conference is at seven-thirty p.m.*
(diecinueve [y] treinta) **horas.**
La boda es a las **15** (quince) **horas.** *The wedding is at three p.m.*

6.F.6 Time expressions: *de la mañana / tarde / noche*

With the 12-hour clock, add whether it is the morning, afternoon, or evening.

Es la una **de la mañana.**   *It's one in the morning.*
Son las cinco **de la tarde.**   *It's five in the afternoon.*
Son las nueve **de la noche.**   *It's nine at night.*

6.G Dates

La fecha

6.G.1 Structure

a. The date is expressed with the verb **ser.** For day, month, and year, cardinal numbers are used with the following structures.

15 de mayo de 2010   Hoy **es** (el) quince de mayo de dos mil diez.   15/05/2010

b. In Spain, the first of the month is expressed with **uno,** but in Latin America, **primero** is used.

Hoy es (el) **uno** de enero.
Hoy es (el) **primero** de enero.   *Today is January first.*

6.G.2 Letters

In letters and other documents, place and date are separated by a comma, like in English. Months can also come before the day's date.

Nueva York, 2 de mayo de 2020   Nueva York, dos de mayo de dos mil veinte
Nueva York, abril 19 de 2010   Nueva York, abril diecinueve de dos mil diez

6.G.3 Years

In Spanish, years are not read as hundreds as they are in English. The year is always read as a cardinal number.

4 de julio de 1776:
Cuatro de julio de mil   *July fourth, seventeen seventy-six*
setecientos setenta y seis

6.G.4 The calendar

In Spain, the calendar goes from Monday to Sunday, but in many Latin American countries the calendar starts with Sunday like in the U.S.

6.G.5 Expressions of time for dates

Todo/a(s), **próximo/a(s)**, **dentro de**, and **en** are commonly used in expressions of time.

◀ **todo:** Determiners 7.C.9

todos los días / meses, **todas las** semanas	*every day/month/week*
todos los años	*every year*
dentro de / en **ocho** días	
dentro de / en **una** semana	*in a week*
dentro de / en **unos** días	*in a few days*
dentro de / en **quince** días	
dentro de / en **dos** semanas	*in two weeks*
la semana **próxima**; el mes/año **próximo**	
la **próxima** semana, el **próximo** mes/año	*next week/month/year*
Mi cumpleaños es dentro de **ocho** días.	*My birthday's in a week.*
La escuela empieza dentro de / en **quince** días.	*School begins in two weeks.*

6.H Age

La edad

6.H.1 Structure

In Spanish, age is expressed with the verb **tener.**

◀ **tener** with age: 29.D

Juliana **tiene** tres años.	*Juliana is three years old.*

6.H.2 Birthdays

The verb **cumplir** describes how many years a person is turning or how old a person is.

Juliana **cumple** tres años hoy.	*Juliana is turning three today.*
	Juliana is three today.

6.H.3 Talking about age

In English, it is common to include age when talking about people, for example, in the news (*A sixty-year-old won the lottery.*) In Spanish, it is not so common to use age when talking about people, except when it is of significance to the context. Note the following age expressions.

Expressions of age	Use
quinceañero/a	Terms used to refer to fifteen-year olds. **La fiesta de quinceañera** or **fiesta de quince años** is a celebration for girls who turn fifteen in Latin America to mark their passage into adulthood.
veinteañero/a	A less common term for people around twenty years of age, primarily used to emphasize that they are still young.
cuarentón/cuarentona cincuentón/cincuentona sesentón/sesentona	Derogatory terms used to refer to men or women over forty, fifty, sixty years of age: *forty-year-old, fifty-year-old, sixty-year-old.*
octogenario/a, nonagenario/a, centenario/a	Neutral terms referring to old age for both sexes: *eighty-year-old, ninety-year-old, hundred-year-old.*

◀ Augmentative suffixes: 2.C.10b

Temperatura

6.I.1 Structure

a. Temperature can be expressed using the following structures.

Hacer and estar with weather
expressions 29.C.1

¿Qué temperatura **hace**?	*What's the temperature?*
Hace tres grados **bajo cero**.	*It's three degrees below zero.*
¿Cuántos grados **hace**?	*How many degrees is it?*
Hace veinte **grados**.	*It's twenty degrees.*
¿A qué temperatura **estamos**?	*What's the temperature (now)?*
Estamos a cero **grados**.	*It's freezing (It's zero degrees).*

b. Temperature is measured in degrees Celsius (**grados Celsius/centígrados**) in Spain and Latin America, except in Puerto Rico, which uses both the system used in the U.S., Fahrenheit (**grados Fahrenheit**), and Celsius.

In Spanish, there should be a space between the number and the degree symbol, and no space between the degree symbol and *C* or *F*.

15 °C es aproximadamente 60 °F.　　　　*15 °C is about 60 °F.*

6.I.2 Words and expressions

temperatura **máxima/mínima**	*highest/lowest temperature*
temperatura **media/promedio**	*average temperature*
temperatura **normal**	*normal temperature*

6.J Idiomatic expressions

6.J.1 The expressions *y pico, y tantos*

In order to express *a bit* in relation to quantities (prices, amounts), the expression *number* + **y pico / y tantos** can be used: **treinta y uno y pico,** (*thirty-one and a bit*). In Chile, the latter expression is preferred because the former is considered taboo.

6.J.2 *Década* and other words for periods of time

Collective numbers and counting
expressions: 6.C

The periods of time **quinquenio** (*5 years*), **decenio** (*10 years*), and **centenio** (*100 years*) only refer to the numbers of years. **Década** (*decade*), **siglo** (*century*), and **milenio** (*millennium*), on the other hand, are specific periods of years. **Edad** and **era/época** are used to refer to long or remote periods of time: **Edad de Hierro** (*Iron Age*), **Era Moderna** (*Modern Times*). The majority of these terms are formal and are used primarily in written language.

Alejandro y Sara vivieron en la **década de los treinta**, en el **siglo XX**.	*Alejandro and Sara lived in the thirties, in the 20th century.*
El **nuevo milenio** trae muchas incógnitas.	*The new millennium brings many unknowns.*
El presupuesto es solamente para un **quinquenio**. Es **quinquenal**.	*The budget is only for a five-year period. It is every five years.*

Práctica

Actividades 1–16, pp. A17–A20

Indefinite quantifiers and pronouns
Cuantificadores y pronombres indefinidos

Chapter 7
Determiners (4)
A. Determiners and pronouns

B. Positive and negative indefinite quantifiers

C. Indefinite quantifiers with only positive forms

D. Indefinite pronouns

E. Common features of indefinite quantifiers and pronouns

F. Regional variations

7.A Determiners and pronouns

Determinantes y pronombres

Within the grammatical category known as determiners, words like **alguno/a(s)** (*some*) and **muchos/as** (*many*) are considered *indefinite quantifiers*. The indefinite articles **un/una** can also be considered indefinite quantifiers. Just like all other determiners, indefinite quantifiers support the noun and make it indefinite when they refer to identity, quantity, or size. In addition to indefinite quantifiers, this chapter also introduces *indefinite pronouns*; both express indefinite references and have negative forms with double negation. Some indefinite quantifiers can function as *determiners*, *pronouns*, and *adverbs*.

Había **mucha** gente. *(determiner)*	*There were a lot of people.*
Necesitaba uno pero compré **muchos**. *(pronoun)*	*I needed one but I bought a lot.*
Mi hermano trabaja **mucho**. *(adverb)*	*My brother works a lot.*

◄ Indefinite quantifiers as adverbs: 7.E.4

7.B Positive and negative indefinite quantifiers

Cuantificadores indefinidos con formas afirmativas y negativas

There are two groups of indefinite quantifiers. One group has both negative and positive forms, as shown below, and the other group has only positive forms (see **7.C**). The majority of quantifiers in these groups can agree in gender and number, but none of them have comparative or superlative forms.

◄ Comparisons: 3.E, Ch. 11

Positive		Negative	
algún, alguno/a	*some/any*	**ningún, ninguno/a**	*no/not any/none*
alguno/a(s)	*some [pl.]*	**ninguno/a(s)**	*no/not any [pl.]*

7.B.1 Double negation of *ninguno/a*

The negative forms **ningún** and **ninguno/a** require a double negation when they are placed after the verb; the same applies to the pronouns **nadie** and **nada**.

¡**No** tienes **ningún** perfil personal actualizado en tu sitio web!	*You don't have an updated personal profile on your website!*
No hay **nadie** en el restaurante.	*There is no one in the restaurant.*

◄ Double negation with **ningún** and **tampoco**: 7.E.1

7.B.2 Algún, alguno/a(s); ningún, ninguno/a

a. Algún and **ningún** function only as determiners and are only used before singular masculine nouns. Before singular feminine nouns that begin with a stressed **a** or **ha**, **algún** is commonly used (**algún arma**), but **alguna** is also possible (**alguna arma**). **Alguno(s)** can be both a pronoun and a determiner. As a determiner, the singular form only appears after the noun. **Alguna(s)** can also function as both a pronoun and a determiner. As a determiner, the singular form can be used before or after a noun. The plural forms **algunos/as** can only be used before a noun.

◄ Other short prenominal adjective forms: **buen, mal, primer, tercer**: 3.D

—¿Hay **algún** cine cerca?	*Are there any movie theaters nearby?*
—No, no hay **ningún** cine cerca.	*No, there are no movie theaters nearby.*
¿Tienes **alguna** propuesta?	*Do you have a suggestion?*
Si hay **algún** problema, avísame.	*If there is any problem, let me know.*
No hay problema **alguno**.	*There is no problem.*
Tengo **algunas** dudas.	*I have some doubts.*

ninguno/a in relative *which*-clauses: 23.D.2e ▶

b. Alguno/a(s) and **ninguno/a** (but *not* **ningunos/as**) can be used with the preposition **de** or a relative clause (*which*-clauses).

Leímos **algunas de las** nuevas novelas.	*We read some of the new novels.*
No hay **ninguna que** nos guste mucho, pero **algunas de ellas** son muy populares.	*There aren't any that we like in particular, but some of them are very popular.*

c. Alguno/a(s) is always placed after the noun in negative sentences. The following pairs of sentences have the same meaning.

No hay alternativa **alguna**.	*There isn't an/any alternative.*
No hay **ninguna** alternativa.	
No habrá viaje **alguno** este año.	*There won't be any trip this year.*
No habrá **ningún** viaje este año.	

d. The plural forms **ningunos/as** can be used before or after the noun in negative sentences, but the form **ninguno/a de** + *plural article* or *pronoun* is more common.

No he visitado **ninguna de las** plataformas de petróleo.	*I haven't visited any of the oil rigs.*

e. Ninguno/a de + *pronoun* is also used in Spanish to express *none of* in English. In such cases, **nadie** can not be used. However, this concept may be expressed with **nadie** when the **de** + *pronoun* is removed.

Ninguna de nosotras tiene vacaciones.	*None of us has vacation.*
Ninguno de ellos sabe español.	*None of them knows any Spanish.*
Nadie sabe español.	*No one knows Spanish.*

7.C Indefinite quantifiers with only positive forms

Cuantificadores indefinidos solo con formas afirmativas

Quantifying adverbs: 10.D ▶

The group of indefinite quantifiers with only positive forms is large. Some refer to the noun's indefinite identity (**cualquiera**), indefinite quantity (**muchos**), or degree (**más, menos**), while some refer to a whole (**todo**) and others to a part of something (**cada**).

cualquiera que + subjunctive: 23.D.2d
Le venderé mi casa a **cualquiera que** pague un buen precio.
I will sell my house to whoever pays the best price.

ambos/as	both	**muchos/as**	many/lots/a lot of
bastante	quite/quite a lot/enough	**otro/a**	another/another one
bastantes	quite/quite a lot/enough [pl.]	**otros/as**	other [pl.]
cada	each/every	**poco/a**	little/bit
cualquier, cualquiera (de)	whichever/whoever/any (of)	**pocos/as**	few
cualesquiera (de)	which/whoever (of)/any	**tanto/a**	so much
demás	rest/remainder	**tantos/as**	so many
demasiado/a	too much	**todo/a**	all/every/whole/everything
demasiados/as	too many [pl.]	**todos/as**	all [pl.]
más	more	**un, una**	a
menos	fewer, less	**unos/as**	some
mucho/a	a lot of/much	**varios/as**	various/several

7.C.1 Form and agreement

Indefinite quantifiers that agree in gender and/or number with the noun cannot be compared the way adjectives can. However, the determiners **mucho, poco,** and **tanto** can take the superlative ending **-ísimo/a: muchísimo/a, poquísimo/a, tantísimo/a.**

mucho - muchísimo:
4.B.3b
Comparison of adjectives: 3.E
Comparison of adverbs: 10.I
Comparisons: Ch. 11

Ambos novios se han casado **varias** veces.	*Both partners have married several times.*
Ella tiene **muchísimos** hijos y él tiene solo **una** hija.	*She has a lot of children and he has only one daughter.*
Todos son muy felices con **tantísima** gente en casa.	*Everyone is very happy with so many people at home.*
Cada familia es diferente.	*Every family is different.*

7.C.2 Positive quantifiers with double placement

Quantifiers with only positive forms are generally placed before the noun, but the following quantifiers can also be placed after the noun. Note that when following the noun, **cualquiera, más,** and **menos** must be determined with **un/a(os)** or **otro/a(s)** (or a cardinal number).

Combination of two determiners: 4.B.6

Bastante(s): 7.C.7

Varios: 7.C.6

bastante(s)	**bastante** dinero	*quite a lot of money*
	dinero **bastante**	*enough money*
vario/a(s)	**varias** galletas	*several cookies*
	galletas **varias**	*an assortment of cookies*
cualquier(a)/ cualesquiera	**cualquier** día	*whichever/any day*
	cualesquiera días	
	un día **cualquiera**	
	unos días **cualesquiera**	
más, menos	**más/menos** pan	*more/less bread*
	un pan **más/menos**	*one more loaf/one loaf less*
	otro pan **más/menos**	*another loaf/another loaf less*
	otros panes **más/menos**	*some more loaves/a few loaves less*

7.C.3 Indefinite quantifiers as pronouns

a. With a few exceptions, all quantifiers can function as a pronoun when the noun to which they refer is not explicitly stated.

Determiners as pronouns: 4.B.2

En Argentina **todo** me gusta. Hay **bastante** que ver y **mucho** que hacer.	*I like everything in Argentina. There's quite a lot to see and do.*

b. The shortened forms **un, algún, ningún** and **cualquier** cannot function as pronouns, while the corresponding longer forms in both singular and plural can: **uno/a(s), alguno/a(s), ninguno/a(s), cualquiera, cualesquiera.**

—¿Hay estudiantes franceses aquí?	*Are there French students here?*
—No, este año no hay **ninguno,** pero a veces vienen **algunos**.	*No, there aren't any this year, but sometimes there are some.*

c. In order to function as pronouns, **demás** must be accompanied by an article (**los, las, lo**) and **cada** must always be used with **uno/a** or a noun.

Dos estudiantes de la clase tienen A en todo. **Los demás,** tienen B.	*Two students in the class have an A in everything. The others have a B.*
Cada uno hizo un gran esfuerzo.	*Every one of them tried very hard.*

d. The examples below show **varios/as, otro/a(s)**, and **poco/a(s)** used as pronouns.

Varios recibieron un premio, **otros** recibieron dos premios y muy **pocos,** muchos premios.

Some of them received one prize, others received two prizes and very few, a lot of prizes.

7.C.4 *Un, uno/a, unos, unas*

Use of indefinite articles: 5.B ▶
Indefinite pronouns: 7.D ▶

a. Only the forms **un, una,** and **unos/as** can be placed before the noun, while **uno** can be only used as an indefinite determiner in the form **uno de los** (*one of the*) before the noun. In any other context, **uno** is used as a pronoun.

b. Un(a) can usually be omitted in negative sentences (*not any*).

No hay policía en la calle.	*There are no policemen on the street.*
Ella no tiene familia.	*She doesn't have any family.*
No tenemos pan en casa.	*We don't have any bread in the house.*

c. Un poco de (*A little*) is used before the noun.

Hace **un poco de** calor aquí.   *It's a little warm here.*

d. Unos/as means *about, approximately* when used before numbers.

El boleto de autobús cuesta **unos** cincuenta dólares.   *The bus ticket costs about fifty dollars.*

7.C.5 *Cualquier, cualquiera, cualesquiera*

a. Before all singular (masculine and feminine) nouns, the shortened form **cualquier** is always used. After both masculine and feminine nouns, only **cualquiera** can be used. When used after the noun, **cualquiera** can also mean *ordinary*.

Cualquier persona puede ser admitida en la universidad.	*Any person can be admitted to the university.*
Él no es una persona **cualquiera**.	*He is not an ordinary person.*
Le pediré un favor a **cualquiera de** mis amigos.	*I will ask any of my friends a favor.*
Cualquiera que llegue tarde no podrá entrar.	*Whoever arrives late will not be allowed in.*

Cualquiera in relative clauses: ▶
15.B.7, 23.D.2d

b. The plural form, **cualesquiera,** is not commonly used.

Cualesquiera (que) sean tus motivos, no estoy de acuerdo con tu decisión.	*Whatever your reasons, I don't agree with your decision.*
Traeme dos libros **cualesquiera**.	*Bring me any two books.*

7.C.6 *Ambos/as, varios/as*

Different meanings of **varios**: ▶
7.C.2

Ambos/as (*Both*) is always plural and can never be followed by **dos**. However, it can be replaced by **los/las dos**. **Ambos/as** can function alone as a pronoun when the noun is not stated. **Varios** expresses a quantity greater than two.

Ambas chicas hablan español.	*Both girls speak Spanish.*
Las dos chicas estudian mucho.	*The two girls study a lot.*
Varias personas son suecas.	*Several people are Swedish.*
Llegaron dos invitados y **ambos** son alemanes.	*Two guests arrived and both are German.*

7.C.7 *Bastante(s)*

This quantifier must agree in number with the noun, and usually precedes it.

Placement of **bastante** after ▶
the noun: 7.C.2

Hay **bastante** gente en el concierto.	*There are quite a lot of people at the concert.*
En este libro hay **bastantes** ejemplos de gramática.	*In this book there are quite a lot of grammar examples.*

Indefinite quantifiers and pronouns • **Chapter 7**

7.C.8 Cada, cada uno/a

a. Cada does not change form and only indicates a part of a whole. It cannot stand alone without a noun. It is used as a pronoun in the form **cada uno/una (de)**. **Todo** + *singular noun* means *every (single) one* and is a synonym for **cada uno de los/las** + *noun*.

Determiners as pronouns: 4.B.2b
Todo: 7.C.9

Cada estudiante debe hacer el trabajo individualmente.	*Every student should do the work individually.*
Revisaremos el contenido de **cada uno de** los contratos.	*We will go through the contents of every one of the contracts.*
Todo contrato/**Cada uno de** los contratos debe estar firmado.	*Every single contract should be signed.*

b. Cada, cada uno de los/las + *noun* brings attention to each member of a group.

Cada animal es único.	*Each animal is unique.*
Cada uno de los animales es único.	*Each of the animals is unique.*

c. In Spanish, periods of time are expressed with **todo: todos los días, todas las semanas. Cada** is used to convey periodical repetition rather than a whole period of time.

Pienso en ti **cada** segundo del día, **todos** los días.	*I think about you every second of the day, every day.*
Hay que tomar la medicina **cada** dos horas.	*The medicine must be taken every two hours.*
Cada vez suben más los precios.	*The prices keep increasing (each time).*

7.C.9 Todo

a. When **todo** indicates something abstract (*everything*), it is an indefinite pronoun.

Todo es muy sencillo.	*It's all very simple.*
¿Lo terminaste **todo**?	*Did you finish everything?*

b. When it refers to an implied noun and appears alone, **todo** is a pronoun and agrees in gender and number with the noun.

—¿Enviaste los paquetes? —Sí, los envié **todos**.	*Did you send all the packages? Yes, I sent them all.*
Dice que no le gusta la polenta, pero siempre se la come **toda**.	*He says he doesn't like polenta, but he always eats it all.*

c. Todo/a + *singular noun* is a synonym for **todos/as los/las** + *plural noun*.

Todo animal es único.	*Every animal is unique.*
Todos los animales son únicos.	*All animals are unique.*

d. Todo lo, todo el, and **toda la** refer to an entire object or something as a whole.

Eso es **todo lo** que sé.	*That's all/everything I know.*
¡**Todo el** año pasó volando!	*The whole year flew by!*
Te querré **toda la** vida.	*I will love you my whole life.*

e. Todo/a un(a) intensifies the noun.

 todo/a un(a): 4.B.6c

Es buenísimo tener **todo un** día libre.	*It's awesome to have a whole day free.*
¡Los glaciares de Alaska son **toda una** maravilla!	*The glaciers in Alaska are all so amazing!*

Determiners as pronouns:
4.B.2b, 4.B.6d

7.C.10 Demás

Demás does not change form and usually needs a plural, definite article when it is placed before a noun. It is often used as a noun with the neuter article **lo** to mean *the rest, the remainder* and with **todo** as an intensifier: **todo lo demás** (*everything else*). On rare occasions, **demás** can be used without an article.

Usted debe firmar **los demás** documentos.	You must sign the rest of the documents.
Dime **todo lo demás**.	Tell me about all the rest/everything else.
Saludos para tu familia y **todos los demás** parientes.	Greetings to your family and all your other relatives.
Los jefes y **demás** colegas vendrán a la fiesta de Navidad.	The bosses and other colleagues will come to the Christmas party.

7.C.11 Demasiado/a(s)

With uncountable nouns (*water, pollution*) **demasiado** means *too much*. With countable nouns, it means *too many*. It can be combined with **poco,** to mean *too little*, but not with **mucho/a(s)**.

Hay **demasiada** contaminación.	There is too much pollution.
Tenéis **demasiadas** cosas que hacer.	You [pl.] have too many things to do.
Se come mucha carne y **demasiado poco** pescado.	They eat a lot of meat and not enough fish.

7.C.12 Más, menos, mucho/a(s), poco/a(s)

These quantifiers are very flexible. Their most important function is in comparisons, but they also form many common expressions. Note the use of **un poco más/menos de, varios**.

Expressions with *más, menos, mucho, poco*	
muchas más horas	many more hours
muchos menos amigos	far fewer friends
un poco más de café	a little more coffee
algunos pocos ejemplos **más**	a few more examples
bastante más dinero	quite a lot more money
bastantes menos cosas	far fewer/very few things
otras cosas **más**	several other things
varias cosas **menos**	fewer things

Invitaron a **mucha más** gente de lo que habían dicho.	They invited a lot more people than they'd said they would.
Tendrías que poner **un poco menos de** chocolate y **un poco más de** azucar.	You should use a little less chocolate and a little more sugar.
No pienso esperar **muchas** horas **más**.	I won't wait many more hours.
Te presto **un** libro **más** y basta.	I'll lend you one more book and that's it.

7.C.13 Otro/a(s)

a. Unlike English, **otro/a** can never be combined with **un(a)**, but it can be placed after the definite article: **el/la otro/a, los/as otros/as** (*the other, the others*). **Otro** is used in many Spanish expressions.

¡**Otra** pizza, por favor!	Another pizza, please!
Te vi **el otro** día.	I saw you the other day.
Este café no es bueno; compra **otra** marca.	This coffee is not good; buy another brand.
Viajaré el lunes y regresaré **al otro** día.	I will travel on Monday and return the following day.

b. Otro/a(s) can be combined with many quantifiers.

Otro/a(s) **with other quantifiers**	
ningún otro estudiante	*no other student*
alguna otra casa	*another house/some other house*
muchos otros países	*many other countries*
cualquier otro día	*any other day*
otro poco de leche	*a little more milk*
otros pocos casos	*a few other cases*
pocas otras personas	*few other people*
varios otros sitios	*several other places*
bastantes otras cosas	*many other things*
todos los otros muebles	*all the other furniture*
todo lo otro	*all the rest*
otra vez **más/menos**	*once more/less*
otras cosas **más/menos**	*some more/fewer things*
otros tres ejemplos	*three other examples*

7.D | Indefinite pronouns

Pronombres indefinidos

7.D.1 Form and placement

Indefinite pronouns can function just like common personal pronouns in a sentence. They do not agree in gender (except **una** for females) and can *never* directly support nouns like the determiners (**algún auto**). **Cada uno/a** (*each one, every*) is included as a compound indefinite pronoun.

◄ **un, uno, una** as indefinite determiners: 7.C.4

Indefinite pronouns			
Positive		**Negative**	
uno (una)	one/someone	**nadie**	no one/nobody
alguien	someone		
algo	something	**nada**	nothing

7.D.2 Features of indefinite pronouns

a. Indefinite pronouns are used with singular verbs. They do not have a plural form. If it is necessary to refer to an indefinite plural group of people, an indefinite quantifier must be used.

◄ Indefinite quantifiers with only positive forms: 7.C

¿Hay **alguien** en casa?	*Is anyone home?*
Tengo que decirte **algo**.	*I have to tell you something.*
Uno no puede saberlo todo.	*One can't know everything.*
Como abogada, **una** trabaja muchas horas diarias.	*As a lawyer, one has to work many hours a day.*

b. The negative forms need double negation when placed after the verb.

◄ Double negation of **ninguno/a**: 7.B.1

No hay **nada**.	*There is nothing/isn't anything.*
No vemos a **nadie** allí.	*We can't see anyone there.*

c. The preposition **a** must be used before indefinite pronouns that refer to a person when they function as objects: **a uno/a, a alguien, a nadie**.

◄ Use of the preposition **a** with direct objects: 12.B.2c, 13.E.2

Ellos no conocen **a nadie**.	*They know no one./They don't know anyone.*
Si **a uno** le gusta el sol, debe ir a Miami.	*Someone who likes the sun ought to go to Miami.*

7.D.3 Uno/a

a. Uno/a is used in impersonal expressions that also imply personal experience. Men use **uno** and women use **una**. However, it is also usual for women to use **uno**.

En la playa puede **uno** acostarse y descansar.	On the beach one can lay down and rest.
Uno se siente satisfecho con un trabajo bien hecho.	One feels satisfied after a job well done.
Aquí se siente **uno** muy bien.	One feels very good here.
Como le dije a mi mamá, **una** a veces tiene que quejarse.	As I told my mom, you have to complain sometimes.

In the left margin: uno in impersonal **se** sentences: 28.E.2b

b. When the noun is not stated, the determiners **unos** and **unas** also function as pronouns.

¿Tienes **unas** tijeras? Sí, tengo **unas** aquí.	Do you have a pair of scissors? Yes, I've got a pair here.

7.D.4 Nadie más

The expression **nadie más** means *nobody else.*

Nadie más tiene buenas notas.	Nobody else has good grades.
No conocemos a **nadie más** que a ti en la ciudad.	We don't know anyone other than you in the city.

7.D.5 Nada

As a pronoun and an adverb, **nada** forms many idiomatic expressions.

Este aparato **no** sirve para **nada**.	This gadget isn't useful for anything.
Tú **no** sirves para **nada**.	You're completely useless.
Tus notas **no** son **nada** buenas.	Your grades aren't good at all.
Luisa **no** es **nada** simpática.	Luisa is not nice at all.
El príncipe se casó **nada menos que** con una plebeya.	The prince married a commoner, no less.
No queremos **nada más**.	We don't want anything else.
¡Por favor, **nada de** tonterías!	Please, none of that silliness!

7.E Common features of indefinite quantifiers and pronouns

Características comunes de determinantes y pronombres indefinidos

In the left margin: Positive and negative indefinite quantifiers: 7.B Indefinite quantifiers with only positive forms: 7.C

7.E.1 Double negation

A special characteristic in the Spanish language is that the negative indefinite determiners **ningún**, **ninguno/a(s)** and the indefinite pronouns **nadie** and **nada** require *double negation* when they are placed after the verb. In this case, **no** or another negative expression must stand before the verb.

No tengo **nada**.	I don't have anything.
Hoy **no** viene **nadie**.	Nobody is coming today.
Tampoco hay **ninguna** explicación.	There isn't any explanation either.

7.E.2 Reference: person or thing?

The indefinite pronouns **alguien** and **nadie** are *only* used for people, while **algo** and **nada** can *only* be used for things. The indefinite determiners **algún, alguno/a, ningún, ninguno/a, cualquier(a), todo/a(s), un, uno/a** and all the other indefinite quantifiers in tables **7.B** and **7.C** can be used for both people and things.

Hoy **no** trabaja **nadie** porque **no** hay **nada** que hacer.

Nobody is working today because there is nothing to do.

Algunos trabajadores creen que **algo** raro sucede en la fábrica.

Some workers believe that something strange is happening in the factory.

Todos los empleados están seguros de que **alguien** sabe la verdad.

All the employees are sure that someone knows the truth.

7.E.3 The preposition *a* before an indefinite pronoun

The preposition **a** must be placed before all indefinite pronouns and indefinite quantifiers which function as direct or indirect objects and refer to people.

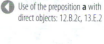
Use of the preposition **a** with direct objects: 12.B.2c, 13.E.2

No conozco **a nadie** en la universidad todavía.

I don't know anyone at the university yet.

Le preguntaré **a algún** estudiante qué actividades hay hoy.

I will ask one of the students what activities there are today.

7.E.4 Indefinite quantifiers and *algo, nada* as adverbs

Algo and **nada** can function as quantifying adverbs. **Tan, tanto, más**, and **menos** are also used as adverbs in comparisons. The adverb **muy** can only be used before adjectives and adverbs, while **mucho** can only be used after the verb.

Comparisons: Ch. 11

Quantifying adverbs: 10.D

Quantifiers and gradable adverbs			
algo	something	**nada**	nothing
mucho, muy	a lot/very	**poco**	little/few
demasiado	too much	**bastante**	quite
tan	as/very/so	**tanto**	so much
más	more	**menos**	less

Trabajo **mucho** y **muy** bien.

I work a lot and very well.

¡Los canadienses esquían **tanto** y son **tan** buenos!

Canadians ski a lot and are very good!

A veces esquío **mucho,** otras veces **poco**.

Sometimes I ski a lot, other times not so much.

Me siento **bastante** bien esquiando, pero **algo** insegura porque mis esquíes no son **nada** modernos.

I feel quite good when I ski, but a bit insecure because my skis aren't very new.

Últimamente en Colorado nieva **menos**.
Antes nevaba **mucho más**.

Recently, it has been snowing less in Colorado. It used to snow a lot more.

7.E.5 *Mismo, propio*

a. The intensifying forms **mismo/a, mismos/as** (*self/selves*) and **propio/a, propios/as** (*own*) are considered *semi-determiners* (**cuasideterminantes**). They are placed after a personal pronoun or proper noun. Both agree in gender and number but do not have comparative or superlative forms. **Propio/a** intensifies possessive determiners and proper nouns (with the definite article): **mi propio auto** (*my own car*); **el propio Juan,** which means the same as **Juan mismo** (*John himself*). **Propio /a** cannot be used with personal pronouns the same way as **mismo/a**.

Adjectives: **mismo** (*same*), comparisons with **el mismo** (*the same*): 11.C.5
Mismo with reflexives: 27.A.2
Expressions with **propio**: 9.D.3e

¿Quieres tener casa **propia**?

Do you want your own house?

Tú mismo debes decidir sobre tu **propia** vida.

You, yourself, should decide about your own life.

b. In both English and Spanish, *self* must follow the pronoun. Note that *self* cannot always be translated as **mismo/a(s),** which can also be an adjective.

él mismo, ella misma, etcétera	*himself, herself, etc.*
el mismo, la misma, los mismos, las mismas	*the same*
mi propio, mi propia, mis propios, mis propias	*my own*

Use of pronoun in contrasts: ▶ 13.A.1b

Por mi parte/Personalmente, me siento rico, pero no tengo ni un centavo.	*I **myself** feel rich, but I don't have a cent to my name.*
Mi blog lo escribo **yo misma/yo sola**.	*I write my blog **myself**.*
Hoy nos visitará el presidente **en persona**.	*Today the president **himself** will visit us.*
Dijo que todo había salido mal, pero **él mismo** se veía contento.	*He said that everything had gone wrong, but he **himself** seemed happy.*
¿Tienes todavía **la misma** dirección?	*Do you still have the same address?*

c. Mismo/a can also intensify a direct or indirect object. **Mismo** can also be used to intensify adverbs such as **ya, ahora, allí**, etc.

Mismo/a with reflexive ▶ pronouns: 27.A.2

¿Os veis a vosotros **mismos** como buenos estudiantes?	*Do you see yourselves as good students?*
¿Te darás a ti **misma** un buen regalo?	*Will you give yourself a good present?*
Ven aquí ya **mismo**.	*Come here right now.*

7.E.6 Sendos

The determiner **sendos/as** (*each*) can only occur before a plural noun and is used in written, formal language.

Los ganadores recibieron **sendos** premios.	*The winners each received a prize.*
Ellos escribieron **sendas** entradas en sus blogs.	*They each wrote their own blog post.*

7.F Regional variations

Variaciones regionales

7.F.1 Más

As an intensifier, **más** is placed after the indefinite pronouns **nada** and **nadie: No hay nada/nadie más.** (*There isn't anything/anyone else.*) In Andalucia, the Caribbean, and in some parts of South America, **más** can occur before **nada** and **nadie** with the same meaning: **No queremos más nada.**

7.F.2 Poca de, (de) a poco, por poco

a. In central regions of Spain, **un poco de** can agree in gender: **una poca de sal.**

b. In everyday language, the Mexican expression **a poco** is common for communicating amazement or disbelief: **¿A poco crees que soy tonta?** (*You surely don't think I'm stupid, do you?*)

c. De a poco / de a poquito(s) (*Little by little*) is a common adverbial expression in Latin America: **Dame la medicina de a poquitos**. (*Give me the medicine little by little.*)

d. Por poco is often used colloquially to mean *almost*.

Por poco me caigo.   *I almost fell.*

7.F.3 Con todo y + clause or noun

This expression, which means *despite*, is commonly used in some Latin American countries and in Northeast Spain.

Con todo y tus disculpas, no te perdono.   *Despite your excuses, I don't forgive you.*

Práctica

 Actividades 1–20, pp. A21–A26

Demonstratives
Demostrativos

8.A   Demonstrative determiners and pronouns

Determinantes y pronombres demostrativos

8.A.1   Structure

Demonstrative determiners and pronouns show where people and objects are in relation to the speaker. English has a two-level system: (*this/that, these/those*), which can sometimes be strengthened with *here* and *there*. Spanish has a three-level system which specifies whether the item is close to the person speaking, close to the person being spoken to, or far away from both.

| Relative placement | Determiners | | | | Pronouns |
| | Masculine | | Feminine | | Neuter |
	Singular	Plural	Singular	Plural	Singular
close to the person speaking	est**e**	est**os**	est**a**	est**as**	**esto**
close to the person being spoken to	es**e**	es**os**	es**a**	es**as**	**eso**
far away from both people	aquel	aquell**os**	aquell**a**	aquell**as**	**aquello**

8.A.2   *Este, ese, aquel*

a. Demonstrative determiners in the singular and plural are usually placed before the noun and agree with it in gender and number. These forms can stand after **todo/a(s),** and before cardinal numbers.

Aquella cas**a** es grande.	*That house (over there) is big.*
Estos tres libr**os** son míos.	*These three books are mine.*
No entiendo **todo eso.**	*I don't understand that.*

 Cardinal numbers: 6.A

Todo: 7.C.9

b. Demonstratives placed after a noun can communicate a condescending or ironic attitude. **Aquel /aquella** has a more neutral attitude than the other forms.

¡No sé qué dice **el** profesor **ese**!	*I don't know what that teacher said!*
El niño **este** no para de hablar.	*That child won't stop talking.*
¡Qué tiempos **aquellos**!	*Those were good times!*

c. Demonstrative determiners with masculine and feminine forms can stand alone (without a noun). In this case, they act as pronouns and they have traditionally carried a written accent to differentiate them from the forms that precede nouns. For years, the written accent was considered a requirement only in cases of ambiguity, such as the one below.

¿Por qué comieron **aquellos** bocadillos?	*Why did they eat those sandwiches?*
¿Por qué comieron **aquéllos** bocadillos?	*Why did they (those people) eat sandwiches?*

The *Nueva ortografía* approved by the RAE in November 2010 still allows the use of the accent in cases of ambiguity. However, it is not a requirement, since the cases of ambiguity are rare and are very easily avoided.

8.A.3 **Reference to time and items in a text**

a. Demonstrative determiners can also refer to events in the past or near future, or to specific items or ideas in a text. **Este/a** and **estos/as** occur in many expressions to refer to the nearest moment in time within the present time period. **Esta mañana, esta tarde,** and **esta noche** are equivalent to **hoy por la mañana, hoy por la tarde,** and **hoy por la noche.**

esta mañana	this morning	esta semana	this week
esta tarde	this afternoon	este mes	this month
esta noche	tonight	este año	this year

En **estos** días voy a trabajar mucho.	I'm going to work a lot these days.
Nos veremos **esta** noche.	We are meeting up tonight.
Este año será difícil.	This year will be difficult.

b. **Ese/a** and **aquel/aquella** refer primarily to the past, but can also refer to the future.

En **esa/aquella** época, todo era mejor.	At that time, everything was better.
Las ventas empiezan a las ocho y, en **ese** momento, abrirán las puertas.	The sales start at eight o'clock and, at that moment, the doors will open.

8.A.4 *Esto, eso, aquello*

a. The neuter demonstratives **esto, eso,** and **aquello** can only function as neuter pronouns.

Esto que me dijiste me dejó preocupada.	What you told me made me worried.
Tengo mucho trabajo y **eso** no me gusta nada.	I have so much work and I don't like that at all.
¿**Aquello** te parece bien?	Does that sound good to you?

b. The neuter demonstratives are mostly used to refer to objects or concepts. When used to refer to people, they can be derogatory, unless the meaning of the demonstrative is actually explained. They are rarely used to refer to animals.

¡**Esto** es mi equipo de trabajo! (*derog.*)	This (thing over here) is my work team!
Mi equipo de trabajo era **eso**, un excelente grupo humano.	My team was that, a wonderful group of people.

Lo que: 15.B.7b ▶ **c.** **Aquello** can replace **lo** in relative clauses. In that case, it does not indicate proximity/distance.

¡Haz **aquello/lo** que te dije!	Do what I told you!

Todo: 7.C.9 ▶ **d.** Neuter demonstratives can be used with **todo**.

Todo esto es mentira.	This is all a lie.

8.A.5 *Aquí, allí*

Adverbs of place: 10.E.1 ▶ A few adverbs naturally go with demonstrative pronouns: **acá/aquí, allí/ahí/allá**.

A estas personas que están **aquí** no las conozco.	These people here, I don't know them.
Ese señor que está **allí** es Luis.	That man there is Luis.

8.B Regional variations

Variaciones regionales

Esto and **este** are often used as fillers in speech, as are expressions such as **pues, ah,** and **eh**.

Este... no sé qué decir...	Well... I don't know what to say...
Luisa, ... **esto**... ¿me prestas dinero?	Luisa, ... um... can I borrow some money?

Práctica

(S) Actividades 1–4, pp. A26–A27

Possessives
Posesivos

9.A Possessive determiners

Determinantes posesivos

Possessives are determiners that express possession or belonging. The short, unstressed forms (**átonos**) are placed before the noun (*prenominal*). The long, stressed forms (**tónicos**) must always be placed after the noun (*postnominal*), but they can also stand alone as pronouns. Possessives always agree with the noun or object that is owned, regardless of placement.

mi libro	*my book*	**el** libro **mío**	*my book*
tus amigos	*your friends*	**los** amigos **tuyos**	*your friends*
nuestra casa	*our house*	**la** casa **nuestra**	*our house*
vuestro país	*your [pl.] country*	**el** país **vuestro**	*your [pl.] country*

9.B Prenominal possessives

Determinantes posesivos prenominales

Short possessives are placed before the noun (the object owned) and only agree in number, except **nuestro** and **vuestro,** which agree in both gender and number. **Tú** and **vos** use **tu(s),** and all 3rd persons, including **usted(es),** use **su(s).**

◀ **cuyo:** 15.A.2, 15.B.1-2, 15.B.6

Prenominal possessives			
	Singular	**Plural**	
yo	mi	mis	*my*
tú	tu	tus	*your*
vos	tu	tus	*your*
usted	su	sus	*your*
él	su	sus	*his*
ella	su	sus	*her*
nosotros/as	nuestr**o/a**	nuestr**os/as**	*our*
vosotros/as	vuestr**o/a**	vuestr**os/as**	*your*
ustedes	su	sus	*your*
ellos/as	su	sus	*their*

mi libro	*my book*	**su** escuela	*your/its/his/her/their school*
mis hermanos	*my siblings*	**sus** escuelas	*your/its/his/her/their schools*
tu casa	*your house*	**nuestra** casa	*our house*
tus libros	*your books*	**nuestras** familias	*our families*
nuestro amigo	*our friend*	**nuestros** amigos	*our friends*
vuestros amigos	*your friends*	**vuestras** casas	*your houses*

9.C Postnominal possessives

Determinantes posesivos posnominales

9.C.1 Structure

Like adjectives, postnominal possessives agree in gender and number with the noun to which they refer.

Postnominal possessives			
	Singular	**Plural**	
yo	mí**o/a**	mí**os/as**	*mine*
tú	tuy**o/a**	tuy**os/as**	*yours*
vos	tuy**o/a**	tuy**os/as**	*yours*
usted	suy**o/a**	suy**os/as**	*yours*
él	suy**o/a**	suy**os/as**	*his*
ella	suy**o/a**	suy**os/as**	*hers*
nosotros/as	nuestr**o/a**	nuestr**os/as**	*ours*
vosotros/as	vuestr**o/a**	vuestr**os/as**	*yours*
ustedes	suy**o/a**	suy**os/as**	*yours*
ellos/as	suy**o/a**	suy**os/as**	*theirs*

Definite article: 5.A.1
Indefinite quantifiers (determiners): 7.B–7.C

9.C.2 **Postnominal forms: use**

a. Postnominal forms must be used when a definite article, an indefinite article, or one or more determiners are placed before the noun.

el libro **mío**	*my book (the book of mine)*	**la** casa **mía**	*my house*
los libros **míos**	*my books*	**las** casas **mías**	*my houses*
un amigo **mío**	*my friend*	**varios** libros **vuestros**	*various books of yours*
todas estas cosas **tuyas**	*all these things of yours*	**bastantes** ideas **nuestras**	*quite a lot of our ideas*
el teléfono **tuyo** es mejor que el mío	*your telephone is better than mine*	**un** compañero **nuestro**	*a schoolmate of ours*

Comparisons with postnominal possessives: 11.B.1f

b. Postnominal possessives can stand alone like pronouns when the noun is not mentioned. They agree in gender and number with the noun they replace and must be used with a definite article.

Este es mi número de teléfono, ¿cuál es **el tuyo**?	*This is my telephone number, what's yours?*
Estos papeles son **los míos** y esos son **los tuyos**.	*These papers are mine and those are yours.*
Haz el pastel con tu receta, no con **la mía**.	*Bake the cake with your recipe, not with mine.*
Esta cámara es **la nuestra**, no **la tuya**.	*This is our camera, not yours.*
Lo tuyo es mío y **lo mío** es tuyo.	*What is yours is mine and what is mine is yours.*
Vuestra casa es muy grande. **La nuestra** es más pequeña.	*Your [pl.] house is very big. Ours is smaller.*

c. With **ser** and **parecer,** postnominal possessives can emphasize ownership without an article or other determiner.

Ese lápiz es **mío**.	*That pencil is mine.*
¿Es **tuyo** todo esto?	*Is all this yours?*
Las demás cosas parecen **mías**.	*The remaining things seem to be mine.*

Combining prenominal and postnominal possessives: 9.D.7

d. In Spanish, when several possessives are put together such as *yours and mine, your or my friend,* a combination of prenominal and postnominal possessives or a combination of *de + subject pronoun* is used.

Mañana vienen **tus** amigos y **los míos**.	*Tomorrow, your friends and mine are coming.*
Las preferencias **de ellos** y **las mías** son iguales.	*Their preferences and mine are the same.*
El carro **de Juan** y **el nuestro** son del mismo modelo.	*Juan's car and ours are the same model.*

e. Postnominal possessives are commonly used instead of compound prepositions made up of *noun + preposition.*

◀ Compound prepositions: 12.A.2b

alrededor de ellos / alrededor **suyo**	*around them*
al lado de ella / al lado **suyo**	*next to her*
en torno a mí / en torno **mío**	*around me*

9.D Features

Características generales

9.D.1 Use of *de + pronoun* to clarify possessor

The possessives **su(s)** and **suyo/a(s)** may refer to something owned by any third person, singular or plural, or by **usted(es)**. If the context is ambiguous or to establish contrast, use **de** + *pronoun* or *noun* to identify the owner clearly.

Benito no lavará su auto sino el **de ella**.	*Benito will not wash his car, but hers.*
La familia **de ellos** es muy grande.	*Their family is very large.*
Ellos son los padres **de Leonor**.	*They are Leonor's parents.*
Estos documentos son **de ustedes**.	*These documents are yours.*
¿Este libro es **de usted**?	*Is this book yours?*

9.D.2 Use of *de nosotros/as* in Latin America

In Latin America, **de** + **nosotros/as** frequently replaces **nuestro/a(s)** in oral and written Spanish.

La casa **de nosotros** es en Texas.	*Our home is in Texas.*
Una prima **de nosotras** vive en Miami.	*A cousin of ours lives in Miami.*
El auto **de nosotros** es un modelo viejo.	*Our car is an old model.*

9.D.3 Uses of *propio*

In Spanish, **propio/a(s)** (*own, of one's own*) can be used before or after a noun, with or without a possessive, and can have several meanings.

a. To stress ownership, place **propio/a(s)** *before* a noun and after a possessive, as in English.

◀ Compared with **mismo**. 7.E.5

Mary vio el robo con **sus propios** ojos.	*Mary saw the robbery with her own eyes.*
Prefiero tener **mi propia** habitación.	*I prefer to have my own room.*
Crea **tu propio** blog.	*Create your own blog.*
Juan construyó **su propia** casa.	*Juan built his own house.*

b. Propio/a(s) is used to express characteristics of people and things. Note the use of **de** + *pronoun* or *noun*.

◀ **Ser** with nouns: 30.B.1

Jugar bien es **propio** de campeones.	*Playing well is the way of champions.*
¡Esa risa es **propia** de Luisa!	*That laughter is typical of Luisa!*
El tango es **propio** de Argentina.	*Tango is typical of Argentina.*
La salsa tiene un ritmo muy **propio**.	*Salsa music has a very unique rhythm.*
Las travesuras son **propias** de los niños.	*Pranks are typical of children.*

c. Propio/a can be a synonym of **mismo/a** + *place.* This use is equivalent to the English *proper.*

◀ Vivo en la **misma** capital.

Vivo en la **propia** capital.	*I live in the capital proper.*

d. Propio/a(s) may be a synonym of *adequate, fitting, proper, correct,* or *suitable,* as in the following examples.

Este diccionario es **propio** para estudiantes.	*This dictionary is suitable for students.*
Te daré botas **propias** para el invierno.	*I will give you a pair of adequate winter boots.*

Other meanings of **propio** : 7.E.5

e. Propio/a appears in many frequent and useful expressions.

Rita vive en su **propio mundo**.	*Rita lives in her own world.*
Estudiamos por **interés propio**.	*We study out of our own interest.*
El acusado actuó en **defensa propia**.	*The accused acted in self-defense.*
Eso lo sé por **experiencia propia**.	*I know that from my own experience.*
Esto lo decides por **cuenta propia**.	*You should decide this on your own.*
Aprendo español a mi **propio ritmo**.	*I learn Spanish at my own pace.*

9.D.4 Article instead of possessives

Ownership expressions with an article: 5.C.7

a. The definite article is used instead of a possessive with parts of the body or personal belongings. However, with verbs like **ser** and **parecer,** the possessive is used to make ownership clear.

¡Niños, tenéis **las** manos sucias!	*Children, your hands are dirty!*
¿Dónde he dejado **las** gafas?	*Where did I leave my glasses?*
Tengo puestos **los** zapatos nuevos.	*I have my new shoes on.*
Mis zapatos son de cuero.	*My shoes are made of leather.*
Tu piel parece muy seca.	*Your skin looks very dry.*

b. The definite article is used instead of the possessive when the verb is reflexive because the reflexive pronoun already indicates the owner.

Tienes que poner**te los** lentes.	*You have to put in your contacts.*
Voy a lavar**me la** cara.	*I am going to wash my face.*
El perro se rasca **el** lomo.	*The dog is scratching his back.*

Verbs like **gustar**: 13.F.3, 17.B.4

c. Verbs that express physical reactions and ailments, such as **arder, doler,** and **picar** are used with indirect object pronouns. The affected part of the body, which is the subject of the sentence, uses a definite article, not a possessive.

¿**Te** arden **los** ojos?	*Do your eyes burn?*
A ellos **les** duelen **los** pies.	*Their feet hurt.*

d. When ownership is not obvious, using the possessives helps to clarify who the owner is.

La madre paseaba con **los/sus** hijos.	*The mother was walking with the/her children.*
Hoy visité a **la/mi** vecina.	*I visited the/my neighbor today.*
La/Mi familia me visitará el Día de Acción de Gracias.	*The/My family will visit me on Thanksgiving.*

9.D.5 *Lo* + possessives

With the neuter article **lo**, the postnominal possessives express general ownership or areas of interest.

Lo tuyo es el arte.	*Art is your thing.*
Lo nuestro no es un secreto.	*Our relationship is not a secret.*
Lo mío es tuyo.	*What's mine is yours.*
Y ahora, cada uno a **lo suyo**.	*And now, it's every man for himself.*
Lo vuestro es la literatura.	*Literature is your [pl.] thing.*

9.D.6 Definite and indefinite meaning of possessives

a. Prenominal possessive forms always refer to a definite object: **mis amigos = los amigos míos** (*my friends*). Postnominal possessive forms are much more flexible and may also convey ownership of unspecified objects or unspecified quantity: **unos/muchos/varios/los otros amigos míos** (*some/many/several/other friends of mine*).

b. Definite articles can never accompany a prenominal possessive because they are already definite, as explained in part **a** above. In this case, postnominal possessives must be used.

Tu trabajo es muy interesante.
El trabajo **tuyo** es muy interesante.

Your work is very interesting.

c. Unlike prenominal possessives, postnominal forms can be used with demonstratives and many indefinite determiners.

◄ Possessive determiners: 9.A

Ese viaje **vuestro** tendrá que esperar.
¡No te diré **ningún** secreto **mío**!
Olvidamos **varias** cosas **nuestras** en el hotel.
¡**Esa** idea **tuya** es fantástica!

That trip of yours will have to wait.
I won't tell you any of my secrets!
We forgot several of our things at the hotel.
That idea of yours is fantastic!

d. The verb **estar** is used with definite nouns while **haber** is used with indefinite nouns. This means that prenominal possessive forms (which are definite) are generally used with **estar** and postnominal forms (which are indefinite) with **haber**. When using postnominal possessives with **estar,** you usually need a definite article or another determiner to express definiteness. Compare the following examples:

◄ Uses of **estar** and **haber**: 29.B.1, 30.C.7

Aquí **están los** cinco dólares **tuyos** y **los** cuatro **míos**.
Aquí **están tus** cinco dólares y **mis** cuatro dólares.
Somos tres hermanos: primero **está mi** hermana mayor que tiene veinte años y luego **está mi** hermano menor que tiene quince.
En el garaje **están mis** libros viejos y hay, además, **varias** cosas **tuyas**.
Aquí **hay** cinco dólares **tuyos** y cuatro **míos**.

Here are your five dollars and my four.
Here are your five dollars and my four dollars.
We are three siblings: first there's my older sister who is twenty years old and then there is my younger brother who is fifteen.
In the garage, there are my old books and there are also several things of yours.
Here are five dollars that are yours and four that are mine.

9.D.7 Combining prenominal and postnominal possessives

Prenominal possessives can be combined with postnominal forms. Several postnominal forms can also be combined, but two prenominal forms can never be combined unless the noun is repeated.

◄ Use of postnominal possessives: 9.C.2d

Los planes **tuyos y míos** son incompatibles.
Hoy vendrán **vuestras** amigas y las **mías**.
Mi cumpleaños y **el tuyo** son el mismo día.
Mi cumpleaños y **tu** cumpleaños son el mismo día.

Your and my plans are incompatible.
Your friends and mine will come today.

My birthday and yours are on the same day.

9.D.8 Use of possessives in vocatives

a. Postnominal possessives are more common than prenominal possessives in vocatives when addressing someone by name, title, or nickname.

¡Querida Alicia mía, escúchame bien!	*My dear Alicia, listen to me very carefully!*
Amigos míos, ¡la cena está servida!	*Dear friends, dinner is served.*
Cariño mío, te extraño.	*I miss you, my dear.*

b. Particularly in Latin America, the prenominal possessives are commonly used in vocatives.

amor **mío**	**mi** amor	*my love*
cielito **mío**	**mi** cielito	*my darling*
corazón **mío**	**mi** corazón	*my darling*
hijo/a **mío/a**	**mi**jito/**mi**jita, **m'**hijito/**m'**hijita	*my son/daughter*

c. In military circles, the norm is to use prenominal possessives with titles. Kings, nobles, cardinals, and the Pope are addressed in similar ways.

mi capitán	*my captain*	**Su** Alteza Real	*Your Royal Highness*
mi general	*my general*	**Su** Excelencia	*Your Excellence*
mi sargento	*my sargeant*	**Su** Santidad	*Your Holiness*
mi soldado	*my soldier*	**Su** Señoría	*Your Honor*

9.E Regional variations

Variaciones regionales

9.E.1 Adverbs of place used with possessives

Compound prepositions: 12.A.2b ▸

a. The following structure with the adverbs **delante** and **detrás** is common in the Spanish-speaking world:

El perro camina **delante de ella**.　　　　*The dog walks in front of her.*

The agreement of the possessive ▸
with a female owner is *not*
accepted in formal speech
in most Spanish-speaking
countries: ***El perro
camina delante** suya*.

b. Although not as common, the possessive expression can be replaced with a postnominal possessive.

El perro camina **delante suyo**.　　　　*The dog walks in front of her.*

Práctica

(S) Actividades 1–12,
pp. A28–A31

Adverbs
Adverbios

10.A Overview

Aspectos generales

Adverbs describe *when, how, where,* and *why* something happens or is done. Adverbs can modify a verb, another adverb, an adjective, or a whole sentence. Adverbs always keep the same form and never agree with any noun or other word in the sentence.

Adverbs can be used together with:		
1. Verbs	Camino **rápidamente**.	*I walk **quickly**.*
2. Other Adverbs	Camino **muy** rápidamente.	*I walk **very** quickly.*
3. Adjectives	Estoy **bastante** cansado.	*I am **quite** tired.*
4. Sentences	**Generalmente**, estudio los lunes.	***Usually**, I study on Mondays.*

10.B Adverbs of time

Adverbios de tiempo

10.B.1 Cuándo, cuando

Question		Answer	
¿cuándo?	*when?*	**cuando**	*when*

Cuándo with a written accent is used in direct and indirect questions. Without a written accent, **cuando** is used in subordinate clauses.

—¿**Cuándo** hacéis las tareas? *When do you [pl.] do your homework?*

—Las hacemos **cuando** podemos. *We do it when we can.*

cuando in subordinate clauses: 23.E.2a
Conjunctions of time: 16.C.3
Relative adverbs: 15.C.1
Indirect questions: 14.B.9, 31.B.6d

10.B.2 Common adverbs of time

ahora	*now*	**entonces**	*then*
antes	*before*	**después**	*after*
		luego	*later*
hoy	*today*	**mañana**	*tomorrow*
		pasado mañana	*day after tomorrow*
		ayer	*yesterday*
		anteayer	*day before yesterday*
		anoche	*last night*
		antenoche	*night before last*
siempre	*always*	**nunca**	*never*
		jamás	*never ever*
tarde	*late*	**temprano**	*early*
todavía, aún	*still*	**todavía no, aún no**	*not yet*
ya	*already, now*	**ya no**	*no longer*
mientras	*while*		

Podemos descansar **después**.	We can rest **later**.
Ana viene **mañana**.	Ana is coming **tomorrow**.
Siempre estudio mucho.	I **always** study a lot.
No estudiaste **ayer**.	You didn't study **yesterday**.
Hoy es martes.	**Today** is Tuesday.
Pronto termino.	I'll finish **soon**.
Escribo **mientras** lees.	I'll write **while** you read.
Primero trabajamos y **luego/después** descansamos.	**First** we'll work and **later/after** we'll rest.
Siempre llegas **antes** y yo **después**.	You always arrive **before** and I arrive **after**.

10.B.3   Nunca, jamás

Nunca and **jamás** mean *never* or, sometimes, *ever*, but **jamás** is more emphatic. They can be used together to make an even stronger negation, **nunca jamás** (*never ever*). These adverbs can come before or after a verb, but both require a double negation when they follow a verb.

Nunca te olvidaré./**No** te olvidaré **nunca**.	I will **never** forget you.
Jamás nos diremos adiós./**No** nos diremos adiós **jamás**.	We will **never** say goodbye.
Nunca jamás te olvidaré./**No** te olvidaré **nunca jamás**.	I will **never** (ever) forget you.

10.B.4   Ya, ya no; todavía, todavía no; aún, aún no

a. Note how these adverbs are used in the following sentences:

Ya lo he pagado todo.	I have **already** paid for everything.
Ya no estudio literatura.	I'm **not** studying literature **anymore**.
Todavía vivo en Nueva York.	I **still** live in New York.
Todavía no hablo bien español.	I **don't** speak Spanish well **yet**.

b. The following are common expressions used with **ya**.

¡**Ya** voy!	*I'm coming!*	**Ya** (lo) sé.	*I already know that.*
¡**Ya** vengo/regreso!	*I'll be right back!*	**Ya** verás/veremos.	*You'll see. / We'll see.*

Diacritical marks: 1.E.6c ▶

c. Aún is a synonym of **todavía**. **Aun** (without an accent) can mean *even*, *also*, or *including*.

Aún vivo en Nueva York.	I **still** live in New York.
Aún no hablo bien español.	I don't speak Spanish well **yet**.
Sigo cansado **aun** después de dormir la siesta.	I am tired **even** after taking a nap.
Todos, **aun** los que al principio se opusieron, apoyaron la decisión.	Everyone supported the decision, **including** those who had initially opposed it.

10.B.5   Después, luego

The adverbs **luego** and **después** are synonyms.

Después/Luego vuelvo.	I'll come back **later**.

10.B.6   Adverbs of frequency

a. These adverbs express how often something happens and can be arranged on a scale where **siempre** and **nunca** are opposites, with adverbs of various frequencies in between.

Adverbial phrases: 10.H ▶

Más frecuencia ←-------------------------------------→ Menos frecuencia							
siempre	*always*	**casi siempre**	*almost always*	**casi nunca**	*almost never*	**nunca, jamás**	*never*
todo/a(s) + *def. article* **+ time**	*every + time*	**muchas veces**	*many times*	**pocas veces**	*a few times*	**nunca jamás**	*never ever*
		a veces, a menudo	*sometimes, once in a while*	**rara vez**	*seldom, rarely*		
		frecuentemente, con (mucha) frecuencia	*frequently*	**con poca frecuencia**	*not frequently*		

Trabajo **todos los días**.   *I work every day.*
Siempre estudio por la mañana.   *I always study in the morning.*
A veces practico el vocabulario.   *Sometimes I practice the vocabulary.*
Casi siempre escribo en mi blog.   *I almost always write in my blog.*
Nunca me canso de chatear.   *I never get tired of chatting.*
Rara vez vamos a la playa.   *We rarely go to the beach.*

b. In addition to these frequency adverbs and expressions, Spanish uses **cada** + *time expression* to emphasize incremental actions or events.

Cada día aprendo más español.   *I learn more Spanish each day.*

10.C   Adverbs of manner

Adverbios de modo

10.C.1   *Cómo, como*

Question		Answer	
¿Cómo?	*How?*	**como**	*as, like*

Cómo with a written accent is used in direct and indirect questions. **Como** is used without a written accent in comparisons and subordinate clauses that express the manner in which something is done.

Como in subordinate clauses: 23.E.1
Relative adverbs: 15.C.1
Cómo: 14.B.6

El clima está tan bueno hoy **como** ayer.   *The weather is just **as** good today as yesterday.*
Viaja **como** quieras, en avión o en tren.   *Travel **as** you wish, by plane or train.*
—¿**Cómo** quieres el café?   ***How** do you want your coffee?*
—¡Exactamente **como** tú lo preparas!   *Exactly **how** you prepare it!*

Conjunctions of comparison: 16.C.8
Expressing manner - **como**: 16.C.9

10.C.2   Common adverbs of manner

bien	*good*	**mal**	*bad*
mejor	*better*	**peor**	*worse*
así	*this way, like this/that*	**regular**	*so-so*

Quiero el café **así**: ¡caliente!   *I want my coffee **like this**: hot!*

The adverb **bien** can be used as adjective: **Ellos son gente bien.** (*They are good people.*) Also in exclamations: **¡Qué bien!** (*That's great!*)

a. The adverbs **bien** and **mal** have their own forms for comparison.
¡Hoy la comida está **peor**!   *The food is **worse** today!*
El clima es **mejor** en verano.   *The climate/weather is **better** in the summer.*

10.C.3 Bien

The adverb **bien** before an adjective acts as an intensifying adverb.

La película es **bien** divertida.	*The film is **quite** funny.*
¡Tienes un auto **bien** bonito!	*You have a **really** nice car!*

10.D Quantifying adverbs

Adverbios de cantidad

10.D.1 Cuánto, cuanto

Cuán is a short form of **cuánto** used mainly in exclamations and can be replaced by **qué**:
¡**Cuán/Qué** listo es este chico!
(*What a bright kid he is!*)

Question		Answer	
¿Cuánto?	*How much?*	**cuanto**	*as much (as)*

a. Cuánto with a written accent is used in direct and indirect questions. **Cuanto** without a written accent in subordinate clauses expresses *quantity* or *degree*.

Indirect questions:
14.B.9, 31.B.6d

—¿**Cuánto** trabajas?	***How much*** *do you work?*
—Trabajo **cuanto** puedo.	*I work **as much as** I can.*

b. In speech and in less formal texts, it is more common to use **todo lo que** (*as much as*) instead of **cuanto**.

Indefinite quantifiers as adverbs: 7.E.4

Trabajo **todo lo que** puedo.	*I work **as much as** I can.*

10.D.2 Other common modifiers and quantifying adverbs

Suficiente = bastante

más *(more)*	← --------------------------------------- →		**menos** *(less)*
demasiado *too much*	**mucho, muy** *a lot, very*	**bastante, suficiente** *enough/quite a lot/quite*	**poco** *little*
tanto, tan *so much*	**casi** *almost*	**apenas** *barely, hardly*	**solo, solamente** *only*

Me comí **casi** todo el paquete.	*I ate **almost** the whole package.*
Apenas tengo dos dólares.	*I **barely** have two dollars.*
Duermes **mucho** y trabajas **poco**.	*You sleep **a lot** and work **little**.*
Solo estudio español.	*I **only** study Spanish.*
Tú trabajas **más** que yo.	*You work **more** than I.*
¡Nieva **tanto** hoy!	*It's snowing **so much** today!*

a. Más, menos, and **tanto** are the most common adverbs used in all types of comparisons.

Comparisons: Ch. 11

Estudiamos **más que** vosotros.	*We study **more than** you [pl.].*
Tengo **menos** dinero **que** antes.	*I have **less** money **than** before.*
Sabes **tanto como** yo.	*You know **as much** as I do.*

b. Casi is mostly used with the present tense in Spanish, while *almost*, in English, can also be used in the past tense.

Casi compro un auto nuevo.	*I **almost** bought a new car.*

c. The adverb **bastante** can stand alone or be combined with other adjectives or adverbs.

Trabajo **bastante**.	I work **quite a lot**.
Mary está **bastante** cansada.	Mary is **quite** tired.
Tu trabajo está **bastante** bien.	Your work is **quite** good.
No comes **bastante**.	You don't eat **enough**.

◀ **Bastante** placed before and after a noun 7.C.2

d. The adverbs **muy, mucho,** and **demasiado** cannot occur together. Note how they are used in English.

Hablas **mucho**.	You talk **a lot**.
Trabajas **demasiado**.	You work **too much**.
Estamos **demasiado** cansados.	We are **too** tired.
El problema es **muy** difícil.	The problem is **very** dificult.

◀ **Demasiado**: 7.C.11

10.E Adverbs of place

Adverbios de lugar

There are two groups of adverbs that express where an action takes place. One group expresses relative distance from the perspective of the speaker. The other group expresses the location of people and things in a room.

10.E.1 Relative distance

Close to the person speaking		Far from the person speaking	
aquí	here	**allí, ahí**	there
acá	here	**allá**	there

a. Aquí and **allí** work similarly to *here* and *there*, and are used primarily to indicate location.

Aquí siempre hace buen tiempo.	It's always good weather here.
Allí están tus libros.	There are your books.

b. Ahí is more general than **allí** and expresses an indefinite location when used with **por**.

Tus zapatos están **por ahí**.	Your shoes are somewhere around there.
—¿Dónde entrenas los domingos?	Where do you train on Sundays?
—**Por ahí**, en la ciudad o en el parque.	Somewhere around there, in the city or the park.

c. Acá and **allá** are often used with verbs of motion. In contrast to **allí,** the adverb **allá** can be used with **más** and **muy.**

Ven **acá**.	Come here.
Isabel va para **allá**.	Isabel is on her way there.
El correo está **más allá**.	The post office is farther away.

10.E.2 Adverbs of place and direction: *adónde/adonde; dónde/donde*

◀ **Donde/adonde**: 16.C.10

Adverbs of place can refer to specific locations of people and things and some of them also indicate direction.

a. These adverbs are used to ask and answer a question about a location or direction.

Question		Answer	
¿adónde?	where?	**adonde**	where (in, on, at)
¿a dónde?	to where?	**a donde**	to where
¿dónde?	where?	**donde**	where

b. Dónde (*where*) is a question adverb which refers to location. **Donde** (*where*) can be used to answer a question with **dónde** and refers to a location already mentioned.

Donde in subordinate
clauses: 23.E.1
Relative adverb **donde**:
15.C.1

—¿**Dónde** vive tu familia?

Where does your family live?

—Vive en la ciudad **donde** nací.

They live in the city **where** I was born.

c. It is common to use *preposition* + **la/el/los/las que** in relative clauses as a synonym for **donde**.

—¿**Dónde** estudias?

Where are you studying?

—En una escuela **en la que** hay buenos maestros.

At a school **where** there are good teachers.

d. Adónde (*To where*) is a question adverb that is used to refer to location with verbs of motion. **Adonde** can be used to answer questions using **adónde**. In this case, **adonde** is a relative adverb referring to a definite location. It can be written as two words: **a dónde, a donde**.

Donde, adonde are used
informally for the meaning *at*
(*somebody's house*):
Estoy donde Juan. *I'm at Juan's.*

—¿**Adónde** viajas en verano?

Where do you travel in the summer?

—Este año iré a Londres, **adonde** viajé el año pasado.

This year I'll go to London, **where** I traveled last year.

—Viajo **a donde** vive mi familia.

I'm going **to where** my family lives.

10.E.3 Other common adverbs of place and direction

Ser, estar with adverbs:
30.C.1, 30.E

The following adverb pairs look similar, but their meanings and uses are different. The adverbs in the *Place* column describe location only. The adverbs in the other column express location relative to a specific *direction*.

Place		Direction	
delante	*in front*	**adelante**	*forward, ahead, in front, at the front*
detrás	*in the back*	**atrás**	*behind, back, at the back*
encima	*on top, over*	**arriba**	*above, up*
debajo	*beneath, underneath*	**abajo**	*below, down*
dentro	*within, inside*	**adentro**	*inside*
fuera	*out, outside*	**afuera**	*outside*
cerca	*close (by)*		
lejos	*far (away)*		
alrededor	*around*		
enfrente	*opposite, in front*		

Prepositional phrases: 12.A.2

a. Adverbs of place that describe location usually form prepositional expressions with **de**: **delante de** (*in front of*), **encima de** (*on top of*), **alrededor de** (*around*), etc. The other group of adverbs cannot be used with **de**.

Delante de la iglesia hay una plaza.

In front of the church there is a square.

Hay mucha gente **dentro de** la iglesia.

There are lots of people inside the church.

b. Only adverbs of place that also convey direction can be used with prepositions indicating movement: **hacia adelante** (*in a forward direction*), **hasta atrás/arriba** (*all the way back/up*), **hacia/para abajo** (*downwards*) and similar expressions.

La chica miraba **para arriba y para abajo**.

The girl looked up and down.

Cerca, lejos: 10.E.3h

c. Adverbs of quantity can modify adverbs of place that indicate direction to describe the degree of distance in a specific direction. Adverbs of place that do not indicate direction *do not accept* adverbs of quantity (except **cerca** and **lejos**).

Adverbs • **Chapter 10**

más adelante	farther on, later	muy abajo	very far down
bastante arriba	very high up	un poco atrás	a little bit behind
muy cerca	very close	mucho más lejos	much farther away
demasiado atrás	too far back	nada lejos	not very far away

 Prepositional phrases: 12.A.2

d. Delante/detrás express location exclusively, while **adelante/atrás** convey a sense of movement or placement (*forward* and *backward*) in addition to location.

El parque está allí **delante**.	*The park is there, right in front.*
El parque está allí **adelante**.	*The park is there, farther on.*
La fuente está **detrás**.	*The fountain is in back.*
La fuente está más **atrás**.	*The fountain is farther back.*
Los niños viajan **atrás** y los adultos **adelante**.	*The children ride in the back and the adults in the front.*

 **Delante** *de usted:* see adverbs of place used with possessives: 9.E.1

e. Arriba and **abajo** express location, but always with a sense of direction, *up* or *down*. Therefore, these two adverbs can be used to mean *upstairs, downstairs* or figuratively as in the expressions: **los de arriba** (*upper class*) and **los de abajo** (*lower class*). **Encima/debajo** express only location.

En el texto, los títulos van **arriba** y las notas van **abajo**.	*In the text, the titles go above and the notes go below.*
En la caja, encuentras los libros **debajo** y los papeles **encima**.	*In the box, you will find the books underneath and the papers on top.*

f. Dentro and **fuera** are not commonly used alone and are usually combined with prepositions to refer to physical or figurative places.

Los rayos X muestran el cuerpo **por dentro**.	*X-rays show the inside of the body.*
Por fuera, la casa se ve chica.	*The house looks small from the outside.*
Hay mucha gente **fuera del** cine.	*There are a lot of people outside the movie theater.*

g. Adentro and **afuera** must be used with an explicit or implied verb of motion.

No te muevas, quédate **afuera**.	*Don't move, stay outside.*
Hace frío, vamos **adentro**.	*It's cold; let's go inside.*

h. Cerca and **lejos** express location only. Adverbs of quantity (**muy, bastante,** etc.) and **de** often accompany these adverbs. They can *never* be used with prepositions of direction.

El centro de la ciudad queda **lejos**.	*The city center is far away.*
Alaska queda **lejos de** Nueva York.	*Alaska is far from New York.*

 Adverbs + **hacia, hasta**: 10.E.3b

10.E.4 **Adverbs of place and prepositions**

There is an important difference between adverbs of place and prepositions. Prepositions must be followed by a noun, while adverbs of place can stand alone.

 Compound prepositions: 12.A.2b

Prepositions	
El perro está **debajo de** la cama.	*The dog is **under** the bed.*
Las cartas están **encima de** la mesa.	*The letters are **on** the table.*

Adverbs of place	
En la caja encuentras los libros **debajo** y los papeles **encima**.	*In the box, you'll find the books **underneath** and the papers **on top**.*

10.F | Positive, negative, and doubting adverbials

Adverbios de afirmación, de negación y de duda

10.F.1 Common positive and negative adverbs

¿no?	right (true)?	¿sí?	yes? is it true?
sí	yes	no	no, not
bueno	good, well	también	also
tal vez, quizás	maybe	tampoco	neither

a. In negative sentences, **no** is always placed before the verb. Note how you answer negatively in Spanish: **No, no...** *No... not.* Both **¿sí?** and **¿no?** are placed at the end of the sentence in order to ask a question, which is equivalent to a *tag question* in English.

—Vives en Chicago, **¿no?**	You live in Chicago, **don't you**?
—**No, no** vivo en Chicago.	**No**, I **don't** live in Chicago.
—**Sí,** vivo en Chicago.	**Yes**, I live in Chicago.

b. In spoken language, it is common to add **sí** in order to add emphasis to a positive statement, especially when contrasting negative and positive statements.

¿Tú **no** quieres ir? ¡Yo **sí** quiero!	You don't want to go? I sure do!

c. **También** is used like the English *also.* **Tampoco** is used in negative sentences to mean *neither.*

Gabriel viene y Carolina **también**.	Gabriel is coming and Carolina too.
Tú **no** quieres ir y yo **tampoco**.	You don't want to go and neither do I.

Use of the subjunctive in independent clauses: 23.B.1

Ojalá: use of the subjunctive: 23.B.2b

d. **Tal vez** and **quizá(s)** are synonyms. Both can be used with the indicative and the subjunctive.

Quizás es/sea Luisa.	It might be Luisa.
Tal vez viajamos/viajemos pronto.	We might go soon.

10.G | Adverbs ending in -*mente*

Adverbios terminados en -*mente*

10.G.1 Structure

Adverbs ending in -*mente*: 1.E.8

The most common adverbs in Spanish end in **-mente** and are formed using the feminine form of an adjective. When the adjective does not have a feminine form, the ending **-mente** is added to the basic form. Adjectives keep written accents when they form adverbs.

Adjectives		Adverbs	
Masculine	**Feminine**	**Adjective + -*mente***	
correcto	correct**a**	correct**amente**	correctly
fácil	fácil	fácil**mente**	easily
feliz	feliz	feliz**mente**	happily

Felizmente, aprobé el examen.	Happily, I passed my exam.
Hablas **correctamente**.	You speak correctly.

Adverbs • **Chapter 10**

10.G.2 Adjectives as adverbs

In modern Spanish, a number of common adjectives are also used as adverbs without the **-mente** ending. Note that these short forms are always masculine and singular.

Respiro **hondo**.	*I'm breathing deeply.*	Juegan **duro**.	*They play hard.*
Escribes **claro**.	*You write clearly.*	Camino **rápido**.	*I walk quickly.*
Juegas **limpio**.	*You're playing fairly.*	Hablan **raro**.	*They speak in a strange way/strangely.*

10.G.3 Placement of adverbs

a. The placement of an adverb in Spanish is flexible. Adverbs that end in **-mente** are almost always placed after the verb. Adverbs that support an adjective or other adverbs are usually placed before the verb.

Laura canta **maravillosamente**.	*Laura sings marvelously.*
Mike **casi siempre** está ocupado.	*Mike is almost always busy.*
La explicación es **poco clara**.	*The explanation is not very clear.*

b. When there are several **-mente** adverbs in a row, only the final adverb keeps the **-mente** ending.

La profesora explica la lección clara, pausada y excelente**mente**.	*The teacher explains the lesson clearly, slowly, and very well.*

10.H Adverbial phrases

Locuciones adverbiales

Adverbial phrases combine adverbs, prepositions, or nouns, and express the same meaning as adverbs: time, manner, quantity, place, assertion, doubt, and negation.

10.H.1 Adverbial phrases vs. adverbs ending in *-mente*

Some common adverbs ending in **-mente** may be replaced by a prepositional expression with the same meaning, formed with the corresponding noun.

Adverb ending in *-mente*	Adverbial phrase	
claramente	con claridad	*clearly*
cortésmente	con cortesía	*courteously*
difícilmente	con dificultad	*with difficulty*
firmemente	con firmeza	*firmly*
locamente	con locura	*madly*
rápidamente	con rapidez	*quickly*
repentinamente	de repente	*suddenly*
sinceramente	con sinceridad	*sincerely*
telefónicamente	por teléfono	*by phone*

a la larga	in the long run	**A la larga**, conseguirás trabajo. *You will get a job in the long run.*
a las mil maravillas	wonderfully	¡Se preparó **a las mil maravillas**! *It was prepared wonderfully!*
a lo grande	luxuriously, in style	Celebrarán la boda **a lo grande**. *They will celebrate their wedding in style.*
a (la) mano	close at hand	Lleva tu pasaporte **a (la) mano**. *Have your passport close at hand.*
a menudo	frequently, often	Viajamos en avión **a menudo**. *We travel frequently by plane.*
a veces	sometimes	**A veces** duermo la siesta. *I take naps sometimes.*
al final	at/in the end	**Al final** decidimos irnos en tren. *In the end, we decided to travel by train.*
alguna vez	sometime (ever)	¿Has ido a México **alguna vez**? *Have you ever been to Mexico?*
con frecuencia	frequently, often	Escribo en Twitter **con frecuencia**. *I write on Twitter frequently.*
de primera mano	firsthand	Sé la noticia **de primera mano**. *I know the news firsthand.*
en algún momento	at some point, sometime	**En algún momento** debes decidirte. *You will have to decide sometime.*
en alguna parte	somewhere	He dejado mis gafas **en alguna parte**. *I left my glasses somewhere.*
en buenas manos	in good hands	Este trabajo está **en buenas manos**. *This job is in good hands.*
en fin	finally, well then	**En fin**, tenemos que irnos ya. *Well then, we have to go now.*
por fin	at last, finally	**Por fin** has terminado el trabajo. *You have finished your work at last.*
por las buenas o por las malas	one way or the other	Tendrás que estudiar **por las buenas o por las malas**. *You will have to study one way or the other.*
por necesidad	out of necessity	Trabajamos **por necesidad**. *We work out of necessity.*
por poco	almost	**Por poco** pierdo el autobús. *I almost missed the bus.*

10.I Comparison of adverbs

Comparación del adverbio

10.I.1 Comparative constructions

Comparisons: Ch. 11
Comparison of adjectives: 3.E

a. Adverbs have a basic, positive form, as well as a comparative form. Most adverbs form the comparative using **más** or **menos**. Some have irregular forms.

Adverbs	Positive	Comparative
Regular	**eficazmente** *efficiently*	**más/menos eficazmente** *more/less efficiently*
Irregular	**bien** *well*	**mejor** *better*
	mal *badly*	**peor** *worse*
	mucho *much/a lot*	**más** *more*
	poco *little/a bit*	**menos** *less*

Actualmente, la gente vive **mejor**.

El médico cree que como **mal**, pero mi hermano come **peor** que yo.

Nowadays, people live better.

The doctor thinks I eat badly, but my brother eats worse than I do.

b. Comparisons using adverbs can be formed with the following structures:

más/menos + *adverb* + **que** or **tan** + *adverb* + **como**

Viajamos **más frecuentemente que** antes.

Leemos **tan bien como** vosotros.

We travel a lot more than before.

We read as well as you [pl.] do.

10.I.2 **Superlative constructions**

a. Absolute superlatives of adverbs can be formed by adding **-mente** to the absolute superlative feminine form of an adjective with an **-ísima** ending. In English, the superlative is reproduced with other intensifying adverbs: *very, unbelievably*, etc.

Superlatives of adverbs: 11.D.2

Adjectives		Adverbs	
Positive	**Superlative**	**Superlative of adjective +** *-mente*	
lento	**lentísima**	**lentísimamente**	*very slowly*
claro	**clarísima**	**clarísimamente**	*very clearly*
fuerte	**fuertísima**	**fuertísimamente**	*very strongly/hard*

¡Explicas todo **clarísimamente**!

Te comportas **tontísimamente**.

You explain everything very clearly!

You're behaving really stupidly.

b. Short adverbs that are identical to masculine singular adjectives take the ending **-ísimo**.

Adjectives as adverbs: 10.G.2

Corre **rápido**.   *He runs fast.*   Corre **rapidísimo**.   *He runs very fast.*

c. Some adverbs that are not derived from adjectives also have absolute superlatives. The absolute superlative keeps the ending of the adverb.

lejos → **lejísimos**   *very far*   cerca → **cerquísima**   *very close*

poco → **poquísimo**   *very little*   mucho → **muchísimo**   *a lot*

Los fines de semana duermo **poquísimo**.

Mis primos viven **lejísimos**.

I sleep very little on weekends.

My cousins live very far away.

d. Relative superlatives can be formed using a comparative form (sometimes preceded by a definite article).

Fue **la pintura más cuidadosamente** realizada.

De todas las pinturas, esta es **la más cuidadosamente realizada**.

Juan es quien **más dedicadamente** trabaja.

*It was **the most carefully** done painting.*

*Of all the paintings, this is **the most carefully done**.*

Juan is the one who works the most diligently.

e. **Lo más/menos** + *adverb* + *adjective/clause* is usually equivalent to the English *as much as* + *adjective/clause* or *as little as* + *adjective/clause*. The adjective most commonly used in this construction is **posible**.

Entreno **lo más frecuentemente posible**.		*I train as much as possible.*	
Trabaja **lo más rápidamente que puede**.		*She works as fast as she can.*	

f. Lo más/menos + *adverb* + *adjective/clause* is also commonly used in time expressions.

Lo más tarde que llegué al trabajo es las diez.	*The latest I arrived to work is ten.*
Hazlo **lo más pronto que puedas**.	*Do it as soon as you can.*

g. When English uses a superlative adverb, Spanish can use either a sentence containing a relative clause or a comparative sentence. Note in the examples below that when using a comparative sentence, the first term is compared with everything/everyone else in the group.

*He runs **the fastest**.*	Él es el que más rápido corre.
	Él corre más rápido que todos.
*We all felt bad, but she felt **the worst**.*	Todos nos sentimos mal, pero ella es la que peor se sintió.
	Todos nos sentimos mal, pero ella se sintió peor que todos.
*She resolved the problem **the most intelligently**.*	Ella es la que resolvió el problema más inteligentemente.
	Ella resolvió el problema más inteligentemente que el resto.

10.J Regional variations

Variaciones regionales

10.J.1 Diminutives

Diminutives, augmentatives, ▶
and pejoratives: 2.C.6, 3.A.4

In Latin America, diminutives of adverbs are common in daily language.

ahora	*now*	ahorita	*right now/in a moment*
allá	*there*	allacito	*over there*
aquí	*here*	aquicito	*exactly here*
después	*later/after*	despuesito	*right away/in just a moment*
enseguida	*soon*	enseguidita	*in a tiny little bit*

10.J.2 *Vale, bien, de acuerdo, claro que sí*

a. In informal daily language, **vale** is used in Spain for questions with the meaning: *Is that OK?, OK?, Is it alright?* The answer may include the same word.

—Nos vemos más tarde, **¿vale?**	*We'll meet up later, OK?*
—**¡Vale!**	*OK!*

b. In Latin America, there are many local variations of *OK.* Some of the most common expressions are **está bien, de acuerdo, dale, sí, ok.**

—Regreso pronto, **¿de acuerdo?**	*I'll be back soon, OK?*
—**¡De acuerdo!**	*OK!*
—Nos juntamos más tarde.	*We'll get together later.*
—**Dale.**	*OK.*

c. In the Spanish-speaking world, some of the most common expressions to express agreement or disagreement and to communicate consent are **claro, claro que sí, claro que no, por supuesto que sí, cómo no, por supuesto que no.**

Práctica

Ⓢ Actividades 1–20,
pp. A32–A37

—¿Puedo abrir la ventana?	*Can I open the window?*
—**¡Claro que sí!** ¡Ábrela!	*Of course! Open it!*
—¿Estás irritada?	*Are you irritated/annoyed?*
—**¡Claro que no!**	*Of course not!*

Comparisons
Comparaciones

11.A Overview

Aspectos generales

Some English adjectives have a comparative form in which *-er* is added to the end (*long, longer*), while others use *more* and *less* (*more/less popular*). English adverbs use *more* and *less* for comparative forms (*more slowly*). Nouns are compared using *as many as, more/fewer than*. Spanish uses a much more regular structure to compare differences and inequalities between objects or people (*nouns, pronouns*), characteristics (*adjectives*), actions (*verbs*), and how the actions happen (*adverbs*).

11.B Comparisons of inequality

Desigualdad

11.B.1 Adjectives, adverbs, nouns, and verbs

a. Inequality is expressed in the following way in Spanish.

Comparisons of adjectives, adverbs, nouns, and verbs		
más (*more*) / **menos** (*less*) +	adjectives/adverbs/nouns/verbs	+ **que** (*than*)

Note that the subject pronoun is always used in comparisons (**yo, tú, él,** etc.).

Adjectives	Las películas son **más *largas*** que las telenovelas.	*Films are longer than soap operas.*
	Antonio es **menos *famoso*** que yo.	*Antonio is less famous than I.*
Adverbs	La impresora grande imprime **más *rápidamente*** que la pequeña.	*The big printer prints more quickly than the little one.*
	Escribo **mejor** en español **que** en francés.	*I write better in Spanish than in French.*
Nouns	Tengo **más *libros*** que Betty.	*I have more books than Betty.*
	Hoy tengo **menos *dinero*** que ayer.	*Today I have less money than yesterday.*
Verbs	***Viajas* más** que yo.	*You travel more than I do.*
	***Entreno* menos que** tú.	*I train less than you.*

b. A number of adjectives and adverbs have irregular comparative forms.

Adjectives		Irregular comparatives	
bueno/a(s)	*good*	**mejor(es)**	*better*
malo/a(s)	*bad/evil*	**peor(es)**	*worse*
joven/jóvenes	*young*	**menor(es)**	*younger*
viejo/a(s)	*old*	**mayor(es)**	*older*

Adverbs		Irregular comparatives	
bien	*well*	**mejor**	*better*
mal	*badly*	**peor**	*worse*
mucho	*a lot/very*	**más**	*more*
poco	*little*	**menos**	*less*

◀ Comparison of adjectives: 3.E

◀ **Inferior** and **superior** are irregular comparatives of **bajo** and **alto**. See table in 11.D.1b.

◀ Comparison of adverbs: 10.I

c. The regular comparative forms of **bueno/a** and **malo/a** can also be used. However, in this case, they exclusively emphasize character judgments.

María es **más buena** que el pan.	*María is a very good person./María is kindness itself.*
María es **mejor** cocinera que su madre.	*María is a better cook than her mother.*

d. Mayor and **menor** are used interchangeably with the regular comparative forms. They are also used as comparative forms of **grande** and **pequeño** when these refer to age.

Carlos es **menor / más joven** que yo.	*Carlos is younger than I am.*

e. Grande and **pequeño** also use **mayor** and **menor** as superlative forms when describing the scope or importance of an issue.

Mi ciudad tiene el **mayor** número de desocupados.	*My city has the largest number of unemployed people.*

f. After **que,** a postnominal possessive always follows a definite article: **el mío, la suya,** etc.

Postnominal possessives: 9.C

Mi auto gasta menos gasolina **que el tuyo**.	*My car consumes less gasoline than yours.*
Nuestras vacaciones son (mucho) más largas **que las vuestras**.	*Our vacations are (much) longer than yours [pl.]*

g. When numbers are compared, **que** is replaced by **de.**

Asisto a **más de** tres clases todos los días.	*I attend more than three classes a day.*
El libro costó **menos de** veinte euros.	*The book cost less than twenty euros.*

Adverbs: mucho, muy: 7.E.4

h. Comparative forms can be strengthened with the help of other adverbs. The most common are **mucho, bastante,** and **(un) poco.** The adverb **muy** cannot be placed before **más** or **menos,** and can only stand before adjectives or adverbs.

El tiempo está hoy **mucho peor** que ayer.	*The weather today is much worse than yesterday.*
Los billetes de avión son **bastante más** caros que los pasajes de tren.	*Plane tickets are quite a lot more expensive than train tickets.*

i. The following comparative expressions indicate that something is different: **diferente a/de, distinto/a(s) + a** (*different from*).

El último libro de Gabo es **diferente a** los otros.	*Gabo's latest book is different from the others.*
Tú eres **distinta a** todas las otras chicas.	*You're different from all the other girls.*

j. In English, comparative forms of an adjective can be used without stating a comparison: *We live in a bigger city in Ecuador. She is married to an older man.* In Spanish this is not possible and such expressions must be said in a different way.

Vivimos en una ciudad **muy/relativamente** grande en Ecuador.	*We live in a very/relatively big city in Ecuador.*

k. In affirmative comparisons, **nadie/ninguno/nunca/nada** express *more/less than anyone, anytime,* etc.

Sois **más** hábiles **que nadie**.	*You [pl.] are more skilled than anyone.*
Podéis bailar **mejor que ninguno**.	*You [pl.] can dance better than anybody.*
Hoy habéis actuado **mejor que nunca**.	*Today you [pl.] have performed better than ever.*

l. The expression **no... más que** in *negative* sentences is not comparative and is equivalent to **no... sino** or **solamente** as in the following examples.

sino: 16.B.1, 16.B.5

No hablo **más que** español.	*I speak nothing but Spanish.*
No hablo **sino** español.	*I speak nothing but Spanish.*
Solamente hablo español.	*I only speak Spanish.*

Comparisons with *de + definite article + que*

a. The second element of a comparison can be a relative clause that refers to the noun in the first term of the comparison. In this case, the second element is introduced by **de** + *definite article* + **que**. The definite article agrees in gender and number with the noun in the first term of the comparison.

más/menos +	*sing. masc. noun* + **del que**	+ *clause*
	sing. fem. noun + **de la que**	
	pl. masc. noun + **de los que**	
	pl. fem. noun + **de las que**	

Gastamos **más** *dinero del* que teníamos. (gastamos dinero; teníamos dinero) | *We spent more money than we had.*

Había **más** *gente* **de** *la* que esperábamos. (había gente; esperábamos gente) | *There were more people than we expected.*

Fuimos a **menos** *museos* **de** *los* que planeábamos visitar. (fuimos a museos; planeábamos visitar museos) | *We went to fewer museums than we had planned to visit.*

Había **menos** *plazas* **de** *las* que hay en mi ciudad. (había plazas; hay plazas) | *There were fewer squares than there are in my home town.*

b. De lo que is used when the second term of a comparison is a clause and the first is a verb, an adjective, or an adverb.

◀ Lo: 5.A.2

Verb	**Trabajó** más **de lo que** esperábamos.	*He worked more than we expected.*
Adjective	Los precios allí son bastante **más** *altos* **de lo que** dice la gente.	*The prices there are a lot higher than people say.*
Adverb	El tiempo pasó **más** *rápidamente* **de lo que** pensábamos.	*The time passed more quickly than we thought.*

c. De lo que can also be used when the first term of the comparison is a noun. In this case, the verb in the second term of the comparison does not refer specifically to the noun in the first term. This occurs particularly with the noun **vez** or when the first term of the comparison expresses a measurement.

Gasté *cinco dólares* **más de lo que** habíamos acordado. | *I spent five dollars more than we had agreed.*

Vine de visita *tres veces* **más de lo que** viniste tú. | *I came to visit three more times than you.*

◀ Multiples: 6.E.2

d. De lo que can also occur when the clause in the second term of the comparison refers to a general concept rather than to the specific noun in the first term of the comparison. In this case, agreement with the noun is also possible.

Gastamos **más** *dinero* **de lo que/del que** pensábamos. (gastamos dinero; pensábamos gastar menos dinero) | *We spent more money than we thought.*

Compare with this sentence, in which **de lo que** cannot be used:

Gastamos **más** *dinero del* que teníamos en el banco. (gastamos dinero; teníamos dinero) | *We spent more money than we had in the bank.*

e. De lo is also used with adjectives like **aconsejable, autorizado, esperado, habitual, justo, necesario, normal, permitido, previsto,** and **requerido.** It is also possible to use **que** in this case.

Trabajé más **de/que lo** esperado. | *I worked harder than expected.*

Me parece más complicado **de/que lo** previsto. | *It seems more complicated than anticipated.*

11.C Comparisons of equality

Igualdad

The structures for comparing similar characteristics, people, and objects depend on what is being compared.

11.C.1 Tan

Adjectives and adverbs are compared in the same way when emphasizing similarities.

tan *(so)* + *adjective/adverb* + **como** *(as)*

Adjectives	Las películas no son **tan** *cortas* **como** las telenovelas.	*Films are not as short as soap operas.*
	Antonio es **tan** *famoso* **como** yo.	*Antonio is as famous as I am.*
Adverbs	La impresora grande imprime **tan** *rápidamente* **como** la pequeña.	*The big printer prints just as quickly as the little one.*
	Escribo **tan** *bien* en español **como** en francés.	*I write as well in Spanish as in French.*

Indefinite quantifiers
(determiners): 7.E.4

11.C.2 Tanto/a(s)

Nouns (people and objects) are compared using the word **tanto/a(s),** which agrees with the noun that follows it.

tanto/a(s) *(as much/many)* + *noun* + **como** *(as)*

Nouns	Tengo **tantos** libros **como** Betty.	*I have as many books as Betty.*
	Hoy, tengo **tanto** dinero **como** ayer.	*Today, I have just as much money as yesterday.*

11.C.3 Tanto

Verbs are compared using **tanto,** which does not change form and is placed after the verb. The verb is implied after **como** and is normally not repeated.

Tanto... como:
16.B.2d

verb + **tanto** *(just as much/as much)* + **como** *(as)*

Verbs	**Viajas tanto como** yo.	*You travel as much as I do.*
	Entreno tanto como tú.	*I train just as much as you.*

11.C.4 Igual/como, tal como

The expression **igual de... que** is used for both adjectives and adverbs. With verbs, **igual que** is used, and with nouns, **igual a** and **(tal) como.**

Adjectives	Rita es **igual de** joven **que** yo. Rita es joven **como** yo.	*Rita is just as young as I.* *Rita is young like me.*
Adverbs	Yo no escribo **igual de** bien **que** tú.	*I don't write as well as you.*
Nouns	Mi camisa es **igual a** / **tal como** la tuya.	*My shirt is just like yours.*
Verbs	Nosotros trabajamos **igual que** / **como** ellos.	*We work just like them.*

11.C.5 *Mismo/a(s)*

Similarity can be expressed using a definite article and **mismo/a(s)** (*the same*).

Tengo **la misma** camisa que tú.	*I have the same shirt as you.*
Tenemos **la misma** camisa.	*We have the same shirt.*
Hago **lo mismo** de siempre.	*I'm doing the same as always.*
Siempre ponen **las mismas** películas año tras año.	*They always show the same films year after year.*

◀ **Mismo:** Other meanings: 7.E.5 and 27.D

11.D Superlatives

El superlativo

Superlatives refer to the highest or lowest grade of a characteristic (adjectives), how something is done (adverbs), or to the greatest or smallest number of people or things (nouns). In English, the superlative is formed with the ending *-est* (*biggest, smallest, youngest*) or with *most, least.*

11.D.1 Adjectives

a. The superlative of adjectives is formed using **el/la/los/las más/menos** + *adjective.*

Me gustan varios deportes, pero el fútbol es **el más interestante**.	*I like many sports, but soccer is the most interesting.*

b. The following adjectives have irregular superlatives.

Adjectives		Comparatives		Superlatives	
alto	high	más alto superior	higher	el más alto el superior supremo	the highest
bajo	low	más bajo inferior	lower	el más bajo el inferior ínfimo	the lowest
bueno	good	más bueno mejor	better	el más bueno el mejor óptimo	the best, optimal
grande	big	más grande mayor	bigger	el más grande el mayor máximo	the biggest, the maximum
malo	bad	más malo peor	worse	el más malo el peor pésimo	the worst
pequeño	small	más pequeño menor	smaller	el más pequeño el menor mínimo	the smallest, the minimum

◀ Comparison of adjectives: 3.E, 11.B.1

◀ **Más bueno** and **más malo** are used exclusively to refer to character traits: 3.E.2b, 11.B.1c

Esta es **la peor** noticia **que** he recibido.	*This is the worst news I've (ever) received.*
Esta película es **la peor que** he visto.	*This film is the worst I've (ever) seen.*
Mario y Carlos son malos diseñadores, pero Pedro es **el peor**.	*Mario and Carlos are bad designers, but Pedro is the worst.*
Mis dos gatitos son buenos como el pan. No muerden ni rasguñan a nadie. Pero el gatito de mi vecino es **el más bueno** de todos.	*My two kittens are very good. They never bite or scratch. But my neighbor's cat is the nicest of all.*
Los resultados no son **óptimos**, pero son aceptables.	*The results are not optimal, but they are acceptable.*

Todo: 7.C.9 ▶

c. It is common to add **todos/as** (*all*) in superlative sentences. **Todos/as** is always plural and agrees in gender with the noun that follows it or with the context of the sentence.

Rita es **la** estudiante **más** joven **de todos/as**.	*Rita is the youngest student of all.*

(**todos:** there are male students in the group; **todas:** all students in the group are female)

Rita es **la más** jóven **de todos** los estudiantes.	*Rita is the youngest of all the students.*
¿Cuál es **la mejor** película **de todo** el festival?	*Which is the best film in the whole festival?*

d. De is used if a group is indicated.

Nueva York es **la** ciudad **más** grande **del** país.	*New York is the biggest city in the country.*
Este libro es **el menos** caro **de** estos.	*This book is the least expensive of these.*

Superlatives with **-ísimo**: 3.E.3 ▶
Absolute superlative
of adverbs: 11.D.2a-b

e. The endings **-ísimo/a(s)** can be added to adjectives or adverbs to form the *absolute superlative*.

grandísimo	*unbelievably big*	**facilísimo**	*very, very easy*

f. The following superlative adjectives are used in daily language.

Agreement of determiners: 4.B.4 ▶

Esa ropa es de **ínfima** calidad.	*Those clothes are of the lowest quality.*
Tu solución no es **óptima**.	*Your solution isn't the best.*
La diferencia es **mínima**.	*The difference is minimal.*
La temperatura **máxima** fue de 3 grados.	*The maximum temperature was 3 degrees.*

g. Comparison of age is made with **mayor/menor,** while peoples' height/size is compared using **alto/bajo** and **grande/pequeño**.

Marcos es **el mayor** de los tres, pero es el más pequeño.	*Marcos is the oldest of the three, but he is the smallest.*
Olivia es **la menor** de la clase pero es la más alta.	*Olivia is the youngest in the class but she is the tallest.*

h. Adjectives can also be strengthened using many adverbs, such as **bien, enormemente, extraordinariamente, terriblemente, impresionantemente, increíblemente, verdaderamente,** and **totalmente**.

Bien as an adverb: 10.C.3 ▶
Adverbs ending in ▶
-mente: 10.G

El problema es **bien** grave.	*The problem is really serious.*
Lucía es **enormemente** rica.	*Lucía is extremely wealthy.*
Eso es **extraordinariamente** extraño.	*That is extraordinarily strange.*
La comida es **terriblemente** mala.	*The food is terribly bad.*
Ella es **impresionantemente** bella.	*She is strikingly beautiful.*
El tráfico está **increíblemente** malo.	*The traffic is incredibly bad.*
Eres **verdaderamente** listo.	*You are truly clever.*
La caja está **totalmente** vacía.	*The box is totally empty.*

11.D.2 Adverbs

Comparison of adverbs: 10.I ▶

a. Absolute superlatives of adverbs ending in **-mente** can be formed by adding **-mente** to the absolute superlative feminine form of an adjective with an **-ísima** ending. Short adverbs that are identical to masculine singular adjectives take the ending **-ísimo**.

Adjectives as adverbs: 10.G.2 ▶

Ríe **locamente**.	*He laughs wildly.*	Ríe **loquísimamente**.	*He laughs extremely wildly.*
Corre **rápido**.	*He runs fast.*	Corre **rapidísimo**.	*He runs very fast.*

b. Some adverbs that are not derived from adjectives also have absolute superlatives. The absolute superlative keeps the ending of the adverb.

Superlative constructions with adverbs: 10.I.2

lejos → lejísimos	*very far*	cerca → cerquísima	*very close*
poco → poquísimo	*very little*	mucho → muchísimo	*a lot*
Vivo **lejísimos**.	*I live very far.*	Comes **poquísimo**.	*You eat very little.*

c. Superlative constructions can be formed using the comparative form (sometimes preceded by a definite article).

Es el caso **más cuidadosamente** investigado.	*It is the most carefully investigated case.*
De todos los casos, este es **el más cuidadosamente** investigado.	*Of all the cases, this one is the most carefully investigated.*
Es el detective que **más cuidadosamente** investiga.	*He is the detective that most carefully investigates.*

d. Lo más/menos + *adverb* + *adjective/clause* is usually equivalent to the English *as much as* + *adjective/clause* or *as little as* + *adjective/clause*. The adjective most commonly used in this construction is **posible**. This is also used in time expressions.

Entreno **lo más frecuentemente** posible.	*I train as much as possible.*
Trabaja **lo más rápidamente** que puede.	*She works as fast as she can.*
Lo más temprano que llego a la oficina es a las ocho.	*The earliest I get to the office is eight o'clock.*

e. The Spanish equivalent of an English sentence that contains a superlative adverb can be a sentence containing a relative clause or a comparative sentence (in which the first term of the comparison is compared with everything/everyone else in the group).

He sings **the best**.	Él es el que mejor canta. Él canta mejor que todos.
He worked **the most tirelessly**.	Él es el que trabajó más incansablemente. Él trabajó más incansablemente que el resto.

11.D.3 *Lo*

The neuter article **lo** forms abstract noun phrases that can also have a superlative meaning.

Use of neuter article **lo** in order to form nouns: 5.A.2

lo mejor	**Lo mejor** del verano es el calor.	*The best thing about summer is the heat.*
lo más increíble	¡Eso es **lo más increíble** de todo!	*That is the most incredible thing of all!*
lo más posible	Debes decir **lo menos posible**.	*You should say as little as possible.*
lo más romántico	La ceremonia fue **lo más romántico** de la boda.	*The ceremony was the most romantic part of the wedding.*
lo peor	Ese libro es **lo peor que** he leído.	*That book is the worst thing I have (ever) read.*
lo más sensato	Eso es **lo más sensato que** puedes hacer.	*It is the most sensible thing to do.*

The subjunctive in relative clauses: 23.D

11.D.4   Superlatives with *que*

a. Besides **de** + *group*, it is possible to form superlative constructions using **más/menos** and the relative pronoun **que**.

Este libro es **el más interesante de** todos los que he leído.	*This is the most interesting book of all the books I have read.*
Este libro es **el más interesante que** jamás haya leído.	*This is the most interesting book (that) I have ever read.*
Es **el libro que más** me gusta.	*It's the book (that) I like best.*

Lo que: 15.B.7b **b.** The neutral **lo** is used instead of **el/la/los/las** when it does not refer to a specific noun. The constructions with **lo que más/menos** are usually translated as *the thing that* or *what*.

El que más me gusta es este libro. (**el** = el libro)	*The one I like best is this book.*
Lo que más me gusta es jugar al tenis. (**lo** = jugar al tenis)	*What I like best is to play tennis.*

c. When the comparison focuses on an adjective or adverb, the adjective or adverb is placed between **más/menos** and **que**.

Lo más valioso que tiene mi país es su gente.	*The most valuable thing my country has is its people.*
Lo más rápidamente que puedes viajar allí es en avión.	*The fastest you can travel there is by plane.*

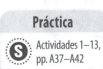

Práctica

Actividades 1–13,
pp. A37–A42

Prepositions
Las preposiciones

12.A Overview

Aspectos generales

Prepositions are words or word phrases that can be placed before a noun to indicate the semantic relationship between that noun and another word in the sentence. They never change form. The majority of prepositions indicate a relationship between two words in terms of time, location, direction, or origin. The meaning depends on the prepositions used and the words linked.

Since Spanish and English use prepositions in different ways, a preposition used in Spanish may not have a direct English translation.

Use of prepositions: 12.B

Examples		
Location	Roberto está **en** Sevilla.	*Roberto is in Sevilla.*
Time	Mi vuelo es **a** la una.	*My flight is at one.*
Ownership	la casa **de** José María	*José María's house*

12.A.1 Simple prepositions

a. As in English, single-word prepositions in Spanish are a limited set. They are the following:

Simple prepositions			
a	*to*	**excepto, salvo**	*except, apart from*
ante	*before*	**hacia**	*toward*
bajo	*under*	**hasta**	*until, till*
con	*with*	**mediante**	*through, by means of*
contra	*against*	**para**	*for, to, in order to, by*
de	*of, to, from*	**por**	*for, because of, by*
desde	*from, since*	**según**	*according to*
durante	*during*	**sin**	*without*
en	*on, in, by, at*	**sobre**	*over, about*
entre	*between*	**tras**	*after, behind*

Verbs with prepositions: 17.B.2

Por favor, siéntate con la espalda **contra** la pared.
Please sit with your back against the wall.

Ángel ha estado viajando **desde** ayer.
Ángel has been traveling since yesterday.

Según Elisa, va a llover.
According to Elisa, it is going to rain.

El perrito corre **tras** su dueño.
The little dog runs after his owner.

b. Spanish prepositions always come between two words and can never end a sentence like in English.

Relative pronouns: 15.A.3b

Rita es la chica **con** la que salgo.
*Rita is the girl I go out **with**.*

c. In English two prepositions can be joined using the coordinating conjunctions *and* or *or*, whereas in Spanish, they appear separately in the sentence. The noun or phrase that the preposition refers to is repeated, but the second instance can be replaced by a pronoun.

Tomo el autobús para ir **a** la escuela **y** regresar **de** la escuela.
*I take the bus **to and from** school.*

Plantaremos árboles **delante de** la casa **o detrás de** ella.
*We will plant trees **in front of or behind** the house.*

d. The words **pro**, **versus**, and **vía** are sometimes counted as prepositions. **Pro** precedes nouns: **grupos *pro* derechos humanos** (*pro-human rights groups*). In Spanish, the meaning of **versus (vs.)** is **contra**, **frente a**; it is only used in formal texts: **las grandes economías *versus* las economías de menor escala** (*large economies vs. lower scale economies*). The preposition **vía** indicates how something is done: the medium, the route, etc.: **El viaje es de San Francisco a Nueva York *vía* Chicago.** (*The trip is from San Francisco to New York, via Chicago*).

12.A.2 Compound prepositions and prepositional phrases

Compound prepositions (**locuciones preposicionales**) are formed either by two simple prepositions: **por entre** (*through*), by a combination of preposition(s) and an adverb: **(por) delante de** (*in front of*), **cerca de** (*near*), or combining preposition(s) and a noun: **en contraste con** (*in contrast with*).

a. Below are examples of expressions formed by groups of single prepositions:

a por: 12.C.1

Compound prepositions: *preposition + preposition*		
a por (*Spain*)	Iremos **a por** café.	*We will go **to get** coffee.*
de a	Nos tocan **de a** tres chocolates a cada uno.	*We get three chocolates **each**.*
de entre	Un día **de entre** semana podré trabajar contigo.	*On any **working day**, I will be able to work with you.*
en contra (de)	No actúes **en contra de** tus propios principios.	*Don't act **against** your own principles.*
	¿Estáis **en contra** mía?	*Are you [pl.] **against** me?*
en pro, **en contra de**	¿Estás **en pro** o **en contra** de la propuesta?	*Are you **for** or **against** the proposal?*
para con	Ella es generosa **para con** todos.	*She is generous **with** everyone.*
por entre	El perro se metió **por entre** los arbustos y se escondió.	*The dog squeezed **in between** the bushes and hid.*

b. The prepositions **de** and **por** form many expressions with adverbs. Some adverbs accept **por** when movement is involved (*around the back of, passing by the front of*, etc.).

Adverbs of place with prepositions: 10.E.3

Compound prepositions: *adverb + preposition*			
(por) delante de	in front of, opposite, across from	**(por) detrás de**	behind, in the back of
enfrente de			
frente a			
al lado de	beside, next to	**lejos de**	far from
cerca de	near, close to		
junto a	close to, next to		
encima de	on top of, on	**debajo de**	under, underneath
por encima de	over	**por debajo de**	
dentro de	in, inside of	**fuera de**	out, outside of
por dentro de		**por fuera de**	
alrededor de	around		
antes de	before	**después de**	after
		luego de	

Prepositions • **Chapter 12**

El autobús pasa **por delante de** la catedral.

La catedral está **enfrente del / frente al** parque.

En el parque, los niños juegan **al lado de** sus madres.

Vivimos **cerca del** centro de la ciudad.

Mis abuelos viven **junto a** nosotros.

Dentro de la casa hay un pequeño patio y **alrededor de** él hay plantas.

La casa se veía vieja **antes de** pintarla. **Después de** pintarla, parece nueva.

The bus passes **in front of** the cathedral.

The cathedral is **opposite** the park.

In the park, the children play **next to** their mothers.

We live **close to** downtown.

My grandparents live **next to** us.

Inside the house there is a small courtyard and there are plants **around** it.

The house looked old **before** it was painted. It looks new **after** painting it.

al lado suyo/mío, etc.: 9.C.2e

antes de que, después de que: 23.E.2

c. There are many prepositional phrases that are formed with *nouns* and *one or more prepositions*, usually **a**, **de**, **en**, **por**, and **con**. Most of these phrases may function in a sentence as prepositions, adverbs, or adverbial transitions.

Prepositional phrases: *preposition + noun (+ preposition)*		
a base de	Las tortillas se preparan **a base de** maíz.	Tortillas are made **with** corn.
a bordo de	Los pasajeros pasaron **a bordo del** avión.	Passengers got **on board** the plane.
a cargo de	La profesora está **a cargo de** la clase.	The teacher is **in charge of** the class.
a causa de	Nos retrasamos **a causa del** mal tiempo.	We were delayed **because of** bad weather.
a costa de	No hagas nada **a costa de** los demás.	Don't do anything **at the expense of** others.
a eso de	Llegaremos **a eso de** las tres de la tarde.	We will arrive **around** three in the afternoon.
a falta de	**A falta de** computadora, escribiré a mano.	*Lacking* a computer, I will write by hand.
a fondo	Estudiaremos los documentos **a fondo**.	We will study the documents **in depth**.
a fuerza de	**A fuerza de** voluntad, has logrado tener éxito.	**Through** willpower, you have managed to succeed.
a la hora de	**A la hora de** pagar, ¿no tienes dinero?	**The time comes** to pay the bill, and you don't have money?
a la sombra de	Ese chico creció **a la sombra de** su famoso padre.	That kid grew up **in the shadow of** his famous father.
a la vez	¿Haces todo **a la vez**?	Do you do everything **at the same time**?
a lo largo de	Fue un hombre ejemplar **a lo largo de** toda su vida.	He was an exemplary man **throughout** his whole life.
a lo mejor	**A lo mejor** va a llover hoy.	**Maybe** it will rain today.
a mediados de	Su pedido llegará **a mediados de** mayo.	Your order will arrive **in mid**-May.
a menudo	Estudiamos en la biblioteca **a menudo**.	We study at the library **often**.
a modo de	Leeré un corto texto **a modo de** introducción.	I will read a short text **by way of** introduction.
a partir de	**A partir del** lunes habrá conciertos mensuales.	**Starting** Monday, there will be monthly concerts.
a pesar de	Compraremos la casa **a pesar del** precio.	We will buy the house **in spite of** the price.
a pie	Los estudiantes van a la universidad **a pie**.	Students go to the university **on foot**.
a principios de	El pago se enviará **a principios de** mes.	The payment will be sent **at the beginning of** the month.
a prueba de	Nuestros productos son **a prueba de** golpes.	Our products are shock**proof**.
a raíz de	**A raíz de** la crisis, los precios han subido.	**As a result of** the crisis, prices have risen.

en pie = *standing*

Al menos = por lo menos ▶

De modo que: use of ▶
subjunctive: 16.C.5c

De repente = de pronto ▶

a razón de	Los precios han subido **a razón del** dos por ciento anual.	*Prices have risen **at a rate of** two percent annually.*
a tiempo	Finalmente, todo se hizo **a tiempo**.	*Finally, everything was done **on time**.*
a veces	**A veces** salimos temprano del trabajo.	***Sometimes** we leave work early.*
al menos	¿Me prestas dinero? ¿**Al menos** cinco dólares?	*Can you lend me some money? **At least** five dollars?*
con base en	El informe se realizó **con base en** datos confiables.	*The report was carried out **based on** reliable data.*
con miras a	Los presidentes se reunirán hoy **con miras a** firmar un acuerdo.	*The presidents will meet today **with the purpose of** signing an agreement.*
con motivo de	La cena es **con motivo de** tu visita.	***The reason for** this dinner is your visit.*
con respecto a	No sé nada **con respecto a** este problema.	*I don't know anything **regarding** this problem.*
de acuerdo con	Estoy **de acuerdo con** tu opinión. **De acuerdo con** el profesor, el examen será pronto.	*I **agree with** your opinion. **According to** the teacher, the exam will be soon.*
de lo contrario	Tengo que anotar tu teléfono, **de lo contrario**, lo olvidaré.	*I have to write down your phone number, **if not**, I will forget it.*
de tal modo que, de modo que	Trabajamos mucho **de tal modo que** todo fue un éxito. Trabaja, **de modo que** tengas éxito.	*We worked **in such a way that** everything was a success. Work hard, **so that** you can succeed.*
de nuevo	¡Qué gusto verte **de nuevo**!	*So good to see you **again**!*
de pie	Debes ponerte/estar **de pie** cuando tocan el himno nacional.	*You should **stand up / be standing** when they play the national anthem.*
de regreso a	¿Cuándo estará usted **de regreso a** su trabajo?	*When will you **be back at** work?*
de repente	Hacía sol y **de repente**, empezó a llover.	*It was sunny and **suddenly**, it started to rain.*
de veras	¡**De veras** sabes mucho sobre cine!	*You **really** know a lot about movies!*
de vez en cuando	Vamos al cine **de vez en cuando**.	*We go to the movies **once in a while**.*
en cuanto a	**En cuanto a** películas, me gustan las comedias.	***Regarding** movies, I like comedies.*
en vez de, en lugar de, en cambio de	¿Prefiere usted café **en lugar / cambio / vez de** té?	*Do you prefer coffee **instead of** tea?*
en cambio	La lechuga me gusta, **en cambio** las verduras no.	*I like lettuce; **on the other hand**, I don't like vegetables.*
enseguida	¡Ven **enseguida**!	*Come here **immediately**!*
en torno a	La clase será **en torno a** la literatura moderna.	*The class will be **about** modern literature.*
frente a frente, cara a cara	Los equipos se encontrarán pronto **frente a frente / cara a cara**.	*The teams will soon meet **face to face**.*
para siempre	El petróleo no durará **para siempre**.	*Oil won't last **forever**.*
por eso	Quiero cuidar el ambiente, **por eso** ¡reciclo!	*I want to take care of the environment, **that's why** I recycle!*
por fin	¡**Por fin** acaba de llegar el autobús!	*The bus has **finally** arrived!*
por lo general	**Por lo general**, en España la cena es tarde.	***In general**, dinner in Spain is late.*
por lo menos	Hace mucho frío, pero **por lo menos** hace sol.	*It's cold, but **at least** it's sunny.*
por otra parte, por otro lado	Mi auto es bueno y, **por otra parte / por otro lado** , no es caro.	*My car is nice and **besides**, it's not expensive.*

Prepositions • **Chapter 12**

por poco	¡**Por poco** olvido tu cumpleaños!	*I **almost** forgot your birthday!*
por supuesto	Este es nuestro mejor precio, **por supuesto**.	*This is our best price, **of course**!*
sin embargo	Esta novela no es popular y, **sin embargo**, es excelente.	*This novel is not very popular. **However**, it's excellent!*

Por poco is generally used with the present indicative.

Sin embargo: 16.B.5

12.B Use of prepositions

Uso de las preposiciones

12.B.1 Overview

a. After a preposition, the pronouns for the first- and second-person singular (**yo**, **tú**) change to **mí**, **ti**, except after the prepositions **entre**, **según**, **excepto**, and **salvo**. After these prepositions, subject pronoun forms are always used: **yo**, **tú**. The pronoun **vos** does not change form after a preposition: **para vos** (*for you*), **con vos** (*with you*).

Vos: 13.B.2, 13.B.5
Pronouns after prepositions: 13.C

Ven, siéntate cerca de **mí**.　　　　*Come and sit down close to me.*
Los libros son para **ti**.　　　　　*The books are for you.*
Esto queda entre **tú** y **yo**.　　　*This stays between you and me.*

b. After the preposition **con**, the first-person singular pronoun **mí** changes to **–migo** and the second-person singular pronoun **ti** changes to **–tigo**. These pronouns are invariable.

—¿Quieres ir al cine **conmigo**?　　*Do you want to go to the movies with me?*
—Sí, quiero ir al cine **contigo**.　　*Yes, I want to go to the movies with you.*

c. The reflexive pronoun **sí** takes the invariable form **consigo** after **con**. **Mismo/misma** can be added for emphasis if the action refers back to the subject.

Sí: 13.C.2, 27.A.2
Mismo: emphasis: 7.E.5, reflexive: 27.A.2, 27.D.1d

¿Lleva usted su licencia de conducir **consigo**?　*Do you carry your driving license with you?*
Pensé que Lisa hablaba **consigo misma**, pero ¡estaba conversando por su celular!　*I thought that Lisa was talking to herself, but she was talking on her cell phone!*

12.B.2 The preposition *a*

a. The preposition **a** is used in the following cases:

Clues for use	Examples	
Time	La cita es **a las tres**.	*The appointment is at three.*
Time that has passed before something happens/happened	Me **gradúo a** los dos años.	*I'll graduate after two years.*
	Me **gradué a** los dos años.	*I graduated after two years.*
Direction with verbs of motion	**Llegamos a** casa.	*We arrived home.*
	Bajamos al primer piso.	*We went down to the first floor.*
	Vamos a la reunión.	*We are going to the meeting.*
Distance from a location	El correo está **a dos calles** de la iglesia.	*The post office is (located) two streets/blocks from the church.*
al + *infinitive*	**Al contar** el dinero, faltaba un dólar.	*When I counted the money, one dollar was missing.*
	Pagué **al recibir** el paquete.	*I paid upon receiving the package.*

Other verb periphrases with the infinitive: 26.C

b. When the preposition **a** is followed by the article **el**, the two words combine to form the contraction **al**.

Voy **al** mercado.	*I'm going to the market.*
Le di la información **al** profesor.	*I gave the information to the professor.*

c. One of the most important uses of the preposition **a** is to mark the indirect object of the sentence and to indicate that the direct object is a person. This use is called *the personal* **a**.

The preposition **a** with a direct object: 13.E.2 and with an indirect object: 13.F.1

The preposition **a** with indefinite pronouns and quantifiers: 7.D.2c, 7.E.3

Clues for use	Examples	
Precedes the direct object when it is a person (or it is personified).	Conozco **a** mis vecinos.	*I know my neighbors.*
	Quiero mucho **a** mi mascota.	*I love my pet very much.*
Must be used before indefinite pronouns when they refer to people: **nadie**, **alguno**, **todos**, etc.	Admiro **a todos** mis profesores.	*I admire all my teachers.*
	Conozco **a algunos** de mis profesores personalmente.	*I have met some of my teachers personally.*
It is omitted when the direct object does not have a determiner.	Necesitamos ingenieros especializados.	*We need specialized engineers.*
It is omitted after **tener** as long as no indefinite pronouns follow it.	Tenemos muchos amigos. No tenemos **a nadie** para ese trabajo.	*We have many friends. We don't have anyone for that job.*
The personal **a** must be used before the indirect object.	Le doy un regalo **a Luis**. Les escribo a **mis amigos**. ¡Agrégale más memoria **a tu PC**!	*I give Luis a gift. I write to my friends. Add more memory to your PC!*

12.B.3 **The preposition** *con*

Con is used in the following ways:

Estar con: 30.C.4

Clues for use	Examples	
To mean *with/together with*	Pablo está **con** sus amigos.	*Pablo is with his friends.*
Use of tools	Escribo **con** el lápiz.	*I write with a pencil.*
With nouns in adverbial phrases of manner	Viajo **con** frecuencia.	*I travel often.*
	Te ayudo **con** gusto.	*I'm happy to help you.*
Condition	**Con** precios tan altos, no puedo comprar nada.	*With such high prices, I can't buy anything.*

12.B.4 **The preposition** *de*

a. De has many uses in Spanish. The most important are shown in the table.

Use of **ser**: 30.B.3

Clues for use	Examples	
Ownership	los zapatos **de** Rita	*Rita's shoes*
	el club **de** los estudiantes	*the students' club*
Nationality	Sois **de** México.	*You [pl.] are from Mexico.*
Direction from a location or origin	El avión llega **de** Vancouver.	*The plane arrives from Vancouver.*
	Salí **de** casa temprano.	*I left home early.*
To express belonging	los estudiantes **de** Washington	*the students from Washington*
	las ventanas **de** la casa	*the windows of the house*
Placed before an infinitive to express purpose	la escoba **de** barrer	*the broom for sweeping*
	la mesa **de** planchar	*the ironing board*
To refer to the material of which an object is made	la caja **de** plástico	*the plastic box*
	la cuchara **de** plata	*the silver spoon*

Prepositions • **Chapter 12**

Clues for use	Examples	
Properties	los estudiantes **de** español	*the students of Spanish*
	el libro **de** química	*the chemistry book*
Physical appearance	la persona **de** gafas	*the person wearing glasses*
	el niño **de** pantalón corto	*the child wearing shorts*
	la casa **de** ventanas verdes	*the house with green windows*
estar de + *new or temporal occupation*	**estar de** profesora/enfermero/ayudante	*to be a teacher/a nurse/an assistant (for now, currently)*
estar de + *noun*: describes conditions	estar **de** mal humor	*to be in a bad mood*
	estar **de** viaje/vacaciones	*to be traveling/on holiday*
	estar **de** regreso	*to be back*
	estar **de** buenas/malas	*to be lucky/unlucky*
	estar **de** visita	*to be visiting*
	estar **de** amigos	*to be friends*

◀ Use of **estar de** to express a temporary profession, work: 30.C.3

b. When the preposition **de** is followed by the article **el**, the two words form the contraction **del**.

El libro **del** que te hablé cuesta 20 dólares.   *The book I talked to you about costs 20 dollars.*

12.B.5 **The preposition** *en*

En is used to express the following relationships:

Clues for use	Example	
Specifies where someone/something is located	Estamos **en** Portugal.	*We're in Portugal.*
	Elisa vive **en** la ciudad.	*Elisa lives in the city.*
	El papel está **en** el cajón.	*The paper is in the drawer.*
	Marta está **en** el dormitorio.	*Marta is in the bedroom.*
	El país está **en** Europa.	*The country is in Europe.*
To mean *on, on top*	La cena está **en** la mesa.	*The dinner is on the table.*
With ordinals and the infinitive in expressions like *the first who…*	Rosa siempre es la primera **en** llegar.	*Rosa is always the first to arrive.*
	Ernesto es el último **en** pagar.	*Ernesto is the last one to pay.*
With months, years, and other time expressions (*not used with days*)	**En** junio hay vacaciones.	*There is vacation in June.*
	Lisa llamó **en** ese instante.	*Lisa called just then.*
	Estaba feliz **en** esa época.	*I was happy during that time.*
Expressions with **estar** + **en**	estar **en** silencio	*to be silent*
	estar **en** la pobreza	*to be poor*
	estar **en** la ignorancia	*to be ignorant*
	estar **en** la cúspide	*to be at the height of fame/wealth/etc.*
	estar **en** la oscuridad	*to be in the dark*

◀ **Estar en** + place: 30.D.1

◀ Llegué **el lunes.**

12.B.6 **The prepositions** *para* **and** *por*

Both **para** and **por** mean *to* or *for* but are often used differently in English and Spanish.

Para		
Clues for use	**Examples**	
With a person: refers to the recipient of something	Llegó una carta **para** ti.	*A letter arrived for you.*
	Hay comida **para** todos.	*There's food for everyone.*
With verbs of motion: provides destination	Hoy salimos **para** Chile.	*We're leaving for Chile today.*
	¿Vas **para** la clase?	*Are you going to the class?*
	Ven **para** acá.	*Come here.*
With activity verbs: provides purpose	Trabajo **para** vivir.	*I work to live.*
	Estudiamos **para** aprender.	*We study to learn.*
	Las discotecas son **para** divertirse.	*Nightclubs are for having fun.*
With expressions of time: provides a deadline or a closing date	El documento es **para** el lunes.	*The document is for Monday.*
	Termino el trabajo **para** las tres.	*I'll finish the job by three o'clock.*
With verbs connected to work/tasks: refers to the employer or a client	Trabajo **para** el gobierno. Escribo **para** la televisión.	*I work for the government. I write for TV.*
To express *for being so,* using the formula **para ser tan** + *adjective/ adverb*	**Para** ser tan joven, es muy maduro.	*For a young guy, he's very mature.*
With *tool* + **ser** + **para**: provides area of use	El lápiz es **para** escribir, no **para** jugar.	*Pencils are for writing, not for playing.*
With **estar para** + *infinitive* to express an impending event	Ya estoy **para** salir.	*I'm ready to leave. / I'm about to leave.*

Use of **ser** + **para**: 30.B.4 ▶

See **estar por** *in chart below.* ▶

Por		
Clues for use	**Examples**	
Refers to cause or justification	Cancelaron el carnaval **por** la lluvia.	*They canceled the carnival because of the rain.*
Describes movements through or around an area	Salimos **por** la puerta principal. Paseáis **por** el parque. Mañana paso **por** tu casa.	*We left through the main door. You stroll through the park. I'll stop by your house tomorrow.*
Provides a time frame	Estaré en Madrid **por** unos días.	*I'll be in Madrid for a few days.*
With communication and transmission: television, telephone, mail, Internet, fax, radio	Envíame el paquete **por** correo. Transmiten los partidos de fútbol **por** radio y televisión. Mi profesor enseña **por** la red. Hablas mucho **por** teléfono.	*Send me the package by mail. They broadcast the soccer games on the radio and TV. My teacher teaches lessons online. You talk a lot on the telephone.*
Describes an exchange	Cambié mi auto viejo **por** uno nuevo. Compramos la bicicleta **por** muy poco dinero.	*I changed my old car for a new one. We bought the bicycle for very little money.*
With **estar** + **por** to express the possibility of doing something in the very near future	**Estoy por** ponerme a estudiar un rato. Ella dice que **está por salir** en cualquier momento.	*I think I'm going to study for a bit. She says she's going to leave at any moment.*

See **estar para** *in chart above.* ▶

98

Prepositions • **Chapter 12**

Shows that someone is acting on behalf of someone else	¿Puedes asistir a la reunión **por** mí?	*Can you attend the meeting instead of/for me?*
With percentages	3%: tres **por** ciento	*three percent*
With verbs of motion in the sense of *collecting, getting*	Vamos **por** los niños a las tres. ¿Vas **por** el periódico?	*We'll pick up the children at three o'clock. Are you going to go get the newspaper?*
Refers to tasks which are still to be done (with **quedar**, **hay**, **tener**)	Quedan/Hay/Tengo varias cuentas **por** pagar.	*There are/I have several bills left to pay.*

12.B.7 Expressing location, direction, and time with prepositions

The following prepositions convey physical or figurative movement from one point to another, as well as periods of time.

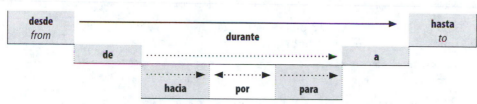

○ Prepositions used with adverbs of place and direction: 10.E.3

a. The preposition pair **desde-hasta** indicates a precise origin and arrival point, while **de-a** conveys a less concrete *from–to* direction. The preposition **por** conveys a *through* movement, while **hacia** and **para** refer to a *forward* destination without any reference to origin.

¿**Para** dónde vas?	***Where*** *are you going?*
Voy **de** la biblioteca **al** gimnasio y **desde** allí tomo el autobús **hasta** el teatro.	*I am going* ***from*** *the library* ***to*** *the gym and* ***from*** *there, I take the bus* ***to*** *the theater.*
El autobús pasa **por** el centro de la ciudad y sigue **hacia** las afueras.	*The bus passes* ***through*** *downtown and continues* ***toward*** *the suburbs.*

b. The prepositions above can also refer to *time*. **Desde-hasta** conveys a limit, while **de-a** only describes a direction in time. **Hacia** is used for approximate time, and **por** forms specific time expressions: **por la mañana**, **por la noche**, **por la tarde**. The preposition **durante** refers to a progressive period of time, while **a** tells the exact time. **En** is used with months and years (not days of the week) and to express how much time is left for something to be completed: **en un mes** (*within/in a month*), **en tres días** (*within/in three days*).

—¿**Para** cuándo terminarás el proyecto?	*(For) when will you finish the project?*
—Lo tendré listo **en** tres días. Hoy martes trabajaré **de** tres **a** cuatro de la tarde y después **desde** mañana **hasta** el viernes. Es decir, trabajaré **durante** tres días.	*I will have it ready* ***within*** *three days. Today, Tuesday, I will work* ***from*** *three* ***to*** *four in the afternoon, and then* ***from*** *tomorrow* ***until*** *Friday. In other words, I will work* ***during*** *three days.*
Terminaré el trabajo **hacia** fines de esta semana. ¡El viernes **por** la tarde, **a** las tres en punto!	*I will finish the work* ***toward*** *the end of this week. Friday* ***in*** *the afternoon* ***at*** *three o'clock!*

c. The preposition pair **ante-tras** describes opposite horizontal locations (*in front of–back of*) and **sobre-bajo** express them vertically (*above–under*), with or without physical contact. **Entre** describes a neutral location *in between* any of these points, also with or without physical contact.

Ante el juez está la acusada y **tras** ella, su familia.	*The accused is* ***before*** *the judge and* ***behind*** *her, her family.*
Sobre la mesa están las pruebas y **bajo** estas, los documentos del juez.	***On*** *the table are the exhibits and* ***under*** *them, the judge's documents.*
Los guardias están de pie **entre** el juez y la acusada.	*The guards are standing* ***between*** *the judge and the accused.*

Compound prepositions: 12.A.2
Adverbs of place and direction:
10.E.3

d. In modern Spanish, the prepositions **ante**, **tras**, and **bajo** are mostly used in idioms, and in formal and figurative language. **Delante de**, **detrás de**, and **debajo de** may replace them if they refer to a *physical* place.

La chica no se rinde **ante** los desafíos.	*The girl doesn't give up when **facing** a challenge.*
Tras la crisis, han aumentado los problemas.	***After** the crisis, the problems have grown.*
Bajo ningún concepto llegues tarde.	*Don't be late **for** any reason at all.*

encima: adverbs of place:
10.E.3

e. Sobre is a synonym of **encima de** only when its reference is a physical place. It can be replaced by **en** only if there is *physical contact* with a horizontal surface. **Contra** implies physical contact *against* a surface (usually vertical) or figuratively, *against* someone or something (a direction, a location, a person, etc.).

La taza de café está **sobre / encima de / en** la mesa.	*The cup of coffee is **on** the table.*
La mesa está **contra** la pared.	*The table is **against** the wall.*
Protégete **contra** el sol.	*Protect yourself **against** the sun.*

f. In addition to location, the preposition **sobre** is often used figuratively. It expresses *about* and *above* or *beyond* a limit (distance, time, quantity, importance, etc.).

El folleto es **sobre** los precios de Internet.	*The brochure is **about** Internet prices.*
Me importas tú **sobre** todas las cosas.	*You matter to me **above** everything else.*

g. The preposition pair **con-sin** (*with–without*) is situational and does not refer to location. **Excepto** and **salvo** (*except*) are synonyms. **Salvo** is formal and used in writing and fixed phrases.

Con mi nuevo teléfono, siempre estoy en la red.	***With** my new phone, I am always online.*
El teléfono es bueno, **excepto** su cámara.	*The phone is good, **except** its camera.*

h. Mediante (*By means of, through*) is formal. Its more common synonyms in Spanish are **con la ayuda de**, **por medio de**, and **a través de**. The preposition **con** may replace it in specific contexts.

Los desacuerdos se resuelven **mediante/con** el diálogo.	*Disagreements are resolved **by means of/ through** dialogue.*
Mediante/Con su colaboración, ayudaremos a muchos niños.	***With** your help, we will help many children.*

12.C Regional variations

Variaciones regionales

12.C.1 *A por*

In Spain, **a por** is used with verbs of motion and nouns (*verb* + **a por** + *noun*) to mean *in search of*. It is sometimes used to clarify meaning. For example, **Voy por agua** could mean *I'm going by water*. But **Voy a por agua** means *I'm going to get some water*.

Voy **a por** la escalera.	*I'm going to get the ladder.*
Pronto iremos **a por** Juan.	*We will pick up Juan soon.*

12.C.2 *Entrar en, entrar a*

The verb **entrar** is usually followed by **en** in Spain and **a** in Latin America.

Entro **en** la sala. (*Spain*) Entro **a la** sala. (*Latin America*)	*I'm going into the living room.*

Práctica

Actividades 1–18,
pp. A42–A47

Personal pronouns
Pronombres personales

Chapter 13

A. Subject pronouns
B. Formal and informal address
C. Pronouns after prepositions
D. Direct and indirect objects
E. Direct object pronouns
F. Indirect object pronouns
G. Placement of direct and indirect object pronouns
H. Repetition of direct and indirect objects

13.A Subject pronouns

Pronombres personales sujeto

Pronouns are words that replace nouns, such as *I, you, me, it, him/her, them*. A pronoun has different forms depending on how it is used in a sentence. The subject form is used when a pronoun is the subject of a sentence.

There are two important regional differences for the subject forms of personal pronouns. In Spain, there are two pronouns for the second-person plural: a formal pronoun, **ustedes**, and an informal one, **vosotros/as**. In Latin America, **ustedes** is used both formally and informally. The other difference is the use of **vos** instead of **tú** for the informal second-person singular pronoun in many areas of Latin America.

Spain			
Singular		**Plural**	
yo	*I*	**nosotros, nosotras**	*we*
tú	*you*	**vosotros, vosotras**	*you*
usted	*you (formal)*	**ustedes**	*you (formal)*
él, ella	*he, she*	**ellos, ellas**	*they*
ello	*it*	(no plural)	

Latin America			
Singular		**Plural**	
yo	*I*	**nosotros, nosotras**	*we*
tú, vos	*you*	**ustedes**	*you*
usted	*you (formal)*		
él, ella	*he, she*	**ellos, ellas**	*they*
ello	*it*	(no plural)	

Map of Spain and Equatorial Guinea: p. xxi
Map of South America: p. xxii
Map of Mexico, Central America and the Caribbean: p. xxiii
Map of **voseo** regions in Latin America: p. 277

Ello: 13.A.2b

13.A.1 Use of the pronoun

a. In Spanish, since the verb ending provides information about the subject, the subject pronoun is often omitted in both written and spoken language.

Habl**o**. *I am talking.*   Habl**amos**. *We are talking.*

Verb forms: 17.A.2b

b. Subject pronouns are used when the subject is unclear. For example, **él/ella/usted** take the same form and **ellos/ellas/ustedes** do as well, so the pronoun is often needed for clarification. Subject pronouns are also used when comparing and contrasting.

Yo soy profesora y **tú** eres dentista.	*I'm a teacher and you're a dentist.*
Ella es simpática; **él** no lo es.	*She's friendly, he's not.*
Nosotros somos profesores y **vosotros** sois médicos.	*We're teachers and you're [pl.] doctors.*
¿Pagan **ustedes** la cuenta o la pagan **ellos**?	*Are you [pl.] paying the bill or are they?*

c. **Usted** and **ustedes** are often abbreviated in written language as **Ud.** and **Uds.**, respectively.

¿Cómo está **Ud.**?	*How are you?*
Les damos a **Uds.** una cordial bienvenida.	*We give you [pl.] a warm welcome.*

esto, eso, aquello: 8.A.4 ▶

13.A.2 It, this/that

a. In order to express a concept or talk about something in general, usually **esto** and **eso** are used.

Eso está bien.	*That is good.*
No comprendemos **esto**.	*We don't understand this.*

b. Ello does not have a plural or other forms. It is a synonym of **eso**.

No pienses en **ello**.	
No pienses en **eso**.	*Don't think about it.*

este/a, ese/a: 8.A.2 ▶

c. Este/a and **ese/a** can replace the subject.

—¿Es importante el Premio Nobel?	*Is the Nobel Prize important?*
—Sí, **ese** es importante.	*Yes, that one is important.*

d. Lo can replace a whole sentence or idea.

—¿Es importante el Premio Nobel?	*Is the Nobel Prize important?*
—Sí, **lo** es.	*Yes, it is.*

13.B Formal and informal address

Formas de tratamiento

In Spanish, we can choose between *formal* and *informal* address for one or several people, but the alternatives differ regionally. The differences can be explained through a historical context. When the Spanish language arrived in the Americas at the end of the 15th century, the informal forms of address for one person were **tú** and **vos**, while **Vuestra Merced** (*Your Grace*) was formal. To address several people, **vos** was also used informally and **Vuestras Mercedes** (*Your Graces*) was the respectful form. Later, in the 17th century, the change in pronunciation of **Vuestra(s) Merced(es)** had already generated the modern formal pronouns **usted** and **ustedes**. At the same time, **vosotros/as** had become the plural informal pronoun to avoid confusion with the singular **vos**, which was used less and less frequently in Spain. By the end of the 18th century, **vos** was no longer used in Spain or its political centers across the Atlantic—Mexico, Peru, and the Caribbean—, where **tú** became the preferred form of address for family and friends. The use of **vos** continued in the rest of the Hispanic world, either as the only informal pronoun (as in Argentina) or together with **tú** (as in Colombia). During the same time period, the use of **vosotros/as** became frequent in parts of Spain, but it never took root in the Hispanic regions of Latin America, the Canary Islands, or parts of Andalusia. Today's forms of address in the Hispanic countries reflect this history.

Vuestra merced became vuesarced, then vusted, and finally, usted. ▶

Subject pronoun chart: 13.A ▶

13.B.1 *Tú - usted*

The use of **tú** for the informal second-person singular is called **tuteo**. In regions that use the **tuteo**, **usted** is the formal address for the second-person singular. In these regions, **tú** is used with close friends and family, while **usted** is used with strangers or those to whom one wishes to show respect. This applies to Spain, Mexico, (except Chiapas), the Caribbean (Puerto Rico, Dominican Republic, most of Cuba, Panama, and the Caribbean coast of Colombia and Venezuela), and many Spanish-speakers in the United States.

Map of Spanish-speakers in the U.S.: p. xxiv ▶

13.B.2 *Vos - usted*

The use of **vos** for the second-person singular, called **voseo**, occurs in many Latin American countries.

a. There are pure **voseo** regions as well as regions where both **tú** and **vos** are used. Argentina, Uruguay, Paraguay, and parts of Central America, Colombia, and Venezuela are pure **voseo** regions.

b. Regions with both **voseo** and **tuteo** are: Bolivia, Chile, Peru, Ecuador, parts of Colombia and Venezuela, and Chiapas (Mexico). In these regions, **usted** is the formal address for the second-person singular. However, the roles of **tú**, **vos**, and **usted** vary. **Usted** might be used to address children or acquaintances (Central America and parts of Colombia), or **vos** might be used with close friends and family, while **tú** is used with other groups. In Argentina and Uruguay, where only **voseo** is used in informal address, **usted** is used in formal address.

c. The publication of the *Nueva gramática* by the Real Academia Española in 2010 treats **voseo** as an integral part of the Spanish language. The increasing use of informal written language on the Internet, in chat rooms, and in social media has helped to make **voseo** more visible as a characteristic of informal communication in many regions of Latin America. In Argentina, Uruguay, Paraguay, Central America, and the **voseo** regions of Colombia, Venezuela, and Ecuador, the pronoun **vos** is used with its own verb forms, some of which are presented in the verb tables in this book. In Chile, the pronoun **vos** itself is not common and its verb forms are slightly different from those mentioned in the verb tables: *¿Cómo estái?*

◀ Map of **voseo** regions in Latin America: p. 277

◀ Voseo. Present indicative, 17.D

d. In all **voseo** regions, **vos** adopted the direct and indirect object pronouns of **tú** (*Te digo a vos. I tell you.*) as well as its possessive and reflexive pronouns (**Vos *te* sentás en *tu* silla.** *You sit in your chair.*).

13.B.3 *Vosotros/as - ustedes*

a. In Spain, there are two plural address forms: the informal **vosotros/as** (for family and friends), and the formal **ustedes** (for strangers and those to whom you wish to show respect).

b. In Latin America, **ustedes**, used with the corresponding **ustedes** verb forms, is the only plural form of address. It is used in both formal and informal contexts. **Vosotros/as** is not used in Latin America except to a very limited degree in specific formal contexts, such as political speeches and religious sermons.

13.B.4 *Nosotros/as, vosotros/as, ellos/as*

For groups consisting of only women, the feminine forms **nosotras**, **vosotras**, and **ellas** are used. For groups consisting of only men, or both women and men, the masculine form is used.

13.B.5 *Tú, vos, usted*

Age, gender, and social status play an important role in the choice of address, and it is important to be aware of local variations, especially in formal contexts. Throughout the Spanish-speaking world, **usted(es)** can be used with strangers, even in **voseo** areas. Those who do not use **vos** in their variant of Spanish can use **tú** with friends and acquaintances in **voseo** areas, but it is an advantage to master the **vos** forms for use in pure **voseo** areas.

Pronombres preposicionales

13.C.1   *Mí, ti, conmigo, contigo*

conmigo/contigo: ▶
12.B.1b, 27.A.2

a. The first- and second-person singular pronouns (**yo** and **tú**) take a new form after a preposition: **mí** and **ti**, respectively. The other pronouns (including **vos**) do not change form after a preposition. After the preposition **con**, **mí** and **ti** change to **–migo** and **–tigo**.

Subject pronoun	Pronouns after prepositions			
	After preposition		**After preposition** *con*	
yo	**mí**	*me*	**conmigo**	*with me*
tú	**ti**	*you*	**contigo**	*with you*

Pronouns after ▶
prepositions: 12.B.1

—¿**Para** quién es el libro?	*Who is the book for?*
—Es **para mí**.	*It's for me.*
—¿Queréis trabajar **para** nosotros?	*Do you [pl.] want to work for us?*
—Sí, queremos trabajar **para** vosotros.	*Yes, we want to work for you [pl.].*
—¿Vas al cine **con** tus amigos?	*Are you going to the movies with your friends?*
—No, hoy voy **sin** ellos.	*No, today I'm going without them.*
—¿Está Isabel **contigo**?	*Is Isabel with you?*
—Sí, Isabel está **conmigo**.	*Yes, Isabel is with me.*

conmigo/contigo/consigo: ▶
12.B.1b–c, 27.A.2

13.C.2   *Sí, consigo*

The *reflexive pronoun* **se** changes to **sí** after a preposition, except after the preposition **con**.

Subject pronoun	Reflexive pronoun	Pronoun after prepositions		
		After preposition	**After preposition** *con*	
él, ella, usted	**se** *self*	**sí**	**consigo**	*with himself, herself, yourself*
ellos, ellas, ustedes				*with themselves*

13.C.3   **With the prepositions** *entre, según*

The subject pronouns **yo** and **tú** are used after the prepositions **entre, según, excepto,** and **salvo**.

Entre **tú** y **yo** hay amor.	*There is love between you and me.*
Según **tú**, tengo un problema.	*According to you, I have a problem.*

13.D **Direct and indirect objects**

Complementos de objeto directo e indirecto

Sentences consist of a subject and a predicate. The verb is part of the predicate, which says something about the subject. In the sentence *I am sleeping,* the verb gives enough information to make the sentence meaningful. In the sentence *I'm giving,* however, more information is needed about the action. An *object* complements the information provided by the verb. In the sentence *I'm giving,* a direct object provides information about *what* is given (for example, *a book*) and an indirect object provides information about *to whom* it is given (for example, *my sister*): *I'm giving **a book** to **my sister**.* Direct and indirect objects can be replaced by object pronouns: *I'm giving **it** to **her**.*

Transitive and ▶
intransitive verbs: 17.B.1

13.E Direct object pronouns

Pronombres de objeto directo

13.E.1 The direct object

The direct object tells *what* or *who* is directly influenced by the action in the sentence.

Leo **el libro**.	*I am reading the book.*
¿Compraste nuevos **zapatos**?	*Did you buy new shoes?*

13.E.2 The preposition *a* before a person

When the direct object is a person, it must be preceded by the preposition **a**. This also applies to indefinite, possessive, and interrogative pronouns.

Conozco **a Griselda**.	*I know Griselda.*
Esperamos **al Sr. Luis Romero**.	*We are waiting for Mr. Luis Romero.*
Visito **a mis papás**.	*I am visiting my parents.*
¿A **quién** vas a visitar en Nueva York?	*Who are you going to visit in New York?*
Visitaré **a algunos** amigos míos.	*I will visit some friends of mine.*
No espero **a nadie**.	*I am not waiting for anyone.*

*The personal **a**: 12.B.2c Use of the preposition **a** when indefinite pronouns and other determiners are direct objects: 7.D.2c and 7.E.3*

13.E.3 Direct object pronouns

a. A direct object can be replaced by a direct object pronoun.

Direct object pronouns		
yo	**me**	*me*
tú, vos	**te**	*you*
usted	**la, lo/le***	*you*
él	**lo/le***	*him*
ella	**la**	*her*
nosotros/as	**nos**	*us*
vosotros/as	**os**	*you*
ustedes	**las, los/les***	*you*
ellos	**los/les***	*them*
ellas	**las**	*them (female)*

The use of **le/les as third-person direct object pronouns is called **leísmo**: 13.E.4*

Me visitan mis amigos.	*My friends are visiting me.*
Te llaman.	*They are calling you.*
Lo espero.	*I am waiting for him/you.*
Las espero.	*I am waiting for you/them.*
Nos invitan.	*They are inviting us.*
Os invito.	*I am inviting you [pl.].*

b. When a preposition is placed before an object pronoun, the pronoun for the first- and second-person singular takes a new form: **mí** and **ti**.

Pronouns after prepositions: 13.C

Nos llaman **a ti** y **a mí**.	*They're calling **you** and **me**.*

13.E.4 *Le/les* **instead of** *lo/los* **as direct object pronouns** - *leísmo*

In Spain, **le/les** is often used as the direct object pronoun for males instead of **lo/los**. In Latin America, **le/les** can occur as the direct object pronoun in some regions, especially with **usted** in sentences that are gender neutral. The use of **le/les** in this case is called **leísmo**.

Conozco **a Juan**.	*I know* **Juan**.
Le conozco. (Spain)	*I know* **him**.
Lo conozco. (Latin America)	

13.F Indirect object pronouns

Pronombres de objeto indirecto

13.F.1 The indirect object

An indirect object is a noun or pronoun that answers the question *to whom* or *for whom* an action is done. Indirect objects can be replaced with the preposition **a** followed by a subject pronoun. The indirect object pronoun is typically used in sentences even when the indirect object also appears.

Le hicimos un favor **a Eric**.	*We did a favor* **for Eric**.
Le hicimos un favor **a él**.	*We did a favor* **for him**.
Le envié una carta **a Eva**.	*I sent a letter* **to Eva**.
Le envié una carta **a ella**.	*I sent a letter* **to her**.

13.F.2 Indirect object pronouns

The indirect object can be replaced by an indirect object pronoun.

Indirect object pronouns		
yo	**me**	*me*
tú, vos	**te**	*you*
usted, él, ella	**le (se)**	*you, him, her*
nosotros/as	**nos**	*us*
vosotros/as	**os**	*you*
ustedes, ellos, ellas	**les (se)**	*you, them*

¿**Te** dio Pedro la noticia?	*Did Pedro give you the news?*
La universidad **os** dio las notas.	*The university gave you [pl.] the grades.*
¿**Le** pago la cuenta?	*Shall I pay the bill for him/her/you?*
¿**Me** dices la verdad?	*Are you telling me the truth?*

13.F.3 Verbs like *gustar*

a. Many Spanish verbs are conjugated using the indirect object pronouns in a similar way as the English expression *It pleases me*. In this sentence, the *grammatical* subject is *it* and the *logical* subject, *I*, is expressed with its object pronoun: *me*. The corresponding Spanish sentence is **Eso me gusta**. In this sentence, **eso** is the grammatical subject, while the logical subject, **yo**, is expressed with the indirect object pronoun: **me**. In the sentence *I like it.*, the grammatical subject is *I* and the object is *it*.

The subject of each sentence is in *italics* in the following examples. Note that **gustar** is conjugated in the third-person singular, **gusta**, when the subject is a verb or a singular noun and in the plural, **gustan**, when the subject is a plural noun.

Nos gusta mucho *caminar.*   *We really like to walk.*

¿Os molesta *el tráfico*?   *Does traffic bother you [pl.]?*

¡Le encantan *los paseos*!   *He/She loves excursions!*

b. The indirect object can be spelled out with **a** + *pronoun / proper noun* for emphasis or clarity, especially in the third person since the indirect object pronoun (**le/les**) is sometimes ambiguous.

A Ramiro le aburre *el teatro.*   *Ramiro finds theater boring.*

A todos nos gustan *las buenas noticias.*   *We all like good news.*

¿Les interesa *la música* **a ustedes**?   *Are you [pl.] interested in music?*

13.G | Placement of direct and indirect object pronouns

Posición de los pronombres de objeto directo e indirecto

13.G.1 Before finite verbs

Direct and indirect object pronouns are placed before a finite verb, or a verb that can stand alone as the main verb in a sentence.

Direct object pronouns	
Nos visitas.	*You're visiting* **us**.

Indirect object pronouns	
Os damos un regalo.	*We're giving* **you** *[pl.] a present.*

Placement of pronouns with non-finite verbal forms: 25.B.4, 25.C.8
Finite and non-finite verbal forms: 17.A.2, 25.A

13.G.2 Finite verbs plus an infinitive or a *gerundio*

a. In verbal expressions with a finite verb plus an infinitive or a **gerundio**, direct and indirect object pronouns can be placed either before the finite verb or attached to the infinitive/**gerundio**.

Direct object pronouns	
Te voy a invitar.	*I'm going to invite you.*
Voy a invitar**te**.	
Nos estáis esperando.	*You're waiting for us.*
Estáis esperándo**nos**.	

Indirect object pronouns	
Os voy a dar una gran noticia.	*I'm going to give you [pl.] some big news.*
Voy a dar**os** una gran noticia.	
Luisa **nos** está preparando la cena.	*Luisa is preparing dinner for us.*
Luisa está preparándo**nos** la cena.	

Verb periphrases with infinitives: 26.B–C
Verb periphrases with the **gerundio**: 26.D

b. When an object pronoun is added to the end of a word, a written accent is added, if necessary, to indicate the stressed syllable.

Accents: 1.E.3

es-pe-**ran**-do   *The word ends in a vowel and the stress falls on the penultimate syllable (**llana**). The word is regular and does not need an accent.*

es-pe-**rán**-do-nos   *The stressed syllable is now the third to last (**esdrújula**) and needs a written accent.*

Impersonal expressions with **ser**: 23.C.8

13.G.3 Impersonal expressions with *ser*

In impersonal expressions with **ser** that are followed by an adjective and the infinitive, the direct and indirect object pronouns are always placed after the infinitive.

Direct object pronouns	
—¿Es bueno estudiar **la lección**?	*Is it good to study **the lesson**?*
—Claro, es bueno estudiar**la**.	*Of course it's good to study **it**.*

Indirect object pronouns	
—¿Es necesario dar**te** instrucciones?	*Is it necessary to give **you** instructions?*
—No, no es necesario dar**me** instrucciones.	*No, it's not necessary to give **me** instructions.*

13.G.4 Compound verb forms with *haber*

Direct and indirect object pronouns must always be placed before the personal forms of **haber** in compound tenses with a past participle.

In all compound forms with **haber**, object pronouns and reflexive pronouns are placed before **haber**. They can never be added to the participle or come after the participle form.

Direct object pronouns	
—¿Dónde está Lisa?	*Where is Lisa?*
—No **la** he visto.	*I haven't seen **her**.*

Indirect object pronouns	
—¿**Te** han dado el dinero?	*Have they given **you** the money?*
—No, no **me** han dado el dinero.	*No, they haven't given **me** the money.*

Placement of pronouns in verb periphrases with: Infinitives: 25.B.4, **Gerundio**: 25.C.8 Object and reflexive pronouns cannot stand after participles: 19.A.1

13.G.5 Indirect and direct object pronouns in the same sentence

a. When both indirect and direct object pronouns occur together, the indirect object pronoun is always first.

—¿Quién **te** regaló **las flores**?	*Who gave you the flowers?*
—Mis amigos **me las** regalaron.	*My friends gave me them/them to me.*

b. Note that the order of the pronouns also applies when both are placed after the infinitive or the **gerundio**.

—¿Quién **te** va a dar **las flores**?	*Who is going to give you flowers?*
—Mis amigos **me las** van a dar.	*My friends are going to give me them / them to me.*
—Mis amigos van a dár**melas**.	

c. The indirect object pronouns **le/les** change to **se** when followed by the direct object pronouns **la(s)** and **lo(s)**.

—¿**Le** enviaste la carta a Pilar?	*Did you send the letter to Pilar?*
—Sí, **se la** envié.	*Yes, I sent it to her.*
—**Les** diste las galletas a los niños?	*Did you give the cookies to the children?*
—No, no **se las** di.	*No, I didn't give them to them.*

13.G.6 With imperatives

Object pronouns are placed *after* the verb in positive imperatives and *before* the verb in negative imperatives. The indirect object pronoun always precedes the direct object. See the following examples with the formal imperative (**usted**).

Placement of pronouns in imperatives: 24.F

Positive	
¡De**me el libro**, por favor!	Please give **me the book**!
¡Dé**melo**, por favor!	Please give **it to me**!

Negative	
¡No **nos** mande **los paquetes** todavía, por favor!	Don't send **the packages to us** yet, please!
¡No **nos los** mande todavía, por favor!	Don't send **them to us** yet, please!

13.H Repetition of direct and indirect objects

Repetición del objeto directo e indirecto

13.H.1 Optional repetition of an object

a. Object pronouns with prepositions (**a mí, a ti, a él**, etc.) can be added after the verb to clarify or emphasize the object. This applies to both the direct and indirect objects and is particularly applicable to **él/ellos, ella(s)**, and **usted(es)**, which have the same indirect object pronouns (**le/les**).

Direct object pronouns	
La respeto.	I respect **her/you**.
La respeto **a usted**, Sra. Jones.	I respect **you**, Mrs. Jones.

Indirect object pronouns	
Les diré la verdad.	I'll tell **them/you** [pl.] the truth.
Les diré la verdad **a ustedes**.	I'll tell **you** [pl.] the truth.

b. An object pronoun with a preposition can also be used for all other persons for extra emphasis.

Direct object pronouns	
Me ven **a mí**.	They see **me**.
Te llaman **a ti**.	They're calling **you**.
Lo espero **a usted**, Sr. Pérez.	I'm waiting for **you**, Mr. Pérez.
Las espero **a ellas**.	I'm waiting for **them**.
Nos invitan **a nosotros**.	They're inviting **us**.
Os invito **a vosotros**.	I'm inviting **you** [pl.].

Indirect object pronouns	
¿**Te** dio Miguel la noticia **a ti**?	Did Miguel tell **you** the news?
Os envié las notas **a vosotros**.	I sent the notes to **you** [pl.].
Le pago la cuenta **a él / a ella / a usted**.	I'll pay the bill for **him/her/you**.
¿**Me** dices la verdad **a mí**?	Are you telling **me** the truth?
Les pido un favor **a ellos**.	I'm asking **them** for a favor.

13.H.2 Necessary repetition of objects

a. When direct or indirect objects in the form of proper nouns or pronouns precede a verb, a corresponding object pronoun is needed *after* the object and *before* the verb.

Direct objects	
A la abuela *la* quiero.	*I love grandma.*
A Juan *lo* visito.	*I am visiting Juan.*
A ti *te* respeto.	*I respect you.*

Indirect objects	
A los chicos *les* doy un regalo.	*I am giving the boys a present.*
A María *le* di mi teléfono.	*I gave María my telephone number.*
A vosotros *os* envío postales.	*I am sending you [pl.] postcards.*

In the examples above, the objects precede the verb: **a la abuela**, **a Juan**, **a ti** (direct objects), and **a los chicos**, **a María**, **a vosotros** (indirect objects). This placement before the verb requires a repetition of the direct or indirect object pronouns.

b. Doubling of object pronouns also applies to things and abstract concepts.

Direct objects	
Esto no **lo** entiendo.	*I don't understand this.*
Tus cartas **las** recibí ayer.	*I got your letters yesterday.*

Indirect objects	
A la pared **le** di una capa de pintura.	*I gave the wall a coat of paint.*
A mi cámara **le** compré más memoria.	*I bought more memory for my camera.*

13.H.3 Indirect objects that communicate personal involvement

In order to communicate that a situation affects someone directly, an indirect object pronoun can be added to the sentence. This object pronoun can be removed without changing the meaning of the sentence.

*This use of the indirect object pronoun is common in Spanish and is called **dativo de interés**.*

¡Cuída**me** bien la casa!   *Take good care of the house (for me)!*

13.H.4 *Todo/a(s)*

Object pronouns are usually repeated when the pronoun **todo/a(s)** is the direct or indirect object in the sentence.

Todo: 7.C.9

La policía **lo** sabe **todo**.	*The police know everything.*
Las invitaron **a todas**.	*They invited all the girls.*
Les enviamos invitaciones **a todos**.	*We sent invitations to everyone.*

13.H.5 Questions and answers

Personal a: 12.B.2c, 13.E.2

Note that the preposition **a** must be included when answering a question with an indirect object pronoun or a direct object pronoun that refers to a person.

—¿A quién llamó Viviana?   *Who did Viviana call?*

—¡**A mí**!   *Me!*

—¿A quiénes les das el regalo?   *Who are you giving the present to?*

—Claro, ¡**a vosotros**!   *To you [pl.], of course!*

Práctica

Actividades 1–16, pp. A48–A52

Questions and question words
Preguntas y palabras interrogativas

Chapter 14

A. Direct questions
B. Interrogatives
C. Exclamations with question words
D. Regional variations

14.A Direct questions

Preguntas directas

In Spanish, the following structures are used to ask a question that requires a *yes*-or-*no* answer.

14.A.1 Change of usual word order

The usual structure of a statement in Spanish is *subject + verb*.

Roberto es estudiante.	*Roberto is a student. (statement)*
Roberto está enfermo.	*Roberto is sick. (statement)*

In questions, the verb is usually placed before the subject. Although the intonation may vary, this word order implies a question.

¿**Es** estudiante **Roberto**?	*Is Roberto a student? (question)*
¿**Está Julia** en casa?	*Is Julia home? (question)*

◀ Emphatic constructions (change of the usual sentence structure): 15.B.8

14.A.2 Intonation

A question can also maintain the usual structure of a statement, *subject + verb*. In this case, the intonation indicates that it is a question.

¿**Pedro está** enfermo?	*Pedro is sick?*
¿**Julia está** en casa?	*Julia is home?*

14.A.3 Tag questions

When the usual statement structure is used, a tag question can be added to the end of the sentence, for example: ¿**no**?, ¿**verdad**?, ¿**no es cierto**?, ¿**no es verdad**?, ¿**no es así**?, ¿**ah**?, ¿**eh**?.

—Hace buen tiempo hoy, ¿**no**?	*It's nice weather today, isn't it?*
—Sí, hace muy buen tiempo.	*Yes, it's very nice weather.*
—Te llamas Alberto, ¿**no es cierto**?	*Your name is Alberto, isn't it?*
—No, me llamo Arturo.	*No, my name is Arturo.*
—Vienes mañana, ¿**verdad**?	*You're coming tomorrow, right?*
—Sí, vengo mañana.	*Yes, I'm coming tomorrow.*

14.B Interrogatives

Interrogativos

14.B.1 Structure

a. Questions that require more than a simple *yes*-or-*no* answer start with an interrogative word. All interrogatives carry an accent.

◀ Relative pronouns: Ch. 15
◀ Adverbs: Ch. 10

Interrogatives		
Qué	*what*	**¿Qué** vas a preparar hoy? *What are you going to prepare today?*
Cuál(es)	*which, what*	**¿Cuál** es tu mejor plato? *Which one is your best dish?*
		¿Cuáles son los ingredientes? *What are the ingredients?*
Quién(es)	*who*	**¿Quiénes** vienen a cenar? *Who is coming to dinner?*
	whom	**¿Con quién** fuiste a la fiesta? *With whom did you go to the party?*
	whose	**¿De quién** es la receta? *Whose recipe is it?*
Cuánto	*how much + verb*	**¿Cuánto** vale la cena? *How much does dinner cost?*
Cuánto/a	*how much + noun*	**¿Cuánta** azúcar quieres? *How much sugar do you want?*
Cuántos/as	*how many + noun*	**¿Cuántos** invitados hay? *How many guests are there?*
Cómo	*how many + noun*	**¿Cómo** está la comida? *How is the food?*
Dónde	*how + verb*	**¿Dónde** está el postre? *Where is the dessert?*
Cuándo	*where*	**¿Cuándo** se sirve la cena? *When is dinner served?*
Por qué	*why*	**¿Por qué** está fría la sopa? *Why is the soup cold?*

Indirect questions:
14.B.9, 31.B.6

b. Interrogatives may also be used with indirect questions.

Van a averiguar **quién** es el chef. · *They are going to find out who is the chef.*

Quisiera saber **cuándo** estará lista la cena. · *I would like to know when dinner will be ready.*

14.B.2 *Qué*

a. Qué (*what, which*) does not change form and can be placed before nouns or verbs.

¿Qué plato prefieres?	*Which dish do you prefer?*
¿Qué quieres beber?	*What do you want to drink?*
¿Qué le pasa a Ramiro?	*What's happening/wrong with Ramiro?*
¿Qué significa eso?	*What does that mean?*
¿Qué opinas?	*What do you think?*

b. Qué is used with the verb **ser** to ask for definitions and explanations.

¿Qué es esto?	*What is this?*
¿Qué son estas cosas?	*What are these things?*
¿Qué es *house* en español?	*What is* house *in Spanish?*

14.B.3 Cuál, cuáles

a. Cuál(es) is used in questions that require choosing something or someone from several concrete alternatives. The choices are usually preceded by a definite article or demonstrative.

¿**Cuáles** son **tus** amigos?	Which (ones) are your friends?
¿**Cuál** era **la** contraseña?	What was the password?
¿**Cuál** quieres, **la** sopa o **la** ensalada?	Which one do you want, the soup or the salad?
Este es tu postre, ¿**cuál** es **el** mío?	This is your dessert, which (one) is mine?

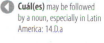 **Cuál(es)** may be followed by a noun, especially in Latin America: 14.D.a

b. If the alternatives in a question are not preceded by a definite article or other determiner (possessive, demonstrative, etc.), the meaning changes and **qué** is more frequent.

¿**Qué** quieres, sopa o ensalada?	What would you like, soup or salad?

Determiners: Ch. 4

c. Cuál(es) de followed by *definite article + noun* or *demonstrative* restricts the choices explicitly.

¿**Cuál de las** ensaladas prefieres?	Which one of the salads do you prefer?
¿**Cuáles de estos** postres son buenos?	Which of these desserts are good?

Demonstratives: Ch. 8

14.B.4 Quién, quiénes

Quién(es) refers only to people. The plural **quiénes** is used if a plural answer is expected.

—¿**Quién** es Luisa?	Who is Luisa?
—Luisa es mi hermana.	Luisa is my sister.
—¿**Quiénes** vienen a cenar?	Who is coming to dinner?
—Vienen Gabi y Rodrigo.	Gabi and Rodrigo are coming.
—¿**De quién** son las botas?	Whose boots are these?
—Son mías.	They are mine.

14.B.5 Cuánto/a(s), cuánto, cuán

a. Cuánto/a (*how much*) and **cuántos/as** (*how many*) agree in gender and number with the noun they modify.

¿Cuán**to** diner**o** necesitamos?	How much money do we need?
¿Cuán**ta** agu**a** mineral quieres?	How much mineral water do you want?
¿Cuán**tas** person**as** vienen hoy?	How many people are coming today?
¿Cuán**tos** plat**os** vamos a servir?	How many dishes are we going to serve?

Adverbs: Ch. 10

b. Use **cuántos/as de** to ask explicitly for the quantity of specific countable nouns.

¿**Cuántos de los** estudiantes están aquí hoy?	How many of the students are here today?
¿**Cuántas de estas** palabras comprendes?	How many of these words do you understand?

c. Cuánto (*how much*) does not change form when it stands alone before a verb.

¿**Cuánto** cuesta la cena?	How much does the dinner cost?
¿**Cuánto** pagaste por el postre?	How much did you pay for the dessert?

d. Cuánto is abbreviated to **cuán** before *adjectives* and sometimes before *adverbs*. Its use is formal and occurs more commonly in exclamations than in questions, where other structures are generally used instead.

¿**Cómo son de caros** los pasajes?	
¿**Cuán caros** son los pasajes?	How expensive are the tickets?

cuánto, cuanto: 10.D.1
cuán = qué tan: 14.B.5e

cómo: 14.B.6

qué tanto, qué tantos: 14.D.c ▶

e. In Latin America, **qué tan**, a common interrogative structure, has the same meaning as **cuán**.

Qué tan + *adjective* or *adverb*	
¿**Qué tan** *caros* son los boletos?	How expensive are the tickets?
¿**Qué tan** *rápidamente* llegas en tren?	How fast do you get there by train?

Adverbs of manner: 10.C ▶
Relative adverbs: 15.C.1

14.B.6 *Cómo*

a. **Cómo** is invariable and can *only* be followed by verbs.

¿**Cómo** estás?	How are you?
¿**Cómo** os parece Barcelona?	How do you [pl.] like Barcelona?
¿**Cómo** se enciende la tele?	How do you turn on the TV?

b. Unlike the Spanish **cómo**, the English *how* may appear before adjectives and adverbs (usually of manner). English sentences with *how + adjective/adverb* must be rephrased in Spanish with other structures. One of these common structures is shown below.

cuán + adjective: 14.B.5d ▶
qué tan + adjective:
14.B.5e, 14.D.b

Cómo + **ser** + **de** + *adjective*	
¿**Cómo es de** *difícil* el problema?	How difficult is the problem?
¿**Cómo son de** *caros* los libros?	How expensive are the books?
¿**Cómo es de** *grande* la ciudad?	How large is the city?

Conjunctions of comparison: ▶
16.C.8

c. **Cuál es** + *noun* or **qué** + *noun* + **tener** are other alternatives. The Spanish noun in these constructions corresponds to the English adjective/adverb in the parallel English structure, *how + adjective/adverb.*

¿**Cómo es de alto** el edificio?	
¿**Cuál es la altura** del edificio?	How **tall** is the building?
¿**Qué altura tiene** el edificio?	
¿**Cómo es de importante** la carta?	
¿**Cuál es la importancia** de la carta?	How **important** is the letter?
¿**Qué importancia tiene** la carta?	

d. *How* questions concerning weight, height, length, and age are asked with specific verbs, instead of using the English structure *how + adjective*.

¿Cuánto **pesa** el bebé?	How much does the baby weigh?
¿Cuánto **pesa** tu portátil?	How heavy is your laptop?
¿Cuánto **miden** las ventanas?	How big are the windows?
¿Cuánto **mide** usted?	How tall are you?
¿Cuántos años **tiene** usted?	How old are you? (What is your age?)
¿Qué edad **tiene** usted?	

e. The purpose of the *how* question in English determines which options are used in Spanish: degree of distance (*how far*), frequency of time (*how often*), degree of a quality (*how well, how tired*), etc. Combinations of adverbs and prepositions with interrogatives, **que** + *noun*, and other structures can convey the same meaning in Spanish as a *how* question in English.

cómo de: 14.B.6b ▶
qué tan: 14.B.5e, 14.D.b
cuán: 14.B.5d

¿**Hasta dónde** vas?	***How far*** are you going?
¿**Cada cuánto** visitas a tu familia?	***How often*** do you visit your family?
¿**Con qué frecuencia** para el autobús?	***How often*** does the bus stop?
¿**A qué distancia** queda?	***How far*** is it?
¿**A qué altura** saltas?	***How high*** can you jump?
¿**A qué velocidad** escribes?	
¿**Cómo** escribes **de** rápido?	***How fast*** can you write?

14.B.7 — Qué tal

a. **Qué tal** is a very informal expression equivalent to **cómo**. It is used as a greeting, to inquire about people and daily events, or to make informal invitations.

¡Hola! ¿**Qué tal**?	*Hi! How are you?*
¿**Qué tal** la película?	*How is/was the movie?*
¿**Qué tal** tu familia?	*How is your family?*
¿**Qué tal** por casa?	*How is everyone at home?*
¿**Qué tal** es Juan como médico?	*How good a doctor is Juan?*
¿**Qué tal** un cafecito?	*How about a coffee?*
¿**Qué tal si** vamos al cine hoy?	*How about going to the movies today?*

b. A question with **qué tal** can be rephrased with **cómo** only if it is followed by a verb.

¿**Qué tal** (está) la comida?	*How is the food?*
¿**Cómo está** la comida?	

14.B.8 — Dónde, cuándo, por qué

a. **Dónde** (*where*), **cuándo** (*when*), and **por qué** (*why*) are invariable and their use is similar to English.

¿**Dónde** vives?	***Where*** *do you live?*
¿**Cuándo** sales para el trabajo?	***When*** *do you leave for work?*
¿**Por qué** regresaste tarde?	***Why*** *did you return so late?*

b. **Dónde** is replaced with **adónde** or **a dónde** with verbs of motion.

¿**Adónde** te mudaste?	*Where did you move to?*

◀ Adverbs of place and direction: 10.E.2

14.B.9 — Indirect questions

Indirect questions are also asked with question words.

◀ Indirect questions: 31.B.6

No sé **qué** quieres.	*I don't know what you want.*
Dime **cómo** estás.	*Tell me how you are.*
Avísame **cuándo** llegas.	*Let me know when you arrive.*
Quiero saber **quién** es tu profesor.	*I want to know who your teacher is.*
Queremos saber **cuánto** dinero hay.	*We want to know how much money there is.*

14.B.10 — El qué, el cómo, el cuánto, el cuándo, el dónde, el porqué

Some common interrogatives can be used as nouns. These nouns are masculine and singular, and carry an accent mark: **el qué, el cómo, el cuánto, el cuándo, el dónde, el porqué**.

No conocemos **el porqué** de la crisis.	*We don't know the reason for the crisis.*
Sabrás **el cuándo** y **el cómo** de la situación después.	*You will find out the when and the how of the situation later.*

14.C Exclamations with question words

Exclamaciones con expresiones interrogativas

Question words with a written accent are also used in exclamations in the following way:

Qué + *noun/ adjective/adverb*	**¡Qué** maravilla!	*How wonderful!*
	¡Qué bonito!	*How beautiful!*
	¡Qué bien!	*Great! (That's wonderful!)*
Cómo + *verb*	**¡Cómo** te quiero!	*I love you so much!*
Cómo + *verb* + **de** + *adj.*	**¡Cómo** es **de** alto!	*It's so tall!*
Cuánto + *verb*	**¡Cuánto** estudias!	*You study a lot!*
Cuánto/a(s) + *noun*	**¡Cuánta** gente!	*So many people! (There were many...)*
	¡Cuántos libros!	*So many books! (There were many...)*
Quién + *verb*	**¡Quién** fuera rico!	*Oh, to be rich!*

Exclamations with the subjunctive: 23.B.2 ▶

Exclamations with the subjunctive: 23.B.2

14.D Regional variations

Variaciones regionales

a. Cuál is more frequently followed by a verb than by a noun, but in many Latin American countries, **cuál** precedes the noun when a choice is implied.

¿De **cuál** país hispano eres?	*Which Hispanic country are you from?*
¿**Cuál** restaurante te gusta más?	*Which restaurant do you like the most?*
¿**Cuáles** recetas vas a preparar?	*Which recipes are you going to prepare?*

cuán: 14.B.5e ▶

b. In Latin America, the following expressions can be used for direct and indirect questions, and exclamations. The intonation of the speaker can determine whether he/she is asking a question or making an exclamation.

Qué tan + *adjective*	¿**Qué tan** bueno es ese café?	*How good is that coffee?*
	¡Qué tan fantástico!	*How fantastic!*
	Me pregunto **qué tan** caro es.	*I wonder how expensive it is.*
Qué tan + *adverb*	¿**Qué tan** bien hablas español?	*How well do you speak Spanish?*
	¡Qué tan bien escribes!	*You write so well!*
Qué tanto + *verb*	¿**Qué tanto** tienes que esperar el autobús?	*How long do you have to wait for the bus?*
	¡Qué tanto trabajas!	*You work so much!*
	Le pregunté **qué tanto** le interesa la política.	*I asked him how interested he is in politics.*

Indirect questions: 14.B.9, 31.B.6 ▶

c. In questions, **cuánto/a(s)** is preferred to **qué tanto/a(s)**, but both expressions can be used in questions and exclamations.

Qué tanto/a(s) + *noun*	¿**Cuánta** gente hay? ¿**Qué tanta** gente hay?	*How many people are there?*
	¡Cuánta gente hay! **¡Qué tanta** gente hay!	*There are so many people!*
	¿**Cuántos** amigos tienes? ¿**Qué tantos** amigos tienes?	*How many friends do you have?*
	¡Cuántos amigos tienes! **¡Qué tantos** amigos tienes!	*You have so many friends!*

d. In the Caribbean, primarily the Dominican Republic, Puerto Rico, and Cuba, it is common to put a subject pronoun before the verb in short **qué** questions.

¿**Qué tú** vas a hacer hoy?	*What are you going to do today?*
¿**Qué tú** quieres?	*What do you want?*

Práctica

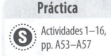

Actividades 1–16, pp. A53–A57

Relative pronouns and adverbs
Pronombres y adverbios relativos

Chapter 15
A. Relative pronouns
B. Choosing relative pronouns
C. Relative adverbs
D. Non-specific relative constructions

15.A Relative pronouns

Pronombres relativos

15.A.1 Structure

A relative pronoun refers to a noun (person, thing, or idea) and can link two descriptions of the noun into a single, complex sentence, made up of a main clause and a *relative clause* or *adjectival clause*.

El profesor enseña español.	*The professor teaches Spanish.*
El profesor es inglés.	*The professor is English.*
El profesor **que** enseña español es inglés.	*The professor who teaches Spanish is English.*

The noun described, **el profesor**, is called the *antecedent* (**antecedente**). The relative pronoun, **que**, introduces a relative clause (**que enseña español**) that refers to the noun.

15.A.2 Spanish relative pronouns

Que is the most common relative pronoun in spoken Spanish. In written language, many other pronouns are used.

> Diacritical marks: 1.E.6

Relative pronouns		Antecedents
que does not change form	*which/who/that*	people, things, ideas
el/la que **el/la cual** article agrees with gender and number of antecedent	*the one/thing which/who/that*	people, things, ideas, whole sentences, actions, events
los/las que **los/las cuales** article agrees with gender and number of antecedent	*those which/who/that*	people, things, ideas, whole sentences, actions, events
lo que, lo cual not used with people, does not change form	*the one/thing which/that*	whole sentences, actions, or events
quien, quienes agrees in number with antecedent	*who*	only people
cuyo/a, cuyos/as expresses ownership or connection, agrees in gender and number with item owned	*whose*	people, things

> **cualquiera:** *anyone*. Indefinite determiners: 7.C.5 and 15.B.7

> **lo que/cual:** Se ofendió mucho, **lo que/cual** me pareció extraño. (*He was very offended, which I thought was strange.*)

> **cuyo/a:** El hombre **cuya** voz es melodiosa. (*The man whose voice is melodious.*)

15.A.3 Important differences between Spanish and English

There are three important differences between English and Spanish relative pronouns:

a. In Spanish, relative pronouns are required, whereas in English they are sometimes optional.

El auto **que** tienes es fabuloso.	*The car **(that)** you have is fabulous.*
¿Es bueno el libro **que** estás leyendo?	*Is the book **(that)** you're reading good?*
No tengo ningún teléfono **que** funcione bien.	*I don't have a phone **that** works well.*

> Use of the subjunctive in relative clauses: 23.D

Prepositions:12.A.1.b ▶

b. In English, a preposition can be placed after the relative pronoun, usually at the end of the sentence, but in Spanish, the preposition must *always* be placed before the relative pronoun.

Spain: **el ordenador** = ▶
the computer

Esta es la computadora **con la que** siempre escribo. | *This is the computer (that) I always write with.*
La casa **en la que** vivimos es pequeña. | *The house (that) we live in is little.*
La chica **con quien / con la que** salgo se llama Anita. | *The girl (that) I go out with is named Anita.*

Personal **a**: 12.B.2c, 13.E.2 ▶

c. In Spanish, when the relative pronoun relates to a person that is a direct or indirect object in the sentence, the preposition **a** must be placed before the relative pronoun.

Pedro fue **a quien** vi ayer. | *It was Pedro I saw yesterday.*
Camila es la estudiante **a quien** le envié la información. | *Camila is the student I sent the information to.*
Janet, **a quien/a la que/a la cual** conozco bien, está de visita. | *Janet, whom I know well, is visiting.*

15.B | Choosing relative pronouns

Elección del pronombre relativo

In order to select an appropriate relative pronoun, the antecedent must first be identified by asking: *Who is the person or what is the thing or idea being described?* In Spanish, the use of the relative pronoun differs depending on whether the clause is *defining* or *non-defining*. If it is non-defining, it is important to note whether the relative pronoun follows a preposition or not.

15.B.1 Non-defining clauses

Comma: 1.F.2 ▶

a. *Non-defining clauses* provide additional information about the antecedent and are always preceded and followed by a comma in Spanish. These clauses are introduced by a relative pronoun (or a relative adverb), sometimes in conjunction with a preposition.

Relative adverbs: 15.C ▶

Mario, **que/quien** siempre llega tarde, no tiene auto. | *Mario, who always arrives late, doesn't have a car.*

Nuestra escuela, **cuya** reputación es excelente, es muy cara. | *Our school, whose reputation is excellent, is very expensive.*

b. When **que** is ambiguous, a *definite article* + **que/cual** can be used to make the antecedent clear.

El señor Juárez y su esposa, **la que/cual** siempre es elegante, llegan hoy. | *Mr. Juárez and his wife, who is always elegant, arrive today.*

15.B.2 Defining clauses

Defining clauses provide information that is necessary for the meaning of a sentence. These are never separated from the antecedent with a comma. Which relative pronoun is used in a defining clause is determined by whether or not a preposition is used.

Choosing relative pronouns in defining clauses		
Relative pronoun	**With a preposition**	**Without a preposition**
que	Yes: after **a, de, en, con**	Yes
el/la/los/las que	Yes	No
el/la/los/las cuales	Yes	No
quien(es)	Yes	No
cuyo/a(s)	Yes	Yes

¿Sabías que cerró el restaurante **en (el) que / en el cual** nos conocimos? | *Did you know that the restaurant where we met has closed?*
El libro **que** me prestaste es muy interesante. | *The book you lent me is very interesting.*
La película **de la cual** hablamos se estrena mañana. | *The movie we talked about opens tomorrow.*

15.B.3 *Que* in defining clauses

a. In defining clauses that do not require a preposition, **que** can be used alone (without an article).

Los amigos **que** tengo son estudiantes.	*The friends (that) I have are students.*
La paz **que** hemos logrado es inestable.	*The peace (that) we've attained is unstable.*
Eso **que** me contaste es muy interesante.	*What you told me is very interesting.*
El rock es la música **que** más me gusta.	*Rock is the music (that) I like best.*

b. Que is generally used with an article after all prepositions, but can be used without the article in defining clauses with the prepositions **a**, **de**, **en**, and **con** when the clause does not refer to a person. This usually occurs only in informal speech.

La ciudad **en (la) que** vivo es grande.	*The city (that) I live in is big.*
El aceite **con (el) que** se preparan las tapas es español.	*The oil (that) you make tapas with is Spanish.*
Los problemas **a (los) que** me refiero son graves.	*The problems I'm referring to are serious.*
La causa **por la que** lucho es justa.	*The cause (that/which) I'm fighting for is just.*
El banco **para el que** trabajo es internacional.	*The bank (that) I work for is international.*

15.B.4 *El/la que/cual, los/las que/cuales* in defining clauses

In defining clauses, these pronouns must always be used *after a preposition* for both people and things. The article must correspond in gender and number with the antecedent.

El señor **al que** llamé no contestó.	*The man I called didn't answer.*	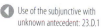 Personal **a**: 12.B.2c, 13.E.2
Los estudiantes **a los que** enseño español son estudiosos.	*The students I teach Spanish to are studious.*	
Las carreteras **por las que** conduzco son peligrosas.	*The roads I drive on are dangerous.*	
La universidad **en la que** estudio queda en Madrid.	*The university I study at is in Madrid.*	
Hoy enviamos las facturas **en las cuales** está toda la información.	*Today we sent the invoices that have all the infomation.*	

15.B.5 *Quien(es)* in defining clauses

Quien(es) cannot be used without a preposition in defining clauses. The preposition **a** is placed before **quien** if the antecedent is a direct or indirect object.

Hablé **con quien** contestó el teléfono.	*I talked to the one/person who answered the telephone.*	
Le escribí **a quien** tú recomendaste.	*I wrote to the one/person you recommended.*	
En Navidad solo les daré regalos **a quienes** más quiero.	*For Christmas, I will only give presents to those I love most.*	
Puedes pedirle ayuda **a quien** quieras.	*You can ask whomever you like for help.*	Use of the subjunctive with unknown antecedent: 23.D.1
Hay que hablar **con quien** pueda resolver el problema.	*You must talk to someone who is able to solve the problem.*	

Cuyo/a(s) is sometimes
referred to as a
relative adjective.

15.B.6 *Cuyo/a(s)*

Cuyo/a(s) is a formal relative pronoun that is only used in written Spanish. It agrees in gender and number with that which is owned and can be used in defining and non-defining clauses. In speech and in less formal texts, **cuyo** is replaced by **que/cual** and the verb **tener**.

Las personas **cuya** nacionalidad es inglesa…	*People whose nationality is English…*
Las personas **que tienen** nacionalidad inglesa…	*People who have English nationality…*

Cualquiera: 7.C.5

15.B.7 Indefinite antecedents

a. El que (*The one who*) refers to a male or an indefinite person and **la que** refers to an indefinite female (in an all female group). **Cualquiera que/quien** (*Whoever*) refers to anyone, without specifying gender.

El que / Cualquiera que / Quien fume aquí, recibirá una multa.	*Anyone who smokes here will get a fine.*

lo que: 8.A.4c, 11.D.4b

b. Lo que (*what, that which*) is a neutral relative pronoun that refers to an indefinite concept (not a person).

Lo que me interesa es la salud.	*What interests me is health.*
Lo que dices es muy importante.	*What you say is very important.*

15.B.8 Emphatic constructions

In English, the description of an event often uses the following structure, especially in a news context: *It was yesterday when…, There was a four-year-old who…, It was here in the city where…* In Spanish, this sentence structure is rare, and only used to emphasize special aspects of an event (time, person, location, manner, etc.).

Common word order in
a sentence: 14.A.1
Other structures using **ser**: 30.B.8
Cuando, donde, and **como**
are relative adverbs. See 15.C.

Fue ayer **cuando** Laura Valle resolvió el problema de los robos en la universidad.	*It was yesterday when Laura Valle solved the problem with the robberies at the university.*
Fue en Londres **donde** sucedieron los hechos.	*It was in London where the events took place.*
Fue Laura Valle **quien** / **la que** lo descubrió todo; no fue Felipe, su jefe.	*It was Laura Valle who discovered it all; it wasn't Felipe, her boss.*
Fue así **como** se supo quién era el culpable.	*That was how it was revealed who the culprit was.*
La manera **como/en la que** lo supe es un secreto.	*The way I found it out is a secret.*

15.B.9 Special cases of agreement

a. In emphatic relative clauses similar to **Yo soy el que/quien**, the verb usually agrees with the relative pronoun (**el que/quien**) and not with the subject of **ser** (**yo**). This also happens with the second person singular (**tú, vos**).

Tú eres *quien* más **trabaja**.	*You are the one who works the most.*
Yo soy *el que* **enseña** español.	*I am the one who teaches Spanish.*
Vos sos *la que* **llamó**.	*You are the one who called.*

This is also the case when the relative clause comes first.

La que **sabe** eres tú.	*The one who knows is you.*

b. The verb may agree with the subject of **ser** (first- or second-person singular) only in informal speech.

Tú eres la que **llegas** tarde.	*You are the one who arrives late.*
Yo soy quien **pagaré** la cuenta.	*I am the one who will pay the bill.*
Vos sos la que no **tenés** tiempo.	*You are the one who doesn't have time.*

c. If the expression **uno/a de los que** (*one of those who...*) is the relative clause, the verb normally follows its subject, the relative pronoun **los/las que** (third-person plural). Sometimes the pronoun **uno/a** is omitted, but the verb in the relative clause still agrees with the plural relative pronoun.

Tú eres **uno** de *los que* **escriben** blogs.	*You are one of those who write blogs.*
Tú eres de *los que* **escriben** blogs.	

d. When the subject of **ser** is a plural pronoun (**nosotros**, **vosotros**), the verb always agrees with it.

Vosotros sois los que **habláis** mejor español.	*You [pl.] are the ones who speak the best Spanish.*
Nosotros somos los que **vendremos**.	*We are the ones who will come.*

15.C Relative adverbs

Adverbios relativos

15.C.1 *Donde, cuando, como*

a. The adverbs **adonde**, **donde**, **cuando**, and **como** can also introduce a relative clause. They are equivalent to **en el/la que** or **en el/la cual** when referring to the *location*, *time*, or *manner* in which an event occurs. They do not change form and do not have a written accent.

La casa **donde** vivo es grande.	*The house I live in is big.*
Me gusta la manera **como** trata a los niños.	*I like the way she treats the kids.*
Extraño la época **cuando** íbamos a la escuela primaria.	*I miss the times when we were in elementary school.*

b. In speech and informal texts, **donde** is often replaced with a preposition of place followed by **el/la/los/las que** when a definite location is being discussed.

La universidad (**en**) **donde / en la que** estudio está en Connecticut.	*The university where I study is in Connecticut.*
Paseamos en un parque **donde / en el que** hay un lago.	*We take walks in a park where there is a lake.*

c. Cuando refers to time in an indicative or subjunctive clause. The subjunctive indicates time in the future.

◀ Use of the subjunctive with conjunctions of time: 23.E.2

Me alegro **cuando** mi abuela viene de visita.	*I am glad when my grandmother visits us.*
Volví a casa **cuando** empezó a llover.	*I went back home when it started to rain.*
Llámame **cuando** tengas tiempo.	*Call me when you have time.*
Te llamaré **cuando** pueda.	*I'll call you when I can.*

d. When there is no explicit antecedent, **donde**, **cuando**, and **como** have traditionally been regarded as conjunctions that introduce an adverbial clause. The current interpretation adopted by the RAE also classifies **donde**, **cuando**, and **como** as relative adverbs when there is no antecedent and refers to these clauses as *free relative adverbial clauses.*

Fui **donde** me dijiste.	*I went where you told me.*
Llegué **cuando** la película había comenzado.	*I arrived when the film had begun.*
Lo pinté **como** tú me pediste.	*I painted it the way you asked me.*

e. Como refers to how something is done and can be replaced with **de la manera que / del modo que**. **Como** is a neutral or less specific word in these clauses, but can be emphasized with the word **tal** (*such*).

Vístete **como / de la manera que** quieras.	*Dress as you want.*
Las cosas **como / del modo que** tú las ves no son ciertas.	*Things the way you see them are not true.*
Debéis escribir los textos **tal como / de la manera que** ha dicho el profesor.	*You [pl.] ought to write the texts just as the professor has said.*

15.D Non-specific relative constructions

Relativos inespecíficos

15.D.1 *(A)dondequiera, cuandoquiera, comoquiera*

a. Non-specific relative constructions are formed combining the indefinite quantifiers **(a)dondequiera, cuandoquiera**, and **comoquiera** with a defining relative clause. These indefinite quantifiers are compound words formed by a relative adverb (**donde, cuando, como**) + **-quiera.** They refer to people and things that are not identified.

Te acompañaré **adondequiera** que vayas.	*I'll go with you wherever you go.*
Cuandoquiera que mi jefe tome una decisión, te aviso.	*When my boss makes a decision, I'll let you know.*
Comoquiera que te llames, yo te voy a decir Pepe.	*Whatever your name is, I'm going to call you Pepe.*

b. Cualquiera also belongs to this group when it precedes a defining relative clause.

Cualquiera que sea tu propuesta, la quiero escuchar.	*Whatever your proposal is, I want to hear it.*

Práctica

Actividades 1–12, pp. A58–A60

Conjunctions
Conjunciones

16.A Overview

Aspectos generales

Conjunctions are words that join elements or clauses together in a sentence. *Coordinating conjunctions* join similar or equal parts of a sentence. *Subordinating conjunctions* make the subordinate clause dependent on the main clause. Conjunctions are invariable and they are a limited set, but two or more words can combine to form conjunctive phrases (**locuciones conjuntivas**).

16.B Coordinating conjunctions

Conjunciones coordinantes

16.B.1 Structure

a. Coordinating conjunctions join together two similar words, expressions, or sentences. Two sentences joined by a coordinating conjunction can each stand alone independently.

Words	En la escuela hay estudiantes **y** profesores.	*At the school there are students **and** teachers.*
Sentences	Podemos ver televisión **o** podemos jugar al ajedrez.	*We can watch TV **or** we can play chess.*

b. The following are the most common coordinating conjunctions in Spanish:

Coordinating conjunctions			
y (e)	and	Isabel **y** Ana estudian **y** trabajan.	*Isabel **and** Ana study **and** work.*
o (u)	or	¿Quieres café **o** té?	*Do you want coffee **or** tea?*
no... ni ni... ni	neither... nor	Hoy **no** llueve **ni** nieva.	*It **neither** rains **nor** snows today.*
pero	but (rather)	Llueve, **pero** no hace frío.	*It's raining, **but** it's not cold.*
sino		**No** quiero café **sino** té.	*I don't want coffee **but** tea instead / rather tea.*

16.B.2 The conjunction *y*

a. The conjunction **y** expresses sum or addition, and can join words or sentences together.

Tenemos tiempo **y** oportunidad.	*We have time and opportunity.*
Estoy feliz **y** satisfecho	*I am happy and satisfied.*
La profesora enseña **y** corrige las tareas.	*The professor teaches and corrects the homework.*

b. When coordinating more than two elements, a comma is used to separate the elements, except before **y**.

Compré peras, manzanas **y** naranjas.	*I bought pears, apples, and oranges.*

c. The conjunction **y** changes to **e** before words that start with **i-** or **hi-**, except when **hi-** is part of a diphthong.

Ana **e I**sabel conversan por teléfono.	*Ana and Isabel are chatting on the phone.*
Mamá siempre lleva aguja **e hi**lo en su bolso.	*Mom always carries a needle and thread in her bag.*
En la acera hay nieve **y hie**lo.	*On the sidewalk there is snow and ice.*

d. *And* can be expressed with the non-inflected **tanto... como** and **y** in Spanish. This formal structure occurs primarily in written Spanish.

Tanto Lisa **como** Pedro vienen hoy.	*Both Lisa and Pedro are coming today.*
El profesor lo explica todo **tanto** rápido, **como** simple **y** claramente.	*The teacher explains everything quickly, simply, and clearly.*
La casa es **tanto** grande **como** bonita **y** moderna.	*The house is big, nice, and modern.*

Comparisons of equality: 11.C.3 ▶

e. Note the difference when comparisons are made using **tan/tanto... como**.

La casa es **tan** grande **como** bonita **y** moderna.	*The house is as big as it is nice and modern.*
Necesitamos **tantos** libros **como** cuadernos **y** calculadoras.	*We need just as many books as notebooks and calculators.*

16.B.3 The conjunction *o*

a. The conjunction **o** expresses two or several alternatives. In Spanish, unlike English, there is no comma before the last element.

Podéis pedir carne, pollo **o** pescado.	*You [pl.] can order beef, chicken, or fish.*

b. The verb is often plural when singular words are joined together with **o**.

Olga **o** Roberto **van** a hablar.	*(Either) Olga or Roberto is going to talk.*

c. Before words that begin with **o** or **ho-**, **u** is used instead.

Tengo siete **u o**cho pesos.	*I have seven or eight pesos.*
¿Regresaste ayer **u ho**y?	*Did you get back yesterday or today?*

d. Traditionally, when **o** appeared between numbers, it was written with an accent mark in order to avoid confusing it with the number zero. According to the RAE's *Nueva ortografía*, modern typography has eliminated the risk of confusing the **o** and the zero. Therefore, the accent mark is no longer used.

Necesitamos 350 **o** 400 pesos.	*We need 350 or 400 pesos.*

e. Bien... bien is used instead of **o... o** to indicate that the options are mutually exclusive. This is mostly used in written language.

Podéis viajar, **bien** en auto, **bien** en tren.	*You [pl.] can travel either by car or train.*
Bien me escribes o **bien** me llamas.	*You can either write or call me.*

f. When **bien** is added to **o... o**, the options are mutually exclusive.

Recibió **o bien** un premio, **o bien** una mención especial.	*He received either an award or a special mention.*

The conjunction *ni*

a. The conjunction **ni** joins negative elements together. It always follows another negation.

Pedro **no** llama **ni** escribe.	*Pedro neither calls nor writes.*
Nunca tenemos pan **ni** leche.	*We never have bread nor milk.*

b. Ni can be placed before each element or just before the last one.

No tenemos leche **ni** azúcar.	*We don't have milk or sugar.*
¡**No** tenemos **ni** leche **ni** azúcar!	*We don't have milk or sugar!*

c. When the compound conjunction **ni... ni** is used to coordinate nouns in the subject, the verb should be plural.

Ni Juan **ni** Marcos **fueron** a la fiesta.	*Neither Juan nor Marcos went to the party.*

16.B.5 *Pero, sino, mas, sin embargo*

a. Pero constrains the meaning of the previous sentence in the same way as *but* in English. **Mas** is a synonym of **pero** that is primarily used in formal texts.

Voy al supermercado, **pero** regreso pronto.	*I'm going to the supermarket, but I'll be back soon.*

b. After a negation, **sino** is used instead of **pero** to indicate and alternate. **Sino que** is used before a finite (conjugated) verb.

La clase **no** es hoy **sino** mañana.	*The class isn't today, but tomorrow.*
No me llamó **sino que** me escribió.	*He didn't call me, but rather he wrote to me.*

c. The expression **sin embargo** has the same meaning as **pero**, but is more formal and mostly used in written language. In formal texts, **sin embargo** is preferred for starting a sentence.

Los precios subieron mucho. **Sin embargo,** los consumidores siguen comprando.	*The prices went up a lot. **However,** consumers continue to buy.*
Los precios subieron mucho, **pero/sin embargo** los consumidores siguen comprando.	*Prices went up a lot, **but/however** consumers continue to buy.*

d. Pero (que) muy does not constrain the meaning. It acts as an intensifier.

El libro es muy **pero (que) muy** difícil.	*The book is very very difficult.*

16.B.6 **Conjunctions that express consequence or introduce an explanation**

Conjunctions that introduce an explanation (**esto es, es decir, o sea**) and conjunctions that express consequence (**por consiguiente, pues, así pues, de manera que,** etc.) are usually grouped with coordinating conjunctions. **Pues** can also be a subordinating conjunction when it expresses cause.

Mi jefe me llamó porque hubo una emergencia. **Por lo tanto/Así pues**, tuve que ir a trabajar el domingo.	*My boss called me because there was an emergency. Therefore, I had to go to work on Sunday.*

16.C Subordinating conjunctions

Conjunciones subordinantes

Subordinate clauses begin with subordinating conjunctions. A subordinate clause (...*if she should come*) is dependent on a main clause (*Nora asked...*) in order to make sense. Subordinating conjunctions form two types of subordinate clauses: **que** clauses (*that* clauses) and adverbial subordinate clauses that are introduced by either simple conjunctions like **porque** (*because*), **aunque** (*although*), or by compound expressions like **tan pronto como** (*as soon as*), **a fin de que** (*in order that*), and others.

Use of the subjunctive in
nominal clauses: 23.C

a. Que is the most common subordinating conjunction in Spanish and is equivalent to *that*.
Que cannot be left out in Spanish.

Main clause	Subordinate clause	Main clause	Subordinate clause
Creo	**que** va a llover.	*I think*	**(that)** *it's going to rain.*
Rosita dijo	**que** está cansada.	*Rosita said*	**(that)** *she's tired.*

Indirect questions, indirect
discourse: 31.B.6

b. Que is often used in colloquial Spanish before an interrogative pronoun. This construction
is not common in written Spanish.

Main clause	Subordinate clause	Main clause	Subordinate clause
Te preguntan	**que cuál** es tu dirección.	*They're asking you*	**what** *your address is.*
Me preguntaron	**que dónde** había ido.	*They asked me*	**where** *I had gone.*

c. In indirect questions without question words, **si** is used. **Que** can precede **si** in colloquial Spanish.

Nos preguntaron (**que**) **si** podíamos ayudar.   *They asked us if we could help.*

16.C.2   **Adverbial subordinate clauses**

Adverbial subordinate clauses begin with conjunctions that express time, manner, purpose,
or other features that elaborate on the action in the main clause.

Use of the subjunctive in
adverbial subordinate
clauses: 23.E

Main clause	Subordinate clause	Main clause	Subordinate clause
Luis se enferma	**cuando** come helado.	*Luis gets sick*	**when** *he eats ice cream.*
Luis estaba bien	**hasta que** comió helado.	*Luis was well/fine*	**until** *he ate ice cream.*
Luis se enfermó	**porque** comió helado.	*Luis got sick*	**because** *he ate ice cream.*
Luis come helado	**aunque** se enferme.	*Luis eats ice cream*	**even though** *he gets sick.*

16.C.3   **Conjunctions of time**

These conjunctions describe when the action happens and introduce temporal subordinate clauses.

Conjunctions of time – *Conjunciones temporales*			
al mismo tiempo que	*at the same time as*	**en cuanto**	*as soon as*
antes de que	*before*	**hasta que**	*until*
apenas	*as soon as*	**mientras (que)**	*while/so long as*
cada vez que	*each time/every time (that)*	**siempre que**	*whenever/always when*
cuando	*when*	**tan pronto como**	*as soon as*
después de que, luego de que	*after/as soon as*	**una vez que**	*as soon as/once*

Use of the subjunctive with
conjunctions of time: 23.E.2

Siempre visito el Museo del Prado **cuando** estoy en Madrid.

I always visit the Prado Museum when I'm in Madrid.

Te llamaré **apenas** termine de estudiar.

I will call you as soon as I finish studying.

Leemos el periódico **mientras** desayunamos.

We read the newspaper while we eat breakfast.

Cada vez que me olvido el paraguas, ¡llueve!

Every time I forget my umbrella, it rains!

Levántate **antes de que** sea tarde.

Get up before it's too late.

16.C.4 Conjunctions of cause

a. Cause is primarily expressed with **porque** in Spanish. The indicative is normally used after conjunctions of cause. If the sentence is negative, the subjunctive can be used.

Use of the subjunctive with conjunctions of cause: 23.E.5

Conjunctions of cause – *Conjunciones causales*		
a causa de que / dado que	puesto que	because (of) / given that / since
porque (como)	ya que	

Rita habla bien español **porque** estudió en Madrid.

Rita speaks Spanish well **because** she studied in Madrid.

No estudio español **porque** esté de moda, sino porque es el idioma de mis abuelos.

I don't study Spanish **because** it's popular, but because it is the language my grandparents spoke.

La casa es cara, **dado que** está en el centro.

The house is expensive **because** it is downtown.

b. Subordinate clauses of cause are usually placed after the main clause. When the cause comes first, **como** is used as the conjunction.

Como Rita estudió en Madrid, habla bien español.

Because/Since Rita studied in Madrid, she speaks Spanish well.

16.C.5 Conjunctions of consequence

a. These conjunctions always follow the main clause and express consequence when used with the indicative. The most common conjunction of consequence is **así que**, but there are several others.

Use of the subjunctive with conjunctions of consequence: 23.E.4

Conjunctions of consequence – *Conjunciones consecutivas*	
así que	
de (tal) forma/manera/modo que	so (that)
de (tal) suerte que	

Mi casa está lejos, **así que** tengo que tomar dos autobuses.

My house is far away, so I have to take two buses.

El profesor no llegó, **de (tal) modo que** ayer no tuvimos clase.

The teacher didn't come, so we didn't have class yesterday.

Ana no tiene trabajo, **de (tal) manera que** tampoco tiene dinero.

Ana doesn't have a job, so she doesn't have any money either.

b. **Tal** can also be used after **forma/modo/manera**.

No encuentro el libro, **de manera tal que** no puedo estudiar.

I can't find the book, so I cannot study.

c. **De (tal) manera** and **de (tal) modo que** followed by the subjunctive express purpose.

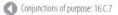
Conjunctions of purpose: 16.C.7

Deben ustedes cumplir la ley, **de tal manera que** no tengan problemas.

You [pl.] must comply with the law so that you [pl.] won't have any problems.

Colgó el cuadro **de tal modo que** le dé la luz.

He hung the painting in such a way that the light would hit it.

Use of the subjunctive with conjunctions of concession: 23.E.6

16.C.6 **Conjunctions of concession**

Clauses introduced by conjunctions of concession express an objection, obstacle, or difficulty for the action in the main clause. This objection or obstacle doesn't alter the action in the main clause as one would expect.

Aun, aún: 1.E.6c

Conjunctions of concession – *Conjunciones concesivas*		
aunque	**a pesar de que**	*although, even though, despite, in spite of*
aun cuando	**pese a que**	

Elena obtiene buenas notas **pese a que** nunca estudia.

Elena gets good grades even though she never studies.

Aunque es joven, Roberto es muy responsable.

Even though he is young, Roberto is very responsible.

A pesar de que la película parece interesante, no sé si la iré a ver.

Despite the fact that the film sounds interesting, I don't know if I'll go see it.

Aun cuando me lo pidiera de rodillas, no iría a la fiesta con él.

Even if he (got down on his knees and) begged me, I wouldn't go to the party with him.

Use of the subjunctive with conjunctions of purpose: 23.E.3

16.C.7 **Conjunctions of purpose**

a. **A fin de que** and **para que** always require the subjunctive. **De manera que** and **de modo que** take the subjunctive when they express purpose. The indicative can be used, but the subordinate clause becomes a clause of consequence. Only subordinate clauses of purpose that begin with **para que** can be placed before the main clause.

Conjunctions of purpose – *Conjunciones de finalidad*	
para que	*in order that, so (that)*
a fin de que, de modo que / de manera que	

Para que tengas buena salud, debes comer bien.

(In order) to have good health, you must eat well.

Debéis planear bien **a fin de que** no tengáis problemas más tarde.

You [pl.] should plan well so you [pl.] don't have problems later.

Te compré entradas para el cine **de modo que** tuvieras algo que hacer el viernes.

I got you movie tickets, so you'd have something to do on Friday.

Conjunctions of consequence: 16.C.5

b. When the indicative is used with **de manera/modo que**, the subordinate clause becomes a clause of consequence. Compare these examples:

Está nevando, **de manera que tienes** que usar botas.

It's snowing, so you have to wear boots.

Te compré un par de botas **de manera que puedas** salir cuando nieva.

I bought you a pair of boots so you can go out when it snows.

16.C.8 Conjunctions of comparison

Comparisons can be made using several structures.

◀ Comparisons: Ch. 11

Conjunctions of comparison – *Conjunciones comparativas*			
más... que	*more... than*	**tanto... como**	*as much... as*
menos... que	*less... than*	**igual... que**	*just as much... as*
tan... como	*as/so... as*	**como, como si...**	*as/like, as if...*

Me preocupo **tanto como** te preocupas tú.   *I worry as much as you do.*
Me habla **como si** yo no supiera nada de política.   *He talks to me as if I knew nothing about politics.*

16.C.9 Expressing manner – *como*

a. The relative adverb **como** describes *how* something is done or happens. Followed by the indicative, it refers to past and present actions. The subjunctive is used to express uncertainty about the way in which the action will be performed, or when the action refers to the future.

◀ Subjunctive in adverbial subordinate clauses: 23.E.1

Escribí el ensayo **como** quería el profesor.   *I wrote the essay the way the teacher wanted.*
Escribiré el ensayo **como** quiera el profesor.   *I will write the essay however the teacher wants.*

b. The expression **como si** is used to talk about assumptions and always precedes a form of the past subjunctive.

Beatriz habla español **como si** fuera española.   *Beatriz speaks Spanish as if she were Spanish.*
Te quejas **como si** el examen hubiera sido difícil.   *You're complaining as if the exam had been difficult.*

16.C.10 Expressing location – *donde/adonde*

The relative adverb **donde** can also act as a conjunction.

Iremos **adonde** querráis.   *We'll go where you [pl.] want.*
Vivo **por donde** está la escuela.   *I live around where the school is.*

◀ **Adonde** is used with verbs of motion: 10.E.2

16.D Conditional conjunctions

Conjunciones condicionales

16.D.1 Conditional clauses

Conditional conjunctions are used to make an assumption about something that will or will not happen. The most important conditional conjunction in Spanish is **si**, although there are others. The subjunctive is used with all conditional conjunctions except with **si**, which has special rules and sometimes takes the indicative, and **siempre que**, which expresses habit (*whenever*) with the indicative and condition with the subjunctive (*as long as*).

◀ Conditional subordinate clauses: 23.E.7

Conditional conjunctions – *Conjunciones condicionales*			
si	*if/whether*	**con tal de que**	*provided that / as long as*
en caso de que	*in case*	**siempre y cuando**	
a menos (de) que	*unless*	**siempre que**	*provided that / as long as / whenever*

Lleva el paraguas **en caso de que** llueva.	*Carry the umbrella **in case** it rains.*
Os escribiré **siempre y cuando** me escribáis.	*I'll write to you [pl.] as long as you [pl.] write to me.*
No podremos ir de paseo **a menos que** tengamos tiempo.	*We will not be able to go for a walk **unless** we have time.*
Siempre que vamos al mercado, compramos demasiado.	***Whenever** we go to the market, we buy too much.*
Iremos al parque, **siempre que** terminemos temprano.	*We will go to the park, **as long as** we finish early.*

16.D.2 Conditional clauses with *si*

a. Spanish distinguishes between real and possible conditional clauses, and *imaginary* (hypothetical) and *counterfactual* (impossible) conditional clauses. Real and possible conditional clauses take the indicative. The subjunctive expresses what is imagined (*If I were rich...*) or impossible (*If the sky were green... ; If I had done it...*).

Conditional clauses with *si*		Result
Real/true	**Si** Luis come helado, *If Luis eats ice cream,*	se enferma. *he gets sick.*
	Si Luis come helado, *If Luis eats ice cream,*	se enfermará. *he will get sick.*
Imagined/hypothetical	**Si** Luis comiera helado, *If Luis ate ice cream,*	se enfermaría. *he would get sick.*
Not fullfilled in the past / impossible	**Si** Luis hubiera comido helado, *If Luis had eaten ice cream,*	se habría enfermado. *he would have gotten sick.*

The past perfect subjunctive ▶ with **-era** (but not **-ese**) can also be used to express the unfulfilled/impossible situation: **Si** Luis hubiera comido helado, se **hubiera** enfermado. Past perfect subjunctive: 22.E

b. When the **si** clause precedes the main clause, a comma is needed. When the **si** clause follows the main clause, no comma is needed.

| **Si me invitas,** allí estaré. | *If you invite me, I'll be there.* |
| Allí estaré **si me invitas.** | *I will be there if you invite me.* |

c. Donde, como, and **mientras** can express a condition when they are followed by the subjunctive.

Donde no **encuentre** trabajo, no tendré dinero.	*If I don't find work, I won't have money.*
Como no me **digas** la verdad, les voy a preguntar a tus padres.	*If you don't tell me the truth, I'm going to ask your parents.*
Mientras yo **tenga** salud, trabajaré diariamente.	*As long as I have my health, I'll work every day.*

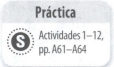

Práctica

Actividades 1–12, pp. A61–A64

The present indicative
Presente de indicativo

17.A Verbs

Verbos

17.A.1 The sentence

a. A sentence is a self-contained unit that relates a subject to a predicate. The predicate is a grammatical expression that designates states, actions, characteristics, etc., that pertain to the subject. The verb is the main element in the predicate. The other elements of the predicate can be nouns or pronouns that function as *objects*, as in Juan tiene **un libro**; adverbs or adverbial expressions that explain the circumstances around the subject's actions, as in Juan comió **rápidamente** or Juan comió **en la cocina**; prepositions that are required by the verb, as in Juan piensa **en** María; and conjunctions, which link sentences, as in Juan comió **porque** su mamá había preparado su plato favorito.

b. The subject can be represented by a pronoun, a name, a noun, or any expression that can replace it.

Determiners and subjects: 4.B.1

Subject	Predicate	
Ellos **Luis y Ana**	estudian	las lecciones todos los días.
Todos los estudiantes de español **Las personas de las que te hablé**	son	excelentes estudiantes.

17.A.2 Verb forms

a. Verbs describe actions: what you do or what happens. Verb forms are divided into two main groups: personal forms that are conjugated (*finite forms*) and non-personal forms (*non-finite*) that cannot be conjugated: infinitives, present participles (**gerundios**), and past participles.

b. Verbs consist of two parts: a stem and an ending. Spanish verbs are divided into three conjugation groups based on their infinitive endings: **-ar**, **-er**, and **-ir**. What remains after dropping the **-ar**, **-er**, or **-ir** ending is the verb stem. Verbs are conjugated in Spanish by changing the infinitive ending to other endings that indicate person, number, time, and mood. For that reason, in Spanish it is not always necessary to include the subject like in English.

cantar *to sing*			
Stem	**Ending**		*Ending indicates:*
cant-	**-o**	*I sing*	present indicative, 1st-person singular
cant-	**-arás**	*you will sing*	simple future, 2nd-person singular
cant-	**-ó**	*he/she sang*	preterite, 3rd-person singular
cant-	**-aríamos**	*we would sing*	conditional, 1st-person plural

17.B Verb objects and complements

Objetos y complementos verbales

17.B.1 Copulative, transitive, and intransitive verbs

a. Verbs are classified into three main categories:

Types	Characteristics	Examples	English
Copulative	links the subject and its complements	María **es** traductora. El agua **está** caliente.	*María is a translator.* *The water is hot.*
Transitive	takes one or more objects	María **habla** español e inglés con su novio. María **hierve** agua.	*María speaks Spanish and English with her boyfriend.* *María boils water.*
Intransitive	does not take a direct object	María **habla** demasiado sobre sus amigas. El agua **hierve** desde hace diez minutos.	*María talks too much about her friends.* *The water has been boiling for ten minutes.*

b. Some verbs can be both transitive and intransitive.

Carlos **habla** portugués.	*Carlos speaks Portuguese.*
Carlos **habla** mucho.	*Carlos speaks a lot.*

17.B.2 Verbs with prepositions

Glosario combinatorio:
pp. 279–322 ▶

a. While some verbs can be followed by a direct object (transitive verbs), others require a prepositional phrase called **complemento de régimen**. Sometimes the same verb can be used with a direct object or with a preposition.

No **creo en** los fantasmas.	*I don't believe in ghosts.*
Disfruté (de) las vacaciones.	*I enjoyed my vacation.*

b. The choice of preposition is not predictable. Verbs with similar meanings might take different prepositions or a direct object. A verb in Spanish might take a preposition that is different from the one required by its English counterpart.

No **confío en** él.	*I don't trust him.*
No **me fío de** él.	*I don't trust him.*
Consiguió diez dólares.	*He got hold of ten dollars.*
Se hizo con diez dólares.	*He got hold of ten dollars.*
Asistí a la conferencia.	*I attended the conference.*

c. The most common prepositions used in **complementos de régimen** are **a, de, en**, and **con**. Verbs that require **por** or **para** are not common.

Preposition	Verb with prepositions			
a	asistir a	*to attend*	jugar a	*to play*
con	encontrarse con	*to meet*	soñar con	*to dream about/of*
de	disfrutar de	*to enjoy*	sufrir de	*to suffer from*
en	confiar en	*to trust*	influir en	*to influence / to have influence on*
por	preocuparse por	*to worry about*	interesarse por	*to be interested in*

The present indicative • **Chapter 17**

¿Asistió usted **a** la conferencia?	*Did you attend the conference?*
¡Disfruta (de) tu tiempo libre!	*Enjoy your free time!*
Jugaremos al ajedrez profesionalmente.	*We will play chess professionally.*
Ellos sueñan con un mundo mejor.	*They dream of a better world.*

d. In most cases, the preposition is followed by a noun or noun phrase. However, many verbs with prepositions can be followed by infinitives.

Me encontré con Marcos.	*I met up with Marcos.*
Soñé con **ella**.	*I dreamt of her.*
Sueño con **ir** a Europa.	*I dream of going to Europe.*

e. Some verbs with prepositions can only be followed by an infinitive. These verbal expressions usually take **a** or **de**.

Verb periphrases with the infinitive: 26.C

verb + preposition + infinitive			
empezar a	*to start*	acabar de	*to finish*
volver a	*to repeat*	tratar de	*to try to*

La película **acaba de empezar**.	*The movie has just begun.*
Traté de alcanzar el autobús.	*I tried to catch the bus.*

17.B.3   Reflexive verbs

Reflexive pronouns and verbs: 27.A

a. Reflexive verbs express the fact that the subject performing the action is also the recipient, directly or indirectly.

Subject	Predicate		
	Reflexive pronoun	**Verb**	**Adverbial expression**
(Yo)	Me	lavo	frecuentemente.

Subject	Predicate			
	Reflexive pronoun	**Verb**	**Direct object**	**Adverbial expression**
(Yo)	Me	lavo	las manos	frecuentemente.

b. Many daily routines are expressed with reflexive verbs.

Reflexive verbs for daily routines: 27.D.1e

Ella **se cepilla** los dientes.	*She brushes her teeth (herself).*
Te pones los zapatos.	*You put on your shoes (yourself).*

c. Verbs that take reflexive pronouns are not always reflexive in meaning.

Reflexive verbs with reciprocal meaning: 27.D.3

Verbs that change meaning: 27.E

Verbs that express change: 27.G

Reciprocal meaning	**Nos** ayuda**mos** siempre.	*We always help each other.*
Change in meaning	Hoy cayeron diez centímetros de nieve. **Se me cayó** el libro.	*Ten centimeters of snow fell today. I dropped the book.*
Physical, social, or mental change	Ana **se casó** con Luis y sus familias **se alegraron**.	*Ana married Luis and their families were happy.*
Verbs of change	Luis **se hizo** ingeniero.	*Luis became an engineer.*

Verbs with prepositions: 17.B.2 ▶

d. Many reflexive verbs require specific prepositions.

Reflexive verbs with prepositions			
atreverse a	*to dare to*	encontrarse con	*to meet up with*
decidirse a	*to decide to*	enojarse con	*to get angry with*
despedirse de	*to say goodbye to*	convertirse en	*to become / turn into*
reírse de	*to laugh at*	interesarse por	*to be/get interested in*

El público **se ríe de** los payasos.	*The audience is laughing at the clowns.*
La chica **se convirtió en** una atleta.	*The girl became an athlete.*
Nos despediremos de ella para siempre.	*We will say goodbye to her forever.*
No **me atrevo a** preguntar qué pasó.	*I don't dare ask what happened.*
¿Dónde **os encontráis con** vuestros amigos?	*Where do you [pl.] meet your friends?*

17.B.4 Verbs like *gustar*

Indirect object pronouns: 13.F ▶
Verbs like **gustar**: 9.D.4, 13.F.3
Reflexive verbs conjugated with an indirect object pronoun: 27.G.2b
Use of the subjunctive in subordinate clauses with verbs like **gustar**: 23.C.3

Pronouns after prepositions: 13.C ▶

a. The Spanish verb **gustar** functions differently from its English counterpart, *to like*. In Spanish, the person or object that is liked is the subject of the sentence and usually appears after the verb. The person that likes something usually appears before the verb and is expressed with an indirect object pronoun. The indirect object is emphasized by adding **a** + *prepositional pronoun*.

Me gusta el helado de chocolate.	*I like chocolate ice cream.*
A mí me gusta el helado de fresa.	*I like strawberry ice cream.*
A mi hermana le gustan los dos.	*My sister likes both.*

b. Since the verb needs to agree with the subject, it agrees with the person or thing that is liked. If the subject is an infinitive, the verb **gustar** is used in the third-person singular form.

A María **le gustan los hombres altos**.   *María likes tall men.*
(**los hombres altos**: *third-person plural subject*; **gustan**: *third-person plural verb*)

A María **le gusta su vecino, Luis**.   *María likes her neighbor, Luis.*
(**su vecino, Luis**: *third-person singular subject*; **gusta**: *third-person singular verb*)

A Marcos y a mí **nos gusta nadar**.   *Marcos and I like swimming / to swim.*
(**nadar** *is an infinitive*: *third-person singular subject*; **gusta**: *third-person singular verb*)

c. Gustar is most commonly used with third-person singular or plural subjects. However, it is possible to use other subjects.

Me **gustaste** desde el momento en que te vi.   *I liked you from the moment I saw you.*
(*implicit subject*: **tú**, *second-person singular*; **gustaste**: *second-person singular*)

¿Te **gusto**?   *Do you like me?*
(*implicit subject*: **yo**, *first-person singular*; **gusto**: *first-person singular*)

Nos **gustáis** mucho.   *We like you a lot.*
(*implicit subject*: **vosotros**, *second-person plural*; **gustáis**: *second-person plural*)

d. Many other Spanish verbs function like **gustar**. Some of these verbs are shown in the table below:

Verbs like *gustar*			
aburrir	*to bore/tire*	enfadar	*to anger*
agradar	*to please/gratify*	entristecer	*to sadden*
alarmar	*to alarm/startle*	entusiasmar	*to delight / carry away*
alegrar	*to be/make happy*	extrañar	*to miss*
apenar	*to distress*	fascinar	*to fascinate*
asustar	*to scare*	fastidiar	*to annoy/bother/upset*
complacer	*to please*	frustrar	*to frustrate*
convenir	*to suit*	importar	*to be important / care about*
desesperar	*to despair/exasperate*	indignar	*to outrage*
disgustar	*to dislike*	interesar	*to interest / be interested in*
divertir	*to amuse/entertain*	irritar	*to irritate*
doler	*to hurt/ache*	molestar	*to bother/annoy*
emocionar	*to thrill/excite*	preocupar	*to worry*
encantar	*to delight/love*	sorprender	*to surprise*

◀ Article instead of possessives with verbs of physical reactions and ailments: 9.D.4

Los fumadores **me irritan**.	*Smokers irritate me.*
La oscuridad **me asusta**.	*Darkness scares me.*
Nos conviene reunirnos mañana.	*It suits us to meet tomorrow.*
¿**Te divierten** las comedias?	*Do comedies amuse you?*
Me alegra que tengas éxito.	*I am happy that you are successful.*
Nos interesa el español.	*We are interested in Spanish. / Spanish interests us.*
Nuestros clientes **nos importan**.	*Our clients are important to us.*

e. Some of these verbs can also be used reflexively.

Me alegro por tu éxito.	*I am happy for your success.*
Nos interesamos por el español.	*We are interested in Spanish.*

17.C Tense and mood

Tiempo y modo

17.C.1 Verb tense

Verb tense tells when an action takes place: past, present, or future. There is not always a direct correlation between the grammatical verb tense and the time expressed in the sentence. For example, the present indicative can convey future actions in Spanish: **Vengo mañana.** (*I'm coming tomorrow.*)

17.C.2 Verb mood

Verb mood tells how the speaker feels about an action. Spanish has three moods like English. Each mood has its own conjugation form and follows specific rules of use.

a. Indicative: Usually expresses facts.

b. Subjunctive: Expresses doubt or uncertainty, feelings or emotions, wishes, preferences, assumptions, the unknown, and imaginary situations or events.

◀ Subjunctive: Ch. 22–23

c. Imperative: Expresses orders and requests.

◀ Imperative: Ch. 24

The present indicative

Presente de indicativo

17.D.1 Regular verbs

a. All three conjugation groups (**-ar, -er, -ir**) have both regular and irregular verbs. Regular verbs do not have any changes in the stem and each conjugation group has its own conjugation patterns.

Map of the spread of **vos** in Latin America: p. 277
Voseo: 13.B.2 , 13.B.5, 17.D.1c–d

Subject pronoun		**cantar** *to sing*	**correr** *to run*	**vivir** *to live*
I	yo	cant**o**	corr**o**	viv**o**
you	tú	cant**as**	corr**es**	viv**es**
you	vos	cant**ás**	corr**és**	viv**ís**
you (formal), he, she	usted, él, ella	cant**a**	corr**e**	viv**e**
we	nosotros/as	cant**amos**	corr**emos**	viv**imos**
you [pl.]	vosotros/as	cant**áis**	corr**éis**	viv**ís**
you [pl.], they	ustedes, ellos/as	cant**an**	corr**en**	viv**en**

b. Verbs ending in **-ar** are the largest group. New verbs are usually formed in Spanish with the **-ar** ending. The following are some of the most common regular verbs.

Regular verbs, present tense: Verb conjugation tables, p. 261

-ar **verbs**				
acabar	*to finish*	ganar	*to win*	pasar	*to pass/spend (time)*
amar	*to love*	investigar	*to investigate*	practicar	*to practice*
bailar	*to dance*	lavar	*to wash*	saltar	*to jump*
buscar	*to look for*	llamar	*to call*	terminar	*to end*
caminar	*to walk*	llegar	*to arrive*	tomar	*to take/drink/eat/have*
comprar	*to buy*	llevar	*to bring/carry*	trabajar	*to work*
desear	*to desire*	mandar	*to order/send*	usar	*to use*
empacar	*to pack*	mirar	*to look*	viajar	*to travel*
escuchar	*to listen*	necesitar	*to need*	visitar	*to visit*

-er **verbs**	
aprender	*to learn*
beber	*to drink*
comer	*to eat*
comprender	*to understand*
creer	*to believe*
leer	*to read*
responder	*to answer*
temer	*to fear*
vender	*to sell*

-ir **verbs**	
abrir	*to open*
asistir	*to attend (something)*
describir	*to describe*
decidir	*to decide*
escribir	*to write*
insistir	*to insist*
permitir	*to permit/allow*
recibir	*to receive*
subir	*to climb/go up*

—¿Qué deportes **practicas**? *Which sports do you play/practice?*
—No **practico** deportes. *I don't play/practice any sports.*
Bailo y **camino** mucho. *I dance and walk a lot.*

c. The verbal forms of **vos** and **vosotros/as** are similar because these two pronouns share a common origin and their verbal forms are regular, even when the verb is stem-changing or has other irregularities. This regularity is especially striking when **vos** forms are compared to the verbal forms of **tú**, which have many irregularities.

vos: 13.B, 13.B.2, 13.B.5

d. In the present indicative, **vos** is conjugated by adding **-ás** to **-ar** verbs, **-és** to **-er** verbs, and **-ís** to **-ir** verbs. There are very few irregular forms: **vos sos** (*you are*). Note that **-ir** verbs have the same endings for **vos** and **vosotros/as**, except for the verb **ir** (*to go*): **vos vas, vosotros/as vais.**

Vos **and** *vosotros/as*: **regular present indicative**			
Personal pronoun	*-ar* **pensar** *to think*	*-er* **tener** *to have*	*-ir* **decir** *to say*
vos	pens**ás**	ten**és**	dec**ís**
vosotros/as	pens**áis**	ten**éis**	dec**ís**

17.D.2 **Verbs with spelling changes in the first-person singular:** *yo*

In Spanish, there are a number of verbs that have spelling changes in order to maintain the right sound pattern when conjugating the verb. The spelling changes always occur in the last letters of the verb stem, before adding the endings. The endings usually are regular, but can be irregular in some cases.

Pronunciation of consonants: 1.C.6

a. Verbs that end in **-cer**, **-cir** and **-ger**, **-gir**, **-guir** have spelling changes in the verb stem, but take regular endings.

Verbs with spelling changes: Verb conjugation tables, pp. 257–276. For **c-z**, see verb patterns 32, 72, 75; for **c-zc**, see verb patterns 14, 15, 43.

-cer, *-cir* **verbs with spelling changes**			
When the verb stem ends in a **vowel**, a **z** is added before the final **c** in the first-person singular.		When the verb stem ends in **n** or **r**, the final **c** becomes a **z** in the first-person singular.	
cono**cer** *to know*	yo cono**zco**	conven**cer** *to convince*	yo conven**zo**
condu**cir** *to drive*	yo condu**zco**	espar**cir** *to spread/sprinkle*	yo espar**zo**

Other *-cer, -cir* **verbs**					
Verbs with **-zco** ending in first-person singular (**yo**)		Verbs with **-zo** ending in first-person singular (**yo**)		Verbs with **-zo** ending in first-person singular with **o → ue** stem change	
agrade**cer**	*to appreciate/thank*	ejer**cer**	*to exercise*	co**cer** → cue**zo**	*to cook*
apete**cer**	*to fancy / feel like*	ven**cer**	*to beat/defeat*	tor**cer** → tuer**zo**	*to twist*
condu**cir**	*to drive*				
dedu**cir**	*to deduce*				
desapare**cer**	*to disappear*				
introdu**cir**	*to introduce*				
recono**cer**	*to recognize*				
tradu**cir**	*to translate*				

—Yo **conduzco** limusinas. ¿En qué trabajas tú?   *I drive limousines. What do you do?*

—**Traduzco** del español al inglés para un canal de televisión.   *I translate from Spanish into English for a TV station.*

b. In the first-person singular, **g** is changed to **j**, but the pronunciation remains the same.

-ger, -gir **verbs with spelling changes**		
Subject pronoun	dirigir *to lead/direct/manage/run*	exigir *to claim/demand*
yo	dirijo	exijo

Other *-ger, -gir* **verbs**			
acoger	*to welcome*	infringir	*to infringe*
afligir	*to afflict*	proteger	*to protect*
corregir	*to correct*	recoger	*to collect / pick up*
elegir	*to choose/elect*	restringir	*to restrict*
escoger	*to choose*	sumergir	*to submerge*
fingir	*to pretend*	surgir	*to emerge*

Corregir and **elegir** also have vowel shifts in the stem: **corrijo, elijo:** 17.D.5 Verb conjugation tables, pp. 257–276. See verb patterns 26, 35, 54.

Dirijo una organización ecológica.	*I manage an ecological organization.*
Recojo y reciclo la basura.	*I collect and recycle the trash.*
Protejo la naturaleza.	*I protect nature.*
Exijo una ciudad más limpia.	*I demand a cleaner city.*

c. The ending **-guir** changes to **g** in the first-person singular, but the pronunciation remains the same.

-guir **verbs with spelling changes**	
Subject pronoun	extinguir *to extinguish / put out (fires)*
yo	extingo

Other *-guir* **verbs**			
conseguir	*to get/obtain/achieve*	proseguir	*to continue*
perseguir	*to pursue/persecute*	seguir	*to follow*

Seguir and **perseguir** also have vowel shifts in the stem: **sigo, persigo:** 17.D.5 Verb Conjugation Tables, pp. 257–276. See verb patterns 36, 64.

Soy policía y persigo a los criminales.	*I am a policeman and I chase criminals.*
No extingo incendios porque no soy bombero.	*I don't put out fires because I'm not a firefighter.*

17.D.3 **Verbs without spelling changes in** *nosotros/as, vosotros/as, vos*

Some verbs have spelling changes in the present in all persons except **nosotros/as**, **vosotros/as**, and **vos**. The present endings are regular.

a. In **-uir** verbs, **i** changes to **y** before **e** or **i** in all forms except **nosotros/as**, **vosotros/as**, and **vos**.

Conjugation of *-uir* **verbs**	
Subject pronoun	construir *to build*
yo	construyo
tú	construyes
vos	construís
usted, él, ella	construye
nosotros/as	construimos
vosotros/as	construís
ustedes, ellos/as	construyen

Verbs with spelling changes: Verb conjugation tables, pp. 257–276. See verb pattern 23.

Other -uir verbs			
constit**uir**	to constitute	h**uir**	to escape/flee
constr**uir**	to build/construct	incl**uir**	to include
contrib**uir**	to contribute	infl**uir**	to influence
destit**uir**	to dismiss	int**uir**	to sense
destr**uir**	to destroy	recl**uir**	to imprison/confine
dismin**uir**	to diminish	reconstr**uir**	to reconstruct
distrib**uir**	to distribute	sustit**uir**	to substitute/replace

La gente **huye** cuando hay un huracán.   *People flee when there is a hurricane.*
Los huracanes **destruyen** las ciudades.   *Hurricanes destroy cities.*

b. Several verbs that end in **-iar** and **-uar** take a written accent on the **-i** and **-ú** except in the
nosotros/as, **vosotros/as**, and **vos** forms.

-iar, -uar **verbs with spelling changes**		
Subject pronoun	env**iar** *to send*	contin**uar** *to continue*
yo	env**ío**	contin**úo**
tú	env**ías**	contin**úas**
vos	env**iás**	contin**uás**
usted, él, ella	env**ía**	contin**úa**
nosotros/as	env**iamos**	contin**uamos**
vosotros/as	env**iáis**	contin**uáis**
ustedes, ellos/as	env**ían**	contin**úan**

Verbs that need an accent:
Verb conjugation tables,
pp. 257–276. For i:í, see verb
patterns 29, 34, 53; for u:ú, see
verb patterns 37, 57, 59.

Other -iar, -uar **verbs**			
acent**uar**	to emphasize	evac**uar**	to evacuate
ampl**iar**	to enlarge/extend	eval**uar**	to evaluate
ans**iar**	to long for	grad**uar**se	to graduate
conf**iar**	to confide/trust	gu**iar**	to guide
deval**uar**	to devalue	insin**uar**	to insinuate
efect**uar**	to carry out / execute	perpet**uar**	to perpetuate
enfr**iar**	to cool down / chill	sit**uar**	to locate

Lucía gu**í**a a los turistas. Ellos conf**í**an en ella.   *Lucía guides the tourists. They trust her.*
Pronto me grad**ú**o como maestra.   *I will graduate as a teacher soon.*

17.D.4   Verbs with diphthongs or vowel shifts in the stem

Several verbs in all three conjugation groups have a systematic vowel shift in the stem.
The stressed vowel in the stem becomes a diphthong or the vowel shifts when the verb is
conjugated. This happens in all verb forms except for **nosotros/as**, **vosotros/as**, and **vos**. Most verbs
with vowel shifts have regular endings, but some are irregular. A few verbs also have an irregular
first-person singular (**yo**) conjugation.

Spanish verbs have several types of diphthongs in the present indicative: **e → ie, o → ue, i → ie**,
and **u → ue**.

Diphthongs: 1.C.2

a. Conjugation of verbs with diphtongs: *e → ie*

	empezar *to begin/start*	**perder** *to lose*	**preferir** *to prefer*
yo	emp**ie**zo	p**ie**rdo	pref**ie**ro
tú	emp**ie**zas	p**ie**rdes	pref**ie**res
vos	empezás	perdés	preferís
usted, él, ella	emp**ie**za	p**ie**rde	pref**ie**re
nosotros/as	empezamos	perdemos	preferimos
vosotros/as	empezáis	perdéis	preferís
ustedes, ellos/as	emp**ie**zan	p**ie**rden	pref**ie**ren

Verbs with diphthongs:
Verb conjugation tables,
pp. 257–276. See verb
patterns 24, 27, 28, 45,
49, 56, 65.

b. Other verbs with diphthongs: *e → ie*

-*ar* **verbs**	
atrav**e**sar	*to cross*
cal**e**ntar	*to warm up*
c**e**rrar	*to close*
com**e**nzar	*to start/begin*
desp**e**rtar	*to wake up*
gob**e**rnar	*to govern*
n**e**gar	*to deny/refuse*
p**e**nsar	*to think*
recom**e**ndar	*to recommend*

-*er* **verbs**	
def**e**nder	*to defend*
desc**e**nder	*to descend*
enc**e**nder	*to light / switch on*
ent**e**nder	*to understand*
qu**e**rer	*to want*

-*ir* **verbs**	
cons**e**ntir	*to consent*
div**e**rtirse	*to have fun*
m**e**ntir	*to lie*
s**e**ntir	*to feel*

¿Qu**ie**res ir al cine hoy?   *Do you want to go to the movies today?*

Lo s**ie**nto, hoy pref**ie**ro estudiar.   *Sorry, I prefer to study today.*

c. Conjugation of verbs with diphthongs: *o → ue*

	contar *to count*	**volver** *to return*	**dormir** *to sleep*
yo	c**ue**nto	v**ue**lvo	d**ue**rmo
tú	c**ue**ntas	v**ue**lves	d**ue**rmes
vos	contás	volvés	dormís
usted, él, ella	c**ue**nta	v**ue**lve	d**ue**rme
nosotros/as	contamos	volvemos	dormimos
vosotros/as	contáis	volvéis	dormís
ustedes, ellos/as	c**ue**ntan	v**ue**lven	d**ue**rmen

Verbs with diphthongs:
Verb conjugation tables,
pp. 257–276. See verb
patterns 6, 9, 16, 25, 44,
50, 61, 67, 72.

d. Other verbs with diphthongs: *o → ue*

-*ar* **verbs**	
alm**o**rzar	*to have lunch*
c**o**star	*to cost*
enc**o**ntrar	*to find*
m**o**strar	*to show*
pr**o**bar	*to try/taste*
rec**o**rdar	*to remember*
s**o**ñar	*to dream*

-*er* **verbs**	
dev**o**lver	*to give back*
ll**o**ver	*to rain*
m**o**ver	*to move*
p**o**der	*to be able*
prom**o**ver	*to promote*
rem**o**ver	*to remove*
res**o**lver	*to resolve*

-*ir* **verbs**	
m**o**rir	*to die*

The present indicative • **Chapter 17**

—¿Cuánto **cue**sta el libro?   *How much does the book cost?*

—No rec**ue**rdo. Unos veinte dólares.   *I don't remember. About twenty dollars.*

e. Conjugation of verbs with diphthongs: *i* → *ie*

	adquirir *to acquire*	inquirir *to inquire*
yo	adqu**ie**ro	inqu**ie**ro
tú	adqu**ie**res	inqu**ie**res
vos	adquirís	inquirís
usted, él, ella	adqu**ie**re	inqu**ie**re
nosotros/as	adquirimos	inquirimos
vosotros/as	adquirís	inquirís
ustedes, ellos/as	adqu**ie**ren	inqu**ie**ren

Verbs with diphthongs: Verb conjugation tables, pp. 257–276. See verb pattern 4.

En la universidad adqu**ie**ro nuevos conocimientos.   *At college, I gain new knowledge.*

f. Conjugation of verbs with diphthongs: *u* → *ue*

	jugar *to play*
yo	j**ue**go
tú	j**ue**gas
vos	jugás
usted, él, ella	j**ue**ga
nosotros/as	jugamos
vosotros/as	jugáis
ustedes, ellos/as	j**ue**gan

Verbs with diphthongs: Verb conjugation tables, pp. 257–276. See verb pattern 41.

Jugar is the only verb with the **u** → **ue** vowel shift.

—¿J**ue**gas algún deporte?   *Do you play any sports?*

—Sí, j**ue**go al fútbol.   *Yes, I play soccer.*

17.D.5 Vowel shifts

Only **-ir** verbs have an **e** → **i** vowel shift in the present indicative.

	pedir *to ask for*
yo	p**i**do
tú	p**i**des
vos	pedís
usted, él, ella	p**i**de
nosotros/as	pedimos
vosotros/as	pedís
ustedes, ellos/as	p**i**den

Verbs with vowel shifts: Verb conjugation tables, pp. 257–276. See verb patterns 20, 26, 48, 58, 64.

Other -ir verbs with vowel shift e → i					
competir	to compete	elegir	to choose	repetir	to repeat
corregir	to correct	impedir	to impede	seguir	to follow
despedir	to dismiss	perseguir	to pursue	servir	to serve

Siempre **p**i**do** tapas en el restaurante español.   *I always order tapas at the Spanish restaurant.*
Allí nunca re**p**i**ten** los mismos platos.   *They never repeat the same dishes there.*

17.D.6 **Irregular verbs in the present indicative**

a. Verbs with the ending –*go* in the first-person singular *(yo)*

	caer *to fall*	hacer *to do/* *make*	salir *to leave /* *go out*	poner *to put*	traer *to bring*	valer *to cost /* *be worth*
yo	cai**go**	ha**go**	sal**go**	pon**go**	trai**go**	val**go**
tú	caes	haces	sales	pones	traes	vales
vos	caés	hacés	salís	ponés	traés	valés
usted, él, ella	cae	hace	sale	pone	trae	vale
nosotros/as	caemos	hacemos	salimos	ponemos	traemos	valemos
vosotros/as	caéis	hacéis	salís	ponéis	traéis	valéis
ustedes, ellos/as	caen	hacen	salen	ponen	traen	valen

Irregular verbs are found alphabetically in the Verb conjugation tables, pp. 257–276. See verb patterns 8, 13, 39, 46, 51, 63, 73, 74, 79.

Other verbs like *poner*			
componer	*to make up / compose*	proponer	*to propose*
disponer	*to dispose/arrange/* *prepare/stipulate*	suponer	*to suppose*

Other verbs like *traer*			
atraer	*to attract*	distraer	*to distract*

Soy un gran esquiador. ¡No **me caigo** nunca!   *I am a great skier. I never fall!*
Me pongo las botas y los esquíes.   *I'm putting on my boots and skis.*
Salgo de casa muy optimista.   *I leave home in an optimistic mood.*
Traigo muchas fotos del paseo.   *I'm bringing many photos from the outing.*

b. Verbs with the ending -*go* in the first-person singular *(yo)*, **and vowel shifts**

	decir *e → i* *to say/tell*	oír *i → y* *to hear*	tener *e → ie* *to have*	venir *e → ie* *to come*
yo	di**go**	oi**go**	ten**go**	ven**go**
tú	d**i**ces	o**y**es	t**ie**nes	v**ie**nes
vos	decís	oís	tenés	venís
usted, él, ella	d**i**ce	o**y**e	t**ie**ne	v**ie**ne
nosotros/as	decimos	oímos	tenemos	venimos
vosotros/as	decís	oís	tenéis	venís
ustedes, ellos/as	d**i**cen	o**y**en	t**ie**nen	v**ie**nen

Other verbs like *decir*					
desdecir	*to deny*	maldecir	*to curse/swear*	predecir	*to predict*

Verb conjugation tables, pp. 257–276. See verb patterns 11, 20, 46, 69, 76.

Other verbs like *tener*					
atenerse	*to abide*	detener	*to detain/stop*	obtener	*to obtain*
contener	*to contain*	mantener	*to maintain*	sostener	*to sustain*

Other verbs like *venir*			
convenir	*to agree/suit*	prevenir	*to prevent*

—¿Qué **dices**? No te **oigo**.   *What are you saying? I can't hear you.*

—**Digo** que no **vengo** mañana.   *I'm saying that I'm not coming tomorrow.*

—No **tengo** tiempo.   *I don't have time.*

c. Verbs with irregular forms in the first-person singular *(yo)*

Verb conjugation tables, pp. 257–276. See verb patterns 12, 19, 62, 77.

	caber *to fit*	dar *to give*	saber *to know*	ver *to see*
yo	**quepo**	**doy**	**sé**	**veo**
tú	cabes	das	sabes	ves
vos	cabés	das	sabés	ves
usted, él, ella	cabe	da	sabe	ve
nosotros/as	cabemos	damos	sabemos	vemos
vosotros/as	cabéis	dais	sabéis	veis
ustedes, ellos/as	caben	dan	saben	ven

—¡No **quepo** aquí!   *I don't fit here!*

—¿Te **doy** más espacio?   *Shall I give you more room?*

—No **sé**. **Veo** que este escritorio es muy estrecho.   *I don't know. I can see that this desk is very narrow.*

d. Completely irregular verbs

The verb **haber** has two conjugation forms: a personal form like the auxiliary verb, *to have*, and an impersonal form with the meaning *there is/are*.

	estar	ser	haber	ir
	to be		*to be, to have*	*to go*
yo	est**oy**	**soy**	**he**	**voy**
tú	est**ás**	**eres**	**has**	**vas**
vos	est**ás**	**sos**	**has**	**vas**
él, ella, usted	est**á**	**es**	**ha**	**va**
nosotros/as	estamos	**somos**	**hemos**	**vamos**
vosotros/as	estáis	**sois**	habéis	**vais**
ustedes, ellos/as	est**án**	**son**	**han**	**van**

—Hola, ¿dónde **estás**?   *Hello, where are you?*

—Hola, **estoy** en la cafetería.   *Hi, I'm in the cafeteria.*

—Ya **voy**. ¡Espérame!   *I'm coming. Wait for me!*

No **he** cenado todavía.   *I haven't eaten dinner yet.*

En la escuela **hay** muchos estudiantes.   *There are many students in the school.*

Verb conjugation tables, pp. 257–276. See verb patterns 33, 38, 40, 66. Impersonal form of **haber**: 29.B.1

17.E Use of the present indicative

Uso del presente de indicativo

17.E.1 Present actions

The present indicative is used for actions that take place in the present: *now, today, this month, this year.*

Estoy aquí.	*I'm here.*
Ahora mismo **salgo**.	*I'm leaving right now.*
Este año **estudio** español.	*I'm studying Spanish this year.*

17.E.2 Habits

Just like in English, the present can be used to express habits. Adverbs or other time expressions emphasize the time period.

Entreno todos los días.	*I train every day.*
Abrimos de 6 de la mañana a 5 de la tarde.	*We open from six in the morning until five in the afternoon.*
Los domingos no **trabajamos**.	*We don't work on Sundays.*

17.E.3 Timeless facts

As in English, the present indicative in Spanish is used in definitions, descriptions, and other timeless statements.

El Sol **es** una estrella.	*The Sun is a star.*
En Chile **se habla** español.	*They speak Spanish in Chile.*
Diez más diez **son** veinte.	*Ten plus ten is twenty.*

The future: Ch. 20 ▶

17.E.4 Present with future meaning

The present can express the future with the help of context or time adverbs.

Mañana **te llamo**.	*I'll call you tomorrow.*
Y ahora, ¿qué **hago**?	*And what do I do now?*
Me **caso** el viernes.	*I'm getting married on Friday.*
¡Ya **vamos**!	*We're coming!*

17.E.5 Historical present

Stories in the past with verbs in the present convey involvement. This approach is common in historical texts and in lively oral stories.

Cristobal Colón **llega** al Nuevo Mundo en 1492.	*Christopher Columbus arrives in the New World in 1492.*
México **se independiza** en 1810.	*Mexico becomes independent in 1810.*
España **pierde** su última colonia en 1898.	*Spain loses its last colony in 1898.*

17.E.6 The present with imperative meaning

The use of the present with imperative meaning primarily occurs in spoken language.

¡**Os calláis** de inmediato!	*Be quiet at once!*
¡Ahora mismo **vienes** aquí!	*Come here at once!*
¡**Escribes** esa carta hoy mismo!	*Write that letter today!*

The present indicative • **Chapter 17**

17.E.7 Confirming present

In spoken questions, the present is used to convey or confirm wishes or requests. Note the corresponding expressions in English.

¿Te **doy** más espacio?	*Shall I give you / Would you like more room?*
¿**Compramos** un helado?	*Shall we / Would you like to buy an ice cream?*
¿**Os recojo** mañana?	*Shall I / Would you like me to pick you [pl.] up tomorrow?*

17.E.8 Time expressions: *desde, desde hace, hace... que*

◀ hace + *time* + **que**, **llevar** + **gerundio** 18.E.11

Verbs in the present can refer to actions from the past that continue into the present. The expressions **desde, desde hace,** and **hace** + *time expression* + **que** indicate this continuity in the present.

¿**Desde** cuándo trabajas en el banco?	*How long have you worked at the bank?*
Trabajo en el banco **desde hace** dos años.	*I have worked at the bank for two years.*
Hace dos años **que** trabajo en el banco.	

17.E.9 Conditional clauses

◀ Indicative or subjunctive in conditional sentences: 16.D.2, 23.E.8

Real and possible conditions in subordinate clauses with **si** are expressed with the present indicative.

Si no **desayuno** bien, siempre me da hambre muy rápido.	*If I don't eat well at breakfast, I always get hungry very quickly.*

17.F The present progressive

El presente progresivo

17.F.1 Progressive tenses

Spanish can express progressive actions in various ways, but **estar**, in any tense, followed by the present participle (**gerundio**), forms the closest equivalent to the English progressive tenses. The Spanish *present progressive* is formed with the present indicative of **estar: Estoy escribiendo**. (*I am writing*.); the *past progressive* is a verb periphrasis formed with the preterite or the imperfect of **estar: Estuve/Estaba escribiendo**. (*I was writing*.); the *future progressive* is formed with the simple future of **estar: Estaré escribiendo**. (*I will be writing*.) All the other tenses (simple and compound) are formed following the same pattern. Although the structure of the progressive tenses in both languages is similar, they aren't always used in the same way.

◀ Formation of the **gerundio**: 25.C

◀ Progressive tenses: 25.C.3, Verb periphrases with the **gerundio**: 26.D

17.F.2 Simple present vs. present progressive

The simple present describes habitual actions. To refer to actions that are not habitual, the present progressive can be used. It is mostly used to emphasize actions that are in progress or are happening *now* or *at this moment*.

Simple present	Present progressive
Elisa **trabaja** desde casa. *Elisa works from home.*	Elisa **está trabajando** desde casa. *Elisa is working from home (lately, now).*
Me duele la rodilla. *My knee hurts.*	**Me está doliendo** la rodilla. *My knee is hurting (right now).*
¿Me **oyes** bien? *Can you hear me well?*	¿Me **estás oyendo** bien? *Can you hear me well (now)?*

Modal verbs: 26.B ▶

17.F.3 Modal verbs

Modal verbs (such as **poder** and **deber**) and **estar** cannot be conjugated in the progressive tenses, but **ser** can, as long as it refers to a temporary situation, usually with passive meaning. This use is limited to formal written language and to current ongoing events.

Passive voice with *ser*	Present progressive
El país **es afectado** por el huracán.	El país **está siendo afectado** por el huracán.
The country is affected by the hurricane.	*The country is being affected by the hurricane.*

17.F.4 Using the present to refer to the future

Progressive tenses: 25.C.3d-f ▶

a. In Spanish, the simple present can be used to refer to the future, while the present progressive is exclusively used to refer to actions that are in progress.

Estoy llegando.	*I am arriving (now).*
Llego mañana.	*I am arriving tomorrow.*
¿Qué estás haciendo?	*What are you doing (now)?*
¿Qué haces mañana?	*What are you doing tomorrow?*

ir a + *infinitive*: 26.C.1 ▶

b. The simple present forms of **ir a** + *infinitive* can be used to refer to the future.

Voy a comprarme un carro.	*I am going to buy myself a car.*
¿**Vas a salir** esta noche?	*Are you going out tonight?*

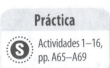

Práctica

(S) Actividades 1–16, pp. A65–A69

The present indicative • **Chapter 17**

The preterite and the imperfect
Pretérito perfecto simple e imperfecto

18.A Past-tense forms and verbal aspect

Formas del pasado y aspecto verbal

18.A.1 Past-tense forms

Spanish has two simple tenses to express the past: the *preterite* and the *imperfect*. Both can be similar to the English preterite, but are used differently, depending on the context.

Spanish preterite	Spanish imperfect	English preterite
Hablaste.	Hablabas.	*You spoke.*
Subiste.	Subías.	*You went up.*

18.A.2 Aspect

a. The Spanish preterite and imperfect tenses convey different *aspects* of actions, events, and states of being, and indicate how they are perceived in relation to time. The preterite action has a starting and/or finishing point and clearly shows that an action took place at a definite time or has been completed. On the other hand, the imperfect action does not have a concrete beginning or end; rather, it expresses an ongoing, habitual, repetitive, or frequent action in the past or an action with an indefinite period of time.

Preterite	Imperfect
Al chico le dio frío cuando caminó a la escuela hoy.	Al chico le daba frío cuando caminaba a la escuela.
The boy got cold when he walked to school today.	*The boy used to get cold when he walked to school.*

b. In English, the simple past tense does not always explicitly distinguish between perfect and imperfect actions. Therefore, the Spanish preterite and imperfect tenses can sometimes be translated the same way into English, even though the meaning of preterite and imperfect actions are different.

El perro **saltó** por encima de la cerca.	*The dog jumped over the fence.*
El perro **saltaba** por encima de la cerca.	*The dog jumped over the fence. (over and over again)*

18.B The preterite

Pretérito perfecto simple

18.B.1 Regular verbs

Regular **-er** and **-ir** verbs have the same endings in the preterite. Note that the **yo**, **usted**, **él**, and **ella** forms carry a written accent. The **tú** and **vos** endings are the same.

	-ar **viajar** to travel	-er **comer** to eat	-ir **salir** to go out
yo	viaj**é**	com**í**	sal**í**
tú/vos	viaj**aste**	com**iste**	sal**iste**
usted, él, ella	viaj**ó**	com**ió**	sal**ió**
nosotros/as	viaj**amos**	com**imos**	sal**imos**
vosotros/as	viaj**asteis**	com**isteis**	sal**isteis**
ustedes, ellos/as	viaj**aron**	com**ieron**	sal**ieron**

Preterite of regular verbs: p. 261

18.B.2 Verbs with spelling changes

Some verbs undergo minor spelling changes in the preterite in order to maintain the correct sound pattern. The endings are regular.

a. First-person singular spelling changes:

	c → qu **buscar** to look for	g → gu **jugar** to play	g → gü **averiguar** to find out / check	z → c **empezar** to start/begin
yo	bus**qué**	ju**gué**	averi**güé**	empe**cé**
tú/vos	buscaste	jugaste	averiguaste	empezaste
usted, él, ella	buscó	jugó	averiguó	empezó
nosotros/as	buscamos	jugamos	averiguamos	empezamos
vosotros/as	buscasteis	jugasteis	averiguasteis	empezasteis
ustedes, ellos/as	buscaron	jugaron	averiguaron	empezaron

Verb conjugation tables, pp. 257–276. For **c:qu**, see verb patterns 71, 78; for **g:gu**, see 41, 42, 45, 61; for **g:gü**, see 10; for **z:c**, see 6, 9, 18, 27, 34.

Ayer bus**qu**é a Carlos todo el día.
Por la noche averi**gü**é su dirección.
Visité a Carlos y ju**gu**é ajedrez con él un rato.

I looked for Carlos all day long yesterday.
At night I found out his address.
I visited Carlos and played chess with him for a while.

c → qu **Verbs like** *buscar*		g → gu **Verbs like** *jugar*	
explicar, expli**qué**	to explain	llegar, lle**gué**	to arrive
practicar, practi**qué**	to practice	pagar, pa**gué**	to pay (for)
tocar, to**qué**	to play (an instrument) / to touch	entregar, entre**gué**	to deliver
sacar, sa**qué**	to take (out) / withdraw	negar, ne**gué**	to deny/refuse
gu → gü **Verbs like** *averiguar*		z → c **Verbs like** *empezar*	
apaciguar, apaci**güé**	to appease/pacify	abrazar, abra**cé**	to hug
atestiguar, atesti**güé**	to attest/testify	alcanzar, alcan**cé**	to reach
desaguar, desa**güé**	to drain	almorzar, almor**cé**	to have lunch
santiguarse, me santi**güé**	to make the sign of the cross	comenzar, comen**cé**	to start/begin

Ayer comen**cé** mis estudios universitarios.
Practi**qu**é la pronunciación con Ana.
Almor**c**é en la cafetería.
Por la tarde sa**qu**é dinero del banco y pa**gu**é los libros nuevos.

I began my college studies yesterday.
I practiced my pronunciation with Ana.
I ate lunch in the cafeteria.
In the afternoon, I withdrew money from the bank and paid for the new books.

The preterite and the imperfect • **Chapter 18**

b. Below are the third-person singular and plural spelling changes:

	caer *to fall*	leer *to read*	concluir *to conclude*	oír *to hear*
yo	caí	leí	concluí	oí
tú/vos	caíste	leíste	concluiste	oíste
usted, él, ella	cayó	leyó	concluyó	oyó
nosotros/as	caímos	leímos	concluimos	oímos
vosotros/as	caísteis	leísteis	concluisteis	oísteis
ustedes, ellos/as	cayeron	leyeron	concluyeron	oyeron

Verb conjugation tables, pp. 257–276. See verb patterns 13, 17, 23, 46.

Verbs like *caer*		Verbs like *leer*	
decaer	*to decay/deteriorate*	creer	*to believe*
recaer	*to have a relapse*	poseer	*to have/own*
		proveer	*to provide/supply*
Verbs like *concluir*			
constituir	*to constitute*	huir	*to escape/flee*
construir	*to build/construct*	incluir	*to include*
contribuir	*to contribute*	influir	*to influence*
destituir	*to dismiss/remove*	intuir	*to sense*
destruir	*to destroy*	recluir	*to imprison*
disminuir	*to diminish*	reconstruir	*to reconstruct*
distribuir	*to distribute*	sustituir	*to substitute/replace*

El gobierno constru**y**ó calles nuevas.   *The government built new roads.*
El ministerio distribu**y**ó los fondos.   *The ministry distributed the funds.*
Los grupos de presión influ**y**eron en la decisión.   *The pressure groups influenced the decision.*

18.B.3 **Verbs with irregular stems**

There are many irregular verbs in the preterite. Many follow predictable patterns.

a. All **-ir** verbs with vowel shifts in the present indicative also have vowel shifts in the third-person singular and plural in the preterite.

Verb conjugation tables, pp. 257–276. See verb patterns 25, 48, 58, 65.

	e → i			o → u
	pedir *to ask for*	reír *to laugh*	sentir *to feel*	dormir *to sleep*
yo	pedí	reí	sentí	dormí
tú/vos	pediste	reíste	sentiste	dormiste
usted, él, ella	p**i**dió	r**i**ó	s**i**ntió	d**u**rmió
nosotros/as	pedimos	reímos	sentimos	dormimos
vosotros/as	pedisteis	reísteis	sentisteis	dormisteis
ustedes, ellos/as	p**i**dieron	r**i**eron	s**i**ntieron	d**u**rmieron

Ayer, en la fiesta, Lisa p**i**dió tapas de jamón.   *At the party yesterday, Lisa ordered ham tapas.*
Sus amigos p**i**dieron la tortilla española.   *Her friends ordered the Spanish omelet.*
Todos se r**i**eron mucho y se s**i**ntieron muy bien.   *Everyone laughed a lot and felt great.*
Nadie d**u**rmió nada.   *Nobody slept at all.*

b. Irregular stems: **u** group

Verb conjugation tables, pp. 257–276. See verb patterns 7, 12, 33, 38, 50, 51, 62, 69.

Personal form of **haber**: Verb conjugation tables, p. 269 Impersonal form of **haber**: 29.B.1

Infinitive	Stem
andar	and**uv**-
caber	c**up**-
estar	est**uv**-
haber	h**ub**-
poder	p**ud**-
poner	p**us**-
saber	s**up**-
tener	t**uv**-

Endings	
Subject	**andar**
yo	anduv**e**
tú/vos	anduv**iste**
usted, él, ella	anduv**o**
nosotros/as	anduv**imos**
vosotros/as	anduv**isteis**
ustedes, ellos/as	anduv**ieron**

Rita **estuvo** muy poco tiempo en Madrid.
Ella no **pudo** visitar el Museo de Bellas Artes.
No **tuve** oportunidad de verla.
Nunca **supe** qué pasó.

Rita was in Madrid for a very short time.
She couldn't visit the Museum of Fine Arts.
I didn't get the chance to see her.
I never found out what happened.

c. Irregular stems: **i** group

Verb conjugation tables, pp. 257–276. See verb patterns 39, 56, 76.

Infinitive	Stem
hacer	h**ic**-
querer	q**uis**-
venir	v**in**-

Endings	
Subject	**hacer**
yo	hic**e**
tú/vos	hic**iste**
usted, él, ella	hiz**o**
nosotros/as	hic**imos**
vosotros/as	hic**isteis**
ustedes, ellos/as	hic**ieron**

Hacer also has a spelling change in the third-person singular: **hizo**.

Patricia no **hizo** nada hoy.
Los invitados no **vinieron** a tiempo.
No **quise** interrumpirte.

Patricia didn't do anything today.
The guests didn't arrive on time.
I didn't want to interrupt you.

d. Irregular stems: **j** group

**Decir also has vowel changes in the stem.

Note that third-person preterite forms drop the **i** in the ending.

Verb conjugation tables, pp. 257–276. See verb patterns 14, 20, 73.

Infinitive	Stem
conducir	condu**j**-
decir*	di**j**-
introducir	introdu**j**-
producir	produ**j**-
traducir	tradu**j**-
traer	tra**j**-

Endings	
Subject	**decir**
yo	dij**e**
tú/vos	dij**iste**
usted, él, ella	dij**o**
nosotros/as	dij**imos**
vosotros/as	dij**isteis**
ustedes, ellos/as	dij**eron**

—¿**Trajiste** suficiente dinero?
—No, no **traje** dinero.

Did you bring enough money?
No, I didn't bring any money.

—¿**Dijisteis** la verdad?
—Sí, **dijimos** toda la verdad.

Did you [pl.] tell the truth?
Yes, we told the whole truth.

18.B.4 Irregular verbs

Ir, **ser**, and **dar** are irregular in the preterite. Note that the verbs **ser** and **ir** have identical conjugation patterns.

The preterite of *ir, ser,* and *dar*		
	ir / ser *to go / to be*	**dar** *to give*
yo	**fui**	**di**
tú/vos	**fuiste**	**diste**
usted, él, ella	**fue**	**dio**
nosotros/as	**fuimos**	**dimos**
vosotros/as	**fuisteis**	**disteis**
ustedes, ellos/as	**fueron**	**dieron**

Verb conjugation tables, pp. 257–276. See verb patterns 19, 40, 66.

—¿**Fuiste** a pasear con Alicia?

—Sí, **di** un paseo con ella.

Did you go for a walk with Alicia?

Yes, I went for a walk with her.

18.C Use of the preterite

Uso del pretérito perfecto simple

In Spanish, the preterite is primarily used in the following ways:

18.C.1 To mark the beginning and end of an action

The Spanish preterite indicates the start, the end, or the completion of events and actions in the past. Specific verbs or expressions like *in the end* or *finally* can be used in English to convey this information about the action.

Escribí las cartas.

¿Cuándo **empezasteis** el semestre?

Finalmente **encontré** mis llaves.

El perro **se bebió** el agua.

I wrote the letters.

When did you [pl.] start the semester?

I finally found my keys.

The dog drank up the water.

18.C.2 To indicate that an action took place in the past

a. Use of the preterite states that an action or situation actually occurred and ended or did not occur in the past.

Fui a Madrid el año pasado.

Las clases **me gustaron** mucho.

Lina no **estuvo** enferma ayer.

Mi abuelo **fue** un gran hombre.

Ayer no **llovió** en Nueva York.

Hubo un incendio en un hotel.

Nosotros **nos quisimos** mucho.

Todo tiempo pasado **fue** mejor.

I went to Madrid last year.

I liked the classes a lot.

Lina was not sick yesterday.

My grandfather was a great man.

Yesterday, it didn't rain in New York.

There was a fire in a hotel.

We loved each other very much.

In the old days, things were better.

b. The preterite is used to state historical facts.

La Constitución de Estados Unidos **fue escrita** en 1787.

Hernán Cortés **llegó** a México en 1521.

Costó mucho ganar la Segunda Guerra Mundial.

La primera Constitución española **se firmó** en 1812.

The United States Constitution was written in 1787.

Hernán Cortés arrived in Mexico in 1521.

It cost a lot to win World War II.

The first Spanish Constitution was signed in 1812.

In the central regions of Spain, Bolivia, and in the north of Argentina, events that have recently occured can be stated using the *present perfect*: **Hoy ha llovido.** *It has rained today.* See Regional variations: 19.C

Passive voice with **ser**: 28.B

18.C.3 To indicate a sequence of events

a. The preterite can be used to describe actions that were part of a list or chain of events. In this context, the preterite marks the end of one action and the beginning of the next.

Rosa **se levantó** temprano. **Se vistió** rápidamente, no **comió** nada y **salió** corriendo a tomar el autobús.

Rosa got up early. She got dressed quickly, didn't eat anything, and rushed out to catch the bus.

b. Using the imperfect in the same context would indicate habitual or repeated actions in the past.

Rosa **se levantaba** temprano, **se vestía** rápidamente, no **comía** nada y **salía** corriendo a tomar el autobús.

Rosa used to get up early, get dressed quickly, eat nothing, and rush out to catch the bus.

18.D The imperfect tense

El pretérito imperfecto

18.D.1 Regular verbs

Most Spanish verbs have regular forms in the imperfect.

Preterite of regular verbs: p. 261 ▶

	-ar **cantar** *to sing*	-er **comer** *to eat*	-ir **vivir** *to live*
yo	cant**aba**	com**ía**	viv**ía**
tú/vos	cant**abas**	com**ías**	viv**ías**
usted, él, ella	cant**aba**	com**ía**	viv**ía**
nosotros/as	cant**ábamos**	com**íamos**	viv**íamos**
vosotros/as	cant**abais**	com**íais**	viv**íais**
ustedes, ellos/as	cant**aban**	com**ían**	viv**ían**

Flora **vivía** en Bogotá.
Tenía muchos amigos allí.
Se sentía muy contenta.

Flora used to live / lived in Bogotá.
She had many friends there.
She felt very happy.

18.D.2 Irregular verbs

Only three verbs are irregular in the imperfect.

Verb conjugation tables, pp. 257–276. See verb patterns 40, 66, 77. ▶

	ser	ir	ver
yo	**era**	**iba**	**veía**
tú/vos	**eras**	**ibas**	**veías**
usted, él, ella	**era**	**iba**	**veía**
nosotros/as	**éramos**	**íbamos**	**veíamos**
vosotros/as	**erais**	**ibais**	**veíais**
ustedes, ellos/as	**eran**	**iban**	**veían**

Todo **era** mejor antes.
Íbamos al parque todos los días.
La gente siempre **se veía** feliz.

Everything was better before.
We would / used to go to the park every day.
People always looked happy.

18.E | Use of the imperfect

Uso del pretérito imperfecto

In Spanish, the imperfect is primarily used in the following ways:

18.E.1 | Scene or backdrop

a. The imperfect can be used to *set the scene* for dynamic past actions. For example, it can be used to describe the time of day, how someone felt, or what was happening when another action occurred.

El sol **brillaba**.	*The sun was shining.*
Me sentía optimista.	*I felt optimistic.*
Había paz en el mundo.	*There was peace in the world.*

b. The descriptions above create the backdrop for specific actions that can be expressed using the preterite.

El sol **brillaba** cuando **viajé** ayer.	*The sun was shining when I traveled yesterday.*
Me sentía optimista y todo **salió** bien.	*I felt optimistic and everything went well.*
Había paz en el mundo, pero todo **cambió** en un instante.	*There was peace in the world, but everything changed in an instant.*

c. In stories, the imperfect is used for a description in the past or to tell about what was happening when a specific action occurred. Punctual time expressions like **de pronto** (*suddenly*) and **en ese momento** (*at that moment*) indicate the beginning of a specific past action that interrupts ongoing actions. This interrupting action is expressed with the preterite.

Había paz en el mundo. El sol **brillaba** y **me sentía** optimista, pero ese mismo día **cambió** mi vida para siempre.	*There was peace in the world. The sun was shining and I felt optimistic, but on that same day my life changed forever.*
Anoche **iba** para mi casa. Todo **parecía** muy tranquilo. **Era** tarde y no **se veía** ni un alma, cuando de pronto **escuché** un grito desgarrador.	*I was on my way home last night. Everything seemed very peaceful. It was late and there wasn't a soul to be seen, when suddenly I heard a bloodcurdling scream.*

18.E.2 | Weather

a. Weather can be described using the imperfect as a backdrop for other actions that are expressed in the preterite.

Ayer **nevaba** mucho cuando **salí**.	*It was snowing a lot yesterday when I went out.*

b. When describing the weather during a specific interval in the past, the preterite can be used.

Ayer **nevó** mucho.	*It snowed a lot yesterday.*

18.E.3 | Age

Like the weather, age is a common backdrop for describing past events, and therefore is often expressed using the imperfect. The verb **tener** is used in the imperfect to indicate that someone *was a certain age* when something happened. The verb **cumplir** is used in the preterite to indicate that someone turned a certain age.

Cuando **tenía** dieciocho años, conocí al amor de mi vida.	*When I was eighteen, I met the love of my life.*	◀ **tener** with age: 29.D
Cuando **cumplí** diecinueve años, todo había terminado ya.	*When I turned nineteen, it (our relationship) was over.*	

18.E.4 Characteristics

The imperfect is used to describe the characteristics of people, things, or conditions in the past.

Luis y yo **nos queríamos** mucho.   Luis and I loved each other a lot.
Mis abuelos **eran** personas extraordinarias.   My grandparents were extraordinary people.

18.E.5 Habits and preferences

With action verbs, the imperfect often describes habits, routines, or events that used to happen repeatedly or at regular intervals in the past. Time expressions such as **todos los días**, **cada año**, **siempre**, etc., are often used to emphasize the repetition of an action.

¿**Ibais** a la escuela todos los días?   Did you [pl.] go to school every day?
¿Te **daban** regalos de Navidad?   Did you use to get Christmas presents?
Me **gustaba** esquiar.   I used to like skiing.

18.E.6 Incomplete action with *ya*

a. After **ya**, the imperfect expresses an action in the past that was about to happen, but was interrupted. **Ir a** + *infinitive* can also be used in the imperfect to express the same thing.

Ya **salía** cuando sonó el teléfono.   I was on my way out when the phone rang.
Iban a salir cuando llegaste.   They were just about to leave when you arrived.

ir a + *infinitive*: 26.C.1 ▶

b. The imperfect can be used to express two or more past actions that used to happen at the same time. Note the significant difference with the use of the preterite.

Siempre **me caía** cuando **montaba** en bicicleta.   I always used to fall when riding my bike.
Me caí cuando **monté** en bicicleta.   I fell when I was riding my bike / rode my bike.

18.E.7 Courtesy

The imperfect can be used to make polite requests.

Quería pedirte una cosa.   I wanted to ask you for something.
Venía a solicitar información. I came to ask for some information.

18.E.8 Dreams and children's games

When children invent games based on fantasy or imagination, the context is created using the *imperfect*. When dreams are talked about, the start of the story is often **Soñé que...** and the rest is told in the *imperfect* and other past structures. The *preterite* is rarely used.

Juguemos a que **estábamos** en una nave   Let's play that we are in a spaceship,
espacial, que tú **eras** un monstruo y que you're a monster and I'm chasing you.
yo te **perseguía**.

Soñé que era el día del examen y que no   I dreamt that it was exam day and that I
había estudiado nada.   hadn't studied anything.

18.E.9 Completed actions with the imperfect

In news reports and historical texts, the imperfect is sometimes used in place of the preterite to describe a completed action. This stylistic choice lends greater immediacy and a descriptive tone to the narration.

La boda real se realizó ayer en La Almudena.   The royal wedding was held yesterday in
Unas horas después, Madrid **celebraba** la boda   La Almudena. Some hours later, Madrid
del siglo con fiestas en toda la ciudad.   celebrated the wedding of the century
                                                with parties all over the city.

Indirect discourse: Ch. 31

18.E.10 Indirect discourse

a. Indirect discourse is a way to report what someone said without using a direct quote. Indirect discourse is expressed using a subordinate clause with **que**. Quotation marks are not used.

Direct discourse	Indirect discourse
Él **dice**: "No tengo dinero". *He says: "I don't have any money."*	Él **dice que** no **tiene** dinero. *He says that he doesn't have any money.*
Tú **dijiste**: "Ella **quiere** viajar". *You said: "She wants to travel."*	Tú **dijiste que** ella **quería** viajar. *You said that she wanted to travel.*
Él **decía**: "Ellas no **saben** nada". *He said: "They don't know anything."*	Él **decía que** ellas no **sabían** nada. *He said that they didn't know anything.*
Ellos **dijeron**: "**Esperamos** que no **suban** los precios". *They said: "We hope the prices won't go up."*	Ellos **dijeron que esperaban** que no **subieran** los precios. *They said that they hoped the prices wouldn't go up.*

When the verbs express will or desire, the subjunctive is used in the subordinate clause, but the structure to express indirect discourse is the same.

b. The imperfect is used in indirect discourse when information or questions that were in the present tense in direct discourse are supplied with the preterite of verbs like **decir**, **preguntar**, **comentar**, or other reporting verbs.

Rita dijo que no **tenía** dinero.	*Rita said she didn't have any money.*
Te pregunté que si **querías** cenar.	*I asked you if you wanted to have dinner.*

c. Ir a + *infinitive* expresses the future in Spanish. The imperfect of **ir** is often used in indirect discourse to describe what someone *was going to do*.

ir a + *infinitive*: 26.C.1

Jaime me contó que **iba** a viajar.	*Jaime told me that he was going to travel.*
Te pregunté que si **ibas** a cenar.	*I asked you if you were going to have dinner.*

18.E.11 Expressions with *hace/hacía* + **period of time** + *que (no)*

a. Hace/Hacía + *period of time* + **que (no)** is used to express *how long since something has* (*not*) *been done*. In affirmative sentences, it is equivalent to the verbal periphrasis **llevar** + *time expression* + **gerundio**. In negative sentences, it is equivalent to **llevar** + *time expression* + **sin** + *infinitive*.

llevar + *time expression* + gerundio: 26.D

Hace tres años **que vivo** en Madrid. **Llevo** tres años **viviendo** en Madrid.	*I have lived in Madrid for three years.*
Hace un año **que no voy** a Londres. **Llevo** un año **sin ir** a Londres.	*It's been a year since I was last in London. / I haven't been in London for a year.*
¡**Hacía** mucho tiempo **que no** te **veía**! ¡**Llevaba** mucho tiempo **sin verte**!	*I hadn't seen you for ages.*

b. The imperfect is often used when you want to express that a certain amount of time is over.

Llevo mucho tiempo **sin verte**.	*Long time no see. (I still haven't seen you.)*
Llevaba mucho tiempo **sin verte**.	*It's been so long since I've seen you. (But now I've seen you.)*

18.E.12 Impersonal constructions *había, hubo*

When the verb **haber** is used to express existence in the past (*there was/were*), it is always conjugated in the third-person singular. The preterite of **haber**, **hubo**, expresses an action or state that has ended, while the imperfect, **había**, describes the existence of something in the past without stating that it ended.

En el siglo XX **hubo** muchas guerras.	*In the 20th century, there were many wars.*
Casi en ningún país **había** paz en esa época.	*Almost no country had peace during that period.*

18.F Verbs that change meaning

Verbos cuyo significado cambia

Some common verbs have different meanings in the preterite and the imperfect. Note that the meaning may also change depending on whether the statement is affirmative or negative.

The examples in this chart describe scenes and narrate events in the story *La siesta del martes* by Gabriel García Márquez.

Saber: 26.B.7 ▶

Querer: 26.B.6 ▶

Poder: 26.B.5 ▶

Verb	Preterite	Imperfect
tener	*to get; to receive* El sacerdote **tuvo** una visita inesperada: la madre y la hermana del difunto. *The priest got an unexpected visit: the mother and the sister of the deceased.*	*to have* La hija **tenía** dificultades para mover la persiana. *The daughter was having a hard time moving the blinds.*
saber	*to find out; to discover* **Supieron** que Carlos se murió el lunes anterior. *They found out that Carlos died the previous Monday.*	*to know* El padre no **sabía** quiénes eran. *The father did not know who they were.*
querer	*to try (without necessarily succeeding)* La mujer **quiso** visitar el cementerio donde estaba enterrado su hijo. *The woman tried to visit the graveyard where her son was buried.*	*to want* La gente del pueblo se asomaba a la ventana porque **quería** ver qué sucedía. *The townspeople looked out their windows because they wanted to see what was happening.*
no querer	*to refuse* La mujer **no quiso** irse de la casa del cura sin verlo. *The woman refused to leave the rectory without seeing him.*	*not to want* La mujer **no quería** despertar al cura. *The woman did not want to wake up the priest.*
conocer	*to meet* Cuando el cura **conoció** a la mujer, se quedó muy sorprendido. *When the priest met the woman, he was very surprised.*	*to know about, to be familiar with* Nadie **conocía** a Carlos en ese pueblo. *Nobody in that town knew Carlos.*
poder	*to manage to do; to succeed in doing* La mujer **pudo** convencer a la hermana del cura de que fuera a buscarlo. *The woman managed to convince the priest's sister to go fetch him.*	*to be able to; to have the ability* En la distancia, **se podía** escuchar la música que tocaba la banda. *The music the band was playing could be heard in the distance.*
no poder	*to be unable to* La chica **no pudo** subir la ventana del tren. *The girl was unable to close the window in the train.*	*to be unable to (in a general sense)* **No se podía** respirar en el tren a causa del calor. *It was so hot inside the train that one could not breathe.*

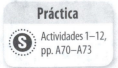

Práctica

Actividades 1–12, pp. A70–A73

The present perfect and the past perfect
Pretérito perfecto compuesto y pluscuamperfecto

19.A The present perfect

Pretérito perfecto compuesto

The present perfect is formed in Spanish with the present indicative of the auxiliary verb **haber** (see table below) and the past participle of the main verb.

¿**Has leído** este libro?   *Have you read this book?*

19.A.1 Regular past participles

a. To form the past participle, the ending **-ado** is added to regular **-ar** verbs and the ending **-ido** is added to regular **-er** and **-ir** verbs. The **tú** and **vos** forms are the same.

Present perfect					
Subject pronoun	**Present indicative of** *haber*	**+**	**Regular past participles**		
			-ar* verbs: *-ado	***-er* and *-ir* verbs: *-ido***	
			hablar	**querer**	**venir**
yo	**he**	**+**	habl**ado**	quer**ido**	ven**ido**
tú/vos	**has**				
usted, él, ella	**ha**				
nosotros/as	**hemos**				
vosotros/as	**habéis**				
ustedes, ellos/as	**han**				

b. In the present perfect, the past participle always ends in **-o**. Unlike in English, in Spanish, words cannot come between **haber** and the past participle. Object and reflexive pronouns must be placed before **haber**.

Siempre **he trabajado** mucho.	*I **have** always **worked** a lot.*
Lo **he buscado** por todos lados.	*I **have looked** for it all over the place.*
Lucas **se ha quedado** dormido.	*Lucas **has overslept**.*

c. When the verb stem of an **-er** or **-ir** verb ends in any vowel except for **-u**, a written accent must be added to the participle, forming the ending **-ido**. The combination of **u + i** usually forms a diphthong and does not have a written accent (const**ru**ido, h**u**ido).

Infinitive	Verb stem	Past participle	
creer	**cre-**	creído	*thought, believed*
leer	**le-**	leído	*read*
oír	**o-**	oído	*heard*
sonreír	**sonre-**	sonreído	*smiled*
traer	**tra-**	traído	*brought*

¿Has **leído** novelas españolas?   *Have you read Spanish novels?*

Compound tenses: Verb conjugation tables, p. 261

The present perfect used to be called the **pretérito perfecto**. Nowadays, it is referred to as **pretérito perfecto compuesto**.

The past participle in passive **ser** clauses: 28.B.3 Compound tenses using **haber**: Verb conjugation tables: p. 261

Diphthongs: 1.C.2, 1.D.2

19.A.2 Irregular past participles

a. A number of verbs have an irregular past participle. Most irregular past participles end in **-to**.

Infinitive	Irregular past participles	
abrir	**abierto**	opened
cubrir	**cubierto**	covered
decir	**dicho**	said, told
describir	**descrito**	described
descubrir	**descubierto**	discovered
escribir	**escrito**	written
hacer	**hecho**	done, made
morir	**muerto**	died
poner	**puesto**	placed
resolver	**resuelto**	resolved
romper	**roto**	broken
satisfacer	**satisfecho**	satisfied
ver	**visto**	seen
volver	**vuelto**	returned

Las tiendas no **han abierto** todavía.   *The shops **haven't opened** yet.*

b. The following three verbs have two equally accepted participles, a regular and an irregular form. Both can be used to form compound tenses and passive sentences. The use of **frito**, **impreso**, and **provisto** is increasing in all Spanish-speaking countries as opposed to the regular participles.

*Passive voice with **ser**: 28.B* ▶

Irregular participles: 25.D.2 ▶

Infinitive	Past participle	
	Regular	Irregular
freír (*to fry*)	fre**ído**	**frito**
imprimir (*to print*)	imprim**ido**	**impreso**
proveer (*to provide*)	prove**ído**	**provisto**

El chef ha **frito (freído)** las cebollas.
Las cebollas han sido **fritas (freídas)** por el chef.

El secretario **ha impreso (imprimido)** la agenda.
La agenda **ha sido impresa (imprimida)** por el secretario.

La agencia de viajes **ha provisto (proveído)** los itinerarios.
Los itinerarios **han sido provistos (proveídos)** por la agencia de viajes.

The chef has fried the onions.
The onions have been fried by the chef.

The secretary has printed the agenda.
The agenda has been printed by the secretary.

The travel agency has provided the itineraries.
The itineraries have been provided by the travel agency.

c. Only the irregular forms can function as adjectives:

las papas *fritas* (*Latin America*)
las patatas *fritas* (*Spain*)   *the potato chips / French fries*
los documentos *impresos*   *the printed documents*
los uniformes *provistos*   *the provided uniforms*

19.B Use of the present perfect

Uso del pretérito perfecto compuesto

The use of the present perfect has regional differences. The following examples show common uses of this tense in most Spanish-speaking regions.

19.B.1 Life experiences – *nunca, alguna vez, hasta ahora, en mi vida*

a. The present perfect can be used to describe life experiences up to the present moment. Adverbs like **alguna vez, nunca, hasta ahora/hoy,** and **en mi vida** (*never before*) are commonly used.

¿Has viajado en barco **alguna vez**?	*Have you ever traveled by boat?*
Nunca he probado el alcohol.	*I have never tried alcohol.*
¡**En mi vida** he estudiado tanto!	*I have never studied so much in my life!*
Hasta ahora, todo **ha salido** bien.	*Everything has gone well until now.*

b. Context usually implies the point in time when the adverb is not explicit.

Amy hace un café delicioso,	*Amy makes a delicious coffee.*
¿lo **has probado** (alguna vez)?	*Have you (ever) tried it?*

19.B.2 Incomplete actions – *todavía no*

The present perfect is used with **todavía no** (*not yet*) to express actions that are not yet complete.

¿**No has salido** todavía?	*Haven't you gone out / left yet?*
No, todavía **no he salido**.	*No, I haven't gone out / left yet.*

19.B.3 Continuous actions – *siempre*

Siempre and other continuous expressions of time like **muchas veces, todos los días,** etc., are used with the present perfect to extend the action into the present. The preterite, in contrast, fixes the action in the past.

Siempre **te he querido**.	*I have always loved you.*
Siempre **te quise**.	*I always loved you.*
Hemos ido al cine todos los días.	*We have been to the movies every day.*
Fuimos al cine todos los días.	*We went to the movies every day.*

19.C Regional variations

Variaciones regionales

The following examples show the major differences when using the present perfect in Spain and Latin America. There are also variations within each of these regions.

19.C.1 Recently completed actions – *ya, por fin, finalmente*

a. Ya (*already*), **por fin** (*in the end*), and **finalmente** (*finally*) indicate completed actions. In Spain, these phrases are usually used with the present perfect, while the preterite is preferred in most parts of Latin America.

Spain	¡Por fin **has llegado**!	*You have finally arrived!*
Latin America	¡Por fin **llegaste**!	

b. Questions and answers with **ya** and **todavía no** are generally used with different verb tenses in Spain and Latin America.

Spain	—¿Ya **has cenado**?	*Have you had dinner yet?*
	—No, **todavía no he cenado**.	*No, I haven't had dinner yet.*
	—Sí, **ya he cenado**.	*Yes, I have already had dinner.*

Latin America	—¿Ya **cenaste**?	*Did you eat dinner yet?*
	—No, **todavía no he cenado**.	*No, I haven't had dinner yet.*
	—Sí, **ya cené**.	*Yes, I already ate dinner.*

c. In central parts of Spain, the present perfect is used to convey actions completed in the near past. The length of this time period in the past can be subjective and is indicated by time expressions such as **hace un momento, este año, hoy,** and so on. This use is also common in the northwest of Argentina and in Bolivia.

Spain (central)	Hace un momento **he visto** a Ernesto.	*I saw Ernesto a short time ago.*
Latin America	Hace un momento **vi** a Ernesto.	

19.C.2 Interpreting time using the present perfect

When the period of time is specified, the present perfect can be interpreted differently in central parts of Spain and in most parts of Latin America.

Spain (central)	Este verano **hemos ido** mucho al cine.	*This summer, we've been to the movies a lot. (The summer is over.)*
Latin America		*This summer, we've been to the movies a lot. (The summer is not over yet.)*

19.C.3 Cause and effect

Cause and effect relationships in the near past are expressed using the present perfect in Spain and the preterite in Latin America.

Spain	—¿Por qué **has llegado** tan tarde hoy?	*Why did you arrive so late today?*
	—¡**He perdido** el autobús!	*I missed the bus!*
Latin America	—¿Por qué **llegaste** tan tarde hoy?	
	—¡**Perdí** el autobús!	

19.D The past perfect

Pretérito pluscuamperfecto

The past perfect is formed using the imperfect of **haber** and the past participle of the main verb: **había hablado** (*I had talked*).

Pluscuamperfecto					
			Regular past participles		
Subject pronoun	Imperfect of *haber*	+	-*ar* verbs: -*ado*	-*er* and -*ir* verbs: -*ido*	
			hablar	querer	venir
yo	había				
tú/vos	habías				
usted, él, ella	había	+	habl**ado**	quer**ido**	ven**ido**
nosotros/as	habíamos				
vosotros/as	habíais				
ustedes, ellos/as	habían				

◀ Compound tenses: Verb conjugation tables, p. 261
Past participles: 19.A, 25.D

19.E Use of the past perfect

Uso del pretérito pluscuamperfecto

19.E.1 Past before the past

In Spanish, the past perfect expresses what someone *had done*, or what *had occurred* before another action or condition in the past.

Cuando Lina llamó, Pedro ya **había llamado**.　　*When Lina called, Pedro had already called.*

19.E.2 Questions and answers with *ya, todavía no* in the past

Antes, aún, nunca, todavía, and **ya** are often used with the past perfect to indicate the order of past actions. These adverbs, as well as pronouns and the word **no**, cannot come between **haber** and the past participle.

—¿Ya **habías estudiado** español cuando viajaste a Santiago?

Had you already studied Spanish when you traveled to Santiago?

—Claro, ya **había estudiado** español y sabía bastante.

Of course, I had already studied Spanish and I knew quite a lot.

—Cuando llegué a Santiago, no **había estudiado** español todavía.

When I arrived in Santiago, I had not studied Spanish yet.

19.E.3 Indirect discourse

In indirect discourse, the preterite becomes the past perfect.

Camilo dijo: "Vi los fiordos chilenos".
Camilo me contó que **había visto** los fiordos chilenos.

Camilo said, "I saw the Chilean fjords."
Camilo told me that he had seen the Chilean fjords.

19.F The *pretérito anterior*

The **pretérito anterior** is formed using the preterite of **haber** and the past participle of the main verb. This form of the past perfect is rare in today's spoken Spanish and is generally used only in written language.

Past participles: 19.A, 25.D

Pretérito anterior					
Subject pronoun	Preterite of *haber*	+	**Regular past participles**		
			-ar **verbs:** *-ado*	*-er* **and** *-ir* **verbs:** *-ido*	
			hablar	**querer**	**venir**
yo	**hube**	+	habl**ado**	quer**ido**	ven**ido**
tú/vos	**hubiste**				
usted, él, ella	**hubo**				
nosotros/as	**hubimos**				
vosotros/as	**hubisteis**				
ustedes, ellos/as	**hubieron**				

19.G Use of the *pretérito anterior*

Uso del pretérito anterior

a. The **pretérito anterior** marks the end of an action that happened before another action in the past.

Cuando **se hubo tomado** la decisión, concluyeron la reunión.

When the decision had been made, they ended the meeting.

b. The **pretérito anterior** can be replaced with the preterite (**pretérito perfecto simple**).

Cuando **se tomó** la decisión, concluyeron la reunión.

When the decision was made, they ended the meeting.

Práctica

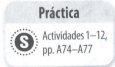

Actividades 1–12, pp. A74–A77

The present perfect and the past perfect • **Chapter 19**

The future
Futuro

20.A Future expressions

Estructuras para expresar el futuro

In Spanish, the future can be expressed using the following structures:

Spanish future expressions		
1. Simple future	Te **devolveré** tus libros muy pronto.	*I will give you back your books very soon.*
2. *ir a* + *infinitive*	**Vamos a construir** una nueva casa.	*We are going to build a new house.*
3. Present indicative	**Regreso** el lunes.	*I am coming back on Monday.* (lit. *I come back on Monday.*)

As you can see above, future actions and events can be expressed in Spanish and English using the simple future and *going to + infinitive* expressions. In English, the present progressive may also refer to a future event or action. Note that the Spanish present progressive *cannot* be used to refer to the future. The simple present, however, can be used in Spanish to refer to the future.

Present progressive: 17.F
Present with future meaning: 17.E.4

Other future expressions: 20.D

20.B The simple future

Futuro simple

The future tense of regular verbs is formed by adding future endings to the infinitive ending. Irregular verbs use the same endings, but have changes in the stems. The **tú** and **vos** endings are the same.

20.B.1 Regular verbs

All regular verbs have a written accent in the future tense except the first-person plural, **nosotros/as**.

Regular verbs: verb conjugation tables, p. 261

	-ar	-er	-ir
yo	trabajar**é**	comer**é**	ir**é**
tú/vos	trabajar**ás**	comer**ás**	ir**ás**
usted, él, ella	trabajar**á**	comer**á**	ir**á**
nosotros/as	trabajar**emos**	comer**emos**	ir**emos**
vosotros/as	trabajar**éis**	comer**éis**	ir**éis**
ustedes, ellos/as	trabajar**án**	comer**án**	ir**án**

20.B.2 Irregular verbs

Few verbs are irregular in the simple future. The verbs that are irregular have a stem change, but take the same endings as regular verbs in the future.

Infinitive	Stem	Infinitive	Stem	Infinitive	Stem
caber	**cabr-**	poder	**podr-**	salir	**saldr-**
decir	**dir-**	poner	**pondr-**	tener	**tendr-**
haber	**habr-**	querer	**querr-**	valer	**valdr-**
hacer	**har-**	saber	**sabr-**	venir	**vendr-**

Verb conjugation tables, pp. 257– 276.

—¿**Vendrás** pronto?   *Will you come soon?*
—Sí, lo **haré**.   *Yes, I will (come).*

20.C | Use of the simple future

Uso del futuro simple

20.C.1 | Future actions

The simple future is generally used to express future actions and events.

¿**Viajaréis** de vacaciones en julio?	Will you [pl.] travel / go away on vacation in July?

20.C.2 | Suppositions

The simple future tense can be used to express suppositions or guesses about present or future actions or states. Whether the present or future is referred to depends on the context.

a. Suppositions about the present:

Assumptions about events in the past: 20.F.2 ▶

—¿Quién **será** ese hombre?	I wonder who that man is? / Who may that man be?
—No lo sé. **Será** alguna persona importante.	I don't know. He may be an important person.

b. Suppositions about the future:

—¿Quién **hará** el trabajo? ¿Tú?	Who will do the job? You?
—¿Yo? No, lo **hará** Rubén. (Supongo que lo **hará** Rubén.)	Me? No, Rubén will do it. (I suppose Rubén will do it.)

20.C.3 | Predictions

The simple future is used in forecasts, horoscopes, and predictions.

Mañana **nevará** en las montañas.	Tomorrow, it will snow in the mountains.
Las personas de Aries **tendrán** una agradable sorpresa esta semana.	People born under Aries will have a pleasant surprise this week.
Predicen que los precios **subirán**.	They predict that prices will go up.
Todo **saldrá** bien, ya **verás**.	Everything will be all right, you'll see.

20.C.4 | Conditional constructions

Conditional conjunctions: 16.D ▶
Conditional si clauses: 23.E.8

The simple future can be used to describe something that will happen under certain imagined conditions. When the condition is seen as possible, it is expressed with the present indicative in a **si** clause.

Si nos ganamos la lotería, **compraremos** la casa.	If we win the lottery, we'll buy the house.

20.C.5 | Decrees

In written language, the simple future is used for laws, regulations, and decrees.

No **matarás**.	Thou shall not kill.

20.C.6 | Impersonal constructions – *habrá*

When **haber** is used as an impersonal verb in the third-person singular of the future tense, it indicates future existence (*there will [not] be*).

No **habrá** reunión mañana.	There won't be a meeting tomorrow.
Habrá vacaciones en julio.	There will be vacation in July.
No **habrá** lluvia mañana.	There won't be rain tomorrow.
Creo que **habrá** tiempo suficiente.	I think there will be enough time.

20.C.7 | Contrast – *shall, will*

a. In American English, the simple future is formed by adding the auxiliary *will*, but pay attention to the following uses of *shall* and its Spanish equivalents:

Communicative function	Spanish	English
Express formal obligation	**Habrá** sanciones.	There **shall** (will) be sanctions.
Express suggestions and requests	¿**Empezamos** (ya)?	**Shall** we start?

b. These Spanish equivalents of *will* are used for making announcements, asking polite questions, offering or refusing to help, ordering in a restaurant, and selecting items in a store.

Se abrirá un nuevo centro comercial.	*A new shopping mall will be opened.*
¿**Asistirá** usted a la reunión?	*Will you attend the meeting?*
¡Yo **abro**!	*I'll get it! (I will open the door.)*
¡Yo no **abro**! (Yo no **abriré**.)	*I won't get it! (I won't open the door.)*
Tráigame una ensalada, por favor.	*I'll have a salad, please.*
Me llevo la blusa roja.	*I'll take the red blouse.*

20.D Other future expressions

Otras expresiones del futuro

20.D.1 *Ir a* + **infinitive**

a. This form is used to express plans or intentions to be carried out immediately or in the very near future.

◀ **Ir a** + infinitive: 26.C.1

—¿Qué **vas a hacer** esta tarde?	*What are you going to do this afternoon?*
—Estoy rendido y **voy a descansar**.	*I'm exhausted and I'm going to rest.*

b. The form **ir a** + *infinitive* describes events which in all likelihood will happen in the near future.

Es muy tarde. ¡**Vas a perder** el tren!	*It's very late. You are going to miss the train!*

c. Ir a + *infinitive* is used in expressions with **ya** to describe an impending event.

Ya **va a empezar** el noticiero.	*The news cast is going to start now.*

20.D.2 The present indicative to express future

The present indicative can only be used to describe future actions if the context refers to the future. Adverbs of time are often part of the sentence.

Las clases **empiezan** mañana.	*School starts tomorrow.*

20.E The future perfect

Futuro compuesto

The future perfect is formed with the simple future of the auxiliary verb **haber** and the past participle of the main verb. **Tú** and **vos** take the same verb form in the future perfect.

◀ Past participles: 19.A.1–2, 25.D

Simple future of *haber*		+	Regular past participles		
			-ar **verbs:** *-ado*	*-er* **and** *-ir* **verbs:** *-ido*	
			hablar	querer	venir
yo	**habré**				
tú/vos	**habrás**				
usted, él, ella	**habrá**	+	habl**ado**	quer**ido**	ven**ido**
nosotros/as	**habremos**				
vosotros/as	**habréis**				
ustedes, ellos/as	**habrán**				

20.F | Use of the future perfect

Uso del futuro compuesto

20.F.1 | A complete action in the future

The future perfect describes an action that will already be complete (*will have happened*) after a specific point in time in the future.

Mañana a esta hora, **habremos regresado** a casa. | By this time tomorrow, we'll have returned home.
En junio, ya **habrás terminado** tus estudios. | By June, you'll have already finished your studies.

20.F.2 | Assumptions about the past

Suppositions about the present or future: 20.C.2

a. The future perfect can express an assumption or guess about the probability of an action or state in the past.

¿Cómo me **habrá ido** en el examen ayer? | I wonder how I did on the exam yesterday?
Jaime no vino a trabajar el lunes. | Jaime didn't come to work on Monday.
¿Dónde **habrá estado**? | Where could he have been?

b. Like the simple future, the future perfect can be used to express distance from past events or reference to other sources.

Según nuestro corresponsal, **habrá habido** muchas personas afectadas por el accidente. | According to our correspondent, many people will have been affected by the accident.

20.F.3 | Conditional constructions

Conditional conjunctions: 16.D
Conditional clauses: 23.E.8

The future perfect expresses what we believe will have happened if a present condition is fulfilled. The **si** clause describing the condition uses the present indicative.

Si no estudias, **habrás perdido** el tiempo en la escuela. | If you don't study, you will have wasted your time at school.

20.F.4 | Impersonal constructions – *habrá habido*

The impersonal form of **haber** (*will have been*) can be used to express assumptions about what could have been.

¿**Habrá habido** algún problema? | Could there have been a problem?
¿**Habrá habido** buenos resultados en el examen? | Could there have been good exam results?

20.G | Regional variations

Variaciones regionales

There are few regional differences in future verb forms in Spanish. It is a bit more common to use **ir a** + *infinitive* in Latin America to refer to both the near and distant future.

Spain	Este año me **graduaré**.	I'm going to / I will graduate this year.
Latin America	Este año me **voy a graduar**.	

Práctica

Actividades 1–12, pp. A77–A80

The conditional
Condicional

21.A The present conditional

Condicional simple

In English, the conditional is expressed with the words *would/should*. In Spanish, the conditional tense is expressed with its own verb forms.

Me alegraría verte de nuevo.	*It would make me happy to see you again.*
Roberto dijo que te **llamaría**.	*Roberto said that he would call you.*

The present conditional of all Spanish verbs is formed by adding the conditional endings to the infinitive endings. The **tú** and **vos** endings are the same.

21.A.1 Regular verbs

All forms have a written accent.

	-ar	-er	-ir
yo	trabajar**ía**	comer**ía**	subir**ía**
tú/vos	trabajar**ías**	comer**ías**	subir**ías**
usted, él, ella	trabajar**ía**	comer**ía**	subir**ía**
nosotros/as	trabajar**íamos**	comer**íamos**	subir**íamos**
vosotros/as	trabajar**íais**	comer**íais**	subir**íais**
ustedes, ellos/as	trabajar**ían**	comer**ían**	subir**ían**

◄ Regular verbs: Verb conjugation tables, p. 261

21.A.2 Irregular verbs

Irregular verbs have the same stem changes in the conditional as in the simple future tense.

◄ Irregular verbs in the simple future: 20.B.2

Infinitive	Stem	Infinitive	Stem
caber	**cabr-**	querer	**querr-**
decir	**dir-**	saber	**sabr-**
haber	**habr-**	salir	**saldr-**
hacer	**har-**	tener	**tendr-**
poder	**podr-**	valer	**valdr-**
poner	**pondr-**	venir	**vendr-**

◄ Irregular verbs are found alphabetically in the Verb conjugation tables, pp. 257–276.

—¿**Podrías** hacerme un favor?	*Could you do me a favor?*
—Lo **haría** si pudiera.	*I would (do it) if I could.*

21.B Use of the present conditional

Uso del condicional simple

21.B.1 Imagined possibility or characterisitic

The present conditional expresses a possibility in the near future.

Llegaríamos más rápido en avión.	*We would arrive faster by plane.*
Estarías mejor en otro trabajo.	*You would be better off at another job.*

21.B.2   Assumptions about the past

The present conditional can be used to express uncertainties or assumptions about the past.

Jaime no vino a trabajar el lunes.	Jaime didn't come to work on Monday.
¿Dónde **estaría**?	Where could/would he have been?
Supongo que hace mil años la gente **hablaría** de forma muy distinta.	I suppose that a thousand years ago people would/could have spoken very differently.
¿Cómo me **iría** en el examen ayer?	I wonder how it went (for me) / I did on my exam yesterday.

21.B.3   Wishes

The present conditional is used with verbs like **gustar, preferir, desear, encantar,** and **alegrar** to express wishes or preferences.

Me encantaría ir al teatro.	I would love to go to the theater.
¿**Te gustaría** estudiar español?	Would you like to study Spanish?

21.B.4   Courtesy

Imperatives: 24.G.3b

The conditional is used to communicate polite inquiries and requests.

¿**Podrías** ayudarme con esto?	Could you help me with this?
¿**Sería** posible realizar la reunión el lunes?	Could/Would it be possible to hold the meeting on Monday?

21.B.5   Advice

The conditional is used to give advice with verbs like **deber** and impersonal expressions like **ser bueno, ser mejor,** and **ser conveniente**.

Subjunctive with impersonal expressions: 23.C.8

Deberíais dejar de fumar.	You [pl.] should stop smoking.
Sería conveniente que fueras al médico.	It would be good if you went to the doctor.
En tu lugar, yo no **haría** eso.	If I were you / If I were in your shoes, I wouldn't do that.

Indirect discourse: Ch. 31

21.B.6   Indirect discourse

The conditional is used to express what *would happen* in the future, from the perspective of a past event.

Has prometido varias veces que **iríamos** de compras hoy.	You have promised several times that we would go shopping today.
Supe que **habría** una conferencia y he venido para escucharla.	I found out that there would be a lecture and I've come to listen to it.

Conditional conjunctions: 16.D
Conditional **si** clauses: 23.E.8

21.B.7   Conditional constructions

The present conditional is used to express what would happen in hypothetical circumstances. The condition is expressed with the imperfect subjunctive in the **si** clause.

The imperfect subjunctive: 22.C

Si no estudiaras, **perderías** el tiempo en la escuela.	If you didn't study, you would waste your time at school.
No me **quedaría** en casa el fin de semana si no tuviera que estudiar.	I wouldn't stay home this weekend if I didn't have to study.
Si pudierais viajar a cualquier parte, ¿adónde **iríais**?	If you [pl.] could travel anywhere, where would you go?

21.B.8 **Impersonal constructions** – *habría*

The present conditional form of **haber, habría** (*there would be*), is used to express the possibility that something could happen or could exist.

Con menor velocidad en las carreteras, **habría** menos accidentes.
With slower speeds on the roads, there would be fewer accidents.

21.C The conditional perfect

Condicional compuesto
The conditional perfect is formed with **habría** + *past participle*.

Conditional of *haber*		+	Regular past participles		
			-*ar* **verbs:** -*ado*	-*er* and -*ir* **verbs:** -*ido*	
			hablar	**querer**	**venir**
yo	**habría**				
tú/vos	**habrías**				
usted, él, ella	**habría**	+	habl**ado**	quer**ido**	ven**ido**
nosotros/as	**habríamos**				
vosotros/as	**habríais**				
ustedes, ellos/as	**habrían**				

◄ Past participles: 19.A.1–2, 25.D

21.D Use of the conditional perfect

Uso del condicional compuesto

21.D.1 Imagined possibility or characterisitic

The conditional perfect can be used to describe an imagined state in contrast to a present situation (what *would [not] have* happened).

Habríamos llegado más rápido en avión. *We would have arrived faster by plane.*
Habrías estado mejor en otro trabajo. *You would have been better off at another job.*
Me aseguraste que hoy, a esta hora, ya **habríamos salido** de compras. *You assured me that today, by this time, we would already have gone out shopping.*
En tu lugar, yo no **habría gastado** tanto dinero en un auto. *If I were you / If I were in your shoes, I wouldn't have spent so much money on a car.*
La semana pasada **habrías podido** comprar mejores boletos. *Last week you would have been able to buy better tickets.*

21.D.2 Conditional constructions

The conditional perfect can also be used to express what would have happened in a hypothetical past circumstance. The circumstance or condition is stated in the **si** clause using the past perfect subjunctive.

◄ Conditional conjunctions: 16.D
Conditional **si** clauses: 23.E.8

◄ The past perfect subjunctive: 22.E

Si hubieras estudiado, no **habrías perdido** el tiempo en la escuela. *If you had studied, you wouldn't have wasted time in school.*
Te **habría invitado** si me hubieras dicho que querías ir. *I would have invited you if you had told me you wanted to go.*

Modal verb periphrases with
the infinitive: 26.B.2 ▶

21.D.3   **English** *should have*

The present conditional of **deber / tener que** + *perfect infinitive* (**haber** + *past participle*) is used to express that something *should have been done.*

Deberías haber estudiado más si querías aprobar el examen.	*You ought to / should have studied more if you wanted to pass the exam.*
Tendrías que haber estudiado más si querías aprobar el examen.	*You should have studied / would have had to study more if you wanted to pass the exam.*

21.D.4   **Impersonal constructions** – *había habido*

The conditional perfect form of **haber**, **habría** (*there would have been*), is used to express the possibility that something *could have existed* or *could have been.*

Con menor velocidad en las carreteras, **habría habido** menos accidentes.	*With slower speeds on the roads, there would have been fewer accidents.*

Práctica

S Actividades 1–13, pp. A81–A84

The subjunctive
Subjuntivo

22.A Overview

Aspectos generales

Verbs have various grammatical properties. One of the most obvious is *tense*, which tells *when* an action takes place: *past*, *present*, or *future*. Another important grammatical property is *mood*, which reflects the *intention* of the speaker. Like English, Spanish has three verb moods: *imperative*, *indicative*, and *subjunctive*. The imperative is used to give commands, the indicative is used to express certainty and objectivity, and the subjunctive is used to express uncertainty and subjectivity, such as doubts, wishes, reactions (i.e., feelings), or imagined realities. The subjunctive mood is rarely used in English, but is essential in Spanish.

The Spanish name for the subjunctive, **subjuntivo**, refers to the dependency of the verb on another element, usually a *governing finite verb*. The governing verb in the sentence generally indicates whether the subjunctive will be used in the dependent clause. When the governing verb communicates a wish (**desear, esperar, necesitar, querer,** etc.), emotion (verbs used with indirect object pronouns, such as **desilusionar, gustar, enojar, encantar, temer,** etc.), impersonal expression (**es bueno que, es fácil que, no conviene que,** etc.), doubt (**dudar, negar,** etc.), or request (**insistir, pedir, prohibir,** etc.), the subjunctive is used.

The governing finite verb: When there is a main clause and a subordinate clause, there are two verbs. The verb in the main clause is the governing finite verb: 23.C

22.B The present subjunctive

Presente de subjuntivo

a. Most of the examples of *subjunctive* used in this chapter appear in groups of three sentences. The first sentence shows the subjunctive in a *nominal* **que**-clause. The second sentence shows the subjunctive in a relative, *adjectival* clause and the third sentence shows the subjunctive in an *adverbial* clause.

Nominal **que**-clause: 23.C
Adjectival clause (relative clause): 23.D
Adverbial clause: 23.E

b. In regions that use **voseo**, the **vos** endings for the present subjunctive can vary. In some areas, the **vos** endings and the **tú** endings are the same: **Quiero que tú/vos salgas de aquí ya mismo.** This is the conjugation presented in this book. The most common **voseo** endings for the present subjunctive are **-és** and **-ás: Quiero que caminés/comás/escribás.** Other regional variations exist as well.

Regional variations: 22.H

Map of **voseo** regions in Latin America: p. 277

22.B.1 Regular verbs

The following endings are added to the verb stem to form the present subjunctive. Note that **-er** and **-ir** verbs have the same endings.

Present subjunctive · regular verbs			
Subject pronoun	**hablar** *to speak/talk*	**comer** *to eat*	**subir** *to go up, to climb*
yo	habl**e**	com**a**	sub**a**
tú/vos	habl**es**	com**as**	sub**as**
usted, él, ella	habl**e**	com**a**	sub**a**
nosotros/as	habl**emos**	com**amos**	sub**amos**
vosotros/as	habl**éis**	com**áis**	sub**áis**
ustedes, ellos/as	habl**en**	com**an**	sub**an**

No es bueno que **hables** cuando comes. *It's not nice to talk with your mouth full (when you're eating).*

Quiero un perrito que no **coma** mucho. *I want a little dog that doesn't eat much.*

¡Compre ya, antes de que **suban** los precios! *Buy now, before the prices go up!*

Present indicative verbs
with spelling changes:
17.D.2 and 17.D.3
Verbs with diphthongs or vowel
shifts: 17.D.4 and 17.D.5

22.B.2 Verbs with a spelling change

Verbs with a spelling change in the first-person singular in the present indicative also have spelling changes in the present subjunctive in order to keep the sound pattern. The verb endings are regular.

a. **-ger, -gir, -guir, -uir** verbs with spelling changes in the present subjunctive:

Ending	Spelling change	Example	First-person singular: *yo* Present indicative	First-person singular: *yo* Present subjunctive
-ger	**g → j**	esco**g**er	esco**j**o	esco**j**a
-gir	**g → j**	ele**g**ir	eli**j**o	eli**j**a
-guir	**gu → g** / **e → i**	extin**gu**ir / se**gu**ir	extin**g**o / si**g**o	extin**g**a / si**g**a
-uir	**ui → y**	constr**ui**r	constru**y**o	constru**y**a

Queremos que **se elija** a un nuevo alcalde.	*We want a new mayor to be elected.*
Los bomberos necesitan equipos que **extingan** mejor los incendios.	*The firemen need equipment that can extinguish fires better.*
Necesitamos fondos para que **se construyan** parques.	*We need funds to build parks.*

b. **-car, -gar, -guar, -zar** verbs with spelling changes in the present subjunctive

The following verbs do not have spelling changes in the present indicative, but do have spelling changes in the present subjunctive, in order to maintain the verb's pronunciation when it is conjugated. The verb endings are regular. Note that several of these verbs also have a diphthong.

Verbs with a spelling change:
Verb conjugation tables,
pp. 257–276. See verb
patterns 10, 18, 42, 71.

Ending	Spelling change	Infinitive	First-person singular: *yo* Present indicative	First-person singular: *yo* Present subjunctive
-car	**c → qu**	to**c**ar	to**c**o	to**qu**e
-gar	**g → gu**	lle**g**ar	lle**g**o	lle**gu**e
-guar	**gu → gü**	averi**gu**ar	averi**gu**o	averi**gü**e
-zar	**z → c**	alcan**z**ar	alcan**z**o	alcan**c**e

More examples of **-car, -gar, -guar, -zar** verbs with spelling changes:

-car		-gar	
bus**c**ar	*to look (for)*	agre**g**ar	*to add*
macha**c**ar	*to crush*	entre**g**ar	*to deliver/turn in*
pi**c**ar	*to bite/sting*	ju**g**ar (**u → ue**)	*to play*
ron**c**ar	*to snore*	ne**g**ar (**e → ie**)	*to deny/refuse*
sa**c**ar	*to take (out)*	pa**g**ar	*to pay (for)*
salpi**c**ar	*to splash*	ro**g**ar (**o → ue**)	*to beg/pray*
-guar		-zar	
apaci**gu**ar	*to appease*	abra**z**ar	*to hug*
desa**gu**ar	*to drain*	almor**z**ar (**o → ue**)	*to have lunch*
men**gu**ar	*to fade/wane*	empe**z**ar (**e → ie**)	*to start/begin*
		endere**z**ar	*to straighten*
		re**z**ar	*to pray*

Pídele al pianista que **toque** nuestra canción.

Quiero viajar en un tren que **llegue**
al centro de París.

Te ayudaré para que **alcances** tus metas.

Ask the pianist to play our song.

I want to take a train that arrives in
downtown Paris.

I will help you so that you reach your goals.

22.B.3 Verbs with accents

Verbs that end in **-iar** and **-uar** take an accent in the present subjunctive just as in the
present indicative.

Present indicative:
Verb conjugation tables, pp.
257–276. For i:í, see verb
patterns 29, 34, 53; for u:ú, see
verb patterns 37, 57, 59.

Ending	Spelling change	Example	First-person singular: *yo*	
			Present indicative	Present subjunctive
-iar	i → í	env**iar**	env**ío**	env**íe**
-uar	u → ú	contin**uar**	contin**úo**	contin**úe**

Other *-iar* and *-uar* verbs			
acent**uar**	to emphasize	evac**uar**	to evacuate
ampl**iar**	to enlarge/extend	eval**uar**	to evaluate
ans**iar**	to long/yearn for	grad**uar**se	to graduate
conf**iar**	to trust	gu**iar**	to guide
deval**uar**	to devalue/depreciate	insin**uar**	to insinuate
efect**uar**	to carry out / execute	perpet**uar**	to perpetuate
enfr**iar**	to cool down / chill	sit**uar**	to situate/locate

Es necesario que **envíes** tu solicitud a tiempo.

Queremos invertir en monedas que no **se devalúen**.

Cuando **te gradúes**, tendrás mejor sueldo.

It's necessary that you send in your application on time.

We want to invest in currencies that won't depreciate.

When you graduate, you'll get a better salary.

22.B.4 Verbs with consonant changes

When the first-person singular is irregular in the present indicative, the present subjunctive is
also irregular. The endings are regular.

a. **-cer** and **-cir** verbs:

Ending	Spelling change	Example	First-person singular: *yo*	
			Present indicative	Present subjunctive
-cer	c → zc	cono**cer**	cono**zco**	cono**zca**
-cir	c → zc	condu**cir**	condu**zco**	condu**zca**

Verb conjugation tables,
pp. 257–276. For c:z, see verb
patterns 32, 72, 75; for c-zc,
see verb patterns 14, 15, 43

Necesito que **se traduzca** la carta.

No hay nadie que **conduzca** bien.

Ven a la fiesta para que **conozcas** a mis amigos.

I need the letter translated.

There's no one who drives well.

Come to the party so you can meet my friends.

b. Verbs with **-g** in the verb stem:

Irregular verbs are found alphabetically in the verb conjugation tables, pp. 257–276. Irregular verbs in the present indicative: 17.D.6

Infinitive		First-person singular: *yo*	
		Present indicative	**Present subjunctive**
decir (**e → i**)	*to say/tell*	**dig**o	**dig**a
ca**e**r (**a → ai**)	*to fall*	**caig**o	**caig**a
hacer	*to do/make*	**hag**o	**hag**a
oír	*to hear*	**oig**o	**oig**a
poner	*to put/place*	**pong**o	**pong**a
salir	*to go out*	**salg**o	**salg**a
tra**e**r (**a → ai**)	*to bring*	**traig**o	**traig**a
tener	*to have*	**teng**o	**teng**a
valer	*to be worth*	**valg**o	**valg**a
venir	*to come*	**veng**o	**veng**a

¡Espero que **haga** un poco de sol hoy!	*I hope there's some sunshine today!*
Compraremos un auto que no **valga** mucho.	*We will buy a car that doesn't cost much.*
Venid a visitarme cuando **tengáis** tiempo.	*Come and visit me when you [pl.] have time.*

22.B.5 *-ar* **and** *-er* **verbs with diphthongs** *e → ie* **and** *o → ue*

All **-ar** and **-er** verbs that have diphthongs or vowel shifts in the present indicative also have them in the present subjunctive. As with the present indicative, the change occurs in all persons except **nosotros/as,** and **vosotros/as.** The endings stay the same.

a. Conjugation of **-ar** and **-er** verbs with diphthong **e → ie**:

	pensar *to think*	**querer** *to want/love*
yo	p**ie**nse	qu**ie**ra
tú/vos	p**ie**nses	qu**ie**ras
usted, él, ella	p**ie**nse	qu**ie**ra
nosotros/as	pensemos	queramos
vosotros/as	penséis	queráis
ustedes, ellos/as	p**ie**nsen	qu**ie**ran

Verb conjugation tables, pp. 257–276. See verb patterns 24, 27, 28, 45, 49, 56, 65.

Other verbs with diphthong *e → ie*			
-ar **verbs**		*-er* **verbs**	
atrav**e**sar	*to cross/go through*	asc**e**nder	*to ascend/rise*
cal**e**ntar	*to warm up / heat*	at**e**nder	*to pay attention*
c**e**rrar	*to close*	def**e**nder	*to defend*
com**e**nzar (**z → c**)	*to start*	desc**e**nder	*to descend/drop*
conf**e**sar	*to confess*	enc**e**nder	*to light / switch on*
desp**e**rtar	*to wake up*	ent**e**nder	*to understand*
emp**e**zar (**z → c**)	*to start*	ext**e**nder	*to extend/spread*
gob**e**rnar	*to govern*	p**e**rder	*to lose/miss*
n**e**gar	*to deny/refuse*	trasc**e**nder	*to become known*
recom**e**ndar	*to recommend*	v**e**rter	*to pour/spill*

¡Esperamos que nos **entendáis**!

Voy a conseguir un reloj que **me despierte** con música.

Enciende la chimenea para que **nos calentemos** un poco.

We hope you [pl.] understand us!

I want to get myself a clock that will wake me up with music.

Light the fire so we can warm up a bit.

b. Conjugation of **-ar** and **-er** verbs with diphthong **o → ue**:

	contar *to relate/count*	**volver** *to return*
yo	cuente	vuelva
tú/vos	cuentes	vuelvas
usted, él, ella	cuente	vuelva
nosotros/as	contemos	volvamos
vosotros/as	contéis	volváis
ustedes, ellos/as	cuenten	vuelvan

Other verbs with diphthong *o → ue*			
-ar verbs		**-er verbs**	
almorzar (**z → c**)	*to have lunch*	devolver	*to give back*
costar	*to cost / be difficult*	llover	*to rain*
encontrar	*to find*	mover	*to move*
mostrar	*to indicate/show*	poder	*to be able to*
probar	*to try/taste*	promover	*to promote*
recordar	*to remember*	remover	*to remove/stir*
soñar	*to dream*	resolver	*to resolve*
volar	*to fly*	soler	*to usually do*

Verb conjugation tables, pp. 257–276. See verb patterns 6, 9, 16, 44, 50, 61, 67, 72.

Es necesario que **recuerdes** tu contraseña.

Haré lo que **pueda** para ayudarte.

Debes tener una buena educación aunque te **cueste** mucho.

You need to remember your password.

I'll do what I can to help you.

You should have a good education even if it's hard work / difficult for you.

c. The verb **oler** (*to smell*) is a unique **o → ue** verb:

huela, huelas, huela, olamos, oláis, huelan

Me gusta que la casa **huela** a flores.

I like the house to smell of flowers.

Verb conjugation tables, pp. 257–276. See verb pattern 47.

22.B.6 **-ir verbs with both diphthong and vowel shift**

All **-ir** verbs with a diphthong in the present indicative also have one in the present subjunctive. In addition, these **-ir** verbs also have a vowel shift in the **nosotros/as** and **vosotros/as** forms.

	e → ie and **e → i** **preferir** *to prefer*	**o → ue** and **o → u** **dormir** *to sleep*
yo	prefiera	duerma
tú/vos	prefieras	duermas
usted, él, ella	prefiera	duerma
nosotros/as	prefiramos	durmamos
vosotros/as	prefiráis	durmáis
ustedes, ellos/as	prefieran	duerman

Verb conjugation tables, pp. 257–276. See verb patterns 25, 65.

Other -ir verbs with diphthong and vowel shifts			
e → ie **and** e → i		o → ue **and** o → u	
divertirse	*to have fun*	morir	*to die*
herir	*to hurt*		
mentir	*to lie*		
sentir	*to feel*		

Me alegra que **te sientas** mejor.   *I'm glad you feel better.*
Prepara el plato que **prefieras**.   *Prepare whichever dish you prefer.*
Acuesta al niño para que **duerma**.   *Put the boy to bed so that he'll sleep.*

22.B.7 The verbs *adquirir* and *jugar*

The verb **adquirir** has the diphthong **i → ie**, but does not have a vowel shift like other irregular **-ir** verbs. The verb **jugar** is an **-ar** verb with a **u → ue** diphthong and the spelling change **g → gu** in the stem.

Verb conjugation tables, pp. 257–276. See verb patterns 4, 41.

	i → ie **adquirir** *to acquire*	u → ue **jugar** *to play*
yo	adqu**ie**ra	j**ue**g**u**e
tú/vos	adqu**ie**ras	j**ue**g**u**es
usted, él, ella	adqu**ie**ra	j**ue**g**u**e
nosotros/as	adquiramos	ju**gu**emos
vosotros/as	adquiráis	ju**gu**éis
ustedes, ellos/as	adqu**ie**ran	j**ue**g**u**en

Es fantástico que mi equipo **juegue** hoy.   *It's fantastic that my team plays/is playing today.*
Apoyaremos al equipo que mejor **juegue**.   *We're going to support the team that plays the best.*
Necesitamos capital para que el equipo **adquiera** más jugadores.   *We need capital so the team acquires/gets more players.*

22.B.8 Completely irregular verbs in the present subjunctive

Diacritical marks: 1.E.6b

The following verbs are irregular in the present subjunctive. Note that **dé** has an accent in order to distinguish the subjunctive form from the preposition **de**.

Verb conjugation tables, pp. 257–276. See verb patterns 19, 33, 38.

	dar *to give*	**estar** *to be*	**haber** *(auxiliary verb)*
yo	**dé**	**esté**	**haya**
tú/vos	**des**	**estés**	**hayas**
usted, él, ella	**dé**	**esté**	**haya**
nosotros/as	**demos**	**estemos**	**hayamos**
vosotros/as	**deis**	**estéis**	**hayáis**
ustedes, ellos/as	**den**	**estén**	**hayan**

	ir *to go*	**saber** *to know*	**ser** *to be*
yo	vaya	sepa	sea
tú/vos	vayas	sepas	seas
usted, él, ella	vaya	sepa	sea
nosotros/as	vayamos	sepamos	seamos
vosotros/as	vayáis	sepáis	seáis
ustedes, ellos/as	vayan	sepan	sean

Verb conjugation tables, pp. 257–276. See verb patterns 40, 62, 66.

Es estupendo que **seas** profesor.

Buscamos a un profesor que **sepa** hablar español.

Puedes empezar en cuanto **estés** listo.

It's great that you're a teacher.

We're looking for a teacher who knows how to speak Spanish.

You can begin as soon as you're ready.

22.C The imperfect subjunctive

Pretérito imperfecto de subjuntivo

22.C.1 Regular verbs

The following endings are added to the verb stem to form the imperfect subjunctive. The **-ra** and **-se** endings are equal in meaning, but the **-ra** ending is more common, especially in Latin America. Note that **nosotros/as** is the only conjugated form which has a written accent and that **-er** and **-ir** verbs have the same endings.

Regular verbs: Verb conjugation tables, p. 261

	hablar *to talk*	**comer** *to eat*	**subir** *to go up*
yo	hablara / hablase	comiera / comiese	subiera / subiese
tú/vos	hablaras / hablases	comieras / comieses	subieras / subieses
usted, él, ella	hablara / hablase	comiera / comiese	subiera / subiese
nosotros/as	habláramos / hablásemos	comiéramos / comiésemos	subiéramos / subiésemos
vosotros/as	hablarais / hablaseis	comierais / comieseis	subierais / subieseis
ustedes, ellos/as	hablaran / hablasen	comieran / comiesen	subieran / subiesen

Me extrañó que nadie **hablara/hablase** español en la clase.

Quería viajar en un teleférico que me **llevara/llevase** hasta la cima de la montaña.

Vimos el menú y salimos de la cafetería sin que nadie **comiera/comiese** nada.

It was strange that nobody spoke Spanish in the class.

I wanted to ride in a cable car that could take me up to the top of the mountain.

We looked at the menu and then left the cafe without eating anything.

22.C.2 Irregular verbs

Many verbs are irregular in the imperfect subjunctive. Irregularities are primarily vowel shifts and consonant changes in the stem. The endings, however, follow a regular pattern. Note that all irregular verbs in the third-person plural of the preterite will also be irregular in the imperfect subjunctive. The most important irregularities are listed in this section.

Irregular verbs in the preterite: 18.B.3 and 18.B.4

a. Verbs with vowel shifts **e → i** and **o → u**:

	e → i **pedir** *to ask for*	o → u **dormir** *to sleep*
yo	p**i**diera/p**i**diese	d**u**rmiera/d**u**rmiese
tú/vos	p**i**dieras/p**i**dieses	d**u**rmieras/d**u**rmieses
usted, él, ella	p**i**diera/p**i**diese	d**u**rmiera/d**u**rmiese
nosotros/as	p**i**diéramos/p**i**diésemos	d**u**rmiéramos/d**u**rmiésemos
vosotros/as	p**i**dierais/p**i**dieseis	d**u**rmierais/d**u**rmieseis
ustedes, ellos/as	p**i**dieran/p**i**diesen	d**u**rmieran/d**u**rmiesen

Verb conjugation tables,
pp. 257–276. See verb
patterns 25, 48, 58, 65.

Other *-ir* **verbs with vowel shifts**		
o → u	m**o**rir	*to die*
e → i	di**v**ertirse	*to have fun*
	h**e**rir	*to hurt*
	m**e**ntir	*to lie*
	r**e**ír	*to laugh*
	s**e**ntir	*to feel*

¡Fue un éxito que la gente **se riera/riese** tanto!

¡Necesitábamos un espectáculo que **nos divirtiera/divirtiese** de verdad!

Todo estaba planeado para que **nos sintiéramos/sintiésemos** bien.

It was a success to see people laughing so much!

We needed a show that truly entertained us!

Everything was planned in such a way as to make us feel good.

b. Verbs with irregular **u**-stem:

Verb conjugation tables,
pp. 257–276. See verb
patterns 7, 12, 33, 38, 50,
51, 62, 69.

Infinitive	Stem
andar	**anduv-**
caber	**cup-**
estar	**estuv-**
haber	**hub-**
poder	**pud-**
poner	**pus-**
saber	**sup-**
tener	**tuv-**

Endings	
yo	**anduv**iera/**anduv**iese
tú/vos	**anduv**ieras/**anduv**ieses
usted, él, ella	**anduv**iera/**anduv**iese
nosotros/as	**anduv**iéramos/**anduv**iésemos
vosotros/as	**anduv**ierais/**anduv**ieseis
ustedes, ellos/as	**anduv**ieran/**anduv**iesen

¡Me gustaría que **tuviéramos/tuviésemos** más dinero!

Necesitábamos un auto que **estuviera/estuviese** en perfecto estado.

Compré un auto grande para que **cupiera/cupiese** toda la familia.

I wish we had more money!

We needed a car in perfect condition.

I bought a big car so the whole family would fit.

The subjunctive • **Chapter 22**

c. Verbs with irregular **i**-stem:

Infinitive	Stem
dar	**di-**
hacer	**hic-**
querer	**quis-**
venir	**vin-**

Endings	
yo	**hic**iera/**hic**iese
tú/vos	**hic**ieras/**hic**ieses
usted, él, ella	**hic**iera/**hic**iese
nosotros/as	**hic**iéramos/**hic**iésemos
vosotros/as	**hic**ierais/**hic**ieseis
ustedes, ellos/as	**hic**ieran/**hic**iesen

Verb conjugation tables, pp. 257–276. See verb patterns 19, 39, 56, 76.

Fue muy molesto que no **vinieras/ vinieses** a la reunión.	It was very annoying that you didn't come to the meeting.
No había nada que yo **quisiera/quisiese**.	There was nothing that I wanted.
Te llamé para que me **dieras/dieses** una explicación.	I called you to get an explanation.

d. Verbs with irregular **y**-stem: **-caer, -eer, -uir, oír**

Infinitive	Stem
caer	**cay-**
leer	**ley-**
concluir	**concluy-**
oír	**oy-**

Endings	
yo	**cay**era/**cay**ese
tú/vos	**cay**eras/**cay**eses
usted, él, ella	**cay**era/**cay**ese
nosotros/as	**cay**éramos/**cay**ésemos
vosotros/as	**cay**erais/**cay**eseis
ustedes, ellos/as	**cay**eran/**cay**esen

Verb conjugation tables, pp. 257–276. See verb patterns 13, 17, 23, 46.

Other verbs with the same spelling changes			
Other verbs like *caer*			
decaer	to decay	recaer	to have a relapse
Other verbs like *leer*			
creer	to believe/think	proveer	to serve/provide
poseer	to have/own	releer	to read again
Other verbs like *concluir*			
constituir	to constitute	construir	to build/construct
contribuir	to contribute	incluir	to include
destituir	to dismiss	influir	to influence
destruir	to destroy	intuir	to sense
disminuir	to diminish	recluir	to imprison
distribuir	to distribute	reconstruir	to reconstruct
huir	to escape/flee	sustituir	to substitute/replace

Fue importante que **reconstruyeran/ reconstruyesen** la ciudad antigua.	It was important to rebuild the ancient part of the city.
No había nada que **disminuyera/ disminuyese** la importancia del proyecto.	There was nothing that would/could diminish the project's significance.
Trabajamos mucho para que el proyecto **concluyera/concluyese** con éxito.	We worked a lot so that the project would be successful.

e. Verbs with irregular **j**-stem:

Verb conjugation tables, pp. 257–276. See verb patterns 14, 20, 73.

Infinitive	Stem
de**c**ir (**e → i**)	di**j**-
traer	tra**j**-
conducir	condu**j**-
introducir	introdu**j**-
producir	produ**j**-
reducir	redu**j**-
traducir	tradu**j**-

Endings	
yo	di**j**era/di**j**ese
tú/vos	di**j**eras/di**j**eses
usted, él, ella	di**j**era/di**j**ese
nosotros/as	di**j**éramos/di**j**ésemos
vosotros/as	di**j**erais/di**j**eseis
ustedes, ellos/as	di**j**eran/di**j**esen

Fue un milagro que no **se produjera/produjese** un accidente.

It was amazing that there wasn't an accident.

No había nadie que **condujera/condujese** bien.

There was nobody who could drive well.

No te creería aunque **dijeras/dijeses** la verdad.

I wouldn't believe you even if you were telling the truth.

f. The imperfect subjunctive of **ir** and **ser**:

Verb conjugation tables, pp. 257–276. See verb patterns 40, 66.

yo	**fuera/fuese**
tú/vos	**fueras/fueses**
usted, él, ella	**fuera/fuese**
nosotros/as	**fuéramos/fuésemos**
vosotros/as	**fuerais/fueseis**
ustedes, ellos/as	**fueran/fuesen**

El director nos pidió que **fuéramos/fuésemos** a la reunión de padres de familia.

The principal asked us to go to the parents' meeting.

Yo quería comprar un auto que **fuera/fuese** seguro y confiable.

I wanted to buy a car that was safe and reliable.

Quería llamarte antes de que **fuera/fuese** demasiado tarde.

I wanted to call you before it was too late.

22.D The present perfect subjunctive

Pretérito perfecto de subjuntivo

The present perfect subjunctive is formed with the present subjunctive of the auxiliary verb **haber** and the past participle of the main verb.

Regular and irregular past participles: 19.A.1 and 19.A.2

Present subjunctive of *haber*		+	Past participle		
			-*ar* **verbs:** -*ado*	-*er* **and** -*ir* **verbs:** -*ido*	
			hablar	querer	venir
yo	**haya**	+	hablado	querido	venido
tú/vos	**hayas**				
usted, él, ella	**haya**				
nosotros/as	**hayamos**				
vosotros/as	**hayáis**				
ustedes, ellos/as	**hayan**				

The subjunctive • **Chapter 22**

Espero que **hayas tenido** un buen viaje.	I hope you have had a good trip.
En mi escuela no hay nadie que **haya reprobado** el examen.	In my school, there is nobody that has failed the exam.
Trabajarás mejor cuando **hayas instalado** una buena conexión a Internet.	You will be able to work better when you have installed a good Internet connection.

22.E The past perfect subjunctive

Pretérito pluscuamperfecto de subjuntivo

The past perfect subjunctive is formed with the imperfect subjunctive of the auxiliary verb **haber** (**hubiera/hubiese**) and the past participle of the main verb.

◄ Regular and irregular past participles: 19.A.1 and 19.A.2

Past perfect subjunctive *haber*		+	Past participle		
			-*ar* **verbs:** -*ado*	-*er* **and** -*ir* **verbs:** -*ido*	
			hablar	**querer**	**venir**
yo	**hub**iera/**hub**iese	+	hablado	querido	venido
tú/vos	**hub**ieras/**hub**ieses				
usted, él, ella	**hub**iera/**hub**iese				
nosotros/as	**hub**iéramos/**hub**iésemos				
vosotros/as	**hub**ierais/**hub**ieseis				
ustedes, ellos/as	**hub**ieran/**hub**iesen				

No pensé que **hubieras/hubieses tenido** un buen viaje.	I didn't think you had had a good trip.
No hubo nadie que **hubiera/hubiese reprobado** el examen.	There was nobody who had failed the exam.
Trabajarías mejor si **hubieras/hubieses instalado** una buena conexión a Internet.	You would work better if you had installed a good Internet connection.

22.F The future simple subjunctive

Futuro de subjuntivo

The future simple subjunctive is no longer used in modern Spanish. It is generally only found in legal texts, laws, and regulations.

a. The future simple subjunctive is formed with the same verb stem as the imperfect subjunctive with the following endings:

◄ Imperfect subjunctive: 22.C

	hablar *to talk*	**comer** *to eat*	**subir** *to go up, to climb*
yo	hablar**e**	comier**e**	subier**e**
tú/vos	hablar**es**	comier**es**	subier**es**
usted, él, ella	hablar**e**	comier**e**	subier**e**
nosotros/as	hablár**emos**	comiér**emos**	subiér**emos**
vosotros/as	hablar**eis**	comier**eis**	subier**eis**
ustedes, ellos/as	hablar**en**	comier**en**	subier**en**

b. Irregular verbs have the same irregularities in the verb stems as the imperfect subjunctive. The endings are the same as they are for regular verbs: **fuere, tuviere, hubiere, hiciere**, etc.

c. In everyday speech, the simple future subjunctive only occurs in proverbs or idiomatic expressions, and in formal speeches of a legal nature.

Habrá multa cualquiera que **fuere** el exceso de velocidad.	*There will be a fine whatever the speed limit violation may be.*
Adonde **fueres,** haz lo que **vieres**.	*When in Rome, do as the Romans do.*
Sea quien **fuere** el embajador, la situación no cambiará.	*Whoever the ambassador is, the situation will not change.*

22.G The future perfect subjunctive

Futuro perfecto de subjuntivo

The future perfect subjunctive is formed with the simple future subjunctive of **haber** and the past participle of the verb: **hubiere hablado**, **hubieres hablado**, etc. This verb tense is used in legal texts, but is not common.

Se aceptarán las solicitudes siempre y cuando **hubieren llegado** antes de expirar el plazo.	*Applications will be accepted as long as they have arrived before the deadline.*

22.H Regional variations

Variaciones regionales

Voseo: 22.B.b

The use of **voseo** forms in the present subjunctive varies regionally. Below are the three main forms:

	1. Voseo (using **tú** form)	2. Voseo (most **voseo** countries)	3. Voseo (Chile)
amar	**ames**	**amés**	**amí(s)**
comer	**comas**	**comás**	**comái(s)**
recibir	**recibas**	**recibás**	**recibái(s)**

Imperative for **vos**: 24.D.1b

Option 2 is common in most **voseo** countries, especially in Central America and the Andean **voseo** countries. In Argentina, it coexists with option 1, while option 2 is the most common for informal negative imperatives (which use the present subjunctive form): **no vayás; no digás**. Option 3 is used primarily in Chile.

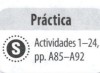

Práctica

(S) Actividades 1–24, pp. A85–A92

Use of the subjunctive
Uso del subjuntivo

23.A Overview

Aspectos generales

The use of the subjunctive in Spanish follows a fairly regular pattern, depending on the type of clause in which it occurs.

23.A.1 Independent clauses

The use of the subjunctive in independent clauses is very limited and occurs mainly in clauses with adverbs of doubt and possibility (where the indicative is also possible) or in exclamations.

23.A.2 Subordinate clauses

The subjunctive occurs primarily in subordinate clauses governed by a main clause. An understanding of the basic structure of subordinate clauses in Spanish is important for using the subjunctive correctly.

There are three main types of subordinate clauses in which the subjunctive is used:

a. *nominal*, or noun, clauses

b. relative, or *adjectival*, clauses

c. *adverbial* clauses

Since the subjunctive is rarely used in English, the translations of examples in this chapter are written to show the nuances of the subjunctive meaning in Spanish.

23.B The subjunctive in independent clauses

El subjuntivo en oraciones independientes

23.B.1 Probability, doubt

In independent clauses with adverbs or other expressions of doubt or possibility such as **quizás, tal vez, posiblemente**, and **probablemente**, both the indicative and the subjunctive can be used. The verb mood used expresses the degree of probability of the outcome. The indicative expresses a higher probability than the subjunctive.

◄ Expressions of doubt with the subjunctive in **que** clauses: 23.C.6
Tal vez/quizás: 10.F.1d

◄ **A lo mejor** (*maybe, perhaps*) is a very common expression for possibility in everyday language.

Subjunctive	Indicative
Posiblemente llegue tarde a casa hoy. *I might arrive/get home late today.*	**Posiblemente** llego tarde a casa hoy. *I'll probably be home late today.*
Quizás fuera gripe lo que tenías. *Maybe you had the flu.*	**Quizás era** gripe lo que tenías. *You probably had the flu.*

23.B.2 Exclamations

a. The subjunctive is *always* used in simple wish clauses in the form of exclamations, usually with **vivir**. In English, this is mostly expressed with *hurrah/hooray, come on,* or *long live!*

¡**Viva** el Barcelona!   *Come on, Barcelona!*

¡**Vivan** los nuevos estudiantes!   *Hooray for the new students!*

¡**Viva** España!   *Long live Spain! / Hooray for Spain!*

Such simple exclamations are accompanied by **que** when expressing wishes or requests. These exclamations can be interpreted as containing an implicit verb of wish or desire (**querer, desear, esperar**) that governs what is said.

¡Que se besen los novios!	*The bride and groom may now kiss!*
¡Que llegue pronto mi amigo!	*I hope my friend arrives soon!*

These simple wish clauses are common in social contexts where expressions of good (or bad) wishes are given.

¡Que tengas un feliz viaje!	*Have a good trip!*
¡Que te vaya bien en el examen!	*Hope the exam goes well!*
¡Que os divirtáis mucho!	*Have a lot of fun!*
¡Que cumplas muchos años más!	*Many happy returns!*
¡Que te parta un rayo!	*Damn you!*

b. The exclamation word **ojalá** comes from the Arabic *in sha'a Allah* meaning *if Allah/God wills*. It is used in the same way as *God willing* in English and expresses a strong desire that something happen. **Ojalá** is used in nominal clauses and is *always* followed by a *subjunctive* tense.

Future	**¡Ojalá** (que) tengas un buen viaje!	*Hope you have a good trip!*
Past	**¡Ojalá** (que) hayas tenido un buen viaje!	*Hope you've had a good trip!*
Counter-factual	**¡Ojalá** (que) hubieras tenido un buen viaje!	*Wish you'd had a good trip!*

23.C The subjunctive in nominal clauses

El subjuntivo en cláusulas subordinadas sustantivas

That-clauses are also called *nominal clauses* because they act in the same way that nouns do and can be the *subject, direct object,* or *indirect object* of the sentence. Nominal clauses in Spanish start with the conjunction **que**, which can never be excluded like *that* can in English.

The verb in the main ▶ clause is the governing finite verb: **espero**.

Main clause	Subordinate clause
Espero	**que** estés bien.
I hope	*(that) you are well.*

The use of the subjunctive in Spanish nominal clauses is always dependent on the meaning of the main governing verb. This verb can fall into one of various verb groups, each with its own rules for the use of subjunctive. The following are the most important verb groups.

23.C.1 Verbs that express want, wish, influence, or necessity

a. The *subjunctive* is always used in nominal clauses when the main verb either directly or indirectly expresses *want, wish, influence,* or *necessity*. Direct expressions can come in the form of orders and decrees, requirements, permission, and prohibition. Indirect expressions include personal wishes, preferences, prayers, hopes, advice, suggestions, recommendations, and necessities. Examples of this type of verb are shown below.

aconsejar	*to advise*	permitir	*to permit/allow*
desear	*to desire*	preferir	*to prefer*
exigir	*to require*	prohibir	*to prohibit*
gustar	*to like*	proponer	*to propose*
impedir	*to impede*	querer	*to want*
insistir	*to insist*	recomendar	*to recommend*
mandar	*to order*	requerir	*to require / call for*

necesitar	to need	rogar	to pray/plead
oponerse	to oppose	solicitar	to request
ordenar	to order/arrange	sugerir	to propose/suggest
pedir	to ask (for)	suplicar	to beg/plead

Te aconsejo que no **fumes**.	I advise you not to smoke.
Le pido a usted que me **ayude**.	I'm asking you to help me.
Te sugiero que no **compres** algo caro.	I suggest you don't buy something expensive.
Recomendamos que **revises** tu correo.	We recommend that you check your mail.
Le solicito que me **envíe** el cheque.	I request that you send me the check.
Os ruego que me **prestéis** dinero.	I beg you [pl.] to lend me money.

b. The expression **hacer que** expresses influence and it should be followed by the subjunctive.

La nieve **hará que** el tráfico **se vuelva** imposible.	The snow will make traffic impossible.

c. The expression **el (hecho de) que** (*the fact that*) is used mostly with the *subjunctive*. This also applies to the abbreviation **que** (*that*). Note that **el que** in this context is not the same as the relative pronoun **el que** (*the one who/that*).

Relative pronouns: 15.A.2

El (hecho de) que suban los precios es bastante común.	(The fact) That prices go up is quite common.
Que todo **sea** tan caro es producto de la globalización.	That everything is so expensive is a result of globalization.
El que te gusten los medios sociales es muy positivo.	(The fact) That you like social media is very positive.

d. When **el hecho de que** is governed by a main verb that means *to know, to be/become clear,* or *to find out,* the indicative can be used.

Nos damos cuenta **del hecho de que / de que** la gente **está** descontenta.	We realize that people are unhappy.

e. The expression **es que** (*it's that*) describes a causal relationship. The *indicative* is used in affirmative clauses and the *subjunctive* in negative subordinate clauses. This expression is an abbreviation of **lo que ocurre/pasa/sucede es que** (*the thing is that*).

lo lógico es que: 23.C.10b

No **es que estemos** aburridos, **es que tenemos** que irnos ya.	It's not that we are bored, it's just that we have to go now.
No **es que** yo no **quiera** ayudarte, **es que** no **puedo**.	It's not that I don't want to help you, I just can't.

23.C.2 *Decir* and other reporting verbs

Indirect discourse: Ch. 31

The verb **decir** and a few others can convey information or express a wish or a request. With these verbs, the *subjunctive* is used when giving an order or when asking for something, and the *indicative* is used when conveying information. The following are examples of reporting verbs.

Direct discourse: 31.A.1
Reporting information and commands: 31.B.2

advertir	to warn	indicar	to indicate
decir	to say/tell	insistir	to insist

Subjunctive	Indicative
Isabel dice que **vengas** pronto.	Isabel dice que **vienes** pronto.
Isabel says that you must come soon.	*Isabel says that you are coming soon.*
La luz roja te indica que **te detengas**.	La luz roja indica que **debes** detenerte.
The red light tells you to stop.	*The red light indicates that you should stop.*
Mis amigos insisten en que **compre** un auto.	Mis amigos insisten en que **necesito** un auto.
My friends insist that I buy a car.	*My friends insist that I need a car.*

23.C.3 **Verbs that express emotions**

Verbs like **gustar**: 17.B.4 ▶

a. The subjunctive is always used in subordinate clauses when the verb in the main clause expresses an emotion or an emotional reaction to something. This happens primarily when a verb expressing emotion (like **gustar**) is inflected with an indirect object pronoun. The subordinate clause describes what a person likes, or finds amazing, frustrating, etc.

Main clause	Subordinate clause
Me alegra	que **tengamos** tantos días libres.
I'm pleased/happy/delighted	*that we have so many free days.*

Other verbs in this group include:

aburrir	*to bore*	enfadar	*to anger*
agradar	*to please*	entristecer	*to sadden*
apenar	*to grieve/sadden*	entusiasmar	*to enthuse/delight*
alarmar	*to alarm*	extrañar	*to surprise*
alegrar	*to please*	fascinar	*to fascinate*
asustar	*to frighten/scare*	fastidiar	*to irritate*
complacer	*to satisfy/please*	frustrar	*to frustrate*
convenir	*to suit*	gustar	*to like*
desesperar	*to exasperate*	importar	*to matter / care about*
disgustar	*to disgust*	indignar	*to infuriate / to make indignant/angry*
divertir	*to amuse*	irritar	*to irritate*
doler	*to hurt/ache*	interesar	*to interest*
emocionar	*to excite*	molestar	*to annoy/bother*
encantar	*to enjoy/love*	sorprender	*to surprise*

Me alegra que nadie **fume** aquí.	*I'm glad that nobody smokes here.*
¿**Os molesta** que **abra** la ventana?	*Do you [pl.] mind if I open the window?*
Nos conviene que la reunión **sea** el martes.	*It's fine with / better for us that the meeting be on Tuesday.*
Me gusta que me **enseñes** a hablar español.	*I like that you teach me to speak Spanish.*

b. Several of the above-mentioned verbs (but not all) can also be used without a subjunctive clause.

Me alegro de/por tu éxito.	*I'm pleased about your success.*
Nos interesamos por el español.	*We're interested in Spanish.*
Nuestros clientes **nos importan**.	*Our clients are important to us.*

23.C.4 **The verb** *sentir* **and other sense verbs**

a. When **sentir** is used with the meaning *to be/feel sorry* in affirmative and negative main clauses, the subjunctive must be used in the subordinate clause. With the indicative, the meaning of **sentir** is *to have a feeling, to feel, to sense*.

Subjunctive	Indicative
Sentimos que no **puedas** asistir al seminario. *We're sorry that you can't attend the seminar.*	**Siento** que **vamos a tener** problemas. *I sense that we're going to have problems.*

b. When sense verbs like **oír, escuchar, ver, percibir, notar,** and **observar** are used in a negative main clause, the subjunctive is usually used in the subordinate clause. The indicative is rarely used in spoken language to state a real and unequivocal physical state in negative clauses.

Subjunctive	Indicative
No oímos que **se acerque** el autobús. *We can't hear that the bus is approaching/coming.*	**Oímos** que **se acerca** el autobús. *We can hear the bus approaching/coming.*
No veo que **haya** desorden en mi habitación. *I don't see that my room is a mess.*	**Veo** que **hay** desorden en mi habitación. *I see that my room is a mess.*

c. The verbs **temer** (*to fear, to be afraid of*) and **esperar** (*to hope, to expect*) are used with the *subjunctive* in negative and affirmative clauses.

La gente **teme** que **suban** los precios.   *People fear that prices will go up.*
No espero que siempre **tengas** tiempo para todo.   *I don't expect you to always have time for everything.*

d. The verb **temer** can also mean *to believe*. With this meaning, the *indicative* can occur with **temer** in affirmative clauses. The verb **esperar** can also express a thought rather than an intention or expectation. In this case, the *indicative* is used (except the present indicative, which cannot be used in this case).

Subjunctive	Indicative
La gente **teme** que **suban** los precios. *People are worried that prices will go up.*	La gente **teme** que **subirán** los precios. *People believe (fearfully) that prices will go up.*
Esperaba que **tuvierais** tiempo en diciembre. *I hoped you [pl.] would have time in December.*	**Esperaba** que **tendríais** tiempo en diciembre. *I imagined you [pl.] would have time in December.*

e. The expression **esperar a que** (*to wait for something to happen*) always requires the subjunctive in both affirmative and negative clauses.

Espero con alegría **a que llegue** el día de la boda.   *I am very much looking forward to the wedding day.*
No esperaré a que te calmes para darte la noticia.   *I won't wait for you to calm down to give you the news.*

23.C.5 Personal opinions, thoughts, and reviews

a. With verbs that express personal opinions, thoughts, and appraisals in negative main clauses, the *subjunctive* is used in the subordinate clause.

no admitir	to not admit	no parecer	to not seem/look like
no conceder	to not concede	no pensar	to not think
no creer	to not believe	no recordar	to not remember
no opinar	to not think/believe	no suponer	to not suppose

No pienso que la lección **sea** fácil.   *I don't think the lesson is easy.*
No sospecho que aquí **haya** nada raro.   *I don't suspect that there is anything strange here.*

b. When the main verb is affirmative, the *indicative* is used in the subordinate clause.

admitir	to admit	parecer	to seem/look like
conceder	to concede	pensar	to think
creer	to believe	recordar	to remember
opinar	to think/believe	suponer	to suppose

Pienso que la lección **es** fácil.　　　　　　　*I think that the lesson is easy.*

Sospecho que aquí **hay** algo raro.　　　　　*I suspect that there is something strange here.*

c. In positive questions, the above-mentioned verbs can be used in spoken language in the *indicative* to signal a desire to confirm or disprove an opinion.

¿Crees que **es** bueno vivir en una ciudad grande?　　*Do you think it's good to live in a big city?*

The adverb **sí/no** makes the use of the subjunctive more probable.

¿Tú sí/no crees que **sea** bueno vivir en una
ciudad tan grande?

*Do you really believe/Don't you believe that
it can be good to live in such a big city?*

d. *Parece*

When **parecer** is used to mean *it seems as if*, the *subjunctive* is used. However, with this expression, the present subjunctive cannot be used. The most common verb tenses used are the imperfect and past perfect subjunctive.

Parece que **estuviéramos** en Navidad.　　*It looks as if / seems like we were in the middle of Christmas.*

No parece que **estuviéramos**
en Navidad.

*It doesn't look as if / seem like we were in the middle
of Christmas.*

como si: 23.E.1e ▶ **Parece** como si **hubiera sido** ayer.　　*It seems as though it was yesterday.*

e. *Comprender, entender*

These two verbs convey a meaning of concession or agreement with something previously said when the subjunctive is used in an affirmative clause. However, with the indicative, they retain the meaning *to understand*. They are always used with the *subjunctive* in negative clauses.

Entiendo que **te sientas** mal, ¡tienes fiebre!　　*I understand that you feel bad; you have a fever!*

Comprendo que la primera respuesta **es** incorrecta.　　*I understand that the first answer is incorrect.*

No **comprendo** que **sea** un error.　　*I don't understand how this could be a mistake.*

23.C.6　Verbs of denial or doubt

a. Verbs that express denial and doubt take the *subjunctive* in both affirmative and negative subordinate clauses.

desconfiar de	to distrust	ignorar	to ignore
dudar	to doubt	negar	to deny

(No) dudo que **digas** la verdad.　　*I (don't) doubt that you're telling the truth.*

(No) niego que **hayamos cometido** un error.　　*I (don't) deny that we have made a mistake.*

La policía **(no) desconfía de** que el testigo
diga la verdad.

*The police (do not) doubt that the witness
is telling the truth.*

b. With statements of absolute certainty, however, **no dudar que** takes the indicative. Note this only applies to the negative form.

No dudo que les **dirás** la verdad.　　

*I don't doubt that you will tell them the truth
(and I am certain of that).*

No dudo en absoluto que siempre **pagas** tus cuentas.　　*I don't doubt at all that you always pay your bills.*

Impersonal expressions
with **ser**: 30.B.6 ▶ ### 23.C.7　Impersonal expressions of certainty

Expressions with **ser/estar** + *adjective/noun* and **haber** + *noun* that convey certainty require the *indicative* in affirmative clauses, and generally the *subjunctive* in negative clauses.

a. Ser (*third-person singular*) + *masculine adjective* + **que**

cierto	*certain*	evidente	*evident*	seguro	*sure*
claro	*clear/obvious*	obvio	*obvious*	verdad	*true*

Es seguro que **habrá** fiesta.   *It's certain that there will be a party.*

No era evidente que **fuera** a ganar el mejor candidato.   *It was not obvious that the best candidate would win.*

b. Estar + *adjective* + **que**

convencido/a de	*convinced (of)*
seguro/a de	*sure (of)*

Estamos seguros de que **lloverá**.   *We're sure it's going to rain.*

¿No estás convencida de que tu decisión **es/sea** correcta?   *Aren't you convinced that your decision is the right one?*

c. Haber (*impersonal conjugation*) + *noun* + **de** + **que**

hay certeza de	*it is certain that*	hay evidencia de	*there is evidence that*
no hay (duda de)	*there's no doubt that*	hay seguridad de	*there's assurance/a guarantee that*

Hay certeza de que el tratamiento **es** bueno.   *It's certain that the treatment is good.*

No hay evidencia de que la medicina **es/sea** efectiva.   *There is no evidence that the medicine is effective.*

23.C.8   Impersonal expressions of wishes, preferences, advice, necessity, decisions, and emotions

Estar with a perfect adjective: 30.C.2

Impersonal expressions with **ser**: 13.G.3, 21.B.5

After impersonal expressions with **ser, estar**, and other verbs that convey wishes, preferences, advice, necessity, decisions, and emotions, the *subjunctive* is used. This applies both to affirmative and negative clauses. The list below shows some of the most common expressions that indicate the use of the *subjunctive* in the subordinate clause.

a. Ser + *singular masculine adjective* + **que**: subjunctive

aconsejable	*advisable*	magnífico	*great, magnificent*
bueno	*good*	malo	*bad*
comprensible	*understandable*	necesario	*necessary*
conveniente	*convenient*	normal	*normal*
dudoso	*doubtful*	peligroso	*dangerous*
esencial	*essential*	probable	*probable/likely*
estupendo	*superb/great/marvelous*	recomendable	*advisable*
fabuloso	*fabulous*	ridículo	*ridiculous*
horroroso	*horrifying*	sospechoso	*suspicious/suspect*
importante	*important*	suficiente	*sufficient*
(in)admisible	*(in)admissible*	terrible	*terrible*
increíble	*incredible*	triste	*sad*
(in)justo	*(un)fair*	urgente	*urgent*
(i)lógico	*(il)logical*	(in)útil	*useful (useless)*

Fue magnífico que nos **dieran** una habitación con vista al mar.   *It was great/magnificent that they gave us a room with a view of the sea.*

Es probable que **haga** buen tiempo mañana.   *It's likely that it'll be nice out tomorrow.*

No es justo que **tengáis** que trabajar doce horas diarias.   *It's not fair that you [pl.] have to work twelve hours a day.*

b. Ser + **mejor/peor /mucho menos/más,** etc. + **que**: subjunctive

mejor	better	peor	worse

Es mejor que **regreses** en avión. It's better/best that you take a flight back.
Fue peor que **mintieras**. It was worse that you lied.
Sería más cómodo que **viajáramos** en tren. It would be more comfortable if we traveled by train.

c. Ser + **un(a)** + *noun* + **que**: subjunctive

error	error/mistake	lástima	pity/shame
fastidio	nuisance	lata	pest/pain
horror	horror	locura	madness
peligro	danger	milagro	miracle
robo	robbery	suerte	luck
costumbre	custom	tontería	silliness/nonsense
delicia	delight/joy	vergüenza	shame/embarrassment

Es una delicia que **nos atiendan** como a reyes. It's a delight to be treated as kings.
¡Fue un milagro que **llamaras**! It was a miracle that you called!
Antes **no era una costumbre** que los hombres **cuidaran** a los niños. In the past, it wasn't customary for men to take care of the children.

d. Estar + *adverb/participle* + **que**: subjunctive

bien	good/fine	permitido	permitted/allowed
decidido	decided	prohibido	prohibited
mal	bad	resuelto	resolved

Está bien que **pagues** con tarjeta. It's fine to pay with a credit card.
Está prohibido que **bebamos** aquí. It's prohibited to drink here.

e. Estar + *adjective* + *preposition* + **que**: subjunctive

Infinitive or subjunctive: 25.B.5 ▶

Verb periphrases with the past participle: 26.E ▶

acostumbrado/a a	accustomed/used to	encantado/a de	glad/delighted to
asustado/a de	afraid of	harto/a de	fed up with / sick of
cansado/a de	tired of	ilusionado/a con	hopeful for
contento/a de	happy/satisfied/content with	orgulloso/a de	proud of
deseoso/a de	longing for/eager to	preocupado/a por	worried about
dispuesto/a a	willing to	satisfecho/a de	satisfied by/with

Estamos hartos de que los vecinos **pongan** la música a todo volumen. We are fed up with the neighbors playing music so loudly.
Estoy satisfecha de que todo **haya salido** bien. I'm satisfied that everything has gone well.

f. Other verbs and expressions that take the subjunctive:

basta con que	it's enough / sufficient that/just	más vale que	it had better/it's better that
da igual que	it doesn't matter / it's the same as	puede (ser) que	it might/could be
da lo mismo que	it makes no difference	vale la pena que	it's worth

Basta con que envíes la solicitud. Just send the request.
Más vale que compréis los boletos de avión con tiempo. You [pl.] had better buy your plane tickets in advance.

23.C.9 Verbs of want: same/different subject

a. When the subject in the main clause and subordinate clause is the same person, the subordinate clause is replaced with the infinitive.

Queremos que **prepares** la cena.	*We want you to prepare dinner.*
Queremos preparar la cena.	*We want to prepare dinner.*
Siento mucho que no **hayas aprobado** el examen.	*I'm so sorry you didn't pass your exam.*
Siento mucho no **haber aprobado** el examen.	*I'm so sorry not to have passed my exam.*

b. In some cases, the subordinate clause can be replaced with the infinitive even when the subjects are different. This happens when an object pronoun in the main clause refers to the same person in the subordinate clause.

La huelga **les impidió** que **viajaran**.	*The strike prevented them from traveling.*
La huelga **les impidió viajar**.	
Te aconsejo que **hagas** más ejercicio.	*I advise you to exercise more.*
Te aconsejo **hacer** más ejercicio.	
Juan **me pidió** que lo **acompañara**.	*Juan asked me to go with him.*
Juan **me pidió acompañarlo**.	
La invité a que **participara** del concurso.	*I invited her to participate in the contest.*
La invité a **participar** del concurso.	

23.C.10 Impersonal expressions with *lo* + adjective/adverb and *lo que*

Lo is a neuter article that is used to form general expressions: **lo bueno** (*the good thing*), **lo mejor** (*the best thing*), **lo que quiero** (*what I want*).

◀ Abstract concepts with **lo:** 5.A.2
Relative pronouns: 15.A.2

a. The *indicative* is used with **lo** expressions that refer to real situations or past events.

Lo + **adjective**	**Indicative**
Lo cierto es *The fact is*	que **estudias** muchísimo. *that you study a lot.*
Lo mejor fue *The best thing was*	que **aprobaste** el examen. *that you passed your exam.*
Lo importante es *The important thing is*	que **eres** inteligente. *that you are intelligent.*

b. The *subjunctive* is used after a number of impersonal expressions that refer to norms, rules, personal reactions, and preferences about what is best, worst, normal, logical, etc.: **lo lógico es que** (*the logical thing [to do] is*), **lo normal es que** (*the normal thing [to do] is*), **lo corriente/común es que** (*the usual thing [to do] is*), and similar expressions. The subjunctive tenses vary based on the tense of **ser**.

Lo + **adjective**	**Subjunctive**
Lo lógico es *The logical thing (to do) is*	que te **llame** yo. *for me to call you.*
Lo más común era *The usual thing we did was*	que **fuéramos** a Torrevieja en verano. *to go to Torrevieja in the summer.*
Lo mejor fue *The best thing was*	que te **conociera**. *meeting you.*

c. In clauses with **lo que** + *verb in the indicative* + **ser**, the subjunctive is used when the verb expresses *a wish, a preference, an order,* or *a necessity*. The indicative is used when referring to something that happens habitually or is a known fact. In these cases, the statement is purely descriptive and there is no wish or necessity on the part of the speaker.

Lo que más me gusta es que nos **sirvas** tapas.	*What I like best is that you serve us tapas.*
Lo que más me gusta es que nunca **hace** frío en Medellín.	*What I like best is that it's never cold in Medellín.*

d. Other common expressions with **lo que** include:

Lo que menos espero es que…	*What I expect least is that…*
Lo único que te pido es que…	*The only thing I ask is that…*
Lo que más necesito es que…	*What I need most is that…*
Lo que no me conviene es que…	*What doesn't suit me is that…*

23.C.11 Tense sequencing

The choice of tense used in a subordinate clause depends on whether the action happened before, at the same time as, or after the action in the main clause.

a. When the *present* or *present perfect subjunctive* appears in the subordinate clause, the present, past, or future is referred to, depending on the tense of the main verb and the context. Some common examples follow.

Main clause		Subordinate clause	
Indicative		Subjunctive	
Present	Te **pido** *I ask you*	**Present**	que no **fumes**. *not to smoke.*
Simple future	Siempre te **pediré** *I will always ask you*		
Present perfect	Te **he pedido** *I have asked you*		
	Me **ha molestado** *It has annoyed me*	**Present perfect**	que **hayas fumado/ fumaras** tanto. *that you have smoked so much.*

b. When the main verb is not in the present, present perfect or future, the verb in the subordinate clause can be in the *imperfect subjunctive*. Choice of tense depends on the context. Some common examples follow.

Main clause		Subordinate clause
Indicative		Imperfect subjunctive
The preterite	Ayer te **pedí** *Yesterday, I asked you*	que no **fumaras**. *not to smoke.*
The imperfect	Antes te **pedía** *I used to ask you*	
Present conditional	Te **pediría** *I would like to ask you*	
Conditional perfect	Te **habría pedido** *I would have asked you*	

23.D The subjunctive in relative clauses

El subjuntivo en subordinadas relativas

Relative clauses (*adjectival clauses*) start with a relative pronoun: **(el, la, los, las) que, quien, (el, la) cual, (los, las) cuales, cuya(s)** or with a relative adverb **(cuando, donde, como, cuanto/todo lo que).** Relative clauses provide a description of the antecedent to which they refer.

Relative pronouns and adverbs: Ch. 15

Main clause (antecedent)	Relative clause (characteristic)
Compra **los libros**	**que necesites.**
Buy the books	*you need.*

In the example above, **los libros** is the antecedent for the relative clause **que necesites.**

The use of the *subjunctive* in the relative clause is always determined by the speaker's perspective of the antecedent. This perspective can be subjective or objective.

23.D.1 Unknown/Known antecedent

a. The *indicative* is used in relative clauses to refer to *specific* people, things, ideas, or events that we already know about. The *subjunctive* is used to refer to something or someone *unknown* that has *imagined* or *wished* characteristics.

Subjunctive: unknown	Indicative: known
Vamos a comprar **una casa** que **tenga** tres dormitorios. *We'd like to buy a house that has three bedrooms.*	Vamos a comprar **una casa** que **tiene** tres dormitorios. *We're going to buy a house that has three bedrooms.*
El hotel contratará a **un chef** que **tenga** experiencia. *The hotel wants to hire a chef who has experience.*	El hotel contratará a **un chef** que **tiene** experiencia. *The hotel is going to hire a chef who has experience.*
Iremos a **un restaurante** que **tenga** buena comida. *We want to go to a restaurant that has good food.*	Iremos a **un restaurante** que **tiene** buena comida. *We're going to a restaurant that has good food.*

b. Verbs like **querer, necesitar, buscar,** and **desear** usually occur in relative clauses that describe *imagined* people, things, events, or situations. The indicative is used to describe *specific* or *concrete* people, things, events, or situations.

Subjunctive: imagined	Indicative: specific
Buscamos **un libro** que **explique** bien el subjuntivo. *We're looking for a book that can explain the subjunctive well.*	Buscamos **el libro** que **explica** bien el subjuntivo. *We're looking for the book that explains the subjunctive well.*
Queríamos **una bebida** que no **tuviera** azúcar. *We'd like a drink that doesn't have sugar.*	Queríamos **la bebida** que no **tiene** azúcar. *We wanted the drink that doesn't have sugar.*

c. The subjunctive is also used in relative clauses with a relative adverb that refers to *unknown* and *non-specific* locations, times, or methods of action. The adverb, or **que** and a suitable preposition, starts the relative clause.

Relative adverbs: 15.C

Subjunctive: unknown	Indicative: known
Iremos a un restaurante **donde/en el que haya** sitio para todos. *We'll go to a restaurant where there is room for everyone.* *(The speaker does not know of a specific restaurant.)*	Iremos a un restaurante **donde/en el que hay** sitio para todos. *We're going to a restaurant where there is room for everyone. (The speaker knows of a specific restaurant.)*
Puedes preparar la cena **como/del modo que quieras**. *You can prepare dinner however you want.* *(The speaker does not know how you want to prepare it.)*	Puedes preparar la cena **como/del modo que quieres**. *You can prepare dinner however you want.* *(The speaker knows how you want to prepare it.)*

Indefinite pronouns: 7.D

Positive and negative indefinite
quantifiers: 7.B

23.D.2 Denied / Non-denied and indefinite antecedent

a. When the main clause indicates or implies that the antecedent does not exist, the subjunctive is used in the subordinate clause.

Negation using *haber*	
Subjunctive: denied/nonexistent	**Indicative: concrete/existing**
En España **no había platos** que **me gustaran** más que el bacalao. *In Spain, there were no dishes I liked more than cod.*	En España **había platos** que **me gustaban** más que el bacalao. *In Spain, there were other dishes I liked more than cod.*
No hay otra persona que me **importe** más que tú. *There is no one more important to me than you.*	**Hay otras personas** que me **importan** más que tú. *There are others who are more important to me than you.*

b. The existence of the antecedent can be denied by negating the whole clause using **nunca**, **jamás**, or other negative expressions such as **en modo alguno** (*in no way / not in any way*), or **en ninguna parte** (*nowhere*).

Negation using *nunca, jamás*	
Subjunctive	**Indicative**
Nunca/Jamás he sido **una persona** que **lea** mucho. *I have never been a person who reads a lot.*	**Siempre** he sido **una persona** que **lee** mucho. *I have always been a person who reads a lot.*
En ninguna parte hay **plataformas petroleras** que **sean** totalmente seguras. *Nowhere are there oil rigs that are completely safe.*	**En muchas partes** hay **plataformas petroleras** que **son** totalmente seguras. *In many places, there are oil rigs that are completely safe.*

c. Affirmative indefinite pronouns and quantifiers used as antecedents describe something or someone that cannot be identified and require the use of the subjunctive. However, the indicative can be used with affirmative indefinite pronouns and quantifiers to indicate that the speaker knows the antecedent but does not want to identify it.

Affirmative indefinite pronouns	
Subjunctive	**Indicative**
¿Hay **algo** que **quieras** decirme? *Is there something you want to say to me?*	¿Hay **algo** que **quieres** decirme? *Is there something specific you want to say to me?*
Quiero **a alguien** que me **quiera**. *I want someone who loves me.*	Quiero **a alguien** que me **quiere**. *I love someone who loves me.*

Indefinite quantifiers with
only positive forms:
cualquiera, *anyone*: 7.C.5

d. Cualquier(a) is used with the subjunctive whether it occurs before the noun or independently as the pronoun.

Cualquier(a) – *anybody/who(m)ever/whichever*	
Subjunctive	
Cualquiera que **tenga** visa puede viajar a España. *Whoever has a visa can travel to Spain.*	Puedes preguntarle la dirección a **cualquier** persona que **encuentres**. *You can ask whomever/anybody you find about the address.*

e. The *subjunctive* must be used when an indefinite pronoun or quantifier is negated: **nadie, nada, ninguno/a(s)**, or **ningún/ninguna** + *noun*.

 Algún, alguno/a(s); ningún, ninguno/a: 7.B.2b

Negative indefinite pronouns/determiners	Affirmative indefinite pronouns/determiners
Subjunctive	**Indicative**
No hay **ningún** equipo que **sea** mejor que el nuestro. *There is no other team that is better than ours.*	Hay **otro** equipo que **es** mejor que el nuestro. *There is another team that is better than ours.*
No existe **nadie** que **juegue** mejor que nosotros. *There is no one else who plays better than us.*	Existe **alguien** que **juega** mejor que nosotros. *There is someone who plays better than us.*
La revista no publicó **nada** que me **interesara** mucho. *The magazine didn't publish anything that interested me.*	La revista publicó **algo** que me **interesó** mucho. *The magazine published something that interested me a lot.*

f. The phrase **el/la/los/las que, quien(es)** (*the one[s] that/who*) is used with the *subjunctive* when it refers to someone or something unknown. Note that this applies to defining relative clauses where **lo/el/la cual** cannot be used.

 Relative pronouns: 15.A

el/la/los/las que, quien(es) – *the one who / those which*	
Subjunctive	**Indicative**
Elena irá con **los que deseen** ir al museo. *Elena will go with anyone who wants to go to the museum.*	Elena irá con **los que desean** ir al museo. *Elena will go with those who want to go to the museum.*
Quienes hayan comprado boletos pueden entrar. *Anyone who has bought tickets can get in.*	**Quienes han comprado** boletos pueden entrar. *Those who (already) have bought tickets can get in.*

g. Clauses with **lo que** take the subjunctive when they refer to something non-specific and the indicative when they refer to something specific.

lo que – *what/whatever*	
Subjunctive	**Indicative**
Lo que digas será muy importante. *Whatever you say will be very important.*	Lo que **dices** es muy importante. *What you say is very important.*

23.D.3 Tense sequencing

The tense of the verbs in the main and relative clauses depends on the context of the sentence. The examples below show some of the most common combinations.

a. When the main verb is in the indicative *present* or *simple future*, the verb in the relative clause is in the *present subjunctive*. When the main verb is in the *present perfect*, the verb in the relative clause is in the *present perfect subjunctive*.

 Subjunctive in adverbial clauses: como, donde, cuando: 23.E.1

Main clause		Relative clause	
Indicative		**Subjunctive**	
Present	**Necesito** una impresora *I need a printer*	**Present**	que **funcione** bien. *that works well.*
Simple future	**Necesitaré** una impresora *I will need a printer*		
Present perfect	Jamás **he tenido** una impresora *I've never had a printer*	**Present perfect**	que **haya funcionado** bien. *that has worked well.*

b. When the main verb is in the indicative and refers to the past, the verb in the subordinate clause is in one of the past forms of the subjunctive. The context determines which tense is used.

Main clause		Relative clause	
Indicative		**Subjunctive**	
Preterite	**Necesité** una impresora *I needed a printer*	**Imperfect**	que **funcionara** bien. *that worked well.*
Imperfect	**Necesitaba** una impresora *I needed a printer*		
Present conditional	**Querría** una impresora *I would like a printer*		
Conditional perfect	**Habría querido** una impresora *I would have liked a printer*		

23.E The subjunctive in adverbial clauses

El subjuntivo en oraciones subordinadas adverbiales

Subordinating conjunctions: 16.C ▶ Adverbial clauses start with adverbial conjunctions that express time, manner, purpose, concession, cause, condition, and other relationships.

23.E.1 Place, manner, quantity

Relative adverbs: 15.C ▶ **a.** In a relative clause, the relative adverbs (**como, donde, cuando**) refer back to the antecedent, which is mentioned and can be identified.

Main clause	Relative clause with antecedent
Estaremos en **un parque** *We'll be in a park*	**donde / en el que podamos** jugar. *where we can play.*

b. When the antecedent is excluded, the adverb does not refer to a specific place, manner, or quantity. These clauses have traditionally been considered adverbial clauses introduced by a conjuction that describe the action (the verb) directly. The *Nueva gramática* regards them as *free relative adverbial clauses* that refer to an implicit antecedent.

Main clause	Adverbial clause
Estaremos *We'll be*	**donde podamos** jugar. *where we can play.*
Vino *He came*	**cuando lo llamamos**. *when we called him.*

c. The *subjunctive* is used in place, manner, and quantity clauses that describe unknown places, methods of action, and quantities/amounts.

como, donde, cuanto, todo lo que	
Subjunctive: unknown	**Indicative: known**
Busca las llaves **donde** las **hayas dejado**. *Look for your keys wherever you left them.*	Busca las llaves **donde** las **dejaste**. *Look for your keys where you left them.*
Resuelvo los problemas **como pueda**. *I resolve problems however I can.*	Resuelvo los problemas **como puedo**. *I resolve problems the way I am able to.*
Ellos harán **cuanto/todo lo que quieran**. *They will do whatever they want.*	Ellos harán **cuanto/todo lo que quieren**. *They will do everything they want.*

d. When the conjunction **como** starts the subordinate clause, the *subjunctive* expresses a condition in a specific context, while the *indicative* expresses a cause.

como	
Subjunctive: condition	**Indicative: cause**
Como no **encuentres** tu pasaporte, no podrás viajar. *If you don't find your passport, you won't be able to travel.*	**Como** no **encuentras** tu pasaporte, no podrás viajar. *Since you can't find your passport, you won't be able to travel.*

e. The conjunctions of manner **como si** and **sin que** always require the *subjunctive* in the subordinate clause. The conjunction **como si** conveys an imagined situation and is used with the *subjunctive* in all tenses except the *present subjunctive*.

como si, sin que	
Subjunctive	
Manuel habla catalán **como si fuera** de Barcelona.	*Manuel speaks Catalan as if he were from Barcelona.*
Manuel aprendió catalán **sin que** nadie le **enseñara**.	*Manuel learned Catalan without anyone teaching him.*

◀ **Parece:** 23.C.5d
◀ Infinitive and **que** -clauses: 23.C.9

f. In exclamations, **ni que** is used with the imperfect subjunctive as an expression of irritation.

No creo lo que dices, ¡**ni que** yo **fuera** tonta!   *I don't believe what you are saying, as if I were stupid!*

23.E.2   Time

Conjunctions of time			
a medida que	*as*	en cuanto	*as soon (as)*
al mismo tiempo que	*at the same time as*	luego (de) que	*after / as soon as*
antes (de) que	*before*	hasta que	*until*
apenas	*as soon as, when just*	mientras (que)	*while (so long as)*
cada vez que	*each time / every time (that)*	según	*according to*
cuando	*when*	siempre que	*whenever (as long as)*
desde que	*since*	tan pronto como	*as soon as / once*
después (de) que	*after / as soon as*	una vez que	*once*

◀ Adverbs of time: 10.B

◀ **mientras** as conditional conjunction: 16.D.2c, 23.E.2b

◀ **cuando** as relative adverb: 15.C.1

a. In general, the *subjunctive* is used in a time clause when the main clause refers to the future. When it does not refer to the future, the *indicative* is used. The examples with **cuando** below illustrate the sequence of time for the majority of time conjunctions. Usually, the subordinate clause comes first.

cuando	
Subjunctive	**Indicative**
Cuando llegue a la oficina, **leeré** mi correo. (Future) *When I get to the office, I'll read my e-mail.*	**Cuando llego** a la oficina, **leo** mi correo. (Present habit) *When I get to the office, I read my e-mail.*
Cuando haya llegado a la oficina, **leeré** mi correo. (Future) *When I have arrived at the office, I'll read my e-mail.*	**Cuando llegué** a la oficina, **leí** mi correo. (Past) *When I got to the office, I read my e-mail.*
Cuando salga de la oficina, **habré leído** mi correo. (Future) *When I leave the office, I will have read my e-mail.*	**Cuando salí** de la oficina, ya **había leído** mi correo. (Past) *When I left the office, I had already read my e-mail.*

Conjunctions of time: 16.C.3

b. Mientras (que) and **siempre que** convey a condition with the *subjunctive* (*if, so/as long as*) and are conjunctions of time with the *indicative*.

mientras, siempre que	
Subjunctive: conditional	**Indicative: time**
Mientras estés enfermo, debes quedarte en casa. *As long as you're sick, you should stay at home.*	**Mientras estás** enfermo, debes quedarte en casa. *While you're sick, you should stay at home.*
Siempre que pidas los boletos con tiempo, pagarás poco. *As long as you book the tickets in advance, you won't pay much.*	**Siempre que pides** tus boletos con tiempo, pagas poco. *When you book the tickets in advance, you don't pay much.*

Antes de que: 16.C.3

c. The conjunction **antes de que** always requires the *subjunctive* in the subordinate clause, but the infinitive can also be used when the subject in the main and subordinate clause is the same. The following conjunctions of time can also be followed by the infinitive: **después de**, **luego de**, and **hasta**. The infinitive follows immediately after conjunctions without **que**.

Infinitive when subject is the same: 23.C.9
Infinitive after a finite verb: 25.B.5

antes de, después/luego de, hasta	
Subjunctive	**Infinitive**
Ven a visitarme **antes de que** yo viaje. *Come and visit me before I travel.*	Ven a visitarme **antes de viajar**. *Come and visit me before you travel.*
¿Podéis quedaros **hasta que terminemos** el trabajo? *Can you [pl.] stay until we've finished the job?*	¿Podéis quedaros **hasta terminar** el trabajo? *Can you [pl.] stay until you've finished the job?*
Os llamaré **después de que regreséis**. *I'll call you [pl.] after you come back.*	Os llamaré **después de regresar**. *I'll call you [pl.] after I come back.*

23.E.3 Purpose, goal

Conjunctions of purpose: 16.C.7

Conjunctions of purpose			
para que	so that	con el fin/objeto/propósito de que	with the aim of
a fin de que	so that	con vistas a que	with a view to

a. Conjunctions of purpose express purpose, intent, goals, and correspond to the English conjunctions *so that, in order that*. The *subjunctive* is used with conjunctions of purpose.

Subjunctive	
La constitución fue modificada **a fin de que** el presidente **pudiera** ser reelecto.	*The constitution was changed so that the president could be re-elected.*

b. Conjunctions of purpose can be followed by the infinitive (without **que**) when the subject in the main and subordinate clause is the same person. Usually a personal pronoun in the main clause will convey who the clause is about.

Subjunctive	Infinitive
Te daré dinero **para que compres** los libros. *I will give you money so that you buy the books.*	Te daré dinero **para comprar** los libros. *I will give you money to buy the books.*

c. With the exception of **para que**, the above-mentioned conjunctions of purpose are mostly used in formal situations and written Spanish.

El gobierno aplicará medidas **con el objeto de que** no **suban** los precios.   *The government will introduce measures with the objective of keeping prices from rising.*

d. The conjunctions **de (tal) modo que, de (tal) manera que,** and **de (tal) forma que** (*so that, in such a way that*) are used with the *subjunctive* to convey purpose. With the *indicative* they convey consequence.

23.E.4 Consequence

Conjunctions of consequence				
de (tal) forma que	*so that, such that, in such a way that*	tan... que	*so... that*	
de (tal) manera que		tal... que		
de (tal) modo que		tanto... que		

Conjunctions of consequence: 16.C.5

a. Conjunctions of consequence express the consequence of a condition using the *indicative*. With the *subjunctive*, they convey purpose.

tal que: 16.C.5b

Mándame un mensaje de texto, **de tal modo que estemos** en contacto.
Text me, so we can keep in touch.

Nos escribimos, **de tal modo que estamos** en contacto.
We write to each other, so we keep in touch.

Subjunctive: purpose	Indicative: consequence
Viaja mucho, **de (tal) modo que conozcas** otras culturas. *Travel a lot, so that you can get to know other cultures.*	Viaja mucho, **de (tal) modo conoces** otras culturas. *Travel a lot, so you get to know other cultures.*
El profesor enseña **de forma que** todos lo/le **entiendan**. *The teacher teaches in a way that allows everyone to understand him.*	El profesor enseña **de forma que** todos lo/le **entienden**. *The teacher teaches in a way that everyone understands him.*

b. After **tan** and **tanto** in an implied comparison, the *indicative* is used. In negative clauses, the *subjunctive* is used.

tan/tanto como: 11.C

Subjunctive: negative	Indicative: affirmative
La nieve no es **tan poca que** no **podamos** esquiar. *There isn't so little snow that we can't ski.*	La nieve es **tan poca que** no **podemos** esquiar. *There's so little snow that we can't ski.*
Los problemas no son **tantos que** yo no **pueda** resolverlos. *The problems are not so many that I can't deal with them.*	Los problemas son **tantos que** no puedo resolverlos. *The problems are so many that I can't deal with them.*

23.E.5 Cause

Conjunctions of cause			
porque	*because*	debido a que	*due to, because*
a causa de que	*because (of)*	puesto que	*since, because*
dado que	*given that*	ya que	*since*

 Conjunctions of cause: 16.C.4

a. Conjunctions of cause in Spanish correspond to the English *because* or *since*. The most common conjunctions of cause are **porque, como,** and **ya que**. In written language, there are more variations.

Indicative: affirmative causes	
Cancelaron los vuelos **debido a que / porque nevaba** mucho.	*The flights were canceled because it was snowing a lot.*
No había buenas habitaciones **dado que / porque era** temporada alta.	*There were no good rooms because it was peak season.*

b. Porque, a causa de que, and **debido a que** are followed by the *subjunctive* when the cause is negated.

Subjunctive: negative causes	Indicative: affirmative causes
Estudio español **no porque sea** obligatorio **sino porque** me gusta. *I study Spanish not because it's mandatory, but because I like it.*	Estudio español **porque es** obligatorio. *I study Spanish because it's mandatory.*

23.E.6   Concession

Conjunctions of concession		
aunque	pese a que	*even if, despite, in spite of, although, whether*
aun cuando	si bien	
a pesar de (que)	y eso que	

Conjunctions of concession: 16.C.6

a. The most common conjunction of concession is **aunque**. The *subjunctive* is used when the subordinate clause conveys something *imagined, not real,* or *in the future*. The *indicative* expresses a fact. The subordinate clause can be placed before the main clause or after it, and the context determines the tense of the subjunctive (*present, imperfect,* or *past perfect*).

Subjunctive: imagined fact	Indicative: real fact
Siempre hablo español **aunque** me **cueste** mucho. *I always speak Spanish even if it is difficult.*	Siempre hablo español **aunque** me **cuesta** mucho. *I always speak Spanish even though it is difficult.*
Aunque me **hubieras hablado** muy rápido en español, te lo habría entendido todo. *Even if you had spoken very quickly to me in Spanish, I would have understood everything.*	**Aunque** me **has hablado** muy rápido en español, te lo he entendido todo. *Although you have spoken very quickly to me in Spanish, I have understood everything.*

b. The expression **por** + *adjective/adverb/noun* + **que** has a meaning of concession and is used with the *subjunctive*.

Por difícil que parezca, el subjuntivo es realmente fácil.	*As hard as it may seem, the subjunctive is really easy.*
Por poco que tengas, siempre puedes ser generoso.	*As little as you may have, you can always be generous.*
Por mucha gente **que venga**, habrá comida para todos.	*Even if a lot of people come, there will be plenty of food for everyone.*

23.E.7   Use of the subjunctive in conditional clauses

Conditional conjunctions: 16.D

Conditional conjunctions			
si	*if*	en caso de que	*in case of*
a no ser que	*if not*	excepto que	*if not*
a menos que	*unless*	siempre y cuando	*if*
con tal (de) que	*provided that / as long as*	siempre que	*provided that / as long as*

a. All conditional conjunctions in the previous table take the subjunctive in the subordinate clause, except the **si** conjunction, which has special rules.

Te llamaré **en caso de que quieras** ir conmigo en el coche.	*I'll call you in case you want to go with me in the car.*
Iremos al cine **con tal de que** la película **sea** buena.	*We'll go to the movies as long as the film is good.*

b. The expression **por si acaso** (*in case*) is very common in everyday speech. It can only be used with the *indicative*.

Lleva ropa de abrigo **por si acaso nieva**.	*Take warm clothes in case it snows.*
Llevaré la tarjeta de crédito **por si acaso necesito** más dinero.	*I will bring my credit card in case I need more money.*

23.E.8 Conditional *si* clauses

A subordinate **si** (*if*) clause conveys a condition, while the main clause expresses the consequence or the result if the condition is fulfilled. The main clause can express a fact, a probability, a hypothetical situation, or an imperative. Each type of clause carries its own rules.

a. *Facts:* When the condition is real and the consequence is certain, both clauses are in the indicative.

Using the *present indicative* in both clauses indicates that the same result happens every time a condition is fulfilled.

Condition: *present indicative*	Result: *present indicative*
Si **trabajas** mucho,	**ganas** dinero.
If you work a lot,	*you earn money.*

Expressing the condition in the *present indicative* and the result in the *future* (*simple future* or **ir a** + *infinitive*) indicates a clear cause-and-effect relationship.

Condition: *present indicative*	Result: *future indicative*
Si **trabajas** mucho,	**ganarás** / **vas a ganar** dinero.
If you work a lot,	*you will earn money.*

Using the *imperfect indicative* in both clauses indicates that something happened each time a condition was fulfilled.

Condition: *imperfect indicative*	Result: *imperfect indicative*
Si **trabajabas** mucho,	**ganabas** dinero.
If you worked a lot,	*you earned money.*

With the *past* or *present perfect*, conditional clauses with **si** usually communicate an assumption about something that happened, has happened, or will have happened because a condition was fulfilled. These assumptions are often expressed as questions.

Condition: *past/present perfect*	Result: *several possible verb tenses*
Si **trabajaste** / **has trabajado** mucho,	**ganaste** / **has ganado** / **habrás ganado** mucho dinero, ¿no?
If you worked/have worked a lot,	*you earned/have earned/must have earned a lot of money, right?*

b. *Probability:* The condition is an assumption and the result is possible.

When the *present conditional* is used in the main clause to express a probable result (*what would happen*) if a condition were fulfilled, the *imperfect subjunctive* is used in the subordinate **si** clause.

Condition: *imperfect subjunctive*	Result: *present conditional*
Si **trabajaras** mucho,	**ganarías** dinero.
If you worked a lot,	*you would earn money.*

c. *Hypothetical:* Both the condition and the result are only assumptions.

To express what could have happened if an imagined condition had been fulfilled, the *past perfect subjunctive* is used in the subordinate **si** clause and the *conditional perfect* in the main clause.

The past perfect subjunctive: ▶ 22.E

Condition: *past perfect subjunctive*	Result: *conditional perfect*
Si **hubieras trabajado** mucho,	**habrías ganado** dinero.
If you had worked a lot,	*you would have earned money.*

Using the past perfect subjunctive in the main clause (**hubieras ganado**) intensifies the assumption that the outcome would have been highly unlikely, but in daily speech the conditional perfect (**habrías ganado**) is preferred. The **-ese** form of the past perfect subjunctive (**hubieses ganado**) is not used in the main clause of a conditional sentence.

Condition: *past perfect subjunctive*	Result: *past perfect subjunctive*
Si **hubieras trabajado** mucho,	**hubieras/habrías ganado** dinero.
If you had worked a lot,	*you could have earned money.*

d. *The imperative in the main clause:* If a condition *is*, *was*, or *will be* fulfilled, the result can be imperative (something that must be done).

Condition: *several possible verb tenses*	Result: *imperative*
Si **trabajas/trabajaste/has trabajado/trabajaras** mucho hoy,	¡**acuéstate** temprano!
If you work/worked/have worked/were going to work a lot today,	*you must go to bed early!*

23.F Regional variations

Variaciones regionales

a. The use of the subjunctive is fairly uniform throughout the Spanish-speaking world. The exception is the use of the *present* subjunctive instead of the *imperfect* subjunctive in nominal clauses in the past. This use occurs mainly in southern parts of Latin America and only when the action in the subordinate clause still pertains to the future.

Indirect discourse: changes in ▶ verb tenses: 31.B.3

Imperfect subjunctive	Present subjunctive
Susana me pidió ayer que **fuera** con ella al centro comercial.	Susana me pidió ayer que **vaya** con ella al centro comercial.
Susana asked me yesterday to go with her to the mall.	

b. The **-ra** and **-se** endings in the imperfect and past perfect subjunctive are equivalent (**hablara, hablase, hubiera/hubiese hablado**), and are used in both Spain and Latin America.

Queríamos una novela que **fuera/fuese** más interesante.

We wanted a novel that was more interesting.

No creía que **hubiera/hubiese** problemas.

I didn't believe that there were problems.

Habría sido bueno que **hubieras/hubieses dejado** de fumar.

It would have been good if you had stopped smoking.

Práctica

Actividades 1–24, pp. A92–A100

The imperative
Imperativo

Chapter 24

A. Formal and informal imperative

B. Affirmative imperative for *tú*

C. Affirmative imperative for *vos* and *vosotros*

D. Negative imperative for *tú*, *vos*, and *vosotros*

E. Imperative forms for *usted*, *ustedes*, and *nosotros*

F. Placement of pronouns

G. Other imperative constructions

H. Imperatives in colloquial expressions

24.A Formal and informal imperative

Imperativo formal e informal

The imperative expresses direct requests or commands with finite (personal) verb forms. Spanish has a formal imperative for **usted** and **ustedes**, an informal imperative for **tú, vos**, and **vosotros**, and reciprocal requests for **nosotros** (*let's*). All negative informal imperatives are the same as the corresponding present subjunctive forms. The affirmative and negative formal imperatives and reciprocal requests for **nosotros** are also formed using the corresponding present subjunctive forms. All conjugation forms that have vowel shifts or diphthongs in the present indicative and the present subjunctive, also have the same changes in the imperative.

24.B Affirmative imperative for *tú*

Imperativo afirmativo de *tú*

24.B.1 Regular affirmative imperatives for *tú*

Regular affirmative forms for **tú** are formed by dropping the **-s** ending in the second-person singular present indicative. Vowel shifts and diphthongs in the present indicative **tú** forms also occur in the imperative.

Regular verbs		Verbs with diphthongs / vowel shifts	
cantar (cantas)	canta	d**o**rmir (duermes)	d**ue**rme
comer (comes)	come	p**e**nsar (piensas)	p**ie**nsa
escribir (escribes)	escribe	p**e**dir (pides)	p**i**de

¡**Habla** más lento, por favor!   *Speak more slowly, please!*

¡**Escribe** un blog!   *Write a blog!*

¡**Piensa** bien las cosas!   *Think carefully about things!*

24.B.2 Irregular affirmative imperatives for *tú*

There are only a few irregular affirmative imperatives for **tú**.

Completely irregular *tú* imperatives			
decir (*to say*)	**di**	salir (*to leave, to go out*)	**sal**
hacer (*to do*)	**haz**	ser (*to be*)	**sé**
ir (*to go*)	**ve**	tener (*to have*)	**ten**
poner (*to put*)	**pon**	venir (*to come*)	**ven**

¡**Sal** a jugar, pero **ten** cuidado con los autos!   *Go out and play, but watch out for cars!*

¡**Ve** y **pon** las cartas en el buzón!   *Go and put the letters in the mailbox!*

Sé valiente y **di** la verdad.   *Be brave and tell the truth.*

Haz lo que te parezca mejor.   *Do what you think is best.*

◄ The present indicative: 17.D

◄ Verbs with vowel shifts/diphthongs: verb conjugation tables, pp. 257–276. See verb patterns 25, 48, 49.

◄ Verb conjugation tables, pp. 257–276

24.C   Affirmative imperative for *vos* and *vosotros*

Imperativo afirmativo de *vos* y *vosotros*

24.C.1   Formation of imperatives for *vos* and *vosotros*

The regular affirmative imperative for **vos** and **vosotros** is formed by dropping the **-r** ending from the infinitive and adding an accent to the final vowel for the **vos** imperative (**cantá**), or adding a **-d** to form the **vosotros** imperative (**cantad**). All informal imperatives are regular, with the exception of the **vos** imperative for the verb **ir**, which uses the imperative form of **andar** (**¡Andá!**).

Affirmative imperative for *vos, vosotros*		vos	vosotros
Verbs			
cant**ar**	canta-	cant**á**	canta**d**
corr**er**	corre-	corr**é**	corre**d**
escrib**ir**	escribi-	escrib**í**	escribi**d**

¡Recordad la contraseña!	*Remember the password!*
Llamá a tu padre.	*Call your father.*
Encendé la luz.	*Turn on the light.*
Andá a buscar a tu hermano.	*Go find your brother.*
Buscad las herramientas.	*Look for the tools.*

24.C.2   Use of the imperative for *vos* and *vosotros*

a. In Spain, **vosotros** is used with its corresponding imperative forms.

¡Venid a visitarme pronto!	*Come and visit me soon!*
Recordad lo que os dije.	*Remember what I told you.*
Proteged la naturaleza.	*Protect nature.*

b. When **vosotros** is used in Latin America as a formal address (to church congregations and less frequently to voters in political speeches), the **vosotros** pronoun and its imperative forms are also used. The structure is identical to that used in Spain for **vosotros**.

¡Ayudad a vuestra parroquia!	*Help your parish!*

c. In the **voseo** regions of Argentina, Uruguay, Paraguay, Costa Rica, Guatemala, Honduras, Nicaragua, El Salvador, Colombia, Venezuela, and Panama, the above-mentioned **vos** imperative is used.

¡Estudiá bien la propuesta!	*Study the proposal well!*
Recordá lo que te dije.	*Remember what I told you.*
Llamá a tu hermano.	*Call your brother.*
Decí la verdad.	*Tell the truth.*

Voseo with the subjunctive: 22.B, 22.H
Map of **voseo** regions in Latin America: p. 277

d. In **voseo** regions in Bolivia, Ecuador, and Chile, the pronoun **vos** is used with the **tú** verb form (**¡Habla, vos!**) in addition to the common form (**¡Hablá, vos!**), or a variant using an **-i** ending (**¡No salgái!**).

24.D Negative imperative for *tú, vos,* **and** *vosotros*

Imperativo negativo de *tú, vos* y *vosotros*

24.D.1 Regular negative imperatives for *tú, vos,* **and** *vosotros*

a. All negative imperative **tú**, **vos** and **vosotros** forms are identical to the conjugation forms of the present subjunctive.

◀ The present subjunctive: 22.B

Negative imperative for *tú, vos, vosotros*			
	cantar	**correr**	**subir**
tú/vos	no cantes	no corras	no subas
vosotros	no cantéis	no corráis	no subáis

b. In regions that use **voseo**, the **vos** endings for the present subjunctive can vary. Since the negative imperative matches the present subjunctive form, several negative imperative forms exist for **vos**. In addition to the conjugation presented in the table above (which matches the **tú** form), another common **voseo** ending for the present subjunctive and negative imperative is **-és/-ás**.

◀ **Voseo** with the subjunctive: 22.B, 22.H

No **cantes/cantés**.　　　No **corras/corrás**.　　　No **subas/subás**.

24.D.2 Irregular negative imperatives for *tú, vos,* **and** *vosotros*

All verbs with vowel shifts and diphthongs keep the irregularities in the informal affirmative and negative imperative forms.

No me **pidas** que mienta.　　　*Don't ask me to lie.*
No **seas** así conmigo.　　　*Don't be like that with me.*
Nunca **hagáis** caso de tonterías.　　　*Never pay attention to such silliness.*

24.E Imperative forms for *usted, ustedes,* **and** *nosotros*

Imperativo de *usted, ustedes* y *nosotros*

Affirmative imperatives for **usted**, **ustedes**, and **nosotros**, and all their negative imperative forms use the corresponding present subjunctive forms. All verbs with vowel shifts and diphthongs in the present subjunctive keep the irregularities in the affirmative and negative imperative forms for **usted**, **ustedes**, and **nosotros**.

◀ The present subjunctive: 22.B

	cantar	**correr**	**subir**
usted	(no) cante	(no) corra	(no) suba
ustedes	(no) canten	(no) corran	(no) suban
nosotros	(no) cantemos	(no) corramos	(no) subamos

No **venga** muy tarde.　　　*Don't come too late.*
Digan la verdad.　　　*Tell the truth.*
Nunca **seamos** descorteses.　　　*Let us never be impolite.*

Posición de los pronombres

All pronouns (reflexive pronouns, direct and indirect object pronouns) are placed *before* negative imperatives and *after* affirmative imperatives. The other rules of pronoun placement also apply here: a) The indirect object pronoun always comes before the direct object pronoun. b) The indirect object pronoun **le** becomes **se** when it appears with a direct object pronoun.

Placement of direct and indirect object pronouns: 13.G.6
Placement of reflexive pronouns: 27.A.1

Necesito tu dirección. ¡Mánda**mela**!	*I need your address. Send it to me!*
Dá**sela** también al profesor y ¡no **se la** des a nadie más!	*Give it to the teacher too, and don't give it to anyone else!*

a. The **-d** ending is dropped from the affirmative **vosotros** imperative when the pronoun **os** is added. This does not happen with other pronouns.

Quita**os** los zapatos antes de entrar.	*Take off your [pl.] shoes before entering.*
Deci**dme** cómo llego allí.	*Tell me how to get there.*

b. In **nosotros** commands, the **-s** ending is dropped before the pronoun **nos**. Also note that **vamos** is generally used instead of **vayamos** (*present subjunctive*).

Sentémo**nos** a descansar.	*Let's sit down and rest.*
Pongámo**nos** a trabajar ya.	*Let's get to work now.*
¡Vámo**nos**!	*Let's go!*

c. The subject pronoun is used with requests only when it is necessary to show a contrast between the people being referred to.

Pon la mesa **tú**, Roberto; ayer la puse **yo**.	*You set the table, Roberto; I did it yesterday.*

24.G Other imperative constructions

Otras expresiones exhortativas

24.G.1 Infinitives

a. In informal everyday language in Spain, the infinitive can also be used with **vosotros** instead of the common imperative.

¡**Ponerse** de pie!	*Stand up!*
¡**Dejaros** de tonterías!	*Stop that nonsense!*

b. Both in Spain and Latin America, an informal request can be strengthened by adding the preposition **a** before the infinitive.

¡**A trabajar**, todo el mundo!	*Everybody, get to work!*
¡**A acostarse**, niños!	*Go to bed, children!*
¡**A entrenarse**, equipo!	*Get training, team!*

24.G.2 Impersonal imperative

a. In contexts where instructions, bans, or commands are expressed to the general public, the *infinitive* is the most common form.

No **fumar**.	*No smoking.*
No **entrar**.	*No entry.*
Leer las instrucciones con cuidado.	*Read the instructions carefully.*
Apagar la luz al salir.	*Turn off the light when you leave.*
¡**Mantener** la calma!	*Stay calm!*

b. Other structures can also be used to express impersonal negative commands. For example, to ban: **Prohibido** + *infinitive* (**Prohibido fumar**) or the imperative for **usted**: **No fume**. Affirmative impersonal commands can also use the imperative for **usted**: **Empuje** (*Push*), **Hale** (*Pull*).

24.G.3 The imperative and politeness

The imperative is softened in everyday language using friendly intonation or by using other verb tenses or expressions. Such softening strategies also occur in English.

a. Verb periphrases with infinitives can be used as imperatives.

¡**Ve a traerme** un cafecito!	*Go and get me a coffee!*
¡**Pongámonos a trabajar**!	*Let's get to work!*
¿**Puedes venir** acá, por favor?	*Can you come here, please?*

 Modal verb periphrases with the infinitive: 26.B

b. Questions with the present conditional of **poder** and **querer** can also be used as imperatives. Adverbs like **ya**, **ahora**, and **inmediatamente** can be added to strengthen the command.

¿**Podrías** contestarme ahora?	*Could you answer me now?*
¿**Querría** usted hacerlo ya?	*Could you do that immediately?*

Present conditional as a polite form: 21.B.4

c. Questions with verbs in the present and statements starting with **A ver** or ending in interrogatives such as ¿**quiere(s)?**, ¿**puede(s)?**, ¿**sí?**, ¿**vale?**, and ¿**eh?**, can soften the imperative as well.

¿**Me dices** tu nombre?	*Can you tell me your name?*
¡**A ver** si terminas pronto!	*Let's see if you can get it done soon!*
Llamas ahora, ¿**vale**?	*Call now, okay?*
¿**Puede decirme** qué hora es?	*Could you tell me what time it is?*
Ayúdame, ¿**eh**?	*Help me, will you?*

d. The expression ¿**Por qué no...?** is extremely common in everyday speech as a polite request, but good intonation is important, as it can easily slip into a reproachful exclamation.

¿**Por qué no** me ayudas?	*Would (Why don't) you help me?*
¿**Por qué no** te callas?	*Would (Why don't) you be quiet?*
¿**Por qué no** te acuestas y descansas un poco?	*Would (Why don't) you lie down and get some rest?*

The subjunctive in independent clauses: 23.B

24.G.4 *Que* + subjunctive

Sentences using the structure **que** + *subjunctive* can be classified as requests (¡**Que siga la fiesta**!), but the verb's meaning can also convey an indirect order or request from someone else (*indirect speech*) using an insistent tone.

Que des una explicación.	*You must give an explanation.*
Que vuelvas a llamar.	*You should / have to call again.*
Que me lo **digas** de nuevo.	*Say it to me again.*
¡**Que** te lo **compres**!	*Go ahead and buy it for yourself!*

El imperativo en expresiones coloquiales

The imperative is also used in common colloquial expressions such as **oye, no me digas, mira**, and **anda ya**. In this case, its meaning is not that of a command or request, but rather an idiomatic expression.

—**Oye**, tengo que ir al mercado ahora.
—¡**No me digas** que te olvidaste del postre!

Listen, I have to go to the market now.
Don't tell me that you forgot the dessert!

—**Oye**, ¿sabes que Eva se va a casar?
—¡**No me digas**!

Hey, did you know that Eva is getting married?
You're kidding! / No way!

Mira que tu opinión me importa.
¡**Anda**! No esperaba verte aquí.

Believe me, your opinion is important to me.
Goodness! I didn't expect to see you here!

—Soy la mejor amiga del mundo.
—¡**Anda ya**!

I am the best friend in the world.
Give me a break! / Come on!

Práctica

 Actividades 1–12, pp. A100–A103

Non-finite verb forms
Formas no personales del verbo

Chapter 25

A. Overview
B. The infinitive
C. The *gerundio*
D. The past participle

25.A Overview

Aspectos generales

In contrast to conjugated personal (*finite*) verb forms, the non-personal (*non-finite*) verb forms are not inflected; they do not change according to the person, number, tense, or mood.

Spanish has three non-finite forms: the *infinitive*, the **gerundio**, and the *past participle*. Although these are verb forms in Spanish, they can have other non-verb functions in a sentence. The infinitive can act as a *noun*, the past participle can act as an *adjective*, and the **gerundio** is primarily used as an *adverb*.

25.A.1 Simple forms

Both the infinitive and the past participle have corresponding forms in English and Spanish, but the **gerundio** does not. The Spanish **gerundio** and the English present participle (the *-ing* form in *I am talking*) are often equated because they form the progressive tense in both languages: **estar leyendo** (*to be reading*). In spite of this similarity, their areas of use are very different. The present participle can be an adjective or an adverb in English (*a **walking** stick; He died **thinking** about his children.*) while the **gerundio** principally functions as an adverb in Spanish. In addition, the words **gerundio** and *gerund* are false cognates. Gerund refers to the nominalization of a verb (***Walking** is good for you.*). In Spanish, the infinitive is used in this case (**Caminar es bueno para la salud**). Therefore, the term **gerundio** is used in this text to refer to this verb form.

◄ Progressive tenses: 17.F.1, 25.C.3, 26.D

Simple forms		
Infinitive	**Past participle**	***Gerundio***
habl**ar** (*to talk / to speak*)	habl**ado** (*spoken*)	habl**ando** (*talking/speaking*)
com**er** (*to eat*)	com**ido** (*eaten*)	com**iendo** (*eating*)
sal**ir** (*to go out / leave*)	sal**ido** (*gone out / left*)	sal**iendo** (*going out / leaving*)

25.A.2 Compound forms

The compound forms of the infinitive and the **gerundio** are formed with **haber** + *past participle*.

◄ Adverbial uses of the **gerundio**: 25.C.5

Perfect infinitive		*Gerundio compuesto*	
haber (*to have*)	habl**ado** (*spoken*)	**habiendo** (*having*)	habl**ado** (*spoken*)
	com**ido** (*eaten*)		com**ido** (*eaten*)
	sal**ido** (*gone out / left*)		sal**ido** (*gone out / left*)

Deberías **haber comido** antes de salir de casa.   *You should have eaten before you left the house.*
Habiendo salido, pudo hacer la llamada.   *Having stepped out, she was able to make the call.*

25.B The infinitive

El infinitivo

The *infinitive* is the base form of the verb. This form can also act as a noun (where English uses the *-ing* gerund form). The infinitive can be the subject or the object of a sentence; it can be modified with articles and other determiners.

The Spanish infinitive can have three endings: **-ar, -er,** or **-ir.** Only a few other Spanish (non-verb) words have these endings: **bazar, bar, néctar, carácter, revólver, mártir, elixir,** etc. Some infinitives that end in **-ir (freír, reír, sonreír)**, have an accent mark.

◄ Verbs: 17.A

25.B.1 The infinitive as a noun

a. The infinitive functions as a noun in non-personal clauses with **ser** or with other verbs where an infinitive is the grammatical subject. The real (logical) subject of the infinitive is not mentioned.

Tener salud importa mucho.	*It is very important to have good health.*
Es necesario **trabajar**.	*It is necessary to work.*

b. The use of the article and other determiners with an infinitive is possible, but is usually only common in written language, idiomatic expressions, and formal contexts. An article or other determiner is mandatory when the infinitive is the subject and is modified with an adjective or a prepositional phrase.

Este eterno llover me tiene harta.	*I'm tired of this never-ending rain.*
El hablar de otras personas no me gusta nada.	*I don't like talking about other people at all.*

c. Since the infinitive retains its verbal characteristics, it can be modified by an adverb when it is the subject or object of a sentence. Likewise, it can be modified by a direct object.

The infinitive with sense verbs: ▶ 25.B.7

Esquiar *bien* es fácil.	*Skiing well is easy.*
Preocuparse *tanto* es totalmente inútil.	*Worrying so much is a complete waste of time.*
Pienso **escribirte** *mucho*.	*I intend to write to you a lot.*
Decirlo es más fácil que **hacerlo**.	*It is easier said than done.*
Estudiar *español* es muy interesante y divertido.	*Studying Spanish is very interesting and fun.*
Quiero recorrer *Latinoamérica* estas vacaciones.	*I want to travel around Latin America over vacation.*

25.B.2 The infinitive with an adverbial function

Conjunctions: Ch.16 ▶
Use of the subjunctive: Ch. 23

a. Para + *infinitive* / **sin** + *infinitive* can start adverbial clauses.

Lo hizo **sin pensar**.	*He did it without thinking.*
Para explicarme, hizo un dibujo.	*To explain it to me, he made a drawing.*

The article **el** after the ▶
preposition **a** is abbreviated to **al**.

b. Al + *infinitive* indicates that an action is happening simultaneously with something else. The order of the clauses can vary and the time of the action is expressed by the conjugated verb.

Al verte, me enamoré.	*Upon seeing you, I fell in love.*

c. The subject of the infinitive must be mentioned explicitly if it is different from the subject in the main clause.

Cierra la puerta al salir **Marta**.	*Close the door when Marta leaves.*
Cierra la puerta al salir.	*Close the door when you leave.*

d. De + *infinitive* is a common expression often used with **ser, seguir**, and **continuar**. It expresses condition or consequence (often negative), assumes a known context, and can have a subject.

De ser tan difíciles las cosas, lo mejor es olvidar el asunto.	*When everything is so difficult, it is best to forget about it.*
De haber continuado así, te habría ido mal.	*If it had continued like that, it would have gone badly for you.*

25.B.3 The infinitive after a noun or adjective

Nouns and adjectives can be modified by a *preposition + infinitive*: **problemas por resolver** (*problems to solve*); **trabajo por hacer** (*work to do*).

Vosotros sois **buenos para jugar** al fútbol.	*You [pl.] are good at playing soccer.*
Hay varios **temas a tratar** en la reunión.	*There are several topics to discuss at the meeting.*
Todavía nos queda **mucho por hacer**.	*We still have a lot to do.*

210   Non-finite verb forms • **Chapter 25**

25.B.4 Placement of pronouns

a. When the infinitive follows an *adjective + preposition*, object pronouns are added to the infinitive.

Las cartas están **listas para enviár***telas*.	*The letters are ready to be sent to you.*
Estoy **contenta de ver***te*.	*I'm glad to see you.*

b. When the infinitive is clearly governed by a finite verb or forms a verb periphrasis (like *ir a + infinitive*), the object or reflexive pronoun is added to the end of the infinitive or before the finite (conjugated) verb.

ir a + *infinitive*: 20.D.1, 26.C.1
Placement of direct and indirect object pronouns: 13.G

La ley tenéis que cumplir**la**.	
La ley **la** tenéis que cumplir.	*The law must be obeyed.*

c. When a reflexive verb is followed by an infinitive, object pronouns are added to the infinitive.

Reflexive pronoun placement: 27.A.1

Me arrepiento de haber**te** mentido.	*I regret lying to you.*
Lina siempre se acuerda de comprar**nos** el diario.	*Lina always remembers to buy us the newspaper.*
¿Te ofreces a ayudar**me**?	*Are you offering to help me?*

25.B.5 The infinitive after a finite verb

a. After a main clause that expresses a wish, an infinitive can be used if the subject in the main clause is referring to him/herself. In this case, the infinitive is *self-referential*, i.e. it refers to the same subject in the main clause. When the person in the main clause is expressing a wish about someone else, a nominal **que** clause is necessary.

The subjunctive in nominal clauses: 23.C.8

Infinitive	Nominal clause
Quiero **ser** feliz.	Quiero **que seas** feliz.
I want to be happy.	*I want you to be happy.*

b. After verbs of doubt (**creer, dudar, estimar**), a nominal **que** clause can replace the infinitive in formal spoken language and in written language (newspaper headlines, speeches, laws), even if the same subject performs the action. The combination **dudar + poder** + *infinitive* is also common in such contexts.

The subjunctive in nominal clauses: 23.C.9

Infinitive	Nominal clause
Creemos saber la razón del problema.	**Creemos que sabemos** la razón del problema.
We think we know the cause of the problem.	*We think that we know the cause of the problem.*
Estimo ganar más dinero en este puesto.	**Estimo que voy a ganar** más dinero en este puesto.
I estimate I'll make more money in this position.	*I estimate that I'll make more money in this position.*
¿**Dudas poder hacerlo**?	¿**Dudas que puedes** hacerlo?
Do you doubt you can do it?	*Do you doubt that you can do it?*

c. Reporting verbs (**decir, asegurar, informar**) in the third-person singular are often followed by **que** clauses even if the infinitive is self-referential. The use of the self-referential infinitive happens with other persons too, but is less common and more formal than a **que** clause.

Reporting verbs: 23.C.2
Indirect discourse: Ch. 31

Infinitive	Nominal clause
El ministro **afirma decir** la verdad.	El ministro **afirma que dice** la verdad.
The minister claims to tell the truth.	*The minister claims that he's telling the truth.*
Informamos haber terminado el proyecto.	**Informamos que terminamos** el proyecto.
We inform you that we have finished the project.	*We inform you that we finished the project.*

d. Most verbs of command (**dejar, permitir, prohibir, recomendar**) are followed by the infinitive, but a **que** clause followed by the subjunctive is also possible.

Infinitive	Nominal clause
No **dejaré salir** a nadie.	No **dejaré que nadie salga**.
I will not have anyone leaving.	*I will not let anyone leave.*
No se te **permitirá viajar** sin visa.	No se te **permitirá que viajes** sin visa.
You won't be allowed to travel without a visa.	*Traveling without a visa won't be allowed.*

25.B.6 The infinitive with verbs of motion

Verb periphrases: 26.B.2
Use of **para** + *infinitive*: 23.E.3b

Verbs of motion such as **venir, bajar, entrar, llegar** are usually followed by the prepositions **a** or **de** + *infinitive*. In these sentences, the verb retains its original meaning of motion and direction in contrast to verb periphrases where the meaning of the finite verb may be lost (**Voy a estudiar**, *I am going to study*).

Ven **a visitarme**.	*Come and visit me.*
Baja **a abrir** la puerta.	*Go downstairs and open the door.*
Vengo **de trabajar**.	*I'm coming from work.*

25.B.7 The infinitive with sense verbs

Gerundio with sense verbs: 25.C.7

Sense verbs (**ver, oír, sentir**) express a punctual action when followed by the *infinitive* and a progressive action when used with the **gerundio**. In such cases, the infinitive always follows the verb without a preposition.

Infinitive	*Gerundio*
Os **oí discutir**.	Os **oí discutiendo**.
I heard you [pl.] argue.	*I heard you [pl.] arguing.*
¿Me **viste llegar** a casa?	¿Me **viste llegando** a casa?
Did you see me arrive home?	*Did you see me arriving home?*

25.B.8 The infinitive as an imperative

Infinitive as an imperative: 24.G.1

a. The use of the infinitive in place of the imperative form of **vosotros** is common in informal contexts in Spain: **¡Venir! ¡Callaros!**

Other imperative constructions: 24.G.1 and 24.G.2

b. In the whole Spanish-speaking world, the infinitive is used in commands, instructions, and signs. In spoken language, it is commonly used with the preposition **a**: **¡A venir todos ya!**

Primero, **conectar** el aparato.	*First, connect the device.*	¡A **trabajar**!	*Let's get to work!*
No **cruzar** la calle.	*Do not cross the street.*	¡A **dormir** ya mismo!	*Go to bed now!*

25.B.9 Verb periphrases with infinitives

Verb periphrases: 26.B

The majority of verb periphrases in Spanish are formed with the infinitive and often with the preposition **a** or **de**.

Vamos a viajar.	*Let's travel.*
Hay que **dejar de fumar**.	*You must stop smoking.*

The Spanish **gerundio** acts as an adverb of manner with an ongoing meaning and, despite a few exceptions, is rarely used as an adjective. It is also used in many verb periphrases. The **gerundio** has both regular and irregular forms.

25.C.1 Regular forms

The ending **-ando** is added to the verb stem of regular **-ar** verbs, and **-iendo** is added to the stem of regular **-er** and **-ir** verbs.

-*ar* **verbs**	-*er* **verbs**	-*ir* **verbs**
habl**ar**	com**er**	sub**ir**
habl**ando**	com**iendo**	sub**iendo**

25.C.2 Irregular forms

Irregular verbs are often **-er** and **-ir** verbs that form the **gerundio** with **-iendo**, but have vowel shifts or consonant changes in the stem. The list below shows some of the most common examples.

◀ Verb conjugation tables, pp. 257–276. See verb patterns 13, 17, 23, 25, 46, 48, 50, 76.

-*uir*, -*eer*, -*aer* **and other verbs**		$e \rightarrow i, o \rightarrow u$ **vowel shift**	
Infinitive	*Gerundio*	**Infinitive**	*Gerundio*
construir	construyendo	p**e**dir	p**i**diendo
leer	leyendo	v**e**nir	v**i**niendo
caer	cayendo	d**o**rmir	d**u**rmiendo
oír	oyendo	p**o**der	p**u**diendo

25.C.3 *Estar* + *gerundio* (progressive tenses)

a. The **gerundio** is combined with the verb **estar** to refer to actions that are ongoing. This verb periphrasis is sometimes referred to as *progressive* or *continuous* tenses.

◀ Progressive tenses: 17.F.1 Verb periphrases with the **gerundio**: 26.D

Estaba trabajando cuando oí la alarma.   *I was working when I heard the alarm.*

b. In Spanish, **estar + gerundio** cannot be used to refer to conditions or states.

Está parado ahí.   *He is standing over there.*

Llevaba un suéter rosado.   *She was wearing a pink sweater.*

c. This verb periphrasis can be used in all indicative and subjunctive mood tenses.

Estar + gerundio: **Indicative mood**		
Present	**Estoy trabajando** en este momento.	*I am working right now.*
Simple future	A las ocho **estaré trabajando**.	*I will be working at eight.*
Preterite	**Estuve cocinando** tres horas.	*I was cooking for three hours.*
Imperfect	**Estaba cocinando** cuando sonó el timbre.	*I was cooking when the doorbell rang.*
Present conditional	Si fuera rica, **estaría viajando** por el mundo.	*If I were rich, I would be traveling around the world.*
Future perfect	Para cuando llegue la pizza, **habré estado esperando** más de una hora.	*By the time the pizza arrives, I will have been waiting for over an hour.*
Present perfect	**He estado pensando** mucho en ti.	*I have been thinking a lot about you.*
Past perfect	Cuando me di cuenta de que era el libro equivocado, ya **había estado leyendo** tres horas.	*When I realized it was the wrong book, I had already been reading for three hours.*
Conditional perfect	**Habría estado estudiando** si hubiera sabido que tenía examen.	*I would have been studying if I had known that I had an exam.*

Estar + *gerundio*: Subjunctive mood		
Present	No creo que **esté durmiendo**.	*I don't think he is sleeping.*
Imperfect	No podía creer que **estuviera dándole** la mano al presidente.	*I couldn't believe I was shaking the president's hand.*
Present perfect	Me extraña que **haya estado trabajando** tantas horas.	*I think it's strange that he's been working so many hours.*
Past perfect	Dudo que **hubiese estado mintiendo**.	*I doubt he had been lying.*

Present with future meaning: 17.E.4
Using the present to refer to the future: 17.F.4

d. In Spanish, the present form of **estar** + **gerundio** is never used to refer to the future.

Llegan mañana.   *They are arriving tomorrow.*
(*Not* *Están llegando mañana.)

e. The future form of **estar** + **gerundio** can be used to express probability about the present, while the conditional form can be used to express probability about the past.

—¿Dónde está Carlos?   *Where is Carlos?*
—**Estará trabajando.**   *He must be working.*

—¿Por qué no vino Carlos?   *Why didn't Carlos come?*
—**Estaría trabajando.**   *He must have been working.*

f. The future perfect of **estar** + **gerundio** can also be used to express probability in the past.

—¿Por qué no atendió el teléfono?   *Why didn't he answer the phone?*
—**Habrá estado durmiendo.**   *He must have been sleeping.*

25.C.4   **Other verb periphrases with the** *gerundio*

Verb periphrases with the
gerundio: 26.D

In addition to **estar**, other verbs can be combined with the **gerundio**. In some cases, the meaning is similar to that of the periphrases with **estar**. In other cases, there are subtle differences.

andar + gerundio	to be + -ing verb	**Andaba pensando** en ir a Punta Cana.	*I was thinking of going to Punta Cana.*
ir + gerundio	to go + -ing verb	**Voy poniendo** la mesa mientras te preparas.	*I'll start setting the table while you get ready.*
llevar/pasarse + time expression + gerundio	to be doing something for + time expression	**Llevo** tres años **estudiando** teatro. **Se pasó** todo el verano **estudiando**.	*I've been studying drama for three years. She has been studying all summer.*
seguir/continuar + gerundio	to keep/continue + -ing verb	**Siguieron planeando** el viaje.	*They kept on planning for the trip.*
venir + gerundio	to be + -ing verb	**Viene pensando** en cambiar de trabajo.	*He has been thinking about changing jobs.*
vivir + gerundio	to keep + -ing verb (habitual or repeated action)	**Vive quejándose.**	*She keeps complaining all the time.*

25.C.5   **Adverbial uses of the** *gerundio*

a. The **gerundio** can function like an adverb. The chart that follows describes the main meanings expressed by the **gerundio**.

Adverbial subordinate clauses: 16.C.2

cause	No **queriendo** escuchar esa conversación, me fui de la reunión.	*Not wanting to listen to that conversation, I left the meeting.*
concession	**Siendo** liberal, sus ideas son un poco conservadoras.	*Being a liberal, his ideas are somewhat conservative.*
condition	**Estando** invitado, sí va.	*If he is invited, he will go.*
manner	Entró **derribando** la puerta.	*He got in by knocking down the door.*
method	Hizo su fortuna **vendiendo** madera.	*He made his fortune selling wood.*
purpose	Me llamó **diciendo** que no iba a venir.	*He called me saying he wasn't going to come.*
simultaneity	Me desperté **queriendo** café.	*I woke up wanting coffee.*

b. To express purpose, the **gerundio** can only be used with verbs of communication. It can be replaced with **para** + *infinitive*.

Conjunctions of purpose: 16.C.7
Adverbial clauses of purpose: 23.E.3
Para + infinitive: 25.B.2b

Le escribió **diciéndole** que la amaba.   *He wrote to her telling her he loved her.*
Le escribió **para decirle** que la amaba.   *He wrote her to tell her that he loved her.*

c. The action expressed by the **gerundio** should happen before, at the same time, or right after the action expressed with the conjugated verb. Although many Spanish speakers use the **gerundio** to refer to an action that happened after (but not *right* after) the action in the main verb, a relative clause is the preferred form in these cases.

Both actions happened at the same time:
Escuchando los anuncios del gobierno, me deprimí.   *Listening to the government announcements, I got depressed.*

The action expressed by the **gerundio** happened before:
Alzando el arco, disparó la flecha.   *Raising the bow, he fired the arrow.*

The action expressed by the **gerundio** happened after:
Aumentaron las tasas de interés **causando** pánico en el mercado.   *Interest rates rose, causing panic in the market.*

Aumentaron las tasas de interés, **lo que causó** pánico en el mercado.   *Interest rates rose, which caused panic in the market.*

d. The **gerundio compuesto** can only refer to actions that happened before the action expressed by the conjugated verb.

Habiendo aprobado el examen, salió a festejar.   *Having passed the exam, he went out to celebrate.*

25.C.6   The *gerundio* vs. the English present participle: adjectival uses

a. Since the **gerundio** normally modifies a verb, the general rule is that it cannot be used as an adjective. Therefore, the English present participle used as an adjective is best replaced by a relative clause, a prepositional phrase, an adjective, or a participle. Sometimes, a completely different structure is needed in Spanish.

there are growing concerns   cada vez preocupa más
suffering people   personas que sufren
growing problems   problemas crecientes / en aumento
swimming pool   pileta de natación / piscina

b. The **gerundio** can be used in picture captions or titles of paintings.

Pablo Picasso, «Mujer **llorando**», 1937.

Pablo Picasso, "Weeping Woman," 1937.

Foto del príncipe heredero **sonriéndoles** a los fotógrafos.

Photo of the crown prince smiling at the photographers.

Mi hermana **enseñándome** a nadar en el verano de 2000.

My sister teaching me to swim, summer 2000.

c. Ardiendo and **hirviendo** can be used as adjectives.

fuego **ardiendo**   *burning fire*   agua **hirviendo**   *boiling water*

25.C.7   Use of the *gerundio* to refer to a direct object

a. With sense verbs like **oír, ver, encontrar, recordar,** and **sentir**, the **gerundio** describes an action performed by the direct object.

Anoche oímos al perro **ladrando**.

Last night we heard the dog barking.

¿No has visto a Sally **bailando**?

Have you not seen Sally dancing?

Hemos encontrado al niño solo y **llorando**.

We found the boy alone and crying.

Siempre recordaré a mi profesora **explicándome** el subjuntivo.

I will always remember my teacher explaining the subjunctive to me.

Placement of the object pronoun: 13.G

b. The **gerundio** can also be used to refer to the object of a verb that expresses a mental or physical representation (**imaginar, recordar**). The **gerundio** should always express an action, never a state.

Me **lo** imaginé **viajando** por el mundo.

I imagined him traveling around the world.

Los recuerdo **hablando** de sus abuelos.

I remember them talking about their grandparents.

Te hacía **viajando** por Europa.

I thought you were traveling around Europe.

No me puedo imaginar **a Carlos bailando** tango.

I cannot imagine Carlos dancing tango.

Recuerdo que Mario tenía problemas.

I remember Mario having problems.

(*Not* *Recuerdo a Mario teniendo problemas.)

25.C.8   Placement of pronouns

a. When the **gerundio** follows a finite verb, the pronoun is placed before the finite verb or is added to the end of the **gerundio**.

(Te estoy escribiendo la carta.)

(I'm writing the letter to you.)

Te la estoy escribiendo. / Estoy escribiéndo**tela**.

I'm writing it to you.

Gerundio with sense verbs: 25.C.7

b. Reflexive and object pronouns must be added to the **gerundio** in clauses with sense verbs and objects.

Te vi bajándo**te** del autobús.

I saw you getting off the bus.

Nos oyeron hablándo**les** en francés a los turistas.

They heard us speaking in French to the tourists.

25.D The past participle

El participio

Present and past perfect: 19.A and 19.D
*Use of the participle in passive **ser** clauses: 28.B*

The past participle forms all the compound forms with the auxiliary verb **haber** (*to have*): **Has hablado.** (*You have spoken.*). With **ser**, the past participle forms passive sentences: **La carta fue escrita.** (*The letter was written.*). Apart from these verb functions, the participle is generally used as an *adjective*.

a. The ending **-ado** is added to the verb stem of regular **-ar** verbs to form the past participle. The ending **-ido** is added to the stem of regular **-er** and **-ir** verbs. Object and reflexive pronouns must *always* be placed before **haber**.

◀ When used as adjectives, past participles agree in gender and number: 3.A.1

hablar → hablado   comer → comido   subir → subido

b. When the verb stem ends in any vowel except **-u**, a written accent is needed on the past participle ending **-ido** (**-er** and **-ir** verbs). The combination of **u + i** usually forms a diphthong and does not have an accent (**construido, huido**).

◀ Accents on vowel combinations: 1.E.4
Hiatus and accentuation: 1.E.5

Infinitive	Verb stem	Past participle	
creer	**cre-**	creído	*thought*
leer	**le-**	leído	*read*
oír	**o-**	oído	*heard*
sonreír	**sonre-**	sonreído	*smiled*
traer	**tra-**	traído	*brought*

25.D.2   **Irregular forms**

A number of verbs have an irregular past participle.

◀ Irregular past participles: 19.A.2

Infinitives	Irregular past participles	
abrir	**abierto**	*opened*
cubrir	**cubierto**	*covered*
decir	**dicho**	*said, told*
descubrir	**descubierto**	*discovered*
escribir	**escrito**	*written*
hacer	**hecho**	*done, made*
morir	**muerto**	*died*
poner	**puesto**	*placed*
resolver	**resuelto**	*resolved*
romper	**roto**	*broken*
satisfacer	**satisfecho**	*satisfied*
ver	**visto**	*seen*
volver	**vuelto**	*returned*

25.D.3   **Past participles with two forms**

a. There are only three Spanish verbs that have two completely equal past participle forms: a regular form and an irregular form that can form all the compound verb tenses with **haber** and passive voice with **ser**.

◀ Passive voice with **ser**: 28.B

Infinitive	Past participle	
	Regular	Irregular
imprimir (*to print*)	imprimido	**impreso**
freír (*to fry*)	freído	**frito**
proveer (*to provide*)	proveído	**provisto**

He **impreso/imprimido** la carta.   *I have printed the letter.*
No hemos **frito/freído** la carne.   *We haven't fried the meat.*
A los viajeros se les ha **provisto/proveído** de todo.   *The travelers have been provided with everything.*

b. In the Spanish-speaking world, **freído** and **provisto** are often used both as a participle and an adjective. The irregular form **impreso** is often used in Latin America both as a participle and an adjective.

El formulario está **impreso**.	*The form is printed.*
Las albóndigas ya están **fritas**.	*The meatballs are already fried.*
La bodega está bien **provista**.	*The wine cellar is well supplied.*

Passive voice with **ser**: 28.B ▶

c. All other Spanish verbs that have two past participle forms use only the regular form in compound tenses with **haber** (**He corregido las cartas.**) and the passive voice with **ser** (**Las cartas han sido corregidas.**). The irregular past participle form is only used as an adjective (**Eso es correcto.**). Below is a list of some of these two-participle verbs with their most common meanings.

Gender and number of ▶
adjectives: 3.A

Infinitives	Participles		Adjectives	
absorber	**absorbido**	*absorbed*	**absorto**	*absorbed/engrossed*
atender	**atendido**	*attended/assisted*	**atento**	*attentive/alert/courteous*
bendecir	**bendecido**	*blessed*	**bendito**	*blessed*
confesar	**confesado**	*confessed*	**confeso**	*self-confessed*
confundir	**confundido**	*confused*	**confuso**	*confused/confusing*
despertar	**despertado**	*awakened*	**despierto**	*awake/bright/alert*
elegir	**elegido**	*chosen/elected*	**electo**	*chosen/elected*
maldecir	**maldecido**	*cursed/damned*	**maldito**	*cursed/damned*
prender	**prendido**	*caught*	**preso**	*imprisoned*
presumir	**presumido**	*presumed*	**presunto**	*presumed/alleged*
soltar	**soltado**	*released / let go*	**suelto**	*loose/fluid/fluent*

Electo is mostly used in Latin ▶
America as an adjective:
el presidente electo
el preso: the prisoner ▶
estar preso: to be imprisoned

25.D.4 Use of the past participle

a. The past participle forms all the compound verb forms with **haber** both in the indicative and the subjunctive moods (**ha salido / haya salido**). The participle form always retains the **-ado/-ido** ending in all compound tenses.

Passive voice with **ser**: 28.B ▶
Estar and passive voice
with **ser**: 28.C.3

b. The past participle is used in the passive voice with **ser**, where it agrees in gender and number with the subject in the sentence.

La novel**a fue escrita** por el escritor.	*The novel was written by the author.*
Las novel**as fueron escritas** por el escritor.	*The novels were written by the author.*

Agreement of the past participle ▶
in verb periphrases: 26.E

c. With **estar**, the past participle conveys the result of an action. Such sentences often correspond to the passive structure with **ser**.

La carta **fue escrita**.	*The letter was written.*
(*passive voice*)	
La carta **está escrita**.	*The letter is written.*
(**estar** + *past participle*)	

Práctica

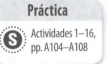

Actividades 1–16,
pp. A104–A108

Verb periphrases and modal verbs
Perífrasis verbales y verbos modales

26.A Overview

Aspectos generales

26.A.1 Verb periphrases

a. *Verb periphrases* (**perífrasis verbales**) are verb combinations made up of an auxiliary verb and a main verb. The main verb always uses a non-personal form: *infinitive*, **gerundio**, or *past participle*.

Volvió a hablar con su hermano.	*He spoke with his brother again.*
Siguió hablando durante toda la reunión.	*He continued talking during the entire meeting.*
Llevo ganados diez premios.	*I have won ten awards (so far).*

b. Auxiliary verbs are usually conjugated, but can also appear in non-personal forms.

Volver a hablar con él fue una alegría.	*Talking to him again was a joy.*
No **pudiendo responder** a la pregunta, se echó a llorar.	*Being unable to answer the question, she began to cry.*

c. Most auxiliary verbs can be used as main verbs.

Volvió a su pueblo.	*He returned to his hometown.*
Sigo su blog todas las semanas.	*I follow your blog every week.*
Llevé a los niños a la fiesta.	*I took the children to the party.*

d. There can be another element, such as a preposition or conjunction, joining the two verbs that form the periphrasis.

Tengo *que* **trabajar** el fin de semana.	*I have to work this weekend.*
Debe *de* **haber llovido** mucho.	*It must have rained a lot.*

e. Not all verb combinations are verb periphrases. In a periphrasis, the meaning of the auxiliary verb is totally or partially different from the meaning of the periphrasis as a whole. In addition, the second verb can never be a direct object of the first.

Tengo que trabajar. (periphrasis – **tener** does not express *possession*)	*I have to work.*
Debo estudiar. (periphrasis – **estudiar** is not the direct object of **debo**)	*I should study.*
Deseo ganar el concurso. Lo deseo. (not a periphrasis – **ganar el concurso** is the direct object of **deseo**)	*I want to win the contest. I want (to win) it.*

26.B Modal verb periphrases with the infinitive

The infinitive: 25.B

Perífrasis modales de infinitivo

26.B.1 Modal auxiliaries

a. Modal auxiliaries express possibility, obligation, necessity, and other aspects of the speaker's attitude towards the action expressed by the main verb.

Modal verbs: 17.F.3

Bailo.	*I dance.*
Puedo bailar.	*I can dance.*
Quiero bailar.	*I want to dance.*

Passive constructions with
se and modal verbs: 28.D.3

26.B.2 Aspect expressed by modal verb periphrases

Modal verb periphrases can express obligation or necessity, possibility, and doubt.

Modal verb periphrases	Aspect expressed	Examples
deber + *infinitive*	obligation	**Debes venir** inmediatamente. *You must come immediately.*
deber de + *infinitive*	doubt or possibility	**Deben de ser** las ocho. *It must be eight o'clock.*
tener que + *infinitive*	obligation	No fui porque **tenía que estudiar**. *I didn't go because I had to study.*
haber de + *infinitive*	obligation	Estos son los documentos que **hemos de darle** al abogado. *These are the documents that we have to give to the lawyer.*
	probability (with perfect infinitive)	Alguien le **ha de haber contado**. *Someone must have told her.*
haber que + *infinitive*	obligation (that cannot be avoided; impersonal: used only in the third-person singular)	**Habrá que sobrellevar** la crisis. *The crisis must be endured.*
poder + *infinitive*	capacity, ability	La cerámica **puede resistir** los cambios de temperatura. *Ceramics can withstand changes in temperature.*
	permission	**Puedes venir** mañana si quieres. *You can come tomorrow if you'd like.*
	assumption	**Podría ser** interesante. *It could be interesting.*
venir a + *infinitive*	approximation	El libro **vino a costarme** unos cien pesos. *The book cost me about 100 pesos.*

26.B.3 Other modal verb periphrases

The following verb periphrases are commonly grouped together with modal verb periphrases.

Modal verb periphrases	Aspect expressed	Examples
parecer + *infinitive*	conjecture	**Parece haber** mucha gente en la fiesta. *There seem to be a lot of people at the party.*
querer + *infinitive*	wish, desire	**Quiero escuchar** música. *I want to listen to music.*
saber + *infinitive*	skill	**Sé hablar** español muy bien. *I know how to speak Spanish very well.*

26.B.4 *Deber / deber de*

a. Deber expresses obligation, but is weaker than **tener que**. **Deber de** only expresses assumption or possibility. In everyday speech, the preposition **de** is often dropped and the meaning becomes ambiguous.

Debes cuidar la naturaleza.	*You should take care of nature.*
Deberías gastar menos.	*You should spend less.*
No **debiste** llegar tarde.	*You shouldn't have arrived late.*
Deberás hacerlo aunque no quieras.	*You should/will do it even though you don't want to.*
Este plato **debe de** ser delicioso.	*This dish must be delicious.*
El huracán **debió de** ser muy fuerte porque hizo mucho daño.	*The hurricane must have been very strong because it caused a lot of damage.*

b. The English *should* is usually translated using the present tense or the conditional of **deber**. However, in many cases it can be translated using the future tense or passive constructions with **se** without a modal auxiliary, particularly in handbooks and other instructions.

You **should** go to the doctor.

Deberías/Debes ir al médico.

When you press the button, you **should hear** a beep.

Al presionar el botón, **escuchará** un sonido.

Al presionar el botón, **se escucha** un sonido.

26.B.5 Poder

a. In the preterite, **poder** conveys that someone succeeded in doing something, while the *imperfect* describes whether a person was able to do something or not.

La puerta estaba cerrada y no **podíamos** entrar.
Finalmente **pudimos** hacerlo.

The door was locked and we couldn't get in.
Finally, we managed to do it.

Verbs that change meaning in the preterite and the imperfect: 18.F

b. The examples below show the use of **poder** in different verb tenses.

Permission or ban	
Todos **podéis** entrar gratis.	All of you [pl.] may go in for free.
¿**Podrías/Puedes** prestarme tu libro?	Could you / Can you lend me your book? / Could I / Can I / May I borrow your book?
No puedes hacer lo que se te ocurra.	You cannot / are not allowed to do whatever you feel like doing.

Possibility/Ability	
¡**No puedo** ponerme las botas!	I can't put my boots on!
Aquí **no se puede** cruzar la calle. ¡Es muy peligroso!	You can't cross the street here. It's very dangerous!
¿**Pudiste** ver la exhibición?	Did you get to see the exhibition?

Assumptions	
Podría ser bueno que vinieras.	It could/might be good if you came.
Eso **pudo/podía** haber sucedido.	It could have happened.
Podrías haber hecho algo.	You could/might have done something.

26.B.6 Querer

Querer is translated differently in the imperfect and the preterite. Notice also the difference in the preterite between **querer** and **no querer**.

Verbs that change meaning in the preterite and the imperfect: 18.F

Quería decirle la verdad, pero no pude.
Quise decirle la verdad, pero no pude.
Me invitaron a salir ayer, pero **no quise**.

I wanted to tell him the truth, but I couldn't.
I tried to tell him the truth, but I couldn't.
I was invited to go out yesterday, but I didn't want to (I refused).

26.B.7 Saber

a. In a verb periphrasis, **saber** indicates that a person has the skills or the knowledge to perform an action. This is independent of being physically, emotionally, or mentally in a state to do it (**poder**).

—¿**Sabes** esquiar?
—Sí, **sé** esquiar, pero **no puedo** hacerlo. Tengo el pie quebrado.

Can you ski?
Yes, I know how to ski, but I can't do it. My foot is broken.

Antes **sabía** hablar bien el español, pero ya **no puedo** hacerlo.

Before I knew how to speak Spanish well, but I can't do it anymore.

Verb periphrases and modal verbs • Chapter 26

b. As a main verb, **saber** is commonly translated as *to know* or *to discover / find out*.

Marcela **sabía** la verdad.   *Marcela knew the truth.*
Marcela **supo** la verdad.   *Marcela discovered / found out the truth.*

Infinitive: 25.B ▸

26.C Other verb periphrases with the infinitive

Otras perífrasis de infinitivo

26.C.1 Verb periphrases that express time

Use of the present to refer ▸
to the future: 17.F.4
Use of the imperfect to
refer to incomplete actions:
18.E.6, 18.E.10c

Verb periphrases	Aspect expressed	Examples
ir a + *infinitive*	future	**Voy a visitar** a mis primos. *I am going to visit my cousins.*
	unexpected action or situation	¡Justo **me fui a enamorar** de ti! *Of all people, I fell in love with you!* ¿Puedes creer que mi auto se quedó sin frenos y **fue a pegarle** precisamente a la Ferrari de mi jefe? *Can you believe that my brakes failed in my car and it went and hit my boss's Ferrari?*
soler + *infinitive*	repetition, habit	**Suelo levantarme** a las seis. *I usually get up at six.*
acostumbrar (a) + *infinitive* (*Lat. Am.*)	repetition, habit	**Acostumbra (a) tomar** el tren a las cinco. *He usually takes the five o'clock train.*
acabar de + *infinitive*	recent action	**Acabo de preparar** la cena. *I just prepared dinner.*
volver a + *infinitive*	repetition	Prometió que no **volverá a decir** mentiras. *He promised that he wouldn't tell lies again.*

26.C.2 Verb periphrases that express a phase

Some verb periphrases refer to the preparation, the beginning, the end, or the interruption of an action.

Verb periphrases	Aspect expressed	Examples
estar por + *infinitive*	preparation	**Estaba por preparar** la cena. *I was about to make dinner.*
comenzar/empezar a + *infinitive*	beginning	**Comenzó/Empezó a llover** en cuanto llegamos. *It began to rain as soon as we arrived.*
ponerse a + *infinitive*	beginning	Cuando terminó el espectáculo, todos **se pusieron a aplaudir**. *When the show was over, everyone began to applaud.*
entrar a + *infinitive*	beginning	Todos **entramos a sospechar** de él. *We all started to suspect him.*
dejar/parar de + *infinitive*	interruption	**Dejó de llover** y salió el sol. *It stopped raining and the sun came out.* ¡**Para de llorar**, por favor! *Stop crying, please!*
acabar/terminar de + *infinitive*	end	**Terminé de cocinar** a las ocho. *I finished cooking at eight o'clock.*
pasar a + *infinitive*	transition	Después de estudiar italiano, **pasé a estudiar** ruso. *After studying Italian, I went on to study Russian.*

Verb periphrases that express a hierarchy or scale

a. Some periphrases with infinitives order an action in a series.

Modal verb periphrases	Aspect expressed	Examples
empezar por + *infinitive*	first action in a series	**Empecé por explicarle** que no me gustaba mi trabajo. *I began by explaining to him that I did not like my job.*
acabar/terminar por + *infinitive*	last action in a series	**Terminé por comprar** el vestido violeta. *I ended up buying the purple dress.*
venir a + *infinitive*	result, outcome	En ese caso, ambas opciones **venían a ser** lo mismo. *In that case, both options turned out to be the same.*

b. **Empezar/acabar/terminar por** + *infinitive* can be replaced by **empezar/acabar/terminar** + **gerundio**.

Acabó por irse.

Acabó yéndose.   *He ended up leaving.*

26.D **Verb periphrases with the** *gerundio*

The **gerundio**: 25.C

   Perífrasis de gerundio

All verb periphrases with the **gerundio** express an ongoing action. Most verbs used as auxiliaries in these periphrases are common verbs of movement (**ir, venir, andar, llevar, pasar, seguir,** etc.).

Verb periphrases	Aspect expressed	Examples
estar + **gerundio**	ongoing action	**Estaba trabajando** cuando me llamaste. *I was working when you called me.*
ir + **gerundio**	incremental process with an end limit/result	Sus problemas de salud **fueron aumentando** hasta que finalmente tuvo que dejar de trabajar. *His health problems kept increasing (getting worse) until he finally had to stop working.*
	beginning of an incremental process	¿Podrías **ir pensando** en temas para el último capítulo? *Could you start thinking about topics for the last chapter?*
venir + **gerundio**	process that began in the past and continues up to the current moment	Nos **venía mintiendo**, pero lo descubrimos. *He had been lying to us, but we found out.* ¡Te **vengo diciendo** que comas mejor! *I've been telling you to eat better!*
andar + **gerundio**	current process that usually happens intermittently	El perro **anda olfateando** todos los árboles. *The dog is going around smelling all the trees.*
llevar + *time expression* + **gerundio**	period of time	**Llevo dos años estudiando** español. *I've been studying Spanish for two years.*
pasar(se) + *time expression* + **gerundio**	current process (more emphatic than **estar** + **gerundio**)	**Se pasó la noche llorando** porque extrañaba a su gatito. *He spent the night crying because he missed his kitten.*
vivir + **gerundio** (*Lat. Am.*)	repeated, constant, or habitual action	Mis vecinos **viven gritando**. No me dejan dormir. *My neighbors are always yelling. They don't let me sleep.*
seguir/continuar + **gerundio**	continued process	Ella **sigue estudiando**. *She is still / keeps on studying.*

Estar + **gerundio** (Progressive tenses): 25.C.3

Past participle: 19.A.1,
19.A.2, 25.D

 26.E | **Verb periphrases with the past participle**

Perífrasis de participio

a. All verb periphrases with the past participle focus on the result of an action or process. The participle agrees in gender and number with the subject, or with the object if there is one.

Estar + *past participle*: 28.C.3

Verb periphrases	Aspect expressed	Examples
estar + *past participle*	resulting state	La carta **está escrita** a mi nombre. *The letter is addressed to me.*
tener + *past participle*	process that has been completed	Eso ya lo **tengo visto**. *I have already looked at that.* Le **tengo prohibido** salir después de las once de la noche. *I have forbidden him to go out after eleven o'clock at night.*
llevar + *past participle*	accumulation up to a certain point in time	**Llevo ganados** cinco premios. *(So far,) I have won five awards.*

The *Nueva gramática* lists only **estar/tener/llevar** + *past participle* as verb periphrases.

b. The following verb phrases are often included with verb periphrases.

dejar + *past participle*	Juan **dejó dicho** que lo llames. *Juan left a message for you to call him.*
encontrarse/hallarse + *past participle*	**Se encuentra muy cansado.** *He is feeling very tired.*
ir + *past participle*	Para marzo ya **iban escritos** cuatro capítulos del libro. *By March, four chapters of the book were already written.*
quedar(se) + *past participle*	**Quedé agotada** después de la fiesta. *I was wiped out after the party.*
resultar + *past participle*	La clase media **resultó beneficiada** por la caída de los precios. *The middle class benefited from the drop in prices.*
seguir + *past participle*	Las calles **siguen vigiladas** por la policía. *The streets continue to be patrolled by the police.*
venir + *past participle*	Las instrucciones **vinieron escritas** en la caja. *The instructions came written on the box.*
verse + *past participle*	Juan **se vio obligado** a partir. *Juan felt obligated to leave.*

Práctica

 Actividades 1–12, pp. A108–A111

Reflexive pronouns and verbs
Pronombres y verbos reflexivos

27.A Structure

Estructura

Reflexive pronouns indicate that the subject is both the doer and the object of the action in a sentence, directly or indirectly: *You* see *yourself* in the mirror. In Spanish, some verbs can only be used reflexively. These verbs are recorded in dictionaries and word lists with the reflexive pronoun **se** after the infinitive ending, like in **lavarse** (*to wash*), **preocuparse** (*to worry*), and **sentirse** (*to feel*). Reflexive pronouns take the same form as object pronouns except for **usted(es)** and the third person: **se**. A different set of pronouns is used after prepositions and is usually followed by the adjective **mismo/a(s)**.

Subject	Reflexive pronouns	lavarse	Translation	After a preposition
yo	**me**	me lavo	*I wash (myself).*	**mí (conmigo)**
tú	**te**	te lavas	*You wash (yourself).*	**ti (contigo)**
vos	**te**	te lavás	*You wash (yourself).*	**vos**
usted, él, ella	**se**	se lava	*You wash (yourself). He/She washes (him/herself).*	**sí, usted/él/ella (consigo)**
nosotros/as	**nos**	nos lavamos	*We wash (ourselves).*	**nosotros/as**
vosotros/as	**os**	os laváis	*You wash (yourselves).*	**vosotros/as**
ustedes, ellos/as	**se**	se lavan	*You/They wash (yourselves/themselves).*	**sí, ustedes/ellos/ellas (consigo)**

Juan **se despierta** temprano.	*Juan wakes up early.*
Mis padres **se preocupan** mucho.	*My parents worry a lot.*
Hazte la pregunta **a ti mismo**.	*Ask the question to yourself.*
Parecía que hablaba **consigo mismo**.	*It seemed he was talking to himself.*

Reflexive verbs: 17.B.3, 27.C
Pronouns after prepositions: 13.C

27.A.1 Placement

a. Reflexive pronouns are placed before the conjugated verb. With verb expressions using the infinitive or **gerundio**, the placement is optional, either before the conjugated verb or after the infinitive/**gerundio**.

Ellos **se** lavan.	*They wash (themselves).*
Ellos **se** van a lavar. Ellos van a lavar**se**.	*They are going to wash (themselves).*
Ellos **se** están lavando. Ellos están lavándo**se**.	*They are washing (themselves).*

b. With compound verb forms using **haber** + *past participle*, the pronoun is always placed before the conjugated verb.

—¿**Os** habéis lavado?	*Have you [pl.] washed (yourselves)?*
—No, no **nos** hemos lavado.	*No, we have not washed (ourselves).*

c. Reflexive pronouns are placed after affirmative imperatives and before negative imperatives.

Lávate las manos antes de la cena.	*Wash your hands before dinner.*
No **te** preocupes por nada.	*Don't worry (yourself) about anything.*

Pronouns after
prepositions: 13.C

mismo/a(s): 7.E.5

27.A.2 Reflexive pronouns after a preposition

a. The forms of the reflexive pronouns used after prepositions (**mí, ti, usted/él/ella, nosotros/as, vosotros/as, ustedes/ellos/as**) can convey a reflexive meaning. After prepositions, the form **sí** can also be used instead of **usted, él/ella, ustedes, ellos/as. Sí** is inherently reflexive. When **mí, ti,** and **sí** follow the preposition **con,** they form **conmigo, contigo,** and **consigo.** The adjective **mismo/a(s)** (*self*) usually follows the pronoun to emphasize the reflexive meaning. It agrees in gender and number with the subject.

Pedro sólo piensa en **sí** mism**o**.	*Pedro only thinks about himself.*
Marina habla **consigo** mism**a**.	*Marina is talking / talks to herself.*

b. Compare these reflexive and non-reflexive uses of pronouns after prepositions.

Reflexive use	Non-reflexive use
Habla **consigo misma**. *She talks to herself.*	Habla **con ella**. *She talks to her.*
Llevaba **consigo** un bastón. *He carried a cane with him.*	Fui al parque **con él**. *I went to the park with him.*
Me lo guardé **para mí misma**. *I kept it for myself.*	Lo guardé **para ella**. *I kept it for her.*
Se lo repitió **a sí/ella misma**. *She repeated it to herself.*	Se lo repitió **a ella**. *He repeated it to her.*

27.B Reciprocal pronouns

Pronombres recíprocos

Different meanings of
reflexive verbs: 27.D

27.B.1 Each other

A plural reflexive pronoun may indicate a *reciprocal* meaning corresponding to the English *each other*.

Mis padres y yo **nos queremos** mucho.	*My parents and I love each other very much.*
Vosotros **os llamáis** todos los días.	*You [pl.] call each other every day.*
Los novios **se abrazan**.	*The couple is hugging each other.*
¿Os habláis vosotros?	*Are you [pl.] talking to each other?*
¿Se escriben tus amigos y tú?	*Do you and your friends write to each other?*

27.B.2 El uno al otro

To emphasize a mutual relationship, **el uno al otro / los unos a los otros** can be added after the verb. The preposition changes according to the preposition required by the verb. The adverbs **mutuamente** (*mutually*) and **recíprocamente** (*reciprocally*) are rarely used. They are more common as adjectives in expressions such as: **El respeto entre nosotros es mutuo/recíproco.** (*The respect between us is mutual/reciprocal*).

Los novios se abrazan **el uno al otro**.	*The couple is hugging each other.*
Se pelean todo el tiempo **el uno con el otro.**	*They fight with each other all the time.*
En Navidad nos damos regalos **los unos a los otros**.	*At Christmas, we give each other gifts.*
Los vecinos se ayudan **mutuamente**.	*Neighbors help each other.*

27.C Reflexive verbs

Verbos reflexivos

Reflexive verbs are conjugated with reflexive pronouns. Many verbs have reflexive and non-reflexive forms. These two conjugation forms for the same verb can result in related or completely different meanings. Spanish verbs that do not have a reflexive meaning but do have a reflexive form are called **verbos pronominales** (*pronominal verbs*).

Reflexive	Non-reflexive
Me **visto** después de bañar*me*. *I get dressed after taking a bath.*	**Visto** a la bebé después de **bañarla**. *I get the baby dressed after bathing her.*
Te **despiertas** temprano. *You wake up early.*	*Te* **despierto** temprano. *I wake you up early.*
Las chicas *se* **levantan** tarde. *The girls get up late.*	Las chicas **levantan** pesas. *The girls lift weights.*
No quiero **despedirme** de ti. *I don't want to say goodbye to you.*	Mi jefe me va a **despedir**. *My boss is going to fire me.*

27.D Different meanings of reflexive verbs

Varios significados de los verbos reflexivos

27.D.1 Reflexive meaning

a. This is the meaning implied when reflexive verbs are discussed. The subject (which must refer to something living) performs the action and is also subject to it. In this case, the singular reflexive intensifier **a sí mismo/a** (*self*) can be added.

Ella **se lava** (a sí misma).	*She is washing (herself).*
El perro **se muerde** la cola (a sí mismo).	*The dog is biting its tail.*

 Reflexive pronouns: 27.A

b. Reflexive verbs and pronouns are used more often in Spanish than in English, although reflexive pronouns are sometimes used in English in a non-reflexive way.

Yo mismo hice la tarea.	*I did the homework **myself**.*
Me voy a **divorciar**.	*I'm going to get divorced.*
¿No **te avergüenzas** de eso?	*Aren't you ashamed of that?*

c. In genuine reflexive verbs, the subject and object refer to the same person. But if an additional object is added to the sentence (for example, **las manos**), the subject is indirectly affected by the action and becomes the indirect object. In this case, the verb is still reflexive.

Los niños **se lavan** las manos.	*The children are washing their hands.*
¿**Te pintaste** las uñas?	*Did you paint your nails?*
Ponte el abrigo.	*Put on your coat.*

Use of article instead of a possessive: 9.D.4

d. In the previous reflexive sentences, it is not common to use the reflexive intensifier (**a mí mismo, a sí mismo**, etc.), but the reflexive action can be emphasized by adding the phrase **por sí mismo/a** or **por sí solo/a** (*himself/herself*).

El abuelo ya no es capaz de levantarse
por sí mismo/solo.

Grandpa can't get up by himself anymore.

e. A number of verbs that describe daily personal care are reflexive. The intensifier **a sí mismo/a** is not needed with these verbs.

Reflexive verbs for daily routines			
acostarse	*to go to bed*	desvestirse	*to get undressed*
afeitarse/rasurarse	*to shave*	maquillarse	*to put on makeup*
dormirse	*to fall asleep*	peinarse	*to comb one's hair*
levantarse	*to get/stand up*	ponerse	*to put on (e.g., clothes)*
bañarse, ducharse	*to take a bath, to take a shower*	quitarse	*to take off (e.g., clothes)*
cepillarse	*to brush (hair or teeth)*	vestirse	*to get dressed*

Nos acostamos tarde.   *We go to bed late.*

Te levantas temprano.   *You get up early.*

Os despertáis a las siete.   *You [pl.] wake up at seven o'clock.*

No puedo **dormirme**.   *I can't fall asleep.*

¿**Te cepillas** los dientes?   *Do you brush your teeth?*

Me ducho y **me visto**.   *I shower and get dressed.*

Ella **se peina** y **se maquilla**.   *She combs her hair and puts on makeup.*

27.D.2   Verbs with only reflexive forms

A few Spanish verbs only have a reflexive form.

Verbs that do not have a reflexive meaning but do have a reflexive form are called **verbos pronominales.**

Verbs with only reflexive forms			
arrepentirse	*to regret*	quejarse	*to complain*
atreverse	*to dare*	jactarse	*to boast*
abstenerse	*to abstain*	suicidarse	*to commit suicide*

El abogado **se jacta** de que nunca ha perdido ni un solo caso. Nadie **se atreve** a **quejarse** de sus servicios.

The lawyer boasts that he has never lost even a single case. Nobody dares to complain about his services.

27.D.3   Reciprocal meaning

el uno al otro: 27.B.2 ▶

a. When two or more people are doing an action and are also the recipients of that action, the meaning is reciprocal (**recíproco**). The reciprocal meaning is emphasized by adding **el uno al otro**, **la una a la otra**, or **mutuamente**. The following verbs are often used with a reciprocal meaning.

Common verbs with reciprocal meaning	
abrazarse	Los novios **se abrazan**. *The couple hugs (each other).*
amarse/quererse	**Nos queremos** desde siempre. *We have always loved each other.*
ayudarse	Mis amigos y yo **nos ayudamos** (**mutuamente**). *My friends and I help each other.*
besarse	En España **nos besamos** al saludar. *In Spain, we kiss when greeting each other.*
comprometerse	¿Vosotros **os** vais a **comprometer**? *Are you [pl.] going to get engaged?*
escribirse	Deberíamos **escribirnos** más. *We should write to each other more.*
hablarse	Mi madre y yo **nos hablamos** a diario. *My mother and I talk to each other every day.*
llevarse bien/mal	**Nos llevamos** bien. *We get along well (with each other).*
mirarse	La madre y el bebé **se miran** a los ojos. *Mother and child are looking into each other's eyes.*
odiarse	Los perros y los gatos **se odian**. *Dogs and cats hate each other.*
pelearse	Algunas personas **se pelean** por todo. *Some people fight about anything.*
tutearse	Nosotros nunca **nos tuteamos**. *We never address each other informally.*
verse	Mis amigos y yo **nos vemos** los sábados. *My friends and I see each other on Saturdays.*

b. English verbs emphasize reciprocal meaning by adding *each other*. Spanish has similar structures with reflexive verbs.

¿**Nos veremos** mañana?   *Will we see each other tomorrow?*

Los jugadores **se reúnen** hoy para entrenar.   *The players are meeting today for training.*

Algunas personas no **se tratan** bien   *Some people don't treat each other well*
y **se pelean** mucho.   *and fight a lot.*

27.D.4   To get (something) done: *mandarse a hacer*

When it is obvious that someone other than the subject is doing the action, **hacerse** (*to get* [*something*] *done*), **mandarse a** (*to have* [*something*] *done*), or similar expressions can be used.

Ella **se hizo construir** una gran casa.   *She had a great house built.*

27.D.5   Verbs that express a complete action

A number of Spanish verbs use the reflexive form and direct object to express that an action is completely fullfilled in relation to the object.

No sé si **creer** todo lo que dices.   *I don't know whether to believe everything you say.*

No sé si **creerme** todo lo que me dices.   *I don't know if I should believe everything you tell me.*

This meaning is conveyed in all verb tenses and used with verbs that express mental and physical activities, such as *to be able to do something perfectly, to learn something by heart, to know somebody inside out, to eat up, to drink up, to climb to the top, to sink to the bottom,* and similar English expressions.

Reflexive verbs that express a complete action	
andarse	**Nos anduvimos** la ciudad entera. *We walked through the whole city.*
aprenderse	¡La profesora **se aprendió** los nombres de pe a pa! *The teacher learned the names from A to Z!*
beberse	¡Ustedes **se bebieron** la limonada hasta la última gota! *You [pl.] drank all the lemonade to the last drop!*
comerse	Y también **se comieron** todas las tapas y los tacos. *And you also finished off (ate up) all the tapas and tacos.*
conocerse	**Me conozco** las calles de Madrid al derecho y al revés. *I know the streets of Madrid inside out.*
creerse	Ellos **se creyeron** todo lo que les dijeron. *They believed everything they were told.*
fumarse	¿Usted **se fuma** toda una cajetilla en un día? *Do you smoke a whole pack in one day?*
leerse	**Nos leemos** el periódico de principio a fin. *We read the newspaper from cover to cover.*
recorrerse	**Nos recorreremos** el país de un extremo a otro. *We'll travel the country from one end to the other.*
saberse	**Os sabéis** la lección al pie de la letra. *You [pl.] know the lesson by heart.*
tomarse	**Tómate** unas vacaciones, te ves cansado. *Take a vacation, you look exhausted.*
tragarse	¿**Te** puedes **tragar** esas píldoras tan grandes? *Can you swallow such big pills?*
verse	**Nos hemos visto** todas las películas de Almodóvar. *We have seen every single Almodóvar movie.*

27.E Verbs that change meaning in the reflexive form

Verbos que cambian de significado en forma reflexiva

Many Spanish verbs have a slightly different meaning when conjugated with a reflexive pronoun.

Non-reflexive	Meaning	Reflexive	Meaning
animar a	*to encourage (to)*	animarse a	*to motivate oneself (to), to dare*
comer	*to eat*	comerse	*to eat up*
decidir	*to decide*	decidirse a/por	*to decide (for oneself) to*
deshacer algo	*to undo something*	deshacerse de	*to get rid of*
jugar	*to play*	jugarse algo	*to gamble*
saltar	*to jump*	saltarse algo	*to skip, ignore*
unir	*to unite*	unirse a	*to join*

¡**Cómete** todas las verduras!	Eat up all your vegetables!
Debes **comer** alimentos sanos.	You must eat healthy food.
Deberías **deshacerte** de tu ropa vieja antes de comprarte nueva.	You should get rid of your old clothes before you buy new ones.
Lo hice mal, así que tengo que **deshacerlo**.	I did it wrong, so I need to undo it.
No **me animo a** contarle la verdad.	I don't dare tell her the truth.
¡Hay que **animar a** nuestro equipo!	We have to encourage our team!
Se jugó a todo o nada y perdió.	He put everything on the line and lost.
Jugó al fútbol toda su vida.	He played soccer all his life.

27.F Reflexive verbs that express involuntary actions

Verbos reflexivos que expresan acciones involuntarias

27.F.1 Involuntary actions

a. The pronominal form can be used, particularly with inanimate objects, to express an action without indicating the person or entity responsible for the action.

Se cayó el vaso.	The glass fell.
Se cerraron las puertas.	The doors (were) closed.
El televisor **se rompió**.	The TV broke.
La ventana **se hizo trizas**.	The window broke into pieces.

b. When an action is perceived as accidental or involuntary, an indirect object pronoun is used to identify the person performing the action or affected by the action.

Estaba hablando con mi hermano y **se me cayó** el teléfono.	I was talking to my brother and I dropped the phone.
Se le rompió su jarrón favorito.	Her favorite vase broke.
Se me cerró la puerta en la cara.	The door (was) closed in my face.
Cuando escuché lo que dijo, **se me fue** el alma a los pies.	When I heard what he said, my heart sank.

c. Constructions like **rompérsele**, **cerrársele**, and **caérsele** can be referred to as *"doubly pronominal,"* since they take both the reflexive pronoun **se** and an indirect object pronoun. Other verbs used in this manner include **ocurrírsele**, **antojársele**, **perdérsele**, **reírsele**, **quedársele**, and **morírsele**.

Se me han ocurrido dos ideas.	I've thought of two ideas.
¿Qué **se te antoja** comer hoy?	What do you feel like eating today?
Se me murió el pececito.	My little fish died.
Cuando le conté la verdad, **se me rio** en la cara.	When I told her the truth, she laughed in my face.
Se nos perdió el gato.	We lost our cat.
Se nos quedaron las llaves adentro.	We left the keys inside.

d. Some of these verbs also have regular pronominal/reflexive uses without the indirect object pronoun. **Antojársele** and **ocurrírsele** can only be used in "doubly pronominal" constructions.

Juan **se rió** mucho.	*Juan laughed a lot.*
Se murió el pececito.	*The little fish died.*
Se perdieron dos niños.	*Two children got lost.*
Las llaves **se quedaron** adentro.	*We left the keys inside. / The keys were left inside.*
Se rompió la llave.	*The key broke.*
Mi hermanita **se cayó**.	*My little sister fell.*

e. Quedar(se) can also be used as a non-pronominal intransitive verb.

Las llaves **quedaron** adentro.	*The keys were left inside.*

27.F.2 *Olvidarse(le)*

The transitive verb **olvidar** can also be used pronominally in two different constructions.

olvidar: **transitive verb**	olvidarse de: **intransitive pronominal verb**	olvidársele algo a alguien: **doubly pronominal verb**
Olvidé su nombre.	Me olvidé de su nombre.	Se me olvidó su nombre.
I forgot his name.		

27.G   Verbs expressing change: *to become*

Verbos de cambio

27.G.1   Change of state

Expressing change and state: 29.E

Verbs that express a shift from one state to another or suggest that a change exists are called *inchoative* verbs. Some of these verbs, such as **emocionarse** (*to get emotional, to be moved*), **envanecerse** (*to become conceited*) and **entristecerse** (*to become sad*), are reflexive, and others, like **envejecer** (*to get old, to age*), **enrojecer** (*to get red, to blush*) are not.

Me emocioné cuando oí las noticias.	*I became emotional when I heard the news.*
La actriz **se entristeció** cuando supo que no había recibido el premio.	*The actress became sad when she found out she had not won the award.*
Juan **envejeció** mucho desde la muerte de su esposa.	*Juan looks a lot older since his wife died.*
Mucha gente **enrojece** cuando la elogian.	*Many people blush when they get compliments.*

27.G.2   Other changes

a. Many reflexive verbs express physical, social, or emotional changes. The table provides some examples. The most important verbs are explained individually after the table.

Reflexive verbs that express change		
Physical position	**Social**	**Emotional**
arrodillarse *to kneel*	**casarse (con)** *to get married (to)*	**alegrarse (de)** *to be happy/glad (about)*
levantarse *to get/ stand up*	**divorciarse (de)** *to get divorced (from)*	**desmotivarse (por)** *to get unmotivated by*
morirse *to die*	**enriquecerse** *to get rich*	**enamorarse (de)** *to fall in love (with)*
moverse *to move*	**graduarse** *to graduate*	**irritarse** *to get irritated*
sentarse *to sit down*	**separarse (de)** *to separate oneself (from)*	**preocuparse (por)** *to worry (about)*

b. Many Spanish verbs that express emotional reactions have two common conjugation forms. One is reflexive and the other is conjugated like **gustar**, with an indirect object pronoun.

Indirect object pronouns: 13.F
Verbs like **gustar**: 1/.B.4

Reflexive form	Conjugation like *gustar*
Me alegro mucho de que vengas. *I'm so happy that you're coming.*	**Me alegra** mucho que vengas. *It makes me happy that you're coming.*
¿**Os preocupáis** por la economía mundial? *Are you [pl.] worried about the world economy?*	¿**Os preocupa** la economía mundial? *Does the world economy worry you [pl.]?*

27.G.3 *Convertirse en* + **noun or nominal expression**

Convertirse en indicates a change that can happen suddenly or after a process, depending on the context. It expresses a significant change, such as a change from boy to man, from a little city to a big city, and so forth.

Nos convertimos en robots con la tecnología.	*Technology turns us into robots.*
La casa **se convierte en** un manicomio cuando Luis hace fiestas.	*The house turns into a madhouse when Luis has parties.*

27.G.4 *Hacerse* + **noun or adjective**

Hacerse expresses changes that happen as a result of a plan or goal.

Mi hermano **se hizo** cura.	*My brother became a priest.*
Los vikingos **se hicieron** poderosos con su superioridad marítima.	*The Vikings became powerful with their maritime superiority.*
Quiero **hacerme** millonario algún día.	*I want to become a millionaire someday.*
Se están haciendo viejos.	*They are becoming/getting old.*

27.G.5 *Ponerse* + **adjective**

Ponerse expresses relatively rapid changes that are often emotional or physically visible.

Mis amigos **se pusieron** verdes de la envidia cuando vieron mi nuevo auto.	*My friends became green with envy when they saw my new car.*
¡No **te pongas** triste!	*Don't be sad!*
Nos pusimos furiosos cuando vimos el desorden.	*We became furious when we saw the mess.*
Me pongo tan contento cuando me visita mi hermana.	*I become so happy when my sister visits me.*

27.G.6 *Quedarse* + **adjective or adverb**

Quedarse expresses a long-term result of a change. The reflexive form is more common in Spain, but has the same meaning as the non-reflexive in Latin America.

¿**(Te) has quedado** triste con la noticia?	*Has the news made you sad? (Are you sad because of the news?)*
Con la crisis, **(nos) quedamos** sin nada.	*Because of the crisis, we were left with nothing.*
Te estás quedando calvo.	*You're becoming/going bald.*
Me quedé muy solo cuando mi novia se fue.	*I became very lonely when my girlfriend left.*

27.G.7 Volverse + *adjective* or *noun*

Volverse expresses primarily a mental or physical change of a certain duration and is more permanent than **ponerse**.

Venezuela **se ha vuelto** un país petrolero muy rico.	*Venezuela has become a very rich oil country.*
Uno no **se vuelve** rico de la noche a la mañana.	*One doesn't become rich overnight.*
Se volvió loca.	*She went mad/crazy.*
La leche **se volvió** agria.	*The milk became sour / went bad.*

27.G.8 Llegar a + *infinitive* + *noun* or *adjective*

This verb periphrasis is the only non-reflexive verb of change. It is used when changes are understood as a longer process and assumes some effort to get to the result.

Nunca **llegaré a ser** famoso.	*I will never become famous.*
Roma **llegó a ser** una gran civilización.	*Rome became a great civilization.*
Es posible que **llegues a tener** éxito.	*It's possible you'll be successful.*

27.G.9 Wishes of change

It is very common to express wishes or plans of change with these verbs.

Ojalá no **se queden** sin casa.	*I hope they are not left without a home.*
Querría que el mundo **llegara a ser** un lugar pacífico.	*I wish the world would become a peaceful place.*
Espero que **nos convirtamos en** grandes amigos.	*I hope that we will become great friends.*

27.G.10 Verb aspect and verbs that express change

a. Verbs that express change are usually used with the perfect tenses (*preterite* and *compound perfect tenses*), which, like the English *to become*, focus on the end result.

Rosa **se ha vuelto** muy antipática.	*Rosa has become very unfriendly.*
Mi ciudad natal **se ha convertido** en una gran metrópoli.	*My hometown has become a big metropolis.*
Se puso furioso cuando le conté la noticia.	*He became furious when I told him the news.*
En la década de 1950, ya **se había convertido** en el hombre más rico de la ciudad.	*By the 1950s, he had already become the richest man in the city.*
Si hubiera estudiado abogacía, **habría llegado a ser** juez.	*If he had studied law, he would have become a judge.*

b. When verbs that express change are used in the *imperfect* or *present* tense, they usually indicate repetition or a description of something that used to happen. Adverbs such as **cada vez más**, **paulatinamente**, and **progresivamente** or the use of the **gerundio** intensify the verb's meaning.

Me parece que la gramática **se vuelve** cada vez más fácil.	*It seems to me that grammar is becoming easier and easier.*
Me ponía furioso cuando me daban una C en el examen.	*I used to become so angry when they would give me a C on an exam.*
En los cuentos de hadas, las ranas **se convertían en** príncipes.	*In fairy tales, frogs turned into princes.*

Práctica

 Actividades 1–16, pp. A112–A116

Passive and impersonal constructions
Estructuras pasivas e impersonales

28.A Active, passive, or impersonal

Activa, pasiva o impersonal

28.A.1 Passive constructions

Active constructions emphasize the person or thing that carries out an action. In contrast, passive constructions emphasize the action itself, rather than the agent. The passive voice states that a subject is *receiving* the action, rather than *doing* the action. The direct object of the active sentence becomes the grammatical subject of the passive sentence. Spanish has two ways to express passive actions: the passive voice with **ser** (**voz pasiva con ser**) and passive constructions with **se** (**pasiva refleja** or **voz pasiva con se**).

Los aztecas **fundaron** Tenochtitlán. (*active*)	The Aztecs founded Tenochtitlan.
Tenochtitlán **fue fundada** por los aztecas. (*passive*)	Tenochtitlan was founded by the Aztecs.
¿Sabes en qué año **se fundó** Tenochtitlán? (*passive*)	Do you know what year Tenochtitlan was founded?

28.A.2 Impersonal constructions

In Spanish, the impersonal **se** (**se impersonal**) expresses the idea of a non-specific subject performing an action. In English, this idea is often expressed using *they, you, people, one*, etc.

En esta oficina **se trabaja** muchísimo.	In this office, people work a lot.
Se habla de su renuncia.	People are talking about his resignation.
Si **se está** tranquilo con uno mismo, **se es** feliz.	If you are at peace with yourself, you are happy.
Se invitó a mucha gente.	Many people were invited.

Unlike the passive constructions with **se**, impersonal constructions with **se** do not have a grammatical subject and the verb is always singular.

28.B Passive voice with *ser*

Voz pasiva con *ser*

28.B.1 The direct object becomes the subject

The passive voice with **ser** can only be formed in Spanish when there is a corresponding active sentence with an *explicit direct object*. The direct object of the active sentence becomes the subject, while the real subject is toned down to *agent* or is removed from the sentence. In the active sentence, the direct object is marked using the preposition **a**. In a passive sentence, this is not necessary since the direct object has become the subject.

◁ Use of **a** with a person as a direct object: 13.E.2

Active voice	Passive voice with *ser*
El rector recibió a los alumnos.	Los alumnos **fueron recibidos** (por el rector).
The principal welcomed the students.	*The students were welcomed (by the principal).*

28.B.2 Verb tenses of *ser* in the passive voice

The verb in the active sentence becomes a *past participle* in the passive sentence and follows **ser** (*to be*), which can generally appear in all verb tenses and moods. However, the passive voice with **ser** is more common in perfect tenses. In the present and imperfect, the passive voice with **ser** expresses repetition or habit.

◁ Regular and irregular *past participle*: 19.A.1, 19.A.2, 25.D

◁ Use of the present indicative: 17.E.2
Use of the imperfect: 18.E.5

Indicative		Subjunctive
El chico es visto	... ha sido visto	Es bueno que el chico sea visto.
... fue visto	... hubo sido visto	Fue bueno que el chico fuera visto.
... era visto	... había sido visto	... fuese visto.
... será visto	... habrá sido visto	... haya sido visto.
... sería visto	... habría sido visto	... hubiera/hubiese sido visto.

Pretérito anterior (hubo sido visto): 19.F

Infinitive	Gerundio
haber sido visto	habiendo sido visto

Una tragedia nuclear como la de Chernóbil no **ha sido vista** nunca.
Muchos creen que podría **haber sido prevenida**.
Las señales de peligro nunca **fueron tomadas** en serio.
Deberían **haberlo sido**.

A nuclear tragedy like Chernobyl has never been seen.
Many believe that it could have been prevented.
The warning signs were never taken seriously.
They should have been.

Use of the past participle: 25.D.4
The past participle in compound tenses: 19.A.1-2

28.B.3 Agreement of past participle

The past participle in the passive voice with **ser** behaves as an adjective and agrees in gender and number with the grammatical subject.

La película fue bien **recibida**.
Las noticias fueron **publicadas** en la red.
El problema debe ser **estudiado**.
Es necesario que **los gastos** sean **controlados**.

The film was well received.
The news was published on the web.
The problem should be studied.
It is necessary that the expenses be monitored.

28.B.4 The agent in the passive voice with *ser*

a. In the passive voice with **ser**, the agent, or *logical subject,* is introduced using **por** + *noun*, *pronoun*, or *clause*.

La contaminación es causada **por nosotros**.
Las reuniones van a ser organizadas **por la ONU**.
Algunas cosas no han sido explicadas **por los responsables**.
El virus ha sido identificado **por los que conocen su ADN**.

Pollution is caused by us.
The meetings are going to be organized by the UN.
A number of things haven't been explained by those responsible.
The virus has been identified by those who recognize its DNA.

b. It is important to distinguish the agent in passive sentences from causal relationships or other contexts that can also be expressed with **por**. Only the first example below indicates the agent.

La velocidad de los autos es controlada **por la policía** (*agent*).
La velocidad de los autos es controlada **por seguridad**.
La velocidad de los autos es controlada **por todo el país**.

The speed limit is monitored by the police.
The speed limit is monitored for safety.
The speed limit is monitored across the country.

28.C | Limitations of the passive voice with *ser*

Limitaciones de la voz pasiva con *ser*

28.C.1 Use of passive voice with *ser*

The passive voice occurs primarily in written formal language, such as in professional articles, contracts, legal documents, etc. It is used to a lesser extent in the news. In cases where the actor or doer is still unknown or not mentioned, passive constructions with **se** are preferred.

Passive constructions with **se**: 28.D
Impersonal **se** sentences: 28.E

28.C.2 The indirect object in the passive voice with *ser*

Only the direct object of an active sentence can become the subject in the passive voice with **ser**. The indirect object can never become the subject. In English, both the direct and indirect object in the active sentence can become the subject in the passive voice.

El premio Nobel de literatura le ha sido otorgado al escritor peruano Mario Vargas Llosa.	*The Noble Prize in Literature was awarded to the Peruvian writer Mario Vargas Llosa.*
Los honorarios me fueron pagados a mí (por el banco).	*The fees were paid to me (by the bank).*
El contrato os será enviado a vosotros (por Marta).	*The contract will be sent to you [pl.] (by Marta).*

28.C.3 *Estar* + *past participle*

The passive voice with **ser** can only be formed with the past participle and not with participle-like adjectives such as **electo/a,** or **bendito/a**. However, these adjectives and past participle forms can convey the result of the action of some verbs by using **estar**.

Past participle: 19.A.1, 19.A.2, 25.D
Verb periphrases with the past participle: 26.E
Estar with a perfect adjective: 30.C.2

Passive sentence with *ser*	Resulting state with *estar*
La novela **ha sido escrita** por un gran narrador. *The novel has been/was written by a great storyteller.*	La novela **está escrita** por un gran narrador. *The novel is written by a great storyteller.*
Las tapas **fueron hechas** por el cocinero. *The tapas were made by the cook.*	Las tapas **están hechas** por el cocinero. *The tapas are made by the cook.*
Los parques **fueron diseñados** por un arquitecto. *The parks were designed by an architect.*	Los parques **están diseñados** por un arquitecto. *The parks are designed by an architect.*

28.D | Passive constructions with *se*

Oraciones pasivas reflejas

28.D.1 The subject in passive constructions with *se*

a. Passive constructions with **se** have an active structure with an *explicit subject* and a *passive meaning*. The subject can be a noun or a clause. The verb agrees with the subject (third-person singular or plural). The verb is always used in the third-person singular if the subject is a clause. Passive constructions with **se** do not have an explicit agent. They are mostly used when the subject (singular or plural) is not a living being. The subjects in the Spanish sentences below are in italics.

El petróleo venezolano **se exporta** a muchos países.	*Venezuelan oil is exported to many countries.*
Los productos **se venden** en todo el mundo.	*The products are sold all over the world.*
Se espera que la situación mejore.	*The situation is expected to improve.*

Indefinite quantifiers: 7.C ▶

b. Indefinite nouns that refer to people can also be the subject of a sentence. The preposition **a** is not necessary here because the noun is *not* the object, but the subject.

Se prefieren personas con experiencia.	*People with experience are preferred.*
Se necesitaban ayudantes.	*They needed assistants. / Assistants were needed.*
Se busca un buen economista.	*They are looking for a good economist. / A good economist is needed.*
Se admitirán muchos estudiantes.	*They will admit many students. / Many students will be admitted.*

Impersonal **se** sentences: 28.E.2 ▶

c. Passive sentences with **se** can also have a clause as the subject. The verb is normally a reporting verb such as **creer, decir, comunicar, informar, saber**, or a verb that provides opinions, beliefs, or knowledge, such as **opinar, creer,** and **saber**. The verb in a passive construction with **se** is *always* inflected in the singular when a clause is the subject.

Anteriormente **se creía** *que* los gnomos realmente existían.	*Previously it was thought that gnomes existed.*
No **se sabía** *dónde* vivían.	*It wasn't known where they lived.*
En las leyendas **se narra** *cómo* los gnomos se convertían en montañas.	*In legends, it is told how the gnomes became mountains.*
Nunca **se sabrá** *si* eso era cierto.	*It will never be known if that was true.*

28.D.2 No agent

Passive constructions with **se** have no agent. The real actor or doer of the action is not mentioned and remains unknown.

Las tradiciones **se conservan** de generación en generación.	*Traditions are preserved (passed on) from generation to generation.*
Los documentos **se imprimen** automáticamente.	*The documents are printed automatically.*

28.D.3 Passive constructions with *se* and modal verbs

Modal verb periphrases with the infinitive: 26.B ▶

In English, modal verbs (*can, could, may, might, must, shall, should, will, would*) are often used to express the passive voice using the construction *modal verb + be + past participle*. In Spanish, the same idea can be conveyed using **se** + *modal verb + infinitive*.

Se podía escuchar todo lo que decían.	*Everything they said could be heard.*
Se debe hacer algo acerca del problema de la contaminación.	*Something should be done about the pollution problem.*

28.D.4 Placement of *se* with verb periphrases

With verb periphrases, **se** is usually placed before the finite verb, but can also be added after the infinitive or **gerundio**.

Las cartas **se** iban a enviar / iban a enviar**se** por correo.	*The letters were going to be sent in the mail.*
El trabajo **se** tiene que hacer / tiene que hacer**se** bien.	*The work must be done well.*
Se está preparando / Está preparándo**se** una gran cena.	*A great dinner is being prepared.*

28.E | Impersonal *se* sentences

Oraciones impersonales con *se*

28.E.1 | Impersonal *se* sentences have no subject

Impersonal **se** sentences have a *passive meaning* and *no grammatical subject*, and the verb *always* appears in the third-person singular. The real actor or doer of the action is assumed to be a living being, but is unknown and indefinite. Like passive constructions with **se**, the impersonal **se** is not the subject, but only a structure used to convey that the meaning is impersonal.

28.E.2 | General statements

a. Impersonal **se** sentences form general statements with verbs that do not take an object (intransitive verbs) such as **vivir, trabajar,** and **llegar,** and with transitive verbs such as **vender, decir,** and **escribir,** when the object is not mentioned. The verb always appears in the third-person singular. The statement's features are described using an adverb or an adverbial expression.

◄ Intransitive verbs: 17.B.1

¡Aquí **se trabaja** con gusto!	*Here, people work with pleasure!*
Sin buena salud, no **se vive** bien.	*Without good health, one can't live well.*
En los blogs **se escribe** muy francamente.	*In blogs, people write very honestly.*

b. In general statements with reflexive verbs, the indefinite pronoun **uno** is used instead of **se.** Both male and female speakers can use **uno.** Female speakers, however, can also use **una.**

◄ Indefinite pronoun **uno/a**: 7.D.3

Con esta música, **uno se duerme** de inmediato.	*One falls asleep immediately to this music.*
Este mapa impide que **uno se pierda** en la ciudad.	*With this map, you can't get lost in the city.*
No es posible **sentarse uno** a leer sin interrupciones.	*It is impossible to sit down and read without interruptions.*
¿Puede **uno marcharse** de aquí a cualquier hora?	*Can one leave at any time?*

c. Ser and **estar** form general statements with impersonal **se** sentences, but this use is limited. General statements with modal verbs are more common (**poder, deber**).

◄ Modal verb periphrases: 26.B

Se está muy bien en lugares tranquilos.	*A good time is had in calm places.*
No siempre **se es** feliz.	*People are not always happy.*
Se puede salir por esta puerta.	*You can go out this door.*
Puede salirse por esta puerta.	

d. If the implicit actor or doer of the action is a woman, it is possible to use a feminine adjective.

Cuando se es **honrado/a**, se llega más lejos.	*If you are honorable, you will go far.*

28.E.3 | Direct objects

a. When the direct object is mentioned and it is a person (proper noun, pronoun), it is preceded by the preposition **a** and the verb is always in the singular.

Se identificará **a los autores** de los robos.	*Those behind the thefts will be identified.*

◄ Use of **a** with a person as a direct object: 13.E.2

b. When the direct object is mentioned and preceded by the preposition **a**, it can also be replaced with an object pronoun. In that case, the direct object pronoun will convey information about the agent's gender: **los/las**. It is common to remove the last remnant of the agent's identity by using **le/les** as direct object pronouns in impersonal **se** constructions.

Other expressions with impersonal meaning: 28.H

Se identificará **a los autores / a las autoras** de los robos.	*Those (male/female) behind the thefts will be identified.*
Se **los/las** identificará.	*They (male/female) will be identified.*
Se **les** identificará.	*They will be identified.*

c. Impersonal **se** sentences can be used with transitive verbs when the direct object is expressed. This use is common in the present tense and appears in signs and ads. (**Se vende casas. Se repara refrigeradores.**) In these cases, the noun is the direct object of the verb and the actor or doer of the action is not stated.

Impersonal *se* **sentence** (*los proyectos*: **direct object**)	
Se aprobó los proyectos.	*The projects were approved.*
Se los aprobó.	*They were approved.*

Passive construction with *se* (*los proyectos*: **subject**)	
Se aprobaron los proyectos.	*The projects were approved.*

28.F The indirect object in passive and impersonal sentences

El objeto indirecto en oraciones pasivas e impersonales

The direct object plays the main role as the grammatical subject in the passive voice with **ser** and in passive constructions with **se**. When the indirect object is explicitly mentioned, it appears in the different sentence types in the following ways.

28.F.1 Active sentence

In a normal active sentence, we can find a subject (**profesor**), a verb (**entregó**), and a direct object (**textos**) as well as an indirect object (**estudiantes**). The objects can be expressed with the corresponding object pronouns.

Placement of direct and indirect object pronouns before conjugated verbs: 13.G.1 Object pronouns with prepositions: 13.H.1b

El profesor les entregó **los textos** a **los estudiantes**.	*The teacher gave the students the texts.*
El profesor **se los** entregó.	*The teacher gave them (to) them.*

28.F.2 Passive voice with *ser*

The real direct object from the sentence above (**textos**) becomes the subject in the passive voice with **ser**. The agent and the references to the indirect object (**les, a los estudiantes**) can be excluded. The indirect object in the active sentence cannot become the subject of the passive voice.

Los textos les fueron entregados a **los estudiantes** (por el profesor).	*The texts were given to the students (by the teacher).*
Los textos les fueron entregados.	*The texts were given to them. (Someone gave them the texts.)*
Los textos fueron entregados.	*The texts were given out. (Someone gave out the texts.)*

28.F.3 Passive constructions with *se*

Passive constructions with **se** have no agent. Information about the indirect object (**les, los estudiantes**) can also be excluded. It is important to note that **se** only indicates that the sentence is impersonal and is not a replacement for the indirect object (**les**), which can be mentioned.

Los textos **se les entregaron** a los estudiantes.	The texts were given to the students. (Someone gave the texts to the students.)
Los textos **se les entregaron**.	The texts were given to them. (Someone gave them the texts.)
Los textos **se entregaron**.	The texts were given out. (Someone gave out the texts.)

28.F.4 Impersonal *se* sentences

In impersonal **se** sentences, the verb appears in the singular and does not have a subject. In general, impersonal **se** sentences occur with intransitive verbs (without objects). When there are both direct and indirect objects, an impersonal **se** sentence would look like this: **Se entregó los textos a los estudiantes**. Such sentences are not common in Spanish, and other solutions are preferred.

Impersonal **se** sentences with direct objects: 28.E.3c
Intransitive verbs: 17.B.1

Passive construction with *se*	Third-person plural
Se entregaron los textos a los estudiantes. / Los textos **se les entregaron** a los estudiantes.	**Les entregaron** los textos a los estudiantes. / **Se los** entregaron.
The texts were given to the students.	*Someone gave the texts to the students. / The texts were given to the students. / They were given to them.*

28.G Comparison of passive constructions with *se* and impersonal *se* constructions

Passive constructions with *se*		Impersonal *se* constructions	
Can only be formed with transitive verbs.	Se enseña inglés.	Can be formed with intransitive or transitive verbs.	Se enseña a hablar mejor. Se vive bien aquí.
The object of the active sentence is the grammatical subject.	Se vendió un cuadro de Picasso. ("un cuadro de Picasso" is the subject of the sentence)	There is no grammatical subject.	Nunca se está seguro en el puesto de trabajo.
The verb can be singular or plural (it must agree with the subject).	Se firmará el tratado. / Se firmarán los acuerdos.	The verb is always singular.	Se firmará los acuerdos. ("los acuerdos" is a direct object; the sentence has no expressed subject)
The indirect object can be expressed.	Se presentaron los textos al jurado. Se le presentaron.	The indirect object can be expressed.	Se presentó los textos al jurado.
Plural direct objects that refer to people and do not have an article can become the subject.	Se buscan nuevos maestros. ("nuevos maestros" is the subject)	When the direct object is a specific person or group of people, the personal **a** is used. The direct object can be replaced by both direct and indirect object pronouns.	Se invitó a los/las nuevos/as maestros/as. ("a los/las nuevos/as maestros/as" is the direct object) Se los/las invitó. Se les invitó.

Impersonal **se** sentences with direct objects: 28.E.3c

Passive constructions with *se*		Impersonal *se* constructions	
The passive subject can be a specific person or group of people when it refers to positions/jobs or to something inherent to a position/job.	Se eligieron los nuevos diputados. Se nombró el nuevo embajador.	*If the direct object is a person, it always requires* **a**. *The verb is always singular.*	Se eligió a los nuevos diputados. Se nombró al nuevo embajador.
The subject can be a noun clause or a reported question. It can also be an infinitive.	Se dice que habrá despidos. Se ha confirmado cómo sucedió el accidente. Se prohíbe fumar.	(***Note:*** *Due to their impersonal meaning, the examples on the left are sometimes interpreted as impersonal* **se** *constructions. However, this text follows the interpretation of the RAE's* Nueva gramática *regarding these structures.*)	

28.H Other expressions with impersonal meaning

Otras expresiones de impersonalidad

a. The following pronouns can be used in an impersonal sense. The most common is the third-person plural, which refers to an impersonal **ellos**.

Impersonal use of the pronoun	
third-person plural	¿Os **atendieron** bien en el restaurante? *Did you [pl.] get good service / Did they serve you well in the restaurant?*
tú	**Tú** nunca **sabes** a qué hora llega el autobús. *You never know when the bus will come.*
la/mucha gente	Que **la gente** crea lo que quiera. *People can think what they want.*
uno/a	**Uno** nunca sabe con seguridad. *One/You can never know/tell with certainty.*

b. Every expression with the impersonal forms of **haber** is impersonal. The verb is only inflected in the singular: *there is / there are*.

Hay problemas.	*There are problems.*	**Hay** paz/guerra.	*There is peace/war.*
Hay mucho.	*There is a lot.*	**Habrá** algo.	*There will be something.*
Hay poco.	*There isn't much.*	No **habrá** nada.	*There won't be anything.*

c. Hacer, ser, and other verbs in expressions of time, weather, and climate are impersonal. The verb is only inflected in the singular.

Hace frío/calor.	*It's cold/hot.*	Ya **era** hora.	*It's about time.*
Es de día/noche.	*It's day/night.*	**Llueve**.	*It's raining. / It rains.*
Es Navidad.	*It's Christmas.*	**Nieva**.	*It's snowing. / It snows.*

d. There are many other verbs that function in the same way, such as:

Importa/Conviene hacerlo.	*It's important/useful to do it.*	**Se trata** de estudiar o no estudiar.	*It's about studying or not studying.*

Práctica

(S) Actividades 1–16, pp. A117–A122

To be and to become
Ser, estar, haber, hacer, tener

29.A Structure: *ser* and *estar*

Estructura de *ser* y *estar*

29.A.1 To be: *ser*

a. *To be* is expressed in Spanish using **ser** and **estar**, but **haber, hacer**, and **tener** are also used to convey *to be*. **Ser** describes the *essential qualities* of the subject while **estar** describes its *condition* or *state*.

b. The verb **ser** cannot be used on its own with the meaning *to exist*, like in the famous Hamlet question **"¿Ser o no ser? Esa es la cuestión"**. A more appropriate modern Spanish translation would have been **"¿Existir o no existir?"**. In very short yes/no questions and answers, however, **ser** can be used to answer, in the sense *it is* or *it's not*, to confirm or deny the identity of an item.

—Este libro **es** tuyo, ¿verdad?	*This book is yours, isn't it?*
—Sí, sí (lo) **es**. /—No, no (lo) **es**.	*Yes, it is. / No, it isn't.*
—¿**Es** Juan el que va allí?	*Is that Juan over there?*
—Sí, sí (lo) **es**. /—No, no (lo) **es**.	*Yes, it is (him). / No, it isn't (him).*

◀ Use of **ser** and **estar**: Ch. 30

29.A.2 To be: *estar*

The verb **estar** can also appear alone in short yes/no questions and used as an answer in the sense *to be present* in a specific or implied location. For example, when a person asks if someone is home or in the office.

—¿**Está** Juan?	*Is Juan there?*
—No, no **está**. / —Sí, sí **está**.	*No, he isn't. / Yes, he is.*

29.B To be: there is, there are

Haber para expresar existencia

◀ Ser, estar, and **haber**: 30.C.7

29.B.1 Impersonal form of *haber*

a. The *impersonal* form of **haber** (*there is / there are; is/are present*) is used instead of **estar** to refer to the existence of non-specific people, things, or concepts.

—¿**Hay** conexión a Internet?	*Is there an Internet connection?*
—Sí, sí **hay**. / —No, no **hay**.	*Yes, there is. / No there isn't.*
—¿**Hay** estudiantes alemanes?	*Are there (any) German students?*
—No, no **hay**. /—Sí, sí **hay**.	*No, there aren't./Yes, there are.*

◀ estar and haber with definite and indefinite possessives: 9.D.6

b. **Haber** cannot be used with subject pronouns or a noun preceded by a determiner. It can be used with indefinite pronouns, determiners, and numbers, except **ambos, cada, los/las demás**, and **cualquiera**.

—¿**Hay** alguien (en casa)?	*Is anyone home?*
—No, no **hay** nadie.	*No, there's nobody home.*
—¿Cuántos estudiantes **hay**?	*How many students are there?*
—**Hay** uno.	*There's one.*

◀ Use of cardinal numbers: 6.B

c. Subject pronouns and nouns with determiners can be used with **estar** in the same situations.

—¿**Están** Laura y Fernando en casa?	*Are Laura and Fernando home?*
—Ella sí **está**, pero él no.	*She's home, but he isn't.*
—Hola, ¿dónde **estás** tú?	*Hello, where are you?*
—**Estoy** en el parque.	*I'm at the park.*
—¿Cuántos de los estudiantes **están** allí?	*How many of the students are there?*
—Tres de ellos **están** aquí.	*Three of them are here.*

29.B.2 Personal form of *haber*

Haber is conjugated as a finite verb in the compound verb forms of the indicative and subjunctive.

¿**Habéis ido** alguna vez a Costa Rica?	*Have you [pl.] ever been to Costa Rica?*
En Ecuador se **ha hablado** quechua por mucho tiempo.	*In Ecuador, Quechua has been spoken for a long time.*

29.C Expressing weather and time: *hacer, estar, ser*

Hacer, estar, ser para expresar clima y horas

Expressing temperature: 6.I.1 ▶

29.C.1 Weather expressions

Hacer and **estar** are used in many weather expressions in which English uses *to be*.

Hace frío.	*It's cold.*	**Hace** sol.	*It's sunny.*
Hace calor.	*It's warm.*	**Hace** mal tiempo.	*It's bad weather.*
Está nublado.	*It's cloudy.*	**Está** lloviendo.	*It's raining.*
Está oscuro.	*It's dark.*	**Está** nevando.	*It's snowing.*

29.C.2 Calendar and time

Ser must be used with the noun: 30.B.1
Time: 5.C.3, 6.F

a. Ser is used with the time, days, months, years, and other periods of time.

Son las tres.	*It's three o'clock.*	**Es** verano.	*It's summer.*
Es lunes.	*It's Monday.*	**Es** 2030.	*It's 2030.*

b. Estar can also be used with days, months, years, and times of the year (but not clock time) as long as there is a preposition before the noun (**a, en**). The verb is inflected in the first-person plural: **nosotros**.

Estamos a lunes.	*It's Monday (finally/now).*
Estamos en marzo.	*We're in March now. / It's March (finally/now).*
Estamos en verano.	*It's summer (finally/now).*
Estamos en 2030.	*It's 2030 (finally/now).*

29.D Expressing age and states: *tener*

Tener para expresar edad y cambios físicos

To turn a certain age: 6.H and 18.E.3 ▶

Tener is used to describe most transient physical states, or to tell age.

Ella **tiene** veinte años.	*She's twenty (years old).*
Él **tiene** hambre/sed/sueño/cansancio/miedo/calor.	*He is hungry/thirsty/sleepy/tired/scared/hot.*

Expresar cambio y estado

29.E.1 **To get / to be: Passive voice with** *ser* **and** *estar + past participle*

a. The passive voice with **ser** is equivalent to the English passive voice with *to be* or *to get*. In this case, the verb expresses a change. The resulting state is described in Spanish with **estar** + *past participle*.

Passive voice with **ser**: 28.B
Verb periphrases with the past participle: 26.E

Las cartas **son** escritas.	*The letters are/get written.*
Las cartas **están** escritas.	*The letters are written.*

b. Together with modal verbs, **ser** and **estar** are used as described in **a** above.

Las cartas **deben / tienen que ser** escritas.	*The letters must be/get written.*
Las cartas **deben / tienen que estar** escritas.	*The letters must be written.*

29.E.2 **To be / to become + infinitive:** *es, fue, era*

While the *present* and the *imperfect* of **ser** are usually translated as *to be* because they describe states, the *preterite* can sometimes be translated as *to become* because it expresses change.

Verbs expressing change: 27.G

La situación **es** imposible de entender.	*The situation is impossible to understand.*
La situación **fue** imposible de entender.	*The situation became impossible to understand.*
La situación **era** imposible de entender.	*The situation was impossible to understand.*

29.E.3 **To become / to turn with weather and time: Spanish equivalents**

Changes in weather, time, days, and years that are expressed with *to become* or *to turn* in English can be reproduced in Spanish in several ways.

Dio la una. / Dieron las tres.	*The clock struck one / three.*
Está amaneciendo. (Amaneció.)	*The sun is rising. (The sun rose.)*
Se hace (hizo) de día.	*It's becoming (It became) daylight.*
Se hace (hizo) de noche. /	*It is (was) getting dark. (It got dark.) /*
Anochece. (Anocheció.)	*The sun is setting. (The sun set.)*
Estamos a lunes. / Ya es lunes.	*It's Monday. / Now/Already it's Monday.*
Se está poniendo (volviendo) frío el tiempo.	*It is getting cold.*
Se puso (Se volvió) frío el tiempo.	*It got cold.*
Es verano (Estamos en verano) de nuevo.	*It's summer again. / We are in summer again.*

29.E.4 **To stay with location:** *quedarse*

To stay can be used in English with adverbs of place. In this case, the meaning in Spanish is expressed using **quedarse** (*to remain/stay*).

Verbs expressing change:
volverse, convertirse:
27.G

Hoy **estamos** en la escuela.	*Today, we're at school.*
Hoy **nos quedamos** en la escuela.	*Today, we're staying at school.*

29.E.5 **To become / to go + adjective:** *quedarse* **and verbs that express change**

a. Changes can also be conveyed with *to become/go + adjective* in English. In Spanish, **quedar(se)**, **ponerse**, and **volverse** can be used.

Verbs expressing
change: 27.G
llegar a ser: 27.G.8

Ella **(se) quedó** ciega.	*She went (was) blind.*
Ella **se volvió** ciega.	*She became blind.*
Se puso loco.	*He went crazy.*
Me puse pálida,	*I became/went pale.*

b. *To become/get + adjective* can be translated using many Spanish reflexive verbs.

alegrarse	to become happy	enojarse	to get angry
callarse	to become quiet	enriquecerse	to become rich
cansarse	to get tired	entristecerse	to get sad
curarse	to get cured	mejorarse	to get better
empobrecerse	to become poor	sonrojarse	to blush

Me alegré mucho cuando recibí la noticia. *I became/got very happy when I got the news.*

No **me canso** de mirar películas. *I don't get tired of watching movies.*

c. In some cases, both the reflexive and the non-reflexive form can be used.

enloquecer(se)   *to go/become mad*

envejecer(se)   *to get/become old*

d. The verb **quedar(se)** cannot be used with a *noun*. Other verbs, such as **convertirse** and **hacerse**, or verb periphrases, such as **llegar a ser**, are used with a noun to express changes.

Los niños **se quedaron** callados. *The children remained quiet.*

Ella **se convirtió** en una excelente abogada. *She became an excellent lawyer.*

Él **llegó a ser** un médico famoso. *Over time, he became a famous doctor.*

Ellos **se hicieron** políticos. *They became politicians.*

Práctica

Actividades 1–7,
pp. A123–A124

Use of *ser* and *estar*
Uso de ser *y* estar

30.A Overview

Aspectos generales

Both **ser** and **estar** mean *to be*, but are used in different ways. In general, **ser** is used to describe the inherent and permanent nature and identity of something. **Estar** is used to describe the condition, state, or location of something; these traits are viewed by the speaker as being circumstantial or temporary, rather than inherent.

Marcos **es** un hombre.	*Marcos is a man.*
Juan **está** cansado.	*Juan is tired.*

30.B Use of *ser*

Usos de *ser*

30.B.1 Noun: *ser*

Only **ser** can be used with nouns (with or without determiners), proper nouns, possessives, personal and indefinite pronouns, and professions.

Soy **Raquel**. Soy **mujer**.	*I'm Raquel. I'm a woman.*
Soy **estudiante**.	*I'm a student.*
Raquel soy **yo**.	*I'm Raquel.*
Soy **una chica** joven.	*I'm a young girl.*
Julio es **mi primo**.	*Julio is my cousin.*
Somos **muchos**.	*We're many. (There's a lot of us.)*
Esto es **algo** importante.	*This is something Important.*

Determiners as subjects/pronouns: 4.B.1–4.B.2
Indefinite pronouns: 7.D
Possessives: 9.C.2c, 9.D.3
Ser with calendar and time: 29.C.2

30.B.2 Adjectives with *ser*: characteristics

Ser describes permanent characteristics that define an individual, an object, or a concept in relation to others of the same kind. The characteristics are perceived as belonging only to the subject. They constitute the subject's identity as an individual or as part of a group.

	Identity: adjective with *ser*		
a.	Appearance	Soy alto. Mis ojos son negros.	*I'm tall. My eyes are black.*
b.	Personality and other qualities	Soy inteligente y trabajador.	*I'm intelligent and hard-working.*
c.	Origin, nationality	Soy español.	*I'm Spanish.*
d.	Belief, ideology, religion	Soy creyente. Soy católico.	*I'm a believer. I'm Catholic.*
e.	Values relating to social norms or constructs	Soy joven y no soy rico. No soy casado.	*I'm young and not rich. I'm not married.*

De: 12.B.4

30.B.3 Description: *ser + de*

Ser + de followed by nouns or pronouns describes characteristics of people and objects, such as origin, ownership, what they consist of, etc.

Eva **es de** Almería.	Eva is from Almería.
Eva **es de** buen humor. (Tiene buen humor.)	Eva is good-natured. (She has a good nature.)
Eva **es de** ojos verdes. (Tiene ojos verdes.)	Eva is green-eyed. (She has green eyes.)
La casa **es de** Eva. Es su casa. La casa es suya.	The house is Eva's. It's her house. The house is hers.
La casa **es de** madera.	The house is made of wood.

30.B.4 Descriptions: *ser para*

Para: 12.B.6

Personal abilities and the purpose of objects can be expressed using **ser** + *adjective* + **para** + *verb*. **Para** + *proper noun* or *pronoun* indicates the receiver.

Ricardo es **bueno para** hablar.	Ricardo is good at talking.
La copiadora es **para copiar**.	The photocopier is for copying.
La fiesta es **para disfrutarla**.	The party is for having fun/enjoying.
El regalo es **para mí/Alejandra**.	The present is for me/Alejandra.

30.B.5 Appearance: *ser + con/a/sin*

The appearance of objects is expressed using **ser** + **con/a/sin.**

Mi blusa es **con/sin botones**.	My blouse has buttons/is without buttons.
La falda es **a rayas**.	The skirt is striped.

30.B.6 Impersonal expressions with *ser*

Impersonal expressions of certainty: 23.C.7

Spanish has many impersonal expressions with **ser** + *noun* or *adjective*.

¿**Es cierto** que sabes inglés?	Is it true that you speak English?
Fue difícil hacerlo.	It was difficult to do.
Es una lástima tener que irnos.	It's a shame that we have to go.

30.B.7 Personal impression: *ser* with indirect object pronouns

Ser can be used with indirect object pronouns and adjectives to express an opinion.

La situación **nos es indiferente**.	The situation makes no difference to us.
Ella **me es** muy **simpática**.	She seems very nice to me.
¿**Te fue difícil** llamarme?	Was it difficult for you to call me?
No les es fácil pagar de contado.	It's not easy for them to pay cash.

30.B.8 Other structures using *ser*

Passive voice with **ser**: 28.B
Emphatic constructions: 15.B.8

Ser is also used in other structures such as the passive voice with **ser: El problema será resuelto**. (*The problem will be solved.*), and emphatic constructions such as **Fue ayer que ocurrió.** (*It was yesterday that it happened.*)

Usos de *estar*

30.C.1 **Adjectives and adverbs with** *estar*: **states**

a. Adjectives that describe changeable physical or social states can be used with **estar**. The use of **estar** suggests that the state is temporary or is not a critical part of the subject's identity. Some adjectives about marital status can be used with **ser** or **estar** with the same meaning: **ser/estar casado, soltero, divorciado.**

◀ Adjectives with **ser**: 30.B.2
Gender and number of adjectives: 3.A

Characteristics: *ser*	**States:** *estar*
El clima **es** inestable. *The weather is unstable.*	El clima **está** inestable. *The weather is (has become) unstable.*
El cielo **es** azul. *The sky is blue.*	El cielo **está** azul. *The sky is blue (today).*
Sandra **es** alegre. *Sandra is a happy person.*	Sandra **está** alegre. *Sandra is happy (at the moment).*
Ella **es** joven. *She is a young person.*	Ella **está** joven. *She is young (still).*
Ella **es** muy pobre. *She is very poor.*	Ella **está** muy pobre. *She is very poor (right now).*

b. Colors, sizes, and other physical characteristics can be described using **estar** when they change in relation to an objective or subjective standard.

Characteristics: *ser*	**States:** *estar*
La esmeralda **es** verde. *The emerald is green.*	Esta pintura **está** muy verde. *This painting is too green.*
El (árbol) bonsái **es** pequeño. *The bonsai (tree) is small.*	Los árboles **están** pequeños. *The trees are (still) small.*
El niño **es** grande y sano. *He is a big and healthy child.*	El niño **está** grande y sano. *The child is big and healthy.*

c. Estar with *adverbs* describes the general state of people and things.

El niño **está** bien ahora. Antes **estaba** peor.   *The child is fine now. He was worse before.*

d. These expressions are used to express how clothes fit:
indirect object pronoun + **está(n)** + *adjective/adverb* (more commonly used in Spain)
indirect object pronoun + **queda(n)** + *adjective/adverb* (more commonly used in the rest of the Spanish-speaking world)

El sombrero **te está / te queda** grande.   *The hat is too big for you.*

e. The expression *indirect object pronoun* + **viene(n)** + *adverb* is used in a similar way.

El lunes **me viene** bien.   *Monday works for me.*

f. Both **ser** and **estar** can be used with the adverb **así**. The choice depends on whether it is an intrinsic characteristic or a temporary state.

Juan **es así**, siempre de mal humor.   *Juan is that way, always in a bad mood.*
Juan **está así** porque perdió su trabajo.   *Juan is that way because he lost his job.*

30.C.2 *Estar* with a *perfect* adjective

Adjectives that convey the result of an action are *perfect* and must be used with **estar**. The most common of such adjectives are the *past participle* forms used in the passive voice with **ser** or those derived from *reflexive verbs* of change (**sentarse, dormirse, despertarse, irritarse**).

The past participle in the passive voice with **ser**: 28.B

Reflexive verbs suggesting change: 27.G

estar + *past participle*: 26.E, 28.C.3

Change	State: *estar*
Las casas **son construidas**. *The houses get built.*	Las casas **están construidas**. *The houses are built.*
El problema **ha sido resuelto**. *The problem has been solved.*	El problema **está resuelto**. *The problem is solved.*
Los niños **se duermen**. *The children are falling asleep.*	Los niños **están dormidos**. *The children are asleep.*
El vaso **se llena**. *The glass is being filled.*	El vaso **está lleno**. *The glass is full.*
Una persona **murió**. *A person died.*	Una persona **está muerta**. *A person is dead.*
El bebé **nació**. *The baby was born.*	El bebé **está vivo**. *The baby is alive.*
Me irrita el ruido. *The noise irritates me.*	**Estoy irritada** por el ruido. *I am irritated by the noise.*
Lisa **se enamoró**. *Lisa fell in love.*	Lisa **está enamorada**. *Lisa is in love.*

30.C.3 *Estar de* + *noun/adjective*

estar de: 12.B.4

With *nouns* or *adjectives* **estar de** denotes states, moods, jobs, professions, or temporary work. **Andar** is an informal synonym in such sentences, while **encontrarse de** is more formal: **Andrea anda / se encuentra de viaje**. (*Andrea is on a trip.*)

Estoy **de viaje**.	*I'm on a trip.*
¿Estáis **de vacaciones**?	*Are you [pl.] on vacation?*
Estamos **de mal humor**.	*We're in a bad mood.*
¿Está usted **de profesor**?	*Are you working as a teacher?*

30.C.4 Idiomatic expressions with *estar*

Use of prepositions: 12.B

Estar is used in many idiomatic expressions.

estar con	No te preocupes, yo **estoy contigo**.	*Don't worry. I'm with you.*
	En eso **estoy con** él. Creo que tiene razón.	*I agree with him on that. I think he is right.*
	Estoy con fiebre.	*I have a fever.*
estar en	**Estoy en** eso.	*I'm working on it.*
estar para	No **estoy para** bromas.	*I don't feel like listening to your jokes.*
estar a punto de	**Estamos a punto de** irnos.	*We are about to leave.*
estar por	**Estoy por** salir.	*I'm about to head out.*
estar que + *verb*	La situación **está que** arde.	*The situation is very volatile.*
	Estoy que no puedo más.	*I'm exhausted. / I'm overwhelmed.*
estar visto	**Está visto** que de literatura no sabes nada.	*It's evident that you don't know anything about literature.*
estar por verse	Lo que va a suceder aún **está por verse**.	*It is still unclear what's going to happen.*

30.C.5 Impersonal expressions with *estar*

Impersonal expressions with **estar** can be formed with *adverbs* and with *adjectives* derived from the *past participle*.

◀ Past participle with
estar: 25.D.4c
Impersonal expressions
with **estar**: 23.C.8d-e

está permitido que	*it is allowed to*	**está mal** que	*it is bad that*
está bien que	*It Is good that*	**está visto** que	*it is clear that*

30.C.6 Estar + gerundio

This *verb periphrasis* refers to continous actions.

◀ estar + gerundio: 25.C.3

Estamos escuchando música.　　　　*We're listening to music.*

30.C.7 Ser, estar, and haber

a. Both **estar** and **haber** can express existence or presence. **Estar** is usually translated as *to be* and refers to the existence or presence of specific objects or people. **Haber** is usually translated as *there is/are* and is used to express existence of an object or person, or occurrence of an event. When using **haber**, the focus is mainly on the existence or occurrence, and the object, person, or event remains unspecified.

◀ Ser, estar, and haber:
29.A–29.C
Estar and **haber** with
definite and indefinite
possessives: 9.D.6d

Hay dos personas esperando al abogado.	*There are two people waiting for the lawyer.*
Las dos personas de las que hablamos **están** en la sala de espera.	*The two people we talked about are in the waiting room.*

b. **Haber** is always used in the singular.

Hubo tres accidentes el fin de semana.	*There were three accidents over the weekend.*
Había mucha nieve.	*There was a lot of snow.*
Dicen que **habrá** tormentas este fin de semana.	*They say there will be storms this weekend.*
Ha habido una pelea.	*There has been a fight.*

c. Both **ser** and **haber** can be used to talk about events. **Haber** points to the occurrence of an unspecified event. **Ser** is used to refer to specific events.

Hubo una fiesta.	*There was a party.*
La fiesta **fue** en un restaurante.	*The party was in a restaurant.*

d. **Estar** and **haber** are usually interchangeable in relative clauses.

Vi los artículos nuevos que **había/estaban** en la tienda.	*I saw the new items that were in the store.*

30.D Ser and estar with location

Ser y estar con lugar

30.D.1 Estar: physical location

Estar implies a concrete physical location or place.

¿Dónde **estarán** mis llaves?	*Where are my keys?*
El auto **está** en el garaje.	*The car is in the garage.*
Las fotos **estaban** en la red.	*The photos were on the web.*
¡Allí **está** el problema!	*There is the problem!*

30.D.2 *Ser* **with location:** *is (located)*

In conversational Spanish, **ser** describes the location of addresses, buildings, cities, countries, and geographical places. A synonym in Spanish is the verb **quedar: ¿Dónde queda Nueva York?** (*Where is New York [located]?*).

Mi casa **es** en Connecticut.	*My house is in Connecticut.*
¿Tu boutique **es** en el centro?	*Is your boutique in the center?*
¡Aquí, nada **es** lejos!	*Here, nothing is far!*

30.D.3 *Ser* **with location:** *to take place*

The location of where events and arrangements *take place* is implied with **ser**. In this case, it is not possible to use **estar**. Corresponding expressions are **tener lugar** (formal) and **celebrar**, which convey a celebration of something.

Quiero que la fiesta **sea** aquí.	*I want the party to be (held) here.*
El partido **será** en Monterrey.	*The match/game will be in Monterrey.*
¿Dónde **va a ser** tu boda?	*Where is your wedding going to be (held)?*
La celebración **fue** en el club.	*The celebration took place at the club.*
Las Fallas **son** en Valencia.	*The Fallas festival is in Valencia.*

30.E Structures with *ser* and *estar*

Estructuras con *ser* y *estar*

		Ser	Estar
Nouns: Ch.2 ▶	Nouns	Él es **profesor**. *He is a teacher.*	Only with **estar de** + *profession*: Él **está de profesor**. *He is working as a teacher.*
Adjectives with **ser** and **estar**: ▶ 30.B.2, 30.C.1	Adjectives	La silla es **cómoda**. *The chair is comfortable.*	La silla está **cómoda**. *The chair feels comfortable.*
Passive voice with **ser**: 28.B ▶ Past participle: 19.A.1, 19.A.2, 25.D	Past participles	Las cuentas **fueron pagadas**. *The bills were paid.*	Las cuentas **están pagadas**. *The bills are paid.*
Prepositions: Ch.12 ▶	Prepositional phrases	Somos **de** Inglaterra. *We are from England.* Esto es **para** comer. *This is for eating.*	Estamos **en** la escuela. *We are in school.* Estamos **sin** dinero. *We are without money.*
Adverbs of place: 10.E ▶	Adverbs	Él es **así**. *He is like that.* La fiesta es **aquí**. *The party is being held here.*	Está **así** porque su hermano está enfermo. *He is (being/feeling) like this because his brother is sick.* Estoy **bien**. *I'm fine.* Estamos **aquí**. *We're here.*
Impersonal expressions with ▶ **ser**: 23.C.7, 23.C.8	Impersonal expressions	**Es importante que** entrenes. *It's important that you train.*	**Está bien que** entrenes. *It's good that you train.*
Emphatic constructions: 15.B.8 ▶	Emphatic constructions	**Es** hoy cuando viajo. *It is today that I travel.* **Fue** eso lo que dije. *That was what I said.*	*Not possible with* **estar**.
estar + **gerundio**: 25.C.3, 26.D ▶	***Gerundio*** (Progressive tenses)	*Not possible with* **ser**.	**Estamos** trabajando. *We're working.*

Práctica

(S) Actividades 1–12, <br> pp. A125–A128

Indirect discourse
Discurso indirecto

Chapter 31
A. Overview
B. Indirect discourse: necessary changes to verb tenses and mood

31.A Overview

Aspectos generales

The ability to relate what we have heard or what we know, think, or believe is important when communicating with other people. Direct and indirect discourse are the strategies used for this purpose.

31.A.1 Direct discourse

Also called *quoted speech*, direct discourse reproduces someone's exact words. In writing, quotation marks indicate that the words enclosed are being reproduced verbatim. Dialogues use a dash for the same purpose. In speech (usually formal), a suitable introductory phrase and proper intonation announces the quotation.

◄ Use of the colon: 1.F.4
Use of the dash: 1.F.7

Direct discourse in writing	Direct discourse in speech
Carlos dice: **"Esta fecha es muy importante para mí"**. *Carlos says: "This date is very important for me."*	Carlos dijo **lo siguiente: " Esta fecha es muy importante para mí".** *Carlos said the following: "This date is very important for me."*

31.A.2 Indirect discourse

Also called *reported speech,* indirect discourse relates someone's statement without quoting their exact words. The structure of the sentence changes to convey the indirect quote. The same structure is used in writing and speech.

◄ **Decir** and other reporting verbs: 23.C.2

Indirect discourse	
Carlos dijo **que esa fecha era muy importante para él.**	*Carlos said (that) that date was very important for him.*

31.B Indirect discourse: necessary changes to verb tenses and mood

Cambios necesarios en el tiempo o modo verbal

31.B.1 Overview

Several sentence components may have to change when reporting someone's words: personal object and reflexive pronouns, possessives, demonstratives, adverbs of time and place, and *especially* the verb tense and/or mood. These changes are determined by the change of perspective needed when reproducing someone else's words in a different context. Usually if the reporting verb is in the present, the verb tenses stay the same.

Uttered on Monday	Iré al cine **mañana**.	*I'll go to the movies tomorrow.*
Reported on Monday	Dice que irá al cine **mañana**.	*He says he'll go to the movies tomorrow.*
Reported on Tuesday	Dijo / Ha dicho que iría al cine **hoy**.	*He (has) said he'd go to the movies today.*
Reported on Wednesday	Dijo que iría al cine **ayer**.	*He said he'd go to the movies yesterday.*
Reported on Sunday	Dijo que iría al cine **el martes**.	*He said he'd go to the movies on Tuesday.*

31.B.2 Reporting information and commands

The most important thing to keep in mind when reporting your own or someone else's statements is whether the statement conveys *information* or transmits a *command*. When reporting information, the mood of the verb does not change. When reporting commands, the imperative is replaced with the subjunctive.

Decir and other reporting ▶ verbs: 23.C.2

Reporting information	Reporting a command
La profesora dice: "Tú siempre **haces** los deberes". → La profesora dice que tú siempre **haces** los deberes.	La profesora dice: "**Haz** los deberes". → La profesora dice que **hagas** los deberes.
The teacher says: "You always do your homework." → The teacher says that you always do your homework.	*The teacher says: "Do your homework." → The teacher says that you should do your homework.*

31.B.3 Changes in verb tenses

a. The following verb tenses change in indirect discourse when the reporting verb is used in the past.

Regional variations in ▶ the use of the subjunctive in nominal clauses: 23.Fa

	Type of change	Direct discourse	Indirect discourse
Indicative	Present → Imperfect	Ella **dijo**: "**Voy** de compras". *She said: "I am going shopping."*	Ella **dijo** que **iba** de compras. *She said that she was going shopping.*
	Preterite → Past perfect	Ella **dijo**: "**Fui** de compras". *She said: "I went shopping."*	Ella **dijo** que **había ido** de compras. *She said that she had gone shopping.*
	Present perfect → Past perfect	Ella **dijo**: "No **he comprado** nada". *She said: "I haven't bought anything."*	Ella **dijo** que no **había comprado** nada. *She said that she hadn't bought anything.*
	Future → Conditional	Ella **dijo**: "**Compraré** algo". *She said: "I will buy something."*	Ella **dijo** que **compraría** algo. *She said that she would buy something.*
	Future perfect → Perfect conditional	Ella **dijo**: "Esta tarde **habré terminado** mis compras". *She said: "I will have finished my shopping this afternoon."*	Ella **dijo** que esta tarde **habría terminado** sus compras. *She said that she would have finished her shopping this afternoon.*
Subjunctive	Present → Imperfect	Ella **dijo**: "**Quiero** que me **acompañes**". *She said: "I want you to go with me."*	Ella **dijo** que **quería** que la **acompañara**. *She said that she wanted me to go with her.*
	Present perfect → Past perfect	Ella **dijo**: "No creo que me **hayan dado** un buen precio". *She said: "I don't believe they gave me a good price."*	Ella **dijo** que no creía que le **hubieran dado** un buen precio. *She said that she did not believe they had given her a good price.*
	Imperative → Imperfect	Ella **dijo**: "¡**Espérame**!" *She said: "Wait for me!"*	Ella **dijo** que la **esperara**. *She said that I should wait for her.*

Ir a: 26.C.1 ▶

b. When reporting a future statement, it is also possible to use the *imperfect* of **ir a** + *infinitive*.

Iré la semana que viene. → Dijo que **iría** la semana siguiente. / Dijo que **iba a ir** la semana siguiente.

I will go next week. → She said she would go next week. / She said she was going to go next week.

31.B.4 Verb tenses that do not change

The following tenses do not change in indirect discourse. However, note that other changes to the sentence may be necessary, such as adding reflexive and object pronouns.

		Direct discourse	Indirect discourse
Indicative	Imperfect	Ella dijo: "**Me gustaban** mucho las tapas". *She said: "I liked tapas a lot."*	Ella dijo que **le gustaban** mucho las tapas. *She said that she used to like tapas a lot.*
	Past perfect	Ella dijo: "Nunca **me había divertido** tanto". *She said: "I'd never had so much fun."*	Ella dijo que nunca **se había divertido** tanto. *She said that she had never had so much fun.*
	Conditional	Ella dijo: "**Tomaría** un crucero". *She said: "I would go on a cruise."*	Ella dijo que **tomaría** un crucero. *She said she would go on a cruise.*
	Conditional perfect	Ella dijo: "**Te habrías divertido** si hubieras venido a la fiesta". *She said: "You would have had fun if you had come to the party."*	Ella dijo que **me habría divertido** si hubiera ido a la fiesta. *She said I would have had fun if I had come to the party.*
Subjunctive	Imperfect	Ella dijo: "Me gustaría que tú **me prepararas** un plato chileno". *She said: "I would like you to prepare a Chilean dish for me."*	Ella dijo que **le** gustaría que **yo le preparara** un plato chileno. *She said that she would like me to prepare a Chilean dish for her.*
	Past perfect	Ella dijo: "**Te** habrías divertido si **hubieras venido** a la fiesta". *She said: "You would have had fun if you had come to the party."*	Ella dijo que **me** habría divertido si **hubiera ido** a la fiesta. *She said I would have had fun if I had come to the party.*

31.B.5 Other necessary changes

a. Retelling and repeating imply a change of perspective and will necessarily require changes in other sentence elements. Spanish and English share these perspectives and the same changes are required.

Direct discourse	Indirect discourse
Ella me dice: "**Te** voy a extrañar mucho". *She tells me: "I am going to miss you a lot."*	Ella dijo que **me** iba a extrañar mucho. *She said she was going to miss me a lot.*
Ella dice: "No puedo poner**me** los zapatos". *She says: "I can't put on my shoes."*	Ella dijo que no podía poner**se** los zapatos. *She said she couldn't put on her shoes.*

b. A change from direct discourse to indirect discourse may also imply a change in time perspective. In addition to changes in verb tenses, adverbs or time expressions may have to change, too.

Direct discourse	Indirect discourse
Fecha: 3 de enero Elena dice: "Publicaré las fotos **mañana**". *Elena says: "I will publish my photos tomorrow."*	Fecha: 15 de enero Elena dijo que publicaría las fotos **al día siguiente**. *Elena said that she would publish her photos the next day.*
Elena dice: "**Anoche** no pude dormir nada". *Elena says: "I couldn't sleep at all last night."*	Elena dijo que no había podido dormir nada **la noche anterior**. *Elena said that she hadn't been able to sleep at all the night before.*

Indirect questions: 14.B.1b, 14.B.9, 16.C.1b–c

a. Questions may be reported indirectly or rephrased to make them more polite. Note that Spanish has the same word order in direct and indirect questions.

	Direct question	Indirect question
Present	—Señor, **¿qué hora es?** *Sir, what time is it?*	—Señor, ¿podría decirme **qué hora es?** *Sir, could you tell me what time it is?*
Past	—¿Qué le **preguntaste** al señor? *What did you ask the man?*	—Le pregunté **qué hora era.** *I asked him what time it was.*

Que before indirect questions: 16.C.1c

b. When reporting *yes/no* questions, **si** introduces the implied question. *If* or *whether* are used in the equivalent construction in English. In informal speech, **que** may be added to the indirect question.

—¿Qué le preguntaste al señor?   *What did you ask the man?*
—Le pregunté (que) **si** sabía la hora.   *I asked him if/whether he knew what time it was.*

Using the future to express conjecture: 20.C.2

c. Verbs referring to mental activity also form statements with **si.**

Me pregunto **si** este producto es bueno.   *I wonder if/whether this product is good.*
No recuerdo **si** la cita es hoy.   *I don't recall if/whether the appointment is today.*

Question words: 1.E.7
Question formation: 14.A–14.B

d. Question words carry an accent in both direct and indirect questions.

—¿**Cuándo** llegará el avión?   *When will the plane arrive?*
—Nadie sabe **cuándo** llegará.   *No one knows when it will arrive.*

—¿**Cómo** se llamará esa chica?   *What is that girl's name?*
—No sé **cómo** se llama ella.   *I don't know what her name is.*

—¿**Dónde** podrán arreglarme el coche?   *Where can my car be fixed?*
—No sabemos **dónde** podrán arreglártelo.   *We don't know where it can be fixed.*

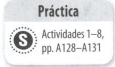

Práctica

S Actividades 1–8, pp. A128–A131

Verb conjugation tables

Pages **261–276** contain verb conjugation patterns. Patterns 1–3 include the simple tenses of three model **-ar, -er,** and **-ir** regular verbs. Patterns 4 to 80 include spell-changing, stem-changing, and irregular verbs. Charts are also provided for the formation of compound tenses (**p. 261**) and **estar + gerundio** periphrases (*progressive tenses*) (**p. 262**). For the formation of reflexive verbs, see **27.A.** To see a list of irregular participles, see **19.A.2** and **25.D.2.**

Spell-changing, stem-changing, and irregular verbs

In patterns 4 to 80, the superscript numbers in parentheses identify the type of irregularity:

[1]Stem-changing verbs (**pensar → pienso**)

[2]Verbs with spelling changes (**recoger → recojo**)

[3]Verbs with accent changes or verbs that require replacing **u** with **ü** (**reunir → reúno; averiguar → averigüé**)

[4]Verbs with unique irregularities (sometimes in addition to stem or spelling changes) (**poner → puse**)

Note: Any form that deviates from the regular verb patterns is indicated in **bold** font.

Voseo

Voseo conjugations are included in the present indicative and in the second person singular informal imperative. These are the **voseo** forms included in the verb charts in the RAE's *Nueva gramática*. For more information about the **voseo**, see **13.B.2, 22.B.b, 24.C,** and **24.D.1.**

tú/vos   hablas/hablás   habla/hablá

Nomenclature

The Spanish names of the verb tenses used in this handbook correspond to the names used in the *Nueva gramática* published by the Real Academia Española.

English terminology used in this handbook	Spanish terminology used in this handbook	Traditional Spanish terminology	Terminology used by Andrés Bello
Simple present	Presente	Presente	Presente
Imperfect	Pretérito imperfecto	Pretérito imperfecto	Copretérito
Preterite	Pretérito perfecto simple	Pretérito indefinido	Pretérito
Present perfect	Pretérito perfecto compuesto	Pretérito perfecto	Antepresente
Past perfect	Pretérito pluscuamperfecto	Pretérito pluscuamperfecto	Antecopretérito
Simple future	Futuro (simple)	Futuro (simple)	Futuro
Future perfect	Futuro compuesto	Futuro compuesto/perfecto	Antefuturo
Present conditional	Condicional (simple)	Condicional simple/presente Potencial simple	Pospretérito
Conditional perfect	Condicional compuesto	Condicional compuesto/perfecto Potencial compuesto/perfecto	Antepospretérito

Tenses not included in the charts

The following tenses are rarely used in contemporary Spanish. They have been excluded from the verb tables in this handbook.

Pretérito anterior (indicativo): See **19.F.**	Cuando **hubo terminado** la fiesta, fuimos a casa.
Futuro simple (subjuntivo): See **22.F.**	Adonde **fueres**, haz lo que vieres.
Futuro compuesto (subjuntivo): See **22.G.**	"Será proclamado Alcalde el concejal que **hubiere obtenido** más votos..."

Negative imperative

The verb forms for the negative imperative are not included in the verb charts. They coincide with the forms of the present subjunctive.

Verb chapters

The following chapters cover verb tense formation and usage.

Indicative	Present	Chapter 17	**Subjunctive**	All tenses – Formation	Chapter 22
	Preterite and Imperfect	Chapter 18			
	Present perfect and Past perfect	Chapter 19		All tenses – Usage	Chapter 23
	Future and Future perfect	Chapter 20			
	Conditional and Conditional perfect	Chapter 21		**Imperative**	Chapter 24

Verbs with stem changes, spelling changes, and irregular verbs

The list below includes common verbs with stem changes, spelling changes, and irregular verbs, as well as the verbs used as models/patterns in the charts on **pp. 261-276**. The number in brackets indicates where in the verb tables you can find the conjugated form of the model verb.

abastecer (*conocer* [15])
aborrecer (*conocer* [15])
abstenerse (*tener* [69])
abstraer (*traer* [73])
acaecer (*conocer* [15])
acentuar (*graduar* [37])
acoger (*proteger* [54])
acontecer (*conocer* [15])
acordar (*contar* [16])
acostar (*contar* [16])
acrecentar (*pensar* [49])
actuar (*graduar* [37])
adherir (*sentir* [65])
adolecer (*conocer* [15])
adormecer (*conocer* [15])
adquirir [4]
aducir (*conducir* [14])
advertir (*sentir* [65])
afligir (*exigir* [35])
ahumar (*rehusar* [57])
airar (*aislar* [5])
aislar [5]
alentar (*pensar* [49])
almorzar [6]
amanecer (*conocer* [15])
amoblar (*contar* [16])
amortiguar (*averiguar* [10])
ampliar (*enviar* [29])
andar [7]
anegar (*negar* [45])
anochecer (*conocer* [15])
apaciguar (*averiguar* [10])
aparecer (*conocer* [15])

apetecer (*conocer* [15])
apretar (*pensar* [49])
aprobar (*contar* [16])
arrepentirse (*sentir* [65])
ascender (*entender* [28])
asentar (*pensar* [49])
asentir (*sentir* [65])
asir [8]
atañer (*tañer* [68])
atardecer (*conocer* [15])
atender (*entender* [28])
atenerse (*tener* [69])
atestiguar (*averiguar* [10])
atraer (*traer* [73])
atravesar (*pensar* [49])
atribuir (*destruir* [23])
aunar (*rehusar* [57])
avergonzar [9]
averiguar [10]
balbucir (*lucir* [43])
bendecir [11]
caber [12]
caer [13]
calentar (*pensar* [49])
cegar (*negar* [45])
ceñir (*teñir* [70])
cerrar (*pensar* [49])
cimentar (*pensar* [49])
cocer (*torcer* [72])
coercer (*vencer* [75])
coger (*proteger* [54])
cohibir (*prohibir* [53])
colgar (*rogar* [61])

comenzar (*empezar* [27])
comer [2]
compadecer (*conocer* [15])
comparecer (*conocer* [15])
competir (*pedir* [48])
comprobar (*contar* [16])
concebir (*pedir* [48])
concernir (*discernir* [24])
concluir (*destruir* [23])
concordar (*contar* [16])
conducir [14]
confesar (*pensar* [49])
confiar (*enviar* [29])
conmover (*mover* [44])
conocer [15]
conseguir (*seguir* [64])
consentir (*sentir* [65])
consolar (*contar* [16])
constituir (*destruir* [23])
construir (*destruir* [23])
contar [16]
contener (*tener* [69])
continuar (*graduar* [37])
contradecir (*predecir* [52])
contraer (*traer* [73])
contrariar (*enviar* [29])
convalecer (*conocer* [15])
convencer (*vencer* [75])
converger (*proteger* [54])
convertir (*sentir* [65])
corregir (*elegir* [26])
corroer (*roer* [60])
costar (*contar* [16])

creer [17]
criar (enviar [29])
cruzar [18]
dar [19]
decaer (caer [13])
decir [20]
deducir (conducir [14])
defender (entender [28])
degollar [21]
delinquir [22]
demoler (mover [44])
demostrar (contar [16])
denegar (negar [45])
derretir (pedir [48])
desafiar (enviar [29])
desaguar (averiguar [10])
desalentar (pensar [49])
desandar (andar [7])
desaparecer (conocer [15])
desasir (asir [8])
descafeinar (aislar [5])
descolgar (rogar [61])
desconsolar (contar [16])
desdecir (predecir [52])
desentenderse (entender [28])
desfallecer (conocer [15])
desfavorecer (conocer [15])
deshacer (hacer [39])
deslucir (lucir [43])
desmerecer (conocer [15])
desoír (oír [46])
despedir (pedir [48])
despertar (pensar [49])
desplegar (negar [45])
desteñir (teñir [70])
destruir [23]
desvestir (pedir [48])
detener (tener [69])
diferir (sentir [65])
digerir (sentir [65])
diluir (destruir [23])
dirigir (exigir [35])
discernir [24]
disentir (sentir [65])
disminuir (destruir [23])
distender (entender [28])
distinguir (extinguir [36])
distraer (traer [73])
distribuir (destruir [23])
divertir (sentir [65])
doler (mover [44])
dormir [25]
efectuar (graduar [37])
ejercer (vencer [75])
elegir [26]
embellecer (conocer [15])

embestir (pedir [48])
emerger (proteger [54])
empalidecer (conocer [15])
emparentar (pensar [49])
empequeñecer (conocer [15])
empezar [27]
empobrecer (conocer [15])
encarecer (conocer [15])
enceguecer (conocer [15])
encender (entender [28])
encerrar (pensar [49])
encontrar (contar [16])
endurecer (conocer [15])
enfriar (enviar [29])
enfurecer (conocer [15])
engullir (zambullir [80])
enloquecer (conocer [15])
enmendar (pensar [49])
enmudecer (conocer [15])
enriquecer (conocer [15])
ensordecer (conocer [15])
entender [28]
enterrar (pensar [49])
entorpecer (conocer [15])
entrelucir (lucir [43])
entreoír (oír [46])
entretener (tener [69])
entristecer (conocer [15])
envejecer (conocer [15])
enviar [29]
equivaler (valer [74])
erguir [30]
errar [31]
escarmentar (pensar [49])
escoger (proteger [54])
esforzar (almorzar [6])
esparcir [32]
espiar (enviar [29])
establecer (conocer [15])
estar [33]
estremecer (conocer [15])
estreñir (teñir [70])
europeizar [34]
evaluar (graduar [37])
exceptuar (graduar [37])
excluir (destruir [23])
exigir [35]
expedir (pedir [48])
extender (entender [28])
extinguir [36]
extraer (traer [73])
fallecer (conocer [15])
favorecer (conocer [15])
fingir (exigir [35])
florecer (conocer [15])
fluir (destruir [23])

fortalecer (conocer [15])
forzar (almorzar [6])
fotografiar (enviar [29])
fraguar (averiguar [10])
fregar (negar [45])
freír (reír [58])
gobernar (pensar [49])
graduar [37]
gruñir (zambullir [80])
guiar (enviar [29])
haber [38]
habituar (graduar [37])
hablar [1]
hacer [39]
helar (pensar [49])
hendir (discernir [24])
herir (sentir [65])
herrar (pensar [49])
hervir (sentir [65])
homogeneizar (europeizar [34])
humedecer (conocer [15])
impedir (pedir [48])
incluir (destruir [23])
inducir (conducir [14])
infligir (exigir [35])
influir (destruir [23])
ingerir (sentir [65])
inquirir (adquirir [4])
insinuar (graduar [37])
instituir (destruir [23])
instruir (destruir [23])
interferir (sentir [65])
introducir (conducir [14])
invernar (pensar [49])
invertir (sentir [65])
investir (pedir [48])
ir [40]
judaizar (europeizar [34])
jugar [41]
leer (creer [17])
liar (enviar [29])
llegar [42]
llover (mover [44])
lucir [43]
malcriar (enviar [29])
maldecir (bendecir [11])
malentender (entender [28])
malherir (sentir [65])
maltraer (traer [73])
manifestar (pensar [49])
mantener (tener [69])
maullar (rehusar [57])
mecer (vencer [75])
medir (pedir [48])
mentir (sentir [65])
merecer (conocer [15])

merendar (*pensar* [49])
moler (*mover* [44])
morder (*mover* [44])
morir (p.p. muerto) (*dormir* [25])
mostrar (*contar* [16])
mover [44]
mugir (*exigir* [35])
mullir (*zambullir* [80])
nacer (*conocer* [15])
negar [45]
nevar (*pensar* [49])
obedecer (*conocer* [15])
obstruir (*destruir* [23])
obtener (*tener* [69])
ofrecer (*conocer* [15])
oír [46]
oler [47]
oscurecer (*conocer* [15])
padecer (*conocer* [15])
palidecer (*conocer* [15])
parecer (*conocer* [15])
pedir [48]
pensar [49]
perder (*entender* [28])
permanecer (*conocer* [15])
perpetuar (*graduar* [37])
perseguir (*seguir* [64])
plegar (*negar* [45])
poblar (*contar* [16])
poder [50]
poner [51]
poseer (*creer* [17])
predecir [52]
preferir (*sentir* [65])
presentir (*sentir* [65])
prevaler (*valer* [74])
probar (*contar* [16])
producir (*conducir* [14])
prohibir [53]
promover (*mover* [44])
proseguir (*seguir* [64])
proteger [54]
proveer (*creer* [17])
pudrir/podrir [55]
quebrar (*pensar* [49])
querer [56]
recaer (*caer* [13])
recoger (*proteger* [54])
recomenzar (*empezar* [27])
reconducir (*conducir* [14])
recordar (*contar* [16])
recostar (*contar* [16])
reducir (*conducir* [14])
reforzar (*almorzar* [6])
refregar (*negar* [45])
regir (*elegir* [26])

rehusar [57]
reír [58]
releer (*creer* [17])
relucir (*lucir* [43])
remendar (*pensar* [49])
remover (*mover* [44])
rendir (*pedir* [48])
renegar (*negar* [45])
reñir (*teñir* [70])
renovar (*contar* [16])
repetir (*pedir* [48])
replegar (*negar* [45])
reproducir (*conducir* [14])
requerir (*sentir* [65])
resarcir (*esparcir* [32])
resolver (p.p. resuelto) (*mover* [44])
restringir (*exigir* [35])
resurgir (*exigir* [35])
retorcer (*torcer* [72])
retrotraer (*traer* [73])
reunir [59]
reventar (*pensar* [49])
revertir (*sentir* [65])
revolcar (*volcar* [78])
robustecer (*conocer* [15])
rociar (*enviar* [29])
rodar (*contar* [16])
roer [60]
rogar [61]
saber [62]
salir [63]
salpimentar (*pensar* [49])
satisfacer (*hacer* [39])
seducir (*conducir* [14])
seguir [64]
sembrar (*pensar* [49])
sentar (*pensar* [49])
sentir [65]
ser [66]
servir (*pedir* [48])
situar (*graduar* [37])
sobrecoger (*proteger* [54])
sobresalir (*salir* [63])
sobreseer (*creer* [17])
sofreír (*reír* [58])
soler [67]
soltar (*contar* [16])
sonar (*contar* [16])
sonreír (*reír* [58])
soñar (*contar* [16])
sosegar (*negar* [45])
sostener (*tener* [69])
subyacer (*yacer* [79])
sugerir (*sentir* [65])
sumergir (*exigir* [35])
surgir (*exigir* [35])

sustituir (*destruir* [23])
sustraer (*traer* [73])
tañer [68]
tatuar (*graduar* [37])
temblar (*pensar* [49])
tener [69]
tentar (*pensar* [49])
teñir [70]
tocar [71]
torcer [72]
tostar (*contar* [16])
traducir (*conducir* [14])
traer [73]
transferir (*sentir* [65])
trascender (*entender* [28])
traslucirse (*lucir* [43])
trastocar (*volcar* [78])
trocar (*volcar* [78])
tropezar (*empezar* [27])
uncir (*esparcir* [32])
urgir (*exigir* [35])
valer [74]
valuar (*graduar* [37])
variar (*enviar* [29])
vencer [75]
venir [76]
ver [77]
verter (*entender* [28])
vestir (*pedir* [48])
vivir [3]
volar (*contar* [16])
volcar [78]
volver (p.p. vuelto) (*mover* [44])
yacer [79]
zambullir [80]
zurcir (*esparcir* [32])

Verb conjugation tables

Regular verbs: simple tenses

Infinitivo / Gerundio / Participio	Pronombres personales	INDICATIVO					SUBJUNTIVO		IMPERATIVO
		Presente	Pretérito imperfecto	Pretérito perfecto simple	Futuro simple	Condicional simple	Presente	Pretérito imperfecto	
1 hablar / hablando / hablado	yo	hablo	hablaba	hablé	hablaré	hablaría	hable	hablara o hablase	
	tú/vos	hablas/hablás	hablabas	hablaste	hablarás	hablarías	hables	hablaras o hablases	habla/hablá
	Ud., él, ella	habla	hablaba	habló	hablará	hablaría	hable	hablara o hablase	hable
	nosotros/as	hablamos	hablábamos	hablamos	hablaremos	hablaríamos	hablemos	habláramos o hablásemos	hablemos
	vosotros/as	habláis	hablabais	hablasteis	hablaréis	hablaríais	habléis	hablarais o hablaseis	hablad
	Uds., ellos/as	hablan	hablaban	hablaron	hablarán	hablarían	hablen	hablaran o hablasen	hablen
2 comer / comiendo / comido	yo	como	comía	comí	comeré	comería	coma	comiera o comiese	
	tú/vos	comes/comés	comías	comiste	comerás	comerías	comas	comieras o comieses	come/comé
	Ud., él, ella	come	comía	comió	comerá	comería	coma	comiera o comiese	coma
	nosotros/as	comemos	comíamos	comimos	comeremos	comeríamos	comamos	comiéramos o comiésemos	comamos
	vosotros/as	coméis	comíais	comisteis	comeréis	comeríais	comáis	comierais o comieseis	comed
	Uds., ellos/as	comen	comían	comieron	comerán	comerían	coman	comieran o comiesen	coman
3 vivir / viviendo / vivido	yo	vivo	vivía	viví	viviré	viviría	viva	viviera o viviese	
	tú/vos	vives/vivís	vivías	viviste	vivirás	vivirías	vivas	vivieras o vivieses	vive/viví
	Ud., él, ella	vive	vivía	vivió	vivirá	viviría	viva	viviera o viviese	viva
	nosotros/as	vivimos	vivíamos	vivimos	viviremos	viviríamos	vivamos	viviéramos o viviésemos	vivamos
	vosotros/as	vivís	vivíais	vivisteis	viviréis	viviríais	viváis	vivierais o vivieseis	vivid
	Uds., ellos/as	viven	vivían	vivieron	vivirán	vivirían	vivan	vivieran o viviesen	vivan

Compound tenses

INDICATIVO

Pretérito perfecto compuesto	Pretérito pluscuamperfecto	Futuro compuesto	Condicional compuesto	
he	había	habré	habría	hablado
has	habías	habrás	habrías	comido
ha	había	habrá	habría	vivido
hemos	habíamos	habremos	habríamos	
habéis	habíais	habréis	habríais	
han	habían	habrán	habrían	

SUBJUNTIVO

Pretérito perfecto compuesto	Pretérito pluscuamperfecto	
haya	hubiera o hubiese	hablado
hayas	hubieras o hubieses	comido
haya	hubiera o hubiese	vivido
hayamos	hubiéramos o hubiésemos	
hayáis	hubierais o hubieseis	
hayan	hubieran o hubiesen	

Estar + gerundio (Progressive tenses)

INDICATIVO

Presente		Pretérito imperfecto		Pretérito perfecto simple		Futuro simple		Condicional simple	
estoy		estaba		estuve		estaré		estaría	
estás		estabas		estuviste		estarás		estarías	
está	hablando	estaba	hablando	estuvo	hablando	estará	hablando	estaría	hablando
estamos	comiendo	estábamos	comiendo	estuvimos	comiendo	estaremos	comiendo	estaríamos	comiendo
estáis	viviendo	estabais	viviendo	estuvisteis	viviendo	estaréis	viviendo	estaríais	viviendo
están		estaban		estuvieron		estarán		estarían	

SUBJUNTIVO

Pretérito perfecto		Pretérito imperfecto	
esté		estuviera o estuviese	
estés		estuvieras o estuvieses	
esté	hablando	estuviera o estuviese	hablando
estemos	comiendo	estuviéramos o estuviésemos	comiendo
estéis	viviendo	estuvierais o estuvieseis	viviendo
estén		estuvieran o estuviesen	

Note: Perfect progressive tenses are formed using a conjugated form of **haber** + **estado** + **gerundio**, as in **he estado comiendo, hubiera estado corriendo**, etc.

Verbs with stem changes, spelling changes, and irregular verbs

Infinitivo / Gerundio Participio	Pronombres personales	INDICATIVO					SUBJUNTIVO		IMPERATIVO
		Presente	Pretérito imperfecto	Pretérito perfecto simple	Futuro simple	Condicional simple	Presente	Pretérito imperfecto	
adquirir [(1)] (i:ie)	yo	**adquiero**	adquiría	adquirí	adquiriré	adquiriría	**adquiera**	adquiriera o adquiriese	
	tú/vos	**adquieres/** adquirís	adquirías	adquiriste	adquirirás	adquirirías	**adquieras**	adquirieras o adquirieses	**adquiere/** adquirí
adquiriendo adquirido	Ud., él, ella	**adquiere**	adquiría	adquirió	adquirirá	adquiriría	**adquiera**	adquiriera o adquiriese	**adquiera**
	nosotros/as	adquirimos	adquiríamos	adquirimos	adquiriremos	adquiriríamos	adquiramos	adquiriéramos o adquiriésemos	adquiramos
	vosotros/as	adquirís	adquiríais	adquiristeis	adquiriréis	adquiriríais	adquiráis	adquirierais o adquirieseis	adquirid
	Uds., ellos/as	**adquieren**	adquirían	adquirieron	adquirirán	adquirirían	**adquieran**	adquirieran o adquiriesen	**adquieran**

Infinitivo / Gerundio / Participio	Pronombres personales	INDICATIVO Presente	Pretérito imperfecto	Pretérito perfecto simple	Futuro simple	Condicional simple	SUBJUNTIVO Presente	Pretérito imperfecto	IMPERATIVO
5 aislar [3] (i:í)	yo	aíslo	aislaba	aislé	aislaré	aislaría	aísle	aislara o aislase	
	tú/vos	aíslas/aislás	aislabas	aislaste	aislarás	aislarías	aísles	aislaras o aislases	aísla/aislá
	Ud., él, ella	aísla	aislaba	aisló	aislará	aislaría	aísle	aislara o aislase	aísle
aislando	nosotros/as	aislamos	aislábamos	aislamos	aislaremos	aislaríamos	aislemos	aisláramos o aislásemos	aislemos
aislado	vosotros/as	aisláis	aislabais	aislasteis	aislaréis	aislaríais	aisléis	aislarais o aislaseis	aislad
	Uds., ellos/as	aíslan	aislaban	aislaron	aislarán	aislarían	aíslen	aislaran o aislasen	aíslen
6 almorzar [1, 2] (o:ue) (z:c)	yo	almuerzo	almorzaba	almorcé	almorzaré	almorzaría	almuerce	almorzara o almorzase	
	tú/vos	almuerzas/almorzás	almorzabas	almorzaste	almorzarás	almorzarías	almuerces	almorzaras o almorzases	almuerza/almorzá
	Ud., él, ella	almuerza	almorzaba	almorzó	almorzará	almorzaría	almuerce	almorzara o almorzase	almuerce
almorzando	nosotros/as	almorzamos	almorzábamos	almorzamos	almorzaremos	almorzaríamos	almorcemos	almorzáramos o almorzásemos	almorcemos
almorzado	vosotros/as	almorzáis	almorzabais	almorzasteis	almorzaréis	almorzaríais	almorcéis	almorzarais o almorzaseis	almorzad
	Uds., ellos/as	almuerzan	almorzaban	almorzaron	almorzarán	almorzarían	almuercen	almorzaran o almorzasen	almuercen
7 andar [4]	yo	ando	andaba	anduve	andaré	andaría	ande	anduviera o anduviese	
	tú/vos	andas/andás	andabas	anduviste	andarás	andarías	andes	anduvieras o anduvieses	anda/andá
	Ud., él, ella	anda	andaba	anduvo	andará	andaría	ande	anduviera o anduviese	ande
andando	nosotros/as	andamos	andábamos	anduvimos	andaremos	andaríamos	andemos	anduviéramos o anduviésemos	andemos
andado	vosotros/as	andáis	andabais	anduvisteis	andaréis	andaríais	andéis	anduvierais o anduvieseis	andad
	Uds., ellos/as	andan	andaban	anduvieron	andarán	andarían	anden	anduvieran o anduviesen	anden
8 asir [4]	yo	asgo	asía	así	asiré	asiría	asga	asiera o asiese	
	tú/vos	ases/asís	asías	asiste	asirás	asirías	asgas	asieras o asieses	ase/así
	Ud., él, ella	ase	asía	asió	asirá	asiría	asga	asiera o asiese	asga
asiendo	nosotros/as	asimos	asíamos	asimos	asiremos	asiríamos	asgamos	asiéramos o asiésemos	asgamos
asido	vosotros/as	asís	asíais	asisteis	asiréis	asiríais	asgáis	asierais o asieseis	asid
	Uds., ellos/as	asen	asían	asieron	asirán	asirían	asgan	asieran o asiesen	asgan
9 avergonzar [1, 2] (cüe) (z:c)	yo	avergüenzo	avergonzaba	avergoncé	avergonzaré	avergonzaría	avergüence	avergonzara o avergonzase	
	tú/vos	avergüenzas/avergonzás	avergonzabas	avergonzaste	avergonzarás	avergonzarías	avergüences	avergonzaras o avergonzases	avergüenza/avergonzá
	Ud., él, ella	avergüenza	avergonzaba	avergonzó	avergonzará	avergonzaría	avergüence	avergonzara o avergonzase	avergüence
avergonzando	nosotros/as	avergonzamos	avergonzábamos	avergonzamos	avergonzaremos	avergonzaríamos	avergoncemos	avergonzáramos o avergonzásemos	avergoncemos
avergonzado	vosotros/as	avergonzáis	avergonzabais	avergonzasteis	avergonzaréis	avergonzaríais	avergoncéis	avergonzarais o avergonzaseis	avergonzad
	Uds., ellos/as	avergüenzan	avergonzaban	avergonzaron	avergonzarán	avergonzarían	avergüencen	avergonzaran o avergonzasen	avergüencen

Infinitivo / Gerundio / Participio	Pronombres personales	INDICATIVO Presente	Pretérito imperfecto	Pretérito perfecto simple	Futuro simple	Condicional simple	SUBJUNTIVO Presente	Pretérito imperfecto	IMPERATIVO
10 averiguar [3] (u:ü)	yo	averiguo	averiguaba	**averigüé**	averiguaré	averiguaría	**averigüe**	averiguara o averiguase	
	tú/vos	averiguas/ averiguás	averiguabas	averiguaste	averiguarás	averiguarías	**averigües**	averiguaras o averiguases	averigua/ averiguá
averiguando averiguado	Ud., él, ella	averigua	averiguaba	averiguó	averiguará	averiguaría	**averigüe**	averiguara o averiguase	**averigüe**
	nosotros/as	averiguamos	averiguábamos	averiguamos	averiguaremos	averiguaríamos	**averigüemos**	averiguáramos o averiguásemos	**averigüemos**
	vosotros/as	averiguáis	averiguabais	averiguasteis	averiguaréis	averiguaríais	**averigüéis**	averiguarais o averiguaseis	averiguad
	Uds., ellos/as	averiguan	averiguaban	averiguaron	averiguarán	averiguarían	**averigüen**	averiguaran o averiguasen	**averigüen**
11 bendecir [4]	yo	**bendigo**	bendecía	**bendije**	bendeciré	bendeciría	**bendiga**	**bendijera o bendijese**	
	tú/vos	**bendices**/ bendecís	bendecías	**bendijiste**	bendecirás	bendecirías	**bendigas**	**bendijeras o bendijeses**	**bendice**/ bendecí
bendiciendo bendecido o **bendito**	Ud., él, ella	**bendice**	bendecía	**bendijo**	bendecirá	bendeciría	**bendiga**	**bendijera o bendijese**	**bendiga**
	nosotros/as	bendecimos	bendecíamos	**bendijimos**	bendeciremos	bendeciríamos	**bendigamos**	**bendijéramos o bendijésemos**	**bendigamos**
	vosotros/as	bendecís	bendecíais	**bendijisteis**	bendeciréis	bendeciríais	**bendigáis**	**bendijerais o bendijeseis**	bendecid
	Uds., ellos/as	**bendicen**	bendecían	**bendijeron**	bendecirán	bendecirían	**bendigan**	**bendijeran o bendijesen**	**bendigan**
12 caber [4]	yo	**quepo**	cabía	cupe	**cabré**	cabría	**quepa**	cupiera o cupiese	
	tú/vos	cabes/cabés	cabías	cupiste	**cabrás**	**cabrías**	**quepas**	cupieras o cupieses	cabe/cabé
cabiendo cabido	Ud., él, ella	cabe	cabía	cupo	**cabrá**	**cabría**	**quepa**	cupiera o cupiese	**quepa**
	nosotros/as	cabemos	cabíamos	cupimos	**cabremos**	**cabríamos**	**quepamos**	cupiéramos o cupiésemos	**quepamos**
	vosotros/as	cabéis	cabíais	cupisteis	**cabréis**	**cabríais**	**quepáis**	cupierais o cupieseis	cabed
	Uds., ellos/as	caben	cabían	cupieron	**cabrán**	**cabrán**	**quepan**	cupieran o cupiesen	**quepan**
13 caer [4] (y)	yo	**caigo**	caía	caí	caeré	caería	**caiga**	cayera o cayese	
	tú/vos	caes/caés	caías	caíste	caerás	caerías	**caigas**	cayeras o cayeses	cae/caé
cayendo caído	Ud., él, ella	cae	caía	**cayó**	caerá	caería	**caiga**	cayera o cayese	**caiga**
	nosotros/as	caemos	caíamos	caímos	caeremos	caeríamos	**caigamos**	cayéramos o cayésemos	**caigamos**
	vosotros/as	caéis	caíais	caísteis	caeréis	caeríais	**caigáis**	cayerais o cayeseis	caed
	Uds., ellos/as	caen	caían	**cayeron**	caerán	caerían	**caigan**	cayeran o cayesen	**caigan**
14 conducir [2] (c:zc)	yo	**conduzco**	conducía	**conduje**	conduciré	conduciría	**conduzca**	**condujera o condujese**	
	tú/vos	conduces/ conducís	conducías	**condujiste**	conducirás	conducirías	**conduzcas**	**condujeras o condujeses**	conduce/conducí
conduciendo conducido	Ud., él, ella	conduce	conducía	**condujo**	conducirá	conduciría	**conduzca**	**condujera o condujese**	**conduzca**
	nosotros/as	conducimos	conducíamos	**condujimos**	conduciremos	conduciríamos	**conduzcamos**	**condujéramos o condujésemos**	**conduzcamos**
	vosotros/as	conducís	conducíais	**condujisteis**	conduciréis	conduciríais	**conduzcáis**	**condujerais o condujeseis**	conducid
	Uds., ellos/as	conducen	conducían	**condujeron**	conducirán	conducirían	**conduzcan**	**condujeran o condujesen**	**conduzcan**

Infinitivo / Gerundio / Participio	Pronombres personales	INDICATIVO					SUBJUNTIVO		IMPERATIVO
		Presente	Pretérito imperfecto	Pretérito perfecto simple	Futuro simple	Condicional simple	Presente	Pretérito imperfecto	
15 conocer (1) (c:zc) / conociendo / conocido	yo	**conozco**	conocía	conocí	conoceré	conocería	**conozca**	conociera o conociese	
	tú/vos	conoces/conocés	conocías	conociste	conocerás	conocerías	**conozcas**	conocieras o conocieses	conoce/conocé
	Ud., él, ella	conoce	conocía	conoció	conocerá	conocería	**conozca**	conociera o conociese	**conozca**
	nosotros/as	conocemos	conocíamos	conocimos	conoceremos	conoceríamos	**conozcamos**	conociéramos o conociésemos	**conozcamos**
	vosotros/as	conocéis	conocíais	conocisteis	conoceréis	conoceríais	**conozcáis**	conocierais o conocieseis	conoced
	Uds., ellos/as	conocen	conocían	conocieron	conocerán	conocerían	**conozcan**	conocieran o conociesen	**conozcan**
16 contar (1) (o:ue) / contando / contado	yo	**cuento**	contaba	conté	contaré	contaría	**cuente**	contara o contase	
	tú/vos	**cuentas**/contás	contabas	contaste	contarás	contarías	**cuentes**	contaras o contases	**cuenta**/contá
	Ud., él, ella	**cuenta**	contaba	contó	contará	contaría	**cuente**	contara o contase	**cuente**
	nosotros/as	contamos	contábamos	contamos	contaremos	contaríamos	contemos	contáramos o contásemos	contemos
	vosotros/as	contáis	contabais	contasteis	contaréis	contaríais	contéis	contarais o contaseis	contad
	Uds., ellos/as	**cuentan**	contaban	contaron	contarán	contarían	**cuenten**	contaran o contasen	**cuenten**
17 creer (3, 4) (y) / **creyendo** / **creído**	yo	creo	creía	creí	creeré	creería	crea	**creyera o creyese**	
	tú/vos	crees/creés	creías	**creíste**	creerás	creerías	creas	**creyeras o creyeses**	cree/creé
	Ud., él, ella	cree	creía	**creyó**	creerá	creería	crea	**creyera o creyese**	crea
	nosotros/as	creemos	creíamos	**creímos**	creeremos	creeríamos	creamos	**creyéramos o creyésemos**	creamos
	vosotros/as	creéis	creíais	**creísteis**	creeréis	creeríais	creáis	**creyerais o creyeseis**	creed
	Uds., ellos/as	creen	creían	**creyeron**	creerán	creerían	crean	**creyeran o creyesen**	crean
18 cruzar (2) (z:c) / cruzando / cruzado	yo	cruzo	cruzaba	**crucé**	cruzaré	cruzaría	**cruce**	cruzara o cruzase	
	tú/vos	cruzas/cruzás	cruzabas	cruzaste	cruzarás	cruzarías	**cruces**	cruzaras o cruzases	cruza/cruzá
	Ud., él, ella	cruza	cruzaba	cruzó	cruzará	cruzaría	**cruce**	cruzara o cruzase	**cruce**
	nosotros/as	cruzamos	cruzábamos	cruzamos	cruzaremos	cruzaríamos	**crucemos**	cruzáramos o cruzásemos	**crucemos**
	vosotros/as	cruzáis	cruzabais	cruzasteis	cruzaréis	cruzaríais	**crucéis**	cruzarais o cruzaseis	cruzad
	Uds., ellos/as	cruzan	cruzaban	cruzaron	cruzarán	cruzarían	**crucen**	cruzaran o cruzasen	**crucen**
19 dar (4) / dando / dado	yo	**doy**	daba	**di**	daré	daría	**dé**	diera o diese	
	tú/vos	das	dabas	**diste**	darás	darías	des	dieras o dieses	da
	Ud., él, ella	da	daba	**dio**	dará	daría	**dé**	diera o diese	**dé**
	nosotros/as	damos	dábamos	**dimos**	daremos	daríamos	demos	diéramos o diésemos	demos
	vosotros/as	**dais**	dabais	**disteis**	daréis	daríais	**deis**	dierais o dieseis	dad
	Uds., ellos/as	dan	daban	**dieron**	darán	darían	den	dieran o diesen	den
20 decir (1,4) (e:i) / **diciendo** / **dicho**	yo	**digo**	decía	**dije**	**diré**	**diría**	**diga**	**dijera o dijese**	
	tú/vos	**dices**/decís	decías	**dijiste**	**dirás**	**dirías**	**digas**	**dijeras o dijeses**	**di**/decí
	Ud., él, ella	**dice**	decía	**dijo**	**dirá**	**diría**	**diga**	**dijera o dijese**	**diga**
	nosotros/as	**decimos**	decíamos	**dijimos**	**diremos**	**diríamos**	**digamos**	**dijéramos o dijésemos**	**digamos**
	vosotros/as	decís	decíais	**dijisteis**	**diréis**	**diríais**	**digáis**	**dijerais o dijeseis**	decid
	Uds., ellos/as	**dicen**	decían	**dijeron**	**dirán**	**dirían**	**digan**	**dijeran o dijesen**	**digan**

Verb conjugation tables

Infinitivo / Gerundio Participio	Pronombres personales	INDICATIVO Presente	Pretérito imperfecto	Pretérito perfecto simple	Futuro simple	Condicional simple	SUBJUNTIVO Presente	Pretérito imperfecto	IMPERATIVO
21 degollar (1, 3) (go:güe) degollando degollado	yo	**degüello**	degollaba	degollé	degollaré	degollaría	**degüelle**	degollara o degollase	
	tú/vos	**degüellas**/degollás	degollabas	degollaste	degollarás	degollarías	**degüelles**	degollaras o degollases	**degüella**/degollá
	Ud., él, ella	**degüella**	degollaba	degolló	degollará	degollaría	**degüelle**	degollara o degollase	**degüelle**
	nosotros/as	degollamos	degollábamos	degollamos	degollaremos	degollaríamos	degollemos	degolláramos o degollásemos	degollemos
	vosotros/as	degolláis	degollabais	degollasteis	degollaréis	degollaríais	degolléis	degollarais o degollaseis	degollad
	Uds., ellos/as	**degüellan**	degollaban	degollaron	degollarán	degollarían	**degüellen**	degollaran o degollasen	**degüellen**
22 delinquir (2) (qu:c) delinquiendo delinquido	yo	**delinco**	delinquía	delinquí	delinquiré	delinquiría	**delinca**	delinquiera o delinquiese	
	tú/vos	delinques/delinquís	delinquías	delinquiste	delinquirás	delinquirías	**delincas**	delinquieras o delinquieses	delinque/delinquí
	Ud., él, ella	delinque	delinquía	delinquió	delinquirá	delinquiría	**delinca**	delinquiera o delinquiese	**delinca**
	nosotros/as	delinquimos	delinquíamos	delinquimos	delinquiremos	delinquiríamos	**delincamos**	delinquiéramos o delinquiésemos	**delincamos**
	vosotros/as	delinquís	delinquíais	delinquisteis	delinquiréis	delinquiríais	**delincáis**	delinquierais o delinquieseis	delinquid
	Uds., ellos/as	delinquen	delinquían	delinquieron	delinquirán	delinquirían	**delincan**	delinquieran o delinquiesen	**delincan**
23 destruir (4) (y) destruyendo destruido	yo	**destruyo**	destruía	destruí	destruiré	destruiría	**destruya**	destruyera o destruyese	
	tú/vos	**destruyes**/destruís	destruías	destruiste	destruirás	destruirías	**destruyas**	destruyeras o destruyeses	**destruye**/destruí
	Ud., él, ella	**destruye**	destruía	**destruyó**	destruirá	destruiría	**destruya**	destruyera o destruyese	**destruya**
	nosotros/as	destruimos	destruíamos	destruimos	destruiremos	destruiríamos	**destruyamos**	**destruyéramos** o **destruyésemos**	**destruyamos**
	vosotros/as	destruís	destruíais	destruisteis	destruiréis	destruiríais	**destruyáis**	**destruyerais** o **destruyeseis**	destruid
	Uds., ellos/as	**destruyen**	destruían	**destruyeron**	destruirán	destruirían	**destruyan**	**destruyeran** o **destruyesen**	**destruyan**
24 discernir (1) (e:ie) discerniendo discernido	yo	**discierno**	discernía	discerní	discerniré	discerniría	**discierna**	discerniera o discerniese	
	tú/vos	**disciernes**/discernís	discernías	discerniste	discernirás	discernirías	**disciernas**	discernieras o discernieses	**discierne**/discerní
	Ud., él, ella	**discierne**	discernía	discernió	discernirá	discerniría	**discierna**	discerniera o discerniese	**discierna**
	nosotros/as	discernimos	discerníamos	discernimos	discerniremos	discerniríamos	discernamos	discerniéramos o discerniésemos	discernamos
	vosotros/as	discernís	discerníais	discernisteis	discerniréis	discerniríais	discernáis	discernierais o discernieseis	discernid
	Uds., ellos/as	**disciernen**	discernían	discernieron	discernirán	discernirían	**disciernan**	discernieran o discerniesen	**disciernan**
25 dormir (1) (o:ue) **durmiendo** dormido	yo	**duermo**	dormía	dormí	dormiré	dormiría	**duerma**	**durmiera** o **durmiese**	
	tú/vos	**duermes**/dormís	dormías	dormiste	dormirás	dormirías	**duermas**	**durmieras** o **durmieses**	**duerme**/dormí
	Ud., él, ella	**duerme**	dormía	**durmió**	dormirá	dormiría	**duerma**	**durmiera** o **durmiese**	**duerma**
	nosotros/as	dormimos	dormíamos	dormimos	dormiremos	dormiríamos	**durmamos**	**durmiéramos** o **durmiésemos**	**durmamos**
	vosotros/as	dormís	dormíais	dormisteis	dormiréis	dormiríais	**durmáis**	**durmierais** o **durmieseis**	dormid
	Uds., ellos/as	**duermen**	dormían	**durmieron**	dormirán	dormirían	**duerman**	**durmieran** o **durmiesen**	**duerman**

Verb conjugation tables

Infinitivo / Gerundio / Participio	Pronombres personales	INDICATIVO Presente	INDICATIVO Pretérito imperfecto	INDICATIVO Pretérito perfecto simple	INDICATIVO Futuro simple	INDICATIVO Condicional simple	SUBJUNTIVO Presente	SUBJUNTIVO Pretérito imperfecto	IMPERATIVO
26 elegir [1,2] (e:i) (g:j) / **eligiendo** / elegido o **electo**	yo	**elijo**	elegía	elegí	elegiré	elegiría	**elija**	**eligiera** o **eligiese**	
	tú/vos	**eliges/elegís**	elegías	elegiste	elegirás	elegirías	**elijas**	**eligieras** o **eligieses**	**elige/elegí**
	Ud., él, ella	**elige**	elegía	**eligió**	elegirá	elegiría	**elija**	**eligiera** o **eligiese**	**elija**
	nosotros/as	elegimos	elegíamos	elegimos	elegiremos	elegiríamos	**elijamos**	**eligiéramos** o **eligiésemos**	**elijamos**
	vosotros/as	elegís	elegíais	elegisteis	elegiréis	elegiríais	**elijáis**	**eligierais** o **eligieseis**	elegid
	Uds., ellos/as	**eligen**	elegían	**eligieron**	elegirán	elegirían	**elijan**	**eligieran** o **eligiesen**	**elijan**
27 empezar [1,2] (e:ie) (z:c) / empezando / empezado	yo	**empiezo**	empezaba	**empecé**	empezaré	empezaría	**empiece**	empezara o empezase	
	tú/vos	**empiezas/** empezás	empezabas	empezaste	empezarás	empezarías	**empieces**	empezaras o empezases	**empieza/** empezá
	Ud., él, ella	**empieza**	empezaba	empezó	empezará	empezaría	**empiece**	empezara o empezase	**empiece**
	nosotros/as	empezamos	empezábamos	empezamos	empezaremos	empezaríamos	**empecemos**	empezáramos o empezásemos	**empecemos**
	vosotros/as	empezáis	empezabais	empezasteis	empezaréis	empezaríais	**empecéis**	empezarais o empezaseis	empezad
	Uds., ellos/as	**empiezan**	empezaban	empezaron	empezarán	empezarían	**empiecen**	empezaran o empezasen	**empiecen**
28 entender [1] (e:ie) / entendiendo / entendido	yo	**entiendo**	entendía	entendí	entenderé	entendería	**entienda**	entendiera o entendiese	
	tú/vos	**entiendes/** entendés	entendías	entendiste	entenderás	entenderías	**entiendas**	entendieras o entendieses	**entiende/** entendé
	Ud., él, ella	**entiende**	entendía	entendió	entenderá	entendería	**entienda**	entendiera o entendiese	**entienda**
	nosotros/as	entendemos	entendíamos	entendimos	entenderemos	entenderíamos	entendamos	entendiéramos o entendiésemos	**entendamos**
	vosotros/as	entendéis	entendíais	entendisteis	entenderéis	entenderíais	entendáis	entendierais o entendieseis	entended
	Uds., ellos/as	**entienden**	entendían	entendieron	entenderán	entenderían	**entiendan**	entendieran o entendiesen	**entiendan**
29 enviar [3] (i:í) / enviando / enviado	yo	**envío**	enviaba	envié	enviaré	enviaría	**envíe**	enviara o enviase	
	tú/vos	**envías/enviás**	enviabas	enviaste	enviarás	enviarías	**envíes**	enviaras o enviases	**envía/enviá**
	Ud., él, ella	**envía**	enviaba	envió	enviará	enviaría	**envíe**	enviara o enviase	**envíe**
	nosotros/as	enviamos	enviábamos	enviamos	enviaremos	enviaríamos	enviemos	enviáramos o enviásemos	enviemos
	vosotros/as	enviáis	enviabais	enviasteis	enviaréis	enviaríais	enviéis	enviarais o enviaseis	enviad
	Uds., ellos/as	**envían**	enviaban	enviaron	enviarán	enviarían	**envíen**	enviaran o enviasen	**envíen**
30 erguir [4] / **irguiendo** / erguido	yo	**irgo o yergo**	erguía	erguí	erguiré	erguiría	**irga o yerga**	**irguiera o irguiese**	
	tú/vos	**irgues o yergues/erguís**	erguías	erguiste	erguirás	erguirías	**irgas o yergas**	**irguieras o irguieses**	**irgue o yergue/** erguí
	Ud., él, ella	**irgue o yergue**	erguía	**irguió**	erguirá	erguiría	**irga o yerga**	**irguiera o irguiese**	**irga o yerga**
	nosotros/as	erguimos	erguíamos	erguimos	erguiremos	erguiríamos	**irgamos o yergamos**	**irguiéramos o irguiésemos**	**irgamos o yergamos**
	vosotros/as	erguís	erguíais	erguisteis	erguiréis	erguiríais	irgáis o yergáis	**irguierais o irguieseis**	erguid
	Uds., ellos/as	**irguen o yerguen**	erguían	**irguieron**	erguirán	erguirían	**irgan o yergan**	**irguieran o irguiesen**	**irgan o yergan**

31 errar [4] (y)
Gerundio: errando — Participio: errado

Pronombres personales	INDICATIVO Presente	Pretérito imperfecto	Pretérito perfecto simple	Futuro simple	Condicional simple	SUBJUNTIVO Presente	Pretérito imperfecto	IMPERATIVO
yo	**yerro** o erro	erraba	erré	erraré	erraría	**yerre** o erre	errara o errase	
tú/vos	**yerras** o erras/errás	errabas	erraste	errarás	errarías	**yerres** o erres	erraras o errases	**yerra** o erra/errá
Ud., él, ella	**yerra** o erra	erraba	erró	errará	erraría	**yerre** o erre	errara o errase	**yerre** o erre
nosotros/as	erramos	errábamos	erramos	erraremos	erraríamos	erremos	erráramos o errásemos	erremos
vosotros/as	erráis	errabais	errasteis	erraréis	erraríais	erréis	errarais o erraseis	errad
Uds., ellos/as	**yerran** o erran	erraban	erraron	errarán	errarían	**yerren** o erren	erraran o errasen	**yerren** o erren

32 esparcir [2] (c:z)
Gerundio: esparciendo — Participio: esparcido

Pronombres personales	INDICATIVO Presente	Pretérito imperfecto	Pretérito perfecto simple	Futuro simple	Condicional simple	SUBJUNTIVO Presente	Pretérito imperfecto	IMPERATIVO
yo	**esparzo**	esparcía	esparcí	esparciré	esparciría	**esparza**	esparciera o esparciese	
tú/vos	esparces/esparcís	esparcías	esparciste	esparcirás	esparcirías	**esparzas**	esparcieras o esparcieses	esparce/esparcí
Ud., él, ella	esparce	esparcía	esparció	esparcirá	esparciría	**esparza**	esparciera o esparciese	**esparza**
nosotros/as	esparcimos	esparcíamos	esparcimos	esparciremos	esparciríamos	**esparzamos**	esparciéramos o esparciésemos	**esparzamos**
vosotros/as	esparcís	esparcíais	esparcisteis	esparciréis	esparciríais	**esparzáis**	esparcierais o esparcieseis	esparcid
Uds., ellos/as	esparcen	esparcían	esparcieron	esparcirán	esparcirían	**esparzan**	esparcieran o esparciesen	**esparzan**

33 estar [4]
Gerundio: estando — Participio: estado

Pronombres personales	INDICATIVO Presente	Pretérito imperfecto	Pretérito perfecto simple	Futuro simple	Condicional simple	SUBJUNTIVO Presente	Pretérito imperfecto	IMPERATIVO
yo	estoy	estaba	**estuve**	estaré	estaría	esté	**estuviera** o **estuviese**	
tú/vos	**estás**	estabas	**estuviste**	estarás	estarías	**estés**	**estuvieras** o **estuvieses**	está
Ud., él, ella	**está**	estaba	**estuvo**	estará	estaría	esté	**estuviera** o **estuviese**	esté
nosotros/as	estamos	estábamos	**estuvimos**	estaremos	estaríamos	estemos	**estuviéramos** o **estuviésemos**	estemos
vosotros/as	estáis	estabais	**estuvisteis**	estaréis	estaríais	estéis	**estuvierais** o **estuvieseis**	estad
Uds., ellos/as	**están**	estaban	**estuvieron**	estarán	estarían	**estén**	**estuvieran** o **estuviesen**	**estén**

34 europeizar [2, 3] (z:c) (i:í)
Gerundio: europeizando — Participio: europeizado

Pronombres personales	INDICATIVO Presente	Pretérito imperfecto	Pretérito perfecto simple	Futuro simple	Condicional simple	SUBJUNTIVO Presente	Pretérito imperfecto	IMPERATIVO
yo	**europeizo**	europeizaba	**europeicé**	europeizaré	europeizaría	**europeice**	europeizara o europeizase	
tú/vos	**europeizas**/europeizás	europeizabas	europeizaste	europeizarás	europeizarías	**europeices**	europeizaras o europeizases	**europeiza**/europeizá
Ud., él, ella	**europeiza**	europeizaba	europeizó	europeizará	europeizaría	**europeice**	europeizara o europeizase	**europeice**
nosotros/as	europeizamos	europeizábamos	europeizamos	europeizaremos	europeizaríamos	**europeicemos**	europeizáramos o europeizásemos	**europeicemos**
vosotros/as	europeizáis	europeizabais	europeizasteis	europeizaréis	europeizaríais	**europeicéis**	europeizarais o europeizaseis	europeizad
Uds., ellos/as	**europeizan**	europeizaban	europeizaron	europeizarán	europeizarían	**europeicen**	europeizaran o europeizasen	**europeicen**

35 exigir [2] (g:j)
Gerundio: exigiendo — Participio: exigido

Pronombres personales	INDICATIVO Presente	Pretérito imperfecto	Pretérito perfecto simple	Futuro simple	Condicional simple	SUBJUNTIVO Presente	Pretérito imperfecto	IMPERATIVO
yo	**exijo**	exigía	exigí	exigiré	exigiría	**exija**	exigiera o exigiese	
tú/vos	exiges/exigís	exigías	exigiste	exigirás	exigirías	**exijas**	exigieras o exigieses	exige/exigí
Ud., él, ella	exige	exigía	exigió	exigirá	exigiría	**exija**	exigiera o exigiese	**exija**
nosotros/as	exigimos	exigíamos	exigimos	exigiremos	exigiríamos	**exijamos**	exigiéramos o exigiésemos	**exijamos**
vosotros/as	exigís	exigíais	exigisteis	exigiréis	exigiríais	**exijáis**	exigierais o exigieseis	exigid
Uds., ellos/as	exigen	exigían	exigieron	exigirán	exigirían	**exijan**	exigieran o exigiesen	**exijan**

36 extinguir [2] (gu:g)
Gerundio: extinguiendo — Participio: extinguido

Pronombres personales	INDICATIVO Presente	Pretérito imperfecto	Pretérito perfecto simple	Futuro simple	Condicional simple	SUBJUNTIVO Presente	Pretérito imperfecto	IMPERATIVO
yo	**extingo**	extinguía	extinguí	extinguiré	extinguiría	**extinga**	extinguiera o extinguiese	
tú/vos	extingues/extinguís	extinguías	extinguiste	extinguirás	extinguirías	**extingas**	extinguieras o extinguieses	extingue/extinguí
Ud., él, ella	extingue	extinguía	extinguió	extinguirá	extinguiría	**extinga**	extinguiera o extinguiese	**extinga**
nosotros/as	extinguimos	extinguíamos	extinguimos	extinguiremos	extinguiríamos	**extingamos**	extinguiéramos o extinguiésemos	**extingamos**
vosotros/as	extinguís	extinguíais	extinguisteis	extinguiréis	extinguiríais	**extingáis**	extinguierais o extinguieseis	extinguid
Uds., ellos/as	extinguen	extinguían	extinguieron	extinguirán	extinguirían	**extingan**	extinguieran o extinguiesen	**extingan**

Infinitivo Gerundio Participio	Pronombres personales	INDICATIVO Presente	Pretérito imperfecto	Pretérito perfecto simple	Futuro simple	Condicional simple	SUBJUNTIVO Presente	Pretérito imperfecto	IMPERATIVO
37 graduar (3) (u:ú) graduando graduado	yo	gradúo	graduaba	gradué	graduaré	graduaría	gradúe	graduara o graduase	
	tú/vos	gradúas/graduás	graduabas	graduaste	graduarás	graduarías	gradúes	graduaras o graduases	gradúa/graduá
	Ud., él, ella	gradúa	graduaba	graduó	graduará	graduaría	gradúe	graduara o graduase	gradúe
	nosotros/as	graduamos	graduábamos	graduamos	graduaremos	graduaríamos	graduemos	graduáramos o graduásemos	graduemos
	vosotros/as	graduáis	graduabais	graduasteis	graduaréis	graduaríais	graduéis	graduarais o graduaseis	graduad
	Uds., ellos/as	gradúan	graduaban	graduaron	graduarán	graduarían	gradúen	graduaran o graduasen	gradúen
38 haber (4) habiendo habido	yo	he	había	hube	habré	habría	haya	hubiera o hubiese	
	tú/vos	has	habías	hubiste	habrás	habrías	hayas	hubieras o hubieses	
	Ud., él, ella	ha	había	hubo	habrá	habría	haya	hubiera o hubiese	
	nosotros/as	hemos	habíamos	hubimos	habremos	habríamos	hayamos	hubiéramos o hubiésemos	
	vosotros/as	habéis	habíais	hubisteis	habréis	habríais	hayáis	hubierais o hubieseis	
	Uds., ellos/as	han	habían	hubieron	habrán	habrían	hayan	hubieran o hubiesen	
39 hacer (4) haciendo hecho	yo	hago	hacía	hice	haré	haría	haga	hiciera o hiciese	
	tú/vos	haces/hacés	hacías	hiciste	harás	harías	hagas	hicieras o hicieses	haz/hacé
	Ud., él, ella	hace	hacía	hizo	hará	haría	haga	hiciera o hiciese	haga
	nosotros/as	hacemos	hacíamos	hicimos	haremos	haríamos	hagamos	hiciéramos o hiciésemos	hagamos
	vosotros/as	hacéis	hacíais	hicisteis	haréis	haríais	hagáis	hicierais o hicieseis	haced
	Uds., ellos/as	hacen	hacían	hicieron	harán	harían	hagan	hicieran o hiciesen	hagan
40 ir (4) yendo ido	yo	voy	iba	fui	iré	iría	vaya	fuera o fuese	
	tú/vos	vas	ibas	fuiste	irás	irías	vayas	fueras o fueses	ve/andá
	Ud., él, ella	va	iba	fue	irá	iría	vaya	fuera o fuese	vaya
	nosotros/as	vamos	íbamos	fuimos	iremos	iríamos	vayamos	fuéramos o fuésemos	vamos
	vosotros/as	vais	ibais	fuisteis	iréis	iríais	vayáis	fuerais o fueseis	id
	Uds., ellos/as	van	iban	fueron	irán	irían	vayan	fueran o fuesen	vayan
41 jugar (1, 2) (u:ue) (g:gu) jugando jugado	yo	juego	jugaba	jugué	jugaré	jugaría	juegue	jugara o jugase	
	tú/vos	juegas/jugás	jugabas	jugaste	jugarás	jugarías	juegues	jugaras o jugases	juega/jugá
	Ud., él, ella	juega	jugaba	jugó	jugará	jugaría	juegue	jugara o jugase	juegue
	nosotros/as	jugamos	jugábamos	jugamos	jugaremos	jugaríamos	juguemos	jugáramos o jugásemos	juguemos
	vosotros/as	jugáis	jugabais	jugasteis	jugaréis	jugaríais	juguéis	jugarais o jugaseis	jugad
	Uds., ellos/as	juegan	jugaban	jugaron	jugarán	jugarían	jueguen	jugaran o jugasen	jueguen
42 llegar (2) (g:gu) llegando llegado	yo	llego	llegaba	llegué	llegaré	llegaría	llegue	llegara o llegase	
	tú/vos	llegas/llegás	llegabas	llegaste	llegarás	llegarías	llegues	llegaras o llegases	llega/llegá
	Ud., él, ella	llega	llegaba	llegó	llegará	llegaría	llegue	llegara o llegase	llegue
	nosotros/as	llegamos	llegábamos	llegamos	llegaremos	llegaríamos	lleguemos	llegáramos o llegásemos	lleguemos
	vosotros/as	llegáis	llegabais	llegasteis	llegaréis	llegaríais	lleguéis	llegarais o llegaseis	llegad
	Uds., ellos/as	llegan	llegaban	llegaron	llegarán	llegarían	lleguen	llegaran o llegasen	lleguen

Infinitivo — Gerundio Participio	Pronombres personales	INDICATIVO Presente	Pretérito imperfecto	Pretérito perfecto simple	Futuro simple	Condicional simple	SUBJUNTIVO Presente	Pretérito imperfecto	IMPERATIVO
43 lucir [1] (c:zc) luciendo lucido	yo	**luzco**	lucía	lucí	luciré	luciría	**luzca**	luciera o luciese	
	tú/vos	luces/lucís	lucías	luciste	lucirás	lucirías	**luzcas**	lucieras o lucieses	luce/lucí
	Ud., él, ella	luce	lucía	lució	lucirá	luciría	**luzca**	luciera o luciese	**luzca**
	nosotros/as	lucimos	lucíamos	lucimos	luciremos	luciríamos	**luzcamos**	luciéramos o luciésemos	**luzcamos**
	vosotros/as	lucís	lucíais	lucisteis	luciréis	luciríais	**luzcáis**	lucierais o lucieseis	lucid
	Uds., ellos/as	lucen	lucían	lucieron	lucirán	lucirían	**luzcan**	lucieran o luciesen	**luzcan**
44 mover [1] (o:ue) moviendo movido	yo	**muevo**	movía	moví	moveré	movería	**mueva**	moviera o moviese	
	tú/vos	**mueves**/movés	movías	moviste	moverás	moverías	**muevas**	movieras o movieses	**mueve**/mové
	Ud., él, ella	**mueve**	movía	movió	moverá	movería	**mueva**	moviera o moviese	**mueva**
	nosotros/as	movemos	movíamos	movimos	moveremos	moveríamos	movamos	moviéramos o moviésemos	movamos
	vosotros/as	movéis	movíais	movisteis	moveréis	moveríais	mováis	movierais o movieseis	moved
	Uds., ellos/as	**mueven**	movían	movieron	moverán	moverían	**muevan**	movieran o moviesen	**muevan**
45 negar [1, 2] (e:ie) (g:gu) negando negado	yo	**niego**	negaba	**negué**	negaré	negaría	**niegue**	negara o negase	
	tú/vos	**niegas**/negás	negabas	negaste	negarás	negarías	**niegues**	negaras o negases	**niega**/negá
	Ud., él, ella	**niega**	negaba	negó	negará	negaría	**niegue**	negara o negase	**niegue**
	nosotros/as	negamos	negábamos	negamos	negaremos	negaríamos	**neguemos**	negáramos o negásemos	**neguemos**
	vosotros/as	negáis	negabais	negasteis	negaréis	negaríais	**neguéis**	negarais o negaseis	negad
	Uds., ellos/as	**niegan**	negaban	negaron	negarán	negarían	**nieguen**	negaran o negasen	**nieguen**
46 oír [3, 4] (y) **oyendo** oído	yo	**oigo**	oía	oí	oiré	oiría	**oiga**	**oyera** o **oyese**	
	tú/vos	**oyes**/oís	oías	**oíste**	oirás	oirías	**oigas**	**oyeras** o **oyeses**	**oye**/oí
	Ud., él, ella	**oye**	oía	**oyó**	oirá	oiría	**oiga**	**oyera** o **oyese**	oiga
	nosotros/as	**oímos**	oíamos	**oímos**	oiremos	oiríamos	**oigamos**	**oyéramos** o **oyésemos**	**oigamos**
	vosotros/as	oís	oíais	**oísteis**	oiréis	oiríais	oigáis	**oyerais** o **oyeseis**	oíd
	Uds., ellos/as	**oyen**	oían	**oyeron**	oirán	oirían	oigan	**oyeran** o **oyesen**	oigan
47 oler [1] (o:hue) oliendo olido	yo	**huelo**	olía	olí	oleré	olería	**huela**	oliera u oliese	
	tú/vos	**hueles**/olés	olías	oliste	olerás	olerías	**huelas**	olieras u olieses	**huele**/olé
	Ud., él, ella	**huele**	olía	olió	olerá	olería	**huela**	oliera u oliese	**huela**
	nosotros/as	olemos	olíamos	olimos	oleremos	oleríamos	olamos	oliéramos u oliésemos	olamos
	vosotros/as	oléis	olíais	olisteis	oleréis	oleríais	oláis	olierais u olieseis	oled
	Uds., ellos/as	**huelen**	olían	olieron	olerán	olerían	**huelan**	olieran u oliesen	**huelan**
48 pedir [1] (e:i) **pidiendo** pedido	yo	**pido**	pedía	pedí	pediré	pediría	**pida**	**pidiera** o **pidiese**	
	tú/vos	**pides**/pedís	pedías	pediste	pedirás	pedirías	**pidas**	**pidieras** o **pidieses**	**pide**/pedí
	Ud., él, ella	**pide**	pedía	**pidió**	pedirá	pediría	**pida**	**pidiera** o **pidiese**	**pida**
	nosotros/as	pedimos	pedíamos	pedimos	pediremos	pediríamos	**pidamos**	**pidiéramos** o **pidiésemos**	**pidamos**
	vosotros/as	pedís	pedíais	pedisteis	pediréis	pediríais	**pidáis**	**pidierais** o **pidieseis**	pedid
	Uds., ellos/as	**piden**	pedían	**pidieron**	pedirán	pedirían	**pidan**	**pidieran** o **pidiesen**	**pidan**

Infinitivo / Gerundio / Participio	Pronombres personales	INDICATIVO					SUBJUNTIVO		IMPERATIVO
		Presente	Pretérito imperfecto	Pretérito perfecto simple	Futuro simple	Condicional simple	Presente	Pretérito imperfecto	
49 pensar [1] (e:ie) / pensando / pensado	yo	**pienso**	pensaba	pensé	pensaré	pensaría	**piense**	pensara o pensase	
	tú/vos	**piensas/pensás**	pensabas	pensaste	pensarás	pensarías	**pienses**	pensaras o pensases	**piensa/pensá**
	Ud., él, ella	**piensa**	pensaba	pensó	pensará	pensaría	**piense**	pensara o pensase	**piense**
	nosotros/as	pensamos	pensábamos	pensamos	pensaremos	pensaríamos	pensemos	pensáramos o pensásemos	pensemos
	vosotros/as	pensáis	pensabais	pensasteis	pensaréis	pensaríais	penséis	pensarais o pensaseis	pensad
	Uds., ellos/as	**piensan**	pensaban	pensaron	pensarán	pensarían	**piensen**	pensaran o pensasen	**piensen**
50 poder [1,4] (o:ue) / pudiendo / podido	yo	**puedo**	podía	**pude**	**podré**	**podría**	**pueda**	**pudiera o pudiese**	
	tú/vos	**puedes/podés**	podías	**pudiste**	**podrás**	**podrías**	**puedas**	**pudieras o pudieses**	**puede/podé**
	Ud., él, ella	**puede**	podía	**pudo**	**podrá**	**podría**	**pueda**	**pudiera o pudiese**	**pueda**
	nosotros/as	podemos	podíamos	**pudimos**	**podremos**	**podríamos**	podamos	**pudiéramos o pudiésemos**	podamos
	vosotros/as	podéis	podíais	**pudisteis**	**podréis**	**podríais**	podáis	**pudierais o pudieseis**	poded
	Uds., ellos/as	**pueden**	podían	**pudieron**	**podrán**	**podrían**	**puedan**	**pudieran o pudiesen**	**puedan**
51 poner [4] / poniendo / **puesto**	yo	**pongo**	ponía	**puse**	**pondré**	**pondría**	**ponga**	pusiera o pusiese	
	tú/vos	pones/ponés	ponías	**pusiste**	**pondrás**	**pondrías**	**pongas**	pusieras o pusieses	**pon/poné**
	Ud., él, ella	pone	ponía	**puso**	**pondrá**	**pondría**	**ponga**	pusiera o pusiese	**ponga**
	nosotros/as	ponemos	poníamos	**pusimos**	**pondremos**	**pondríamos**	**pongamos**	**pusiéramos o pusiésemos**	**pongamos**
	vosotros/as	ponéis	poníais	**pusisteis**	**pondréis**	**pondríais**	**pongáis**	pusierais o pusieseis	poned
	Uds., ellos/as	ponen	ponían	**pusieron**	**pondrán**	**pondrían**	**pongan**	pusieran o pusiesen	**pongan**
52 predecir [1,4] (e:i) / prediciendo / **predicho**	yo	**predigo**	predecía	predije	predeciré o prediré	predeciría o prediría	**prediga**	predijera o predijese	
	tú/vos	**predices/predecís**	predecías	**predijiste**	**predecirás o predirás**	**predecirías o predirías**	**predigas**	**predijeras o predijeses**	**predice/predecí**
	Ud., él, ella	**predice**	predecía	**predijo**	predecirá o predirá	predeciría o prediría	**prediga**	**predijera o predijese**	**prediga**
	nosotros/as	predecimos	predecíamos	**predijimos**	**predeciremos o prediremos**	predeciríamos o prediríamos	**predigamos**	**predijéramos o predijésemos**	**predigamos**
	vosotros/as	predecís	predecíais	**predijisteis**	**predeciréis o prediréis**	predeciríais o prediríais	**predigáis**	**predijerais o predijeseis**	predecid
	Uds., ellos/as	**predicen**	predecían	**predijeron**	predecirán o predirán	predecirían o predirían	**predigan**	**predijeran o predijesen**	**predigan**
53 prohibir [3] (i:í) / prohibiendo / prohibido	yo	**prohíbo**	prohibía	prohibí	prohibiré	prohibiría	**prohíba**	prohibiera o prohibiese	
	tú/vos	**prohíbes/prohibís**	prohibías	prohibiste	prohibirás	prohibirías	**prohíbas**	prohibieras o prohibieses	**prohíbe/prohibís**
	Ud., él, ella	**prohíbe**	prohibía	prohibió	prohibirá	prohibiría	**prohíba**	prohibiera o prohibiese	**prohíba**
	nosotros/as	prohibimos	prohibíamos	prohibimos	prohibiremos	prohibiríamos	prohibamos	prohibiéramos o prohibiésemos	prohibamos
	vosotros/as	prohibís	prohibíais	prohibisteis	prohibiréis	prohibiríais	prohibáis	prohibierais o prohibieseis	prohibid
	Uds., ellos/as	**prohíben**	prohibían	prohibieron	prohibirán	prohibirían	**prohíban**	prohibieran o prohibiesen	**prohíban**

Infinitivo / Gerundio / Participio	Pronombres personales	INDICATIVO Presente	INDICATIVO Pretérito imperfecto	INDICATIVO Pretérito perfecto simple	INDICATIVO Futuro simple	INDICATIVO Condicional simple	SUBJUNTIVO Presente	SUBJUNTIVO Pretérito imperfecto	IMPERATIVO
54 proteger (2) (g:j) / protegiendo / protegido	yo	**protejo**	protegía	protegí	protegeré	protegería	**proteja**	protegiera o protegiese	
	tú/vos	proteges/protegés	protegías	protegiste	protegerás	protegerías	**protejas**	protegieras o protegieses	protege/protegé
	Ud., él, ella	protege	protegía	protegió	protegerá	protegería	**proteja**	protegiera o protegiese	**proteja**
	nosotros/as	protegemos	protegíamos	protegimos	protegeremos	protegeríamos	**protejamos**	protegiéramos o protegiésemos	**protejamos**
	vosotros/as	protegéis	protegíais	protegisteis	protegeréis	protegeríais	**protejáis**	protegierais o protegieseis	proteged
	Uds., ellos/as	protegen	protegían	protegieron	protegerán	protegerían	**protejan**	protegieran o protegiesen	**protejan**
55 pudrir/podrir (4) / pudriendo / podrido	yo	pudro	pudría o podría	pudrí o podrí	pudriré o podriré	pudriría o podriría	pudra	pudriera o pudriese	
	tú/vos	pudres/pudrís	pudrías o podrías	pudriste o podriste	pudrirás o podrirás	pudrirías o podrirías	pudras	pudrieras o pudrieses	pudre/pudrí o podrí
	Ud., él, ella	pudre	pudría o podría	pudrió o podrió	pudrirá o podrirá	pudriría o podriría	pudra	pudriera o pudriese	pudra
	nosotros/as	pudrimos o podrimos	pudríamos o podríamos	pudrimos o podrimos	pudriremos o podriremos	pudriríamos o podriríamos	pudramos	pudriéramos o pudriésemos	pudramos
	vosotros/as	pudrís o podrís	pudríais o podríais	pudristeis o podristeis	pudriréis o podriréis	pudriríais o podriríais	pudráis	pudrierais o pudrieseis	pudrid o podrid
	Uds., ellos/as	pudren	pudrían o podrían	pudrieron o podrieron	pudrirán o podrirán	pudrirían o podrirían	pudran	pudrieran o pudriesen	pudran
56 querer (1,4) (e:ie) / queriendo / querido	yo	**quiero**	quería	quise	**querré**	**querría**	**quiera**	**quisiera** o **quisiese**	
	tú/vos	**quieres**/querés	querías	quisiste	**querrás**	**querrías**	**quieras**	**quisieras** o **quisieses**	**quiere**/queré
	Ud., él, ella	**quiere**	quería	quiso	**querrá**	**querría**	**quiera**	**quisiera** o **quisiese**	**quiera**
	nosotros/as	queremos	queríamos	quisimos	**querremos**	**querríamos**	queramos	**quisiéramos** o **quisiésemos**	queramos
	vosotros/as	queréis	queríais	quisisteis	**querréis**	**querríais**	queráis	**quisierais** o **quisieseis**	quered
	Uds., ellos/as	**quieren**	querían	quisieron	**querrán**	**querrían**	**quieran**	**quisieran** o **quisiesen**	**quieran**
57 rehusar (3) (u:ú) / rehusando / rehusado	yo	**rehúso**	rehusaba	rehusé	rehusaré	rehusaría	**rehúse**	rehusara o rehusase	
	tú/vos	**rehúsas**/rehusás	rehusabas	rehusaste	rehusarás	rehusarías	**rehúses**	rehusaras o rehusases	**rehúsa**/rehusá
	Ud., él, ella	**rehúsa**	rehusaba	rehusó	rehusará	rehusaría	**rehúse**	rehusara o rehusase	**rehúse**
	nosotros/as	rehusamos	rehusábamos	rehusamos	rehusaremos	rehusaríamos	rehusemos	rehusáramos o rehusásemos	rehusemos
	vosotros/as	rehusáis	rehusabais	rehusasteis	rehusaréis	rehusaríais	rehuséis	rehusarais o rehusaseis	rehusad
	Uds., ellos/as	**rehúsan**	rehusaban	rehusaron	rehusarán	rehusarían	**rehúsen**	rehusaran o rehusasen	**rehúsen**
58 reír (1) (e:i) / riendo / reído	yo	**río**	reía	reí	reiré	reiría	**ría**	riera o riese	
	tú/vos	**ríes**/reís	reías	**reíste**	reirás	reirías	**rías**	rieras o rieses	ríe/reí
	Ud., él, ella	**ríe**	reía	**rio**	reirá	reiría	**ría**	riera o riese	ría
	nosotros/as	**reímos**	reíamos	**reímos**	reiremos	reiríamos	**riamos**	**riéramos** o **riésemos**	**riamos**
	vosotros/as	reís	reíais	**reísteis**	reiréis	reiríais	riáis	rierais o rieseis	reíd
	Uds., ellos/as	**ríen**	reían	**rieron**	reirán	reirían	**rían**	rieran o riesen	rían

Infinitivo / Gerundio Participio	Pronombres personales	INDICATIVO Presente	Pretérito imperfecto	Pretérito perfecto simple	Futuro simple	Condicional simple	SUBJUNTIVO Presente	Pretérito imperfecto	IMPERATIVO
59 reunir (3) (uːu) / reuniendo / reunido	yo	reúno	reunía	reuní	reuniré	reuniría	reúna	reuniera o reuniese	
	tú/vos	reúnes/reunís	reunías	reuniste	reunirás	reunirías	reúnas	reunieras o reunieses	reúne/reuní
	Ud., él, ella	reúne	reunía	reunió	reunirá	reuniría	reúna	reuniera o reuniese	reúna
	nosotros/as	reunimos	reuníamos	reunimos	reuniremos	reuniríamos	reunamos	reuniéramos o reuniésemos	reunamos
	vosotros/as	reunís	reuníais	reunisteis	reuniréis	reuniríais	reunáis	reunierais o reunieseis	reunid
	Uds., ellos/as	reúnen	reunían	reunieron	reunirán	reunirían	reúnan	reunieran o reuniesen	reúnan
60 roer (3, 4) (y) / royendo / roído	yo	roo o roigo o royo	roía	roí	roeré	roería	roa o roiga o roya	royera o royese	
	tú/vos	roes/roés	roías	roíste	roerás	roerías	roas o roigas o royas	royeras o royeses	roe/roé
	Ud., él, ella	roe	roía	royó	roerá	roería	roa o roiga o roya	royera o royese	roa o roiga o roya
	nosotros/as	roemos	roíamos	roímos	roeremos	roeríamos	roamos o roigamos o royamos	royéramos o royésemos	roamos o roigamos o royamos
	vosotros/as	roéis	roíais	roísteis	roeréis	roeríais	roáis o roigáis o royáis	royerais o royeseis	roed
	Uds., ellos/as	roen	roían	royeron	roerán	roerían	roan o roigan o royan	royeran o royesen	roan o roigan o royan
61 rogar (1, 2) (o:ue) (g:gu) / rogando / rogado	yo	ruego	rogaba	rogué	rogaré	rogaría	ruegue	rogara o rogase	
	tú/vos	ruegas/rogás	rogabas	rogaste	rogarás	rogarías	ruegues	rogaras o rogases	ruega/rogá
	Ud., él, ella	ruega	rogaba	rogó	rogará	rogaría	ruegue	rogara o rogase	ruegue
	nosotros/as	rogamos	rogábamos	rogamos	rogaremos	rogaríamos	roguemos	rogáramos o rogásemos	roguemos
	vosotros/as	rogáis	rogabais	rogasteis	rogaréis	rogaríais	roguéis	rogarais o rogaseis	rogad
	Uds., ellos/as	ruegan	rogaban	rogaron	rogarán	rogarían	rueguen	rogaran o rogasen	rueguen
62 saber (4) / sabiendo / sabido	yo	sé	sabía	supe	sabré	sabría	sepa	supiera o supiese	
	tú/vos	sabes/sabés	sabías	supiste	sabrás	sabrías	sepas	supieras o supieses	sabe/sabé
	Ud., él, ella	sabe	sabía	supo	sabrá	sabría	sepa	supiera o supiese	sepa
	nosotros/as	sabemos	sabíamos	supimos	sabremos	sabríamos	sepamos	supiéramos o supiésemos	sepamos
	vosotros/as	sabéis	sabíais	supisteis	sabréis	sabríais	sepáis	supierais o supieseis	sabed
	Uds., ellos/as	saben	sabían	supieron	sabrán	sabrían	sepan	supieran o supiesen	sepan
63 salir (4) / saliendo / salido	yo	salgo	salía	salí	saldré	saldría	salga	saliera o saliese	
	tú/vos	sales/salís	salías	saliste	saldrás	saldrías	salgas	salieras o salieses	sal/salí
	Ud., él, ella	sale	salía	salió	saldrá	saldría	salga	saliera o saliese	salga
	nosotros/as	salimos	salíamos	salimos	saldremos	saldríamos	salgamos	saliéramos o saliésemos	salgamos
	vosotros/as	salís	salíais	salisteis	saldréis	saldríais	salgáis	salierais o salieseis	salid
	Uds., ellos/as	salen	salían	salieron	saldrán	saldrían	salgan	salieran o saliesen	salgan

Infinitivo / Gerundio / Participio	Pronombres personales	INDICATIVO Presente	Pretérito imperfecto	Pretérito perfecto simple	Futuro simple	Condicional simple	SUBJUNTIVO Presente	Pretérito imperfecto	IMPERATIVO
64 seguir [(1,2)] (e:i) (gu:g) **siguiendo** seguido	yo	**sigo**	seguía	seguí	seguiré	seguiría	**siga**	**siguiera** o **siguiese**	
	tú/vos	**sigues**/seguís	seguías	seguiste	seguirás	seguirías	**sigas**	**siguieras** o **siguieses**	**sigue**/seguí
	Ud., él, ella	**sigue**	seguía	**siguió**	seguirá	seguiría	**siga**	**siguiera** o **siguiese**	**siga**
	nosotros/as	seguimos	seguíamos	seguimos	seguiremos	seguiríamos	**sigamos**	**siguiéramos** o **siguiésemos**	**sigamos**
	vosotros/as	seguís	seguíais	seguisteis	seguiréis	seguiríais	**sigáis**	**siguierais** o **siguieseis**	seguid
	Uds., ellos/as	**siguen**	seguían	**siguieron**	seguirán	seguirían	**sigan**	**siguieran** o **siguiesen**	**sigan**
65 sentir [(1,4)] (e:ie) **sintiendo** sentido	yo	**siento**	sentía	sentí	sentiré	sentiría	**sienta**	**sintiera** o **sintiese**	
	tú/vos	**sientes**/sentís	sentías	sentiste	sentirás	sentirías	**sientas**	**sintieras** o **sintieses**	**siente**/sentí
	Ud., él, ella	**siente**	sentía	**sintió**	sentirá	sentiría	**sienta**	**sintiera** o **sintiese**	**sienta**
	nosotros/as	sentimos	sentíamos	sentimos	sentiremos	sentiríamos	**sintamos**	**sintiéramos** o **sintiésemos**	**sintamos**
	vosotros/as	sentís	sentíais	sentisteis	sentiréis	sentiríais	**sintáis**	**sintierais** o **sintieseis**	sentid
	Uds., ellos/as	**sienten**	sentían	**sintieron**	sentirán	sentirían	**sientan**	**sintieran** o **sintiesen**	**sientan**
66 ser [(4)] siendo sido	yo	**soy**	**era**	**fui**	seré	sería	**sea**	**fuera** o **fuese**	
	tú/vos	**eres**/sos	**eras**	**fuiste**	serás	serías	**seas**	**fueras** o **fueses**	**sé**
	Ud., él, ella	**es**	**era**	**fue**	será	sería	**sea**	**fuera** o **fuese**	**sea**
	nosotros/as	**somos**	**éramos**	**fuimos**	seremos	seríamos	**seamos**	**fuéramos** o **fuésemos**	**seamos**
	vosotros/as	**sois**	**erais**	**fuisteis**	seréis	seríais	**seáis**	**fuerais** o **fueseis**	**sed**
	Uds., ellos/as	**son**	**eran**	**fueron**	serán	serían	**sean**	**fueran** o **fuesen**	**sean**
67 soler [(1)] (o:ue) soliendo solido	yo	**suelo**	solía				**suela**		
	tú/vos	**sueles**/solés	solías	*soler is a defective verb (it does not exist in certain tenses)			**suelas**		
	Ud., él, ella	**suele**	solía				**suela**		
	nosotros/as	solemos	solíamos				solamos		
	vosotros/as	soléis	solíais				soláis		
	Uds., ellos/as	**suelen**	solían				**suelan**		
68 tañer [(4)] **tañendo** tañido	yo	taño	tañía	tañí	tañeré	tañería	taña	**tañera** o **tañese**	
	tú/vos	tañes/tañés	tañías	tañiste	tañerás	tañerías	tañas	**tañeras** o **tañeses**	tañe/tañé
	Ud., él, ella	tañe	tañía	**tañó**	tañerá	tañería	taña	**tañera** o **tañese**	taña
	nosotros/as	tañemos	tañíamos	tañimos	tañeremos	tañeríamos	tañamos	**tañéramos** o **tañésemos**	tañamos
	vosotros/as	tañéis	tañíais	tañisteis	tañeréis	tañeríais	tañáis	**tañerais** o **tañeseis**	tañed
	Uds., ellos/as	tañen	tañían	**tañeron**	tañerán	tañerían	tañan	**tañeran** o **tañesen**	tañan
69 tener [(1,4)] (e:ie) teniendo tenido	yo	**tengo**	tenía	**tuve**	**tendré**	**tendría**	**tenga**	**tuviera** o **tuviese**	
	tú/vos	**tienes**/tenés	tenías	**tuviste**	**tendrás**	**tendrías**	**tengas**	**tuvieras** o **tuvieses**	**ten**/tené
	Ud., él, ella	**tiene**	tenía	**tuvo**	**tendrá**	**tendría**	**tenga**	**tuviera** o **tuviese**	**tenga**
	nosotros/as	tenemos	teníamos	**tuvimos**	**tendremos**	**tendríamos**	**tengamos**	**tuviéramos** o **tuviésemos**	**tengamos**
	vosotros/as	tenéis	teníais	**tuvisteis**	**tendréis**	**tendríais**	**tengáis**	**tuvierais** o **tuvieseis**	tened
	Uds., ellos/as	**tienen**	tenían	**tuvieron**	**tendrán**	**tendrían**	**tengan**	**tuvieran** o **tuviesen**	**tengan**

70 teñir (1) (e:i) — Gerundio: tiñendo · Participio: teñido

Pronombres personales	INDICATIVO Presente	Pretérito imperfecto	Pretérito perfecto simple	Futuro simple	Condicional simple	SUBJUNTIVO Presente	Pretérito imperfecto	IMPERATIVO
yo	tiño	teñía	teñí	teñiré	teñiría	tiña	tiñera o tiñese	
tú/vos	tiñes/teñís	teñías	teñiste	teñirás	teñirías	tiñas	tiñeras o tiñeses	tiñe/teñí
Ud., él, ella	tiñe	teñía	tiñó	teñirá	teñiría	tiña	tiñera o tiñese	tiña
nosotros/as	teñimos	teñíamos	teñimos	teñiremos	teñiríamos	tiñamos	tiñéramos o tiñésemos	tiñamos
vosotros/as	teñís	teñíais	teñisteis	teñiréis	teñiríais	tiñáis	tiñerais o tiñeseis	teñid
Uds., ellos/as	tiñen	teñían	tiñeron	teñirán	teñirían	tiñan	tiñeran o tiñesen	tiñan

71 tocar (2) (c:qu) — Gerundio: tocando · Participio: tocado

Pronombres personales	INDICATIVO Presente	Pretérito imperfecto	Pretérito perfecto simple	Futuro simple	Condicional simple	SUBJUNTIVO Presente	Pretérito imperfecto	IMPERATIVO
yo	toco	tocaba	toqué	tocaré	tocaría	toque	tocara o tocase	
tú/vos	tocas/tocás	tocabas	tocaste	tocarás	tocarías	toques	tocaras o tocases	toca/tocá
Ud., él, ella	toca	tocaba	tocó	tocará	tocaría	toque	tocara o tocase	toque
nosotros/as	tocamos	tocábamos	tocamos	tocaremos	tocaríamos	toquemos	tocáramos o tocásemos	toquemos
vosotros/as	tocáis	tocabais	tocasteis	tocaréis	tocaríais	toquéis	tocarais o tocaseis	tocad
Uds., ellos/as	tocan	tocaban	tocaron	tocarán	tocarían	toquen	tocaran o tocasen	toquen

72 torcer (1, 2) (o:ue) (c:z) — Gerundio: torciendo · Participio: torcido, tuerto

Pronombres personales	INDICATIVO Presente	Pretérito imperfecto	Pretérito perfecto simple	Futuro simple	Condicional simple	SUBJUNTIVO Presente	Pretérito imperfecto	IMPERATIVO
yo	tuerzo	torcía	torcí	torceré	torcería	tuerza	torciera o torciese	
tú/vos	tuerces/torcés	torcías	torciste	torcerás	torcerías	tuerzas	torcieras o torcieses	tuerce/torcé
Ud., él, ella	tuerce	torcía	torció	torcerá	torcería	tuerza	torciera o torciese	tuerza
nosotros/as	torcemos	torcíamos	torcimos	torceremos	torceríamos	torzamos	torciéramos o torciésemos	torzamos
vosotros/as	torcéis	torcíais	torcisteis	torceréis	torceríais	torzáis	torcierais o torcieseis	torced
Uds., ellos/as	tuercen	torcían	torcieron	torcerán	torcerían	tuerzan	torcieran o torciesen	tuerzan

73 traer (4) — Gerundio: trayendo · Participio: traído

Pronombres personales	INDICATIVO Presente	Pretérito imperfecto	Pretérito perfecto simple	Futuro simple	Condicional simple	SUBJUNTIVO Presente	Pretérito imperfecto	IMPERATIVO
yo	traigo	traía	traje	traeré	traería	traiga	trajera o trajese	
tú/vos	traes/traés	traías	trajiste	traerás	traerías	traigas	trajeras o trajeses	trae/traé
Ud., él, ella	trae	traía	trajo	traerá	traería	traiga	trajera o trajese	traiga
nosotros/as	traemos	traíamos	trajimos	traeremos	traeríamos	traigamos	trajéramos o trajésemos	traigamos
vosotros/as	traéis	traíais	trajisteis	traeréis	traeríais	traigáis	trajerais o trajeseis	traed
Uds., ellos/as	traen	traían	trajeron	traerán	traerían	traigan	trajeran o trajesen	traigan

74 valer (4) — Gerundio: valiendo · Participio: valido

Pronombres personales	INDICATIVO Presente	Pretérito imperfecto	Pretérito perfecto simple	Futuro simple	Condicional simple	SUBJUNTIVO Presente	Pretérito imperfecto	IMPERATIVO
yo	valgo	valía	valí	valdré	valdría	valga	valiera o valiese	
tú/vos	vales/valés	valías	valiste	valdrás	valdrías	valgas	valieras o valieses	vale/valé
Ud., él, ella	vale	valía	valió	valdrá	valdría	valga	valiera o valiese	valga
nosotros/as	valemos	valíamos	valimos	valdremos	valdríamos	valgamos	valiéramos o valiésemos	valgamos
vosotros/as	valéis	valíais	valisteis	valdréis	valdríais	valgáis	valierais o valieseis	valed
Uds., ellos/as	valen	valían	valieron	valdrán	valdrían	valgan	valieran o valiesen	valgan

75 vencer (2) (c:z) — Gerundio: venciendo · Participio: vencido

Pronombres personales	INDICATIVO Presente	Pretérito imperfecto	Pretérito perfecto simple	Futuro simple	Condicional simple	SUBJUNTIVO Presente	Pretérito imperfecto	IMPERATIVO
yo	venzo	vencía	vencí	venceré	vencería	venza	venciera o venciese	
tú/vos	vences/vencés	vencías	venciste	vencerás	vencerías	venzas	vencieras o vencieses	vence/vencé
Ud., él, ella	vence	vencía	venció	vencerá	vencería	venza	venciera o venciese	venza
nosotros/as	vencemos	vencíamos	vencimos	venceremos	venceríamos	venzamos	venciéramos o venciésemos	venzamos
vosotros/as	vencéis	vencíais	vencisteis	venceréis	venceríais	venzáis	vencierais o vencieseis	venced
Uds., ellos/as	vencen	vencían	vencieron	vencerán	vencerían	venzan	vencieran o venciesen	venzan

Infinitivo / Gerundio / Participio	Pronombres personales	INDICATIVO Presente	Pretérito imperfecto	Pretérito perfecto simple	Futuro simple	Condicional simple	SUBJUNTIVO Presente	Pretérito imperfecto	IMPERATIVO
76 venir [1,4] (e:ie) **viniendo** venido	yo	**vengo**	venía	**vine**	**vendré**	**vendría**	**venga**	**viniera** o **viniese**	
	tú/vos	**vienes**/venís	venías	viniste	**vendrás**	**vendrías**	**vengas**	**vinieras** o **vinieses**	**ven**/vení
	Ud., él, ella	**viene**	venía	**vino**	**vendrá**	**vendría**	**venga**	**viniera** o **viniese**	**venga**
	nosotros/as	venimos	veníamos	**vinimos**	**vendremos**	**vendríamos**	**vengamos**	**viniéramos** o **viniésemos**	**vengamos**
	vosotros/as	venís	veníais	**vinisteis**	**vendréis**	**vendríais**	**vengáis**	**vinierais** o **vinieseis**	venid
	Uds., ellos/as	**vienen**	venían	**vinieron**	**vendrán**	**vendrían**	**vengan**	**vinieran** o **viniesen**	**vengan**
77 ver [4] viendo **visto**	yo	**veo**	**veía**	**vi**	veré	vería	**vea**	viera o viese	
	tú/vos	ves	**veías**	viste	verás	verías	**veas**	vieras o vieses	ve
	Ud., él, ella	ve	**veía**	**vio**	verá	vería	**vea**	viera o viese	**vea**
	nosotros/as	vemos	**veíamos**	vimos	veremos	veíamos	**veamos**	viéramos o viésemos	**veamos**
	vosotros/as	**veis**	**veíais**	visteis	veréis	veríais	**veáis**	vierais o vieseis	ved
	Uds., ellos/as	ven	**veían**	vieron	verán	verían	**vean**	vieran o viesen	**vean**
78 volcar [1,2] (o:ue) (c:qu) volcando volcado	yo	**vuelco**	volcaba	**volqué**	volcaré	volcaría	**vuelque**	volcara o volcase	
	tú/vos	**vuelcas**/volcás	volcabas	volcaste	volcarás	volcarías	**vuelques**	volcaras o volcases	**vuelca**/volcá
	Ud., él, ella	**vuelca**	volcaba	volcó	volcará	volcaría	**vuelque**	volcara o volcase	**vuelque**
	nosotros/as	volcamos	volcábamos	volcamos	volcaremos	volcaríamos	**volquemos**	volcáramos o volcásemos	**volquemos**
	vosotros/as	volcáis	volcabais	volcasteis	volcaréis	volcaríais	**volquéis**	volcarais o volcaseis	volcad
	Uds., ellos/as	**vuelcan**	volcaban	volcaron	volcarán	volcarían	**vuelquen**	volcaran o volcasen	**vuelquen**
79 yacer [4] yaciendo yacido	yo	**yazco** o **yazgo** o **yago**	yacía	yací	yaceré	yacería	**yazca** o **yazga** o **yaga**	yaciera o yaciese	
	tú/vos	yaces/yacés	yacías	yaciste	yacerás	yacerías	**yazcas** o **yazgas** o **yagas**	yacieras o yacieses	**yace** o **yaz**/yacé
	Ud., él, ella	yace	yacía	yació	yacerá	yacería	**yazca** o **yazga** o **yaga**	yaciera o yaciese	**yazca** o **yazga** o **yaga**
	nosotros/as	yacemos	yacíamos	yacimos	yaceremos	yaceríamos	**yazcamos** o **yazgamos** o **yagamos**	yaciéramos o yaciésemos	**yazcamos** o **yazgamos** o **yagamos**
	vosotros/as	yacéis	yacíais	yacisteis	yaceréis	yaceríais	**yazcáis** o **yazgáis** o **yagáis**	yacierais o yacieseis	yaced
	Uds., ellos/as	yacen	yacían	yacieron	yacerán	yacerían	**yazcan** o **yazgan** o **yagan**	yacieran o yaciesen	**yazcan** o **yazgan** o **yagan**
80 zambullir [4] **zambullendo** zambullido	yo	zambullo	zambullía	zambullí	zambulliré	zambulliría	zambulla	**zambullera** o **zambullese**	
	tú/vos	zambulles/ zambullís	zambullías	zambulliste	zambullirás	zambullirías	zambullas	**zambulleras** o **zambulleses**	zambulle/ zambullí
	Ud., él, ella	zambulle	zambullía	**zambulló**	zambullirá	zambulliría	zambulla	**zambullera** o **zambullese**	zambulla
	nosotros/as	zambullimos	zambullíamos	zambullimos	zambulliremos	zambulliríamos	zambullamos	**zambulléramos** o **zambullésemos**	zambullamos
	vosotros/as	zambullís	zambullíais	zambullisteis	zambulliréis	zambulliríais	zambulláis	**zambullerais** o **zambulleseis**	zambullid
	Uds., ellos/as	zambullen	zambullían	**zambulleron**	zambullirán	zambullirían	zambullan	**zambulleran** o **zambullesen**	zambullan

El voseo en América Latina

Quesada Pacheco, Miguel Ángel (2002):
"El Español de América". San José, Costa Rica,
Editorial Tecnológica de Costa Rica, p.106.

Glosario combinatorio

In English, you can see somebody *in the flesh*, while in Spanish, you can see someone **en carne y hueso** (lit. *in flesh and bone*). In English, you are *fed up **with** something or someone* and in Spanish, you can be **harto de algo o alguien**. This glossary provides a sample of word combinations like these, which will help expand your vocabulary by giving a glimpse of the common, established word combinations that native speakers use. It will also help you with your grammar by showing that certain verbs take different prepositions from the ones used in English, or that no preposition is needed at all.

These types of word combinations are commonly called *collocations*. Not all word combinations are considered collocations. Many are free combinations with countless options. For example, the phrase **un hermano joven** is a free combination. The adjective, **joven**, can be used together with countless nouns (**un niño joven, una muchacha joven, un profesor joven, una estudiante joven,** etc.). **Un hermano gemelo**, on the other hand, is a collocation. The use of the adjective **gemelo** is restricted to a limited number of nouns.

Lexical collocations usually involve nouns, adjectives, adverbs, and verbs. *Grammatical* collocations usually involve a main word and a preposition or a dependent clause.

Compare these other examples. You can look up these collocations in the glossary!

Free combinations	Collocations
caer en un pozo, caerse en la calle	caer en la cuenta
surtir gasolina, surtir un medicamento	surtir efecto
va al cine, va a la escuela	va de veras

Compare these Spanish and English collocations:

Spanish collocations	English collocations
fuego lento	*low heat*
trabajar **en** algo	*to work **on** something*
hacer la vista gorda	*to turn a blind eye*

How to find collocations in this glossary

Follow these simple rules:

- If there is a noun, look under the noun.
- If there are two nouns, look under the first.
- If there is no noun, look under the adjective.
- If there is no adjective, look under the verb.

In addition, common expressions that are introduced by prepositions are also cross-listed under the preposition.

Abbreviations

adj.	adjective	*f.*	feminine noun	*p.p.*	past participle
adv.	adverb	*fam.*	familiar	*prep.*	preposition
algn	alguien	*form.*	formal	*pron.*	pronoun
Am. L.	Latin America	*m.*	masculine noun	sb	somebody
Arg.	Argentina	*Méx.*	Mexico	sth	something
Esp.	Spain	*pl.*	plural	*v.*	verb

a *prep.* to, at

a altas horas de la madrugada/noche in the wee/small hours of the morning/night

a base de with/of; on the basis of (Esto está hecho a base de verduras.)

a bordo de onboard

a caballo on horseback

a cada rato every so often/often

a cámara lenta in slow motion

a cambio de algo in return for sth

a cargo de, al cargo de in charge of

a causa de because of

a ciegas blindly

a ciencia cierta for sure

a como dé lugar, ~ como diera lugar however possible

a costa de at the expense of (No veo la gracia de reírse a costa de los demás.)

a cucharadas by the spoonful

a cuenta on account

a dieta on a diet

a escondidas secretly, behind sb's back

a eso de around

a este fin, ~ tal fin with this aim

a falta de lacking/for lack of (A falta de un problema, ¡tenemos diez!)

a fin de with the purpose of

a fin de cuentas, al final de cuentas, al fin y al cabo after all

a fondo in depth

a fuego lento on/at/over low heat

a fuerza de by virtue of/because of

a futuro in the future (Deberíamos evaluar los proyectos a futuro.)

a gusto at ease/at home/comfortable (No me siento a gusto aquí.)

a gusto del consumidor *fam.* however you like

a la carrera, ~ las carreras in a hurry

a la derecha (de) to/on the right (Gira a la derecha. Da un paso a la derecha, por favor.)

a la fuerza by force

a la hora de when it is time to (A la hora de escribir, prefiero hacerlo en un lugar tranquilo.)

a la izquierda (de) to/on the left (Si miran a la izquierda, verán uno de los mayores atractivos de la ciudad. María está a la izquierda de Juana.)

a la larga in the long run (Estoy segura de que Pedro, a la larga, comprenderá que es por su bien.)

a la manera de algn sb's way (Hagámoslo a mi manera.)

a la primera de cambio at the first opportunity

a la sombra de in the shadow of

a la vez at the same time

a la vista in sight, on view

a las mil maravillas wonderfully (¡Todo salió a las mil maravillas!)

a lo grande luxuriously, in style (Festejaremos tu cumpleaños a lo grande.)

a lo largo de throughout

a lo loco in a crazy way (Está gastando el dinero a lo loco.)

a lo mejor probably, likely

a los efectos de algo in order to do sth

a manera de algo by way of / as (Traje este dibujo a manera de ejemplo.)

a mano by hand

a (la) mano close at hand (¿Tienes tu planilla a (la) mano?)

a más tardar at the very latest

a mediados de in mid-/by mid- (Voy a retirar las cosas que faltan a mediados del mes que viene.)

a medias halfway/half

a medida que as/when/only (Resolveremos los problemas a medida que vayan surgiendo.)

a menos que unless

a menudo often

a modo de by way of, as (Usó su cuaderno a modo de pantalla.)

a no ser que if not

a nombre de algn addressed to sb

a oscuras in the dark

a partir de from, starting from

a pesar de in spite of

a pie on foot

a poco de algo shortly after sth

a por *Esp.* to go and get (Iré a por ti en dos horas.)

A

a primera hora, ~ última hora first thing/ at the last moment

a principios de at the beginning of (Supongo que nos mudaremos a principios de año.)

a propósito on purpose, by the way (¡Lo hiciste a propósito! Ayer me encontré con Mario; a propósito, me preguntó cuánto vale tu coche.)

a prueba de impervious to sth, resistant (¿Tu reloj es a prueba de agua?)

a raíz de as a result of

a rayas striped

a razón de at a rate of

a regañadientes reluctantly

a renglón seguido immediately afterwards (Las instrucciones se detallan a renglón seguido.)

a sabiendas knowingly

a salvo safe (Mi familia está a salvo, gracias a Dios.)

a simple vista to the naked eye

a solas alone (No me gusta quedarme a solas con ella.)

a su regreso on sb's return

a su vez in turn

a tiempo on time

a todo volumen very loud, at full volume

a tontas y a locas without thinking

a través de through

a trueque de in exchange for

a veces sometimes (A veces me olvido de hacer las compras.)

a ver all right, now, so; let's see (A ver, ¿qué está pasando acá? Llamémoslo a ver qué nos dice.)

a vista de pájaro bird's-eye view

al aire libre outdoors

al descubierto exposed

al día up-to-date

al día siguiente, al otro día on the next day

al efecto, a tal efecto, ~ este efecto for a particular purpose

al fin at last

al final at/in the end (Al final, ¿qué vas a hacer en las vacaciones?)

al igual que just as

al lado de beside, next to

al menos at least

al mismo tiempo que at the same time as

al pie de la letra literally, exactly (Siguieron nuestras instrucciones al pie de la letra.)

al pie de la montaña, ~ los pies de la montaña at the foot of the mountain

al principio at first

al (poco) rato shortly after

al través diagonally

abastecer *v.* to supply

abastecer a algn de algo, ~ a algn con algo to supply sb with sth

abogar *v.* to defend, to fight for

abogar por algn/algo, ~ en favor de algn/ algo to defend sb, to fight for sth (El defensor abogó a favor de los inmigrantes. Toda su vida abogó por los derechos de los trabajadores.)

abstenerse *v.* to abstain

abstenerse de algo to refrain/abstain from sth

abuelo/a *m./f.* grandfather/grandmother

abuelo/a materno/a, ~ paterno/a maternal/paternal grandfather/mother

abundar *v.* to abound

abundar de algo, ~ en algo to abound in

aburrirse *v.* to be bored

aburrirse con algo/algn, ~ de algo/algn, ~ por algo to be bored with sb/sth, to get tired of sb/sth

abusar *v.* **1** to impose, to take advantage, to abuse

abusar de algo to impose on sb (Silvia abusó de mi amabilidad.)

abusar de algn to abuse sb

2 to make excessive use

abusar de algo to make excessive use of sth (No debes abusar del alcohol.)

abuso *m.* abuse, breach

abuso de autoridad, ~ de confianza abuse of authority, breach of trust

acabar *v.* to finish, to end

acabar con algo, ~ de hacer algo to finish sth off, to have just done sth (Acaba con eso de una vez. Acabo de despertarme.)

acabar por algo to end up by doing sth (Este niño acabará por volverme loca.)

nunca acabar never-ending (Esto es un asunto de nunca acabar.)

acceder *v.* **1** to gain access, to access

acceder a algo to gain access to sth; to access sth (He podido acceder a los datos.)

2 to obtain

acceder a un cargo/trabajo to obtain/get a position/job

3 to agree

acceder a algo to agree to sth (Lucas accedió a los deseos de Sara.)

acción *f.* action

acción de armas, ~ de guerra military action

acción de gracias thanksgiving

buena/mala acción good/bad deed

novela/película de acción action novel/movie

pasar a la acción, entrar en ~ to go into action

poner algo en acción to put/turn sth into action

aceptar *v.* to accept

aceptar algo, ~ a algn (como algo) to accept sth/sb (Susana aceptó la oferta. ¿Acepta a Sandro como su legítimo esposo?)

acercarse *v.* to approach

acercarse a algo/algn to approach sth/sb

acercarse algo to come closer (Se acercan las fiestas.)

aconsejar *v.* to advise

aconsejar (algo) a algn to advise/give advice to sb

acordar *v.* **1** to agree

acordar algo con algn to agree to sth with sb

2 to award

acordar algo a algn *Am. L.* to award sth to sb (El premio le fue acordado por unanimidad.)

acordarse *v.* to remember

acordarse de algo/algn to remember sth/sb

acostumbrado/a *adj.* **1** used to

estar acostumbrado/a a algo to be used to sth

2 trained

estar bien/mal acostumbrado/a to be well/badly trained (Lo que pasa es que nos tienen mal acostumbrados.)

acostumbrar *v.* **1** to get used (to)

acostumbrar a algn a algo to get sb used to sth

2 to be accustomed

acostumbrar algo, ~ a algo to be accustomed to/in the habit of doing sth

acostumbrarse *v.* to get used (to)

acostumbrarse a algo/algn to get used to sth/sb

acudir *v.* **1** to attend

acudir a algo to attend sth (Debo acudir a la cita.)

2 to come

acudir en ayuda de algn to come to sb's aid/to help sb (Nadie acudió en su ayuda.)

3 to resort to

acudir a algo/algn to resort to sth/sb (No es necesario acudir a la violencia. Tuvo que acudir a su hermano mayor.)

acuerdo *m.* **1** agreement

estar de acuerdo con algo/algn to agree with sth/sb

estar de acuerdo en algo to agree on sth

hacer algo de común acuerdo to do sth by mutual agreement

llegar a un acuerdo, alcanzar un ~, ponerse de ~ to reach an agreement

2 accordance

de acuerdo con according to, complying with (Procederemos de acuerdo con lo hablado.)

acusar *v.* **1** to blame, to charge

acusar a algn de algo to blame/charge sb for sth

2 to show signs of (Su mirada acusaba cansancio.)

3 to acknowledge

acusar recibo de algo to acknowledge receipt of sth

acuse *m.* acknowledgement

acuse de recibo acknowledgement of receipt (¿Me traes el acuse de recibo firmado, por favor?)

adaptarse *v.* to adapt

adaptarse a algo to adapt to sth

adelantado/a *adj.* advanced
  por adelantado in advance
adelante *adv.* forward
  más adelante farther
además *adv.* besides
  además de apart from (Además de feo,
    es maleducado. Además de ser sabroso,
    es muy saludable.)
administración *f.* administration;
  management
  administración de negocios, ~ de
    empresas business administration
  administración pública civil/public service
admirar *v.* to admire
  admirar algo, ~ a algn to admire sth/sb
admirarse *v.* to be amazed
  admirarse de algo to be amazed at sth
adolecer *v.* to suffer from
  adolecer de algo to suffer from sth
advertir *v.* to warn
  advertir a algn de algo, ~ a algn que
    to warn sb of sth, to warn sb that
    (¿Has advertido a Juan de los riesgos?
    Te advierto que es muy peligroso.)
aficionado/a *m./f.* fan
  ser aficionado a algo to be a fan of sth
agarrarse *v.* **1** to hold on
  agarrarse a algo, ~ de algo to hold
    on to sth
  2 to have a fight
  agarrarse con algn to have a fight with sb
agencia *f.* agency
  agencia de colocaciones
    employment agency
  agencia de contactos dating agency
  agencia de prensa/noticias
    news/press agency
  agencia de publicidad advertising agency
  agencia de viajes travel agency
  agencia inmobiliaria real estate agency
agradar *v.* to appeal
  agradarle algo/algn a algn to be to sb's
    liking (Me agrada tu actitud. Me agrada
    la nueva maestra.)
agradecer *v.* to be grateful, to thank
  agradecerle algo a algn, agradecer a algn
    por algo to thank sb for sth (Te agradezco el
    regalo. Le agradezco por haberme ayudado.)

agua *f.* water
  agua bendita holy water
  agua corriente running water
  agua de lluvia rainwater
  agua de mar seawater
  agua dulce fresh water
  agua mineral (con/sin gas) sparkling/
    mineral water (with/without gas)
  agua oxigenada peroxide
  agua potable drinking water
  agua salada salt water
  aguas servidas/residuales sewage
  como agua para chocolate *Méx.* furious
  estar con el agua al cuello to be up to
    one's neck in problems
  estar más claro que el agua to be
    crystal clear
ahora *adv.* now
  por ahora for the time being
aire *m.* air
  aire acondicionado air conditioning
    (Las habitaciones del hotel tienen
    aire acondicionado.)
  al aire libre outdoors
  en el aire on air
  salir al aire to go out on the air (Nuestro
    programa sale al aire martes y jueves a las
    6 de la tarde.)
alcance *m.* range
  de corto/largo alcance short/long-range
alcanzar *v.* **1** to reach
  alcanzar algo, ~ a algn to reach sth, to
    catch up with sb
  2 to pass
  alcanzar algo a algn to pass sth to sb
  3 to manage to
  alcanzar a hacer algo to manage to do sth
    (No alcancé a terminar el trabajo.)
alegrar *v.* to bring happiness
  alegrar a algn to make sb happy
alegrarse *v.* to be glad, to be happy
  alegrarse de algo, ~ por algo/algn to be
    glad about sth, to be happy for sb
alejarse *v.* to move away
  alejarse de algo/algn to move away
    from sth/sb
alimentar *v.* to feed
  alimentar a algo/algn to feed sth/sb

alimentar algo to fuel sth (Sus comentarios alimentaron el clima de violencia.)

alimentarse *v.* to live, to run

  alimentarse con algo, ~ de algo to live/ run on sth

allí *adv.* there

  de allí en adelante from then on

alma *f.* soul

  alegrarse en el alma to be overjoyed

  alma de la fiesta life/soul of the party

  alma gemela soul mate

  como (un) alma en pena like a lost soul

  con toda el alma with all one's heart

  del alma darling/dearest/best (Es mi amigo del alma.)

  llegarle a algn al alma to be deeply touched by sth (Las palabras del sacerdote me llegaron al alma.)

  sentir algo en el alma to be terribly sorry about sth (Siento en el alma haber sacado ese tema.)

alrededor *adv.* around

  alrededor de around

altura *f.* height

  estar a la altura de las circunstancias to rise to the occasion

  quedar a la altura de algo/algn to be equal to sth/sb

amanecer *v.* to dawn; to wake up/begin at dawn/to start the day (¿A qué hora amanece? ¿Amaneciste bien? Hoy amaneció lloviendo.)

amanecer *m.* dawn, daybreak

amenazar *v.* to threaten

  amenazar (a algn) con algo to threaten (sb) with sth

amigo/a *m./f.* friend

  amigo/a íntimo/a intimate friend

  mejor amigo/a best friend

  (no) ser amigo/a de algo to (not) be fond of sth (No soy muy amigo de las fiestas.)

amo/a *m./f.* master/mistress

  ama de casa housewife

  ama de llaves housekeeper

animarse *v.* to feel like

  animarse a hacer algo to feel like doing sth, to dare (to) do sth

aniversario *m.* anniversary

  aniversario de boda, ~ de bodas wedding anniversary

ansioso/a *adj.* eager

  estar ansioso/a de algo, estar ~ por algo to be anxious/eager to do sth (Estoy ansioso de verlos. Está muy ansiosa por los exámenes.)

anteojos *m.* glasses

  anteojos bifocales bifocals

  anteojos de sol, ~ oscuros sunglasses

antes *adv.* before

  antes de before (Antes de ir a la escuela se detuvo en la plaza.)

  antes de Jesucristo, ~ de Cristo BC

  antes (de) que before (Llámalo antes de que sea tarde. Lo haré antes que me olvide.)

  antes que nada, ~ de nada first of all

antojarse *v.* to feel like

  antojársele algo a algn to feel like/crave sth

apartarse *v.* to separate

  apartarse de algo/algn to separate from sth/sb

apasionarse *v.* to have a passion for

  apasionarse con algo, ~ por algo/algn to have a passion for sth/sb (Mi hijo está apasionado con su nueva guitarra. Marcos está apasionado por esa mujer.)

apetecer *v.* to feel like

  apetecerle algo a algn *Esp.* to feel like (Me apetece un paseo.)

apiadarse *v.* to take pity

  apiadarse de algo/algn to take pity on sth/sb

apoderarse *v.* to seize

  apoderarse de algo/algn to seize sth/sb (El ejército se apoderó del edificio. El miedo se apoderó de todos nosotros.)

apoyar *v.* 1 to rest

  apoyar algo en un lugar to rest sth somewhere

  2 to support

  apoyar a algn (en algo) to support sb (in sth)

  apoyar algo to support sth (El presidente apoyó nuestra causa inmediatamente.)

apoyarse *v.* to lean, to base

  apoyarse en algo, ~ contra algo to lean on sth (Ellos se apoyan mucho en su familia. Se apoyó contra la pared porque estaba mareado.)

aprender *v.* to learn

  aprender a hacer algo to learn to do sth (Debes aprender a escuchar a los demás.)

apresurarse *v.* to hurry

  apresurarse a hacer algo to hurry to do sth (Se apresuraron a dejar todo como estaba.)

  apresurarse en algo to hurry to do sth (Me parece que se apresuró en su respuesta.)

apropiarse *v.* to appropriate

  apropiarse de algo to appropriate sth

aprovechar *v.* to make the best of

aprovecharse *v.* to take advantage

  aprovecharse de algo/algn to take advantage of sth/sb

apuro *m.* rush (¿Por qué tanto apuro para terminar el examen?)

  poner en un apuro to put in a predicament/tight spot (Su comentario me puso en un apuro.)

  tener apuro to be in a hurry; to be urgent (Tengo mucho apuro./El proyecto tiene apuro.)

aquí *adv.* here

  por aquí around here

arrepentirse *v.* to regret

  arrepentirse de algo to regret sth

arriba *adv.* up

  de arriba abajo up and down, from top to bottom

  para arriba y para abajo back and forth

arriesgarse *v.* to risk

  arriesgarse a algo to risk sth/to take a risk

ascender *v.* to rise

  ascender a algo/algn to promote, to be promoted (El grumete ascendió a timonel rápidamente. Parece que van a ascender a Pérez.)

  ascender a un lugar to rise to/reach a place or position

asegurarse *v.* to assure, secure

  asegurarse de algo to assure oneself of sth

asistir *v.* **1** to attend, to witness

  asistir a algo to attend sth, to witness sth (Asistió a la clase. Asistimos a la coronación del rey.)

  2 to assist

  asistir a algn to assist sb (Asistió al médico durante la operación.)

asombrarse *v.* to be amazed

  asombrarse ante algo, ~ con algo, ~ de algo, ~ por algo to be amazed at sth

aspirar *v.* to hope, to seek

  aspirar a algo to hope to become sth (Sandra aspira a convertirse en una cantante famosa.)

  aspirar a la mano de algn to seek sb's hand in marriage

asustado/a *adj.* afraid

  estar asustado/a de to be afraid of

asustar *v.* to frighten

  asustar a algn (con algo) to frighten sb (with sth)

asustarse *v.* to get frightened

  asustarse ante algo, ~ con algo, ~ de algo, ~ por algo to get frightened about sth

atención *f.* attention

  llamar la atención to attract/call attention to

  llamarle a algn la atención sobre algo to draw sb's attention to sth

  prestar atención a algo/algn to pay attention to sth/sb

atender *v.* to pay attention

  atender a algo/algn to pay attention to/ to attend to sth/sb (Debes atender a tus hijos. No atiende a sus deberes.)

atreverse *v.* to dare

  atreverse a algo, ~ con algo to dare to do sth

  atreverse con algn to dare or take on sb

auge *m.* peak

  en auge flourishing

aumento *m.* increase

  aumento de algo increase in sth (Estoy preocupada por su aumento de peso. La policía tomará medidas por el aumento de la violencia en los estadios de fútbol.)

  pedir un aumento, solicitar un ~ to ask for a pay raise

  sufrir un aumento, experimentar un ~ to experience an increase in sth (Los servicios de luz y de gas sufrirán fuertes aumentos. El precio del petróleo experimentó un aumento por tercera semana consecutiva.)

auxilio *m.* help; aid (in an emergency)

  acudir en auxilio de algn to go to sb's aid

  pedir auxilio to ask for help

prestar auxilio to help

primeros auxilios first aid

avance *m.* advance; news summary

avance científico, ~ de la ciencia scientific breakthrough

avance informativo news summary

ave *f.* bird

ave de mal agüero bird of ill omen

ave de paso bird of passage

ave de rapiña bird of prey

aventurarse *v.* to venture

aventurarse a algo, ~ en algo to venture to do sth

aventurarse por un lugar to venture somewhere

avergonzarse *v.* to be ashamed

avergonzarse de algo/algn, ~ por algo/ algn to be ashamed of sth/sb

avisar *v.* to inform

avisar a algn de algo to let sb know about sth

ayudar *v.* to help

ayudar (a algn) a algo, ~ con algo, ~ en algo to help (sb) with sth

B

bajar *v.* to go down

bajar a hacer algo to come down to do sth (¿Cuándo bajará a saludarnos?)

bajar algo de algo, ~ a algn de algo to get sb/sth down from sth (Baja la muñeca de la repisa, por favor. ¿Bajarías al niño del caballo?)

bajar de algo to get off sth (Los pasajeros ya están bajando del avión.)

banda *f.* strip

banda de sonido, ~ sonora soundtrack

banda magnética magnetic strip

basarse *v.* to base

basarse en algo to be based in/on sth

base *f.* base

a base de with/of; on the basis of (Esto está hecho a base de verduras.)

con base en based on

bastar *v.* to be enough

bastar algo (para), ~ con algo (para), ~ a algn algo to be enough (for) (Basta que yo diga algo para que mis hijos hagan

lo contrario. Basta con marcar 911 para obtener ayuda. A mí me basta con tu palabra.)

bastar y sobrar to be more than enough (Con eso basta y sobra.)

batalla *f.* battle

batalla campal pitched battle

dar batalla to cause a lot of problems/grief (Los problemas de salud le han dado mucha batalla.)

de batalla everyday (Son mis zapatos de batalla.)

beca *f.* grant, scholarship

beca de estudios study grant

beca de investigación research grant

boda *f.* wedding, a special anniversary

bodas de oro golden (wedding) anniversary; golden jubilee

bodas de plata silver (wedding) anniversary; silver jubilee

bolsa *f.* **1** bag

bolsa de agua caliente hot-water bottle

bolsa de (la) basura garbage bag

bolsa de compras, ~ de la compra shopping bag

bolsa de dormir sleeping bag

bolsa de hielo ice pack

2 stock market

bolsa de cereales grain exchange

bolsa de comercio commodities exchange

bolsa de valores stock exchange

bordo *m.* board

a bordo de onboard

bote *m.* boat

bote a remos, ~ de remos rowboat

bote inflable inflatable dinghy/raft

bote salvavidas lifeboat

brecha *f.* breach, opening

abrir brecha to break through

brecha generacional generation gap

estar en la brecha to be in the thick of things

seguir en la brecha to stand one's ground

brindar *v.* **1** to toast

brindar (con algo) por algo/algn, ~ a la salud de algn to toast sb/sth

2 to give, to provide

brindar algo a algn to provide sb with sth (Le brindaremos toda la información que necesite.)

broma *f.* joke

celebrar una broma to laugh at a joke

de broma, en ~ as a joke (No le creas, lo dijo en broma. ¿Te asustaste? ¡Era de broma!)

fuera de broma, fuera de bromas, bromas aparte all joking apart/aside

hacerle una broma a algn, gastarle una ~ a algn to play a joke on sb

ni en broma no way

no estar para bromas to not be in the mood for jokes

bromear *v.* to joke

bromear (con algn) sobre algo to joke about sth (with sb)

bueno/a *adj.* good

por las buenas o por las malas one way or the other

burlar *v.* to evade

burlar (a) algo/algn to evade, to get around, to slip past (El delincuente burló la vigilancia y huyó. Marcia burló a su jefe con engaños.)

burlarse *v.* to make fun of

burlarse de algo/algn to make fun of sth/sb

C

caballo *m.* horse

a caballo on horseback

caballo de carrera, ~ de carreras racehorse

caballo de fuerza horsepower

caber *v.* to fit

caber en algo, ~ por un lugar to fit somewhere, to fit through sth

no caber en uno/a mismo/a to be beside oneself

cabo *m.* end

atar los cabos sueltos to tie up the loose ends

dejar cabos sueltos to leave loose ends

llevar algo a cabo to carry sth out

caer *v.* **1** to fall

caer de bruces to fall on one's face

2 to stoop

caer bajo to stoop low

3 to show up

caer de improviso to show up without warning

4 caer bien/mal, ~ en gracia to be liked/disliked, to be fond of

cajero/a *m./f.* cashier

cajero automático, ~ permanente ATM

calidad *f.* quality

calidad de vida standard of living

cámara *f.* camera

cámara de cine film camera

cámara de video video camera

cámara digital digital camera

cámara fotográfica camera

en cámara lenta, a ~ lenta in slow motion

cambiar *v.* to change

cambiar algo a algo, ~ algo en algo to change sth into sth (Necesito cambiar estos dólares a pesos. ¿Me puede cambiar estos bolívares en pesos?)

cambiar algo por algo to change sth for sth

cambiar de algo to change sth (¡Cámbiate de ropa!)

cambiarle algo a algo to change sth in sth (El relojero le cambió la pila a mi reloj.)

cambiarle algo a algn to exchange sth with sb

cambio *m.* **1** change

a la primera de cambio at the first opportunity

cambio de aires, ~ de ambiente change of scenery

2 exchange

a cambio de algo in return for sth

en cambio on the other hand (El vestido azul es feo; el rojo, en cambio, es hermoso.)

en cambio de instead of

camino *m.* way; road

abrir el camino, allanar el ~, preparar el ~ to pave the way

camino vecinal minor/country road

estar camino a algo, estar ~ de algo, estar en el ~ a algo on the way to (Me crucé con él camino al dentista. La vi camino del club. Esa tienda queda en el camino a la escuela.)

estar en camino to be on sb's way (Ya deben estar en camino, no los llames por teléfono.)

por el camino on the way (Vamos, te lo diré por el camino.)

candelero *m.* candlestick

estar en el candelero to be in the limelight

cansado/a *adj.* tired

estar cansado/a de algo to be tired of sth

cansarse *v.* to get tired

cansarse con algo, ~ de algo/algn to get tired of sth (Mi madre se cansa con la rutina. ¿No te cansas de repetir siempre lo mismo?)

capaz *adj.* capable

ser capaz de algo to be capable of sth

cara *f.* face

cara a cara face to face

echar en cara algo a algn to reproach sth to sb (No me eches en cara lo que has hecho por mí.)

carecer *v.* to lack

carecer de algo to lack sth

cargar *v.* **1** to load

cargar a algn de algo to burden sb with sth

cargar algo con algo to load sth with sth

cargar algo en algo to load sth into/onto sth

2 to carry

cargar con algo to carry sth

3 to charge

cargar contra algn to charge against sb

cargo *m.* **1** charge

a cargo de, al ~ de in charge of

hacerse cargo de algo/algn to take charge of sth, to take care of sb

2 position, job

cargo público public office

desempeñar un cargo to hold a position

carne *f.* **1** flesh

carne de cañón cannon fodder

de carne y hueso quite human

en carne propia by personal experience

en carne y hueso in the flesh

2 meat

carne de res beef/red meat

echar toda la carne al asador, poner

toda la ~ al asador to put all one's eggs in one basket

carrera 1 race

a la carrera, a las carreras in a hurry

carrera armamentista, ~ armamentística, ~ de armamentos arms race

carrera contra reloj race against time

2 degree course

seguir una carrera, hacer una ~ to study for a degree

3 career

hacer carrera to carve out/make a career

casarse *v.* to marry; to get married

casarse con algn to marry sb

casarse en primeras/segundas nupcias to marry/remarry

casarse por poder to get married by proxy

caso *m.* **1** case

caso fortuito misadventure

en caso contrario otherwise

en caso de que in case of

en cualquier caso, en todo ~ in any case

no hay/hubo caso there is/was no way

no tiene caso to be pointless

ser un caso perdido to be a hopeless case

2 attention

hacer caso a algn to pay attention to sb

hacer caso de algo to take notice of sth

hacer caso omiso de algo to ignore (Hizo caso omiso de todas las advertencias de su familia.)

casualidad *f.* chance

de casualidad, por ~ by accident

causa *f.* cause

a causa de, por ~ de because of

causa perdida lost cause

ceder *v.* **1** to hand over

ceder algo a algn to hand sth over to sb

2 to give up

ceder en algo to give sth up

3 to give in

ceder a algo, ~ ante algo/algn to give in to sth/sb

celebrar *v.* to celebrate

celebrar algo, ~ por algo to celebrate sth

ceniza *f.* ash

reducir algo a cenizas to reduce sth to ashes

centro *m.* center

  centro comercial shopping mall

  centro de gravedad center of gravity

  centro de mesa centerpiece

  ser el centro de las miradas to have all
    eyes on sb

ceñirse *v.* to stick to

  ceñirse a algo to stick to sth (Deberías
    ceñirte al reglamento.)

cerca *adv.* close

  cerca de near, close to

cerciorarse *v.* to make certain

  cerciorarse de algo to make certain of sth

cerco *m.* siege

  cerco policial police cordon

  levantar el cerco, alzar el ~ to raise
    the siege

  poner cerco a algo to lay siege to sth

cesar *v.* to cease

  cesar de hacer algo to cease doing sth
    (No cesa de insultarnos.)

  sin cesar nonstop (Se trabajó sin cesar en el
    rescate de los mineros.)

charlar *v.* to chat

  **charlar (con algn) de algo, ~ (con algn)
    sobre algo** to chat about sth (with sb)

cheque *m.* check

  cheque de viaje, ~ de viajero
    traveler's check

  cheque en blanco blank check

  cheque sin fondos, ~ sobregirado
    overdrawn check

chocar(se) *v.* to collide

  **chocarse con algo/algn, ~ contra algo/
    algn** to collide/crash against sth/sb

ciencia *f.* science

  a ciencia cierta for sure

  ciencias ocultas occultism

  de ciencia ficción science fiction

  no tiene ninguna ciencia there is nothing
    difficult about it

cinturón *m.*

  cinturón de seguridad seat belt, safety belt

cita *f.* date, appointment

  cita a ciegas blind date

  concertar una cita to arrange an
    appointment

  darse cita to arrange to meet (Se dieron
    cita en la puerta de la iglesia.)

pedir cita to make an appointment

  tener una cita con algn to have an
    appointment/date with sb

citarse *v.* to make an appointment

  citarse con algn to make an appointment
    with sb

coincidir *v.* to agree

  coincidir con algn en algo to agree with
    sb on sth

comentar *v.* to discuss

  comentar algo con algn to discuss sth
    with sb

comenzar *v.* to begin

  comenzar a hacer algo to begin to do sth
    (¿Cuándo comenzarás a trabajar?)

  comenzar por algo to begin by sth
    (Puedes comenzar por pedirme disculpas.)

compadecerse *v.* to take pity on

  compadecerse con algn, ~ de algn to take
    pity on sb

comparar *v.* to compare

  **comparar algo con algo, ~ algo/algn
    a algo/algn, ~ a algn con algn** to
    compare sth/sb with sth/sb else (Estuve
    comparando tu camiseta con la mía y
    la tuya es más grande. Si comparas un
    triángulo a un cuadrado, te darás cuenta.
    ¡Deja de compararme con mi hermano!)

compararse *v.* to compare oneself

  compararse con algn to compare oneself
    to sb

compensar *v.* to compensate

  compensar (a algn) con algo to
    compensate (sb) by doing sth (¿Me
    compensarás con un rico pastel?)

  compensar (a algn) por algo to
    compensate (sb) for sth (Decidimos
    compensarlo por su buen desempeño
    en el trabajo.)

competir *v.* **1** to compete

  **competir con algn por algo, ~ contra algn
    por algo** to compete with/against sb for sth
  2 to rival

  competir en algo to compete in sth (Los dos
    artefactos compiten en calidad y precio.)

complacer *v.* to please

  **complacer a algn con algo, ~ a algn en
    algo** to please sb with sth

complacerse *v.* to take pleasure in

complacerse con algo, ~ de algo, ~ en algo to take pleasure in sth (Nos complace con su visita, Su Señoría. Mi hermana se complace en ayudar a los demás.)

completo/a *adj.* complete

por completo completely

componerse *v.* to be made up

componerse de algo to be made up of sth

comprar *v.* to buy

comprar algo a algn to buy sth from/to sb

comprometerse *v.* **1** to commit

comprometerse a algo, ~ en algo to commit to do sth

2 to get engaged

comprometerse con algn to get engaged with sb

comunicar *v.* **1** to inform, to communicate

comunicar algo a algn to communicate sth to sb

por escrito to be notified in writing

2 comunicar algo con algo to connect sth with sth (Este corredor comunica las habitaciones con la sala de estar.)

comunicarse *v.* to communicate

comunicarse (con algn) mediante algo, ~ (con algn) por algo to communicate (with sb) through sth (Ellos se comunican mediante gestos. Trataré de comunicarme por señas.)

con *prep.* with

con base en based on

con buen pie, ~ el pie derecho with a good start (Creo que no comenzaron con buen pie. Nuestra relación comenzó con el pie derecho.)

con dureza harshly

con el fin de with the purpose of

con erguida frente, ~ la frente bien alta, ~ la frente en alto, ~ la frente levantada with one's head held high

con este fin with this aim

con frecuencia frequently, often (¿Vienes a este bar con frecuencia?)

con la guardia baja with one's guard down

con las propias manos with one's own hands

con mal pie, ~ el pie izquierdo badly

con miras a with the purpose of

con motivo de due to, because of

con permiso with your permission/excuse me

con respecto a regarding

con tal (de) que provided that, as long as

con toda el alma with all one's heart

con toda seriedad seriously

con todas las de la ley rightly (No puedes quejarte, ella te ha ganado con todas las de la ley.)

concentrarse *v.* to concentrate

concentrarse en algo to concentrate on sth

condenar *v.* to condemn

condenar a algn a algo to condemn sb to sth (Su mal carácter lo condenó a la soledad.)

condenar a algn por algo to condemn sb for sth (Lo condenaron por robo.)

confiar *v.* **1** to entrust

confiar algo a algn to entrust sb with sth (Le confío la seguridad de mis hijos.)

2 to trust

confiar en algo/algn to trust sth/sb

3 to confide

confiar algo a algn to confide sth to sb (Me confió sus más oscuras intenciones.)

conflicto *m.* conflict

conflicto armado/bélico armed conflict

conflicto de ideas clash of ideas

conflicto de intereses conflict of interests

conflicto laboral labor dispute

conflicto limítrofe border dispute

conformarse *v.* to be happy

conformarse con poco to be happy with very little

confundir *v.* to mix up

confundir algo con algo, ~ a algn con algn to mix sth/sb up with sth/sb else

confundirse *v.* to mistake

confundirse con algo/algn to mistake sth/sb for sth/sb else

confundirse de algo to get sth wrong (Susana se confundió de coche.)

confundirse en algo to make a mistake in sth

conocer *v.* to know

conocer a algn to know sb

conocer de algo to know about sth

consentir *v.* to agree

consentir algo (a algn) to allow (sb) to do sth (Les consienten todo a sus nietos.)

consentir en algo to agree to sth (El ministro consintió en apoyar al candidato.)

consiguiente *adj.* consequent

por consiguiente therefore

consistir *v.* **1** consist

consistir en algo to consist of sth (La prueba consiste en una serie de actividades prácticas.)

2 to consist of/lie in

consistir en algo to consist of sth (¿En qué consiste la gracia?)

constar *v.* **1** to be stated (La edad no consta en el documento.)

constarle a algn algo to be sure that (Me consta que la carta fue enviada.)

hacer constar/que conste to state (Hagamos constar que pagamos la multa.)

que conste for the record, to set the record straight (Que conste que yo nunca le mentí./Jamás le mentí, que conste.)

2 to consist of

constar de algo to consist of sth (El libro consta de una serie de capítulos.)

consultar *v.* to consult

consultar algo a algn, ~ algo con algn, ~ a algn sobre algo to consult about sth with sb

contar 1 to tell

contar algo a algn to tell sth to sb

2 to count

contar con algo/algn to count on sth/sb

contentarse *v.* to be pleased

contentarse con poco to be pleased with very little

contento/a *adj.* happy

estar contento/a con algo, estar ~ de algo, estar ~ por algo to be happy with/about sth (Estamos contentos con los resultados. ¿Estás contenta de haber ido? Están contentos por la visita del gobernador.)

contestar *v.* to answer, to reply

contestar (a) algo, ~ algo a algn to answer sth to sb

contra *prep.* against

contra reembolso cash on delivery

contrario/a *adj.* opposite

de lo contrario if not/otherwise/on the contrary (Termina tu comida; de lo contrario, te quedarás sin postre.)

contribuir *v.* to contribute

contribuir a algo to contribute to sth (Yo contribuí al progreso de la empresa.)

contribuir con algo to contribute sth (Los vecinos contribuyeron con alimentos y ropa.)

control *m.* control

a control remoto, por ~ remoto by remote control (Funciona a control remoto. Eso se maneja por control remoto.)

control antidoping drug test

control de armas gun control

control de calidad quality control

convalecer *v.* to convalesce

convalecer de algo to convalesce from sth

convencer *v.* to persuade

convencer a algn de algo to persuade sb of sth

convencerse *v.* to believe, to accept

convencerse de algo to accept sth (Debes convencerte de que eso terminó.)

convenir *v.* **1** to agree on

a convenir negotiable (La remuneración es a convenir.)

convenir con algn en algo, ~ con algo to agree on sth with sb (Debo convenir con mi exmarido en los horarios de visita. Convenimos con el dictamen de la auditoría.)

2 to be advisable

convenir a uno algo to be good for sb (Me conviene esperar unos días.)

conversar *v.* to talk

conversar (con algn) de algo, ~ (con algn) sobre algo to talk about sth with sb

convertirse *v.* **1** to turn into

convertirse en algo/algn to turn into sth/sb (Se convirtió en una persona despreciable.)

2 to convert

convertirse a algo to convert to sth (Se convirtió al cristianismo.)

convocar v. **to call, to summon**
  convocar a algn a algo, ~ a algn para algo to summon sb to sth
coro m. chorus
  hacerle coro a algn to back sb up
corredor(a) m./f. **1** runner
  corredor(a) de coches/automóviles race car driver
  corredor(a) de fondo long-distance runner
  corredor(a) de vallas hurdler
  2 agent
  corredor(a) de bolsa stockbroker
  corredor(a) de seguros insurance broker
cosa f. thing
  cualquier cosa anything
  no ser cosa de broma, no ser ~ de risa to not be a joke
  no ser cosa fácil to not be easy (Convencerlo no va a ser cosa fácil.)
  poca cosa hardly anything
costa f. coast, coastline
  a costa de at the expense of (No veo la gracia de reírse a costa de los demás.)
  costas expenses (Después del juicio, tuvo que pagar las costas judiciales.)
costar v. to cost
  costarle a uno algo to lose/to cost one/sb sth (Una pequeña distracción le costó el empleo.)
coste m. cost *Esp.*
costo m. cost *Am. L.*
costumbre f. habit
  como de costumbre, para no perder la ~ as always/usual (Olvidaste tu tarea, para no perder la costumbre. Llegó tarde, como de costumbre.)
  de costumbre usual (Nos vemos en el lugar de costumbre.)
  tener la costumbre de algo, tener algo por ~ to be in the habit of sth
crédito m. credit; loan
  a crédito on credit
  dar crédito a algn/algo to believe (No les dio crédito a mis palabras.)
creer v. to believe
  creer en algn/algo to believe in sb/sth
creerse v. to trust
  creerse de algn *Méx.* to trust sb

crisis f. crisis
  crisis cardíaca heart failure, cardiac arrest
  crisis de identidad identity crisis
  crisis de los cuarenta midlife crisis
  crisis energética energy crisis
  crisis nerviosa nervous breakdown
cuando adv. when
  cada cuando, de ~ en ~ from time to time
  cuando más, ~ mucho at the most
  cuando menos at the least
  cuando quiera whenever (Cuando quiera que llegue el momento.)
cuanto adv. as much as
  cuanto antes as soon as possible
  cuanto más let alone (Es un momento difícil para todos, cuanto más para su esposa.)
  en cuanto as soon (as) (Iré en cuanto pueda.)
  en cuanto a regarding (En cuanto a la inflación, estamos tomando todas las medidas necesarias.)
  por cuanto insofar as
cubierto/a adj. covered
  estar cubierto/a de algo, estar ~ por algo to be covered with sth
cucharada f. spoonful
  a cucharadas by the spoonful
cuenta f. **1** calculation
  a fin de cuentas, al fin de ~ after all
  hacer cuentas, sacar ~ to do calculations
  2 count
  caer en la cuenta de algo, darse ~ de algo to realize sth
  llevar la cuenta to keep count
  más de la cuenta too much (He comido más de la cuenta.)
  3 account
  a cuenta on account
  abrir/cerrar una cuenta to open/close an account
  cuenta a plazo fijo time deposit/fixed-term account
  cuenta corriente (de cheques) checking account
  cuenta de ahorros savings account
  4 consideration
  darse cuenta de algo to realize sth

tener algo en cuenta, tomar algo en ~ to
take sth into account

cuidar *v.* to look after

cuidar algo, ~ a algn, ~ de algo/algn to
look after sth/sb

cuidarse *v.* **1** to take care

cuidarse de algo/algn to take care of sth/sb

2 to avoid

cuidarse de algo to avoid doing sth
(Cuídate de lo que dices por ahí.)

culpa *f.* fault

echarle la culpa de algo a algn to blame
sb for sth

tener la culpa de algo to be sb's fault

culpar *v.* to blame

**culpar a algn de algo, ~ a algn por
algo** to blame sb for sth

culto *m.* worship

rendir culto a algo/algn to worship sth/sb

cumplir *v.* to carry out, fulfill, keep

cumplir con algo/algn to keep
(Yo siempre cumplo con mi palabra.)

D

dar *v.* **1** to find

dar con algo/algn to find sth/sb
(No logro dar con él.)

2 to give

dar algo a algn to give sth to sb

dar de comer a algn to feed sb

3 to hit

dar algo contra algo to hit sth against sth

4 to face

dar a (algo) to face (sth) (Mi ventana
da al jardín.)

de *prep.* of, from

de a each (Nos tocan de a cinco galletas
cada una.)

de a ratos, ~ rato en rato from time to
time

de acuerdo con according to
(Procederemos de acuerdo con
lo hablado.)

de allí en adelante from then on

de broma as a joke (¿Te asustaste?
¡Era de broma!)

**de buen/mal modo, ~ buenos/malos
modos** in a good/bad way

de buena ley genuine (Es oro de buena ley.)

de buena/mala gana willingly/unwillingly

de buena/mala manera in a good/bad way

de carne y hueso quite human

de casualidad by accident

de ciencia ficción science fiction

de corto/largo alcance short-/long-range

de costumbre usual

**de cualquier forma, ~ una u otra forma,
~ todas formas, ~ cualquier manera,
~ todas maneras, ~ cualquier modo,
~ todos modos** anyway, in any case

de cuando en cuando from time to time

de derecha right-wing (Jamás votaré a un
partido de derecha.)

de enfrente across the street

de entre semana working day (No puedo
salir contigo de entre semana, tengo
mucho trabajo.)

de esa manera in that way

de frente face-to-face

de golpe, ~ golpe y porrazo suddenly

de gusto for the fun of it

de izquierda left-wing (Sectores de
izquierda se opusieron a la medida.)

de la derecha on the right (Me gusta
el coche de la derecha.)

de la izquierda on the left (Busca en
el cajón de la izquierda.)

de la mano hand in hand

de lo contrario if not/on the contrary/
otherwise (Termina tu comida; de lo
contrario, te quedarás sin postre.)

de lujo luxury (Iván y Paola se alojarán en
un hotel de lujo durante su luna de miel.)

de mala muerte lousy (No vayas a ese
restaurante, es de mala muerte.)

de manera que so (¿De manera que la
decisión ya está tomada?)

de modo que in such a way that

de nada you're welcome

de ningún modo no way

de ninguna manera certainly not

de nuevo again

de pie standing (Ponte de pie cuando
entre la maestra.)

de plano outright (Se negó de plano a
participar en el negocio.)

de primera mano first hand

de pronto suddenly

de propina tip (¿Cuánto has dejado de propina?)

de regreso a to be back at (¿Cuándo estarás de regreso a la oficina?)

de repente suddenly

de rodillas down on one's knees

de tal modo que, ~ modo que in such a way that (Estudió mucho, de tal modo que aprobó el examen. Ya es tarde, de modo que me voy a casa.)

de través *Méx.* diagonally

de un día para el otro overnight

de un golpe all at once

de una vez (por todas) once and for all

de veras really

de vez en cuando once in a while

de vista by sight (A su hermana la conocemos solo de vista.)

del alma darling/dearest/best (Es mi amigo del alma.)

del mismo modo, de igual modo in the same way

debajo *adv.* under

por debajo de under

debatir *v.* to discuss

debatir (con algn) sobre algo to discuss sth (with sb)

deber *v.* to owe

deber algo a algn to owe sth to sb

decidido/a *adj.* determined

estar decidido a algo to be determined to do sth

decidir *v.* to decide

decidir sobre algo to make a decision about sth

decidirse *v.* to decide, to dedicate

decidirse a hacer algo to decide to do sth

decidirse por algo to decide on sth

dedicar *v.* to devote, to dedicate

dedicar algo a algn to devote sth to sb (Debes dedicarle más tiempo a tu familia.)

dedicarse *v.* to devote

dedicarse a algo to devote oneself to sth

defender *v.* to defend

defender algo, ~ a algn to defend sth/sb

defenderse *v.* to defend oneself

defenderse de algo/algn to defend oneself against sth/sb

degenerar *v.* to degenerate

degenerar en algo to degenerate/lead into sth

dejar *v.* **1** to stop

dejar de hacer algo to stop doing sth

2 to leave

dejar a algn to leave sb

dejar algo mucho que desear to leave much to be desired

3 to let, to allow

dejar a algn hacer algo to let sb do sth

4 to fail

dejar de hacer algo to give up/stop doing sth/to fail to do sth (No dejes de llamarme cuando llegues.)

delante *adv.* ahead

por delante ahead (Aún nos queda mucho por delante.)

por delante de in front of, opposite (Ayer pasé por delante de tu casa.)

deliberar *v.* to deliberate

deliberar sobre algo to deliberate on sth

delito *m.* crime

cometer un delito, incurrir en un ~ to commit a crime

demandar *v.* **1** to require (Esta tarea demanda mucha concentración.)

2 to sue

demandar por daños y perjuicios to sue for damages

demás *pron.* the rest

estar por demás hacer algo there is no point in doing sth

lo demás, los/las ~ the rest

por demás extremely (Te comportas de una manera por demás grosera.)

por lo demás apart from that

y demás and the like (Se aceptan perros, gatos y demás.)

demora *f.* delay

sin demora without delay

dentro *adv.* inside

por dentro de in, inside of

depender *v.* **1** to depend

depender de algo/algn to depend on sth/sb

2 to report

depender de algn to report to sb

derecha *f.* right

a la derecha (de) to/on the right (of) (Gira a la derecha. Da un paso a la derecha, por favor.)

de derecha right-wing (Jamás votaré a un partido de derecha.)

de la derecha on the right (Me gusta el coche de la derecha.)

descansar *v.* **1** to take a break

descansar de algo/algn to take a break from sth/sb (Necesitaba descansar de los niños por un día.)

2 to rest upon

descansar en algo, ~ sobre algo to rest upon sth (Su pierna descansaba sobre unas almohadas.)

desconfiar *v.* to mistrust

desconfiar de algo/algn to mistrust sth/sb

descubierto/a *adj.* exposed

al descubierto exposed (Sus numerosas estafas quedaron al descubierto.)

desde *prep.* since

desde el principio, ~ un principio from the beginning

desear *v.* to wish

desear algo (a algn) to wish sb sth

desembocar *v.* to culminate

desembocar en algo to culminate in sth

deseoso/a *adj.* anxious/eager

estar deseoso/a de to be anxious/eager about

desgracia *f.* misfortune

por desgracia unfortunately

deshacerse *v.* to get rid

deshacerse de algo/algn to get rid of sth/sb

desistir *v.* to give up

desistir de algo, ~ en algo to give up sth (Desistió de vender su casa. Nunca desistió en su empeño por ser el mejor de la clase.)

despedir *v.* **1** to see off

despedir a algn to see sb off

2 to fire

despedir a algn to fire sb

despedirse *v.* to say goodbye

despedirse de algo/algn to say goodbye to sth/sb

desposeer *v.* to strip

desposeer a algn de algo to strip sb of sth

desprenderse 1 to let go

desprenderse de algo/algn to let go of sth/sb (Deberías desprenderte de los objetos que ya no usas.)

2 to emerge

desprenderse de algo to emerge from sth (Los datos se desprenden de una serie de encuestas.)

después *adv.* later

después de Jesucristo, ~ de Cristo AD

después de todo after all

después (de) que after, as soon as (Después de que hablé contigo, encendí el televisor.)

destinar *v.* to allocate

destinar algo a algo, ~ algo para algo to set sth aside for sth

detalle *m.* **1** detail

al detalle retail (Esa tienda vende al detalle.)

con todo detalle in great detail

dar detalles to go into details

entrar en detalles to go into details

2 little gift; nice gesture (Estuvo en París y me trajo un detallecito.)

¡Qué detalle! How thoughtful!

tener un detalle con algn to do sth nice for sb (¿Puedes creer que después de que lo ayudé tanto no tuvo ningún detalle conmigo?)

detenerse *v.* **1** to stop

detenerse a hacer algo to stop to do sth

2 to dwell

detenerse en algo to dwell on sth (Concéntrate en lo importante, no te detengas en detalles.)

detrás *adv.* behind

(por) detrás de behind, in the back of

devolver *v.* to return

devolver algo a algn to return sth to sb

día *m.* day

al día up-to-date

al día siguiente, al otro ~ on the next day

de un día para otro overnight

día de por medio *Am. L.* every other day

día festivo public holiday

día hábil, ~ laborable working day

día tras día day after day

hoy en día nowadays

diente *m.* tooth

armado hasta los dientes armed to the teeth

diente de ajo garlic clove

diente de leche baby tooth

salirle los dientes a algn to be teething (¡Ya le está saliendo el primer dientito!)

dieta *f.* diet

dieta habitual staple diet

estar/ponerse a dieta to be/go on a diet

diferir *v.* **1** to differ

diferir de algo to differ from sth (Su nuevo trabajo difiere de los anteriores.)

2 to disagree

diferir de algn, ~ entre sí to disagree with sb

difícil *adj.* difficult

ser algn difícil to be difficult (Es una persona muy difícil.)

ser difícil de hacer to be difficult to do (Es una asignatura muy difícil de estudiar.)

Dios *m.* God

Dios mediante God willing

Dios mío/santo for Heaven's sake

por Dios for Heaven's sake

si Dios quiere God willing

dirigir *v.* to address

dirigir algo a algn to address sth to sb

dirigirse *v.* **1** to head for

dirigirse a un lugar to head for a place

2 to address

dirigirse a algn to address sb

discrepar *v.* to disagree

discrepar (con algn) en algo, ~ (con algn) sobre algo to disagree (with sb) on sth

disculparse *v.* to apologize

disculparse (ante/con algn) de algo, ~ (ante/con algn) por algo to apologize (to sb) for sth

discutir *v.* to argue

discutir con algn por algo, ~ con algn sobre algo to argue with sb about sth

discutirle algo a algn to argue sth with sb

disfrutar *v.* to enjoy

disfrutar de algo to enjoy sth

disgustado/a *adj.* annoyed

estar disgustado/a con algn, estar ~ por algo to be annoyed with sb/sth

disgustar *v.* to dislike

disgustarle algo/algn (a algn) to dislike sth/sb

disgustarse *v.* to get upset

disgustarse con algo, ~ por algo to get upset because of sth

disponer *v.* to possess

disponer de algo/algn to have sth/sb at one's disposal

disponerse *v.* to prepare

disponerse a hacer algo, ~ para hacer algo to prepare to do sth

dispuesto/a *adj.* willing

estar dispuesto/a a to be willing to

distanciarse *v.* to distance

distanciarse de algo/algn to distance oneself from sth/sb

distinguir *v.* **1** to differentiate

distinguir algo de algo to tell sth from sth else

2 to honor

distinguir a algn con algo to honor sb with sth

distinguirse *v.* to stand out

distinguirse en algo to stand out in sth

distinguirse por algo to stand out for sth

disuadir *v.* to dissuade

disuadir a algn con algo to dissuade sb with sth

disuadir a algn de algo to dissuade sb from sth

divorciarse *v.* to get divorced

divorciarse de algn to get divorced from sb

doler *v.* to hurt

dolerle a uno/a algo to have a pain somewhere (Me duele la cabeza.)

dominio *f.* **1** mastery

ser de dominio público to be public knowledge

tener dominio de uno/a mismo/a to have self-control

tener el dominio de algo to have command of sth

2 field

entrar en el dominio de algo to be in the field of sth (Eso entra en el dominio de la Economía.)

duda *f.* doubt

  sin duda without (a) doubt

dudar *v.* **1** to doubt

  dudar de algo/algn to doubt sth/sb

  2 to hesitate

  dudar en hacer algo to hesitate in doing sth (No dudes en llamarme si necesitas algo.)

dureza *f.* harshness

  con dureza harshly

E

echar *v.* **1** to dismiss/fire

  echar a algn to dismiss/fire sb

  2 to start

  echar a andar algo to start sth

  3 to miss

  echar de menos algo, ~ de menos a algn to miss sth/sb

echarse *v.* to start

  echarse a hacer algo to start to do sth (Los niños se echaron a llorar.)

edad *f.* age

  desde temprana edad from an early age

  edad adulta, mayoría de ~ adulthood

  edad escolar school age

  sacarse la edad, quitarse la ~ to make out that sb is younger

  ser de edad to be elderly

  ser de edad madura, ser de mediana ~ to be middle-aged

efectivo *m.* cash

  en efectivo (in) cash

efecto *m.* **1** effect

  efecto invernadero greenhouse effect

  efecto retroactivo backdated

  efecto secundario side effect

  efectos especiales/sonoros special/sound effects

  en efecto in fact

  estar bajo los efectos de algo to be under the influence of sth

  hacer efecto, tener ~ to take effect (Esos medicamentos ya no me hacen efecto. La nueva ley tendrá efecto a partir del año próximo.)

surtir efecto to have an effect

  2 purpose

  a los efectos de algo in order to do sth

  al efecto, a tal ~, a este ~ for a particular purpose

ejemplo *m.* example

  por ejemplo for example

embargo *m.* seizure/embargo

  sin embargo however

empeñarse *v.* to strive, to insist

  empeñarse en hacer algo to strive to do sth, to insist on doing sth (Debes empeñarte en lograr tus objetivos. Mi padre se empeñó en que fuera a visitarlo.)

empezar *v.* to begin

  empezar a to begin to

  empezar por, ~ con to begin with

en *prep.* in, inside, on

  en algún momento at some point, sometime

  en alguna parte somewhere

  en auge flourishing

  en broma as a joke (No le creas, lo dijo en broma.)

  en buenas manos in good hands (Me marcho, pero los dejo en buenas manos.)

  en cámara lenta in slow motion

  en cambio however

  en carne propia by personal experience

  en carne y hueso in the flesh

  en caso contrario otherwise

  en caso de que in case of

  en cierto modo in a way

  en contra (de) against (No tengo nada en contra de tus compañeros de trabajo. Te recomiendo no ponerte en su contra.)

  en cualquier caso, ~ todo caso in any case

  en cuanto as soon (as)

  en cuanto a regarding

  en cuanto a algo/algn as regards sth/sb (En cuanto a la inflación, estamos tomando todas las medidas necesarias.)

  en efectivo (in) cash

  en el aire on air

  en el futuro, ~ lo futuro in the future (En el futuro, envía los trabajos por correo electrónico. En lo futuro, sé más organizado con los archivos.)

en especie, ~ especies in kind

en fin finally, well then (En fin, creo que eso es todo.)

en frente de in front of

en la margen derecha/izquierda on the right/left bank (En la margen izquierda del río hay más árboles que en la margen derecha.)

en lontananza *form.* in the distance

en (propia) mano hand delivery

en nombre de algo/algn in the name of sth/sb

en pie to be up (awake), to be on one's feet, to be valid (Estuve en pie todo el día. Lo único que quedó en pie fue la antigua capilla. ¿Sabes si la oferta sigue en pie?)

en pie de guerra ready for war

en (un) principio in the beginning

en pro o en contra (de), ~ pro y ~ contra for or against (Hay muchas opiniones en pro y en contra de nuestra propuesta.)

en punto o'clock/on the dot

en razón de because of (No debes discriminar en razón de la edad o la raza de las personas.)

en resumen all in all/in summary

en seguida right away

en suma in short

en torno a about (El argumento de la película gira en torno a las relaciones amorosas.)

en vez de, ~ lugar de, ~ cambio de instead of

en virtud de in virtue of

en vista de que in view of the fact that

enamorado/a *adj.* in love

estar enamorado/a de algn to be in love with sb

enamorarse *v.* to fall in love

enamorarse de algo/algn to fall in love with sth/sb

encantado/a *adj.* glad/enchanted

estar encantado de to be glad about/ pleased with

encantar *v.* to love, to really like; to enchant/put a spell on

encantarle a algn algo to love sth (Me encantan tus zapatos.)

encargar *v.* to ask

encargar algo a algn to ask sb to do sth (Me encargó una botella de vino. Le encargamos a José que cuidara de nuestras plantas.)

encargarse *v.* to take care

encargarse de algo to take care of sth

encariñarse *v.* to get attached

encariñarse con algo/algn to get attached to sth/sb

encima *adv.* on top

encima de on top of, on

por encima de over

encomendar *v.* to entrust

encomendar algo a algn to entrust sth to sb (Le encomendaron el sector administrativo.)

encontrar *v.* to find

encontrar algo, ~ a algn to find sth/sb

encontrarse *v.* to meet

encontrarse con algn to find sb

enemigo/a *adj.* enemy

ser enemigo/a de algo to be against sth (Soy enemigo de la violencia.)

enemistado/a *adj.* estranged

estar enemistado/a con algn to be estranged from sb

energía *f.* energy, power

energía atómica atomic power

energía eólica wind energy

energía hidráulica water power

energía nuclear nuclear energy

energía renovable renewable energy

energía solar solar energy

enfadarse *v.* to get angry

enfadarse con algn por algo to get angry at sb for sth

enfermar *v.* **1** to get ill

enfermar de algo *Esp.* to get ill

2 to drive mad *Am. L.* (¡Me enferma esa actitud!)

enfermarse *v.* to get ill

enfermarse de algo *Am. L.* to get ill

enfrentar *v.* to confront

enfrentar a algn con algn to bring sb face-to-face with sb

enfrentar algo, ~ a algn to face sth/sb

enfrentarse *v.* to confront

enfrentarse a algo to face sth

enfrentarse a algn, ~ con algn to confront sb

enfrente *adv.* **1** opposite

de enfrente across the street

enfrente de in front of, opposite

2 in front

enfrente de algo in front of sth

enojar *v.* to anger

enojar a algn algo to make sb angry

enojarse *v.* to get angry

enojarse con algn por algo to get angry at sb for sth

enorgullecerse *v.* to be proud

enorgullecerse de algo/algn, ~ por algo to be proud of sth/sb

enseguida *adv.* immediately (Te llamaré enseguida.)

enseñar *v.* **1** to teach

enseñar algo a algn to teach sth to sb

2 to show

enseñar algo a algn to show sth to sb

entender *v.* to understand

entender algo, ~ a algn to understand sth/sb

entender de algo to know all about sth

entenderle algo a algn to understand sth sb does (Discúlpame, pero no te entiendo la letra.)

entenderse *v.* **1** to communicate

entenderse con algn to communicate with sb (Se entiende con su primo por señas.)

2 to get along

entenderse con algn to get along with sb (¡Qué suerte que los chicos se entienden!)

3 to deal

entenderse con algn to deal with sb (Es mejor entenderse con el encargado.)

enterarse *v.* to hear, to find out

enterarse de algo to find out about sth

entero/a *adj.* whole

por entero completely

entrar *v.* **1** to go into

entrar a algo *Am. L.* to go into a place (Nunca he entrado a ese cine.)

entrar en algo to go into sth (Entremos en ese banco. No quiere entrar en razón.)

2 to enter

entrar en algo to enter sth (Entramos en una nueva etapa.)

3 to start

entrar a hacer algo to start to do sth (¿A qué hora entras a trabajar?)

entrar como algo to start as sth (Quieren que entre a la editorial como traductora.)

entre *prep.* between

entre horas between meals (No comas golosinas entre horas.)

entregarse *v.* **1** to devote

entregarse a algo/algn to devote oneself to sth/sb

2 to give

entregarse a algo/algn to give oneself over to sth/sb

entristecerse *v.* to grow sad

entristecerse por algo, ~ con algo, ~ a causa de algo to grow sad because of sth

entrometerse *v.* to meddle

entrometerse en algo to meddle in sth

entusiasmarse *v.* to get excited

entusiasmarse por algo, ~ con algo/ algn to get excited about sth/sb

enviar *v.* to send

enviar a algn por algo/algn to send sb out for sth/sb

enviar algo a algn to send sth to sb

envidiar *v.* to envy

envidiar algo a algn to envy sb because of sth

equivocarse *v.* to be wrong, to make a mistake

equivocarse en algo, ~ con algo/algn to be wrong/to make a mistake about sth/sb

escalera *f.* ladder, staircase

escalera caracol, ~ de caracol, ~ espiral spiral staircase

escalera de emergencia fire escape

escalera de mano ladder

escalera mecánica escalator

escandalizarse *v.* to be shocked

escandalizarse por algo to be shocked about sth

esconderse *v.* to hide

esconderse de algo/algn to hide from sth/sb

escondido/a *adj.* hidden

a escondidas secretly, behind sb's back

escribir *v.* to write

escribir a máquina to type

escribir algo a algn to write sth to sb

escribir sobre algo to write about sth

escribirse *v.* to write

escribirse con algn to write to each other

escuchar *v.* to hear

escuchar algo de algn, ~ algo sobre algn to hear sth about sb

esforzarse *v.* to strive

esforzarse en algo, ~ por algo to strive to do sth

eso *pron.* that

a eso de around (Llegué a eso de las ocho.)

por eso that's why

especializarse *v.* to major, to specialize

especializarse en algo to major/specialize in sth

especie *f.* 1 kind

en especie, en especies in kind

ser una especie de algo to be a sort of

2 species

especie en peligro (de extinción) endangered species

especie humana human race

especie protegida protected species

especular *v.* to speculate

especular sobre algo to speculate about sth

esperar *v.* 1 to wait

esperar algo, ~ a algn to wait for sth/sb

2 to hope (Espero que no llueva.)

estación *f.* station

estación de autobuses, ~ de ómnibus bus station

estación de bomberos fire station

estación de policía police station

estación de tren, ~ de trenes train station

estación del metro, ~ del subterráneo subway station

estafar *v.* to defraud/con/rip off

estafar (algo) a algn to defraud sb (out of sth)

estrella *f.* star

estrella de cine movie star

estrella de mar starfish

estrella en ascenso rising star

estrella fugaz shooting star

tener buena/mala estrella to be (born) lucky/unlucky

ver (las) estrellas to see stars

estudiar *v.* to study

estudiar algo to study sth

estudiar para algo to study for sth

evitar *v.* to avoid

evitar algo, ~ a algn to avoid sth/sb

exaltarse *v.* to get worked up

exaltarse por algo to get worked up about sth

exhortar *v.* to urge

exhortar a algn a hacer algo to urge sb to do sth (Los exhortó a continuar con su tarea.)

exigir *v.* to demand

exigir algo a algn to demand sth from sb

exponer *v.* 1 to expose

exponer algo a algo, ~ a algn a algo to expose sth/sb to sth (Es una tela muy delicada, no debes exponerla al sol.)

2 to explain, to describe

exponer algo a algn to explain sth to sb (Marcelo le expuso el problema claramente.)

exponerse *v.* to expose oneself

exponerse a algo to expose oneself to sth (No sé por qué te expones a esos peligros.)

extrañar *v.* to miss

extrañar algo, ~ a algn to miss sth/sb

extrañarse *v.* to be surprised

extrañarse de algo to be surprised at sth

F

fácil *adj.* easy

ser fácil de hacer to be easy to do (Es muy fácil de convencer.)

falta *f.* 1 lack

a falta de lacking/for lack of (A falta de un problema, ¡tenemos diez!)

echar algo en falta to be lacking (Aquí lo que se echa en falta es interés por el trabajo.)

falta de algo lack of sth

falta de educación bad manners

falta de pago nonpayment

2 fail

sin falta without fail

3 mistake

falta de ortografía spelling mistake

faltar *v.* to be missing

  faltarle algo a algn, ~ algn a algn to be in want of sth/sb (*A ese muchacho le falta un objetivo en la vida. Le falta un amigo que lo aconseje.*)

familia *f.* family

  de buena familia from a good family

  familia de acogida foster family

  familia numerosa large family

  familia política in-laws

  sentirse como en familia to feel at home

  tener familia to have children (*Mi prima tuvo familia la semana pasada.*)

  venirle/ser de familia to run in the family

familiarizarse *v.* to become familiar

  familiarizarse con algo to become familiar with sth

fascinar *v.* to fascinate

  fascinar a algn to fascinate sb (*Me fascinan los cuentos de terror.*)

felicitar *v.* to congratulate

  felicitar a algn por algo to congratulate sb on sth

fiarse *v.* to trust

  fiarse de algo/algn to trust sth/sb

fijarse *v.* to notice

  fijarse en algo/algn to notice sth/sb

fin *m.* **1** end

  al fin, por ~ at last

  al fin y al cabo after all

  el fin del mundo the end of the world

  en fin finally, well then

  fin de semana weekend

  poner fin a algo to put an end to sth

  por fin finally

  2 purpose

  a este fin, a tal ~, con este ~ with this aim

  con el fin de, a ~ de with the purpose of

  el fin de algo the purpose of sth

  sin fines de lucro, sin fines lucrativos not-for-profit

  un fin en sí mismo an end in itself

final *m.* end

  al final at/in the end

fondo *m.* depth

  a fondo in depth

forma *f.* **1** shape

  en plena forma in top form

  estar en forma, mantenerse en ~ to be/keep fit

  tomar forma to take shape

  2 way

  de cualquier forma, de una ~ o de otra, de todas formas anyway, in any case

  forma de pago method of payment

  forma de ser the way sb is

fortuna *f.* fortune

  amasar una fortuna, hacer una ~ to make a fortune

  por fortuna fortunately

  probar fortuna to try one's luck

frecuencia *f.* frequency

  con frecuencia frequently, often (*¿Vienes a este bar con frecuencia?*)

frente *f.* **1** forehead

  con erguida frente, con la ~ bien alta, con la ~ en alto, con la ~ levantada with one's head held high

  de frente, frente a ~ face-to-face

  2 front

  el frente de algo the front of sth

  estar al frente de algo to be in charge of sth

  hacer frente a algo/algn to face up to sth/sb

  hacer un frente común to form a united front

  3 *adv.* opposite

  frente a in front of, opposite

fuego *m.* fire

  a fuego lento on/at/over low heat

  abrir fuego contra algo/algn, abrir ~ sobre algo/algn open fire on sth/sb

  estar entre dos fuegos to be between a rock and a hard place

  fuego a discreción fire at will

  fuegos artificiales, ~ de artificio fireworks

  jugar con fuego to play with fire

  prender fuego a algo, pegar ~ a algo to set sth on fire

  sofocar el fuego to put out the fire

fuera *adv.* outside

  fuera de out/outside of

  por fuera de out/outside of

fuerza *f.* strength, force
a fuerza de by (dint of)
a la fuerza by force
fuerza bruta brute force
fuerza de gravedad force of gravity
fuerza de trabajo workforce
fuerza de voluntad willpower
fuerza pública, fuerzas del orden, fuerzas de orden público police
por fuerza necessarily
por fuerza mayor, por causas de ~ mayor force majeure
fundarse *v.* to base
fundarse en algo to be based on sth (¿En qué se fundan tus sospechas?)
futuro *m.* future
con/sin futuro sth/sb with good/no prospects (Es una profesión sin futuro. Ese es un muchacho con futuro.)
en el futuro, en lo ~, a ~ in the future (En el futuro, envía los trabajos por correo electrónico. En lo futuro, sé más organizado con los archivos. Deberíamos evaluar los proyectos a futuro.)
futuro cercano, ~ próximo near future
no tener ningún futuro to have no future (Con esta crisis, nuestra empresa no tiene ningún futuro.)

G

gana *f.* desire
de buena/mala gana willingly/unwillingly
tener ganas de hacer algo, sentir ~ de hacer algo to feel like doing sth
ganar *v.* to win, to beat
ganar a algn en algo to beat sb in sth (No quiero jugar contigo, siempre me ganas en todo.)
ganar a algn para algo to win sb over to sth (Su intención es ganar al directorio para nuestro proyecto.)
general *adj.* general
por lo general in general
genio *m.* **1** temper
tener buen/mal genio, estar de buen/mal ~ to be even-/bad-tempered
2 genius
ser un genio con algo, ser un genio de

algo to be a genius at/very talented in sth (María es un genio con la pelota. Juan es un genio de las letras.)
gestión *f.* **1** process; procedure (Estoy haciendo las gestiones para abrir una tienda de ropa.)
2 management
gestión de proyectos project management
3 (*pl.*) negotiations
golpe *m.* **1** knock, blow
de golpe, de ~ y porrazo suddenly
de un golpe all at once
2 punch, hit
golpe bajo hit below the belt
golpe de efecto dramatic effect
golpe de estado coup d'état
golpe de fortuna, ~ de suerte stroke of luck
gozar *v.* to enjoy
gozar de algo to enjoy sth (Mi abuela goza de buena salud, gracias a Dios.)
gracia *f.* grace
no verle la gracia a algo to not find sth funny (No le veo la gracia a sus chistes.)
grande *adj.* big, large
a lo grande luxuriously, in style (Festejaremos tu cumpleaños a lo grande.)
guardia *f.* guard
bajar la guardia to lower one's guard
con la guardia baja with one's guard down
estar de guardia to be on duty/on call
guardia de seguridad security guard
guardia municipal, ~ urbana police/municipal guard
guiarse *v.* to follow
guiarse por algo to follow sth (Nos guiamos por un antiguo mapa.)
gustar *v.* to like
gustar de algo, ~ a uno algo/algn to like sb/sth
gusto *m.* **1** taste
a gusto del consumidor *fam.* however you like
hacer algo a gusto, hacer algo al ~ to do sth as you please
tener buen/mal gusto to have good/bad taste

tener gusto a algo to taste of sth

2 pleasure

a gusto at ease (No me siento
a gusto aquí.)

con mucho gusto with pleasure

**darle el gusto a algn, hacerle el ~ a
algn** to indulge sb

de gusto, por ~ for the fun of it

mucho gusto, tanto ~ nice to meet you

tener el gusto de algo to be pleased
to do sth

**tomarle el gusto a algo, agarrarle el ~ a
algo** to get to like sth

habituarse *v.* to get used to

habituarse a algo to get used to sth

hablar *v.* to talk

hablar a algn to talk to sb

**hablar acerca de algo/algn, ~ de algo/
algn, ~ sobre algo/algn** to talk about
sth/sb

hablar de más to talk too much

ni hablar no way (¿Lo harías? ¡Ni hablar!)

hacer *v.* to do

hacer algo por algn to do sth for sb

hacerse *v.* to become

hacerse de algo/algn to become of sb/sth
(¿Qué se hizo del coche que tenías? No
sé qué se hizo de Juan, hace años que no
lo veo.)

harto/a *adj.* fed up

estar harto/a de to be fed up with

hasta *prep.* until

hasta ahora, ~ la fecha, ~ el momento so far

hasta entonces until then

hasta que until (Hasta que llegue a casa,
no estaré tranquilo.)

hasta tanto until such time as

no... hasta not until

hermano/a *m./f.* brother/sister

**hermano/a gemelo/a, hermano/a
mellizo/a** twin brother/sister

hermano/a mayor/menor older/younger
brother/sister

medio/a hermano/a half brother/sister

hijo/a *m./f.* son/daughter

como cualquier hijo de vecino, como

todo ~ de vecino like everybody else

hijo/a adoptivo/a adopted son/daughter

hijo/a ilegítimo/a illegitimate
son/daughter

hijo/a único/a only child

hincapié *m.* emphasis

hacer hincapié en algo to emphasize sth

hora *f.* hour; time

a altas horas de la madrugada/noche in
the wee/small hours of the morning/night

a la hora de when it is time to
(A la hora de escribir, prefiero hacerlo en
un lugar tranquilo.)

a primera hora, a última ~ first thing, at
the last moment

dar la hora, decir la ~ to tell the time

entre horas between meals (No
comas golosinas entre horas.)

ser hora de to be time to

ya ser hora de to be about time (Ya era
hora de que volvieras.)

horario *m.* schedule

horario de trabajo work schedule

horno *m.* oven

horno de microondas microwave oven

huelga *f.* strike

declararse en huelga to go on strike

estar de huelga, estar en ~ to be on strike

huelga de brazos caídos sit-down strike

huelga de hambre hunger strike

huir *v.* to run away, to flee

huir de algo/algn to run away from sth/sb

huirle a algn to avoid sb

idea *f.* idea

hacerse a la idea de algo to come to terms
with sth

idéntico/a *adj.* identical

ser idéntico/a a algn to be identical to sb

igual *adj.* equal

al igual que just as

da igual que doesn't matter

igual a algo/algn, ~ que algo/algn the
same as sth/sb (Mi brazalete es igual al
tuyo. Es igual que su madre.)

igual de algo the same as (Está igual de
alta que la última vez que la vi.)

ser igual algo que algo, dar ~ algo que algo (two or more things) to be equal/ the same

ilusionado/a *adj.* hopeful

estar ilusionado/a con to be hopeful for

ilusionarse *v.* to be excited

ilusionarse con algo/algn to be excited about sth/sb

impedir *v.* to prevent

impedir a algn hacer algo to prevent sb from doing sth

importar *v.* to care

importarle algo a algn to care about sth

impuesto *m.* tax

evasión de impuestos tax evasion

impuesto a/sobre la renta income tax

impuesto al valor agregado/añadido, ~ sobre el valor agregado/añadido value-added tax

impuesto directo/indirecto direct/ indirect tax

libre de impuestos tax-free

imputar *v.* to attribute/charge/hold responsible

imputarle algo a algn to attribute sth to sb

indemnizar *v.* to compensate

indemnizar a algn con algo to give sth to sb in compensation

indemnizar a algn por algo to compensate sb for sth

indignar *v.* to outrage

indignar algo a algn to be outraged by sth (Esa decisión ha indignado a todos los vecinos.)

indignarse *v.* to be outraged, to become indignant

indignarse con algn por algo to get angry at sb for sth

inducir *v.* to lead

inducir a algn a algo to lead sb to do sth (Las declaraciones del político pueden inducir a la gente a la venganza.)

inferir *v.* to infer

inferir algo de algo to infer sth from sth (Eso es lo que se infiere de las pruebas.)

influir *v.* to influence

influir en algo/algn, ~ a algn en algo to influence sth/sb

informar *v.* to inform

informar a algn de algo, ~ a algn sobre algo to inform sb of sth

informarse *v.* to inquire

informarse de algo, ~ sobre algo to inquire about sth

ingresar *v.* to join, to enter

ingresar en algo, ~ a algo to join sth

inmiscuirse *v.* to interfere, to meddle

inmiscuirse en algo to interfere in sth

inscribirse *v.* to register

inscribirse dentro de algo to register within sth (Esta medida se inscribe dentro de nuestra política de inmigración.)

inscribirse en algo to enroll in/sign up for sth

insistir *v.* to insist

insistir en algo, ~ sobre algo to insist on sth

inspirarse *v.* to be inspired

inspirarse en algo to be inspired by sth

instar *v.* to urge

instar a algn a algo to urge sb to do sth

interés *m.* interest

de interés + [*adj.*], of + [*adj.*] + interest (Es un programa de interés humano/político.)

despertar (el) interés to arouse interest (El experimento despertó mucho interés.)

poner interés en algo to take interest in sth

por el interés de algn for sb's own interest (Lo hizo por su propio interés.)

tener interés en algo to be interested in sth

interesar *v.* to concern, to interest

interesar a algn en algo to interest sb in sth (Logré interesarlo en nuestra idea.)

interesar algo/algn a algn to be interested in sth/sb (A mí no me interesa lo que piensan los demás. A Juan no le interesan los chismes.)

interesarse *v.* to take interest

interesarse en algo/algn, ~ por algo/ algn to take interest in sth/sb

invitar *v.* to invite

invitar a algn a algo to invite sb to sth

ir *v.* to go

  ir a hacer algo to go to do sth

  ir (a) por algo/algn to go to get sth/sb

irritar *v.* to annoy

  irritar a algn algo to annoy sb (Me irrita su personalidad.)

  irritar a algn con algo to annoy sb with sth (Marcela irritó a su hermana con sus insultos.)

irritarse *v.* to get annoyed

  irritarse con algo, ~ por algo to get annoyed at sth (Se irritó por lo que dije. Siempre se irrita con las críticas de sus colegas.)

irse *v.* to leave

  irse de un lugar to leave a place

izquierda *f.* left

  a la izquierda (de) to/on the left (of) (Si miran a la izquierda, verán uno de los mayores atractivos de la ciudad. María está a la izquierda de Juana.)

  de izquierda left-wing (Sectores de izquierda se opusieron a la medida.)

  de la izquierda on the left (Busca en el cajón de la izquierda.)

J

jactarse *v.* to brag

  jactarse de algo to brag about sth

juego *m.* **1** game

  estar algo en juego to be at stake (No puedo hacer eso, mi carrera está en juego.)

  juego de azar game of chance

  juego de ingenio guessing game

  juego de mesa, ~ de tablero, ~ de salón board game

  juego de palabras pun

  poner algo en juego to bring sth to bear (No voy a poner en juego nuestro futuro.)

  2 play

  juego limpio/sucio fair/foul play

  seguirle el juego a algn to play along with sb

  ser un juego de niños to be a child's game

  3 set

  hacer juego con algo to match sth

  juego de llaves set of keys

juego de té/café tea/coffee set

jugar *v.* to play

  jugar a algo to play sth (¿Quieres jugar al avioncito?)

  jugar con algo/algn to play with sth/sb (Estás jugando con tu futuro. ¡Estoy harta de que juegues conmigo!)

  jugar contra algo/algn to play against sth/sb (Mañana jugaremos contra un equipo muy bueno.)

jugarse *v.* to risk

  jugarse algo to put sth at risk (¿No ves que me estoy jugando el puesto con esto?)

juicio *m.* **1** judgment; sense

  estar en su sano juicio to be in one's right mind

  juicio de valor value judgement

  perder el juicio to go out of one's mind, to go crazy

  tener poco juicio to not be very sensible

  2 opinion

  a juicio de algn in sb's opinion (A mi juicio, lo que hizo está mal.)

  dejar algo al juicio de algn to leave sth up to sb (Dejo la decisión a tu juicio.)

  3 trial

  ir a juicio to go to court

  juicio político political trial

  llevar a juicio to take to court

junto *adv.* close to

  junto a close to, next to

jurar *v.* to swear (Juro que soy inocente.)

  jurar por algo/algn to swear to sth/sb (Lo juró por sus hijos. Le juró por Dios que era cierto.)

justificar *v.* to justify, to excuse

  justificar a algn to make excuses for sb (No intentes justificarlo, es un irresponsable.)

  justificar algo to justify sth (Debes justificar todas tus ausencias.)

juzgar *v.* to judge

  a juzgar por algo judging by

  juzgar algo, ~ a algn por algo to judge sth/sb for sth

  juzgar por uno mismo to judge for oneself

L

lado *m.* side
  al lado de beside, next to
  por otro lado on the other hand
lamentar *v.* to regret (Lamento lo sucedido.)
lamentarse *v.* to deplore; to complain
  lamentarse de algo/algn to deplore sth/sb, to complain about sth/sb (Me lamento de la falta de interés de los jóvenes por la lectura.)
largo/a *adj.* long
  a la larga in the long run (Estoy segura de que Pedro, a la larga, comprenderá que es por su bien.)
  a lo largo de throughout
lástima *f.* **1** shame, pity
  darle lástima a algn to be a shame (Me da lástima dejar esta casa.)
  ¡Qué lástima! What a pity!
  2 sympathy
  sentir lástima por algn to feel sorry for sb (Siento lástima por esa pobre madre.)
lejos *adv.* far
  lejos de far from
lente *m./f.* lens
  lentes de contacto (duro/a(s), blando/a(s)) (hard/soft) contact lenses
ley *f.* law
  con todas las de la ley rightly (No puedes quejarte, ella te ha ganado con todas las de la ley.)
  conforme la ley, según dispone la ~ in accordance with the law
  de buena ley genuine (Es oro de buena ley.)
  la ley de la selva, la ~ de la jungla the law of the jungle
  ley de la oferta y la demanda law of supply and demand
  ley de ventaja advantage
  ley seca Prohibition
  promulgar/dictar una ley to promulgate/enact a law
  violar la ley to break the law
libertad *f.* freedom, liberty
  dejar a algn en libertad to free/release sb
  libertad bajo fianza, ~ bajo palabra, ~ provisional bail
  libertad condicional parole

libertad de cátedra academic freedom
  libertad de conciencia freedom of conscience
  libertad de cultos, ~ de culto freedom of worship
  libertad de expresión, ~ de palabra freedom of expression/speech
  libertad de prensa freedom of the press
libre *adj.* free
  libre de hacer algo free to do sth (Eres libre de decir lo que quieras.)
limitarse *v.* to merely (do)
  limitarse a algo to merely do sth (Por favor, limítese a responder la pregunta.)
limosna *f.* alms
  dar limosna to give money (to beggars)
  pedir limosna to beg
  vivir de limosnas to live off begging
limpio/a *adj.* clean
  limpio/a de algo purified of, unblemished by (Es un producto limpio de impurezas.)
  pasar algo en limpio, pasar algo a ~ to make a clean copy of sth
  sacar algo en limpio to get sth clear
listo/a *adj.* ready
  estar listo para algo to be ready to do sth
llanto *m.* crying
  romper en llanto to burst into tears
llave *f.* **1** key
  bajo siete llaves hidden away
  la llave de oro, las llaves de la ciudad the keys to the city
  llave de contacto, ~ de encendido ignition key
  llave en mano for immediate occupancy (Nos especializamos en construir casas llave en mano.)
  llave inglesa monkey wrench
  llave maestra master key
  2 valve
  llave de paso stopcock, main valve
  llave del gas gas jet
llegar *v.* **1** to arrive
  llegar a un lugar to arrive somewhere
  2 to become
  llegar a ser algo to become sth/sb (Si sigue así, Agustín llegará a ser un gran escritor.)
llenar *v.* to fill

llenar a algn de algo to fill sb with sth
(El embarazo los llenó de alegría.)

llenar algo de algo, ~ algo con algo to
fill sth with sth

llenarse *v.* to fill

llenarse de algo, ~ algo de algo to fill with
sth (La maceta se llenó de insectos. Los
ojos se le llenaron de lágrimas.)

llevar *v.* to bring

llevar algo a algn to bring sth to sb

llevarle... años a algn to be... years older
than sb

llevarse *v.* **1** to take away

llevarse algo, ~ a algn to take sth/sb away
2 to get along

llevarse bien/mal con algn to get along/
to not get along with sb

loco/a *adj.* **1** crazy

a lo loco in a crazy way (Está gastando el
dinero a lo loco.)

**estar loco/a con algo, estar ~ de algo,
estar ~ por algo/algn** to be crazy with/
from sth/for sth/sb (Está loco con sus
novelas. Está loca de alegría. Está loco por
su novia.)

loco/a de atar, ~ de remate to be
stark raving mad
2 anxious

estar loco/a por algo to be most anxious
to do sth (Estamos locos por comenzar
a entrenar.)

lograr *v.* to succeed, to achieve sth (Creo
que lo lograrás.)

lontananza *f.* distance

en lontananza in the distance

lotería *f.* lottery

ganarse la lotería, sacarse la ~ to win
the lottery

sacarse la lotería con algn to strike it
lucky with sb

ser una lotería to be a lottery (Comprar un
apartamento en ese barrio es una lotería.)

tocarle la lotería a algn to win the lottery

luchar *v.* to fight

luchar contra algo to fight against sth
(Está luchando contra una enfermedad
muy grave.)

luchar por algo/algn to fight for sth/sb
(Luchamos por los derechos de
los ciudadanos.)

luego *adv.* after
luego de after

lugar *m.* place

a como dé lugar, a como diera ~ *Am. L.*
however possible

dar lugar a algo to provoke sth (Eso dará
lugar a disputas.)

dejar a algn en mal lugar to put sb in an
awkward position

en lugar de instead of

lugar común cliché (Este discurso está
lleno de prejuicios y lugares comunes.)

sin lugar a dudas without a doubt

tener lugar to take place

lujo *m.* luxury

con lujo de detalles with a wealth of detail

darse el lujo de, permitirse el ~ de to have
the satisfaction of

de lujo luxury (Iván y Paola se alojarán en
un hotel de lujo durante su luna de miel.)

luna *f.* moon

estar con luna, estar de ~ to be in a foul/
bad mood

**estar en la luna (de Valencia), vivir en la
~ (de Valencia)** to have one's head in
the clouds

luna creciente waxing moon

luna de miel honeymoon

luna llena full moon

luna menguante waning moon

luna nueva new moon

luto *m.* mourning

estar de luto por algn to be in mourning
for sb

guardar luto a algn to be mourning for sb

ir de luto, llevar ~ to wear mourning
clothes

luto riguroso deep mourning

ponerse de luto to go into mourning

quitarse el luto to come out of mourning

M

madrugada *f.* early morning

de madrugada early in the morning
(Llegamos de madrugada.)

madrugar *v.* to get/wake up very early

mal *m.* **1** evil

mal menor lesser of two evils
2 illness

echarle el mal de ojo a algn, darle el ~ de ojo a algn to give sb the evil eye

mal de altura, mal de las alturas altitude sickness

mal de Alzheimer/de Chagas/de Parkinson/de San Vito Alzheimer's/Chagas'/Parkinson's/Huntington's disease

mal de amores lovesickness

mal *adj./adv.* bad

estar mal de algo to be short of sth (Desde que Juan se quedó sin trabajo, la familia ha estado muy mal de dinero.)

nada mal not bad at all

malo/a *adj.* bad

mandar *v.* 1 to send

mandar a algn to send sb

mandar algo a algn to send sth to sb

2 to order

mandar a algn a hacer algo to order sb to do sth (¡No me mandes a callar!)

manera *f.* way

a la manera de algn sb's way (Hagámoslo a mi manera.)

a manera de algo by way of (Traje este dibujo a manera de ejemplo.)

de buena/mala manera in a good/bad way

de cualquier manera, de todas maneras anyway, in any case

de esa manera in that way

de manera que so (¿De manera que la decisión ya está tomada?)

de ninguna manera certainly not

manga *f.* sleeve

sacar algo de la manga off the top of one's head

mano *f.* hand

a (la) mano close at hand (¿Tienes tu planilla a (la) mano?)

a mano by hand

con las propias manos with sb's own hands

de la mano hand in hand

de primera mano firsthand

dejar algo en las manos de algn to leave sth in the hands of sb

en buenas manos in good hands (Me marcho, pero los dejo en buenas manos.)

en (propia) mano hand delivery

ir de mano en ~, pasar de ~ en ~ to pass around

irse algo de las manos to get out of hand

levantar la mano to put one's hand up

manos en alto, arriba las manos, manos arriba hands up

tender una mano, ofrecer una ~, dar una ~, echar una ~ to lend a hand

tomarle la mano a algo, agarrarle la ~ a algo to get the hang of sth

maravilla *f.* wonder

a las mil maravillas wonderfully (¡Todo salió a las mil maravillas!)

maravillarse *v.* to be amazed/astonished

maravillarse de algo/algn, ~ con algo/algn, ~ ante algo to be amazed at sth/sb

margen *f.* bank, side *m.* margin

estar al margen de la sociedad/ley to be on the fringes of society/the law

ganar por un amplio/estrecho margen to win by a comfortable/narrow margin

mantenerse al margen de algo to keep out of sth

margen de beneficio, ~ comercial, ~ de ganancias profit margin

margen de error margin of error

margen de tolerancia range of tolerance

nota al margen margin note

mayor *adj.* greater, older

por mayor wholesale

mediados *m.* middle

a mediados de in the middle of (Voy a retirar las cosas que faltan a mediados del mes que viene.)

medida *f.* measure

a medida que as (Resolveremos los problemas a medida que vayan surgiendo.)

medio/a *adj.* half

a medias halfway

meditar *v.* to meditate

meditar sobre algo to meditate on sth

mejor *adj.* better

a lo mejor maybe

menor *adj.* lesser

por menor retail

menos *adj.* less

a menos que unless

al menos at least

por lo menos at least

menudo/a *adj.* small, slight (Es un hombre muy menudo.)

  a menudo often

  menudo... *Esp.* what a…, such a… (¡Menudo lío! ¡Caí en menuda trampa!)

mercado *m.* market

  mercado al aire libre open-air market

  mercado cambiario, ~ de divisas foreign exchange market

  mercado de abastos, ~ de abasto market

  mercado de las pulgas, ~ de pulgas flea market

  mercado negro black market

  mercado persa bazaar

mesa *f.* table

  bendecir la mesa to say grace

  levantar la mesa, quitar la ~, recoger la ~ to clear the table

  mesa auxiliar side table

  mesa de centro, ~ ratona coffee table

  mesa de comedor/cocina dining room/ kitchen table

  mesa de dibujo drawing board

  mesa de negociaciones, ~ negociadora negotiating table

  mesa de noche, ~ de luz bedside table

  mesa plegable folding table

  poner la mesa to set the table

  sentarse a la mesa to sit at the table

meta *f.* **1** finish line

  llegar a la meta to reach the finish line

  2 aim

  alcanzar una meta to reach a goal

  ponerse algo por meta to set oneself a goal

  tener una meta, trazarse una ~ to set a goal for oneself

meterse *v.* **1** to get involved

  meterse en algo to get involved in sth

  2 to pick on

  meterse con algn to pick on sb

  3 to become

  meterse a algo to become sth (Juan se metió a periodista pero no sabe escribir bien.)

miedo *m.* fear

  tener miedo a algo/algn to be afraid of sb/sth

  tener miedo de algo to be afraid of sth

mira *f.* view

  con miras a with the purpose of

mismo/a *adj.* same

  dar lo mismo que to make no difference

misterio *m.* mystery

  dejarse de misterio to stop being mysterious (¡Dejaos ya de tanto misterio y contadnos cuándo os vais a casar!)

  novela de misterio mystery novel

moda *f.* fashion

  estar a la moda, estar de ~, ponerse de ~ to be in fashion

  estar de última moda to be very fashionable

  estar pasado de moda to be out of fashion

  ir a la moda to be trendy

modo *m.* way, manner

  a modo de by way of (Usó su cuaderno a modo de pantalla.)

  de buen/mal modo, de buenos/malos modos in a good/bad way

  de cualquier modo, de todos modos anyway, in any case

  de modo que in such a way that

  de ningún modo no way

  de tal modo que, de ~ que so (that) (Estudió mucho, de tal modo que aprobó el examen. Ya es tarde, de modo que me voy a casa.)

  del mismo modo, de igual ~ in the same way

  en cierto modo in a way

  modo de empleo instructions for use

  ni modo not a chance

  no es modo de hacer las cosas no way of going about things

molestar *v.* to bother

  molestar a algn to bother sb

molestarse *v.* **1** to get upset

  molestarse con algn por algo to get upset with sb for sth

  2 to take the trouble

  molestarse en hacer algo to take the trouble to do sth

momento *m.* moment

  en algún momento at some point, sometime

morirse *v.* to die

  morirse de algo to die of sth, to be really hungry, thirsty… (Se murió de pulmonía. ¡Me muero de hambre!)

morirse por algo to die for sth (¡Me
muero por conocerlo personalmente!)

motivo *m.* reason

con motivo de the reason for

por motivos de fuerza mayor force
majeure

por ningún motivo under no
circumstances

mozo/a *m./f.* **1** young man/woman

buen mozo, buena moza good-looking
boy/girl

2 waiter/waitress *Arg.*

muela *f.* molar; back tooth

muela de juicio wisdom tooth

muerte *f.* death

amenaza de muerte death threat

de mala muerte lousy (No vayas a ese
restaurante, es de mala muerte.)

estar condenado a muerte to be sentenced
to death

hacer algo a muerte to do sth to death

herido de muerte fatally wounded

muerto/a *adj.* dead

muerto/a de cansancio, ~ de sueño
dead-tired

muerto/a de frío freezing

muerto/a de hambre starving

muerto/a de miedo frightened to death

muerto/a de risa dying of laughter

N

nada *pron.* nothing

como si nada as if it were nothing

de nada, por ~ you're welcome

nada de algo not to need any of sth (No
necesitamos nada de combustible.)

nada de nada not a thing

necesidad *f.* need

por necesidad out of necessity

negar *v.* to deny

negar algo a algn to deny sth to sb

negarse *v.* to refuse, to deny

negarse a hacer algo to refuse to do sth

negarse algo to deny oneself sth (Se niega
todo para que su hija pueda estudiar.)

negociar *v.* to negotiate

negociar algo con algn to negotiate sth
with sb

nombre *m.* name

a nombre de algn addressed to sb

en nombre de algo/algn in the name
of sth/sb

no tener nombre to be beyond belief
(Lo que has hecho no tiene nombre.)

nombre artístico stage name

nombre completo full name

nombre de guerra, ~ de batalla
alias, pseudonym

nombre de mujer/varón girl's/boy's name

nombre de pila first name

notar *v.* to notice

hacerse notar to draw attention to oneself

notar algo to notice sth

nube *f.* cloud

por las nubes sky-high (Los precios están
por las nubes.)

nuevo/a *adj.* new

de nuevo again

O

obligar *v.* to force

obligar a algn a hacer algo to force sb to
do sth

obra *f.* work

**obra benéfica, ~ de beneficencia, ~ de
caridad** act of charity

obra de arte work of art

obra de consulta reference book

obra de teatro theater play

obra maestra masterpiece

obstinarse *v.* to insist

obstinarse en algo to insist on sth (Se
obstina en dificultar las cosas.)

ocuparse *v.* to be in charge

ocuparse de algo/algn to be in charge of
sth/sb

ofender *v.* to offend

ofender a algn to offend sb

ofenderse *v.* to be offended

ofenderse con algn por algo to be
offended with sb because of sth

ojo *m.* eye

a los ojos de la sociedad in the eyes
of society

guiñar el ojo to wink

¡Ojo! Be careful!, Watch out!

tener (buen) ojo to be sharp (Mi hermano tiene muy buen ojo para estas cosas.)

oler *v.* to smell

oler a algo to smell like sth (La habitación olía a jazmines.)

oler algo to smell sth (Huele este perfume, es francés.)

olvidarse *v.* to forget

olvidarse de algo/algn to forget about sth/sb

olvidársele algo a algn to forget about sth

opinar *v.* to have an opinion

opinar (algo) de algo/algn, ~ sobre algo/algn to have an opinion about sth/sb (¿Qué opinas de la reforma económica? El ministro opinó sobre las nuevas medidas. Pablo opina que su nuevo jefe es un tirano.)

opinión *f.* opinion

cambiar de opinión to change sb's mind (Mi hermano cambió de opinión sobre las vacaciones.)

oponerse *v.* to oppose

oponerse a algo/algn to oppose sth/sb

optar *v.* to choose

optar por algo to choose sth

ordenar *v.* to order

ordenar algo a algn to order sb to do sth

orgulloso/a *adj.* proud

estar orgulloso/a de to be proud of

oscuro/a *adj.* dark

a oscuras in the dark

P

padecer *v.* to suffer

padecer de algo to suffer from sth

pagar *v.* to pay

pagar al contado, ~ en efectivo to pay in cash

pagar algo a algn to pay sth to sb

pagar algo con algo to pay for sth with sth

pagar (algo) por algo to pay (sth) for sth

para *prep.* for, to

no ser para tanto to not exaggerate/to not be so bad (No te quejes por eso, que no es para tanto.)

para con with (Son muy buenos para con los niños.)

para siempre forever

parada *f.* stop

parada de autobús, ~ de ómnibus bus stop

parada de metro subway stop

parada de taxi taxi stand

parecer *v.* **1** to look like

al parecer, ~ que apparently, evidently, it would seem/appear

2 to have an opinion

a mi parecer in my opinion

parecer mentira to seem impossible

parecerse *v.* to be like

no parecerse en nada a algo/algn not to be/look alike at all

parecerse a algo/algn to be/look like sth/sb

parecido/a *adj.* **1** similar

ser parecido/a a algo/algn to be similar to sth/sb

2 good-looking

ser bien/mal parecido/a to be good-/bad-looking

pareja *f.* **1** couple; pair

formar parejas to get into pairs

vivir en pareja to live together

2 partner

la pareja the other one (No encuentro la pareja de este calcetín.)

tener pareja to have a partner (Después de tanto tiempo de soltería, finalmente tengo pareja.)

parte *f.* part

en alguna parte somewhere

por otra parte besides (La película es interesante y, por otra parte, no tengo nada que hacer.)

participar *v.* to take part

participar en algo to take part in sth

partido *m.* game, match

sacar partido de algo to take advantage of sth

tomar partido to take sides

partir *v.* to leave

a partir de starting

pasaje *m.* ticket

pasaje de ida one-way ticket

pasaje de ida y vuelta round-trip ticket

sacar un pasaje to buy a ticket

paseo *m.* walk

estar de paseo to be visiting

mandar a algn a paseo to tell sb
to get lost

paseo marítimo esplanade

paso *m.* **1** passage, passing; path

dicho sea de paso by the way (Dicho sea
de paso, te queda muy bien ese color.)

el paso del tiempo the passage of time

2 way

abrir paso to make way

abrirse paso to make one's way

ceder el paso to yield

cerrar el paso to block the way

3 pass

paso fronterizo border crossing

4 step

a pasos agigantados by leaps and bounds

con paso firme firmly, purposefully

dar un paso en falso to stumble; to make
a false move

paso a paso step-by-step

5 rate, speed

a este paso at this rate

a paso de hormiga/tortuga at a
snail's pace

pata *f.* leg

estirar la pata *fam.* to kick the bucket

meter la pata *fam.* to put one's foot in
one's mouth

pata delantera/trasera front/hind leg

patas para arriba *fam.* upside down

saltar en una pata to jump for joy

paz *f.* peace

**dejar en paz algo, dejar en ~ a algn, dejar
a algn vivir en ~** to let sth/sb alone

descansar en paz rest in peace

estar en paz, quedar en ~ *fam.* to be
at peace

firmar la paz to sign a peace agreement

hacer las paces to make up

pedir *v.* to ask; to request

pedir algo a algn to ask sb (for) sth
(Pidió un adelanto a su jefe. Pidió a su
secretaria que escribiera una carta.)

pedir algo por algo to ask sth for sth
(¿Cuánto pide por la bicicleta?)

pedir prestado to borrow

pelearse *v.* to quarrel

pelearse con algn por algo to quarrel with
sb over sth

pelo *m.* hair

**andar con los pelos de punta, estar con
los ~ de punta** to be in a real state

caérsele el pelo a algn to lose one's hair

cortarle el pelo a algn to cut sb's hair

cortarse el pelo to have one's hair cut

no tener ni un pelo de tonto to not be a fool

no tener pelos en la lengua to not mince
one's words

pelo lacio, ~ liso straight hair

pelo rizado curly hair

ponerle a algn los pelos de punta to make
sb's hair stand on end

por un pelo just (¡Nos salvamos por
un pelo!)

traído por los pelos, traído de los ~
far-fetched

pena *f.* sorrow

vale la pena que it's worth it that/to (Vale
la pena que te esfuerces, tendrás una
buena recompensa.)

pensar *v.* to think

pensar algo de algn to think sth of sb
(Pienso que Susana es muy cruel.)

pensar en algo/algn to think about sth/sb

percatarse *v.* to notice

percatarse de algo to notice sth

permiso *m.* permission

dar permiso, pedir ~ to give/ask for
permission

(con) permiso excuse me

permitir *v.* to allow

permitir algo a algn to allow sb to do sth

persistir *v.* to persist

persistir en algo to persist in sth

pertenecer *v.* to belong

pertenecer a algn to belong to sb (Este
reloj le pertenecía a mi bisabuelo.)

pesar *m.* regret, sorrow

a pesar de, pese a in spite of

mal que le pese a algn whether sb likes
it or not

pie *m.* foot

a pie on foot

al pie de la letra literally, exactly (Siguieron
nuestras instrucciones al pie de la letra.)

al pie de la montaña, a los pies de la montaña at the foot of the mountain

con buen pie, con el ~ derecho to get off to a good start (Creo que no comenzaron con buen pie. Nuestra relación comenzó con el pie derecho.)

con mal pie, con el ~ izquierdo badly

dar pie a algo to give rise to sth

dar pie con bola *fam.* to get sth right (Últimamente todo me sale mal, no doy pie con bola.)

de pie standing (Ponte de pie cuando entre la maestra.)

en pie to be up (awake), to be on one's feet, to be standing (Estuve en pie todo el día. Lo único que quedó en pie fue la antigua capilla. ¿Sabes si la oferta sigue en pie?)

en pie de guerra ready for war

hacer pie to be able to touch the bottom (No puedo hacer pie en esa piscina.)

nacer de pie to be born lucky

nota a pie de página, nota al ~ de página footnote

perder pie, no hacer ~ to get out of one's depth (Si pierdes pie, llámame enseguida.)

pie de fotografía caption

pie de imprenta imprint

pie equino clubfoot

pie plano flat foot

pila *f.* **1** battery

funcionar a pila(s), funcionar con pila(s) to run on batteries

2 pile, loads

pila de algo, pilas de algo mountains of sth

plano *m.* flat

de plano outright (Se negó de plano a participar en el negocio.)

plantado/a *adj.* planted

dejar plantado/a a algn to stand sb up (¡No puedo creer que te dejara plantado!)

plantado de algo planted with sth (El campo está plantado de trigo.)

plazo *m.* **1** period

corto plazo short-term

dar un plazo to give a deadline (Nos dieron un plazo de 30 días para comenzar a pagar.)

largo plazo long-term

medio plazo, mediano ~ middle-term

2 installment

pagar a plazos to pay in installments

poco *pron.* little

a poco de algo shortly after sth

dentro de poco soon

poco antes de algo shortly before sth

poco y nada very little, to hardly do sth (Hicieron poco y nada por sus compañeros.)

por poco almost (¡Por poco le creo sus mentiras!)

poder *v.* to be possible

puede (ser) que might/could be (Puede ser que salgamos campeones este año, estamos jugando bien. Puede que mañana llegue tarde a casa, tengo una reunión con mi jefa.)

poner *v.* **1** to put

poner algo en marcha to start sth

poner algo / a algn en un lugar to put sth somewhere, to put sb in his/her place

2 to make

poner a algn de una manera to make sb feel some way (Ese poema me pone triste.)

ponerse *v.* to begin

ponerse a hacer algo to begin to (Ponte a hacer la tarea ahora mismo.)

por *prep.* by, for, in

por adelantado in advance

por ahora for the time being

por aquí around here

por casualidad by accident

por causa de because of

por completo, ~ entero completely

por consiguiente, ~ lo tanto therefore

por cuanto insofar as

por delante ahead (Aún nos queda mucho por delante.)

por delante de in front of, opposite (Ayer pasé por delante de tu casa.)

por demás extremely (Te comportas de una manera por demás grosera.)

por dentro de in, inside of

por desgracia unfortunately

por detrás de behind, in the back of

por Dios for heaven's sake

por ejemplo for example

por el camino on the way (Vamos, te lo cuento por el camino.)

por el principio at the beginning

por encima de over

por entre in between (Los niños se metieron por entre los invitados y los perdimos de vista.)

por escrito in writing

por eso that's why

por fin finally

por fortuna fortunately

por fuera de out, outside of

por fuerza necessarily

por fuerza mayor, ~ causas de fuerza mayor, ~ motivos de fuerza mayor force majeure

por gusto for the fun of it

por las buenas o por las malas one way or the other

por las nubes sky-high

por lo demás apart from that

por lo general, ~ regla general in general

por lo menos at least

por lo pronto, ~ de pronto, ~ el pronto for a start

por lo tanto therefore

por lo visto apparently

por mayor wholesale

por menor retail

por nada you're welcome

por necesidad out of necessity

por ningún motivo under no circumstances

por otra parte, ~ otro lado besides (La película es interesante y, por otra parte, no tengo nada que hacer.)

por poco almost (¡Por poco le creo sus mentiras!)

por principio on principle

por siempre jamás forever and ever

por suerte luckily

por supuesto of course

por un pelo just (¡Nos salvamos por un pelo!)

por... vez for the... time

preferir *v.* to prefer

preferir algo a algo to prefer sth to sth

preguntar *v.* to ask

preguntar algo a algn to ask sb sth

preguntar (a algn) por algo/algn to ask (sb) about sth/sb

preocupado/a *adj.* worried

estar preocupado/a por to be worried about

preocupar *v.* to be worried

preocupar a algn to be worried about sth

preocuparse *v.* to worry

preocuparse de algo to take interest in sth (No se preocupó más del tema.)

preocuparse por algo/algn to worry about sth/sb (Estoy preocupada por la educación de mis hijos.)

prescindir *v.* **1** to do without

prescindir de algo/algn to do without sth/sb

prescindir de los servicios de algn to dispense with sb's services

2 to disregard

prescindir de algo to disregard sth

3 to dispense

prescindir de algo to dispense of sth (Decidió prescindir de los detalles.)

presenciar *v.* to witness

presenciar algo to witness sth

prestar *v.* to lend

prestar algo a algn to lend sth to sb

primero/a *adj.* first

ser el/la primero/a en hacer algo to be the first one to do sth (Eres el primero en ocuparse de los niños.)

principio *m.* **1** beginning

a principios de at the beginning of (Supongo que nos mudaremos a principios de año.)

al principio at first

desde el principio, desde un ~ from the beginning

en (un) principio in the beginning

por el principio at the beginning

2 principle

cuestión de principios question of principles

por principio on principle

ser algn de principios to be someone with principles

prisa *f.* haste

correr prisa to be in a rush

darse prisa to hurry

privar *v.* to deprive

privar a algn de algo to deprive sb of sth

privarse *v.* to deprive oneself

privarse de algo to deprive oneself of sth

procurar *v.* 1 to try, to aim to/at

procurar hacer algo to try to do sth
(Procura terminar el proyecto esta semana.)
2 to obtain

procurar algo para algn to obtain sth for
sb (Procuraremos alimentos
para los refugiados.)

prohibir *v.* to ban/forbid

prohibirle a algn algo to forbid sb
to do sth

prohibirle algo a algn to ban sb from
doing sth

pronto *adv.* soon

de pronto suddenly

¡hasta pronto! see you soon!

lo más pronto posible as soon as possible

por lo pronto, por de ~, por el ~ for
a start

tan pronto como as soon as, once

propina *f.* tip

dar propina to tip

de propina tip (¿Cuánto has dejado
de propina?)

dejar una propina to leave a tip

proponer *v.* to propose, suggest

**proponer a algn para algo, ~ a algn como
algo** to propose, suggest sb as sth

proponer algo a algn to propose sth to sb

proporcionar *v.* to provide

proporcionar algo a algn to provide sb
with sth (Me proporcionó todos los
materiales necesarios.)

propósito *m.* intention

a propósito on purpose, by the way
(¡Lo hiciste a propósito! Ayer me encontré
con Mario; a propósito, me preguntó
cuánto vale tu coche.)

propósito de enmienda a promise to
mend one's ways

sin propósito aimlessly

tener buenos propósitos to have
good intentions

proteger *v.* to protect

**proteger algo de algo/algn, ~ a algn de
algo/algn, ~ algo contra algo** to protect
sth/sb from/against sth/sb

protegerse *v.* to protect oneself

**protegerse de algo/algn, ~ contra
algo/algn** to protect oneself from/against
sth/sb

protestar *v.* to complain

protestar contra algo/algn to protest
against sth (Los manifestantes protestan
contra el gobierno.)

protestar por algo to complain about sth
(Protestan por la falta de trabajo.)

provecho *m.* benefit

sacar provecho de algo to benefit from sth

prueba *f.* proof

a prueba de impervious to, resistant (¿Tu
reloj es a prueba de agua?)

punto *m.* point

**anotarse un punto con algo, marcarse un
~ con algo** to get ten out of ten on sth

en punto o'clock/on the dot

estar a punto de hacer algo to be about to
do sth

poner punto final a algo to end

punto álgido culminating point, climax
(La crisis económica alcanzó su
punto álgido.)

punto de apoyo fulcrum

punto decimal decimal point

punto final period

punto y aparte period, new paragraph

punto y coma semicolon

punto y seguido period

puntos suspensivos ellipsis

Q

quedar *v.* 1 to fit

quedarle algo bien/mal a algn to fit well/
badly (¿Me queda mal el vestido?)
2 to cause an impression

quedar bien/mal con algn to make a
good/bad impression on sb (No quiero
quedar mal con mis suegros.)
3 to agree

quedar en algo con algn to agree to do sth
with sb (Quedamos en no volver a hablar
del tema.)

quedarse *v.* to keep

  quedarse con algo to keep sth

  quedarse dormido to oversleep

quejarse *v.* to complain

  quejarse de algo/algn to complain about sb/sth (¿De qué te quejas? No deja de quejarse de sus vecinos.)

  quejarse por algo, ~ de algo to complain of sth (Marta se queja por el costo de vida. Tu hijo se queja de un fuerte dolor de muelas.)

quiebra *f.* bankruptcy

  declararse en quiebra, irse a la ~ to go bankrupt

quitar *v.* to take off

  quitar algo a algn to take sth from sb

rabo *m.* tail

  con el rabo entre las piernas, con el ~ entre las patas with one's tail between one's legs

raíz *f.* root

  a raíz de as a result of

  echar raíces to take roots

  raíz cuadrada/cúbica square/cube root

rato *m.* while

  a cada rato the whole time

  al (poco) rato shortly thereafter

  de a rato, de a ratos, de ~ en ~ from time to time

  hace rato for some time

  pasar el rato to spend time/hang out

  ratos libres, ~ de ocio spare time

  tener para rato to be a while

raya *f.* **1** line

  a rayas striped

  pasarse de la raya to overstep the mark, to go too far, to push one's luck

  tener a algn a raya, mantener a algn a ~ to keep sb under control

  2 part

  llevar raya al medio/al costado to part one's hair in the middle/to one side

razón *f.* **1** reason

  atender razones, atenerse a ~, avenirse a ~ to listen to reason

  darle la razón a algn to admit sb is right

en razón de because of (No debes discriminar en razón de la edad o la raza de las personas.)

  entrar en razón to see reason

  perder la razón to lose one's mind

  razón de ser raison d'être/reason for being (¡Esta masacre no tiene razón de ser!)

  razón social registered name

  tener (la) razón, llevar la ~ to be right

  2 rate

  a razón de at a rate of

  3 information

  dar razón de algo/algn to give information about sth/sb

rechazar *v.* to reject

  rechazar a algn por algo to reject sb for sth

  rechazar algo a algn to reject sth from sb

reclamar *v.* to claim, to demand

  reclamar algo de algn to demand sth from sb

recomendar *v.* to recommend

  recomendar algo a algn to recommend sth to sb

recompensar *v.* to reward

  recompensar a algn por algo to reward sb for sth (Deberías recompensar a tus alumnos por su esfuerzo.)

reconciliarse *v.* to reconcile

  reconciliarse con algo to become reconciled to sth (Se reconcilió con su idea de la familia.)

  reconciliarse con algn to make up with sb (Marcia se reconcilió con su marido.)

recordar *v.* to remind

  recordar algo a algn to remind sb of sth

recuperarse *v.* to recover

  recuperarse de algo to recover from sth

recurso *m.* **1** resource

  agotar todos los recursos to exhaust all the options

  como último recurso as a last resource

  recurso natural, recursos naturales natural resource(s)

  recursos económicos economic/financial resources

  recursos energéticos energy resources

  recursos humanos human resources

sin recursos with no means/without resources

2 appeal

interponer/presentar un recurso to file an appeal

red *f.* net

caer en las redes de algn to be trapped by sb

reembolso *m.* refund

contra reembolso cash on delivery

referir *v.* **1** to tell

referir algo a algn to tell sth to sb (Nos refirió sus experiencias como maestro rural.)

2 to refer

referir a algn a algo to refer sb to sth (Nos refirió al segundo párrafo de la nota.)

referirse *v.* to refer

referirse a algo/algn to refer to sth/sb (No entiendo a qué te refieres. No me estaba refiriendo a ti.)

reflexionar *v.* to reflect

reflexionar sobre algo/algn to think about sth/sb

refugiado/a *adj.* refugee

refugiado/a político/a political refugee

refugiado/a de guerra war refugee

regalar *v.* to give as a gift

regalar algo a algn to give sth to sb as a gift

regañadientes *adv.* reluctantly

a regañadientes reluctantly

regla *f.* rule

por regla general in general

regreso *m.* return

a su regreso on sb's return

de regreso a back at/to (¿Cuándo estarás de regreso a la oficina?)

emprender el regreso to set off on the return trip

reírse *v.* to laugh

reírse de algo/algn to laugh at sth/sb

reírse por algo to laugh because of sth

remedio *m.* **1** remedy

santo remedio to do the trick (¿Tienes tos? Prepara un vaso de leche tibia con miel y santo remedio.)

2 solution

no tener remedio to be hopeless/to

have no solution (Olvídalo, nuestro matrimonio no tiene remedio.)

3 option

no tener más remedio que, no quedar más ~ que, no haber más ~ que, no haber otro ~ que to have no option but to

renglón *m.* line

a renglón seguido immediately afterwards (Las instrucciones se detallan a renglón seguido.)

renunciar *v.* **1** to resign

renunciar a algo to resign from sth (Renunció a su trabajo y salió a recorrer el mundo.)

2 to renounce

renunciar a algo to renounce sth (Decidimos renunciar a la lucha armada.)

reñir *v.* to quarrel

reñir con algn to quarrel with sb

reojo *m.* the corner of the eye

mirar de reojo a algn to look at sb out of the corner of one's eye

repente *adv.* suddenly

de repente suddenly

repercutir *v.* **1** to impact

repercutir en algo/algn to have an impact on sth/sb

2 to pass on

repercutir algo en algn, ~ sobre algn to pass sth on to sb

reponerse *v.* to recover

reponerse de algo to recover from sth

reprochar *v.* to reproach

reprochar algo a algn to reproach sb for sth

reputación *f.* reputation

tener reputación de to have a reputation as (Tiene reputación de buen cocinero.)

resentirse *v.* to get upset

resentirse con algn por algo to get upset with sb because of sth

resignarse *v.* to resign oneself

resignarse a algo to resign oneself to sth

resistirse *v.* to be reluctant, to resist

resistirse a algo to resist sth

respecto *m.* matter, regard

con respecto a regarding

respetar *v.* to respect

respetar a algn por algo to respect sb
for sth

responder *v.* to answer

**responder algo a algn, responder a
algo** to answer sb about sth

responder por algo/algn to be held
responsible

responsabilizar *v.* to blame

responsabilizar a algn de algo to blame
sb for sth (La víctima responsabilizó a la
policía del fracaso de la operación.)

responsable *adj.* responsible

ser responsable de algo to be responsible
for sth

resumen *m.* summary

en resumen all in all

hacer un resumen to summarize

reunirse *v.* to meet

reunirse con algn to meet with sb

revista *f.* **1** magazine

revista de chistes comic book

revista de modas fashion magazine

revista del corazón *Esp.* gossip magazine

2 revue

teatro de revista vaudeville-style comedy

3 review

pasar revista a algo to review sth

rivalizar *v.* to compete

rivalizar con algn por algo to compete
with sb on sth

rodilla *f.* knee

de rodillas down on one's knees

hincar la rodilla to go down on
one's knee

pedir algo de rodillas to beg on
one's knees

rogar *v.* to beg

rogar algo a algn to beg sb for sth

romper *v.* to break

romper algo to break sth

romper con algn to break up with sb

S

saber *v.* **1** to know

(de) haberlo sabido had sb known

**saber algo de algo/algn, ~ algo sobre
algo/algn** to know sth about sth/sb
(Mi padre sabe algo de física. ¿Sabes algo

de Mariano? ¿Alguien sabe algo
sobre la fiesta?)

2 to taste

saber a algo to taste like sth (Esto sabe
a nueces.)

sabiendas *adv.* knowingly

a sabiendas knowingly

salida *f.* exit; way out

no verle salida a algo not to see a way
out of sth (No le veo la salida a
este problema.)

salir *v.* **1** to leave

salir de algo to leave from sth

salir para algo to leave for sth (Salgo para
Colombia esta misma noche.)

salir por algo to leave via sth (¡No querrás
que salga por la chimenea!)

2 to go

salir a algo to go out onto/into/for (Salieron
al balcón. ¿Salimos a comer?)

salir con algn to go out with sb

3 to take after

salir a algn to take after sb (El bebé salió a
su padre.)

saludar *v.* to greet

saludar a algn to greet sb

salvo *adv.*

a salvo safe (Mi familia está a salvo, gracias
a Dios.)

ponerse a salvo to reach safety

satisfecho/a *adj.* satisfied

estar satisfecho/a de to be satisfied
by/with

seguir *v.* to follow

seguir algo, ~ a algn to follow sth/sb

seguro/a *adj.* **1** safe

hacer algo sobre seguro to play safe
with sth

2 sure

estar seguro/a de algo to be sure about sth

sentado/a *adj.* seated

esperar sentado/a to not hold sb's breath

sentido *m.* **1** sense

sentido común common sense

sentido de algo sense of sth (Su sentido
del deber es admirable.)

sentido de (la) orientación sense of
direction

tener sentido to make sense
2 consciousness
perder el sentido to lose consciousness
recobrar el sentido to regain consciousness
sentir *v.* **1** to feel
sentir algo hacia algn, ~ algo por algo/ algn to feel sth for sth/sb
2 to regret
sentir algo to regret sth (Siento mucho haberte dicho eso.)
sentirse 1 to feel
sentirse bien/mal to feel well/ill
2 to be offended
sentirse con algn *Méx.* to be offended with sb (Está sentida con su hermana porque le mintió.)
ser *v.* to be
a no ser que if not, unless
ser de algo/algn to become (¿Qué fue del aumento que te iban a dar? ¿Qué será de nuestros amigos?)
ser *m.* being
el ser y la nada being and nothingness
ser humano human being
ser sobrenatural supernatural being
ser vivo, ~ viviente living being
serie *f.* series
coches/motores de serie production cars/ engines
fuera de serie out of this world
producción en serie, fabricación en ~ mass production
serie numérica numerical sequence
seriedad *f.* seriousness
con toda seriedad seriously
falta de seriedad irresponsibility, lack of seriousness
servir *v.* to serve
servir a algo/algn to serve sth/sb
siempre *adv.* always
casi siempre almost always
como siempre as usual
¡hasta siempre! farewell!
para siempre forever
por siempre jamás forever and ever
siempre que whenever, provided that (Me viene a visitar siempre que puede. Te ayudaré, siempre que prometas contarme toda la verdad.)

siempre y cuando if (Iré siempre y cuando me acompañes.)
silencio *m.* silence
guardar silencio to keep silent
sin *prep.* without
sin cesar nonstop
sin demora without delay
sin embargo however
sin falta without fail
sin fines de lucro, ~ fines lucrativos not-for-profit
sin lugar a dudas, ~ duda without a doubt
sin propósito aimlessly
sobrar *v.* to have in excess
sobrar algo a algn to have sth in excess (Les sobraba el dinero.)
solidarizarse *v.* to support
solidarizarse con algo/algn to support sth/ sb (Nos solidarizamos con su reclamo. La presidenta se solidarizó con los trabajadores despedidos.)
solo/a *adj.* alone
a solas alone (No me gusta quedarme a solas con ella.)
sombra *f.* shadow
a la sombra de in the shadow of
soñar to dream
soñar con algo/algn to dream about sth/sb
sorprender *v.* to surprise
sorprender a algn con algo to surprise sb with sth
sorprenderse *v.* to be surprised
sorprenderse de algo, ~ por algo to be surprised about sth
sospechar *v.* to suspect
sospechar algo, ~ de algn to suspect sth/sb
subasta *f.* auction
sacar algo a subasta to put sth up for auction
subir *v.* to get on
subir a algo to get on/onto sth
suceder *v.* to happen
suceder algo a algn for sth to happen to sb
suerte *f.* **1** chance
caer en suerte, tocar en ~ for something to fall to sb's lot

echar algo a la suerte, echar algo a suertes to toss a coin for sth

la suerte está echada the die is cast

2 luck

buena/mala suerte good/bad luck

desear buena suerte a algn to wish luck to sb

estar de suerte to be in luck

por suerte luckily

probar suerte to try one's luck

traer buena/mala suerte, dar buena/mala ~ to bring good/bad luck

sufrir to suffer

sufrir de algo to suffer from sth

sufrir por algo/algn to suffer because of sth/sb

sugerir *v.* to suggest

sugerir algo a algn to suggest sth to sb

suma *f.* sum

en suma in short

suplicar *v.* to beg, to implore

suplicar a algn por algo/algn to beg sb to do sth

supuesto/a *adj.* so-called

por supuesto of course

sustituir *v.* to replace

sustituir a algn to replace sb

sustituir algo con algo, ~ algo por algo to replace sth with sth

T

tablón *m.* board

tablón de anuncios bulletin board

taller *m.* workshop, garage

taller mecánico, ~ de reparación garage

tanto *pron.* so, so much

otro tanto the same

por (lo) tanto therefore

tanto... como... both... and...

tardar *v.* to take (time)

a más tardar at the very latest

tardar en algo to take a long time to

tarde *adv.* late

hacerse tarde to be getting late

más vale tarde que nunca better late than never

ser tarde para algo to be too late for sth

tarde o temprano sooner or later

tarjeta *f.* card

tarjeta de crédito credit card

tarjeta de débito debit card

tarjeta postal postcard

tasa *f.* **1** tax; fee (Debo pagar las tasas.)

2 rate

tasa de desempleo unemployment rate

tasa de interés interest rate

tasa de mortalidad/natalidad mortality rate/birthrate

telón *m.* curtain

telón de fondo background

temer *v.* to fear

temer a algo/algn to be afraid of sth/sb

temer por algo/algn to fear for sth/sb

tender *v.* to tend

tender a algo to tend to sth (Siempre tiendo a preocuparme por todo.)

tener *v.* to have

tener que ver to pertain/have sth to do (No tiene nada que ver con este asunto.)

terminar *v.* to finish

terminar con algo/algn to finish with sth/sb

terminar de hacer algo to finish sth

tiempo *m.* time

a tiempo on time

al mismo tiempo que at the same time as

tiempo libre free time

tirar *v.* **1** to throw

tirar algo a algn to throw sth to sb, to throw sth at sb

2 to pull

tirar de algo to pull sth

3 to shoot

tirar a dar to shoot to wound

tirar a matar to shoot to kill

tirar a traición to shoot in the back

tomar *v.* to take

tomar a algn por algo to take sb for sth (A nadie le gusta que lo tomen por tonto.)

tono *m.* pitch, tone

estar a tono con to keep up with, to be in tune with

fuera de tono inappropriate, out of place

no venir a tono to be out of place

subido de tono risqué

tonto/a *adj.* silly

a tontas y a locas without thinking

toparse *v.* to encounter

toparse con algo/algn to run into sth/sb

torno *m.* about, around

en torno a around (El argumento de la película gira en torno a las relaciones amorosas.)

trabajar *v.* to work

trabajar en algo, ~ con algo to work on/in/with sth

trabajar para algn to work for sb

trabajar por algo to work for sth

traducir *v.* to translate

traducir algo a algo to translate sth into sth

transformarse *v.* to become

transformarse en algo/algn to become sth/sb

transporte *m.* transportation

transporte aéreo air freight

transporte marítimo shipping

transporte público public transportation

tratar *v.* **1** to try

tratar de hacer algo to try to do sth

2 to treat

tratar bien/mal a algn to treat sb well/bad

3 to deal

tratar con algn to deal with sb

4 to call

tratar a algn de algo to call sb sth (¡Me trató de mentiroso!)

tratarse *v.* **1** to socialize

tratarse con algn to socialize with sb

2 to address

tratarse con respeto to show respect for each other, to treat (each) other with respect

tratarse de usted/tú to address each other as "usted"/"tú"

3 to be about

tratarse de to be about (¿De qué se trata la novela?)

través *adv.* across

a través de through

al través diagonally

de través *Méx.* diagonally

trepar *v.* to climb

trepar a algo, ~ por algo to climb up sth

treparse *v.* to climb

treparse a algo to climb sth

tropezar *v.* **1** to stumble

tropezar con algo to stumble over sth (Se tropezó con la silla.)

2 to run into

tropezar con algo/algn to run into sth/sb (¿A que no sabes con quién me tropecé hoy?)

trueque *m.* barter

a trueque de in exchange for

U

último/a *adj.* last

ser el/la último/a en hacer algo to be the last one to do sth (Fue el último en dejar el barco.)

V

vacilar *v.* to hesitate

vacilar en algo to hesitate to do sth (No vaciló en la respuesta.)

vacilar entre algo y algo to hesitate over sth (Estoy vacilando entre seguir con este empleo y buscar uno nuevo.)

valer *v.* **1** to be worth

más vale que had better/it's better that (Más vale que traigas lo que te pedí la semana pasada.)

valer más/menos to be more/less valuable

2 to be useful

valer de algo a algn to be useful (Mis protestas no valieron de nada.)

valer para algo to be good at sth

valerse *v.* **1** to use

valerse de algo/algn to use sth/sb

2 to manage

valerse por uno/a mismo/a to manage on one's own (No puede valerse por sí misma.)

vanguardia *f.* vanguard; avant-garde

estar/ir a la vanguardia (de algo) to be at the forefront (of sth)

vengar *v.* to avenge

vengar algo to avenge sth

vengarse *v.* to take revenge

vengarse de algo, ~ de algn por algo to take revenge (on sb) for sth

ver *v.* to see

a ver all right, now, so; let's see (A ver, ¿qué está pasando acá? Llamémoslo a ver qué nos dice.)

veras *f. pl.* something true (Lo dijo entre veras y bromas.)

de veras really (Te lo digo de veras.)

vestirse *v.* to get dressed; to dress up

vestirse de algo to dress up as sth

vez *f.* time

a la vez at the same time

a su vez in turn

a veces sometimes (A veces me olvido de hacer las compras.)

alguna vez sometime (Deberíamos invitarlos a cenar alguna vez.)

cada vez que each/every time (that)

de una vez (por todas) once and for all

de vez en cuando once in a while

en vez de instead of

por... vez for the... time

una vez que once (Una vez que termines la tarea, podrás jugar con la computadora.)

una y otra vez time after time

vilo *adv.* in the air

estar en vilo, seguir en ~ to be in the air

levantar a algn en vilo to lift sb up off the ground

mantenerse en vilo to be in suspense

virtud *f.* virtue

en virtud de by virtue of

virtudes curativas healing powers

vista *f.* sight

a la vista at sight

a primera vista at first sight

a simple vista to the naked eye

a vista de pájaro bird's-eye view

de vista by sight (A su hermana la conocemos solo de vista.)

en vista de que in view of

estar con la vista puesta en algo/algn, tener la ~ puesta en algo/algn to have one's eye on sth/sb

hacer la vista gorda to turn a blind eye

perder algo de vista, perder a algn de ~ to lose sight of sth/sb

perderse de vista to disappear from view

saltar a la vista the first thing that hits you/stands out

tener algo en vista, tener a algn en ~ to have sth/sb in view/mind

vistazo *m.* look

dar/echar un vistazo a algo to have a quick look at sth (Échale un vistazo al modelo y dime qué te parece.)

visto *p.p.* seen

por lo visto apparently

volumen *m.* volume

a todo volumen at full volume

subir/bajar el volumen to turn the volume up/down

volumen de ventas volume of sales

volver *v.* to do again

volver a hacer algo to do sth again

votar *v.* to vote

votar a algn, ~ por algn to vote for sb

votar a favor de algo, ~ en contra de algo to vote for/against sth

voz *f.* voice

cambiar de voz, mudar de ~ to change one's voice

correr la voz to spread the word

dar la voz de alarma to raise the alarm

1. Lee la conversación telefónica entre Pablo y su bisabuela. Luego, elige la opción correcta. `1.D`

PABLO ¡Hola, abuela! ¿Cómo estás? ¡Habla Pablo, tu bisnieto!

ABUELA ¿Mi qué? No se oye muy bien...

PABLO Tu (1) _____ (bi-snie-to / bis-nie-to / bis-niet-o). Te estoy llamando desde Alicante.

ABUELA ¿Desde dónde?

PABLO (2) _____ (A-li-can-te / A-li-cant-e / Ali-ca-nte). ¿Recibiste una postal mía, una con muchas flores?

ABUELA ¿Con muchas qué?

PABLO Con muchas (3) _____ (fl-o-res / flo-res / flor-es). La compré en una tienda muy linda.

ABUELA ¿La qué?

PABLO La (4) _____ (co-mpré / comp-ré / com-pré) en una tienda. Bueno, quería decirte que estoy muy bien aquí. La gente es muy amable y no hay ningún problema.

ABUELA ¿Qué dijiste sobre un poema?

PABLO No, dije (5) _____ (pro-blem-a / pro-ble-ma / prob-le-ma).

ABUELA Bueno, te mando un beso y llámame de nuevo, querido Javier.

PABLO ¡Pero si soy (6) _____ (Pa-blo / Pab-lo / Pa-bl-o)!

2. Eres editor(a) en un periódico y debes corregir la forma en que se separaron en sílabas las palabras. `1.D`

> **¿Quieres ser mi compañera de** (1) **v-** _____
> **iaje?** Me llamo Daniel y soy un (2) ho- _____
> mbre de treinta y dos años de (3) eda- _____
> d. Busco una mujer joven que (4) qu- _____
> iera ir de vacaciones pronto a (5) Eur- _____
> opa y que le guste mucho ver (6) ciud- _____
> ades nuevas y visitar muchos (7) mus- _____
> eos. Si le interesara, no dude en (8) ll- _____
> amarme. ¡Hasta pronto!

3. Indica con _Sí_ o _No_ si es posible separar en sílabas las vocales subrayadas. Si respondes _Sí_, muestra cómo lo harías. `1.D`

1. p<u>ia</u>no _____
2. c<u>ua</u>dro _____
3. f<u>eo</u> _____
4. c<u>ao</u>s _____
5. <u>ai</u>re _____
6. r<u>ue</u>da _____
7. t<u>ea</u>tro _____
8. barr<u>io</u> _____

4. Síntesis Separa en sílabas estas palabras. `1.D`

1. cepillo _____
2. excelente _____
3. pantalones _____
4. poeta _____
5. cielo _____
6. hacia _____
7. suave _____
8. aprender _____
9. empleado _____
10. oxígeno _____
11. empresa _____
12. Paraguay _____
13. anochecer _____
14. callejón _____
15. carruaje _____

5. ¿Con o sin tilde? Lee esta carta y decide si estas palabras llevan tilde o no. `1.E`

Querida Juana:

(1) _____ (Te / Té) escribo desde Medellín. ¡Estamos tan cerca! No (2) _____ (se / sé) cuántos días me quedaré aquí, pero espero que puedas venir a visitarme. ¿Quieres que te (3) _____ (de / dé) mi número de teléfono? (4) _____ (Si / Sí) quieres, puedes llamarme por las tardes. (5) _____ (Tu / Tú) sí que me has dado tu teléfono, ¿verdad? Hasta pronto.

(6) _____ (Tu / Tú) amiga, Paula

6. Ordena las palabras en esta tabla según sean llanas, agudas o esdrújulas. `1.E`

| balón | álbum | silla | ballets | lágrimas | césped | árbol |
| palabra | razón | ídolos | cómpramelo | estoy | rápido | pasión |

Llanas	Agudas	Esdrújulas

7. Forma las palabras. Recuerda colocar o quitar la tilde si es necesario. `1.E`

1. trae + los = _____
2. póster + es = _____
3. devuelve + los = _____
4. récord + s = _____
5. tomate + s = _____
6. inglés + es = _____
7. colección + es = _____
8. come + los = _____

8. En estas oraciones hay palabras que deberían llevar tilde. ¡Corrígelas! `1.E`

1. ¿Hoy es miercoles o jueves? _____
2. Hace ocho dias que nadie me llama. ¡Me siento sola! _____
3. Papá, regalanos camisetas de baloncesto para Navidad. ¡Por favor! _____
4. ¿Quieres venir a tomar un te a casa? _____
5. ¡Cuántos arboles hay en este bosque! _____
6. La profesora me dijo que este calculo estaba mal. ¿Pero dónde está el error? _____

9. En estas palabras, indica dónde está el hiato (si es que lo hay) y qué tipo de vocales lo forman: *fuertes* **(F) y** *débiles* **(D).** `1.E`

1. oído _____
2. maíz _____
3. aeroplano _____
4. compañía _____
5. cooperar _____
6. repetía _____
7. Mediterráneo _____
8. reescribir _____
9. Luis _____
10. zanahoria _____
11. león _____
12. tío _____

10. Lee la historia de Martín e indica al menos seis palabras que tengan hiato. `1.E`

Hace poco estuve con Raúl, un gran amigo mío. Siempre lo veo los fines de semana, pero esta vez nos vimos aunque era lunes. Me contó que tuvo una pelea con su novia, María. Dice que incluso le mandó a su casa un ramo de flores con un poema, pero sin buenos resultados. La realidad es que yo tampoco creo que haya una solución. Espero que ella lo llame y se reconcilien un día de estos.

11. ¿Con o sin tilde? En cada oración, hay una palabra con un error. Corrígela. `1.E`

1. Él hermano de Carla todavía no sabe escribir. _____

2. ¡Cuántas veces té he dicho que no tires los papeles al piso! _____

3. Aún si tuviera dinero, no compraría una casa en la playa. _____

4. No debo engordar mas. De lo contrario, podría afectar mi salud. _____

5. ¡Ya se cómo resolver este problema! _____

6. Sí vamos a la playa, debemos llevar sombrero y protección solar. _____

7. ¡Este libro es para tí! _____

8. Señora, la operación de su marido fué exitosa. _____

9. Éstas sillas son muy económicas, ¡no pierda esta oportunidad! _____

10. ¡Te ví ayer en el parque! Estabas con tu amigo José. _____

12. Completa el aviso publicitario con los pronombres interrogativos y exclamativos de la lista. `1.E`

cómo	como	quién	quien	dónde	donde	que	qué

¿(1) _____ no soñó alguna vez con una luna de miel (2) _____ sea inolvidable? Podemos ayudarte a planear tu viaje tal (3) _____ lo desees, ¡con (4) _____ hayas elegido para pasar el resto de tu vida! ¿(5) _____ preferirías pasar tu luna de miel? ¿(6) _____ prefieres: playa, montañas o campo? Te damos consejos sobre los mejores lugares (7) _____ podrás disfrutar del romance. ¿(8) _____ puedes comunicarte con nosotros? Llámanos al 435 423 847 o visita nuestra página web (www.lunasllenasdemiel.com).

13. Usa los adjetivos de la lista para reescribir estas oraciones con un adverbio que termine en -*mente*. `1.E`

atento	frecuente	público	rápido	sincero	teórico

1. Marta corrió <u>con rapidez</u> hasta la cocina. ¡Su comida se estaba quemando! _____

2. Lee cada frase <u>con atención</u> y encontrarás el error. _____

3. Debes cepillarte los dientes <u>con frecuencia</u> para no tener caries. _____

4. Dímelo <u>con sinceridad</u>, ¿te gusta mi nuevo corte de cabello? _____

5. <u>En teoría</u>, nada debería salir mal. Pero no siempre es así. _____

6. No me gusta que me llames "Juanita" <u>en público</u>, mamá. Dime "Juana", por favor. _____

14. Escribe el singular o el plural de estas palabras. `1.E`

1. _____ → márgenes

2. aborigen → _____

3. _____ → condiciones

4. _____ → manteles

5. árbol → _____

6. _____ → intereses

7. _____ → meses

8. _____ → atunes

15. El señor González es un empresario con muchas actividades. Completa las oraciones con la opción correcta. `1.E`

6:00 a.m. El señor González salió de su casa y su (1) _____ lo llevó al club.
a. chofer   b. chófer   c. Ambas opciones son posibles.

7:30 a.m. Después de hacer ejercicio y jugar al (2) _____, se dio una ducha y se dirigió a su trabajo.
a. fútbol   b. futbol   c. Ambas opciones son posibles.

10:30 a.m. González habló por teléfono con un empleado sobre un reporte (3) _____ de América Latina.
a. economico-social   b. económico-social   c. Ambas opciones son posibles.

1:30 p.m. González le escribe un correo electrónico a su secretaria. El asunto dice: "¿(4) _____ MI ALMUERZO?"
a. DONDE ESTA   b. DÓNDE ESTÁ   c. DONDE ESTÁ

4:00 p.m. González sube al (5) _____ piso del edificio y se reúne con sus empleados.
a. décimoséptimo   b. décimoseptimo   c. decimoséptimo

6:00 p.m. González les comunica a sus empleados que, debido a la mala situación (6) _____, debe despedir al 50% de su plantilla.
a. político-económica   b. politico-economica   c. político-economica

16. Coloca la tilde donde haga falta. Como ayuda, las sílabas tónicas están subrayadas. `1.E`

1. pais	6. corazones	11. actriz	16. poesia
2. amplio	7. dimelo	12. holandes	17. fisico-quimico
3. gramatica	8. actuar	13. debiles	18. cantalo
4. hacia	9. dime	14. creeme	19. veintitres
5. razon	10. vi	15. sutilmente	20. aquello

17. El teclado de la computadora de Julia funciona muy mal. ¡No escribe las comas! Ayuda a Julia a corregir el correo electrónico que escribe a su amiga, Guadalupe. `1.F`

De:	julia@micorreo.com
Para:	guadalupe@micorreo.com
Asunto:	Bienvenida

Hola Guadalupe:

¡Bienvenida a Córdoba amiga! ¡Qué bien que ya estés en la ciudad! No veo la hora de encontrarnos pero estoy un poco ocupada: por las mañanas voy a un curso de cocina. Estoy muy contenta con el curso. La profesora que es tan buena onda resultó ser mi vecina. ¿Puedes creerlo?

¿Te parece que mañana nos veamos? Podemos dar un paseo en barco ir a museos y caminar en el parque. Allá hace frío pero aquí calor. Para mí todo fue tan genial cuando llegué a esta ciudad. ¡Te encantará conocerla!

Un abrazo muy grande

Julia

18. Lee lo que escribió Lucía en su diario de viaje. Completa su relato con la opción correcta. `1.F`

Santiago de Chile_____ (; / . / ,) (1)
3 de febrero de 2010

Este es mi último día en Santiago y he visto todo lo que quería ver_____ (: / , / ;) (2) la Plaza de Armas, el mercado central, el centro financiero y el teatro municipal. Para mí_____ (; / , / :) (3) lo más increíble de esta ciudad es que tanta gente vive en ella. Santiago_____ (; / , / :) (4) que fue

fundada en el siglo XVI_____ (; / , / :) (5) ¡hoy tiene 6_____ (; / , / :) (6) 6 millones de habitantes! Otra cosa que me encantó sobre esta ciudad fue la gente. ¡Conocí a personas tan amables! Por ejemplo, a Juanita, la cocinera del hostal _____ (: / , / :) (7) a Pablo, el vendedor de periódicos_____ (: / , / :) (8) y a Esther, la camarera de un bar.

Espero volver algún día... ¡y pronto!

19. Lee las oraciones y complétalas con los elementos del recuadro. `1.F`

> ...   ()   —   —   « »   :   -

1. La asociación franco_____alemana de Lima hoy celebra su centenario.
2. Juan me miró a los ojos y me dijo_____"Quiero casarme contigo."
3. _____¡Hola, Carlos! Cuánto tiempo sin vernos.
   _____¡Hola, Manuela! Un gusto verte de nuevo.
4. Este año leí muchos poemas, pero el que más me gustó fue _____Al callarse_____, de Pablo Neruda.
5. Compramos tantas cosas para la fiesta: dulces, decoración, bebidas, comida_____
6. En Buenos Aires_____ la capital de Argentina_____ hay cada vez más turistas.

20. Corrige la puntuación en estas oraciones. `1.F`

1. Hoy hace tanto calor, ¡verdad!
2. El prefijo —anti significa "contrario".
3. Sara, Paula, Gastón, José, y Pedro fueron al cine el domingo.
4. El jefe de Silvina (que se llama Juan Carlos (igual que el rey de España) no quiere que sus empleados lleguen ni un minuto tarde al trabajo.
5. Lee los capítulos 1.5 y resúmelos en una hoja.
6. Mi hermana que siempre está de mal humor hoy estaba sonriente.
7. —Vienes a la fiesta?
   —Sí si me invitas.
8. Hola. Roberto. Cómo estás?

21. Ricardo visitó con sus compañeros de clase la Ciudad de México. Completa su relato con la opción correcta. `1.G`

El (1) _____ (Lunes / lunes) pasado visité por primera vez el (2) _____ (Distrito Federal / distrito federal), la capital de México. Yo no lo sabía, pero es la octava ciudad más rica del mundo: ¡su (3) _____ (PBI / Pbi) es de 315 000 millones de dólares! Los (4) _____ (Mexicanos / mexicanos) son muy simpáticos y serviciales. El señor (5) _____ (del Valle / Del Valle), el guía de nuestra excursión, no era de México, sino de (6) _____ (el Salvador / El Salvador). Creo que lo que más me interesó de esta excursión fue visitar la (7) _____ (Universidad nacional autónoma de México / Universidad Nacional Autónoma de México). Sí, ¡la famosa (8) _____ (UNAM / Unam)! Ojalá que pueda estudiar allí dentro de unos años.

22. A estas palabras les falta una letra. Elige la opción correcta para cada palabra. `1.G`

1. (v/V) _____aca
2. (B/b) _____olivianos
3. (P/p) _____rovincia
4. (O/o) _____toño
5. (a/A) _____mazónico
6. (V/v) _____alencia
7. (t/T) _____ijuana
8. (F/f) _____ebrero

23. En estas oraciones no se usan correctamente las mayúsculas. Corrige los errores. `1.G`

1. Mi mamá nació en milán, pero no sabe hablar bien Italiano.
2. La gente fuera de españa no dice "euskadi", sino "país Vasco".
3. El estrecho de Magallanes es un paso marítimo ubicado al sur de sudamérica.
4. El Reino de arabia saudita limita con Jordania y Kuwait, entre otros países.
5. El Río Amazonas tiene un gran caudal de agua.
6. una de las grandes capitales de la moda es parís.
7. La Ciudad de Río De Janeiro es mi ciudad favorita.

24. Síntesis Une los elementos de las dos columnas para formar oraciones. `1.D–1.G`

1. En una enumeración, antes de la *y*,
2. Las estaciones del año
3. Para expresar duda, inseguridad o temor,
4. Son ejemplos de palabras con acento diacrítico
5. Los acrónimos de cuatro letras o menos
6. En algunos países, para expresar un decimal,
7. Son ejemplos de palabras con hiato
8. Antes de las citas textuales
9. Son ejemplos de palabras con triptongo

a. *maestro* y *coexistir.*
b. *aún* y *té.*
c. no se usa la coma.
d. se usa la coma.
e. se usan los puntos suspensivos.
f. se usan los dos puntos.
g. *Paraguay* y *Uruguay.*
h. se escriben en mayúscula.
i. se escriben en minúscula.

Practice more at **vhlcentral.com.**

Nouns

Chapter 2

1. Coloca estos sustantivos en la columna adecuada. `2.A`

fiscal	comediante	representante	malabarista	ciclista	gerenta
profesora	portero	delfín	pájaro	poeta	yegua
artista	nuera	escritor	cirujana	bailarín	toro

Masculino	Femenino	Masculino/Femenino

2. Cambia el género de estos sustantivos. `2.A`

1. el accionista → _____
2. la madrina → _____
3. el periodista → _____
4. el cuñado → _____
5. el joven → _____
6. la yegua → _____

7. la doctora → _____
8. el cocodrilo macho → _____
9. la modelo → _____
10. el emperador → _____
11. el gallo → _____
12. la suegra → _____

3. Lara escribió una composición para la escuela. Complétala con el artículo correspondiente (*la* para femenino, *el* para masculino). `2.A`

Tema: (1) _____ barrio donde vivo

Mi barrio es muy pequeño. Todo (2) _____ vecindario se conoce. Por (3) _____ tarde, todos los niños jugamos en (4) _____ calle. (5) _____ verdad es que todo es muy tranquilo. Solo debemos tener cuidado con (6) _____ tranvía y los coches.

Tenemos muchos lugares para divertirnos. Por ejemplo, (7) _____ cine. Durante (8) _____ fin de semana, en (9) _____ programa hay películas infantiles. Si no hay una película interesante, vemos (10) _____ televisión o escuchamos (11) _____ radio. Pero (12) _____ parque es mi lugar favorito.

En nuestra cuadra, viven muchas familias de distintos países. (13) _____ mitad de ellas viene de Latinoamérica. Lo cierto es que es muy divertido, porque somos todos diferentes, pero (14) _____ comunicación es muy buena siempre.

4. Elige la palabra que no tiene el mismo género que las otras del grupo. `2.A`

1. realidad   mal   poesía   foto
2. dolor   sol   corazón   luz
3. canción   diente   papel   cielo
4. heroína   problema   flor   libertad
5. inteligencia   gente   fantasma   calle
6. día   rol   color   sinceridad

7. muerte   confirmación   ayuda   mapa
8. amor   solicitud   viuda   cara
9. amanecer   poder   lunes   vejez
10. dilema   drama   idea   síntoma
11. rojo   enero   Barcelona   Pacífico
12. tabú   rubí   clase   cine

5. Elige la opción correcta para completar estas oraciones. `2.A`

1. _____ (La orden/El orden) vino directamente del jefe. Debemos obedecerle.

2. En la misa, _____ (la cura/el cura) rezó por la paz en el mundo.

3. Silvio, ¿puedes ayudarme? Tengo solo _____ (una pendiente/un pendiente) y se hace tarde para ir a la fiesta.

4. _____ (La Everest/El Everest) es una montaña que mide más de 8000 metros de altura.

5. Sin dudas, _____ (la rosa/el rosa) es mi color favorito para los vestidos de mis muñecas.

6. Me golpeé y ahora me duelen mucho _____ (la frente/el frente) y los ojos.

6. Lee esta descripción sobre la ciudad de Bogotá. Elige la opción correcta. `2.A`

1. La ciudad de Bogotá es _____ capital de la República de Colombia.
   a. la   b. el

2. Está ubicada en _____ centro del país.
   a. la   b. el

3. Tiene _____ población de casi siete millones de habitantes.
   a. una   b. un

4. La ciudad ofrece _____ gran cantidad de museos, teatros y bibliotecas.
   a. una   b. un

5. _____ Bogotá es el río más extenso de los alrededores de la ciudad.
   a. La   b. El

6. _____ orquídea es la flor que se usa como símbolo de Bogotá.
   a. La   b. El

7. Los lugares turísticos más importantes son _____ jardín botánico, el observatorio nacional y el mirador La Calera.
   a. la   b. el

8. _____ azul predomina en la bandera de esta ciudad.
   a. La   b. El

7. Escribe el plural de estas palabras. `2.B`

1. vela _____
2. perro _____
3. canción _____
4. paquete _____
5. emoción _____

6. coche _____
7. papá _____
8. tren _____
9. pez _____
10. mujer _____

11. día _____
12. país _____
13. policía _____
14. reloj _____
15. viernes _____

8. Completa las oraciones con las palabras de la lista. Atención: ¡debes usarlas en plural! `2.B`

| ratón | pared | señor | club | corazón | voz | paz | bus |

1. _____, pueden pasar al salón. La directora los espera.

2. ¡Cuántas historias de _____ rotos!

3. Hay _____ que nos llevan a Buenos Aires por un precio muy económico.

4. Hagamos las _____. No quiero más discusiones.

5. Los _____ de fútbol importantes tienen estadios gigantes.

6. Escucho _____ de niños gritando ¡y no puedo dormir!

7. Ten cuidado. Por la noche, siempre hay _____ en la cocina.

8. Quiero pintar las _____ de color rojo. ¿Qué te parece?

9. Marca los plurales en cada frase e indica si son *regulares* (R) o *irregulares* (I). `2.B`

1. Los miércoles jugamos a las cartas. _____

2. Mi tía compra los mejores tés en la tienda de la esquina. _____

3. En el tribunal, los jueces trabajan hasta la media tarde. _____

4. ¡Quiero comprarme esos pantalones! _____

5. Los paréntesis se usan para encerrar información que amplía la de la oración principal. _____

6. El profesor corrige las tesis de sus alumnos. _____

7. Me encantan los rubíes. _____

8. Con la computadora, puedes contar los caracteres de un texto fácilmente. _____

10. En cada oración, elige la opción correcta. `2.B`

1. El plural de *virus* es _____.
   a. *virus*   b. *viruses*
2. El singular de *cumpleaños* es _____.
   a. *cumpleaño*   b. *cumpleaños*
3. El plural de *crisis* es _____.
   a. *crisises*   b. *crisis*
4. El plural de *compás* es _____.
   a. *compás*   b. *compases*
5. El plural de *comedor* es _____.
   a. *comedores*   b. *comedors*
6. El plural de *régimen* es _____.
   a. *régimenes*   b. *regímenes*

11. Indica si estos sustantivos existen en plural y singular, o solamente en plural. `2.B`

1. oasis _____
2. nupcias _____
3. gafas _____
4. prismáticos _____
5. víveres _____
6. tabúes _____
7. análisis _____
8. imágenes _____
9. jueves _____
10. tijeras _____
11. vacaciones _____
12. afueras _____

12. Corrige este aviso publicitario. Hay 10 errores. `2.B`

> **¡Buscamos jovenes con gana de aprender!**
>
> ¿Tienes entre 18 y 23 año y eres estudiante de Administración con espíritus emprendedor? ¿Quieres ganar experiencia y trabajar en la vacación? GREA es una empresa que se encuentra en el alrededor de la ciudad de Panamá y ofrece muchos beneficio para sus empleados. El trabajo es de cuatro hora diarias y ofrecemos interesantes condición de contratación. Si te interesa la propuesta, envíanos tu currículums por correo electrónico.

13. Cecilia nos cuenta cómo se sintió la primera vez que viajó en avión. Completa el relato con la opción correcta. `2.C`

Mi primer viaje en avión

El viernes pasado fue la primera vez que viajé en avión. Pero fue un viaje (1) _____ (cortito / cortote), porque duró solo media hora. No puedo mentirles, siempre les tuve algo de (2) _____ (miedito / miedazo) a los aviones.

El avión era enorme. Tenía unas (3) _____ (alitas / alotas) y dos (4) _____ (turbinitas / turbinotas). Pero, por dentro, todo era distinto. En cada fila, había muchos (5) _____ (asientotes / asientitos) donde mi papá casi no podía sentarse y (6) _____ (ventanitas / ventanotas) que no me dejaban ver nada. ¡Parecía un (7) _____ (juguetito / juguetote)!

Cuando despegó, mi mamá me tomó la (8) _____ (manita / manota) y me dijo que me quedara (9) _____ (tranquilita / tranquilota). Mi hermano Daniel, que tiene solo tres años, se comportaba como un verdadero chico (10) _____ (grandote / grandecito). ¡Hasta quería ir a la cabina del piloto! Por suerte, el vuelo estuvo muy bien. Incluso pudimos ver unos (11) _____ (dibujotes / dibujitos) animados en una (12) _____ (pantallita / pantallota) que estaba en frente de cada asiento. ¡No veo la hora de volver a volar!

14. Gabriela está celosa de su hermana que acaba de nacer. Completa el correo electrónico que le escribe a su amiga Estela. `2.C`

Hola, Estela:

¿Cómo estás? Te escribo porque tengo un (1) _____ (problemón / problemita) y estoy tan triste. Hace un mes que nació mi (2) _____ (hermanucha / hermanita), Sandra, y, al parecer, ya no le importo a nadie. Es verdad que Sandra nació un poco (3) _____ (debilita / debilota). Ahora está más (4) _____ (fuertucha / fuertecita), pero sigue siendo el centro de atención. Debe ser porque tiene unos (5) _____ (ojitos / ojazos) azules. ¡Son los ojos más grandes que he visto! También sus pequeñas (6) _____ (manitas / manotas) son tan dulces. Quiero que (7) _____ (mamaza / mamita) me preste atención de nuevo. ¿Qué puedo hacer? ¡Gracias por tu (8) _____ (ayudita / ayudota)!

Gabriela

15. Síntesis Decide si estas afirmaciones son ciertas o falsas. Si son falsas, corrígelas. `2.A–2.D`

Cierto	Falso	
☐	☐	1. Es correcto decir *la serpiente hembra*.
☐	☐	2. Son despectivos *casucha, peliculón* y *flacucho*.
☐	☐	3. *Yerno* es el femenino de *nuera*.
☐	☐	4. En algunos países hispanohablantes, *azúcar* es masculino; y en otros, es femenino.
☐	☐	5. Los diminutivos de *pez, carro* y *bebé* son *pezecito, carrito* y *bebito*.
☐	☐	6. *Enseres* solamente puede usarse en plural.
☐	☐	7. Es incorrecto usar *parienta* como femenino de *pariente*.
☐	☐	8. El aumentativo **-ito** indica afecto cuando uno se dirige a personas queridas.
☐	☐	9. El aumentativo de *nariz* es *narizota*.
☐	☐	10. *Perrazo* es un aumentativo.

16. Síntesis Elige la palabra que no pertenece al grupo. ¡Presta atención al género y al número! `2.A–2.D`

1. solterón   cincuentón   cuarentón   camión
2. viernes   veces   lunes   análisis
3. princesa   suegra   poeta   emperatriz
4. almirante   representante   mariscal   abogado
5. programa   dilema   problema   arena
6. enero   jueves   rojo   flor
7. cita   playita   manchita   pastillita
8. dosis   tesis   crisis   bis
9. baldes   padres   callejones   asistentes
10. clima   panorama   pasaje   madre

Practice more at **vhlcentral.com.**

1. Reescribe las oraciones colocando las partes subrayadas en femenino. 3.A

1. El líder anarquista nació en 1898. _____
2. El niño danzarín salta y salta sin parar. _____
3. El doctor alemán ahora vive en París. _____
4. Un ejecutivo importante renunció a su cargo. _____
5. He perdido mi gato negrote, mi juguete favorito. _____
6. El empleado gentil atiende a los clientes con una sonrisa. _____
7. El niño feliz jugaba en las hamacas del parque. _____
8. El fanático acosador no dejaba tranquila a la cantante. _____

2. Reescribe los sustantivos y adjetivos según las instrucciones. 3.A

1. sabor agradable → (plural) _____
2. perro particular → (femenino) _____
3. profesor conservador → (femenino) _____
4. niño albanés → (femenino) _____
5. político burgués → (femenino, plural) _____
6. salón posterior → (plural) _____
7. rostro paliducho → (plural) _____
8. joven bribón → (femenino) _____
9. plato tentador → (plural) _____
10. coche veloz → (plural) _____
11. publicación periódica → (plural) _____
12. aborigen guaraní → (plural) _____

3. Julieta y Martina deciden qué vestir para la fiesta de graduación. Completa la conversación con los adjetivos en el género y número adecuados. 3.B

JULIETA ¿Tienes una idea (1) _____ (claro) de qué vestirás para la graduación?

MARTINA Sí, tengo una falda y unos zapatos (2) _____ (rojo) que me gustaría combinar con una blusa y una cartera (3) _____ (anaranjado).

JULIETA ¿No te parece que con algo (4) _____ (blanco) quedaría mejor? ¿O unos (5) _____ (bonito) zapatos y falda de color amarillo?

MARTINA No sé, siempre me gustaron las vestimentas (6) _____ (colorido).

JULIETA Mira, yo podría prestarte un vestido con flores (7) _____ (amarillo) claro y tirantes (8) _____ (rojo).

MARTINA ¡Perfecto! Y podría entonces usar mis zapatos y cartera (9) _____ (verde).

JULIETA ¿Puedo verlos?

MARTINA Sí, aquí están. Y, ¿cómo luzco?

JULIETA ¡Como un (10) _____ (impactante) arco iris!

4. Francisco escribió un poema para su novia, Andrea. Completa el poema con los adjetivos y asegúrate de que el género y el número sean los adecuados. `3.B`

Tienes unos (1) _____ (hermoso) y (2) _____ (grande) ojos,

y una mirada y sonrisa (3) _____ (bondadoso).

Unas cejas y cabellos (4) _____ (pelirrojo)...

Y una voz tan (5) _____ (fabuloso).

Y yo, un ser (6) _____ (afortunado), como pocos,

miro esas pupilas y pestañas (7) _____ (esplendoroso),

y, con mi corazón en pleno alboroto,

deseo que un buen día seas mi esposa.

5. En cada oración decide si el adjetivo entre paréntesis debe ir antes o después del sustantivo. `3.C`

1. Todos dicen que es lindo, pero, para mí, es un _____ perro _____. (feíto)

2. Compré un _____ libro _____ en una feria de artículos usados. (agotado)

3. La _____ revista _____ *Saludables siempre* se publica cada dos meses. (médica)

4. La _____ película _____ del famoso director no tuvo el éxito esperado. (última)

5. Disculpe, señora, ya no tenemos más ese juguete. Se vendió como _____ pan _____. (caliente)

6. La _____ organización _____ lucha por los derechos de los trabajadores. (sindical)

7. La _____ situación _____ de ese país empeora día a día. (social)

8. Juana es una _____ amiga _____. Siempre me ayuda cuando lo necesito. (buena)

6. Olivia escribió una carta al editor del periódico local. Decide si la ubicación de los adjetivos es adecuada. Si no lo es, corrígela. `3.C`

Editor estimado:

En la provincia oriental de Recodo, conseguir un digno trabajo es duro. La oficina laboral no ofrece una amable atención. Lo que es peor, los empleados maleducados se ríen de la gente en su cara propia. La realidad cruda es que no hay puestos de trabajo disponibles. Sin embargo, todos están en derecho pleno de ser tratados cordialmente.

Le pido que comunique esta situación a las nacionales autoridades.

Saludos,

Olivia P.

7. Ordena los elementos para armar una oración que tenga sentido. `3.C`

1. En realidad, | concurso | tienen posibilidades | ambos | de ganar | participantes | famoso | el
   En realidad, ... _____

2. Pedí | pañuelo | un | expresamente | azul | que me enviaran
   Pedí... _____

3. muchas | romance | que buscan | personas | un | Hay | veraniego
   Hay... _____

4. nocturna | activa | deportistas | tienen | una | vida | Pocos
   Pocos... _____

5. mediterránea | calor | en esta | Hace | playa | tanto
   Hace... _____

6. principal | edificio | en la | El | concurrida | calle Posadas | se encuentra
   El... _____

8. Completa las oraciones con el adjetivo y el sustantivo en el orden correcto. Cada palabra puede usarse una sola vez. `3.C`

menor	buen	ciertas	alta	noticias	lenguas	tensión	gusto
gran	malas	único	santo	padre	hijo	amigo	hermana

1. No sé compartir mis juguetes. Debe ser porque soy _____ _____.
2. ¡Qué bien decorada que está la casa! Ella tiene _____ _____.
3. ¡Cuidado con esos cables! ¡Son de _____ _____!
4. A menudo al Papa se lo denomina _____ _____.
5. No escuches lo que dicen las _____ _____.
6. Un amigo que está a tu lado en momentos difíciles es un _____ _____.
7. Mamá, no puede ser, siempre es lo mismo con mi _____ _____.
8. No te preocupes, no sabemos si son _____ _____.

9. Lee el resumen de un capítulo de la novela *Caballero a caballo* y complétalo. Asegúrate de que el género y el número de los adjetivos sean los adecuados. `3.D`

En el (1) _____ (primero) capítulo de esta (2) _____ (grande) novela, conocemos al (3) _____ (bueno) caballero José de Salamanca, quien emprende un largo viaje en busca de su futura esposa. En la (4) _____ (tercero) jornada, se encuentra con la imagen de (5) _____ (Santo) Diego, quien le aconseja que no siga con su búsqueda, porque podría ser peligroso para su corazón. José de Salamanca no hace caso al supuesto (6) _____ (malo) augurio y sigue adelante. En la (7) _____ (cuarto) jornada de su travesía, recibe una (8) _____ (malo) noticia. Sus (9) _____ (grande) esperanzas se destrozan cuando se entera de que su princesa ya es la esposa del conde de Aranjuez.

10. Dos hermanas discuten sobre sus habitaciones. Completa el diálogo usando comparativos y superlativos. `3.E`

MARIEL Mi ventana es (1) _____ (+ / grande) que la tuya.

CONSTANZA Te equivocas; mi ventana es (2) _____ (+ / grande) de la casa.

MARIEL Mi habitación es (3) _____ (+ / luminosa) que la tuya.

CONSTANZA ¡De ninguna manera! La mía es (4) _____ (+ / luminosa) del primer piso.

MARIEL Y mi cama es (5) _____ (+ / buena) que la tuya.

CONSTANZA ¿En qué mundo vives? Mi cama (6) _____ (+ / buena) de todas.

MARIEL Pero, ¿has visto qué tranquila que es mi habitación? Es (7) _____ (− / ruidosa) que la tuya.

CONSTANZA Imposible. La mía es (8) _____ (− / ruidosa) de la casa.

MARIEL Claro, tú crees que siempre tienes la razón, porque eres la hermana (9) _____ (+ / vieja).

CONSTANZA ¿Ves? Me dices eso porque te aprovechas de ser (10) _____ (+ / joven) de la familia.

MARIEL Uy, ¡qué aburrida que eres, Constanza!

CONSTANZA No, ¡tú eres (11) _____ (+ / aburrida) del mundo!

11. Elige la opción correcta para completar cada oración. `3.E`

1. Juan es _____ de los tres hermanos.
   a. el mayor   b. el más viejo   c. a y b

2. Carlos es _____ en matemáticas que Marta.
   a. más bueno   b. mejor   c. mayor

3. El libro es _____ de lo que pensaba.
   a. más bueno   b. mejor   c. menor

4. El accidente fue _____ de lo que imaginábamos.
   a. más malo   b. peor   c. el peor

5. Mi hermana es _____ que mi hermano. Ella nunca miente y siempre me ayuda.
   a. mejor   b. la más buena   c. más buena

12. ¡Qué exagerada que es Eloísa! Completa las oraciones con el superlativo usando el sufijo *-ísimo/a*. `3.E`

1. Paula dice que su perro es muy flaco, pero el mío es _____.

2. Concepción me contó que su hermano es muy tonto, pero el mío es _____.

3. Catalina siempre se queja de que su mochila es muy pesada, pero la mía es _____.

4. Mi hermana Sara dice que ella es muy ordenada, pero yo soy _____.

5. Clara cree que su profesora es muy simpática, pero la mía es _____.

6. A Joan la película le pareció muy triste, pero a mí me pareció _____.

7. Eva dice que tiene muchos amigos, pero yo tengo _____.

8. Y mi mamá dice que soy muy exagerada, ¡pero yo digo que soy _____!

13. Síntesis Indica qué ejemplo(s) corresponde(n) a cada afirmación. `3.A–3.E`

a. un problema técnico	g. el niño debilucho
b. una gran mujer	h. una forma mejor
c. las niñas y mujeres contentas	i. un hombre narigón
d. la primera vez	j. el caso más importante
e. el defensor ecologista	k. las casas y jardines caros
f. el pobre hombre	l. un diario político-económico

1. Algunos adjetivos no varían con el género.

2. Algunos adjetivos se apocopan (abrevian) cuando van delante de un sustantivo.

3. Algunos adjetivos no se apocopan (abrevian) cuando van delante de un sustantivo femenino.

4. Algunos adjetivos cambian de significado según estén delante o detrás de un sustantivo.

5. Algunos adjetivos solo tienen una posición posible.

6. Algunos adjetivos tienen comparativos irregulares.

7. La mayoría de los adjetivos tienen superlativos regulares.

8. Cuando hay varios sustantivos de distinto género antes de un adjetivo, este último toma la forma masculina en plural.

9. Cuando hay varios sustantivos de igual género, el adjetivo toma el mismo género en plural.

10. Algunos sustantivos forman adjetivos al agregar un sufijo aumentativo.

11. Los adjetivos con sufijos apreciativos se colocan después del sustantivo.

Practice more at **vhlcentral.com**.

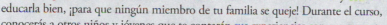
1. Lee el artículo que se publicó en el periódico escolar. Marca los determinantes que aparecen en él. `4.A–4.B`

Amo educado, perro educado

¿Te gustan las mascotas? ¿Siempre quisiste tener una, pero tu mamá piensa que es demasiado trabajo? ¡Tenemos tu solución!

Somos un equipo de veterinarios que trabaja en un albergue con muchos perros abandonados. Algunos perros son cachorros, pero otros son más grandecitos. Estos animalitos buscan amor: ¡sabemos que tú puedes dárselo!

Sabemos que cuidar de un perro no es fácil y muchas madres no quieren encargarse de él. Por eso, te ofrecemos un curso introductorio al cuidado de animales: aprenderás cómo satisfacer todas las necesidades de tu mascota y cómo educarla bien, ¡para que ningún miembro de tu familia se queje! Durante el curso, conocerás a otros niños y jóvenes que te contarán sus experiencias con sus mascotas. Cada uno de ellos tiene historias fantásticas: de amor, de momentos inolvidables, pero también de bastante sacrificio. Por último, cuando hayas acabado el curso y aún tengas muchas ganas de tener un perro, te daremos uno en adopción. El año pasado, cuarenta mascotas encontraron un hogar feliz... ¿Qué esperas? Visita nuestro sitio web www.educaryadoptarperros.com y nos pondremos en contacto contigo.

---

2. Para cada ejemplo, decide si la palabra subrayada funciona como *determinante*, *pronombre* o *adverbio*. `4.A–4.B`

Ejemplo	Determinante (con sustantivo explícito)	Pronombre (determinante con sustantivo implícito)	Adverbio
1. Las grandes capitales tienen <u>muchos</u> problemas de contaminación.			
2. Comí <u>demasiado</u> esta noche. Mañana debería comer cosas más livianas.			
3. <u>Esta</u> es la última vez que limpio la cocina después de que tú cocinas.			
4. Ya tienes <u>bastantes</u> discusiones con tu jefe... ¡haz las paces de una vez!			
5. Cuando esta casa sea <u>mía</u>, ¡haré fiestas todas las noches!			
6. ¡<u>Alguien</u> me quiere! Tengo una llamada perdida en mi teléfono celular.			
7. ¿Siempre de compras? Tienes que ahorrar. ¡No compres <u>más</u>!			
8. Con <u>tanto</u> humo de cigarrillo, no puedo respirar bien.			
9. Algunos compañeros son amables; pero <u>otros</u>, no.			
10. ¡<u>Esta</u> oportunidad de hacerme famoso es única!			
11. ¿Conoces el trabalenguas que se llama "<u>Tres</u> tristes tigres"?			
12. "<u>Menos</u> televisión y más estudio", me dijo la maestra.			
13. <u>Aquella</u> es mi novia. ¿Acaso no es hermosa?			
14. No hables <u>tanto</u>: ¡estamos en la biblioteca!			
15. <u>Pocas</u> veces me duermo después de las doce de la noche.			
16. ¡Qué hermosa noche! ¡<u>Tantas</u> estrellas!			

*Practice more at **vhlcentral.com.***

Actividades

1. Completa la conversación con el artículo definido adecuado. `5.A`

1. ¡Cuántas veces te dije que no uses mi ropa. ¡Usa _____ tuya!

2. Hoy a _____ cuatro de la tarde podríamos ir al cine, ¿no?

3. En _____ Estados Unidos, la gente no duerme la siesta; pero en _____ Salvador, sí.

4. Me encantan las manzanas, sobre todo _____ verdes.

5. Mis vecinos, _____ Rodríguez, van de vacaciones todos los años a México.

6. Dile a _____ señora Pérez que no podremos ir a la cena _____ jueves.

2. Elige la opción correcta en esta conversación. `5.B`

PABLO ¿Qué podríamos regalarles a tus padres para su aniversario de casados?

MARÍA No sé, no tengo (1) _____ (la/una/otra) idea clara.

PABLO Quizás podríamos comprarles (2) _____ (un/unos/otro) juego de platos; los que les regalamos hace (3) _____ (un/otro/unos) años se rompieron durante la mudanza. ¿Te acuerdas?

MARÍA Sí, es verdad. Pero, ¿cuánto dinero tenemos?

PABLO Creo que (4) _____ (un/otros/unos) ciento cincuenta dólares.

MARÍA Bien, el juego de platos me parece (5) _____ (un/otra/una) buena idea.

3. Completa esta carta con el artículo correspondiente. Si no es necesario usar un artículo, escribe X. `5.B–5.C`

Estimado (1) _____ doctor Pérez:

Quiero hacerle (2) _____ consulta. Estoy de vacaciones con mi hijo Joaquín en (3) _____ Perú desde hace (4) _____ días. Desde ayer, al niño le duele (5) _____ cabeza y tiene fiebre. ¿Puede ser por (6) _____ vacuna que le dio antes del viaje? ¿O tal vez por (7) _____ calurosa que es esta ciudad?

Ayer fuimos a (8) _____ hospital en Lima y (9) _____ médico me dijo que no es nada grave (*serious*). Pero yo quería preguntarle a usted, porque es su pediatra. No hay consejos como (10) _____ suyos.

Muchas gracias por su ayuda,

Paula Sánchez

4. Síntesis Completa el anuncio con las palabras de la lista. `5`

del	el	la	las	los	otra	un	un

Nuevo club escolar de artes marciales

Somos (1) _____ grupo de alumnos (2) _____ noveno año de la escuela Campos Verdes y queremos organizar un club de aficionados a (3) _____ artes marciales.

¿Practicas taekwon-do, karate o alguna (4) _____ arte marcial? ¿Quizás (5) _____ arte marcial que no conocemos?

Estamos en (6) _____ gimnasio de (7) _____ escuela todos (8) _____ jueves por la tarde. ¡Ven, que queremos conocerte!

🔊 Practice more at **vhlcentral.com.**

1. Escribe estos números en letras. `6.A–6.B`

1. 28 _____
2. 132 _____
3. 1200 _____
4. 19 _____
5. 44 _____

6. 102 _____
7. 333 _____
8. 1 000 000 _____
9. 1981 _____
10. 57 _____

2. Reescribe las oraciones usando números. `6.A–6.B`

1. Camila nació el tres de agosto de mil novecientos ochenta y tres.
_____

2. Tardaron ciento tres años en construir este castillo.
_____

3. Para el lunes próximo, tengo que leer doscientas veintiuna páginas.
_____

4. El empresario tiene un millón cuatrocientos mil dólares.
_____

5. Necesitamos vender veintinueve mil unidades este mes.
_____

6. El gobierno dio un subsidio de quinientos ocho dólares a cada vecino por la inundación.
_____

7. Debo devolverte setecientos noventa y un pesos antes del treinta de enero.
_____

8. Debido a la tormenta, se cayeron mil treinta y tres árboles.
_____

3. Reescribe las oraciones usando numerales colectivos. `6.C`

1. Hoy la tienda vendió <u>veinte</u> pares de zapatos en una tarde.
_____

2. En México, hay más de <u>treinta</u> periódicos distintos.
_____

3. Cuando ahorre más dinero, me compraré <u>cien</u> lápices de colores.
_____

4. Si compro <u>diez</u> camisetas, cada una cuesta $8,59.
_____

5. Sí, me llevaré <u>doce</u> rosas.
_____

6. Asistieron al congreso <u>sesenta</u> especialistas.
_____

7. ¡Hay más de <u>mil</u> lugares que quiero visitar!
_____

4. Cintia fue al mercado con su madre. Completa la conversación con las palabras de la lista. `6.C`

con	más	es igual a	un	por ciento	y	coma

CINTIA ¿Cuánto costó toda la compra?

MADRE En total, costó diez dólares (1) _____ cincuenta y cinco centavos.

CINTIA Ah, pensé que era más dinero. ¿Estás segura?

MADRE Sí, las verduras costaron ocho dólares; y la carne, cuatro (2) _____ cincuenta (3) _____ cinco centavos.

CINTIA Pero... ocho (4) _____ cuatro (5) _____ cincuenta y cinco (6) _____ doce (7) _____ cincuenta y cinco.

MADRE ¡Qué brillante que es mi hija! Me olvidé del descuento que hizo el verdulero.

CINTIA ¿Quizás (8) _____ veinticinco (9) _____ de descuento?

MADRE Increíble. ¡Ojalá tuviera (10) _____ diez (11) _____ de tu inteligencia!

5. Forma oraciones con elementos de las tres columnas. `6.D`

1. No puede ser: es la	centenario	hombre que se casó en la familia.
2. No sé qué regalarles a los abuelos para su	quinta	vez que lavo los platos.
3. Daniel fue el	milenaria	pieza se encuentra en el Museo Nacional.
4. El 30 de mayo es el	primer	de la fundación de mi pueblo.
5. Luis	trigésimo	era llamado "El Rey Sol".
6. En la actualidad, la	catorce	aniversario de casados.

6. Elige la opción correcta para completar las oraciones. `6.D`

1. El _____ (milenario/millonario) Juan Rodríguez pasa sus vacaciones en Mallorca.

2. La _____ (tercera/tercer) oportunidad es la última.

3. El papa Juan Pablo _____ (dos/segundo) murió en 2005.

4. $\frac{1}{100}$ es un _____ (centésimo/milésimo).

5. En su _____ (trigésimo/treintavo) aniversario, la empresa realizará una gran fiesta.

6. En total, corrí diez vueltas, pero en la _____ (quinta/quincuagésima), paré a descansar un rato.

7. Enrique _____ (ocho/octavo) pertenecía a la casa Tudor.

8. En el _____ (décimo primero/décimo primer) piso, vive mi abuela Porota.

7. Escribe las fracciones en las dos formas posibles. `6.E`

1. 1/2 _____ _____   4. 4/5 _____ _____

2. 1/13 _____ _____   5. 1/8 _____ _____

3. 1/4 _____ _____   6. 2/4 _____ _____

8. Lee la receta y corrígela. En total, hay siete errores. `6.D–6.E`

Cocina rápida: Recetas "en una millonésima segundo"

Hoy: Galletitas navideñas

Mezcle medias taza de azúcar con 250 gramos de harina (es decir, un cuarto kilo de harina). Derrita una quinta del paquete de mantequilla al fuego. Agregue la mantequilla a la primer mezcla. Estire la masa sobre una superficie plana y amásela. Colóquela en la nevera durante un cuarta de hora. Retire la masa y córtela en ocho partes iguales. Tome cada noveno y estírelo con un palo de amasar. Decórelos al gusto y llévelos al horno durante medio hora.

9. ¿Qué hora es? Escríbela de todas las maneras posibles. `6.F`

1. _____
_____
_____

4. _____
_____

2. _____
_____
_____

5. _____
_____
_____

3. _____
_____
_____

6. _____
_____
_____

10. Hoy es lunes y Marcos mira el calendario de esta semana. Escribe respuestas completas de acuerdo con el contenido del calendario. Debes escribir todos los números en letras. `6.F–6.G`

Lunes 1/10	Martes 2/10	Miércoles 3/10	Jueves 4/10	Viernes 5/10
8:40 a.m. Escuela	8.40 a.m. Escuela	8:40 a.m. Escuela	8:40 a.m. Escuela	8:40 a.m. Escuela
4:30 p.m. Natación	6:15 p.m. Regalo para la abuela	11:30 a.m. Examen de español		7:30 p.m. Cumpleaños de la abuela
		2:30 p.m. Dentista		

1. ¿Qué fecha es hoy?

2. ¿Qué sucede el tres de octubre?

3. ¿Qué debe hacer Marcos todos los días?

4. ¿A qué hora debe comprar el regalo para la abuela?

5. ¿A qué hora va a la escuela?

6. ¿Qué debe hacer el miércoles a las dos y media de la tarde?

7. ¿En qué fecha y a qué hora es la fiesta de cumpleaños de la abuela?

8. ¿Qué debe hacer Marcos en la tarde del lunes?

11. Completa la historia de Martina con las palabras de la lista. `6.H`

tenga	cumple	quinceañera	setentón	sesentona
cumplí	ser	sexagenaria	veinteañera	

Un año más

Ayer (1) _____ quince años. La semana que viene, como toda (2) _____, celebro mi cumpleaños con una gran fiesta. Invité a cincuenta personas, entre familiares y amigos. El mismo día de la fiesta, mi abuela (3) _____ sesenta años. En broma, le digo que es una (4) _____, pero ella me dice que es una (5) _____ en perfecto estado físico.

Ella me contó que, cuando ella era una (6) _____, había muchos jóvenes que estaban enamorados de ella. Pero ahora, solo tiene un vecino (7) _____ que la invita todos los domingos a bailar tango. ¡Qué graciosa que es mi abuela! Espero ser igual de divertida cuando (8) _____ su edad.

12. Lee el pronóstico del tiempo y escribe las preguntas para las respuestas dadas. `6.I`

Hoy	Mañana	Pasado mañana
Temperatura: 10 °C	Temperatura: −1 °C/4 °C	Temperatura: −3 °C/8 °C

1. ¿_____? Hoy hace 10 °C.

2. ¿_____? Mañana será de −1 °C.

3. ¿_____? Mañana será de 4 °C.

4. ¿_____? Serán de −3 °C y 8 °C.

5. ¿_____? No, aquí medimos la temperatura en grados centígrados.

13. Síntesis Elige la palabra que no pertenece al grupo. `6.B–6.J`

1. decenas   docenas   décadas   veintenas

2. tercio   cuarto   quinto   media

3. trigésimo   sexagésimo   décimo   veintiséis

4. máxima   mínima   promedio   próxima

5. cumplir   tener   celebrar   ser

6. sesentón   octogenario   veinteañero   quinceañero

7. décadas   siglos   milenios   millones

8. y veinte   y quince   y medio   y treinta

14. Síntesis Elige la opción correcta en cada oración. `6.B–6.J`

1. En la _____ de Hierro, comenzaron a fabricarse armas y herramientas de hierro.
   a. Época   b. Edad

2. Una _____ de huevos son diez huevos.
   a. decena   b. docena

3. Había _____ de personas en el festival.
   a. trescientos   b. cientos

4. _____ una y cuarto, nos encontramos en la estación.
   a. A las   b. A la

5. Debes llegar a las dos _____ diez, porque a las dos en punto sale el tren.
   a. menos   b. y

6. En España, se dice "_____ de enero".
   a. primero   b. uno

7. Hoy estamos a cero _____.
   a. grados   b. grado

8. Un plan quinquenal dura _____ años.
   a. cinco   b. quince

15. Síntesis Clasifica las palabras de la lista en la categoría apropiada. `6.B–6.J`

| billón | cuarentena | decena | doceava parte | millar | trescientos | un quinto |
| ciento uno | cuatro octavos | décimo cuarto | mil uno | quinto | trigésimo | la mitad |

Colectivos	Cardinales	Ordinales	Fraccionarios

16. Síntesis Escribe la palabra que corresponde a cada definición. `6.B–6.J`

1. período de mil años _____

2. la mitad de algo _____

3. que ocupa el lugar número diez en una serie ordenada de elementos _____

4. persona de más de diecinueve años y menos de treinta _____

5. una parte de las trece iguales en que se divide un todo _____

6. llegar a tener un número entero de años o meses _____

7. que ocupa el lugar número cien en una serie ordenada de elementos _____

8. que ha cumplido ochenta años y aún no ha llegado a los noventa _____

Practice more at **vhlcentral.com.**

1. Escribe las preguntas a estas respuestas. Asegúrate de incluir cuantificadores indefinidos en ellas. `7.A– 7.B`

1. ¿_____? No, ninguna de mis amigas vive en Perú.

2. ¿_____? Sí, hay un parque de diversiones cerca.

3. ¿_____? No, ningún compañero reprobó el examen.

4. ¿_____? No, ninguno de nosotros comerá esta comida.

5. ¿_____? Sí, comeré algunas frutas antes de dormir.

6. ¿_____? Sí, encontraré alguna oficina abierta en este barrio.

2. Completa las oraciones con las palabras de la lista. Atención: hay dos palabras que no debes usar. `7.B`

algún	alguno	algunos	nada	ningún	ningunas	ninguna	ninguno

1. No tienes _____ posibilidad de ganar la lotería. ¡Mejor ponte a trabajar!

2. _____ de los hombres de esta oficina está casado.

3. ¿Conoces _____ lugar divertido para ir de vacaciones?

4. No tengo _____ gafas de ese color. Mañana me compraré unas.

5. ¿_____ de ustedes podrá ir a la feria medieval? ¡Todos están ocupadísimos!

6. No hay _____ problema, podemos posponer la cita para la semana próxima.

3. Compara las oraciones y decide cuál es correcta. Es posible que ambas oraciones sean correctas. `7.B`

1. _____ a. ¿Conoces el nombre de alguna arma de fuego?
   b. ¿Conoces el nombre de algún arma de fuego?

2. _____ a. Nadie de ellos tiene cabello oscuro.
   b. Ninguno de ellos tiene cabello oscuro.

3. _____ a. No encuentro mis llaves por ningún sitio.
   b. No encuentro mis llaves por ninguno sitio.

4. _____ a. ¿Alguna vez vendrás a visitarme?
   b. ¿Algún vez vendrás a visitarme?

5. _____ a. No había blusa alguna que me gustara.
   b. No había ninguna blusa que me gustara.

4. Reordena las oraciones de forma correcta. `7.B`

1. para mí / No habrá / alguno / regalo / en este cumpleaños

_____

2. de los / en el sur de Brasil / algunos / campos / Iré a

_____

3. No, / come / de ellos / carne / ninguno

_____

4. chico / nos guste / hay / ningún / que / No

_____

5. Veré / que viven / en Colombia / a / parientes / algunos

_____

6. ¿? / mexicana / este año / maestra / alguna / Tendremos

_____

7. vestidos / algunos / mejores / de los / Nos probamos

_____

Actividades

5. Lee la carta que escribió Francisca a su amiga. Indica cuáles son los cuantificadores indefinidos que solo tienen forma positiva. `7.C`

> Querida Eva:
>
> ¡Te extraño cada día más! ¿Cuándo podremos vernos? Ya sé que tenemos muchas actividades, pero deberíamos encontrarnos cualquier día de estos.
>
> ¿Sería demasiado estrés que nos viéramos el miércoles? Los demás días de la semana trabajo hasta muy tarde. En todo caso, podríamos coordinar para hacer las compras juntas u otra cosa que quieras.
>
> Deberíamos vernos alguna vez antes de fin de año, ¿no?
>
> Espero una respuesta pronto,
> Francisca

6. Para cada ejemplo, indica si el cuantificador debe concordar en género y/o número con el sustantivo. `7.C`

Ejemplo	Sí	No
1. Ante **alguna** duda, consulte con su médico de cabecera.		
2. **Cada** uno ordena su habitación.		
3. Tengo **muchísimo** sueño.		
4. Hay **varias** alumnas que son excelentes deportistas.		
5. Habrá **más** contaminación si no cuidamos el planeta.		
6. Compra **menos** dulces la próxima vez.		

7. Inserta el cuantificador en el lugar adecuado de la oración. `7.C`

1. En nuestra tienda, le ofrecemos recetas: desde platos elaborados hasta platos rápidos. (varias)
   _____

2. Con dos kilos, me veré mejor. (menos)
   _____

3. Cinco días y comienzan las vacaciones. (más)
   _____

4. Tengo sueño: mejor hablemos mañana. (bastante)
   _____

5. Un día llegarás a casa y estaré esperándote con una gran sorpresa. (cualquiera)
   _____

6. Hay cosas que tenemos que hablar. Necesitamos más tiempo. (varias)
   _____

8. En estos ejemplos, indica si el cuantificador indefinido funciona como pronombre o no. `7.C`

1. Quería comprar libros, pero ninguno me pareció interesante. _____

2. Busquemos unas películas buenas y mirémoslas. _____

3. No me decido todavía: cualquiera me viene bien. _____

4. Algunos amigos de Juan viven en México. _____

5. Comunícate con cualquier integrante de nuestro personal. _____

6. ¡Todo me sale mal! _____

7. Al final, me arrepentí de comprar la cámara. No es necesario tener una. _____

8. La vecina de la esquina es amable; las demás, no. _____

9. Julia y Joaquín hablan sobre su ciudad. Completa la conversación con las palabras de la lista. Si no es necesario agregar una palabra, indícalo con una X. `7.C`

> cualquier   cualquiera   cualquiera de   un   una   unos

JULIA ¿Vivirías para siempre en nuestra ciudad?

JOAQUÍN Sí, me encanta. Además, no podría vivir en (1) _____ de los pueblos cercanos.

JULIA Mmm... no sé, nuestra ciudad no tiene (2) _____ playa. Tampoco tiene (3) _____ bosque.

JOAQUÍN Pienso que el clima es ideal aquí. Hace (4) _____ poco de calor en el verano, pero no demasiado.

JULIA Puede ser... De (5) _____ manera, debo quedarme hasta que termine la escuela.

JOAQUÍN Sí, y para eso faltan (6) _____ cuatro años.

JULIA Es verdad, pero podría ir pensando en mudarme a (7) _____ las ciudades que tienen universidades importantes.

JOAQUÍN No es (8) _____ mala idea. Además, ¡tiempo es lo que nos sobra!

10. Para cada oración, elige la opción correcta. En algunos casos, ambas respuestas son correctas. `7.C`

1. Carmen y Sandra van a escuelas diferentes, pero _____ (ambas / cada una) juegan en el mismo equipo de hockey.

2. Ya tengo _____ (bastantes/demás) problemas con aprender francés. ¡Aprender también chino sería demasiado!

3. _____ (Todos/Ambos) los estudiantes deben hacer la tarea para el lunes próximo.

4. _____ (Ambos / Los tres) perros deben ir a la veterinaria: Pipo y Colita, hoy; y Huesito, mañana.

5. Estudié _____ (cada una de / todas) las lecciones del libro, de la primera a la última.

6. _____ (Cada semana / Todas las semanas) tengo clases de música.

7. Mi médico dijo que es saludable comer _____ (cada/durante) cuatro horas.

11. Contesta las preguntas con respuestas completas usando la palabra entre paréntesis. `7.C`

1. ¿Compraste las cosas que aparecían en la lista? Sí, _____ (todas).

2. ¿Esos pueblos son iguales entre sí? No, _____ (cada).

3. ¿Has estudiado para el examen? Sí, _____ (todo).

4. ¿Eres un experto en motocicletas? Sí, _____ (todo un).

5. ¿Me has contado todos los detalles de la boda? Sí, _____ (todo lo).

12. Elige la opción correcta para completar estas oraciones. `7.C`

1. No te preocupes, me encargaré de todo _____ (lo/los) demás.

2. Yo quería ir de viaje de estudios al sur, pero _____ (lo/las) demás eligieron el viaje al norte.

3. Necesito mucho _____ (menos / menos de) tiempo, ¡seis días son más que suficientes!

4. Si hago un poco _____ (más / más de) esfuerzo, me aceptarán en la universidad que quiera.

5. Tengo que arreglar _____ (otros detalles más / otros más detalles) y podremos irnos.

6. ¿Te acuerdas de que _____ (el otro / un otro) día hablamos sobre este tema?

7. Trabajemos _____ (otras tres / tres otras) horas y vámonos al parque.

8. El café no está muy dulce: quiero _____ (otro poco / otro poco de) azúcar.

13. Reemplaza las palabras subrayadas por un pronombre indefinido. `7.D`

1. ¿Hay alguna persona que hable alemán aquí? _____

2. Ninguna persona viene de Colombia. _____

3. Al momento de elegir una playa en toda Latinoamérica,
   una persona elegiría una playa de Brasil. _____

4. Ninguna persona puede ayudarme. _____

5. No viajes con ninguna cosa que sea de valor. _____

6. Hay una cosa que debes saber. _____

14. Convierte estas oraciones afirmativas en negativas. `7.D`

1. ¿Hay alguien que sea español? _____

2. Yo tenía que decirte algo. _____

3. Escucho algo cuando hablo por teléfono. _____

4. Tú conoces a alguien que puede venir. _____

5. Me cuenta mucho sobre su abuelo, Pedro. _____

15. Reescribe este relato de forma impersonal usando el pronombre *uno* en lugar del pronombre de la segunda persona del singular. `7.D`

Posibles soluciones para el insomnio

Muchas personas sufren de insomnio ocasionalmente. ¿Pero qué puedes hacer cuando esto se convierte en un problema frecuente?

Puedes hacer ejercicio por la tarde, aunque no demasiado tarde. De lo contrario, al momento de dormir, tienes un ritmo demasiado acelerado y no puedes conciliar el sueño.

Otra opción es no tomar bebidas con mucha cafeína. Cuando tomas mucho café o bebidas energéticas, estás más alerta y no puedes dormirte con tanta facilidad.

Muchos médicos recomiendan que no tengas un televisor en la habitación. Es mejor que la habitación sea un lugar donde solamente duermas.

Y, por último, debes intentar tener horarios regulares, es decir, una rutina.

16. ¿*Nada* o *nadie*? Completa las oraciones. `7.D`

1. La vendedora de la tienda no fue _____ amable al atenderme.

2. No quiero a _____ más que a ti.

3. No tengo fuerzas para _____. Es mejor que descanse más.

4. El pronóstico no es _____ bueno: el paciente deberá quedarse en el hospital un largo tiempo.

5. ¿Tienes más hambre? Yo no quiero _____ más.

6. ¿Adivina quién me invitó a su cumpleaños? ¡_____ menos que el embajador de México!

17. Cada vez que Patricia dice algo, Diego la contradice. Escribe los comentarios de Diego usando la palabra entre paréntesis. `7.E`

1. **PATRICIA** Tu mamá siempre habla mucho.
   DIEGO _____ (poco).

2. **PATRICIA** Es bastante seguro que yo gane una beca.
   DIEGO _____ (nada).

3. **PATRICIA** En el último año, la economía de nuestro país creció mucho menos, en comparación con años anteriores.
   DIEGO _____ (más).

4. **PATRICIA** Este resfriado no es nada grave.
   DIEGO _____ (bastante).

5. **PATRICIA** Hace mucho que dejaste de trabajar.
   DIEGO _____ (tanto).

18. Completa este folleto con la forma correcta de *mismo* o *propio*. `7.E`

¡Baje de peso ya!

¿No se siente cómodo con su (1) _____ cuerpo? ¿Tiene unos kilitos de más que lo hacen sentirse inseguro? ¡Siéntase bien consigo (2) _____ en treinta días! Gracias al revolucionario tratamiento que ofrecemos, bajará sus kilos de más de forma fácil y saludable, a su (3) _____ ritmo.

Nuestro método es totalmente distinto de los demás: sin pastillas, sin mentiras, sin recetas mágicas. Se trata de buscar en uno (4) _____ las fuerzas y ganas para darle un rumbo nuevo a su (5) _____ vida. Llame ahora (6) _____ y le regalaremos un video explicativo donde podrá ver testimonios de muchos de nuestros clientes satisfechos.

19. Síntesis Une los elementos de las dos columnas para formar oraciones. `7.B–7.E`

1. No tengo ningún _____
2. Algún _____
3. No hay forma _____
4. Creo que hay bastantes _____
5. Ya tengo bastante _____
6. Elige cualquiera de _____
7. Me ha dicho que en todo _____
8. Debes mirar a cada _____
9. Fue mi propia _____
10. Creo que he aprendido _____
11. Mi novio me dijo algo _____

a. con mis problemas. ¡No puedo solucionar los tuyos!
b. lugares donde podríamos festejar tu cumpleaños.
c. momento de tranquilidad.
d. lado de la calle antes de cruzar.
e. madre la que me contó la verdad.
f. día seré rico y dejaré de trabajar.
g. momento estará conmigo.
h. alguna de entrar sin saber el código secreto.
i. mucho esta tarde.
j. las blusas; todas son hermosas.
k. muy dulce.

20. Síntesis Decide a qué ejemplo hace referencia cada explicación. `7.B–7.E`

_____ 1. No tienes ninguna mascota.

_____ 2. ¿Hay algún problema?

_____ 3. Me gusta todo en esta tienda.

_____ 4. Me quedan unos cinco mil dólares en la cuenta.

_____ 5. Ambas sillas pertenecen a Marta.

_____ 6. Cada calle tiene un nombre distinto.

_____ 7. Uno debe cuidar su salud siempre.

_____ 8. Carla y Javier recibieron sendos galardones.

a. Es un cuantificador que se usa siempre en plural y que puede reemplazarse por "los/las dos".

b. Es un cuantificador que se usa en lugar de "aproximadamente" antes de un número.

c. Es un determinante que significa "uno cada uno" y se usa en el lenguaje escrito.

d. Este cuantificador se abrevia antes de sustantivos masculinos en singular.

e. Es un cuantificador que no concuerda en género ni en número con el sustantivo y solo indica una parte de un todo.

f. Esta forma negativa requiere una doble negación cuando se encuentra después del verbo.

g. Se usa cuando el hablante necesita expresarse de una forma impersonal.

h. Es un cuantificador indefinido que, en este caso, se usa como pronombre.

Practice more at **vhlcentral.com.**

Demonstratives | **Chapter 8**

1. Carlos está en la zapatería y quiere comprarse calzado nuevo. Observa las imágenes y completa las oraciones de la vendedora con determinantes demostrativos. `8.A`

1. _____ zapatos son clásicos y elegantes, ¿le quedan cómodos?

2. Si quiere algo más moderno, tiene _____ zapatos marrones, con rayas marrón claro, que están en el exhibidor.

3. O, si busca algo más informal, puedo ofrecerle _____ zapatillas color beige, están a un precio muy razonable.

4. ¿O prefiere _____ zapatos negros que le ofrecí al principio?

5. Me gustan los zapatos clásicos, llevo _____.

2. Martín está en la habitación que tenía cuando era niño. Completa la descripción con las palabras de la lista. `8.A`

| aquellos | esas | esos | esta | aquel | eso | este | estas |

(1) _____ era mi habitación. Todo (2) _____ espacio de aquí era únicamente para mí, ¿no es genial? (3) _____ repisas que ves aquí están repletas de mis cómics favoritos. En (4) _____ cajones que están detrás de las repisas están mis juguetes de cuando era niño. Y (5) _____ oso gigante que ves al fondo es el primer peluche que me regalaron. Y mira (6) _____ marrón que se ve por la ventana. Es un edificio de oficinas bastante feo. Allí antes había una casa de madera. ¡Qué tiempos (7) _____! Nos pasábamos allí todo el verano. ¡(8) _____ eran aventuras de verdad!

3. Elige la opción correcta para completar el artículo periodístico. `8.A`

Accidente automovilístico

(1) _____ (Aquella/Esta) madrugada, alrededor de las 5:30 a.m., dos coches chocaron en la intersección de las calles Colina y San Petersburgo. Según testigos, el conductor del coche azul cruzó la avenida con el semáforo en rojo. Los registros policiales indican que (2) _____ (esto/esta) no es la primera vez que este conductor comete una infracción de (3) _____ (esto/este) tipo. (4) _____ (Este/Aquel) tampoco es el primer accidente en esta intersección.

En la escena del accidente, un vecino, Francisco Gómez, declaró: "(5) _____ (Ese/Esto) ya pasó varias veces antes. (6) _____ (Aquel/Aquello) semáforo no está bien sincronizado con (7) _____ (aquel/aquello)".

Las autoridades de seguridad vial están analizando (8) _____ (eso/este) y otros casos de accidentes por cruzar semáforos en rojo. Sin embargo, afirman que (9) _____ (estas/estos) son casos de negligencia, y no de problemas técnicos.

4. **Síntesis** Completa las oraciones con demostrativos. `8.A–8.B`

1. La niña _____ que está allí no deja de mirarme: ¿qué querrá de mí?

2. _____ tres piedras que tengo en la mano son muy valiosas.

3. ¿Ves _____ que se mueve en el fondo del jardín? ¡Es mi perro!

4. Recibí dos veces la misma factura. Mira aquí: _____ esta semana; y aquella, la semana pasada.

5. ¿Cómo armo _____? No entiendo las instrucciones.

6. _____... no sé la respuesta... no hice la tarea.

7. ¡Ay! ¡Ojalá tuviera tu edad! En _____ tiempos, todo parecía posible.

8. _____ vez no me olvidaré de llevar mi pasaporte.

9. Mira aquí: todo _____ lo gané trabajando... ¡trabajando muchísimo!

Practice more at **vhlcentral.com.**

1. Completa la conversación con los determinantes posesivos correspondientes. `9.B`

MAMÁ ¿Has hecho (1) _____ tarea?

ANDRÉS Por supuesto, mamá. (2) _____ maestro es muy estricto.

MAMÁ ¿Y has ordenado (3) _____ habitación? Mañana viene (4) _____ amigo... ¿cómo se llama?

ANDRÉS Julio. Sí, mamá, hasta guardé todos (5) _____ juegos en el armario.

MAMÁ Bien hecho. Pero, ¿qué hiciste con (6) _____ camiseta de fútbol? Mañana debes llevarla a la escuela.

ANDRÉS No te preocupes, mamita. (7) _____ entrenador tiene todas (8) _____ camisetas en (9) _____ casa.

MAMÁ Así me gusta. ¡Solamente deseo que (10) _____ vidas sean ordenadas!

ANDRÉS ¡Sí, mamá! Y ya lo sabes, ¡(11) _____ deseos son órdenes!

2. Completa las oraciones con los determinantes posesivos correspondientes. `9.C`

1. No encuentro varios cuadernos _____ (yo). ¿Sabes dónde pueden estar?

2. Ayer me llamó una compañera _____ (tú).

3. En el periódico, publicaron muchos artículos _____ (nosotros).

4. ¿Te gustan las novelas de Paulo Coelho? Compré unos libros _____ (él) a un precio muy bueno.

5. ¿Qué haremos con todos estos juguetes _____ (tú) cuando crezcas? Podríamos donarlos.

6. ¡Cómo extraño usar esas zapatillas _____ (yo)! Eran hermosas, ¿te acuerdas?

7. Un profesor _____ (nosotros) nos recomendó esta universidad.

8. En la fiesta, conocí a unos amigos _____ (él).

9. Esas amigas _____ (vosotros) que vinieron de visita son muy simpáticas.

10. ¿Estos libros de contabilidad son _____ (ustedes)?

3. Reescribe estas oraciones cambiando los posesivos según la persona entre paréntesis. `9.B–9.C`

1. Esa compañera tuya no deja de llamar a casa. (vosotros)
_____

2. Varios profesores míos dieron clases en universidades importantes del extranjero. (tú)
_____

3. Nuestras madres hablan tanto. Con razón, nuestros padres miran tanta televisión. (ellos)
_____

4. ¿Puedes alquilar un DVD en la tienda de tu barrio? (yo)
_____

5. Tus zapatos están sucios. Es necesario lavarlos antes de guardarlos en tu armario. (vosotros)
_____

6. Sus perros se llaman Guardián y Sultán, ¿no? Esos nombres no podrían ser más que idea suya. (tú)
_____

Actividades

4. Completa las oraciones con los posesivos de la lista. `9.B–9.C`

| suya | míos | vuestro | mi | tus | sus | nuestros | tuyos |

1. Carla, _____ padres llamaron preocupados. ¡Quieren saber dónde estás!

2. Unos vecinos _____ se quejaron porque mi perro ladra. ¡Qué intolerancia hay en mi barrio!

3. Mis padres son más viejos que los _____.

4. _____ compañera de cuarto, Alicia, estudia toda la noche y no me deja dormir.

5. Estos son _____ derechos como estudiantes. ¡Solamente nosotros podemos defenderlos!

6. ¿Has visto lo linda que es Paula? ¡_____ ojos son impactantes!

7. Es claro que Flavia organizó la fiesta sorpresa. Todo esto es obra _____.

8. Esto es _____, ¿no? Recuerdo que lo habéis dejado en mi casa.

5. Clasifica estos determinantes posesivos según puedan usarse como prenominales, posnominales o ambos. `9.B–9.C`

Determinante	Prenominal	Posnominal	Pre/posnominal
1. su			
2. míos			
3. vuestros			
4. suyos			
5. nuestra			
6. tus			
7. mis			
8. tuya			
9. vuestra			
10. nuestros			

6. Una amiga tuya empezó con sus clases de español hace muy poco. Ayúdala a corregir su tarea. Elige la opción correcta. `9.B–9.C`

Mis regalos de Navidad

Finalmente llegó la Navidad. (1) _____ (Tus/Mis) papás me dieron muchos regalos.

Bueno, primero, (2) _____ (su/mi) hermano, Pablo, abrió su regalo: un espectacular rompecabezas. Siempre fue (3) _____ (su/mi) sueño tener uno, y se le hizo realidad. Después fue mi turno. A diferencia de Pablo, el único deseo (4) _____ (suyo/mío) era una sencilla muñeca Patsy, ya sabes, la que sale en la televisión. Vi cuatro cajas, que parecían todas cosas (5) _____ (tuyas/mías) porque tenían mi nombre en ellas. En la primera caja, había una muñeca Patsy. Y en las demás, todos (6) _____ (sus/vuestros) accesorios. ¡Sí, y todo era (7) _____ (mío/nuestro)!

En fin, pasé todo (8) _____ (su/mi) fin de semana jugando con mi muñeca Patsy, ¡y con todos (9) _____ (sus/tus) vestidos y zapatos!

7. Reescribe cada frase diciendo exactamente a quién pertenece cada cosa. `9.D`

Regalos para adolescentes
Sugerencia: *Sol y lluvia*

En este libro, encontramos los relatos de Amparo, una hermosa y simpática joven que vive en una pequeña ciudad en el sur de (1) su país natal, Chile. Pero, al cabo de los primeros capítulos, en (2) su diario, es claro que (3) su vida no es de color de rosa: Amparo se encuentra con muchos problemas sin solución.

El autor de *Sol y lluvia*, Facundo Quesada, presentó (4) su libro y dio una conferencia de prensa. En (5) palabras suyas: "Esta historia es ideal para lectores adolescentes, porque pueden identificarse con Amparo. Al leer (6) su diario, ellos se dan cuenta de que no son de otro planeta: que tanto en (7) su vida como en (8) las suyas hay alegrías y tristezas, pero todo tiene una solución". Por esta razón y muchas otras, les recomendamos este libro para (9) sus hijos de entre doce y dieciséis años.

1. _____	4. _____	7. _____
2. _____	5. _____	8. _____
3. _____	6. _____	9. _____

8. Completa las oraciones con *propio, propia, propios* o *propias*. Decide si va antes o después del sustantivo. `9.D`

1. Te lo digo por _____ experiencia _____: cuida tus pertenencias en el aeropuerto.

2. Carina vive en su _____ mundo _____ y nunca presta atención en clase.

3. No puede ser que no me creas: ¡lo he visto con mis _____ ojos _____!

4. Le recomiendo ese abrigo que está en la vidriera: es una _____ chaqueta _____ para el invierno.

5. Yo tengo _____ habitación _____. ¿Y tú? ¿Compartes tu habitación con tu hermana?

6. Ella trabaja por _____ cuenta _____, pero antes era empleada de una tienda.

9. Luciana va al médico. Completa la conversación con determinantes posesivos o artículos definidos. `9.D`

LUCIANA Hola, doctor. Le cuento (1) _____ inquietud: me pica (2) _____ lunar (*mole*) que tengo aquí en (3) _____ brazo. Además, (4) _____ piel es muy blanca.

MÉDICO Bueno, Luciana, primero unas preguntitas. ¿En (5) _____ familia, hay casos de cáncer?

LUCIANA No, nadie tuvo cáncer.

MÉDICO ¿Te duele (6) _____ lunar?

LUCIANA No, no me duele, pero a veces me pica (7) _____ piel de alrededor.

MÉDICO Mmm... Bueno, haremos un examen el lunes que viene.

LUCIANA Bien, déjeme ver (8) _____ agenda... Perfecto, pero, ¿qué puedo hacer para solucionar la picazón?

MÉDICO Es importante que no te rasques (9) _____ piel.

LUCIANA Sí...

MÉDICO Ponte protector solar en (10) _____ brazos antes de salir de (11) _____ hogar.

LUCIANA ¿Solamente allí?

MÉDICO Bueno, lo ideal es que te pongas protector en todo (12) _____ cuerpo.

LUCIANA Perfecto, entonces me cuido (13) _____ lunar hasta la próxima visita.

MÉDICO Luciana, ¡eres (14) _____ mejor paciente!

10. Completa las oraciones con las frases de la lista. 9.D

| mi amiga | mi general | mi papá | auto nuestro |
| valijas nuestras | tus bufandas | botas tuyas | |

1. ¿Recuerdas ese _____ que se descomponía en los días más importantes?

2. Aquí hay unas _____ de color marrón. ¿Las quieres todavía?

3. Para mi cumpleaños, vinieron _____ y la tuya.

4. Estaré listo a las 7 de la mañana, _____, como buen sargento que soy.

5. Mi tía tiene 46 años, y luego está _____, que tiene 43.

6. Aquí están _____ favoritas. ¿Qué hago con ellas?

7. En la casa de Andrea tenemos varias _____ que debemos buscar.

11. Síntesis Decide si estas oraciones son correctas. Corrige las incorrectas. 9.A–9.E

1. Tengo las gafas siempre sucias. Debería limpiarlas más a menudo. _____

2. Mira, allí están tus libros. Los míos están aquí. _____

3. Sabes que te adoro, mi querida Eva. _____

4. Mi y tu hermano se llaman igual. _____

5. En país tuyo, ¿ahora es invierno o verano? _____

6. Mañana vendrá la tía, ¡no la tuya! _____

7. Me duele mucho mi cabeza. ¿Qué hago? _____

8. El abogado del delincuente declaró que el ataque fue en propia defensa. _____

9. Alteza Real mía, le aseguro que todos los pobladores lo admiran. _____

10. Es posible que recibas alguna carta mía la semana que viene. _____

12. Síntesis Completa la historia con la opción correcta. 9.A–9.E

De alumno a alumno

¿No consigues (1) _____ (tus/los) libros que te han pedido? ¿No sabes cómo hacer (2) _____ (las tareas tuyas / tus tareas)? No te rompas más (3) _____ (la/tu) cabeza tratando de hacerlas por (4) _____ (propia cuenta / cuenta propia).

¡Ofrecemos (5) _____ (una solución propia / tu solución) para estudiantes de primer año!

Somos un grupo de estudiantes de quinto año a punto de graduarnos y queremos que todos (6) _____ (vuestros compañeros / nuestros compañeros) de escuela tengan el mismo éxito que hemos tenido nosotros. Bajo el lema (*motto*) "Lo (7) _____ (mío/tuyo) es (8) _____ (mío/tuyo)", donamos nuestros libros y apuntes, y ayudamos a quienes tengan dificultades en matemáticas, ciencias y literatura. Puedes encontrarnos en el aula 43, justo enfrente (9) _____ (de la mía / de la tuya).

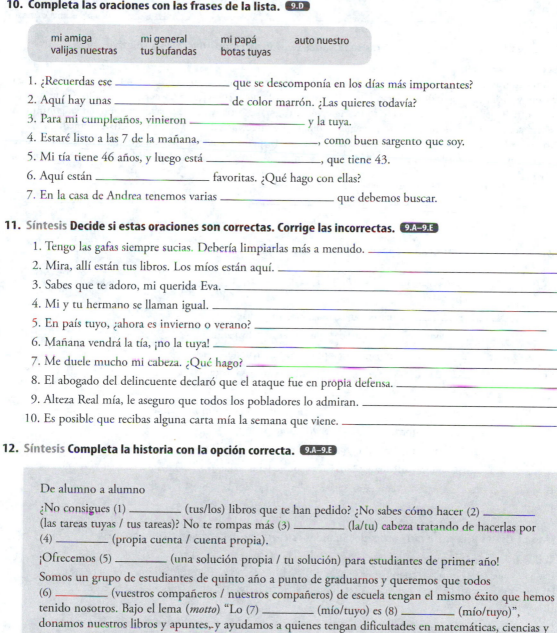 Practice more at **vhlcentral.com.**

1. Lee este texto e indica si las palabras subrayadas se utilizan como adverbios o adjetivos. `10.A`

El tren en Internet

¡Ahora comprar sus billetes de tren es muy (1) <u>fácil</u>! Ingrese en nuestro sitio web. En el buscador de horarios, elija la hora y el día en el que desea viajar. Luego, busque la tarifa que (2) <u>mejor</u> se adecue a su bolsillo. Cuando la encuentre, haga clic (3) <u>rápidamente</u> sobre la opción escogida. No tiene (4) <u>demasiado</u> tiempo: en cinco minutos deberá concretar su compra. (5) <u>Ahora</u> pague su billete. Le ofrecemos una (6) <u>amplia</u> variedad de medios de pago. No olvide ingresar una dirección de correo electrónico, a la que le enviaremos (7) <u>inmediatamente</u> el billete que deberá imprimir. Preséntese en la estación (8) <u>pocos</u> minutos antes de la salida del tren... ¡y (9) asunto <u>arreglado</u>!

1. _____   4. _____   7. _____
2. _____   5. _____   8. _____
3. _____   6. _____   9. _____

2. Completa las oraciones con las palabras de la lista. `10.B`

| temprano | cuándo | pasado mañana | nunca | antes | cuando | ya (3) | tarde | después |

1. Dime _____ estarás en tu casa y pasaré a visitarte.

2. _____ hace frío, uso bufanda y guantes muy abrigados.

3. _____ de los relámpagos, siempre se oye un trueno.

4. _____ de salir del país, verifica que tienes tu pasaporte.

5. Mañana es miércoles y _____ es jueves.

6. ¡Te despiertas demasiado _____! ¡Hoy es domingo y son las 7 a.m.!

7. _____ o temprano verás que tengo razón.

8. _____ no tengo más dinero. ¡Tendré que pedirles un poco a mis padres!

9. _____ jamás adivinarías a quién encontré en la calle.

10. _____ sabes la respuesta... ¡para qué me preguntas!

11. _____ verás qué divertida es esta amiga mía.

3. María Luisa es una chica muy ocupada. Completa su relato con la opción correcta. `10.B`

Todos los días tengo algo para hacer por las tardes, después de la escuela. Es decir, (1) _____ (casi siempre / casi nunca) tengo tiempo libre. (2) _____ (Nunca/Siempre) me encontrarás en casa por las tardes. Si quieres verme, tendrás que ir al club, porque estoy allí (3) _____ (frecuentemente / rara vez).

(4) _____ (A veces / Pocas veces) me gustaría quedarme en casa, pero sé que es importante entrenar y socializar... ¡y no hay nada mejor que el club para eso! Bueno, entonces si quieres que nos veamos, (5) _____ (siempre/nunca) me busques en casa... ¡ya sabes dónde estoy (6) _____ (con poca frecuencia / con mucha frecuencia)!

4. Elige la opción correcta para cada oración. `10.C`

1. _____ (Cómo/Como) me dijiste, compré las flores más lindas para Susana.

2. Cada día me siento _____ (mal/peor): este remedio no cura mi tos.

3. Bate los huevos de esta manera, _____ (cómo/como) te estoy mostrando.

4. Esta carne no está _____ (bien/mejor) cocinada. ¡Parece cruda!

5. La próxima vez elegiré _____ (mejor/así) el destino de mis vacaciones.

6. Tu amiga es _____ (mal/bien) simpática. Invítala a todas nuestras fiestas.

5. Completa la conversación con _bien, mejor, así, cómo y como_. `10.C`

REBECA ¡Qué (1) _____! Si te mudas cerca de casa, podremos vernos todas las tardes.

CAMILA Sí… Me encantaría que fuera (2) _____; pero no sé (3) _____ haré para encontrar un apartamento a buen precio y bien ubicado.

REBECA Es verdad, aquí la gente vive (4) _____; por las noches siempre hay movimiento y todos quieren vivir aquí.

CAMILA Quizás sería (5) _____ buscar un apartamento en otro barrio, (6) _____ dijo mi madre.

REBECA No te preocupes, ya encontraremos un apartamento (7) _____ bonito para ti.

CAMILA ¡(8) _____ me gusta! Con esta actitud tan positiva, ¡encontraremos uno genial!

6. Cecilia siempre contradice a su madre. Reescribe las oraciones usando el adverbio adecuado. `10.D`

1. **MADRE** En el supermercado debemos comprar mucho.

   CECILIA _____

2. **MADRE** Tardaremos más que la semana pasada.

   CECILIA _____

3. **MADRE** Nos llevará demasiado tiempo.

   CECILIA _____

4. **MADRE** ¡Tendremos que pagar tanto por un taxi!

   CECILIA _____

5. **MADRE** Será mejor comprar poco para todo el mes.

   CECILIA _____

7. Completa las oraciones con las palabras de la lista. `10.D`

muy	todo lo que	casi	demasiado	cuánto	bastante	cuanto

1. Mi instructor de yoga se entrena _____. Creo que eso no es saludable.

2. _____ rompo mi computadora por llevarla en una mochila inadecuada.

3. No sabes _____ extrañé a mi perro durante las vacaciones.

4. Tu jefa nueva es _____ simpática. Mucho mejor que la anterior, ¿no?

5. _____ más aprendo matemáticas, más mejoro en geometría.

6. Me resulta _____ difícil estudiar más de dos horas seguidas.

7. Te juro que hice _____ pude para comprarte un regalo, pero no encontré nada adecuado para ti.

8. ¿*Aquí, allí* o *allá*? Completa el relato de Cintia. `10.E`

¡Cómo me gusta mi ciudad nueva! (1) _____ puedo hacer mucho más que en Lobres, mi pueblo anterior. Es verdad que Lobres era más tranquilo. (2) _____ no nos preocupábamos por cerrar con llave las puertas de los carros o cerrar las ventanas por la noche. (3) _____ es diferente: tenemos que tener más cuidado con nuestros bolsos en la calle y estar más atentos. Lo bueno de vivir (4) _____ es que todos los días hay actividades: ir al cine, a museos, ver espectáculos al aire libre, de todo... Y por suerte siempre puedo volver a Lobres cuando quiero. Voy para (5) _____ una vez cada quince días a ver a mis padres. (6) _____ comemos muy rico, dormimos la siesta y disfrutamos de la tranquilidad del pueblo.

9. Escribe las preguntas para estas respuestas. Debes usar *dónde* o *adónde*. `10.E`

> **Modelo**
>
> ¿Dónde naciste?
> Yo nací <u>en Guatemala</u>.

1. _____
   Iremos <u>al centro comercial</u> para comprar regalos.

2. _____
   Nos encontraremos <u>en el restaurante chino</u> a las 10 p.m.

3. _____
   Juana podrá dormir <u>en mi cuarto</u>.

4. _____
   Por la mañana, viajaremos <u>a Jaén</u>.

5. _____
   El avión aterrizará <u>en el aeropuerto internacional</u>.

6. _____
   Iremos a comer <u>a la casa de la abuela</u>.

10. Elige la opción correcta para cada oración. `10.E`

1. ¡La camisa azul está _____ (delante/adelante) de tus ojos. ¿Cómo no la ves?

2. ¡Cuidado! Si das dos pasos hacia _____ (detrás/atrás), pisarás al gato.

3. Ven _____ (dentro/adentro). Hace mucho frío para estar allí.

4. _____ (Debajo/Abajo) de esa cama, encontrarás muchas cajas.

5. Mira hacia _____ (encima/arriba): el techo tiene mucha humedad.

6. _____ (Dentro/Adentro) de la tienda, la temperatura es óptima.

11. Une las oraciones de las columnas para que tengan sentido. `10.E`

1. Verás que más _____   a. cerca de los carros; es peligroso.

2. No camines muy _____   b. lejos de lo que pensábamos.

3. No estamos nada _____   c. fuera del teatro.

4. El teatro estaba mucho más _____   d. lejos del museo de la ciudad. ¡Tenemos que ir!

5. No te quedes demasiado _____   e. atrás: ¡te perderé de vista!

6. Es verdad: por _____   f. adelante hay una tienda con un cartel anaranjado.

7. Hay mucha gente esperando _____   g. fuera, ella parece una persona dura.

12. Completa las oraciones con adverbios negativos, afirmativos o de duda. `10.F`

| no | quizás | sí | también | tampoco |

1. Qué bien que vendrás al cine. Te gustan las palomitas de maíz, ¿_____?
2. _____ que iremos a la fiesta esta noche.
3. _____ termine de leer el libro este fin de semana... pero no estoy segura.
4. ¡Somos de la misma ciudad! Yo _____ vivo en Nueva York.
5. _____, mi madre vendrá por la tarde. ¿Necesitas hablar únicamente con ella?
6. Camila _____ tendrá vacaciones. Nos quedaremos las dos en la oficina.

13. Reemplaza las palabras subrayadas con adverbios terminados en -*mente*. `10.G–10.H`

1. Me di cuenta de que estaba enamorada de él con locura. _____
2. De repente, todos se habían ido ¡y yo estaba sola! _____
3. Te lo digo con sinceridad: ese vestido no es bonito. _____
4. Podríamos comunicarnos por teléfono, ¿te parece mejor? _____
5. La exhibición salió de maravilla. Ojalá hubieras venido. _____
6. Creo con firmeza en los ideales de nuestro partido. _____
7. Hazlo con tranquilidad y sin apuro. _____
8. Debes tratar a todos con cortesía. _____
9. Ahora sí que lo veo con claridad. _____

14. Decide si estas oraciones son correctas. Si no lo son, corrígelas. `10.G–10.H`

1. Los jugadores corrieron muy rápido detrás de la pelota. _____
2. Julieta increíblemente canta. _____
3. Subimos la montaña lentamente y cuidadosamente. _____
4. Habla más claro, que no te entiendo. _____
5. Debes respirar hondo cuando corres. _____
6. Has respondido correctomente. _____

15. Une las locuciones adverbiales con su significado. `10.H`

_____ 1. a lo grande	a. finalmente
_____ 2. a menudo	b. con todo lujo
_____ 3. en buenas manos	c. a cargo de alguien responsable
_____ 4. por fin	d. bueno...
_____ 5. en fin	e. casi
_____ 6. de primera mano	f. con frecuencia
_____ 7. por poco	g. por experiencia propia
_____ 8. a la larga	h. a largo plazo

16. Reescribe las oraciones usando el comparativo. `10.I`

1. Por la tarde, yo trabajo bien. Por la noche, trabajo muy bien.
Por la noche… _____

2. Claudia dormía mal. Claudia ahora duerme bien.
Claudia ahora… _____

3. Este año peso poco. El año pasado pesaba mucho.
Este año… _____

4. Andrés lee rápido. Juan lee muy rápido.
Andrés… _____

5. En España, se vive bien. En Francia, se vive muy bien.
En España… _____

6. Mi hermana estudia frecuentemente. Mi hermano estudia muy pocas veces.
Mi hermana… _____

17. Simón es muy exagerado. Completa las oraciones usando el superlativo. `10.I`

1. Este hombre conduce lento.
No, este hombre _____.

2. Dormimos tranquilamente toda la noche.
No, dormimos _____.

3. Ulises comió mucho en casa.
No, Ulises _____.

4. Isabel respondió las preguntas inteligentemente.
No, Isabel _____.

5. Como no sabía el camino, Paula llegó tarde.
No, como _____.

6. Nuestros padres vinieron pronto cuando conocieron la noticia.
No, nuestros padres _____.

18. Síntesis Clasifica estos adverbios según su clase. `10.A–10.I`

Adverbios	Tiempo	Modo	Cantidad	Lugar
1. nunca				
2. bastante				
3. allí				
4. rápidamente				
5. cerca				
6. rara vez				
7. mañana				
8. mucho				
9. peor				
10. con frecuencia				
11. poco				
12. delante				
13. tranquilamente				

Actividades

19. Síntesis **Completa las oraciones con las palabras de la lista.** `10.A–10.B`

allá	jamás	cuándo	suficiente	como
muy	primero	tampoco	bien	dónde

1. No quieres ir al cine y _____ al teatro. ¿Qué quieres hacer entonces?

2. _____ haría una excursión por la montaña. Sabes que tengo fobia a las arañas.

3. _____ cortas la cebolla y luego la fríes.

4. La peluquería está más _____.

5. Estudia _____ bien este tema: seguramente será importante para el examen.

6. He comprado un teléfono _____ pequeño.

7. Ya he comido _____, creo que no comeré postre.

8. ¿A _____ vamos esta noche?

9. Haré la comida _____ tú me digas.

10. La maestra nos dijo exactamente _____ entregar la tarea.

20. Síntesis **Corrige el texto. Hay ocho errores.** `10.A–10.B`

¿Qué es el mundo laboral?

¿No sabes donde buscar trabajo? ¿No sabes cuanto dinero deberías ganar? Allí te ayudaremos.

_____

Somos un grupo de ex alumnos de tu escuela y queremos ayudarte a conocer un poco menos el mercado laboral. Tampoco queremos contarte sobre nuestros trabajos y como los conseguimos.

_____

_____

Apúntate a las reuniones que realizamos semanal en la sala de conferencias de la escuela. Te esperamos, ¿si?

_____

_____

🔧 Practice more at **vhlcentral.com.**

Comparison 🔊   **Chapter 11**

1. Completa las oraciones usando el comparativo. `11.B`

1. El autobús es rápido.
   El tren es muy rápido.
   El tren _____.

2. En Buenos Aires, hace calor.
   En Lima, hace mucho calor.
   En Lima, _____.

3. La maestra de biología es joven.
   La maestra de matemáticas es muy joven.
   La maestra de matemáticas _____.

4. Juana es buena en voleibol.
   Carina es muy buena en voleibol.
   Juana _____.

5. Por la mañana llovió poco.
   Por la tarde llovió mucho.
   Por la mañana _____.

6. *Shrek* es mala.
   Shrek 2 es muy mala.
   Shrek 2 _____.

2. Haz comparaciones entre Martín y Susana. Sigue el modelo. `11.B`

> **Modelo**
>
> Martín comió poco.
> Susana comió mucho.
> *Martín comió menos que Susana.*
> *Susana comió más que Martín.*

1. Martín corre 15 minutos por día.
   Susana corre 30 minutos por día.

   _____

   _____

2. Martín tiene dos perros.
   Susana tiene un perro.

   _____

   _____

3. Martín duerme 8 horas.
   Susana duerme 9 horas.

   _____

   _____

4. Martín tiene un promedio de 8.
   Susana tiene un promedio de 9.

   _____

   _____

5. Martín hizo dos tortas.
   Susana hizo una torta.

   _____

   _____

6. Martín es alto.
   Susana es baja.

   _____

   _____

3. Identifica cuáles de estos adjetivos y adverbios tienen comparativos irregulares. Escribe las formas irregulares. `11.B`

1. malo _____
2. rápido _____
3. poco _____
4. viejo (edad) _____

5. sucio _____
6. oscuro _____
7. llano _____
8. mucho _____

9. alto _____
10. ordenado _____
11. blando _____
12. bueno _____

4. Reescribe las oraciones usando las expresiones entre paréntesis. `11.B`

1. En agosto, tengo aproximadamente dos semanas de vacaciones. (más de)

   _____

2. Durante el verano, voy más seguido al parque. (bastante)

   _____

3. Vivimos en un barrio céntrico. (relativamente)

   _____

4. Cuando estoy a dieta, bebo solamente agua mineral. (más que)

   _____

5. Dormí la siesta y ahora tengo poco sueño. (menos)

   _____

6. Mis manos son más delicadas que tus manos. (tuyas)

   _____

7. Mis horarios actuales son distintos a los que tenía antes. (diferentes)

   _____

5. Completa las oraciones con las opciones de la lista. `11.B`

de (2)	de lo que
que (3)	de los que
	de las que

1. Me gusta más _____ pensaba.

2. Tengo más trabajo _____ tú.

3. Asisto a más _____ seis clases en la universidad.

4. Hoy me siento peor _____ ayer.

5. Compré más libros _____ tenía pensado.

6. Fotografié más plazas _____ pensaba.

7. A veces duermo menos _____ lo necesario.

8. No juego más _____ fútbol.

6. Cecilia comenzó las clases y no para de quejarse. Completa su relato con las palabras de la lista. `11.B`

tal como	misma	tanto	mismo	tantas
tan	igual	como	tan	tan

¡Qué día!

Otra vez comenzaron las clases. Debo ir todos los días de 9 a.m. a 12 p.m. y luego de 3 p.m. a 5 p.m. ¡Es increíble tener que estar (1) _____ horas en un mismo lugar! ¡Tengo (2) _____ poco tiempo libre!

La maestra no es la (3) _____ que el año pasado. Ahora tenemos a la señorita Gómez, que es (4) _____ de aburrida que la señorita Albornoz, y nos hace trabajar (5) _____ como quiere. Y lo peor es que siempre nos manda hacer lo (6) _____ que hicimos el año pasado.

Solamente espero que este año no se me haga (7) _____ largo (8) _____ el año pasado. (9) _____ dijo mamá, no debería ser (10) _____ pesimista. Y tiene razón: mirándolo del lado positivo, ya falta un día menos para que terminen las clases.

7. Forma oraciones lógicas combinando elementos de las tres columnas. `11.C`

1. La historia no fue tal	tanto	como sea posible estas vacaciones.
2. Tamara tiene	tantos	de alta que yo.
3. Debo leer	igual	me la contaste. Fue más trágica.
4. Conduce exactamente a la	como	rápido como puedas, antes de que se enfríe.
5. Estela es	misma	mala suerte.
6. No entiendo cómo pude tener	tanta	velocidad que indica el cartel.
7. Come tu tarta	tan	libros que no ha leído aún.

8. Reescribe las oraciones usando el superlativo. `11.D`

> **Modelo**
>
> Este auto es mejor que el resto de los autos. (todos)
> *Este auto es el mejor de todos.*

1. Los productos de nuestra compañía son mejores que los de la competencia. (mercado)

   _____

2. Sebastián es más alto que los compañeros de su clase. (clase)

   _____

3. Este sofá tiene una calidad peor que los demás sofás. (todos)

   _____

4. La música de esta radio es mejor que la de otras radios del país. (país)

   _____

5. Juanito es más pequeño que sus hermanos. (familia)

   _____

6. Mis ensaladas son más deliciosas que las demás. (concurso de cocina)

   _____

7. Mi padre es más viejo que los demás padres. (todos)

   _____

9. Completa este anuncio publicitario con las palabras de la lista. `11.D`

verdaderamente	novedosísimo	lo más	lo mejor (2)	pequeñísimo
óptimo	ínfimo	practiquísimo	extraordinariamente	

Chaumanchas

En esta oportunidad, le ofrecemos *Chaumanchas*, el (1) _____ quitamanchas de bolsillo. Gracias a su envase (2) _____ pequeño, puede llevarlo con usted adonde vaya. Este quitamanchas es (3) _____ para madres de niños que se manchan todo el tiempo o para personas que viajan por negocios. *Chaumanchas* tiene una efectividad (4) _____ increíble: elimina manchas de aceite, grasa, tinta, ¡y muchísimas más!

¡Llame ya! ¡Le enviaremos este producto (5) _____ rápido posible! De esta manera, recibirá (6) _____ del mercado directamente en su hogar. Y (7) _____ de todo: con la compra de este (8) _____ producto, recibirá gratis un (9) _____ cepillo quitamanchas. *Chaumanchas*, el máximo poder quitamanchas en un (10) _____ envase.

10. Isabel contradice a su hermana Eugenia. Completa la conversación con expresiones que indiquen igualdad o desigualdad. `11.B-11.C`

EUGENIA ¿Qué te pareció la fiesta de ayer? Para mí, fue la mejor del año.

ISABEL De ninguna manera, (1) _____.

EUGENIA Pero había más invitados que en la fiesta de Juan. Eso no lo puedes negar...

ISABEL No, había (2) _____ que en esa fiesta.

EUGENIA Y la música era todo el tiempo distinta.

ISABEL No, era siempre (3) _____.

EUGENIA ¡Y bailamos muchísimo!

ISABEL ¡No, (4) _____!

EUGENIA Ay, Isabel, parece que no estuvimos en la misma fiesta. ¡Nunca me divertí tanto!

ISABEL No, ¡nunca (5) _____!

EUGENIA ¿Y la comida? Yo comí muchísimo, ¿y tú?

ISABEL Yo comí (6) _____ y no bebí (7) _____ un vaso de agua.

EUGENIA ¡Qué increíble que seamos hermanas!

ISABEL ¡Sí! Es increíble que seamos de la (8) _____ familia!

11. Cambia las comparaciones usando la palabra entre paréntesis. `11.B-11.C`

1. Catalina es más alta que su madre. (igual)

   _____

2. Tatiana tiene más vestidos que sus amigas. (tantos)

   _____

3. Mis notas son tan buenas como las tuyas. (mejores)

   _____

4. La primera parte de esta película es peor que la segunda. (tan)

   _____

5. Tú no comes más que yo. (tanto)

   _____

6. Mis calcetines son tal como los tuyos. (diferentes)

   _____

12. Síntesis Completa estas oraciones con los comparativos y superlativos que se dan en las opciones. `11.B-11.D`

1. Caminar es _____ agotador que andar en bicicleta.
   a. tan   b. más   c. tanto

2. Cómprate un colchón _____ que el que tienes y dormirás muy bien.
   a. más bueno   b. óptimo   c. mejor

3. Mi reproductor de MP3 es el más pequeño _____ he visto hasta ahora.
   a. que   b. como   c. de

4. Tienes más _____ cien películas en tu mediateca.
   a. que   b. como   c. de

5. Cristina es la empleada que _____ contacto tiene con los clientes.
   a. mejor   b. más   c. buenísimo

6. El fútbol es totalmente distinto _____ los demás deportes.
   a. de   b. a   c. que

7. Esta casa es _____ que las de los alrededores.
   a. mayor   b. más antigua c. menor

8. Aprender chino es más difícil _____ pensaba.
   a. de los que   b. de lo que   c. que

13. **Síntesis** Escribe oraciones a partir de las indicaciones dadas. `11.B–11.D`

> **Modelo**
>
> Las zapatillas de esta marca son buenas. + / el mercado
> *Las zapatillas de esta marca son las mejores del mercado.*

1. Roma es una ciudad romántica. – / Venecia

   _____

2. El carro azul es muy elegante. = / el carro rojo

   _____

3. Esta vendedora es realmente encantadora. + / el mundo

   _____

4. La tarea de hoy es fácil. – / la tarea de ayer

   _____

5. Este periódico es más conocido que el resto. + / el país

   _____

6. Puedo comprar tantos zapatos como tú. – / tú

   _____

7. Tus tartas son las mejores que he probado. = / tartas de mi madre

   _____

8. Las calles de Madrid son anchísimas. + / toda Europa

   _____

Practice more at **vhlcentral.com**.

Prepositions · Chapter 12

1. **Completa el artículo con las preposiciones de la lista.** `12.A`

| para | excepto | durante | de | hasta | desde | entre | tras | sobre |

Un lugar inolvidable

(1) _____ todos aquellos que desean pasar unas vacaciones de lujo, les recomendamos el hotel *Mar azul*. Este hotel se encuentra (2) _____ la costa del océano Atlántico y posee más de doscientas habitaciones. (3) _____ el siglo XX, allí se hospedaron innumerables famosos (4) _____ la farándula (*show business*) de América Latina; (5) _____ ellos, Luis Miguel y Santana.

(6) _____ 2004 (7) _____ 2006, el hotel permaneció cerrado al público por reformas. (8) _____ las remodelaciones, *Mar azul* reabrió sus puertas, (9) _____ las zonas de sauna y masajes, que se abrieron en 2007.

Desde entonces, el grandioso hotel alberga diariamente a más de 300 huéspedes.

2. Reescribe las oraciones usando las palabras de la lista. Haz los cambios necesarios. `12.A`

> pro   vía   versus (2)   o   y

1. Hoy en la televisión podremos ver el partido del Real Madrid <u>contra</u> el Barcelona.
   _____

2. Fui a París. <u>Camino a París pasé por</u> Londres.
   _____

3. Tobías trabaja para una organización que está <u>a favor de los</u> derechos de los animales.
   _____

4. <u>Arriba de</u> la nevera hay suciedad. <u>Debajo de</u> la nevera hay suciedad.
   _____

5. Mira el gráfico del precio de alquiler <u>frente al</u> precio de compra.
   _____

6. ¿Nos encontramos <u>enfrente del</u> gimnasio? ¿Nos encontramos <u>detrás del</u> gimnasio?
   _____

3. Combina elementos de las tres columnas para formar oraciones. `12.A`

1. Yo no tengo nada en	sin	un boleto.
2. Seamos sinceras,	entre	de su cama.
3. Mi casa está muy	contra	él y tú hay problemas.
4. Me encanta dormir la siesta	bajo	de tus amigos.
5. No puedes subir al autobús	sobre	el naranjo.
6. El papel de carta está	debajo	el escritorio.
7. Mi hermana cree que hay monstruos	lejos	del parque de diversiones.

4. Observa el mapa y completa la carta que escribió Yolanda con las preposiciones de la lista. `12.A`

> en   sobre   lejos de   al lado de   cerca de   hasta   delante de   de

Querida Claudia:

¿Cómo estás? Te escribo para contarte sobre mi barrio nuevo... ¡que me encanta!

Vivo en una casa en la esquina (1) _____ la calle Latina y la avenida América. (2) _____ mi casita, a la izquierda, está la escuela; y, a la derecha, la biblioteca. (3) _____ la avenida América, no muy (4) _____ mi casa, está el parque Robles. (5) _____ este parque, está el hospital. La semana pasada fuimos allí con mi mamá porque ella no se sentía muy bien. Mientras ella estaba con el médico, fui (6) _____ el kiosco, que queda justo (7) _____ diagonal al hospital, y me compré un refresco. Y, como estaba tan (8) _____ la heladería, me compré también un helado.

¿No te parece genial? ¡Es un barrio que tiene todo!

Espero que vengas a visitarme pronto.

Saludos,

Yolanda

Actividades

5. Reordena las oraciones para que tengan sentido. `12.A`

1. estoy / pro / de la / Yo /reforma constitucional / en _____
2. por / entre / gato / se perdió / El / las malezas _____
3. tu demora, / A / causa / el tren / de / perdimos _____
4. fue / a / Carola / una / por / barra de pan _____
5. Willy / Tengo / para / con / una obligación _____
6. y negra / es roja / fuera / por / dentro / La chaqueta / por _____
7. cuanto / En / a / deberás comprar / los zapatos, / unos nuevos _____
8. las entrevistas / Son / mejores / cara / cara / a _____
9. general, / las películas / lo / prefiero / de terror / Por _____
10. regreso / leche / Compraremos / de / al hostal _____

6. Completa las oraciones con la preposición correcta. `12.B`

1. Llegamos a Boston _____ las ocho.
2. Vi _____ Juan en el parque.
3. Necesito una tabla _____ planchar nueva.
4. No llegué a horario _____ tu culpa.
5. Si no tienes el ensayo listo _____ el jueves, el profesor te quitará un punto.
6. Se movía _____ mucha lentitud.
7. Parece que este carro estuviera hecho _____ plástico.

7. Vuelve a leer las oraciones de la _actividad 6_. Decide a qué preposición hace referencia cada explicación. `12.B`

1. Se usa para referirse a una causa o justificación. _____
2. Se usa para referirse a una fecha límite. _____
3. Se usa antes de un verbo para expresar propósito. _____
4. Se usa con sustantivos en locuciones adverbiales de modo. _____
5. Se usa con objetos directos cuando refieren a personas. _____
6. Se usa para referirse al material con el que están fabricados los objetos. _____
7. Se usa para referirse a una hora determinada. _____

8. Reescribe estas oraciones usando la preposición entre paréntesis. `12.B`

1. Karina cortó el papel usando una tijera. (con)

_____

2. Isabela tiene nacionalidad española. (de)

_____

3. Tengo mal humor. (de)

_____

4. Llegó una carta destinada a ti. (para)

_____

5. La señora que tiene cabello rubio se quedó dormida. (de)

_____

6. Debido a este aumento de salario, podré ahorrar un poco más de dinero. (con)

_____

7. Cuando llegué, tú ya estabas dormida. (a)

_____

Actividades

9. Completa estas oraciones con *a, de, con* y *en*. `12.B`

1. La pescadería está _____ dos cuadras de mi casa.

2. La cita es _____ las cuatro de la tarde.

3. Debes estar _____ silencio. La abuela duerme la siesta.

4. _____ gusto, te ayudo a poner la mesa.

5. Todas estas son carteras _____ Rocío.

6. Deja de hablar por teléfono _____ tu novio. ¡La factura será carísima!

7. Escríbele un mensaje de texto _____ Juan y dile que llegaremos tarde.

8. El maestro _____ español nos da muchísima tarea.

9. _____ agosto, iremos a las montañas.

10. _____ los nueve años, viajé por primera vez a *Disneyworld*.

10. Completa este anuncio con *de, a* o *con*. Incluye el artículo o el pronombre personal si corresponde. `12.B`

Feria (1) _____ **las Naciones**: miles de culturas en un solo lugar
(2) _____ 20 (3) _____ 29 (4) _____ agosto, en el centro (5) _____ exposiciones
de la Ciudad de Buenos Aires, podrás visitar la Feria de las Naciones. Allí podrás comprar
productos (6) _____ todos los países (7) _____ mundo: salchichas (8) _____ Alemania,
perfumes de Francia y mucho más. ¡Es como si estuvieras de viaje por todo el mundo!
Ven ¡y trae (9) _____ tus amigos!

11. ¿*Para* o *por*? Completa las oraciones con la preposición correcta. `12.B`

1. No tengo tiempo _____ ir de compras contigo.

2. _____ las tardes, estudio muchísimo.

3. _____ el dolor de garganta, te recomiendo que tomes un té con miel.

4. _____ fin, estamos de vacaciones. Necesito descansar de la escuela.

5. Lucía trabaja _____ una compañía farmacéutica.

6. _____ mí, esa película fue la mejor del año.

7. ¿Viajas _____ placer?

8. La biblioteca es un lugar _____ leer, ¡silencio!

12. ¿Con *a* o sin *a*? Decide si es necesario usar *a* en cada una de estas oraciones. Si no es necesario, escribe X. `12.B`

1. Julia conoce _____ todos sus clientes.

2. ¿Por qué le trajiste flores _____ Paula si no es una ocasión especial?

3. Se buscan _____ profesores de física.

4. Tengo _____ demasiados compañeros de trabajo. No puedo invitarlos _____ todos.

5. Nos dijo el mecánico que debemos ponerle aceite _____ la motocicleta.

6. ¡Cuánto extraño _____ mi casa!

7. ¡Cómo me gustaría visitar _____ Ulises!

13. Elige la opción correcta en cada oración. `12.B`

1. ¿_____ (Para/De) dónde vienes?

2. _____ (Desde/De) mañana, me despertaré todos los días a las 7 a.m.

3. Recuerda pasar _____ (por/entre) la panadería antes de venir a casa.

4. Camina _____ (tras/hasta) la esquina. Cuando estés allí, dobla a la izquierda.

5. La tienda está abierta _____ (de/desde) 3 a 8.

6. ¿_____ (De/Para) dónde vamos esta noche?

7. _____ (Durante/En) tres días, llegarán mis padres.

8. La bicicleta está apoyada _____ (contra / encima de) la pared.

9. _____ (Salvo/Con) nuestra ayuda, usted podrá conseguir un puesto de trabajo.

10. _____ (Ante/Tras) una tormenta, siempre llega la calma.

14. Síntesis Completa las oraciones con las palabras de la lista. Escribe X si no se necesita una preposición. `12.A–12.C`

> sin   de   desde   hasta   para   entre   en   por

1. _____ el momento, no hay pruebas de que los extraterrestres existan.

2. _____ dudas, aprobaremos este examen.

3. _____ la farmacia y la carnicería, está la verdulería.

4. ¿Llegó un correo electrónico _____ mí?

5. _____ estos motivos, no quiero ir de vacaciones con ella.

6. La boda se celebró _____ la iglesia de San Pablo.

7. ¿Se puede vivir _____ la caridad?

8. ¿Conoces _____ la casa de Juan?

15. Síntesis Elige la preposición correcta para completar estas oraciones. `12.A–12.C`

1. _____ tu ayuda, no podremos salvar el planeta.
   a. Con   b. Sin   c. En

2. _____ La Habana, verás qué amable que es la gente.
   a. De   b. En   c. Hasta

3. Hay un teléfono _____ la oficina de la directora.
   a. de   b. en   c. entre

4. _____ el año pasado, vivimos en este edificio.
   a. Desde   b. De   c. Entre

5. ¿Cuál es la diferencia _____ *casar* y *cazar*?
   a. en   b. de   c. entre

6. _____ la lluvia, tuvimos que quedarnos en casa.
   a. De   b. Sin   c. Por

7. _____ Guadalajara, hay 1000 kilómetros.
   a. Hasta   b. Entre   c. De

8. _____ María, todos quieren comer pastel.
   a. Durante   b. Excepto   c. Sin

16. Síntesis Completa las oraciones con preposiciones simples o compuestas. `12.A–12.C`

1. _____ regreso a casa, me topé con una manifestación.

2. Los presidentes se reunieron con miras _____ resolver la situación.

3. Aunque este es un país rico, hay mucha gente que vive _____ la pobreza.

4. No sé qué le pasa. Está _____ muy mal humor.

5. Las discrepancias se resuelven _____ el diálogo.

6. Deja la correspondencia _____ la mesa, junto al teléfono.

17. Síntesis Relaciona los ejemplos con las explicaciones. `12.A–12.C`

_____ 1. Se refiere a la ubicación de algo o alguien.

_____ 2. Se refiere al destinatario de algo.

_____ 3. Se usa para expresar un propósito con verbos de actividad.

_____ 4. Se usa para mostrar que alguien hace algo en tu lugar.

_____ 5. Se usa con verbos de movimiento y sustantivos en España.

_____ 6. En España, se usa otra preposición para esta misma frase.

_____ 7. Se usa para expresar posesión.

_____ 8. Se usa con el verbo **estar** para describir condiciones.

_____ 9. Se usa con el verbo **estar** para expresar un trabajo temporario.

a. Aprendo español **para** hablar bien con mis parientes de México.

b. **En** Barcelona, encontrarás gente de todo el mundo.

c. Mis amigos están **de** visita hasta el primero de octubre.

d. Hay un mensaje **para** ti. Léelo.

e. ¿Podrías buscar a Juanito **por** mí?

f. Florencia está **de** camarera en el bar de la esquina.

g. ¿La policía viene **a por** mí? ¡Yo no hice nada!

h. No me interesan las vidas **de** los famosos.

i. Entré **a** la casa y se cortó la luz.

18. Síntesis Completa los espacios en blanco con la preposición (simple o compuesta) adecuada. Como pista, tienes la primera letra de cada una. `12.A–12.C`

1. H_____ la playa, hay dos kilómetros.

2. S_____ mi madre, "al que madruga, Dios lo ayuda".

3. C_____ tu casa, vive la profesora de matemáticas.

4. J_____ mis amigos, organizaré una gran fiesta de cumpleaños.

5. H_____ fines del siglo veinte, se inventó el Bluetooth.

6. E_____ marzo y junio, aquí es otoño.

7. T_____ esa expresión dura, se esconde una persona muy amable.

8. E_____ Juan, todos tienen menos de dieciocho años.

9. E_____ esa época, todos trabajábamos en la misma empresa.

10. Quiero salir c_____ en una cita.

11. C_____ ese vestido, llamarás la atención de todos los invitados.

12. Josefina es siempre la primera e_____ terminar los exámenes.

13. Entré e_____ la estación de metro y compré un boleto.

Practice more at **vhlcentral.com.**

Actividades

1. Reemplaza el texto subrayado con el pronombre adecuado. `13.A–13.B`

1. Camila y yo jugamos a las cartas toda la tarde. _____

2. ¿Sofía viene a la fiesta de fin de año? _____

3. Sandra y Facundo están durmiendo. _____

4. La abuela vendrá de visita el fin de semana. _____

5. Mi esposa y yo formamos una familia hermosa. _____

6. Romina y Laura son estudiantes de quinto año. _____

7. Mi hermana, mi padre y yo iremos de vacaciones a las montañas. _____

8. No pienses en los costos. La calidad es lo importante. _____

2. ¿Formal o informal? Decide quién dice cada frase. `13.A–13.B`

____ 1. Le prometo que, de ahora en adelante, llegaré temprano todos los días.

____ 2. ¿Podría decirme dónde está la juguetería, por favor?

____ 3. No me molestes más, ¿acaso no ves que estoy estudiando?

____ 4. Vosotros debéis respetar las reglas.

____ 5. Ustedes prometieron organizar competencias deportivas para nosotros.

____ 6. ¿Quieres darme tu teléfono celular?

a. un empleado a su jefe

b. un niño a su hermano

c. una niña a un anciano

d. un director de escuela a los alumnos

e. una amiga a otra

f. un alumno a las autoridades escolares

3. Reescribe las oraciones reemplazando el pronombre subrayado por el pronombre entre paréntesis. `13.A–13.C`

1. Vosotros habéis jugado muy bien esta tarde. (nosotros) _____

2. La empresa está satisfecha con ella. (tú) _____

3. Ustedes siempre tienen muchas vacaciones. (vosotros) _____

4. Para él, las tareas son fáciles. (usted) _____

5. Entre nosotros, hay muy buena comunicación. (ellos) _____

6. Ustedes son estudiantes, ¿verdad? (ellas) _____

4. Completa las oraciones con las palabras de la lista. `13.A–13.C`

vosotros	él	mí	conmigo
yo	tú (2)	ti	consigo

1. ¿Vas _____ o voy yo al supermercado?

2. Para _____, este programa de televisión es muy malo. Pero es solo mi opinión, obviamente.

3. Carlos no está contento _____ mismo.

4. Entre Gabriela y _____ hay muchos conflictos. Debemos hablar sobre eso.

5. Según _____, todos deberíamos trabajar de lunes a lunes.

6. Rita es colombiana y _____ eres venezolano, ¿no?

7. _____ sabéis que es importante mantener la imagen de la empresa.

8. Tengo un regalo hermoso para _____. Te encantará.

9. _____ vivirás tranquila. Verás que soy una persona muy tranquila.

5. Reescribe las oraciones reemplazando el objeto directo por el pronombre correspondiente. `13.E`

1. Roberto compró naranjas en el mercado central. _____

2. Llamamos al abuelo porque lo extrañábamos. _____

3. Julia estudió muy bien la lección de gramática. _____

4. Finalmente la policía atrapó al ladrón. _____

5. Gonzalo buscó sus zapatillas debajo de la mesa. _____

6. Los obreros comen el almuerzo a las dos de la tarde. _____

7. Constanza y Sofía les compran flores a sus madres. _____

8. Traje los libros de la biblioteca. _____

6. Escribe la pregunta o la respuesta según corresponda. `13.E`

> **Modelo**
>
> ¿A quién viste en la fiesta?   ¿ _Qué cocinaste_ ?
> _Vi a tu hermana._ (tu hermana)   Cociné un pollo al horno.

1. ¿A quién invitamos a nuestra fiesta de aniversario? _____ (todos nuestros amigos)

2. ¿_____ esta noche? Conocí a los padres de Estela.

3. ¿_____ hacer? Prefiero descansar un poco y luego ir a un museo.

4. ¿A quién ama tu hermana? _____ (su novio)

5. ¿Qué tipo de libros lees? _____ (novelas románticas)

6. ¿A quién has llamado por teléfono? _____ (tú)

7. ¿Qué ciudades visitaste? _____ (París y Roma)

8. ¿_____ esta noche? Visitamos a tus primos.

7. Usa los fragmentos para escribir oraciones, reemplazando el objeto indirecto por el pronombre correspondiente. `13.F`

1. Julia / dio / una bufanda / a su hermana _____

2. dijiste / mentiras / a tus compañeros de clase _____

3. ellos / contaron historias de terror / a nuestros hermanos _____

4. el camarero / recomendó / una paella a los turistas _____

5. tu madre / mostró / al cliente / la habitación _____

6. hoy leerás / a tu hermanito / un cuento de hadas _____

7. pedí / dinero / a mis padres _____

8. Lee el relato de Josefina. Primero, marca todos los pronombres de objetos indirectos. Luego indica el sujeto de esas oraciones. `13.F`

Soy una persona un poco complicada. No me gusta salir de casa. Me molesta mucho el ruido de los carros y motocicletas. Por eso, prefiero estar en casa.

Me gusta leer novelas: sobre todo, me interesan las novelas románticas. Además, me encanta ver comedias en la televisión. Ojalá algún día encuentre a mi pareja ideal. Un hombre a quien le guste mirar televisión conmigo, le interesen las noticias de la actualidad y le encante cocinar. ¿Os parecen demasiado grandes mis expectativas?

9. Reordena las oraciones. `13.G`

1. la ceremonia / invitaré / a / Los / religiosa _____

2. espera / en / la esquina / Claudia / te _____

3. gran sorpresa / daré / una / Les _____

4. tres entradas / nos / Emilia / para el teatro / compró _____

5. su / me / regalará / Omar / cámara de fotos antigua _____

6. a su casa / Los / de inmediato / llamaré _____

7. ¿? / para armar / das / Me / las instrucciones / la cama _____

10. Reescribe las oraciones. Sigue el modelo como ejemplo. `13.G`

> **Modelo**
>
> Te voy a enseñar inglés.
> *Voy a enseñarte inglés.*

1. ¿Nos estás preparando la merienda?

   _____

2. Yo podría ayudarte con tus tareas.

   _____

3. Lucía me va a acompañar hasta la esquina.

   _____

4. El público está alentándolos.

   _____

5. La directora les va a enviar una carta de recomendación.

   _____

6. Estamos dándoles excelentes ideas para hacer un negocio.

   _____

11. Lucas te hace muchas preguntas. Contéstalas usando el pronombre adecuado. `13.G`

1. **LUCAS** Falta poco para la fiesta. ¿Has comprado toda la decoración?

   TÚ Sí, _____.

2. **LUCAS** ¿Sería bueno decorar las ventanas?

   TÚ Sí, _____.

3. **LUCAS** ¿Has mandado las invitaciones?

   TÚ Sí, _____.

4. **LUCAS** ¿Has llamado a los invitados para confirmar su presencia?

   TÚ No, aún _____.

5. **LUCAS** ¿Me darás pronto la lista de invitados?

   TÚ Sí, _____.

6. **LUCAS** ¿Necesitas mi ayuda?

   TÚ ¡Gracias! Pero no _____.

12. Matías tiene una lista de quehaceres que le dejó su mamá. Completa los comentarios que escribe Matías junto a cada quehacer usando pronombres para los objetos directos e indirectos. `13.G`

○ HACER TAREA ✓	Ya la he hecho.
LLAMAR TÍA ✓ (1)	
ARREGLAR COMPUTADORA ✖ (2)	
LLEVAR PAQUETE JUANA ✖ (3)	
BUSCAR PERRO ✓ (4)	
DAR COMIDA PERRO ✖ (5)	
DEVOLVER SILLA VECINO ✓ (6)	

13. Une los ejemplos con las explicaciones. `13.H`

_____ 1. Se repite el objeto para enfatizar su identidad.

_____ 2. Se debe repetir el objeto cuando los nombres propios están antepuestos al verbo.

_____ 3. Se repite el objeto cuando hace referencia a cosas.

_____ 4. Se repite el objeto cuando se hace referencia a conceptos abstractos.

_____ 5. Se repite el objeto para indicar que la situación afecta a alguien directamente.

a. ¡Cuídame muy bien a mi perrito!

b. Tienen que comprarle más memoria a mi computadora.

c. A Marta la vemos todos los jueves.

d. Todo esto jamás podremos recordarlo.

e. A mí no me mientes, ¿verdad?

14. Síntesis Elige el ejemplo que no se corresponde con los demás. `13.A–13.H`

1. _____
   a. Nosotros somos profesionales.
   b. Ustedes son argentinos.
   c. Vosotros sois extranjeros.

2. _____
   a. Llamé a Francisco ayer.
   b. Invitamos a todos nuestros amigos.
   c. Se la envié la semana pasada.

3. _____
   a. Contigo soy feliz.
   b. Ella no tiene problemas conmigo.
   c. Según ella, yo luzco mayor de lo que soy.

4. _____
   a. A nadie le interesa jugar al póker.
   b. A Juana la quiero mucho.
   c. A mi madre le encanta ir de compras.

5. _____
   a. Se lo daré mañana.
   b. Pronto se venderá la casa.
   c. Se lo he dicho mil veces.

6. _____
   a. No nos despierte muy temprano, por favor.
   b. Llámenme después de las 10 de la mañana.
   c. A mí me quieres, ¿no?

15. **Síntesis Corrige las oraciones que son incorrectas.** `13.A–13.H`

1. Traje muchas flores para tú.

   _____

2. ¿Te molestan mis ronquidos?

   _____

3. Os daré un regalo si te portas bien, Juana.

   _____

4. Vosotros ya habéis hécholo.

   _____

5. Yo la llevo a ella a su casa, no te preocupes.

   _____

6. A Daniela le conozco de la universidad.

   _____

7. A ti te aprecio mucho.

   _____

8. Mis tíos las me regalaron para Navidad.

   _____

16. **Síntesis Completa la carta de Santiago con las palabras de la lista.** `13.A–13.H`

> nos   les (2)   os (2)   me (2)   le   ti   vos

Queridos Juan y Alfredo:

Os escribo porque a mis tíos se (1) _____ ocurrió una idea perfecta para un negocio: ¡un servicio de piscinas móviles! Ya sé que probablemente no (2) _____ parecerá algo viable, pero si tan solo leyerais el plan de negocios que ellos escribieron... ¡es fantástico!

La idea (3) _____ vino a la mente un día de verano, de muchísimo calor. Mi tía (4) _____ dijo a mi tío:

—¿A (5) _____ te gustaría tener una piscina en casa?

Y, mi tío, que es argentino, le contestó con su tono característico:

—A mí (6) _____ parece que a (7) _____ el calor te hace mal... ¿no ves que no tenemos espacio?

Desde ese momento, no dejaron de pensar en tener una piscina, hasta que un día ambos se miraron entre sí, y se dijeron:

—¿Y si (8) _____ trajeran una piscina a nuestra casa?

Bueno, el plan de negocios es muy largo, pero si queréis, (9) _____ lo mando por correo postal.

¿(10) _____ enviaríais vuestras direcciones?

Saludos y hasta pronto,

Santiago

Practice more at **vhlcentral.com.**

Chapter 14

1. Reordena las oraciones. Usa las mayúsculas como ayuda. 14.A

1. a comer, / ¿ / no es así / viene / ? / Úrsula

   _____

2. hizo / frío, / verdad / Ayer /¿ / ?

   _____

3. ¿ / Karina / Duerme / todavía / ?

   _____

4. ¿ / toman / ? / Ustedes / el avión / de las 12, / no

   _____

5. Tiene / las notas / el profesor / del examen / ¿ / ?

   _____

6. Sabe / que / Florencia / la llamé / ¿ / ?

   _____

2. Escribe dos tipos de preguntas posibles para estas respuestas, como en el modelo. 14.A

> **Modelo**
>
> *¿Corrió Juana la maratón?*
> *Juana corrió la maratón, ¿no es cierto?*
> Sí, Juana corrió la maratón.

1. _____

   _____

   No, mi hermana no tiene quince años.

2. _____

   _____

   Sí, hoy debo ir a la escuela.

3. _____

   _____

   No, ellos no harán las compras hoy.

4. _____

   _____

   Sí, la primavera en nuestro país comienza el 21 de septiembre.

5. _____

   _____

   No, el edificio no fue construido en 1980.

6. _____

   _____

   No, no quiero pastel.

3. **Sabrina está en una entrevista de trabajo. Completa las preguntas del entrevistador con *qué*, *cuál* o *cuáles*.** `14.B`

ENTREVISTADOR Buenos días, ¿(1) _____ es su nombre?

SABRINA Me llamo Sabrina Pérez Garrido.

ENTREVISTADOR ¿(2) _____ son sus aptitudes para este trabajo?

SABRINA Bueno... soy estudiante de administración, hablo español e inglés, y tengo un buen dominio de la informática.

ENTREVISTADOR Bien, ¿(3) _____ piensa sobre esta compañía?

SABRINA Pienso que es una compañía de gran nivel, con una buena política de recursos humanos y una gran reputación a nivel mundial.

ENTREVISTADOR ¿(4) _____ son sus pasatiempos?

SABRINA Me gusta leer, hacer deportes y tomar fotografías.

ENTREVISTADOR ¿(5) _____ tipo de trabajo espera hacer para nosotros?

SABRINA Me gustaría ser asistente de directorio.

ENTREVISTADOR Bien, ¿(6) _____ son sus expectativas salariales?

SABRINA No sé exactamente... escucho ofertas.

ENTREVISTADOR Por último, ¿(7) _____ es su número de teléfono?

SABRINA 309-987-0008.

ENTREVISTADOR La llamaremos en cuanto tengamos novedades.

4. **En cada pregunta, elige la opción correcta.** `14.B`

1. ¿_____ (Quién/Cuál/Quiénes) fue el libertador de Venezuela?
   Simón Bolívar.

2. ¿_____ (Quién/Cuál/Quiénes) es tu fecha de nacimiento?
   El 30 de octubre de 1992.

3. ¿_____ (Qué/Cuál/Quiénes) fueron a tu cumpleaños?
   Mi tía Estela, mis padres y casi todos mis amigos.

4. ¿_____ (Quién/Cuál/Quiénes) era Marilyn Monroe?
   Era una actriz estadounidense.

5. ¿_____ (Quién/Cuál/Qué) estás viendo en la tele?
   Una película de terror.

6. ¿_____ (Quién/Cuál/Quiénes) viven en esta casa?
   Solamente Víctor y su perro.

7. ¿_____ (Quién/Cuál/Qué) llamó por teléfono?
   Tu jefe.

8. ¿_____ (Quién/Cuál/Cuáles) es tu apellido?
   Fernández.

5. **Completa las preguntas con el pronombre interrogativo adecuado.** `14.B`

1. ¿Cuá_____ kilos de tomates quiere, señora?

2. ¿Cuá_____ días de vacaciones tenemos?

3. ¿Cuá_____ costó la compra en el supermercado?

4. ¿Cuá_____ café has bebido hoy?

5. ¿Cuá_____ empleados tiene la compañía?

6. ¿Cuá_____ lejos está la próxima gasolinera?

7. ¿Cuá_____ trabajaste la semana pasada?

8. ¿Cuá_____ eficaz es este medicamento?

6. Reescribe estas preguntas usando *cómo*. `14.B`

1. ¿Cuán difícil es el problema?
   _____

2. ¿Cuán grande es la habitación?
   _____

3. ¿Qué altura tiene tu padre?
   _____

4. ¿Qué tal te sientes esta tarde?
   _____

5. ¿Qué te parece nuestro apartamento nuevo?
   _____

6. ¿Cuál es el peso de la lavadora?
   _____

7. Completa esta conversación con las palabras de la lista. `14.B`

cuánto	qué	qué tal	cuántos	cómo	cuáles	cuán

VENDEDOR Buenos días. ¿(1) _____?

CLIENTE Muy bien, gracias, ¿y usted?

VENDEDOR Bien, gracias. ¿(2) _____ le puedo ofrecer?

CLIENTE Bueno, quisiera tomates. ¿(3) _____ me recomienda?

VENDEDOR Mire, hoy trajeron unos que están a buen precio. ¿(4) _____ kilos quiere?

CLIENTE ¿(5) _____ son de grandes?

VENDEDOR Son para ensalada, de tamaño medio.

CLIENTE Bien, entonces un kilo, por favor.

VENDEDOR Aquí tiene.

CLIENTE ¿(6) _____ le debo?

VENDEDOR Tres con cincuenta.

CLIENTE Aquí tiene. ¡Hasta luego!

8. Escribe las preguntas indirectas para estas preguntas directas. `14.B`

1. ¿Quién es tu cantante favorito?
   Quiero saber _____.

2. ¿Cuántos años tiene Joaquín?
   Dime _____.

3. ¿Cuánto dinero hay en la cuenta?
   Dile a Carlos _____.

4. ¿Cómo se llama la persona que me espera?
   Recuerda decirme _____.

5. ¿Cuánto tiempo horneas la torta?
   Por favor, dime _____.

6. ¿Cuál es tu número de teléfono?
   Quisiera saber _____.

7. ¿Qué te gustaría beber en la cena?
   Quiero saber _____.

9. Une los elementos de las tres columnas para formar preguntas. `14.B`

1. ¿Qué	años	haces deportes?
2. ¿De qué	altura	debes renovar tu licencia de conducir?
3. ¿Con qué	frecuencia	es tu camiseta?
4. ¿Cada cuántos	talla	de rápido?
5. ¿A qué	nadas	sobre el nivel del mar está la ciudad de Quito?
6. ¿Cómo	distancia	hay entre tu casa y la mía?

10. Reescribe las oraciones usando la palabra entre paréntesis. `14.B`

1. Ismael quiere saber la razón de su despido. (porqué)
_____

2. Dime el lugar en que viste tu teléfono por última vez. (dónde)
_____

3. ¿A qué hora vendrás a buscarme? (cuándo)
_____

4. ¿De qué manera puedo contactar contigo? (cómo)
_____

5. ¿Por qué razón no viniste a mi fiesta de cumpleaños? (por qué)
_____

6. ¿Cómo está la comida que preparé? (qué tal)
_____

11. Elige la opción correcta para cada oración. `14.B`

1. ¿_____ (A qué / Cuánta / Cuál) distancia está el hospital?

2. Realmente no sé _____ (porqué / cuándo / por qué) no me despertaste esta mañana.

3. ¿_____ (Cuál / Qué tal / Cómo) tus cosas? Hace tanto que no nos vemos.

4. ¿_____ (Hasta dónde / Dónde / Hasta cuándo) vas? Quizás puedo llevarte con el carro.

5. ¿_____ (Cómo/Cuán/Cuánto) son de caras esas bicicletas? Me gustaría comprar una nueva.

6. ¿_____ (Cuáles/Qué/Cuál) son tus zapatos, los verdes o los negros?

7. Desconozco totalmente el _____ (cuándo/cómo/porqué) del funcionamiento de las redes inalámbricas. Es una tecnología que no logro comprender.

12. Decide si las siguientes oraciones son correctas. Si no lo son, corrígelas. `14.B`

1. Explícame como ir hasta el centro de la ciudad. _____

2. ¿Qué tal si tomamos un café en este bar? _____

3. ¿Cuánto años tienes? _____

4. ¿Que es *alacena* en inglés? _____

5. ¿Cuánta personas van al cine los fines de semana? _____

6. ¿Qué grande es la cocina? _____

7. Dime el por qué de tu visita. _____

13. Ricardo está de vacaciones y está maravillado con todo lo que ve. Completa las exclamaciones de Ricardo. `14.C`

> **Modelo**
>
> Ricardo piensa: Los parques de esta ciudad son grandes.
> Ricardo dice: *¡Qué grandes que son los parques de esta ciudad!*

1. Ricardo piensa: Hay tantas flores en este parque.
Ricardo dice: _____

2. Ricardo piensa: Este barrio es muy elegante.
Ricardo dice: _____

3. Ricardo piensa: Los restaurantes son tan caros.
Ricardo dice: _____

4. Ricardo piensa: Las calles son tan limpias.
Ricardo dice: _____

5. Ricardo piensa: Me gustaría vivir en esta ciudad.
Ricardo dice: _____

6. Ricardo piensa: Ojalá fuera rico para vivir aquí.
Ricardo dice: _____

14. Une los elementos de las dos columnas para formar oraciones. `14.D`

1. ¿Qué tanta _____   a. tenemos que esperar para que deje de llover?

2. ¡Qué tanto _____   b. discoteca te gusta más?

3. ¡Qué tantos _____   c. animales hay en este zoológico!

4. ¿Qué tanto _____   d. ciudad vienes?

5. ¿De cuál _____   e. hablas! No te callas un segundo.

6. ¿Cuál _____   f. gente hay en el concierto?

15. Síntesis Cristina es una famosa cantante. Completa la entrevista que le hicieron con las palabras de la lista. `14.A–14.D`

| cuántos | cómo | cuál | no es cierto | qué tal | cuándo | qué (3) |

CONDUCTOR Ante todo, Cristina, muchas gracias por darnos esta entrevista. ¿(1) _____ fue tu última entrevista televisiva?

CRISTINA La última fue en agosto de este año. Estuve de gira por todo el país y casi no he tenido tiempo para entrevistas.

CONDUCTOR ¿(2) _____ tu gira? ¿Estás contenta?

CRISTINA La verdad es que fue muy intensa. Muchísimos conciertos, muchas ciudades.

CONDUCTOR ¿(3) _____ fue la reacción del público ante este nuevo espectáculo que presentaste?

CRISTINA Mi público es muy efusivo: cantan, aplauden, bailan. Evidentemente les gustó, pero eso es lo que uno siempre espera, ¿(4) _____?

CONDUCTOR Sí, pero sabemos también que tuviste una convocatoria increíble en tus conciertos. ¿(5) _____ espectadores tuviste?

CRISTINA No sabría decirte... ¡Pero no te imaginas con (6) _____ rapidez se agotaron las entradas!

CONDUCTOR ¡(7) _____ me alegro por ti!

CRISTINA Gracias. Ahora estoy preparando mi nuevo disco.

CONDUCTOR ¿(8) _____ tanto tendremos que esperar para escucharlo?

CRISTINA En dos meses saldrá a la venta. Espero que les guste.

CONDUCTOR Muchas gracias, Cristina. Y no te imaginas con (9) _____ ansias esperamos tu nueva producción.

16. Síntesis Une los ejemplos con las explicaciones. `14.A–14.D`

_____ 1. Es una estructura afirmativa seguida de una pregunta.

_____ 2. Es una pregunta para dar a elegir a alguien entre varias alternativas concretas.

_____ 3. Es una pregunta cuyo pronombre interrogativo concuerda en género y número con el sustantivo que modifica.

_____ 4. Es una abreviación de *cuánto* y se usa antes de adjetivos.

_____ 5. Es una pregunta con estructura afirmativa.

_____ 6. Es un pronombre interrogativo que no varía en género ni en número cuando está seguido por verbos.

_____ 7. Es una expresión que se usa en Latinoamérica para decir *cuántos*.

a. ¿Cuánto costó la computadora?

b. ¿Cuántos kilos de patatas has comprado?

c. Explícame por qué no llegaste a horario.

d. ¡Qué tantos primos tienes!

e. ¿Qué prefieres beber, agua o jugo?

f. ¿Cuán pesado es tu equipaje?

g. Aquí hace demasiado calor, ¿no?

Practice more at **vhlcentral.com**.

1. Marca los antecedentes de los pronombres relativos. En el caso de *cuyo/a*, subraya también la frase con la que concuerda. `15.A`

Mujer busca marido

Me llamo Olivia y tengo 44 años. Busco a un hombre que tenga entre 45 y 55 años y que esté dispuesto a formar una pareja estable.

Me gustaría tener una pareja que no tenga hijos, preferentemente. Me gustan los hombres altos, elegantes y formales.

Soy activa y llevo una vida que podría definir como tranquila. Trabajo durante la semana y los fines de semana hago actividades al aire libre. El estilo de vida que llevo es un poco costoso, por lo tanto, preferiría un hombre cuyo salario sea superior o igual al mío.

Si eres un hombre que tiene estas cualidades, no dudes en llamar al teléfono que aparece abajo.

2. Reordena los elementos para formar oraciones lógicas. `15.A`

1. que / es la mujer / Lucila / las flores / me dio _____

2. donde / un lugar / puedo comprar / Encontré / productos orgánicos _____
   _____

3. que / Te / una mujer / ha llamado / se llama Elisa _____

4. Os gustó / que / os di / ¿ / el regalo / ? _____

5. donde / El barrio / está / vivo / muy lejos del centro _____

6. que / en el bar / Nos encontramos / te indiqué _____

3. Une los elementos de las tres columnas para formar oraciones. `15.A`

1. Las tareas	quienes	currículum sea mejor.
2. La tienda	que	puerta es azul es demasiado oscura.
3. Todas las estudiantes	cuyo	hablé me recomendaron el mismo libro.
4. La habitación	con las que	me olvidé el paraguas está cerrada.
5. Contrataremos a la candidata	cuya	cenamos anoche nos han invitado a su casa.
6. Los amigos con los	donde	te encargué deben estar terminadas antes del 20 de junio.

4. Decide si las oraciones son correctas. Si no lo son, corrígelas. `15.A`

1. Le presento al empleado fue contratado la semana pasada. _____

2. La escuela quien está en la esquina es muy buena. _____

3. Los alumnos que tengan buenas calificaciones podrán recibir becas. _____

4. Elige la bufanda donde más te guste. _____

5. Daniela, quien conocí en la escuela, ahora trabaja conmigo. _____

6. Beberé lo que tú bebas. _____

5. Decide si estas proposiciones relativas son explicativas (*non-defining*) (ND) o especificativas (*defining*) (D). `15.B`

_____ 1. Gastón, quien nunca duerme la siesta, siempre se va a dormir a las 8 de la noche.

_____ 2. Las noches que son despejadas son las más frías.

_____ 3. Me encanta la playa a la que fuimos la semana pasada.

_____ 4. Mi bicicleta nueva, la cual compré en el mercado de las pulgas, funciona de maravilla.

_____ 5. Los libros que compré ayer son carísimos.

_____ 6. La niña a la que saludé es nuestra vecina.

6. Completa las oraciones con *que, el que* y *la que*. `15.B`

1. La situación en _____ estoy no es muy agradable.

2. Los colores _____ más me gustan son el rojo y el azul.

3. El banco en _____ estoy sentado es incómodo.

4. Las mujeres _____ trabajan conmigo son súper amables.

5. La discoteca en _____ te conocí es la mejor del pueblo.

6. Te diré el motivo por _____ no vine.

7. No le cuentes a nadie la idea _____ te di.

7. Combina las dos oraciones usando el pronombre relativo entre paréntesis. `15.B`

1. París tiene muchos puentes. París es mi ciudad favorita. (que)

_____

2. La profesora se llama Silvia. Conocí a esta profesora ayer. (quien)

_____

3. Trabajé para una empresa durante 20 años. La empresa está ahora en quiebra. (cual)

_____

4. La semana que viene viajaré a Europa. Europa es mi continente favorito. (cual)

_____

5. Mañana jugaré baloncesto. No he jugado jamás antes al baloncesto. (cual)

_____

8. Completa las oraciones con las palabras de la lista. `15.B`

| lo que | quienes | cualquiera | cuyo | quien | que (2) |

1. Las personas _____ número de documento termine en 8 deberán presentarse el día lunes.

2. _____ quiera comer rico y barato vendrá a nuestro restaurante.

3. El _____ conduzca sin prudencia recibirá una sanción.

4. _____ más me interesa es la historia.

5. Todos los países _____ forman la Unión Europea tienen proyectos en común.

6. Me agradan las personas con _____ puedo hablar sobre literatura.

9. **Reescribe las oraciones. Como ayuda, tienes las primeras palabras.** `15.B`

1. Yo lavaré los platos. Soy yo _____.

2. El jefe pagará una parte de los despidos. Es el jefe _____.

3. Comimos una exquisita paella en Valencia. Fue en Valencia _____.

4. Cervantes escribió *Don Quijote de la Mancha*. Fue Cervantes _____.

5. Ganamos la competencia el fin de semana pasado. Fue el fin de semana pasado _____.

6. Los estudiantes tienen demasiados reclamos. Son los estudiantes _____.

10. **Reescribe las oraciones usando adverbios relativos.** `15.C`

1. La ciudad en la que vivo tiene 200.000 habitantes. _____

2. Lo haré del modo en que tú me has dicho._____

3. En la época en que nací, mis padres vivían en el extranjero._____

4. Ella siempre me ha dado todo lo que tenía. _____

5. Me gusta la manera en que crecen esas flores. _____

11. **Síntesis Elige la opción correcta para cada oración.** `15.A–15.D`

1. No me gusta nada la manera _____ me hablas.
   a. la que   b. en la que   c. que

2. Como dice el dicho: "A _____ madruga, Dios lo ayuda".
   a. los   b. que   c. quien

3. Cecilia _____ es una excelente compañera de trabajo.
   a. , quien es amiga de María,
   b. quien es amiga de María
   c. cuyo cabello es rubio

4. Mañana no tengo que trabajar, _____ me alegra muchísimo.
   a. el que   b. que   c. lo cual

5. El químico _____ se fabricó este material es tóxico.
   a. con quien   b. con el que   c. cuyo

6. Te invitaré _____ que vaya de vacaciones.
   a. donde   b. adondequiera   c. adonde

7. El hombre _____ hablabas es el embajador de China.
   a. con que   b. con quien   c. quien

12. **Síntesis Completa las oraciones con el pronombre relativo o el adverbio relativo correcto.** `15.A–15.C`

1. Para la época _____ se fundó esta ciudad, la economía era básicamente ganadera.

2. Este periódico, _____ nombre es *La Tribuna*, es uno de los más importantes del país.

3. Ayer conocí a tu padre, de _____ me hablaste tanto.

4. El mismo día _____ choqué con el carro, tú perdiste tu vuelo a Colombia.

5. El doctor _____ me atendió la semana pasada hoy está de vacaciones.

6. La Navidad más divertida _____ pasé fue la de 1998.

7. Te presentaré a las personas con _____ trabajo.

8. La casa _____ vivo es de alquiler.

9. Hoy me levanté muy temprano, _____ es un gran esfuerzo para mí.

10. Mi mejor amiga, _____ es fotógrafa, trabaja mucho.

11. El modo _____ trabaja mi hermano es muy particular.

12. Vimos una casa _____ muros estaban cubiertos de hierba.

Practice more at **vhlcentral.com.**

1. Completa las oraciones con las conjunciones coordinantes de la lista. `16.B`

> ni... ni...   e   pues   sino   no... ni...   y   pero

1. Cuando lleguemos a casa, comeremos frutas _____ chocolates.

2. Mis padres se ducharán _____ irán a hacer las compras.

3. Ese vestido _____ es amarillo _____ naranja: es rosado.

4. _____ crudo, _____ demasiado cocido; quiero que el pavo esté en el punto justo.

5. Llegamos a tiempo a la fiesta, _____ nos olvidamos del regalo para el cumpleañero.

6. No es tu padre _____ tú quien debe hacer la tarea.

7. Voy a ducharme, _____ he hecho deportes ¡y no quiero oler mal!

2. En cada oración, decide cuál es la conjunción coordinante adecuada (*y/o*). `16.B`

1. Tenemos entre cuatro _____ cinco dólares; no sé exactamente cuántos.

2. Bien comes ya mismo _____ esperas hasta las cuatro de la tarde.

3. Mi computadora nueva tiene cámara web _____ pantalla de 17 pulgadas.

4. Por cinco dólares puedes comprar una hamburguesa con patatas fritas, ya sea con un refresco _____ con un zumo, tú eliges.

5. Sara es la cantante; _____ tú, el guitarrista.

6. ¿Cuándo _____ dónde nos encontraremos con Raquel? Pásame la información por mensaje de texto, por favor.

7. Se lo dices tú _____ se lo digo yo.

3. Completa la carta con la opción correcta. `16.B`

> Querida Gabriela:
>
> No sabes cuánto te extraño. Hace apenas un mes que te fuiste a vivir al D.F., (1) _____ (pero/pues) me parece que fue hace un año. (2) _____ (Ni/Tanto) Guadalupe (3) _____ (ni/como) yo te echamos de menos (4) _____ (pues/y) nos gustaría que volvieras pronto; (5) _____ (sin embargo / sino) sabemos que México es tu país favorito (6) _____ (y/e) que eres feliz allí.
>
> Por aquí todo sigue igual: (7) _____ (no/ni) peor (8) _____ (no/ni) mejor. Tenemos siete (9) _____ (o/u) ocho compañeros de clase nuevos, muy simpáticos todos. Uno de ellos habla a la perfección (10) _____ (tan / tanto) inglés como francés (11) _____ (y/o) español, (12) _____ (pero/pues) su madre es francesa, su padre es mexicano y él nació en Estados Unidos.
>
> Recuerda que, si quieres hablar con nosotras, nos puedes contactar (13) _____ (bien/ni) por chat, (14) _____ (sino/bien) por Skype.
>
> ¡Un abrazo fuerte!
>
> Milena

Actividades

4. En esta conversación indica las conjunciones subordinantes. `16.C`

PACIENTE Buenos días, doctor Pérez.

DOCTOR Buenos días. Dígame: ¿qué lo trae por aquí?

PACIENTE A ver... desde hace dos días, cuando me levanto, me duele mucho el estómago.

DOCTOR Me ha dicho que le duele el estómago. ¿Suele comer alimentos poco saludables?

PACIENTE No... pero, pensándolo mejor, aunque no coma nada me duele la barriga. Eso sí, bebo café, me encanta.

DOCTOR Entonces usted no come, pero toma café. ¿Cuántas tazas toma por día?

PACIENTE Tomo solamente dos o tres en cuanto llego al trabajo, dos más una vez que tengo un tiempito libre, y tres más por la tarde porque me da sueño trabajar tanto.

DOCTOR ¡Y después me pregunta que cuál es el motivo de su dolor de estómago!

PACIENTE Creo que tiene razón, doctor. Debería tomar el café con un chorrito de leche, ¿no?

DOCTOR Mire, como usted no mide cuánto café toma, se lo prohibiré totalmente. Siempre que sienta ganas de tomarse un cafecito, tómese un té o, mucho mejor, un vaso de agua, de manera que su estómago no siga empeorando.

PACIENTE Muchas gracias, doctor.

DOCTOR ¡Cuídese! Adiós.

5. Reescribe las oraciones para que contengan cláusulas sustantivas (*nominal clauses*). `16.C`

> **Modelo**
>
> Tengo frío. (dice/Rosa)
> *Rosa dice que tiene frío.*

1. ¿Cuál es tu número de teléfono? (pregunta/Leonel)
   _____

2. ¿Tienes el correo electrónico de Carla? (pregunta/José)
   _____

3. El lechero vendrá a las nueve. (creen/Juan y Marina)
   _____

4. ¿Has oído el timbre? (pregunta/Estela)
   _____

5. Me gustaría dormir la siesta. (dice/Mirta)
   _____

6. Indica si estas oraciones contienen conjunciones subordinantes temporales o causales. `16.C`

1. Antes de que llegaras, estaba hablando por teléfono con Luis. _____

2. Llegué tarde al trabajo, ya que perdí el tren de las 8. _____

3. Como no me has llamado, te llamo yo a ti. _____

4. Tan pronto como empezó la tormenta, la gente se refugió en las tiendas. _____

5. Cada vez que voy a visitarte, me esperas con una comida riquísima. _____

6. Dado que no se han cumplido las reglas, todos tendrán sus respectivas sanciones. _____

7. Puesto que vuestros perros ladran día y noche, deberéis mudaros a otro lugar. _____

8. Mientras tú cocinas, yo lavo la ropa. _____

7. En cada oración, elige la opción correcta. `16.C`

1. Compré muchas frutas y verduras, _____ (de manera que / dado que) tendremos la nevera llenísima.

2. Venderemos nuestro carro, _____ (de modo que / puesto que) casi no lo usamos.

3. Tengo muchísimo sueño, _____ (porque / así que) dormiré un rato, ¿sí?

4. Alejandra quiere ir a la playa, _____ (de modo que / porque) quiere disfrutar de este hermoso día.

5. El supermercado está cerrado, _____ (así que / puesto que) tendremos que comer en el restaurante.

6. Mis compañeros de apartamento organizaron una fiesta en el parque, el fin de semana _____ (a causa de que / de modo que) no tengamos que limpiar nuestro apartamento al día siguiente.

8. Une las oraciones usando las conjunciones dadas. `16.C`

> **Modelo**
>
> Mis amigos son muy graciosos. Sin embargo, yo nunca me divierto con ellos.
> (aunque) *Aunque mis amigos son muy graciosos, yo nunca me divierto con ellos.*

1. Estudio muchísimo la gramática española. Sin embargo, siempre cometo los mismos errores.
(a pesar de que) _____

2. Trabajaré mucho hoy. Por lo tanto, mañana podré descansar.
(de modo que) _____

3. Martín cocina. Parece un experto.
(como si) _____

4. Julia trabaja mucho. Patricia trabaja las mismas horas que Julia.
(tanto... como) _____

5. Iremos a pasear. Iremos al lugar que tú quieras.
(donde) _____

6. Quieres comer dulces. Antes debes comerte toda la comida.
(para que) _____

7. Yo como una gran cantidad de verduras. Tú comes tantas verduras como yo.
(igual,,, que) _____

8. Debes ahorrar. Solamente así podrás comprar tu propia casa.
(a fin de que) _____

9. En cada oración, elige la opción correcta. `16.D`

1. _____ dejes de quejarte porque la casa está sucia, mañana limpiaré hasta el último rincón.
a. A menos que   b. En caso de que   c. Con tal de que

2. _____ el precio de los productos orgánicos no suba, seguiré comprándolos.
a. Si   b. Con tal de que   c. Siempre y cuando

3. Los trabajadores no volverán a sus puestos de trabajo _____ les paguen los salarios atrasados.
a. a menos que   b. en caso de que   c. si

4. _____ tengo tiempo, hago deportes.
a. Con tal de que   b. En caso de que   c. Siempre que

5. _____ haya un incendio, baje por las escaleras.
a. En caso de que   b. Siempre y cuando   c. Si

6. _____ no me llamas por mi cumpleaños, me enojaré muchísimo.
a. A menos que   b. Si   c. Siempre que

7. _____ yo pueda trabajar, no te faltará nada.
a. A menos que   b. Mientras   c. Si

8. _____ no elijas algo muy costoso, te compraré un regalo.
a. A menos que   b. Si   c. Siempre que

10. **Indica si las condiciones son (a) reales/posibles, (b) probables/hipotéticas o (c) imposibles.** `16.D`

_____ 1. Si me acompañaras a la fiesta, ganaríamos el premio a la pareja de la noche.

_____ 2. Te invitaremos a cenar solamente si nos prometes que serás puntual.

_____ 3. Si tuvieras una mascota, comprenderías la responsabilidad de tener un animal a tu cargo.

_____ 4. Los abuelos no te habrían regalado ese CD si hubieran sabido que ya lo tenías.

_____ 5. Si saliera el sol, iríamos a patinar al parque.

_____ 6. Si mis hijos tienen clases por la mañana, podré anotarme en el curso de cerámica.

_____ 7. Nunca se lo habría contado a Silvia si me hubieras dicho que era un secreto.

_____ 8. Si haces ejercicio, te mantienes en forma.

11. **Síntesis Une las frases para formar oraciones lógicas.** `16.B–16.D`

1. Aunque odio los teléfonos móviles, _____

2. Siempre que hago una pausa, _____

3. Para que mi jefe no se enfade, _____

4. Me quedé sin batería en el teléfono, _____

5. Sin querer borré todos los contactos, _____

6. Como borré todos los contactos, _____

7. Ahora sé cómo usar el teléfono, _____

a. en mi trabajo me piden que tenga uno.

b. de modo que mi jefe no pudo comunicarse conmigo.

c. así que no tengo excusas para no estar en contacto con mi jefe.

d. porque no sabía usar el teléfono.

e. mi jefe me dio un papel con todos los teléfonos.

f. mi jefe me llama por teléfono.

g. debo devolver sus llamadas de inmediato.

12. **Síntesis Completa las oraciones con las conjunciones de la lista. Hay dos conjunciones que no debes usar.** `16.B–16.D`

al mismo tiempo que	cada vez que	ni	pero	que si	sino
antes de que	cuando	o	pues	si	tanto... como
así que	en caso de que	para que	que	sin embargo	y

1. Mamá me aseguró _____ Papá Noel vendría si me portaba bien.

2. El señor González no es tu amigo, _____ tu profesor, _____ háblale con respeto.

3. El secretario no redactó la carta _____ organizó las reuniones, _____ lo despidieron.

4. _____ dieran las doce, Cenicienta debía volver a su casa.

5. _____ la fiesta sea un éxito, debemos hacer mucha publicidad.

6. _____ no puedas venir, por favor, avísanos con antelación.

7. _____ hace frío, me gusta quedarme en casa y ver películas.

8. _____ pones atención, verás que aprenderás más rápido.

9. _____ te vas de vacaciones, la oficina es un caos.

10. No sé si reír _____ llorar.

11. Mis padres no llegaron aún. _____, avisaron que vendrían temprano.

12. No puedo salir esta tarde, _____ debo trabajar.

13. Adriana lavó la ropa, limpió la casa _____ preparó la cena.

14. Tengo muchos días de vacaciones, _____ me tomaré solamente una semana.

15. _____ Melisa _____ Romina y Mariela son maestras.

Practice more at **vhlcentral.com.**

1. Indica si los verbos en este texto son *copulativos*, *transitivos* o *intransitivos*. Escríbelos en la columna correcta. `17.B`

El famoso actor Julio Suárez, quien **protagonizó** telenovelas como *Amar es vivir* y *Enamorados siempre*, **sufrió** ayer un accidente de tránsito cuando **conducía** por el centro de Bogotá. Aunque Suárez no **tuvo** lesiones graves, el acompañante del artista aún **está** en el Hospital Central.

El accidente **sucedió** a las 20 horas del lunes 3 de agosto, cuando otro conductor **hizo** un giro peligroso para **ingresar** a una gasolinera y **chocó** el vehículo del prestigioso actor.

Suárez **está** preocupado por la salud de su amigo, a quien **conoció** cuando **era** aún un actor desconocido. "Les **pido** a los conductores que **sean** más prudentes al **conducir**", exclamó el artista.

Copulativo	Transitivo	Intransitivo

2. En cada oración, elige la opción correcta. `17.B`

1. ¡Cuántas veces soñé _____ (por/con) una fiesta como esta!

2. Horacio siempre se interesó _____ (por/en) la arquitectura de la ciudad.

3. ¿Confirmaste que asistiremos _____ (a/en) la reunión escolar?

4. ¡Ojalá quisieras jugar _____ (con/a) las cartas conmigo!

5. Volveremos _____ (a/en) vernos la semana que viene.

6. Mis padres se han encontrado _____ (en/con) los tuyos en el supermercado.

7. ¿Habéis disfrutado _____ (de/con) la playa?

3. En cada oración, elige la opción correcta. `17.B`

1. Juliana _____ de las escaleras y tuvo que ir al hospital.
   a. cayó   b. se cayó

2. No _____ despertarte: ¡dormías tan plácidamente!
   a. me atreví   b. me atreví a

3. Ayer _____ demasiado tarde.
   a. despertamos   b. nos despertamos

4. Quiero que _____ a la abuela hasta que yo vuelva.
   a. cuides   b. te cuides

5. Por favor, ¡_____ esa barba! ¡No te queda bien!
   a. afeita   b. aféitate

6. Estaba preparando la comida y _____ el dedo con un cuchillo.
   a. corté   b. me corté

7. No _____ la ropa y ahora no tenemos ni un par de calcetines limpios.
   a. lavamos   b. nos lavamos

4. Reescribe las oraciones usando el verbo entre paréntesis. `17.B`

1. Los alumnos detestan hacer la tarea. (disgustar)

_____

2. ¿No te sientes triste por la despedida de Flor? (entristecer)

_____

3. Adoro ir a las montañas en invierno. (fascinar)

_____

4. ¡Qué sorpresa tu visita! (sorprender)

_____

5. Tengo miedo de los fantasmas. (asustar)

_____

6. Para mí, es muy divertido ir de compras. (divertir)

_____

5. Conjuga estos verbos en presente de indicativo. `17.D`

1. completar (nosotros) _____   5. insistir (ella) _____

2. cumplir (vosotros) _____   6. leer (yo) _____

3. beber (tú) _____   7. responder (él) _____

4. viajar (ellos) _____   8. investigar (vos) _____

6. Completa las oraciones usando los verbos de la lista conjugados en presente de indicativo. `17.D`

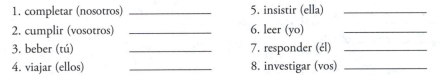

| conseguir | cocer | ejercer | exigir | introducir | traducir | recoger |

1. ¿_____ (yo) la moneda en esta ranura?

2. ¿Cuánto tiempo _____ (yo) esta pasta?

3. Te _____ que me ayudes a limpiar la casa.

4. _____ (yo) la profesión desde hace veinte años.

5. Yo _____ los juguetes y tú los guardas en el armario.

6. No _____ (yo) olvidarte: sueño contigo todas las noches.

7. ¿Cómo _____ (yo) esta palabra? No se me ocurre cómo hacerlo.

7. Reescribe las oraciones usando el pronombre indicado. `17.D`

1. ¿Por qué incluyes a Juana en tu lista de invitados, pero no a mí? (vos)

_____

_____

2. ¿Continuáis con las clases de guitarra? (tú)

_____

3. No confiamos en el criterio de Emiliano. (yo)

_____

4. Siempre perdéis el hilo de la conversación. (ellos)

_____

5. Nosotros te defendemos si pasa algo. (yo)

_____

6. Volvemos a las nueve y media de la noche. (ellos)

_____

7. Te pedimos un gran favor. (yo)

_____

8. **Completa el texto con los verbos conjugados en presente de indicativo.** `17.D`

decidir	convertirse	comenzar	recordar	afligir	acostarse	repetirse
situarse	perseguir	soñar	contar	empezar	deducir	

El martes que viene se estrenará en todas las salas del país la película *La escuela*. Este drama (1) _____ con la participación de estrellas, como el joven actor Tomás Rapal y la ya consagrada Gabriela Perotti.

La historia (2) _____ en un pequeño pueblo y es protagonizada por un niño llamado Juan que (3) _____ el año en una escuela nueva. Ese primer día de clases (4) _____ en una pesadilla, porque sus compañeros lo maltratan y lo (5) _____ por los pasillos de la escuela.

Esa noche, cuando Juan (6) _____ en la cama, (7) _____ hacer todo lo posible para que sus compañeros lo acepten. Sin embargo, al día siguiente, Juan nota que la situación del día anterior (8) _____. Al final del día, Juan (9) _____ que no será fácil enfrentarse a sus compañeros y que debe hacer algo para adaptarse a la nueva escuela.

Así (10) _____ esta magnífica historia: un niño que (11) _____ con ser aceptado. Sin duda, esta situación nos (12) _____ nuestra niñez y los problemas que (13) _____ a los más pequeños en esta difícil etapa de la vida. Una película totalmente recomendable para ver en familia.

9. **Completa las oraciones según lo que dice el calendario con los verbos conjugados en presente de indicativo.** `17.D`

○	**Lunes**
	9:30 poner a lavar ropa
	11:00 salir de paseo con la abuela
	15:00 traer al perro de la veterinaria
	17:00 hacer resumen de literatura
	20:00 componer canción para Paola
	22:00 proponer casamiento a Paola

Bueno, hoy es un día muy especial y complicado, pero ya tengo todo organizado en mi mente. Si a las 9:30 (1) _____ a lavar la ropa, a las 10:30 puedo colgarla, justo cuando (2) _____ de paseo con la abuela. Después de una larga caminata con ella, (3) _____ a casa al perro que está en la veterinaria. Duermo una breve siesta y a las 17:00 (4) _____ el resumen de literatura. Después, me baño y me visto bien elegante con mi ropa recién lavada. A las 20:00, uso toda mi inspiración y le (5) _____ una canción a Paola. Con esa canción, le (6) _____ casamiento. ¡No hay forma de que diga que no!

10. **Completa las oraciones con los verbos conjugados en presente de indicativo.** `17.D`

1. No te _____ (oír) bien si no hablas claro.

2. La escultura _____ (tener) más de trescientos años.

3. ¿Finalmente _____ (venir) tu familia a visitarte?

4. Tú siempre _____ (maldecir) cuando conduces. No debes hacerlo frente a los niños.

5. O te _____ (atener) a las reglas de la casa o te buscas otro lugar donde vivir.

6. Cuando _____ (decir, yo) algo, quiero que me escuches.

7. ¿Los bebés _____ (oír) también cuando están en la panza de su mamá?

11. Escribe oraciones completas siguiendo el modelo. 17.D

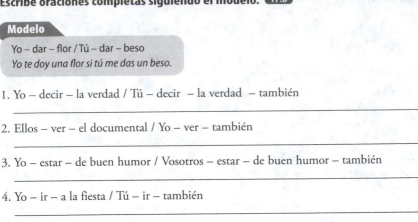

Modelo
Yo – dar – flor / Tú – dar – beso
Yo te doy una flor si tú me das un beso.

1. Yo – decir – la verdad / Tú – decir – la verdad – también
____

2. Ellos – ver – el documental / Yo – ver – también
____

3. Yo – estar – de buen humor / Vosotros – estar – de buen humor – también
____

4. Yo – ir – a la fiesta / Tú – ir – también
____

5. Yo – traer – pastel / Vosotros – traer – un regalo
____

12. Para cada oración, indica por qué se utiliza el presente de indicativo. 17.E

Ejemplos	Acciones presentes	Costumbres	Hechos intemporales
1. Este mes hago ejercicios en el parque.			
2. La Luna es un satélite de la Tierra.			
3. Cuatro más ocho son doce.			
4. A las 7 abre la panadería.			
5. Por la noche, comemos en el salón.			
6. En Argentina, se habla español.			
7. Ahora mismo llamo a la tía.			

13. Para cada oración, indica por qué se utiliza el presente de indicativo. 17.E

____ 1. En 1816, se declara la independencia de Argentina.
a. presente histórico b. hechos intemporales

____ 2. El domingo cocino un riquísimo pollo.
a. presente para dar órdenes b. presente para referirse al futuro

____ 3. ¿Te doy dinero para el metro?
a. presente para dar órdenes b. presente de confirmación

____ 4. Si duermo mal, estoy cansadísimo al día siguiente.
a. cláusulas condicionales b. hechos intemporales

____ 5. ¡Ya mismo dejas lo que haces y vienes aquí!
a. presente para dar órdenes b. presente para referirse al futuro

____ 6. ¿Tomamos un café?
a. presente de confirmación b. presente para referirse al futuro

14. **Une las frases para formar oraciones lógicas.** `17.F`

1. Gonzalo trabaja en una fábrica _____
2. Los niños leen cuentos de terror _____
3. Ulises está trabajando _____
4. Estoy llegando a tu casa, _____
5. Los profesores están leyendo tu examen _____
6. Llego tarde, _____
7. Mis colegas están viajando a Europa _____
8. Te escribo por correo electrónico _____
9. Estoy trabajando en mi tesis _____

a. y no quiere que lo molesten ahora.
b. y siempre tienen miedo a la hora de dormir.
c. baja a abrirme la puerta.
d. y además estudia ingeniería.
e. no me esperes para comer.
f. y no pueden creer los errores ortográficos que tiene.
g. la semana que viene.
h. y espero terminarla pronto.
i. en este momento porque tienen que ir a una conferencia en Madrid.

15. **Síntesis** **Completa las oraciones con el verbo conjugado en presente o presente progresivo.** `17.A–17.F`

1. A Elena le _____ (encantar) las flores rojas.
2. Roberto _____ (casarse) con Susana en mayo.
3. _____ (llamar, yo) a la puerta, ¡pero no me abres! ¿Por qué?
4. Por el contexto, _____ (deducir, yo) que ese término está relacionado con la física.
5. Todavía _____ (elegir, yo) qué voy a comer. ¿Tú ya elegiste?
6. Tu recuerdo me _____ (perseguir) día y noche.
7. Mi esposa y yo _____ (construir) una casa en el bosque. En noviembre, estará terminada.
8. ¿Por qué no _____ (empezar, tú) a cocinar mientras yo limpio el comedor?
9. En este momento no _____ (poder, yo) atenderte.
10. Mi amiga _____ (llegar) de Australia la semana que viene.
11. No puede atender el teléfono porque en este instante _____ (domir).
12. Si no _____ (descansar), te vas a enfermar.

16. **Síntesis** **Conjuga estos verbos en presente y presente progresivo. Si no es posible conjugar el verbo en presente progresivo, coloca una X.** `17.A–17.F`

1. perder (ellos)   _____   _____
2. atravesar (yo)   _____   _____
3. querer (ellos)   _____   _____
4. costar (él)   _____   _____
5. poder (vos)   _____   _____
6. promover (yo)   _____   _____
7. confesar (nosotros) _____   _____
8. estar (vosotros)   _____   _____
9. destruir (tú)   _____   _____
10. oír (ella)   _____   _____
11. deber (tú)   _____   _____
12. salir (yo)   _____   _____

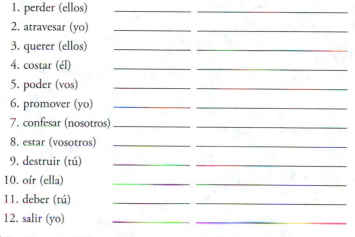

Practice more at **vhlcentral.com.**

1. Lee el texto e indica los verbos conjugados en pretérito perfecto simple. 18.B

Libros perdidos

Me llamo Francisco y el día lunes 23 de agosto tuve una clase en el aula 213. Estuve allí desde las 9 a.m. hasta las 12 p.m. Cuando salí, me olvidé un bolso con libros debajo de la silla. Son un libro de Matemáticas, otro de Física y uno de Química; los compré en la librería universitaria y escribí mi nombre en la primera hoja.

Si alguien los encontró, les pido que me escriban o me llamen al teléfono que aparece abajo.

¡Muchas gracias!
Teléfono: 932 80 394
Correo electrónico: francisco_gutierrez@universidad.edu

2. Completa las oraciones usando el pretérito perfecto simple. 18.B

1. Ayer yo _jugué_ (jugar) al fútbol durante tres horas.
2. Yo ya te _expliqué_ (explicar) tres veces el argumento de la película.
3. El lunes yo _toqué_ (tocar) el timbre de tu casa, pero nadie _contestó_ (contestar).
4. _Se cayó_ (caerse) aceite al piso. Ten cuidado.
5. Es increíble lo rápido que _se reconstruyó_ (reconstruirse) la ciudad después de la inundación.
6. Carolina _se sintió_ (sentirse) mal todo el día y ahora está en el hospital.
7. ¿Quién _puso_ (poner) un calcetín en la nevera?
8. El chofer _condujo_ (conducir) a una velocidad superior a la permitida.

3. Reescribe las oraciones con el pronombre entre paréntesis. 18.B

1. Cristina averiguó el teléfono del chico que vio en el autobús. (yo)
   _____
2. ¿Por qué llegaron tarde tus compañeros? (tú)
   _____
3. ¿Oíste tú también un ruido fuerte? (él)
   _____
4. Dormimos muy bien anoche. (ellos)
   _____
5. Nunca supimos el motivo del incendio. (yo)
   _____
6. Carla y Juan hicieron la comida. (ella)
   _____
7. Ayer fui a la estación de tren para comprar los boletos. (nosotros)
   _____

4. Escribe estos verbos en pretérito imperfecto. 18.D

1. (yo) estuve _estaba_
2. (yo) duermo _dormía_
3. (tú) comiste _comías_
4. (nosotros) vivimos _vivíamos_
5. (nosotros) somos _éramos_
6. (nosotros) vemos _veíamos_
7. (vosotros) fuisteis _ibais_
8. (ellos) compraron _compraban_
9. (nosotros) estamos _estábamos_
10. (yo) supe _sabía_

5. Decide si las explicaciones hacen referencia al pretérito perfecto simple (PPS) o al pretérito imperfecto (PI). Luego une las explicaciones con los ejemplos. `18.B–18.E`

Explicación	Ejemplo
PPS 1. Se usa para constatar datos históricos. *B*	a. Ya iba a llamarte cuando sonó el timbre.
PI 2. Se usa para expresar cómo solía ser una persona en el pasado. *E*	b. El famoso pintor nació el 3 de mayo de 1599.
PI 3. Se usa para expresar una acción en el pasado que no sucedió debido a una interrupción. *A*	c. El autobús se descompuso en el medio de la ruta.
PI 4. Se usa para enfatizar la simultaneidad de dos acciones en el pasado. *D*	d. Mi novio siempre me regalaba flores cuando venía a visitarme.
PI 5. Se usa para expresar cortesía. *F*	e. Mi bisabuelo era amable, simpático y muy culto.
PPS 6. Se usa para indicar que algo sucedió en el pasado. *C*	f. Quería pedirle un favor.
PPS 7. Se usa para enfatizar el fin de una acción y el comienzo de otra. *H*	g. Hace cinco años que vivo en este barrio.
8. Se usa como perífrasis del verbo *llevar + gerundio*. *G*	h. Ese día salí de casa a las 10, tomé el autobús a las 11 y llegué al trabajo a tiempo.

6. Elige la opción correcta. `18.B–18.E`

1. ¿Qué día ___visitaste___ (visitabas/~~visitaste~~) el museo? Me pareció haberte visto.
2. Cuando ___cumplí___ (cumplí/cumplía) ocho años, me regalaron mi primera bicicleta.
3. Cuando era estudiante, ___me despertaba___ (me desperté / ~~me despertaba~~) temprano y ___desayunaba___ (desayuné/desayunaba) con mucha tranquilidad.
4. El día ___estaba___ (fue/estaba) soleado, pero de repente ___se nubló___ (se nublaba / ~~se nubló~~) y ___comenzó___ (comenzaba/~~comenzó~~) a llover.
5. Juguemos a que ___teníamos___ (~~teníamos~~/tuvimos) una gran mansión para nosotras y que ___éramos___ (fuimos/~~éramos~~) millonarias.
6. Cuando ___iba___ (fui/iba) a salir de casa ___me acordé___ (~~me acordé~~ / me acordaba) de que era el cumpleaños de mi madre.
7. Mi primera maestra ___se llamaba___ (se llamó / se llamaba) Claudia.
8. A las ocho de la mañana, ___había___ (hubo/había) sol, pero igualmente ___decidí___ (decidí/decidía) no ir al parque.
9. ___Iba___ (Fui/~~Iba~~) camino a casa cuando ___me encontré___ (~~me encontré~~ / me encontraba) con Pedro.

7. ¿Pretérito perfecto simple o pretérito imperfecto? Decide qué tiempo verbal debes usar y completa las oraciones con los verbos de la lista. `18.B–18.E`

> aliviar ~~decir~~ ~~haber~~ ir (2) ~~sacar~~ ~~ser~~
> ~~dar~~ ~~doler~~ ~~hacer~~ ~~llegar~~ ~~sentarse~~

El martes pasado (1) ___fui___ al dentista porque me (2) ___dolía___ la muela. ¡(3) ___Hacía___ tanto que no (4) ___iba___ al dentista! Por suerte, no (5) ___había___ mucha gente en la sala de espera. En cuanto (6) ___me senté___ en el sillón, el dentista me (7) ___dio___ una inyección con anestesia que (8) ___alivió___ totalmente el dolor. Después, me (9) ___dijo___ que abriera bien grande la boca ¡y me (10) ___sacó___ la muela! ¡Todo (11) ___fue___ tan rápido que no (12) ___llegué___ a tener miedo!

8. Escoge la forma correcta de los verbos en la composición de Eduardo. `18.B–18.E`

Mi escuela nueva

El 7 de septiembre de 2010 (1) ___*fui*___ (**iba/fui**) por primera vez a mi escuela nueva. Me (2) ___*impactaba*___ (**impactaba/impactó**) la belleza del edificio: tiene tres pisos, dos jardines gigantes y una cancha de fútbol propia. Cuando (3) ___*entré*___ (**entraba/entré**) en la clase, todos mis compañeros me saludaron con una sonrisa. La directora incluso me (4) ___*dio*___ (**daba/dio**) un regalo de bienvenida. Cuando (5) ___*terminó*___ (**terminaba/terminó**) la clase, mis compañeros me (6) ___*invitaron*___ (**invitaban/invitaron**) a tomar un helado. En mi escuela anterior, mis compañeros (7) ___*eran*___ (**eran/fueron**) aburridos y antipáticos. ¡Qué suerte que (8) ___*decidía*___ (**decidía/decidí**) cambiarme de escuela! Estoy contentísimo.

9. Catalina está enojada con su mejor amigo, Tomás. Completa las oraciones. `18.E`

> **Modelo**
>
> Tomás dijo: "Quiero que vengas a visitarme".
> Catalina: Me dijiste que *querías que fuera a visitarte*, pero después no parecías tan contento de verme.

1. Tomás dijo: "Es muy importante que seas puntual".
   Catalina: Me dijiste que _____,
   pero cuando llegué a tu casa, ¡no estabas!

2. Tomás dijo: "Tengo una sorpresa para ti".
   Catalina: Me dijiste que _____,
   pero todo era una mentira.

3. Tomás dijo: "Prefiero estar a solas contigo porque hace mucho que no nos vemos".
   Catalina: Me dijiste que _____,
   pero invitaste a tres amigos más.

4. Tomás dijo: "Espero ver todas las fotos de tus últimas vacaciones".
   Catalina: Me dijiste que _____,
   ¡pero te aburriste a la segunda foto!

5. Tomás dijo: "Hace tres meses que no paso tiempo con amigos".
   Catalina: Me dijiste que _____,
   ¡pero un amigo tuyo me dijo que diste una fiesta el sábado pasado!

6. Tomás dijo: "Eres mi mejor amiga".
   Catalina: Me dijiste que _____,
   ¡pero tus acciones dicen lo contrario!

10. Completa las oraciones con el verbo conjugado en pretérito perfecto simple o pretérito imperfecto. `18.F`

1. Finalmente, el caballo _____ (poder) adelantarse y ganó la carrera.

2. Nuestros vecinos no _____ (querer) hacer un fondo común para las reparaciones del edificio.

3. Ayer discutimos con Fernando, porque él _____ (querer) ir al cine y yo no.

4. Cuando conocí a Marta, en 2010, ella _____ (tener) un novio que se llamaba Omar.

5. ¿Recuerdas el club del barrio? Allí siempre se _____ (poder) jugar al baloncesto y al fútbol incluso sin ser socio.

6. Ayer _____ (saber, yo) que me contrataron para trabajar en la tienda de juguetes más grande del país.

7. ¿Recuerdas cuántos años _____ (tener, nosotros) cuando nos mudamos a esta casa?

11. Síntesis Completa las oraciones con los verbos de la lista en el tiempo verbal indicado. `18.A–18.F`

Pretérito perfecto simple	Pretérito imperfecto
haber	ir
traducir	saber
oír	ser
pedir	haber
hacer	preparar

1. La directora nos _____ que nos comportáramos bien durante la ceremonia escolar.

2. Yo no _____ que tenías 18 años. ¡Pareces mayor!

3. ¿Quiénes _____ esta torta? ¡Está riquísima!

4. Graciela _____ al inglés este libro sobre historia sudamericana.

5. Cuando _____ a llamarte, se cortó la luz.

6. La abuela siempre nos _____ el desayuno.

7. De pronto, _____ un ruido y salté de la cama.

8. Soñé que _____ una famosísima actriz.

9. En los años sesenta, _____ un gran movimiento de liberación femenina.

10. En esa época, _____ mucha gente que no sabía leer.

12. Síntesis Completa el relato de Diego con el pretérito perfecto simple o el pretérito imperfecto. `18.A–18.F`

Pilar y yo (1) _____ (conocerse) en el primer año de la escuela primaria cuando (2) _____ (tener) seis años y desde ese momento no nos separamos nunca. Este año (3) _____ (decidir) festejar nuestros cumpleaños juntos. Pilar (4) _____ (enviar) todas las invitaciones y yo (5) _____ (comprar) las comida y las bebidas.

En el día de la fiesta el sol (6) _____ (brillar) y casi no (7) _____ (hacer) frío. (8) _____ (Parecer) que todo iba a salir perfecto. Sin embargo, nadie (9) _____ (aparecer) a la hora esperada. Pilar y yo no (10) _____ (saber) por qué la gente no había venido.

De pronto, ambos (11) _____ (correr) a buscar las invitaciones. Cuando las (12) _____ (leer), ¡no (13) _____ (poder) creerlo! ¡La hora (14) _____ (ser) incorrecta!

Por suerte, dos horas después (15) _____ (comenzar) a llegar los invitados. La fiesta (16) _____ (estar) genial. (17) _____ (Hacer) mucho tiempo que no (18) _____ (divertirse) tanto en una fiesta de cumpleaños.

🔊 Practice more at **vhlcentral.com**.

Actividades

1. Completa las oraciones con los verbos conjugados en pretérito perfecto compuesto. `19.A`

   1. Magdalena _____ (estudiar) toda la tarde.

   2. Todavía no _____ (terminar) mis tareas.

   3. ¡Por fin los trabajadores _____ (recibir) un aumento de sueldo!

   4. Vosotros ya _____ (esperar) demasiado.

   5. Las autoridades _____ (actuar) de forma muy responsable.

   6. Roberto _____ (llegar) hace un momento.

   7. Nuestro jefe nos _____ (invitar) a una conferencia en Las Bahamas.

2. Reordena las oraciones y conjuga los verbos en pretérito perfecto compuesto. `19.A`

   1. ¿ / comer (tú) / Alguna vez / paella / ?

   _____

   2. no / vender / Lucía / todavía / su bicicleta

   _____

   3. Este año / en / esta zona / transformarse / un centro financiero

   _____

   4. En mi vida / un carro / tener / rojo

   _____

   5. ¿ / cuál será / mostrarte / tu oficina / Tus jefes / ?

   _____

   6. ¡ / te / de mí / Tan pronto / olvidar / !

   _____

3. Indica qué verbos tienen participios regulares y cuáles tienen participios pasados irregulares o las dos opciones. Escribe los participios. `19.A`

comprar	sonreír	concurrir	ver	crecer	resolver
estar	leer	descubrir	freír	aumentar	morir

Regulares	Irregulares

4. Completa las oraciones conjugando los verbos en pretérito perfecto compuesto. `19.A`

   1. El músico aún no _____ (componer) la canción que le pidió el director de cine.

   2. ¿_____ (Leer, vosotros) bien qué dice ese cartel?

   3. Veo que ya _____ (volver, tú).

   4. ¿Quién _____ (abrir) la puerta?

   5. Mi madre _____ (traer) unas flores hermosas.

   6. ¿Dónde _____ (poner) Olivia el azúcar?

   7. Hasta ahora, los estudiantes no _____ (resolver) el problema matemático.

5. Decide por qué en estas oraciones se utiliza el pretérito perfecto compuesto. Indica *acción continua*, *acción incompleta* o *experiencia*, según el caso. **19.B**

Ejemplos	Explicación
1. ¿Has dormido alguna vez en una tienda de campaña?	
2. Hemos ido al centro comercial todos los días.	
3. Todavía no he conseguido hablar con mi abuela.	
4. ¡En mi vida he comido tanto como hoy!	
5. Juana está realmente bella hoy, ¿la has visto?	
6. Siempre he querido tener un pececito.	
7. Hasta hoy, no hemos tenido problema alguno.	
8. Muchas veces nos hemos ido a dormir sin comer.	
9. Lorena está haciendo dieta, pero aún no ha podido bajar de peso.	

6. Une las oraciones con sus contextos. **19.B**

_____ 1. He olvidado cerrar la ventana de mi habitación.

_____ 2. La semana pasada olvidé cerrar la ventana de mi habitación.

_____ 3. Mamá ha ido a sus clases de guitarra esta mañana.

_____ 4. Mamá fue a clases de guitarra la semana pasada.

_____ 5. La alumna nueva ha llegado hace unos minutos.

_____ 6. La alumna nueva llegó a la escuela.

a. Me ha dicho que está feliz con su profesor nuevo.

b. No le gustaron y ahora quiere ir a clases de piano.

c. Ahora llueve y seguramente ha entrado agua.

d. Sería bueno saludarla y darle la bienvenida a la escuela.

e. Ahora sé que debo asegurarme de que esté cerrada.

f. Unos minutos después, ya tenía varios amigos.

7. Señala en la conversación telefónica los casos en que los latinoamericanos usarían el pretérito simple. Luego escribe esos verbos en pretérito simple al final de cada párrafo. **19.C**

LUPE ¿Hola?

ANDREA Hola, Lupe, soy Andrea. ¡Por fin te he encontrado en casa! ¿Cómo estás? _____

LUPE Bien, un poco ocupada, pero dime.

ANDREA Hace unos minutos he visto a Tomás en la estación de tren. Me contó que jamás ha tomado un avión en su vida. No entiendo cómo puede viajar siempre en tren o en autobús... ¡se tarda tanto en llegar! Por ejemplo, este año, ¡que ya se acabó! con mi madre hemos viajado en más de ocho ocasiones desde Lima hasta Buenos Aires en avión. ¿Te imaginas un viaje así en autobús? _____

LUPE No, no podría imaginármelo.

ANDREA ¿Y ya te he contado que hace unos días vi en el aeropuerto a tu profesora de música? Nunca he hablado con ella, pero tampoco lo haría: no parece muy simpática. _____

LUPE Andrea, lamento interrumpirte, pero todavía no he cocinado, ni me he duchado y tengo que irme a las clases de cerámica. _____

ANDREA Sí, sí, no te preocupes. Yo ya he cocinado, he lavado los platos y ahora estoy mirando un programa de chismes sobre famosos. _____

LUPE En serio, Andrea. ¡Tengo que irme!

ANDREA Bueno, bueno. Te mando un beso y nos vemos. ¡Chau!

8. Completa las oraciones usando el pluscuamperfecto. `19.D`

1. Cuando llegué, todos los autobuses ya _____ (salir).

2. Nunca _____ (imaginar) que algo así podía sucederme.

3. Una semana antes, nosotros _____ (recibir) una carta de la tía, en la que decía que estaba muy bien de salud.

4. Mi hermanito no _____ (entender) la letra de la canción hasta que yo se la expliqué.

5. No pudimos viajar porque _____ (olvidar) el pasaporte en casa.

6. Roberto nos dijo que su perro _____ (comerse) su tarea de matemáticas.

7. Hasta ese momento, jamás _____ (probar, nosotros) el helado con sabor a café.

9. Indica por qué se utiliza el pluscuamperfecto en estas oraciones. Escribe el número de la oración en la columna correcta. `19.E`

Pasado antes del pasado	Discurso indirecto

1. El cliente llamó al camarero y le dijo que había visto una mosca en su sopa.

2. No, todavía no había recibido tu mensaje cuando me llamaste.

3. Nos preguntaron si habíamos notado algún cambio en la casa.

4. Llegaste justo cuando yo había salido de casa.

5. ¿Ya habías conocido a Francisco cuando te graduaste?

6. Invitamos a Eduardo a una fiesta, pero nos dijo que la noche anterior no había dormido mucho y estaba cansado.

7. ¿Vosotros os habíais mudado ya cuando vine a vivir a Chile?

10. Modifica las oraciones usando el pluscuamperfecto. `19.E`

> **Modelo**
>
> Me fui de casa y luego tú llegaste. (cuando)
> *Cuando llegaste a casa, yo ya me había ido.*

1. Apagué mi teléfono móvil y luego tú me llamaste. (cuando)

   _____

2. Nos levantamos de la cama y luego sonó el despertador. (cuando)

   _____

3. Laura estudió mucho y luego aprobó el examen. (porque)

   _____

4. Natalia dejó la dieta y luego subió de peso. (porque)

   _____

5. Terminamos de comer y luego llegó Raúl. (cuando)

   _____

6. Pablo se rompió la pierna esquiando y luego no pudo ir a la fiesta. (porque)

   _____

11. Síntesis Une las frases para armar oraciones lógicas. `19.A–19.D`

1. Todavía no me _____
2. Sin duda, este último año _____
3. Al buscar mi bolso, me di cuenta de que _____
4. Le pregunté al camarero si _____
5. Me contestó que, cuando ocurrió el hecho, él todavía no _____
6. Hasta ahora, nadie _____
7. Jamás me _____

a. me lo habían robado.
b. había empezado su turno.
c. he sentido tan indefensa como hoy.
d. ha encontrado mi bolso ni al ladrón.
e. he tenido mucha mala suerte.
f. he recuperado de esta amarga situación por la que pasé.
g. había visto a alguien sospechoso.

12. Síntesis Completa las oraciones con pretérito perfecto compuesto o pluscuamperfecto. `19.A–19.D`

1. Todavía no _____ (encontrar) al amor de mi vida. ¿Lo encontraré algún día?
2. Siempre _____ (anhelar) tener un carro; pero, ahora que lo tengo, no lo uso.
3. El doctor me dijo que yo _____ (cometer) un error al no consultar antes por mi dolor de espalda.
4. ¿No _____ (terminar) tu tarea todavía? Ya llega el profesor.
5. _____ (dormir, nosotros) todos los días hasta las once de la mañana. Deberíamos despertarnos más temprano.
6. _____ (nevar) muchísimo y por eso no podíamos usar las bicicletas.
7. Ella solamente quería saber si tú _____ (limpiarse) los pies antes de entrar a la casa.
8. Hasta ahora, ya _____ (tomar, yo) cinco clases de salsa.
9. Julián no me _____ (devolver) el libro de matemáticas. Lo llamaré para pedírselo.
10. Todos _____ (imprimir) sus ensayos, ¡pero yo no! Por suerte, corrí a casa y lo imprimí de inmediato.

Practice more at **vhlcentral.com**.

The future   **Chapter 20**

1. Completa las oraciones con el futuro simple. `20.B`

1. El famoso artista _____ (dar) un gran concierto en México.
2. ¿La abuela _____ (cocinar) para nosotros el domingo?
3. ¿Quién me _____ (ayudar) con la mudanza?
4. Los periodistas dicen que el pueblo _____ (elegir) al candidato conservador.
5. Si te comes toda la comida, te _____ (regalar, yo) un riquísimo chocolate.
6. Las reuniones se _____ (cancelar) hasta nuevo aviso.
7. Según los expertos, los precios de los alimentos _____ (subir) un tres por ciento este año.

2. Para cada verbo, indica cuál es la raíz usada para conjugarlo en futuro simple. `20.B`

1. hacer _____   6. saber _____
2. salir _____   7. caber _____
3. valer _____   8. poner _____
4. tener _____   9. haber _____
5. venir _____   10. querer _____

3. Completa el texto con los verbos de la lista conjugados en futuro simple. `20.B`

> querer   poder   hacer   venir   salir   tener   valer

Cuando sea grande, (1) _____ muchísimo dinero y compraré una casa que (2) _____ millones de dólares. (3) _____ fiestas a las que (4) _____ muchísimas personas de todas partes del mundo. Seré tan famoso que (5) _____ en las portadas de todas las revistas y todos los medios (6) _____ hacerme entrevistas. Pero la gran pregunta es: ¿cómo (7) _____ ganar tanto dinero?

4. En cada oración, indica por qué se usa el futuro simple. `20.C`

> a. acciones futuras   b. suposiciones sobre el presente   c. leyes/reglas
> d. suposiciones sobre el futuro   e. pronósticos   f. consecuencias en el futuro

1. ¿Quién será esa chica que nos está saludando? _____

2. Seguramente Estela será nuestra profesora de matemáticas este año. _____

3. Si trabajáis mucho, tendréis muy buenas notas. _____

4. Los trabajadores dispondrán de un día de vacaciones por cada veinte días trabajados. _____

5. Este fin de semana, lloverá en el norte del país. _____

6. ¿Volverás a Chile algún día? _____

5. En estas oraciones, indica por qué se emplea el futuro simple. `20.C`

1. Creo que mañana entregarán las notas del examen.
   a. suposición sobre el futuro   b. acción en el futuro

2. Las personas de este signo conocerán a mucha gente este año.
   a. predicción   b. consecuencia en el futuro

3. No robarás.
   a. acción en el futuro   b. leyes/reglas

4. No habrá trenes mañana debido a la huelga general.
   a. suposición sobre el presente   b. acción en el futuro

5. Este año iré de vacaciones al Caribe.
   a. acción en el futuro   b. suposición sobre el futuro

6. Alicia estará en la plaza. Ve y fíjate.
   a. suposición sobre el presente   b. suposición sobre el futuro

6. Une los elementos de las dos columnas para formar oraciones lógicas. `20.C`

1. Hoy yo _____   a. estaré invitado a la boda?
2. Por favor, tráigame _____   b. un hospital nuevo en 2021.
3. ¿Le compramos _____   c. un vaso de agua.
4. Seré _____   d. penas de hasta ocho años por ese delito.
5. Habrá _____   e. lavo los platos, ¿sí?
6. ¿Yo también _____   f. un regalo?
7. Me llevo _____   g. rico algún día, sin duda.
8. Se construirá _____   h. esa bufanda colorida.

7. En cada oración, indica la opción que refleja el uso más frecuente en español. `20.D`

1. a. Ya empezará la película.
   b. Ya va a empezar la película.

2. a. Llámame más tarde; ahora voy a comer.
   b. Llámame más tarde; ahora comeré.

3. a. ¿Qué harás después del trabajo?
   b. ¿Qué vas a hacer después del trabajo?

4. a. No te apoyes contra la pared recién pintada. Te vas a manchar la ropa.
   b. No te apoyes contra la pared recién pintada. Te mancharás la ropa.

5. a. Apaga tu teléfono celular. Ya empezará la función.
   b. Apaga tu teléfono celular. Ya va a empezar la función.

6. a. Mañana tengo una cita con Cristina.
   b. Mañana tendré una cita con Cristina.

8. Une las oraciones con las explicaciones. `20.D`

_____ 1. ¿Vas a comerte toda la ensalada?

_____ 2. Casi no hay más helado. Si no te apuras, vas a quedarte sin nada.

_____ 3. Mañana a las doce viene la abuela.

_____ 4. Ya vendrá tu madre, no llores más.

_____ 5. Ya van a abrir los negocios.

a. Se describe una acción explicitándose mediante adverbios que tendrá lugar en el futuro.

b. Se expresa una suposición.

c. Se expresa una intención de algo que se hará inmediatamente.

d. Se describe un evento con gran probabilidad de suceder de inmediato.

e. Se describe una acción o un hecho inminente.

9. Completa las oraciones con los verbos conjugados en futuro perfecto. `20.E`

1. El lunes a esta hora, _____ (terminar, nosotros) la mudanza.

2. ¿Dónde _____ (quedar) mi cepillo de dientes? No lo veo por ningún lado.

3. ¿_____ (Haber) disturbios después del partido de fútbol?

4. Si no asistes a las clases de francés, _____ (desperdiciar) el dinero que pagaste.

5. ¡Qué increíble! Dentro de un mes, _____ (graduarse, nosotros).

6. ¿_____ (Llamar) alguien mientras no estuvimos en casa?

7. Mario _____ (cansarse) de esperar. Por eso, se fue sin nosotros.

8. Cuando me vieron con esa camiseta, _____ (pensar) que soy fanático de Boca Juniors.

9. Ana ya _____ (conseguir) entradas. Por eso no te llamó para comprar tu entrada extra.

10. Si trabajais este verano, antes de graduaros ya _____ (obtener) experiencia laboral.

11. Para cuando lleguemos, ya _____ (acabarse) la fiesta.

12. No sé exactamente cuántos kilos de carne compré, pero _____ (comprar) unos cinco o seis kilos.

Actividades

10. **En cada oración, elige la opción correcta.** `20.F`

1. Ya _____ (comeremos / habremos comido) en cualquier momento.

2. ¿A Lucas le _____ (habrá gustado / gustará) realmente mi regalo? No parecía demasiado sorprendido al abrirlo.

3. Según las encuestas, el candidato liberal _____ (habrá obtenido / obtendrá) un cincuenta por ciento de los votos.

4. ¿Quién _____ (se encargará / se habrá encargado) de la decoración del salón? Es realmente una obra de arte.

5. Según el periódico, mañana _____ (lloverá / habrá llovido) por la tarde.

6. Si haces ejercicio, _____ (tendrás / habrás tenido) una vida más saludable.

7. Creo que _____ (habrá / habrá habido) muchísimo para ver en la exposición de mañana.

8. ¿Dónde _____ (irá / habrá ido) tu hermana? Hace un ratito estaba aquí.

11. **Completa las oraciones con el futuro simple o el futuro compuesto. Hay tres verbos que no debes usar.** `20.F`

| inventar | dormir | nacer | saber | valer | contar | estar | jugar | venir | subir |

1. ¿Te das cuenta de que dentro de una hora ya _____ más de cuatro horas seguidas? En lugar de eso, deberías estudiar más.

2. ¿Cuánto _____ esa hermosa blusa?

3. ¿_____ tu hermana a cenar? Ya lleva una hora de retraso.

4. Si el doctor está en lo cierto, en agosto _____ tu hermanita; por lo que tendrás compañera de cuarto.

5. ¿Piensas que los precios _____ en diciembre por la Navidad?

6. ¿Vanesa le _____ la verdad a su madre sobre sus malas calificaciones? Yo no lo creo, porque su madre dice a todos que su hija es la mejor alumna de la clase.

7. Si nos acostamos temprano, mañana _____ más descansados.

12. **Síntesis Lee el texto y elige la forma verbal más apropiada.** `20.B–20.F`

Planes para estas vacaciones

Si todo sale bien, dentro de quince días (1) _____ (estaré / habré estado) en Río de Janeiro, disfrutando de la playa y de la compañía de mis amigos. Pero primero tengo que hacer varias cosas.

Esta semana (2) _____ (tengo / tendré) una reunión con mi jefe para pedirle que me aumente el sueldo y me dé algunos días más de vacaciones. Seguramente me (3) _____ (habrá dicho / dirá) que no al principio; pero después de una hora, (4) _____ (acepta / aceptará) mi pedido. Pensándolo bien, ahora mismo lo (5) _____ (llamaré / voy a llamar) para adelantar la reunión.

La semana que viene ya (6) _____ (habré recibido / recibiré) mi aumento de sueldo y con ese dinero (7) _____ (podré / puedo) comprar los pasajes de avión y los regalos para mis amigos. A Juanita quiero comprarle un libro con fotos de San Francisco; y a Pablo, una camiseta de béisbol. Estoy segura de que (8) _____ (quedarán / van a quedar) boquiabiertos con los regalos.

Por último, espero que el tiempo sea bueno. Según el pronóstico, (9) _____ (habrá llovido / lloverá) muy poco. Espero que así sea, porque de lo contrario (10) _____ (habré gastado / gastaré) muchísimo dinero para estar todo el día dentro del hotel.

Practice more at **vhlcentral.com.**

1. Completa las oraciones con los verbos conjugados en el condicional simple. 21.A

1. ¿__________ (Tener, tú) una manta de más? No encuentro la mía y tengo frío.
2. Si hiciéramos ejercicio, __________ (poder, nosotros) ir de excursión a las montañas.
3. ¿Te __________ (gustar) venir a cenar a mi casa?
4. Si me preguntaras a mí, no __________ (saber) qué decirte.
5. La mujer policía nos dijo que el tren __________ (pasar) a las 17 horas.
6. ¿Crees que __________ (valer) la pena comprar una bicicleta nueva?
7. __________ (Deber, tú) trabajar menos horas. Luces muy cansado.
8. __________ (Querer) vender mi carro. ¿Cuánto dinero me __________ (dar, usted) por él?

2. Completa las oraciones con los verbos de la lista conjugados en el condicional simple. 21.A

saber	vivir	ser	decir	poner	caber	querer	valer

1. ¿Crees que este sofá __________ en mi habitación?
2. Si supieras la verdad, ¿me la __________?
3. Si tuviera más espacio en el comedor, __________ aquí una mesa para ocho personas.
4. __________ conveniente que no gastaras tanto dinero en tecnología.
5. Constanza __________ tener más tiempo libre para hacer deportes.
6. ¿Crees que tus padres __________ en un pueblo pequeño?
7. Me robaron el canasto de la bicicleta. ¿Quién __________ un canasto tan viejo y roto?
8. ¿__________ acompañarme a la fiesta el viernes? Puedo pasarte a buscar.
9. Si estuviéramos en tu situación, no __________ qué hacer.
10. ¿Crees que __________ la pena invertir en acciones de esa compañía?
11. ¿Qué le __________ a vuestro actor favorito?
12. Acabo de comprar este cuadro y no sé dónde se vería mejor. ¿Usted dónde lo __________?

3. ¿Consejo, suposición o deseo? Decide por qué Juanita usa el condicional presente en estas oraciones. 21.B

1. ¿Te gustaría que te regalara una planta para tu graduación? __________
2. ¿Cómo le iría a Tamara en su primer día de clases? __________
3. Preferiría quedarme en casa. __________
4. Deberíais ordenar vuestras habitaciones: vendrán los abuelos este fin de semana. __________
5. Sería mejor que llegues temprano. Necesito ayuda en la cocina. __________
6. Se cree que los griegos tendrían un sistema de comunicación eficiente. __________
7. A nosotros nos gustaría pintar la cocina de color verde. ¿Qué te parece la idea? __________
8. Yo en tu lugar, seguiría con las clases de pintura. ¡Eres un genio para las artes! __________

4. Lucas piensa mucho sobre su vida. Completa las oraciones de forma lógica y conjuga el verbo entre paréntesis. `21.B`

1. Si estudiara más español, _____
2. Si tuviera más dinero, _____
3. Si mis amigos fueran más deportistas, _____
4. Si mi madre me diera más libertad, _____
5. Si tuviera videojuegos nuevos, _____
6. Si no tuviera que ir a la escuela tan temprano, _____
7. Si me encontrara con mi banda de música favorita, _____

a. _____ (armar) un equipo de fútbol.
b. _____ (poder) viajar a México.
c. _____ (comprar) más videojuegos.
d. _____ (dormir) más horas.
e. _____ (salir) hasta tarde con mis amigos.
f. _____ (venir) más amigos a visitarme.
g. les _____ (decir) que me encanta su música.

5. Estela le da consejos a su hermanita que está enferma. Completa las oraciones con los verbos conjugados en el condicional simple. `21.B`

Modelo

(mejor / ponerse una bufanda)
Sería mejor que te pusieras una bufanda.

1. (en tu lugar / tomar mucho té)
   _____

2. (yo que tú / quedar en cama)
   _____

3. (deber / dormir más por la noche)
   _____

4. (en tu lugar / ir al médico)
   _____

5. (yo que tú / no tomar medicamentos)
   _____

6. (en tu lugar / estar contenta por no ir a la escuela)
   _____

6. Une las explicaciones sobre el condicional simple con los ejemplos. `21.B`

1. Se usa para expresar deseos. _____
2. Se usa para dar consejos y sugerencias. _____
3. Se usa para expresar cortesía. _____
4. Se usa para expresar duda o probabilidad en el pasado. _____
5. Se usa para expresar un futuro desde un punto de vista pasado. _____
6. Se usa para hacer una invitación. _____

a. No sé a qué hora nos acostamos anoche. Serían las dos de la mañana.
b. Deberías hablar más español que inglés. Así aprenderás más rápido.
c. Me gustaría viajar al Congo.
d. Nos prometiste que nos llamarías al mediodía.
e. ¿Querrías ir al cine conmigo?
f. ¿Te importaría cerrar la ventana?

7. Completa las oraciones con los verbos conjugados en condicional compuesto. `21.C`

1. Si hubiera tenido más tiempo, _____ (hacer) las compras.

2. Si nos hubiéramos conocido antes, quizás _____ (ser) marido y mujer.

3. Si Olivia no se hubiera mudado a otro barrio, _____ (compartir) muchas más tardes juntas.

4. Me _____ (ir) mejor en el examen si me hubiera preparado mejor.

5. Yo en tu lugar, no _____ (comer) tanto. Ahora te duele la barriga.

6. Con tu ayuda, _____ (tardar, nosotros) mucho menos en hacer la mudanza. ¡Pero no nos ayudaste!

7. Me _____ (gustar) pasar más tiempo con vosotros; pero tuve que trabajar muchísimo.

8. Decide si el condicional compuesto se usa para expresar (a) *una situación imaginaria que contrasta con el presente* **o (b)** *una circunstancia hipotética del pasado.* `21.D`

1. Sin el cinturón de seguridad, el accidente habría sido mucho más grave. _____

2. Te habría invitado a la fiesta si hubiera sabido que estabas en la ciudad. _____

3. Si hubiera estado en tu lugar, yo habría visitado más museos. _____

4. Me aseguraste que, para esta fecha, tendrías el trabajo terminado. _____

5. Si Pamela hubiera llevado una vianda para el viaje, no habría tenido que pagar ocho dólares por un chocolate. _____

6. Si Pedro hubiera sabido que estaba enferma, me habría llamado. _____

7. Seguramente tú habrías cenado en casa si sabías que había comida. _____

9. Escoge la forma correcta del verbo en el aviso publicitario. `21.D`

¿Qué (1) _____ (pasaría / habría pasado) si usted hubiera sabido los números de la pasada lotería de Navidad? ¿Se imagina cómo habría sido su vida? Piense cuántas casas (2) _____ (compraría / habría comprado) con ese dinero.

Pero, claro, usted jamás (3) _____ (ganaría / habría ganado) la lotería porque no tenía... ¡la fabulosa BOLA DE CRISTAL®! El revolucionario producto que adivina el futuro.

Usted que ahora está solo, si hubiera tenido la BOLA DE CRISTAL®, (4) _____ (sabría / habría sabido) dónde encontrar al amor de su vida. ¡Incluso (5) _____ (habría tenido / tendría) al alcance de su mano todas las técnicas para conquistarlo!

Por eso, no siga perdiendo el tiempo. Deje atrás su pasado lleno de tristezas ¡y compre ya la BOLA DE CRISTAL®! ¡Debería (6) _____ (haberlo hecho / hacerlo) hace tiempo!

Llame ya al teléfono que aparece en pantalla y termine con sus incertidumbres.

10. Síntesis Completa las oraciones con los verbos conjugados en condicional simple o condicional compuesto, según corresponda. `21.A–21.D`

1. Si hubieras llevado el teléfono móvil, no _____ (tener, nosotros) este desencuentro.

2. Si fuera de vacaciones a Chile, me _____ (gustar) conocer Valparaíso.

3. Yo te _____ (regalar) otro libro si hubiera sabido que este ya lo tenías.

4. Con un mayor control del tránsito, la gente _____ (conducir) a la velocidad permitida.

5. ¿_____ (Votar) a ese candidato si hubieras sabido que solamente decía mentiras?

6. ¿_____ (Votar, tú) de nuevo por Justo Juárez si se presentara a elecciones?

7. Tú _____ (deber) dicho la verdad desde un principio, las cosas serían más claras entre nosotros ahora. ¡Pero no lo son!

11. Síntesis En cada oración, elige la opción correcta. 21.A–21.D

1. No te preocupes, de todas maneras, ellos no ________ nuestra propuesta. Tenían muchas otras mejores.
   a. habrían aceptado b. aceptarían
2. ¿________ volver a casa ahora o más tarde? Haremos lo que tú quieras.
   a. Habrías preferido b. Preferirías
3. Si me hubieras avisado, ________ una comida vegetariana.
   a. habría cocinado b. cocinaría
4. ¿________ estudiar más tiempo español antes de ir a Guatemala? Yo creo que fue el momento ideal para ti.
   a. Habrías preferido b. Preferirías
5. Si hubiera sabido que dormías, no ________ la puerta.
   a. habría tocado b. tocaría
6. Otra vez llegamos tarde. ________ menos en metro.
   a. Tardaríamos b. Habríamos tardado
7. Supe que ________ una exposición de tu pintor favorito y corrí a decírtelo.
   a. habría b. habría habido
8. ¡________ prestarte dinero si tanta falta te hacía!
   a. Podría b. Habría podido
9. ¿Dónde ________ Natalia ayer por la tarde? No estaba en la oficina.
   a. estaría b. habría estado

12. Síntesis Decide si debes usar el condicional simple o el condicional compuesto. 21.A–21.D

1. Si supieras el esfuerzo que me costó aprender español, ¡no ____________ (decir) que hablo mal!
2. ¿Te ____________ (gustar) casarte conmigo? ¡Te amo tanto!
3. Nuestras mascotas ____________ (ser) más obedientes si les hubiéramos enseñado modales a tiempo.
4. ¿____________ (ser) posible reservar una habitación para dos personas?
5. Las autoridades confirmaron que ____________ (solucionar) la crisis energética para comienzos de 2019.
6. ¿Cuánto crees que ____________(valer) el alquiler de un apartamento como este?
7. Con una buena política de salud, este invierno ____________ (haber) menos enfermos de gripe. Pero como ves, no fue así.
8. En tu lugar, yo no ____________ (escribir) en los bancos de la escuela. Ahora te castigarán por ello.

13. Síntesis Explica qué habrías hecho tú en estas situaciones. Usa las frases de la lista. 21.A–21.D

echarle la culpa a otro camarero	llamar al cerrajero
pedir disculpas	decirle que la pintura era buena

1. ________________
____

2. ________________
____

3. ________________
____

4. ________________
____

Practice more at **vhlcentral.com.**

1. Lee el texto e indica si los verbos subrayados están en modo indicativo (I) o subjuntivo (S). `22.A`

Querida Lucía:

Te escribo porque (1) _____ tengo un gran dilema. (2) _____ Me gustaría tener una mascota, ya sea un gato o un perro. Probablemente (3) _____ busque un gato, porque son más independientes y no (4) _____ necesitan tanto cuidado.

En todo caso, dudo que mis padres (5) _____ acepten mi propuesta. Por eso, (6) _____ voy a buscar la forma de convencerlos. ¿Se te (7) _____ ocurren buenos argumentos que (8) _____ puedan convencerlos?

También pensé en llegar un día a casa con un gato o perro sin hacer muchas preguntas antes. Pero no (9) _____ quiero que mi mamá (10) _____ se enoje y (11) _____ me grite durante todo un día. ¿Qué (12) _____ me recomiendas que (13) _____ haga? Quiero tener una mascota y sé que (14) _____ podré hacerme cargo de ella.

Hasta pronto,
Raúl

2. Completa las oraciones con los verbos de la lista conjugados en presente de subjuntivo. `22.B`

> ladrar   escribir   vivir   correr   desempeñarse   charlar   transmitir

1. El entrenador espera que el equipo _____ mejor en este partido.

2. Por más que _____ (tú), no podrás escaparte de mí.

3. ¿Hay algún canal de televisión que _____ el partido en directo?

4. Me gustaría que _____ (nosotros) con más tranquilidad.

5. ¿Conoces algún animal que _____ más de cien años?

6. La dueña del apartamento no quiere un perro que _____ si está solo.

7. Mi hermana me pide siempre que le _____ un correo electrónico cada semana.

3. Silvina le explica a su amiga las actividades que deben hacer para la próxima clase. Completa las oraciones siguiendo el modelo. `22.B`

> **Modelo**
>
> **PROFESORA** Mañana deberán llegar temprano a clase.
> **SILVINA** La profesora quiere que *mañana lleguemos temprano a clase.*

1. **PROFESORA** Deberán aprender de memoria el himno nacional.
   SILVINA La profesora quiere que _____.

2. **PROFESORA** Cada uno pasará al frente y lo cantará.
   SILVINA Ella quiere que cada uno _____.

3. **PROFESORA** Si lo desean, pueden cantar el himno en parejas.
   SILVINA Nos ha permitido que _____.

4. **PROFESORA** No deberán cometer ni un solo error al cantar la letra.
   SILVINA Ella no admitirá que _____.

5. **PROFESORA** Posiblemente la directora los escuchará cantar.
   SILVINA Dijo que es posible que _____.

6. **PROFESORA** Si todo sale bien, los mejores cantantes formarán parte del coro.
   SILVINA Ella espera que _____.

4. Completa las oraciones con el verbo conjugado en presente de subjuntivo. `22.B`

1. Antes de que _____ (empezar) la función, deberán apagar sus teléfonos móviles.

2. Es mejor que tú _____ (escoger) el regalo que prefieras. No conozco realmente tus gustos.

3. Espero que el pueblo _____ (elegir) bien a su futuro presidente.

4. Tu padre y yo no queremos que tus amigos _____ (seguir) llamando a la hora de comer.

5. Los profesores nos recomiendan que _____ (buscar, nosotros) la bibliografía en sitios de Internet confiables.

6. Estela no cree que Julia _____ (tener) las llaves de nuestra casa. ¿Quién podría tenerlas entonces?

7. Los jueces no permiten que sus vidas privadas _____ (influir) en sus trabajos.

8. Una posibilidad es que _____ (dedicarse) a dar clases de matemáticas. Así podrás ganar dinero extra.

5. Completa la nota que escribió Renata a su hermanita menor con los verbos conjugados en presente de subjuntivo. `22.B`

destruir	cargar	agregar	salir	seguir	apagar	conseguir	alcanzar	tocar

Querida hermanita:

Sé que ya sabes cómo cuidar a mi tortuga, pero quiero asegurarme de que todo (1) _____ bien.

Ante todo, te ruego que no (2) _____ el plato de Manuelita con demasiada lechuga. Ella come muy poco. Otra cosa importante: te sugiero que (3) _____ agua fresca al bebedero todas las mañanas.

Recuerda que a ella no le gusta que la (4) _____ demasiado. No es muy cariñosa y además se asusta cuando viene alguien nuevo. Por la noche, es mejor que (5) _____ la luz, así ella duerme mejor.

Sobre las puertas, mantenlas cerradas para que ella no (6) _____ las plantas que me regaló la abuela. Sé que quizás exagero, pero no quiero que Manuelita (7) _____ esas plantas con flores tan lindas.

Ojalá que (8) _____ recordar todo lo que te expliqué y te agradezco muchísimo tu ayuda. Sé que es mucho pedir que (9) _____ mis instrucciones al pie de la letra, pero sabes que Manuelita es como mi hija y quiero que siempre esté bien.

¡Nos vemos el lunes!
Renata

6. Conjuga estos verbos irregulares en presente de subjuntivo en la persona indicada. `22.B`

> **Modelo**
>
> salir – 1.ª persona del singular: *salga*

1. traer – 2.ª persona del singular _____

2. insinuar – 3.ª persona del plural _____

3. enviar – 3.ª persona del singular _____

4. guiar – 1.ª persona del plural _____

5. conocer – 1.ª persona del singular _____

6. decir – 3.ª persona del singular _____

7. valer – 3.ª persona del plural _____

8. tener – 2.ª persona del plural _____

7. Completa las oraciones con los verbos que sean irregulares o tengan cambios ortográficos en presente de subjuntivo. `22.B`

oír	mencionar	conducir	prestar	escuchar	decir
agrandar	evaluar	poner	ampliar	determinar	manejar

1. Ojalá _____ (ellos) esta carretera. Es muy angosta y hay muchos accidentes de tránsito.

2. Es mejor que le _____ al pintor que vienes de parte mía. Así te hará un descuento.

3. Esperemos que el gobierno pronto _____ los daños producidos por la catástrofe y _____ en marcha un plan de recuperación de los bosques quemados.

4. No estoy seguro de que la abuela _____ bien la música. Quizás deberíamos subir el volumen.

5. Necesito que _____ atención a lo que te digo.

6. Te prohíbo que _____ a una velocidad mayor a la permitida.

8. Juancito contradice siempre a su amiga, Teresa. Completa lo que dice, siguiendo el modelo. `22.B`

Modelo

TERESA Las clases comenzarán a las doce.
JUANCITO No es verdad que *las clases comiencen a las doce.*

1. **TERESA** Empieza a estudiar veinte días antes del examen.
JUANCITO No es necesario que _____.

2. **TERESA** Te contaré una historia increíble.
JUANCITO No quiero que me _____.

3. **TERESA** Seguramente la comida costará unos veinte dólares.
JUANCITO No creo que _____.

4. **TERESA** Llueve muchísimo.
JUANCITO No puede ser que _____.

5. **TERESA** Te despertaré a las nueve con el desayuno.
JUANCITO No quiero que me _____.

6. **TERESA** Probablemente te devolveré los libros a fin de mes.
JUANCITO Es poco probable que me _____.

9. Reescribe las oraciones usando la persona indicada entre paréntesis. `22.B`

1. Es mejor que no pensemos en cosas negativas.
(yo) _____

2. Cuando descendáis las escaleras, veréis a la derecha una gran puerta. Esa es la cocina.
(tú) _____

3. Los profesores no pretenden que entiendas todo el texto; solo la idea principal.
(nosotros) _____

4. La niña insiste en que sus padres le cuenten un cuento cada noche.
(vos) _____

5. Haremos todo lo que podamos para recaudar dinero para los pobres.
(tú) _____

6. Quiero que oláis el nuevo perfume que me compré.
(tú) _____

10. Completa las oraciones con los verbos de la lista. `22.B`

| dormir (2) | morir | divertirse | herir | preferir |

1. Es posible que Lucas _____ volver a casa más temprano. Mejor dale las llaves a él.

2. Quiero que _____ tiempo suficiente, así podréis estar atentos en el seminario de mañana.

3. Le pusimos un bozal al perro para que no _____ a los niños.

4. Ojalá que _____ en la fiesta de Guido.

5. Otra posibilidad es que _____ (nosotros) en una tienda de campaña. Creo que sería lo más económico.

6. El día que mi perro _____ será el día más triste de mi vida.

11. Completa las tablas con los verbos conjugados en presente de subjuntivo. `22.B`

Pronombre	adquirir	jugar
yo	(1)	juegue
tú, vos	(2)	(6)
usted, él, ella	(3)	(7)
nosotros/as	(4)	juguemos
vosotros/as	adquiráis	(8)
ustedes, ellos/as	(5)	(9)

12. Construye oraciones negativas usando el presente de subjuntivo. `22.B`

> **Modelo**
>
> Creo que Juan tiene miedo a las arañas.
> No creo que Juan *tenga miedo a las arañas*.

1. Me parece que llueve.
   No me parece que _____.

2. La policía piensa que el asesino todavía está en los alrededores de la escena del crimen.
   La policía no piensa que _____.

3. Creo que Luis recuerda el día en que nos conocimos.
   No creo que Luis _____.

4. Estoy segura de que ellos prefieren ir de vacaciones a la playa.
   No estoy segura de que ellos _____.

5. Sandra se sabe de memoria toda la lección.
   No creo que Sandra _____.

6. Creo que hoy llego a tiempo para ver la telenovela.
   No creo que _____.

7. Me parece que Juan y Carlos van a venir a la fiesta.
   No creo que _____.

8. Estoy segura que vosotros podéis participar en el evento.
   No creo que _____.

13. Completa el artículo con los verbos conjugados en presente de subjuntivo. `22.B`

> adquirir   divertirse   enfriarse   volver   pensar   guiar   costar   organizar   querer   dormir

"Acampar es incómodo"

Aquí ofrecemos consejos sobre cómo acampar, justamente para quienes (1) _____ que acampar es un sufrimiento.

- Es importante que realmente (2) _____ (ustedes) ir de campamento. Ir a regañadientes (*reluctantly*) o porque no tienen reserva de hotel es un mal comienzo.

- Si eligen un campamento libre, hablen con un guardaparques que los (3) _____ y siempre tengan a mano un mapa de la zona.

- Les recomendamos que (4) _____ (ustedes) un equipamiento adecuado para el clima del lugar al que vayan. Quizás el equipo (5) _____ más de lo que habían presupuestado; pero un equipamiento bueno es siempre una buena inversión.

- Es fundamental que (6) _____ (ustedes) el campamento: separar las áreas donde comerán, dormirán o descansarán.

- Cuando (7) _____ (ustedes), les recomendamos abrigarse bien la cabeza y los pies. No queremos que estas zonas (8) _____, porque luego es muy difícil recuperar el calor.

Esperamos que (9) _____ (ustedes) en su próximo campamento ¡y que (10) _____ (ustedes) a hacerlo una y otra vez!

14. Indica qué oraciones incluyen verbos conjugados en pretérito imperfecto de subjuntivo. Subráyalos. `22.C`

1. Espero que la temperatura sea agradable este fin de semana. No quiero llevar mucho abrigo.

2. Me pareció raro que no te comieras toda tu comida.

3. Me gustaría que hablásemos a solas sobre este tema.

4. Si los trabajadores pidieran un aumento de sueldo, con gusto se lo daría.

5. Es mejor que no haya postre. Ya comimos demasiado.

6. ¡Ojalá pudiéramos ir de vacaciones a Cusco este verano!

7. No creo que sepas todas las respuestas. ¡Solamente el profesor las sabe!

8. Te pedí que te cambiases la camisa. ¡Esa está sucia!

15. El pretérito imperfecto de subjuntivo tiene dos formas. Escribe junto a cada verbo las dos formas correspondientes a la primera persona del singular. `22.C`

1. subir _____ _____
2. pedir _____ _____
3. caber _____ _____
4. ser _____ _____
5. poner _____ _____
6. lastimar _____ _____
7. hacer _____ _____

8. concluir _____ _____
9. desear _____ _____
10. querer _____ _____
11. poseer _____ _____
12. decir _____ _____
13. ir _____ _____

16. Completa las oraciones con los verbos conjugados en pretérito imperfecto de subjuntivo. `22.C`

1. Si yo _____ (hablar) quechua, podría ser traductor en una comunidad indígena.

2. ¡Cómo me gustaría que _____ (viajar, nosotros) a la India!

3. Hasta ayer necesitaba un empleado que _____ (trabajar) por las tardes.

4. Habíamos preparado todo para que los agasajados _____ (sorprenderse) al entrar.

5. Compré comida para que _____ (cocinar, nosotros) juntos.

6. Fue fundamental para el rescate que los bomberos _____ (llegar) de inmediato.

17. Conjuga estos verbos en pretérito imperfecto de subjuntivo. `22.C`

1. divertir (yo) _____

2. saber (nosotros) _____

3. tener (ellos) _____

4. caer (vosotros) _____

5. leer (tú) _____

6. producir (ella) _____

7. ser (ustedes) _____

8. distribuir (ellos) _____

9. dar (yo) _____

10. hacer (él) _____

18. Reescribe las oraciones usando el pretérito imperfecto de subjuntivo. `22.C`

1. Te pido que me prestes atención.
   Te pedí que _____.

2. Podemos ir al cine si realmente quieres.
   Podríamos ir al cine si realmente _____.

3. Te llamo para que me incluyas en tu lista de invitados.
   Te llamé para _____.

4. No quiero que destruyan ese edificio antiguo tan hermoso.
   No quería _____.

5. Me alegra que puedas venir a nuestra fiesta.
   Me alegró _____.

6. Quiero que te sientas como en casa.
   Quería que _____.

7. Julia nos recomienda que tengamos cuidado con nuestros bolsos.
   Julia nos recomendó _____.

8. Le recomiendo que vaya a esa panadería y que pruebe las galletas de limón.
   Le recomendé _____.

19. Escribe los verbos en pretérito perfecto de subjuntivo. `22.D`

1. tardar (ellos) _____

2. ser (nosotros) _____

3. compartir (vosotros) _____

4. pedir (ustedes) _____

5. beber (yo) _____

6. escribir (tú) _____

7. probar (ella) _____

8. descubrir (nosotros) _____

9. traducir (ellos) _____

10. jugar (vos) _____

20. Completa las oraciones conjugando los verbos en el pretérito perfecto de subjuntivo. `22.D`

1. No es verdad que _____ (querer) leer tu diario íntimo. Jamás lo haríamos.

2. Nos alegra tanto que _____ (venir, ustedes).

3. Esperamos que _____ (pasar, usted) un día estupendo en nuestro spa.

4. No dudo que Julieta _____ (preguntar) por Martín. Todos sabemos que ella está enamorada de él.

5. En mi familia no hay nadie que _____ (divorciarse).

6. Verás que la escuela te parecerá más fácil una vez que _____ (aprobar) los primeros exámenes.

21. Indica qué oraciones incluyen verbos conjugados en pretérito pluscuamperfecto de subjuntivo. Subráyalos. `22.E`

1. Si hubieras llegado temprano a casa, no te habrías perdido el exquisito postre que hizo Camila.

2. No sabía que hoy era tu cumpleaños.

3. Cuando hayan aprendido todas las palabras, les haré una pequeña prueba.

4. Entre mis amigos, no encontré a nadie que hubiera ido a Quito.

5. Me habría bastado con que me hubieras mandado un mensaje de texto. Estuve esperándote dos horas bajo la lluvia.

6. Si hubiésemos salido antes, no habríamos perdido el tren.

7. No pensé que hubieses disfrutado la fiesta tanto como yo.

8. Nunca pensé que pudiese haber tanta gente allí.

9. Te habría invitado a la fiesta si hubiera sabido que ya habías vuelto de tu viaje.

22. Completa las oraciones con el verbo conjugado en el pretérito pluscuamperfecto de subjuntivo. `22.E`

1. Si tan solo _____ (saber) que querías ir a la playa, te habría invitado.

2. Si _____ (conocer) antes a tu hermana, la habría invitado a mi casamiento.

3. ¡Ojalá _____ (poder, nosotros) trabajar en esta escuela!

4. Si vosotros _____ (subir) a la torre, habríais visto toda la ciudad.

5. Si _____ (cerrar, tú) la puerta, el gato no se habría escapado.

6. En toda la universidad no encontré a dos profesores que _____ (graduarse) después de 1990.

23. Completa las oraciones conjugando los verbos en el tiempo verbal indicado. `22.F–22.G`

1. Cualquiera _____ (ser) la nacionalidad de los turistas, se deberán solicitar los pasaportes en todos los casos. (futuro del subjuntivo)

2. Se tendrán en cuenta aquellos currículos que se _____ (recibir) antes del 20 de agosto. (futuro perfecto del subjuntivo)

3. A donde _____ (ir), haz lo que _____ (ver). (futuro del subjuntivo)

4. Quien _____ (tener) algo en contra de esta unión, ya no podrá evitarla. (futuro perfecto del subjuntivo)

5. Sea quien _____ (ser) el culpable de este delito, deberá pagar por ello. (futuro del subjuntivo)

24. Síntesis **Identifica los verbos en subjuntivo e indica en qué tiempo están conjugados.** `22.A–22.H`

1. Que te haya invitado a comer a casa no significa que no tengas que ayudarme a cocinar. _____

2. Vaya a donde fuere, el fantasma de mis pesadillas me persigue. _____

3. Ojalá nos divirtamos en la casa de Paula. _____

4. Hicimos muchísimo para que todo saliera tal como lo planeamos. _____

5. Si tu hermana nos pidiera ayuda, seríamos los primeros en ayudarla. _____

6. Hicimos comidas sin carne para que los vegetarianos pudiesen disfrutar del banquete. _____

7. Me pareció tan extraño que Tamara no fuera a clase. _____

8. Quien hubiere desobedecido a las autoridades será castigado con ocho años de prisión. _____

9. Por más que hayas sido elegido como mejor compañero, deberás estudiar muchísimo para pasar de año. _____

Practice more at **vhlcentral.com.**

Use of the subjunctive | Chapter 23

1. Completa las oraciones con los verbos de la lista conjugados en subjuntivo. `23.B`

cambiar	cumplir
avisar	venir
divertir	llegar
regalar	reconciliarse

1. ¡Que te _____ muchísimo en la fiesta!

2. ¡Ojalá me _____ la muñeca que tanto quiero! Creo que ellos ya saben qué quiero.

3. ¡Ojalá nos _____ antes sobre el retraso del tren! Habríamos aprovechado para ver más la ciudad.

4. ¡Que _____ muchísimos años más, hermanita!

5. Posiblemente _____ de visita la tía Carolina. Ábrele la puerta, ¿sí?

6. Quizás el gobierno _____ su política económica en los próximos años.

7. Ojalá que _____ . Hacen muy buena pareja.

8. Posiblemente (nosotros) _____ tarde mañana a causa del tráfico.

2. Une las frases para formar oraciones lógicas. `23.B`

1. Ojalá Roberto no traiga postre de chocolate; ____   a. así que yo no compraré nada.
2. Ojalá Roberto no hubiera traído una tarta de limón: ____   b. de la cena que hice.
3. Probablemente Roberto compre algo de postre, ____   c. el que trajo la torta de naranja.
4. Quizás fuera Roberto ____   d. siempre estar conmigo.
5. Ojalá Roberto haya disfrutado ____   e. yo ya compré uno.
6. Ojalá Roberto disfrute ____   f. me la comí toda y ahora me duele la barriga.

3. Sofía le da consejos a su amiga Elena. Escribe oraciones siguiendo el modelo. `23.C`

Modelo

Estudia después de cada clase. (insistir)
Insisto en que estudies después de cada clase.

1. Sé puntual. (sugerir)
   Sugiero que seas puntual.

2. Ayuda a tus compañeros. (aconsejar)
   Aconsejo que ayudes a tus compañeros

3. Siempre haz los ejercicios de matemáticas. (recomendar)
   Recomiendo que siempre hagas los ejercicios de matemáticas

4. Llámame por la tarde si tienes preguntas. (pedir)
   Pido que me llames por la tarde si tienes preguntas

5. ¡Presta atención a mis consejos! (rogar)
   Ruego que prestes atención a mis consejos.

6. Recuerda todo lo que te digo. (necesitar)
   Necesito que recuerdes todo lo que te digo.

4. Completa las oraciones con un elemento de cada lista. `23.C`

que	elegir
el que	retrasarse
es que	tener
hace que	aprobar
el hecho de que	bajar

1. La huelga del transporte _____ todos los vuelos _____.

2. _____ no _____ el examen no es excusa para bajar los brazos. ¡Te queda medio año por delante!

3. _____ te _____ "mejor compañero" habla muy bien de ti.

4. _____ _____ los precios no es algo muy frecuente en este país.

5. No _____ yo _____ poco dinero, es que todo aquí es muy caro.

5. Lee estas oraciones y decide si en cada caso se expresa deseo o se brinda información. `23.C`

1. Agustina insistió en que le trajeran un café. _____

2. Manuela le gritó a su hermana que se quedara tranquila. _____

3. Mi novia insiste en que soy el chico más lindo del mundo. _____

4. El policía me indicó que estacionara. _____

5. Las autoridades afirmaron que los pasajeros están a salvo. _____

6. Insisto en que me dejen hablar con un abogado. _____

7. Te advierto que no me hagas enojar. _____

8. Mi padre sostiene que él tiene la razón. _____

6. Reescribe las oraciones siguiendo el modelo. `23.C`

> **Modelo**
>
> ¿Te visitan tus padres? ¡Cuánto me alegra!
> *Me alegra que te visiten tus padres.*

1. ¿Te robaron la maleta? ¡Qué indignante! _____

2. ¿Estás fumando? ¡Cómo me molesta! _____

3. ¿Los vecinos están haciendo una fiesta? ¡Cómo me enfada eso! _____

4. ¿Has perdido el tren? ¡Cuánto lo lamento! _____

5. ¿Has ganado la lotería? ¡Qué sorpresa! _____

7. En cada oración, elige la opción correcta. `23.C`

1. Ya no oímos cuando _____ los vecinos. Usamos protectores en los oídos por la noche.
   a. griten   b. gritan

2. Temo que la inyección me _____. ¡Mira lo grande que es la aguja!
   a. duele   b. dolerá

3. Esperaba con ansias a que me _____ sobre la beca.
   a. contestan   b. contestaran

4. Creo que la camarera _____ muy amable.
   a. es   b. sea

5. No pienso que la profesora nos _____ buenas notas.
   a. da   b. dé

6. Parece como si _____ ocho grados bajo cero.
   a. hace   b. hiciera

7. ¿Piensas que _____ mejor esperar a que bajen los precios?
   a. es   b. sea

8. Presiento que esto _____ en un gran problema pronto.
   a. se convierta   b. se convertirá

8. Fabián es un chico que lo cuestiona todo. Completa las oraciones con los verbos conjugados en indicativo o subjuntivo según corresponda. `23.C`

1. Desconfío de que me _____ (has contado / hayas contado) la verdad sobre tus calificaciones.

2. Pero no dudo en absoluto que _____ (seas/eres) una buena persona.

3. Aunque no niego que _____ (haya pensado / he pensado) lo contrario.

4. Es cierto también que esto ya _____ (ha sucedido / haya sucedido) antes.

5. No hay certeza alguna de que _____ (vayas/vas) a cambiar de actitud.

6. Pero, al fin y al cabo, estoy convencido de que nuestra amistad _____ (sobreviva/sobrevivirá) a este conflicto.

7. Te aconsejo que _____ (dejas/dejes) de fumar.

8. Admito que no _____ (haya leído / he leído) ese libro.

9. Fue muy importante que nos _____ (dijeras/dijiste) la verdad.

10. Estoy muy acostumbrado a que los vecinos _____ (hagan/hacen) mucho ruido.

9. Tomás critica la forma de actuar de sus compañeros de grupo. Completa las oraciones con los verbos conjugados en subjuntivo. `23.C`

De:	tomasito@email.com
Para:	leandroj@email.com, vanesam@email.com
Asunto:	El trabajo en grupo

Fue increíble que se (1) _comportaran_ (comportar) de esa manera la clase pasada. No es justo que yo siempre (2) _tenga_ (tener) que hacer las tareas por ustedes. ¡Es terrible que (3) _piensen_ (pensar) de esa manera!

Tú, Leandro. Fue un error que no (4) _vinieras_ (venir) a la reunión del sábado pasado. No era el trato que solo un miembro del grupo (5) _trabajara_ (trabajar) por todos. Está bien que ahora (6) _quieres_ (querer) compensar tu error, pero ya es demasiado tarde.

Y tú, Vanesa, ¿acaso estás acostumbrada a que la gente te (7) _espera_ (esperar)? Estoy harto de que (8) _lleguen_ (llegar) tarde a todas las reuniones.

A los dos, les repito lo que ya les dije la semana pasada: más vale que (9) _____ (cambiar) de actitud. Me da igual que la profesora los (10) _____ (desaprobar): si esto no cambia, le contaré todo.

10. Une las frases para formar oraciones lógicas. `23.C`

1. Queríamos _E_
2. Te aconsejamos _B_
3. A tus padres les ha molestado _A_
4. A los empleados les molesta _F_
5. Es la tercera vez que les pido _C_
6. Ayer Julio nos pidió dos veces _G_
7. La lluvia les impidió _D_

a. que no hayamos limpiado la casa después de la reunión.
b. que no descuides tu bolso.
c. que limpien la sala después de usarla.
d. ir de excursión a la montaña.
e. ir al cine y ver la película nueva de vampiros.
f. que los clientes no saluden al entrar.
g. que no habláramos muy alto.

11. Reescribe las oraciones usando _lo_ + _adjetivo/adverbio_ y _lo que_. `23.C`

1. Pasa a buscarme tú. Eso es lo lógico.
_____

2. Eres realmente hermosa. Eso es lo cierto.
_____

3. La gente es simpática. Eso es lo más común.
_____

4. El tren llegó a horario. Eso fue lo más normal.
_____

5. Por suerte, no nos robaron. Eso habría sido lo peor.
_____

6. El sistema de transporte funciona muy mal. Eso es lo que veo.
_____

7. Has aprobado el examen. Eso es lo bueno.
_____

8. Escribes inglés perfectamente aunque no es tu primer idioma. Eso es lo más interesante.
_____

12. Para cada oración, elige la opción correcta. `23.D`

1. La junta directiva elegirá a un delegado que es muy responsable.
   a. La junta también tomará en cuenta la experiencia de los candidatos en esa área.
   b. Se llama Juan Carlos Gómez y tiene experiencia en esa área.

2. Buscamos un sillón que tenga dos metros de largo.
   a. En el comedor, no nos entraría uno más grande.
   b. Lo vimos la semana pasada en un catálogo.

3. Los niños quieren un muñeco que dice frases en español.
   a. Se llama "Sr. Caballín", pero no lo encuentro en ninguna juguetería.
   b. Les compraré el primero que vea.

4. Te llevaré a un museo donde haya una exposición de arte.
   a. He estado allí antes y he visto exposiciones súper interesantes.
   b. Seguramente encontraremos uno por aquí cerca.

5. Necesito un diccionario que tenga imágenes.
   a. Lo vi en Internet y ahora no recuerdo el nombre.
   b. Creo que me ayudaría a memorizar las palabras más rápido.

13. En cada oración, elige la opción correcta. `23.D`

1. _____ (Jamás/Siempre) he sido una alumna que tiene buenas notas.

2. _____ (En ninguna parte / En muchas partes) del mundo hay aeropuertos donde se pueda fumar.

3. En tu casa _____ (no había / había) un par de cuadros que me encantaban.

4. _____ (No existe nadie / Existe alguien) que pueda resolver este acertijo.

5. Quiero una bufanda. Cómprame _____ (cualquiera/una) que cuesta menos de 8 dólares y que vi ayer en la vidriera.

6. Contrata a cualquiera que _____ (pueda trabajar / puede trabajar) los fines de semana.

7. Busco a la persona que _____ (quiera/quiere) alquilar mi habitación. Su nombre es Manuel, pero no recuerdo su apellido.

14. Completa las oraciones con los verbos conjugados en indicativo o subjuntivo. `23.C–23.D`

1. Lo que _____ (decidir) Marta será respetado por todos.

2. Ahora lo que más _____ (necesitar, nosotros) es un buen colchón.

3. A mi cumpleaños estarán invitados los que me _____ (llamar) para saludarme.

4. Quienes _____ (hacer) la reserva del asiento tienen una plaza asegurada.

5. Lo que no me conviene es que _____ (subir) la tasa de interés.

6. Lo que más nos gusta es que nos _____ (regalar) videojuegos.

7. Quienes te _____ (acabar) de saludar son los vecinos del primer piso.

8. Me gustaría tener una casa que _____ (tener) una piscina climatizada en la sala, pero no creo que exista.

9. Nunca he conocido a nadie que le _____ (gustar) comer comida picante en el desayuno.

10. En Argentina, no había comida que me _____ (encantar) más que el asado.

15. Reescribe las oraciones siguiendo el modelo. `23.D`

> **Modelo**
>
> Necesito un par de tijeras que corten bien.
> Jamás he tenido *un par de tijeras que hayan cortado bien.*

1. Busco a un hombre que sea cariñoso.
   Buscaba _____.

2. Quiero estudiar una profesión que me haga feliz.
   Habría querido _____.

3. Necesito un par de lentes que cuesten menos de 90 dólares.
   Necesitaba _____.

4. Quiero tener amigos que sean sociables.
   Habría querido _____.

5. Busco un libro que sea en inglés.
   Buscaba _____.

16. Une los elementos de las tres columnas para formar oraciones lógicas. `23.E`

1. Nos encontraremos en un bar	como	podamos conectarnos a Internet.
2. Dinos un nombre	cuanto	la dejó el conserje.
3. Estaré en la plaza	en el que	tú quieras.
4. Haz las cosas	donde	quieren.
5. Ellos comen	que	te guste mucho.
6. Busca la maleta	en la que	nos conocimos.

17. Reescribe las oraciones usando la conjunción entre paréntesis. `23.E`

1. Juan Manuel habla castellano como un español. (como si fuera)

   _____

2. Hice la tarea y nadie me ayudó. (sin que)

   _____

3. Si no llegas a horario, me habré ido. (como)

   _____

4. Dado que no tienes dinero, te prestaré un poco. (como)

   _____

5. ¡Ni loca te presto dinero! (ni que)

   _____

18. **Lee la carta de Joaquín y elige la opción correcta.** `23.E`

> Querida Alicia:
> ¿Cómo estás? Luego de (1) _____ (que reciba/recibir) tu mensaje de texto, me quedé un poco preocupado. Imagínate que, tan pronto como lo (2) _____ (leyera/leí), corrí hasta este cibercafé para comunicarme contigo.
> ¿Estás más tranquila? ¡Qué mala suerte con estos ladrones! Pero cuántas veces te dije que, cada vez que (3) _____ (camines/caminas) por el centro, lleves tu bolso delante de ti. Estas son las cosas que pasan cuando (4) _____ (descuidas/descuides) tus pertenencias. Te recomiendo que vayas a la comisaría ya mismo. Después de que (5) _____ (hagas/haces) la denuncia, la policía comenzará a buscar tus documentos. Hasta que (6) _____ (recuperes/recuperas) tu pasaporte, usa tu documento de identidad mexicano. Por favor, apenas (7) _____ (lees/leas) mi mensaje, llámame por teléfono.
>
> Un abrazo,
> Joaquín

19. **Completa las oraciones con las conjunciones de la lista.** `23.E`

> tanto que   a causa de que   para   tan ... que   porque (2)   a fin de que

1. Ando en bicicleta no _____ me guste, sino _____ no perjudica el medio ambiente.
2. _____ no haya desempleo, el gobierno puso en marcha un plan de generación de puestos de trabajo.
3. Llovía _____ no pudimos ir al concierto.
4. La probabilidad de ganar el concurso no es _____ baja _____ debamos desanimarnos.
5. _____ perdimos el autobús, ahora tenemos que esperar dos horas.
6. Tengo que pedir un crédito _____ comprar la casa.

20. **Reescribe las oraciones usando la conjunción entre paréntesis.** `23.E`

1. No tengo hambre, pero comeré una porción de pizza. (si bien)
   _____
2. No me invitaron a la fiesta. De todas maneras, no habría ido a esa fiesta. (aunque)
   _____
3. Podría venir mucha gente a la fiesta. Sin embargo, habrá lugar para todos. (por + *sustantivo* + que)
   _____
4. Hacía mucho calor. Sin embargo, los niños jugaron en el parque. (pese a que)
   _____
5. No compraría esa casa aun teniendo el dinero. (aunque)
   _____
6. Ni siquiera viviendo en Barcelona me sería fácil aprender catalán. (aun cuando)
   _____

21. Escribe oraciones a partir de las frases dadas. Conjuga los verbos en subjuntivo o indicativo, según corresponda. `23.E`

1. Podrías venir a cenar a casa _____
   (a no ser que / ya / tener / planes)

2. Lleva el paraguas _____
   (por si acaso / llover)

3. Compré bebida de más _____
   (en caso de que / esta noche / venir / más invitados)

4. Solo serás exitoso _____
   (si / esforzarte)

5. Habrías llegado a tiempo _____
   (si / el metro / funcionar / bien)

6. Si anoche saliste hasta las 4 de la madrugada, _____
   (hoy / no / deber / quejarte)

7. Si me dijeras que ganaste la lotería, _____
   (yo / no / creerte)

22. Síntesis Completa el texto con la opción correcta. `23.A–23.E`

¿Que cuáles (1) _____ (son/sean) mis sueños? ¡Qué pregunta! Bueno, esperaba que me (2) _____ (hagas/hicieras) una pregunta más concreta.

A ver... No es que (3) _____ (haya/hay) algo con lo que sueñe en realidad. Me gusta vivir el momento y disfrutar del día a día. Pero, para ser sincera, a veces sueño con encontrar a un hombre que me (4) _____ (quiere/quiera) y a quien yo (5) _____ (quiera/quiero). Sería tan romántico estar en pareja ¡y para toda la vida! Quizás yo (6) _____ (sea/soy) un poco ingenua, pero para mí es muy importante saber que la otra persona se (7) _____ (compromete/comprometa) a tener una relación de muy largo plazo.

Y hablando de sueños o ambiciones... ¡ojalá (8) _____ (tenga/tuviera) un trabajo mejor! Deseo estar en una empresa donde me (9) _____ (paguen/pagaran) más y (10) _____ (tenga/tuviera) que trabajar menos. ¡Eso sí que no creo que se (11) _____ (haga/hace) realidad! Pero soñar no cuesta nada.

23. Síntesis Completa las oraciones con las palabras o frases de la lista. `23.A–23.E`

No siento	Que	Es aconsejable	Comprendo	Estoy convencido
Es sorprendente	El que	Siento	Parece como si	

1. ¡_____ duerman bien!

2. _____ que no gasten dinero en hoteles caros.

3. _____ hayas sido amable conmigo hoy no me dice nada.

4. _____ que hoy será un gran día.

5. _____ que nos espere un futuro brillante.

6. _____ la gente no tuviera ganas de trabajar.

7. _____ que no hayas llegado a tiempo. El tránsito en esta ciudad es un caos.

8. _____ de que seremos los vencedores.

9. _____ que una actriz tan mala recibiera un Oscar.

24. Síntesis Une los ejemplos con las explicaciones. `23.A–23.E`

_____ 1. Dormiré en una cama que sea cómoda.

_____ 2. Lo lógico es que durmamos en una tienda de campaña.

_____ 3. No había una sola persona que hablara español.

_____ 4. Mientras sigas comportándote mal en clase, jamás tendrás buenas notas.

_____ 5. Los precios son tan altos que no podemos comprar ni un café.

_____ 6. Por si acaso no me despierto, llámame por teléfono por la mañana.

_____ 7. Si tocas el fuego, te quemarás.

_____ 8. El pueblo desconfía de que el gobernador sea honesto.

a. Usamos el subjuntivo con expresiones que hacen referencia a normas, reglas o preferencias consideradas las mejores, las peores, etc.

b. Usamos el subjuntivo en proposiciones temporales cuando la oración hace referencia a una acción futura.

c. Usamos el subjuntivo en proposiciones relativas cuando nos referimos a algo cuyas características imaginamos o deseamos.

d. Usamos el indicativo para expresar una condición cuando la relación condición-resultado es segura.

e. Usamos el indicativo siempre con esta expresión.

f. Usamos el subjuntivo cuando afirmamos que el antecedente de la proposición relativa no existe.

g. Usamos el indicativo en comparaciones implícitas.

h. Usamos el subjuntivo con verbos que expresan duda, tanto en proposiciones subordinadas afirmativas como negativas.

Practice more at **vhlcentral.com.**

The imperative | Chapter 24

1. Completa las oraciones con el verbo conjugado en imperativo afirmativo de _tú_. `24.B`

1. _____ (descansar) unas horas y te paso a buscar a las 8.

2. _____ (limpiar) tus gafas. ¡Están muy sucias!

3. _____ (comer) toda tu comida si quieres el postre.

4. _____ (esperar) hasta que venga la abuela.

5. _____ (leer) en voz alta las primeras frases del libro.

6. _____ (ordenar) la habitación: ¡es un desastre!

7. _____ (ir) a visitar a tus abuelos.

8. _____ (poner) las bolsas sobre la mesa.

9. _____ (tener) bien a mano el pasaporte.

10. _____ (comprar) este libro. Te lo recomiendo.

2. Reescribe las oraciones con el verbo conjugado en imperativo afirmativo de tú. `24.B`

1. Tienes que venir a casa a buscar el DVD. ¡_____!

2. Tienes que ser amable con tus compañeros de clase. ¡_____!

3. Tienes que poner cada libro en su lugar. ¡_____!

4. Tienes que hacer todo lo que yo te digo. ¡_____!

5. Tienes que ir a la farmacia ya mismo. ¡_____!

6. Tienes que decir "permiso" antes de entrar. ¡_____!

3. Eres jefe de redacción del periódico escolar. Contesta las preguntas de tus compañeros. `24.C`

> **Modelo**
>
> **COMPAÑEROS** ¿Debemos escribir artículos?
> (No, corregir | artículos | redactados)
> **TÚ** *No, corregid los artículos redactados.*

1. **COMPAÑEROS** ¿Debemos entrevistar al director?
   (No, entrevistar | profesor de música)
   TÚ _____

2. **COMPAÑEROS** ¿Llamamos por teléfono al profesor de música?
   (No, enviar | mensaje electrónico)
   TÚ _____

3. **COMPAÑEROS** ¿Debemos pensar en preguntas sobre música contemporánea?
   (No, hacer | preguntas | música clásica)
   TÚ _____

4. **COMPAÑEROS** ¿Debemos escribir el artículo para el lunes?
   (No, escribir | artículo | miércoles)
   TÚ _____

5. **COMPAÑEROS** ¿Podemos hacer un descanso ahora?
   (Sí, descansar | una hora)
   TÚ _____

4. Una amiga argentina te da consejos para cuando llegues a Buenos Aires. Escribe sus mandatos usando el imperativo afirmativo de *vos*. `24.C`

1. (tener cuidado con tus maletas) _____

2. (comprar un mapa en la estación) _____

3. (preguntar dónde tomar el autobús 152) _____

4. (ser simpática con el chofer del autobús) _____

5. (buscar la calle Juramento) _____

6. (tocar el timbre del apartamento 1B) _____

5. Reescribe las oraciones en imperativo negativo. `24.D`

1. Haz ejercicio cuatro veces por semana. _____

2. Leed todos los libros de la biblioteca. _____

3. Tirad los periódicos viejos a la basura. _____

4. Sé cordial con los turistas. _____

5. Aparca tu carro enfrente de mi casa. _____

6. Venid a cenar a casa. _____

7. Sal de ahí. _____

8. Ayudad a vuestros amigos. _____

6. Completa las oraciones con los verbos de la lista conjugados en imperativo de *usted, ustedes* o *nosotros*. `24.E`

decir	jugar	hacer	pedir	respetar	subir	tomar

1. Hoy no _____ a la pelota. Ayer practicamos demasiadas horas.

2. _____ el tren de las 8:50, profesor. Lo esperaré en la estación.

3. Alumnos, _____ las normas de la escuela; de lo contrario, habrá sanciones para todos.

4. No _____ que somos estudiantes. Es mejor que crean que somos profesionales.

5. _____ lo que quiera, señor Juárez. La empresa pagará la cuenta del restaurante.

6. _____ hasta el quinto piso. Allí los estará esperando la coordinadora.

7. Jamás _____ trampa en la competencia deportiva. El entrenador se enojaría muchísimo con nosotros.

7. Escribe las oraciones siguiendo el ejemplo. `24.F`

> **Modelo**
>
> ¿Me traes una bebida?
> *Tráeme una bebida.*
> *Tráemela.*

1. ¿Nos das un abrazo?
   _____
   _____

2. ¿Os quitáis el abrigo?
   _____
   _____

3. ¿Me cortas el cabello?
   _____
   _____

4. ¿Nos regalas unas rosas?
   _____
   _____

5. ¿Me manda una postal, señorita Álvarez?
   _____
   _____

8. Completa los consejos de salud que da el Doctor Salvador a sus televidentes. `24.B–24.F`

Buenos días, damas y caballeros. Hoy hablaremos sobre cómo llevar una vida saludable.

Si quieren vivir durante mucho tiempo y gozar de buena salud, sigan mis consejos. Primero, no (1) _____ (fumar) más. El cigarrillo causa cáncer de pulmón a ustedes y a quienes los rodean. ¡(2) _____ (Decidirse) de una vez y (3) _____ (terminar) con ese vicio! Segundo, (4) _____ (olvidarse) de las comidas con gran contenido graso y, además, ¡(5) _____ (hacer) deporte! (6) _____ (Caminar), (7) _____ (correr), lo que ustedes quieran... ¡y no (8) _____ (mirar) tanta televisión! Por último, (9) _____ (dormir), como mínimo, ocho horas diarias.

¡(10) _____ (Ser) inteligentes y (11) _____ (cuidarse)! ¡Hasta la próxima!

9. Completa los mandatos del cocinero español a sus empleados. `24.B–24.F`

Julia y Lucía, (1) _____ (cortar) la zanahoria en tiritas muy finas. Tú, Marcelo, (2) _____ (tener) más cuidado cuando lavas las patatas: tienen tierra todavía. Y tú, Ester, (3) _____ (ir) al depósito y (4) _____ (traer) dos kilos de cebollas. (5) _____ (Deber, vosotros) prestar atención a lo que os digo. ¡No (6) _____ (distraerse, vosotros)!

¡(7) _____ (Hacer, nosotros) de este restaurante el mejor de toda España! Y ahora, (8) _____ (poner) manos a la obra.

10. **Reescribe las oraciones usando la estructura indicada entre paréntesis.** `24.G`

1. ¡Venid a casa ya mismo!
   (infinitivo) _____

2. Lea el prospecto del medicamento.
   (imperativo impersonal) _____

3. ¡Trabajen duro!
   (A + infinitivo) _____

4. ¡Tomad un plato cada uno!
   (infinitivo) _____

5. Prohibido adelantarse.
   (imperativo negativo de tú) _____

6. ¡Poner más empeño!
   (imperativo afirmativo de vosotros) _____

11. **Eres nuevo en la oficina y quieres ser muy amable. Reescribe las oraciones usando los comienzos indicados.** `24.G`

1. ¡Hagan silencio!
   ¿Podrían_____?

2. ¡A trabajar, todos!
   ¡Pongámonos_____!

3. ¡Dame el teléfono de este cliente!
   ¿Me_____?

4. ¡Cállate la boca!
   ¡A ver_____!

5. ¡Ayúdame con los paquetes!
   ¿Por qué_____?

6. ¡Paga el café que te compré!
   Que_____.

12. **Síntesis La directora, Tomás y sus padres tienen una reunión. Completa los mandatos informales (dirigidos a Tomás) y formales (dirigidos a sus padres).** `24.B–24.G`

ayudarlo con las tareas para el hogar	molestar a tus compañeros
enseñarle buenos modales	prestar atención a la clase
llegar puntualmente	recompensarlo con dinero

Tomás, (1) _____ o te quedarás fuera de la escuela. Y a ustedes, les pido por favor, (2) _____ a Tomás. Le contesta mal a todos los profesores y eso es inadmisible. Otra cosa, Tomás, (3) _____. La profesora Menéndez se queja de que no sabes ni siquiera en qué asignatura estás.

Y, usted, señor Pérez, no (4) _____. Es evidente que Tomás no es el autor de frases como "La situación político-financiera de Azerbaiyán es inverosímil".

Ah, me olvidaba: ¡no (5) _____ cuando aprueba un examen, señores padres! Él tiene el deber de estudiar... ¡sin recibir nada a cambio!

Por último, Tomás, ¡no (6) _____! Te quedarás sin amigos en poco tiempo.

Practice more at **vhlcentral.com.**

1. Completa la tabla clasificando las formas no personales de los verbos que aparecen en el texto. `25.A`

> Querida Natalia:
>
> Desde hace dos años, mi familia viene festejando Halloween, también llamada "Noche de Brujas". Nos encanta disfrazarnos de personajes que dan miedo. Claro, tener el mejor disfraz no es fácil. El año pasado estuve diseñando mi traje durante una semana. Pero al probármelo, me quedaba demasiado ajustado, por lo que terminé comprando un disfraz ya confeccionado en una tienda.
>
> Este año tengo mucho por hacer. ¿Quieres ayudarme? Por lo visto, deberé tener más cuidado cuando haga mi disfraz. Si estás decidida a ayudarme, todas las sugerencias serán bien recibidas.
>
> Avísame qué te parece lo que te he propuesto.
>
> ¡Hasta pronto!
>
> Leandro

Infinitivo	Gerundio	Participio

2. Reemplaza el texto subrayado por una frase con infinitivo. `25.B`

1. El sonido de las campanas no me dejó dormir.
   _____

2. La caminata es una buena forma de ejercicio.
   _____

3. La compra de la casa nos llenó de deudas.
   _____

4. No es bueno que beba refrescos.
   _____

5. El baile me divierte.
   _____

6. Te recomiendo que comas frutas y verduras.
   _____

3. Reescribe las oraciones usando el infinitivo. `25.B`

1. Me alegré tanto cuando te vi.
   Al _____.

2. Si hubieras estudiado más, hoy tendrías mejores calificaciones.
   De _____.

3. Cuando amaneció, la playa estaba desierta.
   Al _____.

4. Si es tan complicado el viaje, mejor nos quedamos aquí.
   De _____.

5. Cuando llegue Juan, llámame por teléfono.
   Al _____.

6. Si hubiéramos seguido caminando, habríamos llegado al muelle.
   De _____.

Actividades

4. En cada oración, elige la opción correcta. `25.B`

1. Me gustaría _____ alegre.
   a. estar   b. que yo esté   c. Ambas opciones son posibles.

2. No permitiremos _____ sin entrada.
   a. que ingresen   b. ingresar   c. Ambas opciones son posibles.

3. Lucía está cansada y quiere _____ la siesta.
   a. dormir   b. que ella duerma   c. Ambas opciones son posibles.

4. El delincuente se declaró inocente. El testigo asegura _____.
   a. mentir   b. que miente   c. Ambas opciones son posibles.

5. No se te permitirá _____ con tanto equipaje.
   a. que viajes   b. viajar   c. Ambas opciones son posibles.

6. Tenemos muchos asuntos _____.
   a. por discutir   b. que debemos discutir c. Ambas opciones son posibles.

5. Une las frases para formar oraciones lógicas. `25.B`

1. Te dije que salieras _____   a. de correr.

2. Eran las seis cuando vine _____   b. gritar y vinimos corriendo.

3. Te oímos _____   c. caminando de la mano.

4. Por favor, no _____   d. a cerrar el negocio.

5. Nos vieron _____   e. molestar.

6. Vamos _____   f. a abrirme la puerta cuando llegara.

6. Completa las oraciones combinando los verbos de ambas listas. `25.C`

andar	seguir		bajar	necesitar
llevar	terminar		comer	pensar
quedar	venir		ir	trabajar

1. Por más que me digas que es malo para la salud, yo _____ _____ carne.

2. Ayer me _____ _____ en lo que me dijiste. ¿De veras te quieres mudar?

3. Mi padre _____ treinta años _____ en la misma compañía. ¡Es increíble!

4. Emilio _____ _____ de peso desde el verano pasado. ¡Parece que va a desaparecer!

5. Al final, los estudiantes _____ _____ a Cancún en su viaje de estudios.

6. Mi hermana _____ _____ una bicicleta nueva. Le regalaré una para su cumpleaños.

7. Clasifica los ejemplos de gerundio según los usos mencionados en la lista. `25.C`

a. causa	b. concesión	c. condición	d. método	e. modo	f. propósito	g. simultaneidad

1. Siendo tan jóvenes, parecen muy responsables. ___   5. Me dormí pensando en el problema. ___

2. Lloviendo mañana, iremos al cine en vez de al parque. ___ 6. No queriendo ver a Juan, me fui de la fiesta. ___

3. Los alumnos salieron corriendo de la escuela. ___   7. Pablo se hizo famoso cantando boleros. ___

4. Nos llamaron diciendo que había huelga. ___

8. Reescribe las oraciones usando el gerundio. `25.C`

1. El jefe nos llamó para decirnos que estábamos despedidos.
   _____

2. Como no te encontré, me fui a casa.
   _____

3. Mientras caminábamos, cantábamos.
   _____

4. Como vi que no había comida, decidí irme al mercado.
   _____

5. Si presionas el botón de ese modo, lo romperás.
   _____

6. Me quebré la pierna mientras practicaba esquí.
   _____

9. En cada oración, elige la opción correcta. `25.C`

1. En la tienda, había dos cajas _____ (conteniendo/que contenían) rompecabezas de mil piezas.
2. ¿No me ves? ¡Estoy _____ (parando/parado) frente a ti!
3. El autobús chocó contra un árbol _____ (resultando heridos los pasajeros/habiendo esquivado una vaca).
4. Cocina la pasta en agua _____ (que hierve/hirviendo) durante cinco minutos.
5. No me puedo imaginar a mi abuelo _____ (cantando/cantar) en una banda de rock.
6. Me encanta la foto de tu madre _____ (abrazando/que abraza) a tu padre.
7. La policía salió en busca del delincuente _____ (capturándolo/y lo capturó) unos minutos después.

10. Completa el relato de Cristina con el participio adecuado del verbo entre paréntesis. `25.D`

Hoy me he (1) _____ (despertar) muy (2) _____ (confundir). Soñé que era (3) _____ (elegir) presidenta del país. Sí, como has (4) _____ (oír). Lo más (5) _____ (confundir) de todo era que yo nunca me había (6) _____ (presentar) a elecciones. Después de haber (7) _____ (asumir) el cargo, me acusaban de ser una gobernante (8) _____ (corromper), que había (9) _____ (robar) millones de dólares al pueblo. Después de un juicio de cinco minutos y sin prueba alguna, estaba (10) _____ (prender) de por vida.
Por suerte, en cuanto estuve lo suficientemente (11) _____ (despertar), me di cuenta de que estaba (12) _____ (sanar) y (13) _____ (salvar).

11. Escribe oraciones siguiendo el modelo. `25.D`

> **Modelo**
>
> Se ha cocinado un pollo.
> *El pollo está cocinado.*

1. Se ha redactado la renuncia.
   _____

2. Se ha divorciado Julia.
   _____

3. Se han casado Juan y Paula.
   _____

4. Se ha soltado al perro.
   _____

5. Se ha corregido el ensayo.
   _____

6. Se ha resuelto el problema.
   _____

12. En cada oración, elige la opción correcta. 25.D

1. Los comentarios _____ realizados por usuarios anónimos.
   a. son   b. están

2. El enigma _____ resuelto por el famoso científico Juan Carlos Luz.
   a. será   b. estará

3. La tienda _____ abierta de 8 a 12.
   a. está   b. fue

4. La paciente _____ atendida por la doctora Pérez.
   a. ha sido   b. ha estado

5. La ciudad _____ conquistada por los indígenas en 1450.
   a. ha estado   b. ha sido

6. El templo _____ construido de piedras y lodo.
   a. está   b. es

7. Las clases _____ suspendidas hasta nuevo aviso.
   a. han estado   b. han sido

13. Síntesis Completa el artículo con la forma no personal adecuada de los verbos de la lista. 25.A–25.D

| decidir | golpear | liberar | presumir | quedarse | recibir | ser |

Carlos Castaño, el (1) _____ asesino de la cantante Úrsula Gómez, ha sido (2) _____ en el día de ayer. (3) _____ declarado inocente por el jurado, Castaño ahora ha (4) _____ hacerle juicio al Estado. Dos días antes, el jurado había (5) _____ una carta de una vecina de Gómez. En ella, la vecina describe que vio a una mujer (6) _____ a Gómez la noche del 8 de diciembre. Al (7) _____ sin sospechosos, la policía ha reanudado la búsqueda.

14. Síntesis Completa las oraciones con la forma no personal del verbo entre paréntesis. 25.A–25.D

1. Nadie se hace rico _____ (vender) artesanías.

2. De _____ (continuar) la huelga, no podremos viajar a Alicante.

3. Segundo, _____ (desconectar) el suministro eléctrico.

4. Quiero comprar el cuadro que se llama "Mujer _____ (tejer)".

5. Me encanta el refrán que dice "A lo _____ (hacer), pecho".

6. _____ (pagar) con la tarjeta de crédito, te endeudarás sin saberlo.

7. Juan camina _____ (mover) los brazos de un lado al otro.

8. Al _____ (oír) la puerta, el gato se escondió debajo del sofá.

15. Síntesis Une las frases para formar oraciones lógicas. 25.A–25.D

1. No soy capaz _____   a. acordándome de cuánto te gustan.

2. Compré fresas _____   b. comiendo palomitas de maíz.

3. Vimos una película _____   c. de dormir en una tienda de campaña.

4. A la tienda, entró una mujer _____   d. al sentarme en la silla.

5. Cómo me gusta _____   e. el cantar de los pájaros.

6. Me quedé dormida _____   f. atenta a las palabras de su amiga.

7. Luciana estaba _____   g. dando gritos y saltando.

16. Síntesis Une los ejemplos con las explicaciones. `25.A–25.D`

1. Para expresar propósito, el gerundio solamente puede usarse con verbos de comunicación.

2. Los verbos de movimiento como este siempre llevan la preposición **a** o **de**.

3. Por lo general, se usa el infinitivo junto a verbos de deseo para indicar que el sujeto de la acción deseada es quien expresa el deseo.

4. Solo hay tres verbos en español que permiten formar tiempos compuestos con el participio regular o el irregular. Solo la forma irregular se usa como adjetivo.

5. Se puede usar el gerundio para referirse al objeto de los verbos que expresan una representación, ya sea mental o física.

6. Esta estructura funciona como un adverbio para indicar que la acción está ocurriendo paralelamente a otra.

7. Los sustantivos y adjetivos pueden ser modificados por una preposición más infinitivo.

8. Hay verbos que al parecer tienen dos formas de participio pasado, pero se emplea el participio regular para formar tiempos compuestos con **haber**.

a. Baja a recibir el pedido del supermercado, por favor.

b. He impreso el pasaje del tren en la casa de Irma.

c. Al salir, cerré la puerta.

d. Nuestra prima nos escribió contándonos que se casaba.

e. Quiero ganar la lotería.

f. ¡Tenemos tantas cosas por hacer!

g. Me imagino a Marina patinando sobre hielo ¡y me da risa!

h. Nunca he sido tan bien atendido en un restaurante.

Practice more at **vhlcentral.com.**

Verb periphrases and modal verbs

Chapter 26

1. Completa las oraciones con los verbos modales de la lista. `26.B`

deber (2)   tener (2)   haber (3)   poder (2)   venir (2)

1. Esta mesa no _____ a costar más de 300 dólares, ¿la compramos?

2. ¿_____ probar la ensalada? Se ve tan rica y tengo tanta hambre.

3. No tenemos otra opción: _____ de sacar esa muela, aunque no quieras.

4. Lucía _____ de haberse quedado dormida. Son las 10 y todavía no ha llegado al trabajo.

5. Los alumnos _____ de asistir, como mínimo, a un 75% de las clases.

6. Como las habitaciones de todos los hoteles estaban reservadas, mis padres _____ que dormir en el auto.

7. _____ de ser tres o cuatro los que aún no han pagado la cuota del club. No estoy segura.

8. Elisa y tú _____ hacer la presentación de Historia para el miércoles próximo.

9. Al final, los arreglos de la casa _____ a costarnos más de dos mil pesos.

10. Me quedé en casa porque _____ que estudiar para el examen.

11. ¿Sabías que las bolsas de plástico _____ causar la muerte de muchas mascotas que se meten en ellas y se asfixian?

2. En cada oración, elige la opción correcta. `26.B`

1. No _____ (deberías/debes de) salir tan desabrigada si tienes tos.

2. ¿Finalmente _____ (pudiste/podías) hablar con María? Yo la llamé varias veces y me atendió el contestador.

3. ¡Esta bici es el mejor regalo! Siempre _____ (quería/quise) tener una bicicleta amarilla.

4. ¿_____ (Debes/Sabes) hablar alemán? Hay una clienta que necesita ayuda ¡y no habla ni un poquito de español!

5. Cuando encienda la lavadora, _____ (debería titilar/titilará) una luz verde.

6. No _____ (debías/debiste) haberle puesto tanta sal a la ensalada. ¡Es imposible comerla!

7. En las montañas, _____ (parece/puede) haber mucha nieve. Es un día perfecto para esquiar.

8. Por supuesto que sé montar en bicicleta, pero hoy no _____ (puedo/debo de) hacerlo. ¡Me duele la rodilla!

3. Decide si estos ejemplos de perífrasis verbales expresan _tiempo_, una _fase_ o una _serie_. `26.C`

1. Juana se puso a llorar en cuanto vio a su hija en el traje de novia. _____

2. Empezaremos por meter toda la ropa en cajas. Luego, las rotularemos. _____

3. No acostumbramos beber café por las mañanas. _____

4. ¡Deja de llamarme por teléfono! _____

5. Volveremos a vernos pronto, ¿no? _____

6. Todo nuestro trabajo vino a resultar en vano. ¡Todo por no leer bien las instrucciones! _____

7. Cuando llegaste, estaba por escribirte un mensaje de texto. _____

8. ¡Justo vengo a olvidarme el trabajo de Historia en casa! _____

4. Completa la carta con las perífrasis verbales del cuadro. `26.C`

volveré a	fui a	para de	puso a	acababa de	empiezo por	suelo	terminaré por

Querida hermana:

¿Cómo estás? (1) _____ decirte que te extraño muchísimo. Bien sabes que yo no (2) _____ quejarme, pero estos primeros días aquí en Chile no han sido fáciles.

No te imaginas qué frío que es el clima aquí. ¡No (3) _____ llover! Ayer (4) _____ salir de casa, muy bien vestida para ir a una entrevista y, de pronto, se (5) _____ llover a cántaros. Por supuesto, no (6) _____ salir sin paraguas.

Otra cosa, mi compañera de cuarto es muy maleducada. Nunca limpia, tampoco cocina y me trata mal. ¡Qué mala suerte que tengo! ¿Cómo (7) _____ parar a esta habitación?

Bueno, veré qué hago en las próximas semanas. Seguramente (8) _____ mudarme a otra habitación.

Un gran abrazo,

Tu hermana menor

5. Une los elementos de las tres columnas para formar oraciones lógicas. `26.C`

1. Después de probar con el canto,	volvería a	estudiar pintura.
2. En esas dos horas, el profesor no	dejó de	robar en la tienda.
3. Me juró que no	iría a	comer dulces, ¡pero este bombón es tentador!
4. Un rato después de salir el sol,	suelo	hablar ni un segundo.
5. Es verdad que no	pasé a	hacer las compras por iniciativa propia.
6. Natalia nunca	entró a	nublarse y a la media hora llovía sin parar.

6. Usa los verbos de la lista para formar perífrasis verbales de gerundio de los verbos entre paréntesis. `26.D`

andar   estar   ir   venir   llevar   seguir   vivir   pasarse

1. ¿Te das cuenta de que _____ (hablar) por teléfono desde que llegué?

2. Mi madre _____ (criticar) a todas sus vecinas. ¡Es insoportable!

3. El perro _____ toda la tarde _____ (ladrar) y los vecinos se quejaron.

4. Los impuestos _____ (aumentar) hasta que fue casi imposible pagarlos.

5. ¡Hace cuánto que te _____ (pedir) que arregles el grifo de la cocina!

6. Mi padre _____ (necesitar) una corbata nueva. Se la regalaré para su cumpleaños.

7. Juana _____ (vivir) dos años en Ecuador.

8. Yo _____ (trabajar) hasta las 8 de la noche. ¿Tú qué quieres hacer?

7. En cada oración, elige la opción correcta. `26.D`

1. Finalmente, _____ (terminé/anduve) comprando la chaqueta amarilla. La azul no me convencía del todo.

2. La falta de agua potable _____ (anda/continúa) siendo el problema más grave de las zonas más pobres del país.

3. Tomás _____ (sigue/lleva) buscando trabajo unos cuatro meses.

4. La paciente _____ (va/está) recuperándose de la operación. Por favor, déjenla dormir.

5. _____ (Sigo/Llevo) esperando el llamado de Pablo.

6. El niñito ese _____ (está/vive) molestando en clase. Hablaré con sus padres.

8. Une las explicaciones con los ejemplos. `26.D`

1. Expresa un proceso en aumento que tiene un límite o resultado.

2. Expresa una acción constante, habitual o que se repite.

3. Expresa una acción referida a un período de tiempo.

4. Expresa un proceso en curso que se da intermitentemente.

5. Expresa un proceso que comenzó en el pasado y continúa hasta ahora.

6. Expresa un proceso en curso, pero es más enfático que **estar** + **gerundio**.

a._____ Llevo tres horas esperándote en la esquina. ¿Dónde te metiste?

b._____ La humedad de esa pared fue creciendo hasta que finalmente el dueño decidió repararla.

c._____ Mi primita se pasó toda la tarde llorando por su mamá.

d._____ Ya nos venía pareciendo que faltaba dinero de la caja y ahora descubrimos que el vendedor nos robaba.

e._____ Juan y su novia viven peleándose por cualquier cosa.

f._____ Lucas anda preguntando por ti. ¿Por qué no lo llamas?

9. **Reescribe las oraciones usando perífrasis de participio.** `26.E`

1. Mamá le prohibió a Luisito que use vasos de vidrio. (tener) _____

2. Gonzalo ha ganado tres carreras. (llevar) _____

3. Mis amigos han comprado las entradas para mañana. (tener) _____

4. Este director ha dirigido más de veinte películas. (llevar) _____

5. La carta se escribió con tinta roja. (estar) _____

6. Ya escribí veinte capítulos del libro. (llevar) _____

10. **Completa las oraciones con perífrasis verbales usando los verbos de la lista.** `26.E`

| tener (2) | ver | seguir | quedar (2) | estar | venir |

1. La profesora _____ encantada con tu trabajo final. Seguramente te pondrá una buena nota.

2. Ya _____ preparado todo para el concierto de esta noche.

3. El nombre de la empresa _____ impreso en los sobres. No hace falta escribir nada.

4. _____ decidido que se cerrará el restaurante hasta el verano próximo.

5. Federica _____ preocupada por la salud de su perrito. Hace una semana que está enfermo.

6. Mis padres _____ pensado ir de vacaciones al Caribe.

7. Te _____ dicho que me llames con tiempo antes de pasar por casa.

8. Al final, nos _____ obligados a tomar una decisión drástica.

11. **Síntesis Completa las perífrasis con el infinitivo, participio o gerundio de los verbos de la lista.** `26.B–26.E`

| tener | perjudicar | gastar | ver | despertarte | dormir (2) |

1. Perdona, no quería _____. ¡Te llamaré más tarde!

2. Marta está _____ desde las 2 de la tarde.

3. Todos resultamos _____ por la crisis económica.

4. No suelo _____ la siesta, ¡pero hoy estaba tan cansada!

5. Sigo _____ pesadillas con fantasmas. ¡Todo por ver esa película!

6. Llevamos _____ demasiado dinero en este negocio.

7. Acabo de _____ a la chica más linda del mundo.

12. **Síntesis Une las explicaciones con los ejemplos.** `26.B–26.E`

___ 1. Indica una acción que está a punto de empezar.

___ 2. Indica una acción que se está desarrollando.

___ 3. Indica una acción acabada.

___ 4. Indica una acción considerada como resultado.

___ 5. Indica una acción que se repite varias veces.

___ 6. Indica una obligación.

___ 7. Indica una posibilidad.

___ 8. Indica el punto justo de conclusión de una acción.

a. Nadia dejó de leer porque le dolía la cabeza.

b. Estaba por cocinar algo cuando apareciste con una pizza.

c. Suelo comer un yogur como cena.

d. Puedo comerme tres platos de sopa cuando tengo hambre.

e. Hemos de vender más de veinte productos por día.

f. Me estoy rompiendo la cabeza con este crucigrama.

g. Terminamos de tomar el café y nos vamos, ¿sí?

h. Tengo estudiada toda la lección uno.

Practice more at **vhlcentral.com**.

1. Indica los pronombres y verbos reflexivos. `27.A`

> Juan:
>
> Hoy me desperté a las siete de la mañana. Apenas escuché el despertador, me senté en la cama y te llamé por teléfono para despertarte. El teléfono sonó, sonó y sonó, pero no atendiste.
>
> Como todavía era temprano, no me preocupé y decidí darme un baño largo. Después, me cepillé los dientes y me peiné.
>
> Dos minutos después de salir de la ducha, me di cuenta de mi error: ¡me había equivocado de número de teléfono! Ahora me siento tan mal por esta situación. Llegaste tarde al trabajo, tu jefe se enojó contigo y casi pierdes tu trabajo.
>
> ¡Espero que sepas disculparme!
>
> Lucas

2. Escribe las oraciones usando pronombres y verbos reflexivos. `27.A`

> **Modelo**
> dormirse / yo / 8.00 p.m.
> *Me duermo a las 8.00 p.m.*
> *Me voy a dormir/Voy a dormirme a las 8.00 p.m.*

1. afeitarse / Oscar / 9.00 a.m.
   _____
   _____

2. reunirse / ellos / miércoles
   _____
   _____

3. reírse / vosotros / mucho
   _____
   _____

4. pelearse / nosotros / nunca
   _____
   _____

5. ponerse / Gabriela / tacones
   _____
   _____

3. Reescribe las oraciones usando *el uno al otro, los unos a los otros*, etc. `27.B`

1. Juan e Isabel se apoyan mutuamente.
   _____

2. Los alumnos y los profesores siempre se critican mutuamente.
   _____

3. Federica y su amiga se respetan mutuamente.
   _____

4. Los trabajadores se ayudan mutuamente.
   _____

5. Mi madre y mi hermana se miraron entre sí con tristeza.
   _____

4. Indica si estos ejemplos contienen verbos reflexivos. Escribe *sí* o *no*. 27.C–27.D

1. Me he maquillado demasiado, ¿no? _____

2. Juan durmió al niño y comenzó a estudiar. _____

3. ¿Te manchaste la camisa otra vez? _____

4. Despiértenme a las nueve. _____

5. Quita tus cosas de mi armario. _____

6. Los invitados deberán vestirse de etiqueta. _____

5. En cada oración, elige la opción correcta. 27.C–27.D

1. Florencia se bañó _____ rápidamente y salió al cine.
   a. a sí misma   b. X

2. El pobre perrito ya no puede levantarse _____.
   a. por sí mismo   b. X

3. Mi hermano no sabe defenderse _____.
   a. X   b. por sí solo

4. Me acosté _____ muy temprano.
   a. a mí mismo   b. X

5. ¿El niño ya es capaz de ducharse _____?
   a. por sí mismo   b. X

6. ¿A qué hora te despiertas _____ para ir a trabajar?
   a. X   b. a ti misma

7. Una vez que crezca, la niña podrá vestirse _____.
   a. X   b. por sí sola

6. Clasifica los verbos según sean únicamente reflexivos o no. 27.C–27.D

arrepentirse	cansarse	desvivirse
jactarse	lavarse	quemarse
comportarse	conocerse	dignarse
odiarse	quejarse	rebelarse

Únicamente reflexivos	Reflexivos/No reflexivos

7. Completa las oraciones con los verbos de la lista. Agrega el pronombre adecuado a cada verbo. `27.C–27.D`

apoyar	aprender	casar	confesar	duchar	reunir	odiar
abrazar	arrepentir	comprometer	conocer	escribir (2)	mirar	pelear

1. Los enamorados _____ a los ojos y _____ su amor.

2. Estamos tan contentos. _____ el 20 de octubre y _____ el 1.º de diciembre.

3. Los hermanos siempre _____ mutuamente.

4. María y Julia _____ todo el día y sin ningún motivo.

5. Es algo muy raro, pero mi perro y mi gato no _____.

6. Quiero que _____ más seguido. Sé que vivimos lejos, pero queremos estar comunicados, ¿no es así?

7. Las amigas _____ cuando se reencontraron después de tantos años.

8. Aníbal _____ con agua fría porque se había acabado el agua caliente.

9. No es verdad que Ana _____ todos los nombres la primera vez que los oyó.

10. Los directivos _____ la semana próxima para analizar las nuevas propuestas.

11. Ellos _____ cuando eran niños y _____ cartas desde entonces.

12. No _____ de haberle dicho la verdad, aunque no le haya gustado oírla.

8. Completa las oraciones usando los verbos de la lista para expresar una acción "completa". `27.C–27.D`

andar	comer	conocer	creer	saber

1. _____ todos los restaurantes vegetarianos de la ciudad.

2. ¿De veras _____ lo que dice mi hermanita? ¡No seas tonta!

3. Cuando tienen hambre, esos niños _____ tres platos de sopa cada uno.

4. Andrea _____ de memoria los nombres de todas las actrices de la telenovela.

5. ¿_____ toda Barcelona? Supongo que estás cansada.

9. Une los ejemplos con las explicaciones. `27.C–27.D`

_____ 1. Es un verbo que implica reciprocidad.

_____ 2. Es un verbo que solamente puede ser reflexivo.

_____ 3. Es un verbo que expresa una acción "completa".

_____ 4. Es un verbo que implica que uno mismo no realizó la acción.

_____ 5. Es un verbo cuyo sujeto es afectado indirectamente por la acción y, por lo tanto, se convierte en objeto indirecto.

a. ¡De qué color más raro te teñiste el cabello!

b. Me aprendí todo el vocabulario para el examen.

c. Las mujeres no nos llevamos bien entre nosotras.

d. ¡Te quejas y te quejas todo el día!

e. ¡Qué lindo vestido que me mandé a hacer!

10. En cada oración, elige la opción correcta. `27.E`

1. _____ (Anima/Anímate) a tu amiga a que venga a la fiesta.

2. _____ (Me decidí/Decidí) no comprar una casa en las montañas.

3. Josefina _____ (se saltó/saltó) el almuerzo: piensa que así podrá adelgazar más rápido.

4. _____ (Jugamos/Nos jugamos) el pellejo en este partido. ¡Debemos ganarlo sí o sí!

5. No _____ (te deshagas/deshagas) el trabajo que con tanto esfuerzo logramos hacer.

6. ¡_____ (Cómanse/Coman) todo el chocolate! A mí no me gusta.

11. Escribe las respuestas usando reflexivos que expresan acciones involuntarias. `27.F`

> **Modelo**
>
> ¿Qué le pasó a la botella? (romper)
> *Se rompió.*

1. ¿Qué le pasó a tu motocicleta? (descomponer)

   _____

2. ¿Qué le pasó a la batería de tu teléfono? (descargar)

   _____

3. ¿Qué les pasó a los adornos que te regalé? (caer)

   _____

4. ¿Qué le pasó al ovillo de lana? (enredar)

   _____

5. ¿Qué les pasó a los edificios? (derrumbar)

   _____

12. Escribe oraciones siguiendo el modelo. `27.F`

> **Modelo**
>
> Se descompuso la radio. (yo)
> *Se me descompuso la radio.*

1. Se quebró la madera. (tú)

   _____

2. Se cerró la puerta. (él)

   _____

3. Se rompió la tetera. (yo)

   _____

4. Se derramó la leche. (nosotros)

   _____

5. Se agotó la batería. (mi auto)

   _____

6. Olvido siempre los nombres.

   _____

7. Esos hermanitos siempre pierden las llaves.

   _____

13. Completa las oraciones con verbos que expresen cambio. Como pista, tienes los adjetivos que corresponden a dichos verbos. `27.G`

| emocionado/a | enamorado/a | muerto/a | rico/a | rojo/a | separado/a |

1. Cuando se dio cuenta de que todos lo miraban, Juan _____.
2. Mi madre _____ tanto cuando nos graduamos.
3. Mi gato _____ en 2005.
4. Los empresarios _____ a raíz del aumento de los bienes inmuebles.
5. Las adolescentes pronto _____ de la estrella de la música pop.
6. La diputada _____ de su marido y ahora se ve más feliz.

14. Reescribe las oraciones usando el verbo entre paréntesis. `27.G`

1. La oficina es un caos cuando tú no estás. (convertirse)

   _____

2. Tu pececito se entristece apenas sales de la sala. (ponerse)

   _____

3. Mi prima se enriqueció con su tienda de perfumes. (hacerse)

   _____

4. La mala noticia me preocupa todavía. (quedarse)

   _____

5. Ahora Madrid es una ciudad muy cara. (volverse)

   _____

6. Algún día, seré muy rico. (llegar a ser)

   _____

15. Síntesis En cada oración, elige la opción correcta. `27.A–27.G`

1. El ladrón _____ de los objetos robados.
   a. se deshizo   b. deshizo

2. El cabello _____ cada día más.
   a. se cae   b. se me cae

3. ¡Qué tonta soy! _____ los libros en casa.
   a. Se me olvidaron   b. Se olvidaron

4. Juan es tan ingenuo. _____ todo lo que le dicen.
   a. Cree   b. Se cree

5. _____ que vendrías más temprano.
   a. Se me ocurrió   b. Me ocurrió

6. Isabela _____ al bebé y se puso a leer.
   a. se acostó   b. acostó

16. Síntesis Decide qué oración es la intrusa. `27.A–27.G`

1. a. Me leí el libro en una tarde.
   b. Me caí de las escaleras.
   c. Me conozco Venezuela de cabo a rabo.

2. a. No te atreviste a llamarme.
   b. El jefe se dignó a subir los salarios.
   c. La empresa se declaró en quiebra.

3. a. Luisa se operó el lunes.
   b. La ventana se abrió.
   c. El vidrio se rompió.

4. a. Has avergonzado a tu hermana.
   b. El delincuente burló la guardia policial.
   c. ¿Te has burlado de mí?

5. a. Nos casamos en junio.
   b. Te irritaste un poco, ¿no?
   c. Se me olvidó traer dinero.

6. a. ¡Se hizo demasiado tarde!
   b. Se volvió para decirme algo.
   c. El barrio se ha vuelto un lugar concurrido.

Practice more at **vhlcentral.com.**

1. Convierte las oraciones en oraciones pasivas con ser. `28.B–28.C`

1. El Senado aprobó hoy la ley de alimentos orgánicos.

   _____

2. Miles de fanáticos vieron el partido.

   _____

3. La crítica elogió el documental *La selva hoy*.

   _____

4. Los arqueólogos chilenos descubrieron tres tumbas egipcias.

   _____

5. La policía controló la identidad de los pasajeros.

   _____

6. Ambos países firmarán un acuerdo de cooperación.

   _____

2. En cada oración, elige la opción correcta. `28.B–28.C`

1. La prensa de los Estados Unidos _____ muy _____ por no ser imparcial.
   a. fueron/criticados   b. fue/criticada

2. Las cartas que escribió la niña _____ hace dos semanas.
   a. fue enviada   b. fueron enviadas

3. La habitación ya _____ por el señor vestido de azul.
   a. ha sido pagada   b. ha sido pagado

4. Carina _____ mejor compañera por todos sus compañeros.
   a. fue elegida   b. fue electa

5. El contrato de trabajo y el acuerdo de confidencialidad _____ por todas las partes interesadas.
   a. será firmado   b. serán firmados

6. La fila de prioridad de embarque _____ por todos los pasajeros.
   a. deberá ser respetada   b. deberá ser respetado

3. Reordena los elementos para formar oraciones completas. `28.B–28.C`

1. cruelmente / por / fueron / Los animalitos / tratados / el cazador / .

   _____

2. información / serán / con 50.000 dólares / Quienes den / recompensados / .

   _____

3. los lectores / fueron / enviados / Los periódicos / a / esta tarde / .

   _____

4. El problema / el jefe del departamento / había sido / por / resuelto / .

   _____

5. por / diseñado y confeccionado / El vestido de novia / fue / el afamado diseñador / .

   _____

6. fue / El conserje / despertado / los visitantes / por / .

   _____

4. Reescribe las oraciones en voz pasiva siguiendo el modelo. `28.B–28.C`

> **Modelo**
>
> Juan cambiará la lámpara de la cocina.
> *La lámpara de la cocina será cambiada por Juan.*
> *La lámpara ya esta cambiada.*

1. La policía prenderá al delincuente.

   _____

   _____

2. Mi madre hará el pastel para mi cumpleaños.

   _____

   _____

3. Ulises redactará una carta de queja.

   _____

   _____

4. Todos los trabajadores pagarán los aportes jubilatorios.

   _____

   _____

5. El directorio de la compañía publicará la revista *Novedades empresariales*.

   _____

   _____

5. Escribe las oraciones siguiendo el modelo. `28.D`

> **Modelo**
>
> Café: hacer - servir
> *Primero, se hace el café. Luego, se lo sirve.*

1. Papas: pelar - cortar

   _____

2. Tarta: hornear - probar

   _____

3. Casa: construir - pintar

   _____

4. Bombilla de luz: apagar - cambiar

   _____

5. Paciente: llamar - examinar

   _____

6. Cabello: lavar - cortar

   _____

7. Galletas: decorar - hornear

   _____

Actividades

6. Lee las tareas que tienen los cadetes de primer año de la academia militar y completa las oraciones. `28.D`

Lunes	Martes	Miércoles	Jueves	Viernes	Sábado
limpiar el pasillo	ordenar las habitaciones	lavar la ropa	preparar la cena	planchar las camisas	disfrutar el día

1. El lunes se debe _____.
2. El martes _____.
3. _____.
4. _____.
5. _____.
6. _____.

7. Completa las oraciones con los verbos de la lista. Deberás elegir entre oraciones pasivas con ser y oraciones pasivas reflejas. `28.B–28.D`

> detener   saber   mojar   firmar   reparar   aceptar   agregar

1. La antena de mi casa está rota y _____ por un profesional la semana que viene.
2. _____ todas las solicitudes que cumplan con los requisitos.
3. La lavadora no funciona sin detergente. Antes de encenderla, _____ las pastillas en este recipiente.
4. Ayer dejé abierta la ventana de la habitación y _____ todos mis apuntes con la lluvia.
5. Las prescripciones de medicamentos siempre _____ por los médicos.
6. Según la policía, _____ a los responsables del crimen en el transcurso de esta semana.
7. No _____ aún dónde está el dinero robado.

8. Elige la opción correcta para completar cada oración. `28.B–28.D`

1. Ayer vi que, en el restaurante de la esquina, _____ camareros. ¿Te interesa?
   a. se buscan   b. se busca   c. Ambas opciones son posibles.
2. _____ que al final del cuento el príncipe siempre conquista el corazón de la mujer de sus sueños.
   a. Se supone   b. Se suponen   c. Ambas opciones son posibles.
3. Esta enfermedad ya _____ por los expertos de nuestro país.
   a. ha sido estudiada   b. se ha estudiado   c. Ambas opciones son posibles.
4. Los detalles de la reunión _____ durante esta semana.
   a. se prepararán   b. serán preparados   c. Ambas opciones son posibles.
5. La naranja es la fruta que más _____ en España.
   a. se exporta   b. se exportan   c. Ambas opciones son posibles.
6. Las instrucciones _____ con antelación.
   a. deberían comunicarse   b. se deberían comunicar   c. Ambas opciones son posibles.
7. Las cuentas del hogar _____ por correo electrónico a la brevedad.
   a. se envía   b. se envían   c. Ambas opciones son posibles.

9. Escribe oraciones siguiendo el modelo. `28.E`

> **Modelo**
>
> pincel - pintar. *Con el pincel, se pinta.*
> oficina - trabajar. *En la oficina, se trabaja.*

1. cuchillo - cortar

_____

2. pimienta - condimentar

_____

3. cuchara - probar

_____

4. tenedor - comer

_____

5. lápiz - escribir

_____

6. ayuntamiento - debatir

_____

7. escuela - aprender

_____

8. comedor - comer

_____

10. Reescribe las construcciones impersonales subrayadas usando el pronombre indefinido *uno/a* o el pronombre *se,* según corresponda. `28.E`

1. "¡En esta cama, se puede dormir tan bien!", dijo Juan. _____
2. "Si se está tranquilo, se puede trabajar mejor", dijo Lucas. _____
3. En esta tienda una puede comprar lo que quiera. _____
4. "¡Qué bien que se vive en esta ciudad!", dijo Sara. _____
5. "A la estación, se llega en veinte minutos", dijo mi hermana. _____
6. "En la clase de baile, se transpira muchísimo", dijo Julio. _____

11. Escribe oraciones siguiendo el modelo. `28.E`

> **Modelo**
>
> Los pasajeros serán controlados al subir al autobús.
> *Se controlará a los pasajeros al subir al autobús.*
> *Se los controlará al subir al autobús.*

1. Las mujeres son maltratadas en ese país.

_____
_____

2. Los peatones deben ser respetados.

_____
_____

3. Las enfermeras son contratadas por un año.

_____
_____

4. Todo el pueblo es encuestado cada diez años.

_____
_____

5. Los trabajadores son evaluados cada trimestre.

_____
_____

12. En el siguiente texto, indica dónde está expresado el objeto indirecto. `28.F`

Primero, se redactaron las normas de seguridad. Una vez redactadas, la gerencia se las enseñó a los miembros del departamento de documentación. Cuando estaban listas, se las enviaron a todos los trabajadores de la planta.

Hubo diversas reacciones de parte de los trabajadores. Se le informó a la gerencia que muchas de las normas eran obsoletas y se le advirtió que debían hacerse modificaciones con urgencia.

Ahora se han reformado las normas. Mañana por la tarde se las presentará al gerente general. Esta vez seguramente se las aprobará sin objeciones.

13. Decide si estas oraciones son construcciones pasivas con *se* o impersonales con *se*. `28.G`

1. En el instituto que está cerca de casa se enseñan más de veinte idiomas. _____

2. Jamás se supo el origen de esa donación. _____

3. Se contratan camareros con experiencia. _____

4. Cuando se estudia, se aprueba sin problemas. _____

5. Se dicen muchas mentiras en la prensa amarilla. _____

6. Se elogió a nuestra directora en el discurso de inauguración. _____

7. Se vendieron más de cuarenta videojuegos en un día. _____

8. Se cree cada vez menos en los gobernantes. _____

9. Nunca se supo el porqué de su decisión. _____

10. Aquí se trabaja muchísimo. _____

14. Reescribe las oraciones usando la pista entre paréntesis. `28.H`

1. Nunca se sabe cómo estará el tiempo al día siguiente. (uno)

_____

2. Se hace lo que se puede. (gente)

_____

3. Es conveniente tener un botiquín de primeros auxilios. (convenir)

_____

4. No se puede respirar en esta habitación llena de humo. (una)

_____

5. Se te han enviado dos postales. (tercera persona del plural)

_____

6. Ha caído muchísima lluvia en la última semana. (llover)

_____

7. Abundan los libros sobre historia medieval en esta biblioteca. (haber)

_____

8. El clima está frío en esa época del año. (hacer)

_____

9. Te recomiendo que estudies mucho para el examen. (convenir)

_____

15. **Completa las oraciones con las palabras de la lista.** `28.H`

| habían | es | había | han | hay | hubo | era |

1. _____ demasiada nieve y no podemos salir de casa.

2. ¿_____ problemas entre Martín y tú? Veo que ya no se hablan.

3. Este mes, se _____ vendido más de mil ejemplares de la novela.

4. Mis artículos _____ sido publicados en la revista *Lugares* ¡y yo no me había enterado!

5. _____ tanto sol que tuve que ponerme a la sombra.

6. _____ invierno, pero parece primavera.

7. ¡Ya _____ hora de que me llamaras!

16. **Síntesis Elige la opción con construcción pasiva o impersonal que tenga el mismo significado que la oración original.** `28.B–28.H`

1. Reformaron los hoteles por los festejos de fin de año.
   a. Los festejos de fin de año reformaron los hoteles.
   b. Se reformaron los hoteles por los festejos de fin de año.

2. La película fue galardonada con ocho estatuillas.
   a. Se galardonó la película con ocho estatuillas.
   b. Ocho estatuillas galardonaron la película.

3. Uno se puede perder muy fácilmente en este bosque.
   a. En este bosque, uno puede ser perdido fácilmente.
   b. Puedes perderte fácilmente en este bosque.

4. Los investigadores persiguieron al asesino día y noche.
   a. El asesino fue perseguido por los investigadores día y noche.
   b. Se persiguió al asesino día y noche.

5. Los mejores deportistas serán premiados por su desempeño.
   a. Se premiará por su desempeño a los mejores deportistas.
   b. Los mejores deportistas premiarán por su desempeño.

6. El titular deberá firmar los cheques de viajero.
   a. Los cheques de viajero deberán ser firmados por el titular.
   b. Se deberá firmar los cheques de viajero.

7. Lo condenaron injustamente.
   a. Se lo condenó injustamente.
   b. Uno se condenó injustamente.

8. Los conductores fueron multados por exceso de velocidad.
   a. Se multó a los conductores por exceso de velocidad.
   b. El exceso de velocidad multó a los conductores.

Practice more at **vhlcentral.com.**

1. Completa la conversación con los verbos *haber* o *estar*. `29.B`

LUCIANO Hola, soy Luciano, ¿(1) _____ Paula?

JOSEFINA Aquí no (2) _____ ninguna Paula, debes haberte equivocado de número de teléfono.

LUCIANO Seguramente (3) _____ un malentendido.

JOSEFINA Mira, yo vivo aquí y puedo asegurarte que no (4) _____ nadie en esta casa que se llame así.

LUCIANO ¿(5) _____ alguna posibilidad de que estés confundida?

JOSEFINA ¡No (6) _____ posibilidad alguna! Vivo con mi compañera de piso ¡y no se llama Paula!

LUCIANO ¿Y (7) _____ tu compañera contigo ahora?

JOSEFINA No, ahora (8) _____ en la universidad.

LUCIANO Bueno, dile que llamó Luciano y que se (9) _____ olvidado unos libros con su nombre en el aula.

JOSEFINA ¿Paula? ¿No será Laura?

LUCIANO "Laura", "Paula", ¡qué más da! ¡(10) _____ una letra de diferencia!

2. En cada oración, elige la opción correcta. `29.C`

1. _____ (Está/Es) oscuro y _____ (es/son) las 4 de la tarde. ¡Qué feo es el invierno!

2. ¿_____ (Será/Estará) nevando en la montaña ahora?

3. _____ (Es/Estamos) a martes y Juan todavía no ha pagado el alquiler.

4. ¡Esas camisas ya no se usan! _____ (Estamos/Es) en 2010, ¡no en 1980!

5. Ayer _____ (estuvo/fue) nublado y las fotos salieron muy oscuras.

6. _____ (Es/Son) la una: ¿dónde está Carlos?

7. ¿Hoy _____ (estamos/es) lunes o martes?

3. Julián lleva un diario donde escribe sobre las cosas que le pasan todos los días. Completa el diario con las palabras de la lista. `29.C`

está	hizo	estuvo	estamos	son
es	hace	hubo (2)	hará	es

Hoy (1) _____ 8 de julio y (2) _____ las tres de la tarde. A pesar de que (3) _____ verano, (4) _____ mucho frío afuera y (5) _____ lloviendo a cántaros.

Ayer también (6) _____ mal tiempo. (7) _____ nublado y (8) _____ mucho viento.

¡Qué mal! Hoy (9) _____ a viernes y en toda la semana no (10) _____ ni un solo día lindo.

¿(11) _____ menos frío mañana? Me fijaré ya mismo en el pronóstico.

4. Completa las oraciones con la conjugación apropiada de *ser*, *estar* o *tener*. `29.D`

1. Ayer no dormí bien y ahora _____ muchísimo sueño.

2. Ema _____ veinte años menor que Graciela.

3. El perro seguramente _____ hambriento. Dale un poco de comida.

4. ¿Los niños les _____ miedo todavía a los payasos?

5. Este edificio _____ más de doscientos años, ¿puedes creerlo?

6. ¡Qué cansada que _____! Mejor me quedaré en casa.

7. ¿_____ calor? Si os parece, bajaré la calefacción un poco.

5. Traduce las siguientes oraciones usando como ayuda la palabra entre paréntesis. `29.E`

1. It's becoming night.

_____ (hacer).

2. It turned cold.

_____ (ponerse).

3. The clock struck five.

_____ (dar).

4. It's winter again.

_____ (de nuevo).

5. Now it's Friday.

_____ (ya).

6. It became day.

_____ (hacer).

6. Traduce las siguientes oraciones siguiendo el modelo. `29.E`

> **Modelo**
> He went pale.
> *Empalideció.*
> *Se puso pálido.*

1. She blushed.

_____

_____

2. She became happy.

_____

_____

3. My grandfather became rich.

_____

_____

4. I got better.

_____

_____

5. They got sad.

_____

_____

6. We became quiet.

_____

_____

7. He went crazy.

_____

_____

7. Síntesis En cada oración, elige la opción correcta. `29.B–29.E`

1. ¿_____ (Está/Hay) alguien que se llame Ángela en tu clase?

2. José ya _____ (tiene/es) veinticuatro años.

3. Mi hermanito _____ (es/está) cansado.

4. Las lámparas _____ (están/fueron) destruidas por vándalos.

5. En verano, _____ (se hace/anochece) de noche muy tarde.

6. _____ (Estamos/Es) en abril y todavía los árboles no tienen hojas.

7. Hoy _____ (estuve/me quedé) en casa porque me dolía la barriga.

8. Sara se _____ (volvió/puso) tan triste cuando vio que te habías ido.

9. La música _____ (fue/era) tan alta que no podíamos hablar entre nosotros.

10. ¿_____ (Están/Hay) Silvia y Susana en la escuela?

Practice more at **vhlcentral.com.**

1. Completa las oraciones con las preposiciones de la lista. `30.B`

> a   de   sin   para   con

1. Me llamo Juliana y soy _____ Medellín, Colombia.
2. Esta casa es ideal _____ hacer una fiesta, ¿no te parece?
3. Como dice mi abuela, mi hermanita es _____ buen comer.
4. ¡Todos esos regalos son _____ ti!
5. ¿Viste un bolso azul? Es _____ lunares blancos.
6. No me gustan los bolsos que son _____ cremallera. ¡Son un imán para los ladrones!
7. El mantel que me regalaron es _____ cuadros.

2. Reescribe estas oraciones usando *ser* y las palabras entre paréntesis. `30.B`

1. La hermana de Juan me parece muy amable. (me)
   _____

2. ¿De veras sabes andar a caballo? (cierto)
   _____

3. ¡Siento tanto que no nos hayamos visto! (lástima)
   _____

4. Profesora, nos pareció muy difícil hacer la tarea. (nos)
   _____

5. Para mí, no es fácil dormir con la luz del día. (me)
   _____

6. Nací en Bogotá y viví ahí hasta los quince años. (de)
   _____

7. Marcos habla muy bien inglés. (bueno)
   _____

8. Construyeron la casa con madera. (de)
   _____

3. Une las frases para formar oraciones lógicas. `30.C`

1. Luis está _____
2. En este restaurante, no está _____
3. En Alemania, está _____
4. La directora está _____
5. Guillermo, estoy _____
6. En la oficina, la cosa está _____
7. Solo por dos meses, Romina está _____

a. que arde... mejor hablaré con mi jefe mañana.
b. por llegar a tu casa. ¿Bajas a abrirme la puerta?
c. permitido fumar, ¿no ves el cartel?
d. de camarera en el bar de la esquina.
e. con mucha tos. Le llevaré un té.
f. mal visto saludar con un beso a alguien que acabas de conocer.
g. de vacaciones durante todo enero. Llámala por teléfono si es algo urgente.

4. Reescribe las oraciones usando *estar* y la preposición indicada. `30.C`

1. Nos acompaña nuestro queridísimo Presidente. (con)

_____

2. Tengo dolor de garganta desde hace una semana. (con)

_____

3. Casi salgo de casa sin las llaves. (a punto de)

_____

4. Pronto comenzarán las obras del metro nuevo. (por)

_____

5. Mi padre siempre fue partidario de los liberales. (con)

_____

6. Justo iba a comprarte una camisa del mismo color. (por)

_____

5. ¿*Ser* o *estar*? En cada oración, elige la opción correcta. `30.B–30.C`

1. Mira, los dedos de mis manos _____ azules por el frío.
   a. son   ~~b. están~~

2. Ese pantalón te _____ muy grande. ¿No ves que se te cae cuando caminas?
   a. es   ~~b. está~~

3. Las cosas en esta casa _____ así. Si no te gusta, puedes irte a otro lado.
   ~~a. son~~   b. están

4. Natalia _____ de muy mal humor ahora. Mejor habla con ella mañana.
   ~~a. está~~   b. es

5. ¡_____ cansado de ser el único que limpia en esta casa!
   a. Soy   ~~b. Estoy~~

6. ¡Qué grande que _____ tu hija! ¡Cuánto ha crecido en el último verano!
   a. es   ~~b. está~~

7. Te conviene comprar una cama que _____ de madera aunque cueste más que las de metal.
   ~~a. sea~~   b. esté

6. Completa el texto con *ser* o *estar* según corresponda. `30.B–30.C`

¡Qué linda que (1) _____es_____ (es/está) Barcelona! Sin duda, ahora (2) _____está_____ (está/es) entre mis ciudades favoritas para vivir.

El clima (3) _____es_____ (está/es) caluroso en verano, pero no muy frío en invierno. Además, (4) _____está_____ (es/está) la playa ahí nomás. ¿Qué más se puede pedir?

También me encanta la gente, que siempre (5) _____está_____ (está/es) de buen humor para atendernos. (6) _____Es_____ (Es/Está) como estar en casa. ¡(7) _____Estoy_____ (Estoy/Soy) muerta de ganas de mudarme a esta ciudad!

7. En cada oración, elige entre *ser* o *estar*, según corresponda. `30.B–30.C`

1. Hace un rato que no escucho las voces de Juanito y Pedrito. Ya _____ (serán/estarán) dormidos.

2. ¿Sabes de quién _____ (está/es) enamorada Isabel?

3. La decisión _____ (fue/estuvo) aceptada por toda la empresa.

4. ¿Creías que _____ (era/estaba) satisfecha con mis notas? ¡De ninguna manera!

5. ¡Qué triste que _____ (es/está) el perrito! ¿Le pasa algo?

6. ¡Hoy sí que _____ (estás/eres) trabajadora, Paula! No paras ni un minuto.

7. ¿_____ (Es/Está) verdad que lanzarás un disco nuevo el año que viene?

8. ¿*Haber* o *estar*? Completa la conversación con la opción correcta. `30.C`

SABRINA Sabes que en la esquina (1) _____ (está/hay) un parque gigante, ¿no?

TERESA ¿Estás segura? ¿En qué esquina (2) _____ (está/hay)?

SABRINA En la esquina de la avenida Naciones Unidas y Terrazas.

TERESA Ah, sí, ¿a qué venía eso?

SABRINA Allí (3) _____ (hay/está) un concierto esta tarde.

TERESA Genial. ¿(4) _____ (Habrá/Habrán) bandas conocidas?

SABRINA No lo sé, pero el año pasado (5) _____ (hubo/estuvo) muy bien.

TERESA ¿Y sabes si (6) _____ (estará/habrá) lluvia?

SABRINA Mmm... dicen que (7) _____ (habrá/estará) nuboso, pero no muy frío.

TERESA Perfecto. ¿Y tienes entradas? (8) _____ (Hay/Están) dos compañeras de la uni que vendrán a casa a comer y me gustaría ir con ellas.

SABRINA ¡Por supuesto! La entrada es libre y (9) _____ (está/hay) abierto a todo el público.

9. Une las frases para formar oraciones lógicas. `30.D`

1. Mi casa está _____   a. la fiesta de aniversario de los abuelos.

2. Dime dónde será _____   b. en Pamplona, en junio. ¿Quieres que vayamos?

3. Lucía, estoy _____   c. muy lejos de la tuya.

4. Los sanfermines son _____   d. aquí en la esquina, ¿no me ves?

5. Las flores están _____   e. en el auto. Tráelas, por favor.

10. Síntesis En cada oración, elige la opción correcta. `30.B–30.E`

1. La cama _____ (está/es) muy cara ahora. La semana pasada el precio era menor.

2. _____ (Es/Está) importante que vengas a la reunión del jueves.

3. ¿_____ (Estabas/Eras) durmiendo? ¡Discúlpame!

4. _____ (Fue/Estuvo) Francisco quien te llamó ayer, no Federico.

5. Por suerte, la comida ya _____ (está/es) hecha. En un minuto podremos comer.

6. Quiero que _____ (seamos/estemos) felices para toda la vida.

7. _____ (Es/Está) perfecto que estudies mucho, pero también tienes que descansar un poco.

11. Síntesis Completa las oraciones con los verbos de la lista. `30.B–30.E`

estábamos	están	fue	son (2)	estuvo
ha	está (2)	será	hubo	es

1. Marina _____ abogada, pero ahora _____ de profesora de historia en una escuela.

2. _____ evidente que _____ problemas de organización en el desfile del mes pasado. Este mes será diferente.

3. ¿El perro _____ en mi habitación? Las paredes _____ llenas de barro.

4. Aunque los novios _____ de Buenos Aires, la boda _____ en Córdoba.

5. _____ en el cine cuando nos llamaste. _____ prohibido usar el teléfono celular allí.

6. _____ habido muchas peleas entre ellos, pero hoy _____ muy amigos.

12. Rodrigo no sabe bien cuándo usar _ser_ y _estar_. Ayúdalo a terminar su texto con los verbos adecuados. `30.B–30.E`

Mi equipo de fútbol favorito

(1) _____ (Está/Es) sabido que en España hay dos equipos de fútbol muy importantes: el Real Madrid y el F.C. Barcelona. El problema (2) _____ (es/está) que yo (3) _____ (soy/estoy) del Real Madrid, a pesar de (4) _____ (estar/ser) de la ciudad de Barcelona. Me (5) _____ (es/está) tan difícil vivir en Barcelona ¡y ver cómo las banderas del Barcelona (6) _____ (son/están) hasta en la sopa! Por eso, (7) _____ (soy/estoy) a punto de lanzar una campaña para reclutar más fanáticos del Real en Barcelona. Si (8) _____ (eres/estás) conmigo, envíame un mensaje electrónico a mejormadrid@barcelona.es

 Practice more at **vhlcentral.com.**

Indirect discourse

Chapter 31

1. Escribe las oraciones en discurso indirecto siguiendo el modelo. `31.B`

Modelo

(viernes) Lucía dijo: "No iré a la fiesta de mañana".
(Hoy es sábado.) *Lucía dijo que no irá a la fiesta de hoy.*

1. (martes) Tu hermana dijo: "Anoche dormí doce horas".
   (Hoy es viernes.) _____

2. (viernes) La profesora nos dijo: "Estudien para el examen de la semana que viene".
   (Hoy es sábado.) _____

3. (lunes) El presidente dijo: "Me entrevistaré con el presidente ecuatoriano pasado mañana".
   (Hoy es miércoles.) _____

4. (domingo) Juana me dijo: "Nos veremos el martes por la noche".
   (Hoy es lunes.) _____

5. (viernes) Mi tutor me dijo: "Mañana no tendremos clases".
   (Hoy es domingo.) _____

2. Decide si en estas oraciones se da información (I) o una orden (O). Luego, escribe las oraciones en discurso indirecto. `31.B`

1. "Pase y mire sin compromiso". _____ _____

2. "Por favor, no se siente allí". _____ _____

3. "Los pantalones están en oferta". _____ _____

4. "Llévese dos pantalones por 20 dólares". _____ _____

5. "La tienda cierra a las nueve". _____ _____

6. "Apúrese a comprar". _____ _____

7. "Le agradezco su visita". _____ _____

Actividades

3. **Lee el mensaje electrónico que escribió Daniela y completa la nota de Emilio a Juan reescribiendo las oraciones en discurso indirecto.** `31.B`

> ¡Hola!
> ¡Estoy tan feliz porque nos vemos mañana! Llegaré a las nueve y media a la Estación del Sur. Te esperaré en las escaleras del edificio principal. ¡No te olvides de pasar a buscarme! No he tenido vacaciones con amigos desde 2006. Quiero que disfrutemos lo máximo posible. Llama a Juan y avísale sobre mi llegada.
> Daniela

> Juan:
> Hoy recibí un correo electrónico de Daniela.
> 1. Dijo que _____
> 2. Me confirmó que _____
> 3. Dijo que _____ y que _____
> 4. Luego explicó que _____ y que _____ lo máximo posible.
> 5. Por último, me pidió _____ y que _____
> Saludos,
> Emilio

4. **En cada oración, elige la conjugación apropiada del verbo.** `31.B`

1. Andrés dijo: "Quiero que me ayudes con la tarea".
   Andrés dijo que quería que lo _____ (ayudar/ayudara) con la tarea.

2. Los niños dijeron: "Iremos al parque por la tarde".
   Los niños dijeron que _____ (irían/iríamos) al parque por la tarde.

3. José y Roberto me dijeron: "Haz la presentación por nosotros".
   José y Roberto me dijeron que _____ (hiciste/hiciera) la presentación por ellos.

4. Sandra nos dijo: "He olvidado las llaves dentro de mi casa".
   Sandra nos dijo que se _____ (hubiera olvidado/había olvidado) las llaves dentro de su casa.

5. La directora dijo: "No me parece que ustedes se hayan comportado bien".
   La directora dijo que no le parecía que ustedes se _____ (habían/hubieran) comportado bien".

6. Mi madre dijo: "Voy a la peluquería y vuelvo en una hora".
   Mi madre dijo que _____ (iría/iba) a la peluquería y que _____ (volvería/volvía) en una hora.

7. Mi hermano me dijo: "Son las seis. Te llamo en una hora".
   Mi hermano me dijo que _____ (serían/eran) las seis y que me _____ (llamaría/llamaba) en una hora.

8. El doctor me dijo: "Toma el jarabe".
   El doctor me dijo que _____ (tomara/hubiese tomado) el jarabe.

5. Elige la opción correcta para transcribir cada oración en discurso indirecto. `31.B`

1. Él dijo: "Nunca había desaprobado un examen".
   a. Él dijo que nunca había desaprobado un examen.
   b. Él dijo que nunca hubiera desaprobado un examen.

2. Tú me dijiste: "Me encantaría que me fueras a buscar al aeropuerto".
   a. Tú me dijiste que te encantaría que te vaya a buscar al aeropuerto.
   b. Tú me dijiste que te encantaría que te fuera a buscar al aeropuerto.

3. El vecino nos dijo: "No hagan más ruido: no puedo dormir".
   a. El vecino nos dijo que no hagan más ruido porque no podía dormir.
   b. El vecino nos dijo que no hiciéramos más ruido porque no podía dormir.

4. Laura nos dijo: "Me caí de la bicicleta".
   a. Laura nos dijo que se había caído de la bicicleta.
   b. Laura nos dijo que se cayó de la bicicleta.

5. Los clientes de la mesa dos dijeron: "Nos gustaban más los platos del cocinero anterior".
   a. Los clientes de la mesa dos dijeron que les habían gustado más los platos que hacía el cocinero anterior.
   b. Los clientes de la mesa dos dijeron que les gustaban más los platos que hacía el cocinero anterior.

6. Él dijo: "En una hora habré terminado de trabajar y estaré de vacaciones".
   a. Él dijo que en una hora habría terminado de trabajar y estará de vacaciones.
   b. Él dijo que en una hora habría terminado de trabajar y estaría de vacaciones.

7. Juan me explicó: "No te puedo contar la verdad porque me voy a meter en problemas".
   a. Juan me explicó que no me podría contar la verdad porque se metería en problemas.
   b. Juan me explicó que no me podía contar la verdad porque se iba a meter en problemas.

8. Mariela me dijo: "Si no quieres venir, no vengas".
   a. Mariela me dijo que, si no quería ir, no fuese.
   b. Mariela me dijo que, si no quisiera ir, no fuera.

6. Une las oraciones en discurso directo con las oraciones en discurso indirecto. Hay tres oraciones en discurso indirecto que no debes usar. `31.B`

_____ 1. Él dijo: "Me duelen los pies".

_____ 2. Ella dijo: "Quisiera una sopa".

_____ 3. Él dijo: "Mañana nos despertaremos temprano".

_____ 4. Ella dijo: "Anoche escuché ruidos raros".

_____ 5. Él dijo: "Aún no se ha secado mi ropa".

_____ 6. Ella dijo: "Ahora quiero una sopa".

a. Él dijo que había escuchado ruidos raros la noche anterior.

b. Él dijo que le dolían los pies.

c. Él dijo que aún no se había secado su ropa.

d. Ella dijo que había escuchado ruidos raros la noche anterior.

e. Él dijo que mañana se despertarían temprano.

f. Ella dijo que quería una sopa.

g. Ella dijo que en ese momento quería una sopa.

h. Él dijo que al día siguiente se despertarían temprano.

i. Él dijo que aún no se había secado mi ropa.

7. Reordena los elementos para formular preguntas indirectas. `31.B`

1. ¿ / está / podría / dónde / el correo más cercano / decirme / Señora, / ?

   _____

2. mi papá / me pasa a buscar / si / a las cinco / No recuerdo / o / a las seis / .

   _____

3. ¿ / cumple /cuándo / años / Sabes / Cristina / ?

   _____

4. si / Me pregunto / es / esta película / divertida / .

   _____

5. si / no / tenía calor / Le / con esa chaqueta / pregunté / .

   _____

6. era / el nombre / supe / cuál / Nunca / de esa chica tan bonita / .

   _____

7. ¿ / hora / decirme / a qué / Puedes / comeremos / ?

   _____

8. Completa las oraciones para transformar el discurso directo en indirecto. `31.A–31.B`

1. ¿Cuánto tiempo se tarda para llegar en tren a Barcelona?
   Me gustaría saber _____.

2. ¡He perdido mi cartera!
   Marina me dijo _____.

3. ¡No me molestes más!
   Cecilia me pidió _____.

4. Señor, ¿cómo será el tiempo mañana?
   Le pregunté al señor _____.

5. Señora, ¿tiene cambio de veinte dólares?
   Señora, quisiera saber _____.

6. Ayer trabajé hasta las diez de la noche.
   Mi hermana me contó _____.

7. Nunca había tenido un accidente de tránsito.
   Mi tío me dijo _____.

8. Nos gustaría que nos mostraras las fotos de tu viaje.
   Mis padres me pidieron _____.

9. Si hubiéramos tenido tiempo, te habríamos visitado.
   Mis primos me dijeron _____.

10. Compraría una computadora nueva si tuviera dinero ahorrado.
    Le expliqué a mi jefe _____.

Practice more at **vhlcentral.com.**

Actividades

Index

Image credits

About the author

Ana Beatriz Chiquito is a Professor of Spanish at the University of Bergen, Norway, and for nearly twenty years has been affiliated with the Center for Educational Computing Initiatives at MIT as a Visiting Research Engineer. Professor Chiquito holds degrees in Linguistics, Social Sciences, and Teacher Education, and has been a Visiting Professor at the University of Massachusetts, Boston; the Universidad Católica de Quito; the Universidad de Costa Rica; the Norwegian School of Economics and Business Administration; and at the UNDP Program in Public Administration in Ecuador. Professor Chiquito has extensive international experience designing and developing e-learning applications for language education at all levels and for over thirty years has led research projects in Spanish linguistics, sociolinguistics, and e-learning in Latin America, Spain, Norway, and the United States. She has also co-authored several textbooks and e-learning applications for Spanish as a foreign language for the U.S. and European markets. A native of Colombia, she now divides her time between the Boston area and Norway.